Russian Imperialism Revisited

This book examines the nature of Russia's relations with the former Soviet states (FSS), in particular with countries which formed the Commonwealth of Independent States, in order to assess whether there has been a resurgence of Russian imperialism since the collapse of the USSR.

The book sets out to determine whether Russian leaders have attempted to restore a sphere of influence over the former Soviet republics or whether Russia's policies reflect a genuine desire to establish normal state-to-state relations with the new states. It adopts a comprehensive approach, analysing Russia's policies towards the FSS across a broad range of areas: energy, trade and investment; military assistance, security provision and peacekeeping; conflict management, political support, and alliance formation. While not denying the Kremlin's assertive role in the FSS, this book challenges the assumption that Russia has always intended to restore a sphere of influence over its 'Near Abroad'. Rather, it argues that Russia's policies are much more complex, multi-faceted, and often more incoherent than is often assumed. In essence, Russia's actions generally reflect a combination of legitimate state interests, enduring Soviet legacies, and genuine concerns over events unfolding along Russia's borders. This book also shows that, at times, Great-Power nostalgia and a real difficulty with discarding Russia's imperial legacy shapes Russia's behaviour towards the FSS.

This book will be of great interest to students of Russian politics and foreign policy, east European politics, and International Relations in general.

Domitilla Sagramoso is a Lecturer in Security and Development at the Department of War Studies, King's College London, UK.

Contemporary Security Studies
Series Editors: James Gow and Rachel Kerr
King's College London

This series focuses on new research across the spectrum of international peace and security, in an era where each year throws up multiple examples of conflicts that present new security challenges in the world around them.

Quasi-State Entities and International Criminal Justice
Legitimising narratives and counter-narratives
Ernst Dijxhoorn

George W. Bush's Foreign Policies
Principles and Pragmatism
Donette Murray, David Brown and Martin A. Smith

Power Relations in the Twenty-First Century
Mapping a Multipolar World?
Edited by Donette Murray and David Brown

Deterring Russia in Europe
Defence Strategies for Neighbouring States
Edited by Nora Vanaga and Toms Rostoks

British Defence in the 21st Century
John Louth and Trevor Taylor

Cultures of Counterterrorism
French and Italian Responses to Terrorism after 9/11
Silvia D'Amto

Russian Imperialism Revisited
From Disengagement to Hegemony
Domitilla Sagramoso

For more information about this series, please visit: www.routledge.com/Contemporary-Security-Studies/book-series/CSS

Russian Imperialism Revisited
From Disengagement to Hegemony

Domitilla Sagramoso

LONDON AND NEW YORK

First published 2020
by Routledge
2 Park Square, Milton Park, Abingdon, Oxon OX14 4RN

and by Routledge
52 Vanderbilt Avenue, New York, NY 10017

Routledge is an imprint of the Taylor & Francis Group, an informa business

© 2020 Domitilla Sagramoso

The right of Domitilla Sagramoso to be identified as author of this work has been asserted by her in accordance with sections 77 and 78 of the Copyright, Designs and Patents Act 1988.

All rights reserved. No part of this book may be reprinted or reproduced or utilised in any form or by any electronic, mechanical, or other means, now known or hereafter invented, including photocopying and recording, or in any information storage or retrieval system, without permission in writing from the publishers.

Trademark notice: Product or corporate names may be trademarks or registered trademarks, and are used only for identification and explanation without intent to infringe.

British Library Cataloguing-in-Publication Data
A catalogue record for this book is available from the British Library

Library of Congress Cataloging-in-Publication Data
Names: Sagramoso, Domitilla, author.
Title: Russian imperialism revisited : from disengagement to hegemony / Domitilla Sagramoso.
Description: Abingdon, Oxon : Routledge, 2020. | Series: Contemporary security studies | Includes bibliographical references and index.
Identifiers: LCCN 2019052724 (print) | LCCN 2019052725 (ebook) | ISBN 9780415562270 (hbk) | ISBN 9780203861806 (ebk)
Subjects: LCSH: Russia (Federation)–Territorial expansion. | Russia (Federation)–Relations–Former Soviet republics. | Former Soviet republics–Relations–Russia (Federation) | Commonwealth of Independent States. | Imperialism.
Classification: LCC DK510.764 .S238 2020 (print) | LCC DK510.764 (ebook) | DDC 327.47–dc23
LC record available at https://lccn.loc.gov/2019052724
LC ebook record available at https://lccn.loc.gov/2019052725

ISBN: 978-0-415-56227-0 (hbk)
ISBN: 978-0-203-86180-6 (ebk)

Typeset in Times New Roman
by Wearset Ltd, Boldon, Tyne and Wear

Contents

List of maps vii
List of tables viii
Preface ix
Acknowledgements xii
List of abbreviations xiii

Introduction 1

1 What is Russia? Russia's foreign policy orientation under Yeltsin 21

2 Russia and the Commonwealth of Independent States 44

3 CIS integration under Yevgeny Primakov: Russia's post-imperial model 70

4 Russia's CIS gas trade during Yeltsin's Presidencies: towards market-based relations? 94

5 The outbreak of military conflicts: Russia's difficulties in discarding its Imperial legacy 111

6 Vladimir Putin at the helm of Russia: a return of Russia's Hegemony? 131

7 CIS economic integration gathers speed 153

8 Vladimir Putin strengthens CIS military integration: a new military bloc emerges 179

9	Separatist conflicts in Eurasia: Russia's hegemonic power is reinforced	210
10	From Putin to Medvedev … and back to Putin: Whither Russia?	233
11	The Eurasian Economic Union: A neo-Imperial Paradigm?	248
12	Russia's CIS gas trade: an instrument of Russia's hegemony?	278
13	The Russian–Georgian War and its aftermath: Russia's neo-empire	304
14	The annexation of Crimea and the war in Ukraine's Donbass: Russia's neo-empire expands	329
15	Conclusion	342
	Index	357

Maps

1 Russia and The Commonwealth of Independent States   xvi
2 The Caucasus and Central Asia   xvi
3 The Commonwealth of Independent States – European Russia   xvii

'Courtesy of the University of Texas Libraries, The University of Texas at Austin.'

Tables

7.1 Intra-EvrAzES growth in trade, in percentages, between 2000 and 2003, and average GDP growth between 2000 and 2003 — 159
7.2 Intra-EvrAzES growth in trade, in percentages, between 2003 and 2008, and average GDP growth between 2003 and 2008 — 159
7.3 Percentage of Exports and Imports of EvrAzES members to the CU, as percentage of EvraAzES members' total trade — 160
7.4 Percentage of Exports and Imports of EvrAzES members to the CU, as a percentage of EvraAzES members' total trade — 161

Preface

Over the past 10 years the world has witnessed the emergence of an increasingly resurgent, and many would rightly argue, a highly unpredictable Russia, under the leadership of President Vladimir Putin both as President and as Prime Minister of Russia. The Kremlin's decision to invade Georgia in the summer of 2008 and, more significantly, its annexation of Ukraine's Crimea in 2014 have transformed Russia from a country upholding the status quo into a revisionist Power, ready to alter internationally recognised borders through the use of force. Russia's aggressive actions resulted in the acquisition of neighbouring territory and the escalation of tensions in the eastern regions of Ukraine, which, in turn, led to the outbreak of large-scale fighting in the Donbass region. This belligerent behaviour caught many Western decisions-makers, journalists and pundits by surprise. It raised the spectre of Russia's military actions expanding further beyond its current borders. Although direct military confrontation with Europe and the United States was avoided, relations between Russia and the West became extremely strained leading many experts, maybe appropriately, to talk of the re-emergence of a new 'Cold War' with Russia. More significantly, serious concerns were raised over the risk that Russia would use its military and economic might – primarily its abundance of energy resources – to restore the former Soviet Union in a new shape and form.

The break-up of the Soviet Union in 1991 led to a profound transformation of the Eurasian geo-strategic landscape – the continent saw the emergence of a significantly reduced Russian state, surrounded by a series of politically and economically fragile newly independent countries. This new geopolitical predicament raised the possibility that Russia, having lost vast amounts of land and over 25 million ethnic nationals, would find it hard to consider the former Soviet republics as sovereign entities, and would instead, attempt to restore its hegemony over the entire former USSR. The outcome of this dilemma, whether or not Russia would be able to discard its imperial legacy and would prove ready to treat its former 'colonies' as new independent states, remains unresolved. Yet it is crucial as it determines the geopolitical nature of Eurasia and the lines of its future destiny. More significantly, how Russia operates in the former Soviet space helps to shape and define Russia's geo-strategic role both regionally and globally. It is this essential predicament that this book is trying to unlock.

While not denying the Kremlin's assertive role in the former Soviet space, this book challenges the assumption that Russia has always been intent on restoring a sphere of influence on its 'near abroad'. It disputes the view that Russian leaders have always had a clear policy and a vision of creating an 'informal empire' in the Near Abroad – to be understood as an area, composed of former colonies, over which the dominant country or former imperial centre has a substantial capacity to influence developments, and over which other countries are denied a hegemonic presence. It argues, instead, that Russia's policies towards the former Soviet space have generally been much more complex and multi-faceted than is assumed, and often have been characterised by incoherency, especially during the 1990s under President Boris Yeltsin. These policies generally reflect a combination of legitimate state interests, enduring Soviet legacies, and genuine concerns over events unfolding along Russia's borders. This book demonstrates that, more often than not, Russia's policies reflect a real apprehension over the growing foreign, primarily Western, presence in the area, which is perceived as intended to reduce Russia's influence in its neighbouring countries and weaken Russia itself. This book, however, also shows that Great-Power nostalgia and a genuine difficulty of discarding Russia's imperial legacy continues to shape Russia's behaviour in the former Soviet space. Nonetheless, the longing for Empire is not always a determining factor of Russian policy-making in this region, although it has become more salient in the past decade under Putin's leadership.

Events such as the war in South Ossetia and the annexation of Crimea by Russia highlight the need for a dispassionate and sober analysis of Russia's policies in what it calls its 'near abroad', in order properly to guide the actions of political leaders in global capitals. Recent analysis of Russia's foreign policies towards the West in general and to the former Soviet states, in particular, has tended to take a very sensationalist view of Russia's behaviour. While many of Russia's actions justifiably alarm Western countries, a more rigorous and impartial analysis of Russia's policies towards countries in the former Soviet space is nevertheless required, in order to inform and guide government decision-making. In essence, that is the main purpose of this book. By looking carefully at the drivers and motivations behind foreign-policy formulation, the type of policies implemented, and the policy results obtained, this book hopes to provide a more accurate analysis of Russian actions in the former Soviet space. It examines in detail the variety of actors involved in decision-making, the array of instruments used, and the complexity of the values and ideas that currently drive and have driven Russian elites when formulating policy towards the former Soviet countries.

More importantly, this book adopts a comprehensive and all-encompassing approach covering a broad range of areas – energy, trade and investment; military assistance, security provision and peacekeeping; and conflict management and diplomacy. Rather than looking at Russia's policies towards each former Soviet state individually, it addresses the topic on a thematic basis, covering military, political, economic, institutional aspects, in order to achieve a more comprehensive and accurate analysis of Russia's policies towards the former Soviet states as a whole. Furthermore, the book covers the Yeltsin, the three Putin presidencies (until 2017), and the Medvedev interregnum, in order to get a better understanding of developments in the former Soviet space throughout the past decades until today. The book's strength lies not only in its original approach to the topic, but also in the depth of its analysis, as it relies on the thorough and substantive research conducted by the author over the past decade.

Domitilla Sagramoso
London, United Kingdom

Acknowledgements

This book draws upon the vast amount of research on Russian foreign policy that lends insight into these issues. I therefore wish to acknowledge all of the scholars who have made contributions to this field in recent years. I am also particularly indebted to James Gow who provided me with extremely valuable advice on the overall structure and thrust of the work. I am also very grateful to Malcolm Murfett who shared his views on the book and gave me strong encouragement during the last phases of this project. A special thanks also goes to Andrew Humphrys at Routledge for his continued and ongoing support for this project. I am also indebted to Michael Rainsborough and Mats Berdal at the Department of War Studies for their continued support for my work.

I would also like to thank all those who helped me during my several trips to Russia and the former Soviet space. I am particularly indebted to many officials and experts who shared with me their views on the topic, including – but not only – Dmitry Trenin, Aleksandr Nikitin, Andrei Zagorsky, Alex Rondeli and his team, Stepan Safariyan and Georgi Engelhardt. A special thanks goes to Maksim Yusin for his insightful contributions which have helped me better understand the topic throughout the years.

Abbreviations

AA	Association Agreement
ABM	Anti-Ballistic Missile
AIE	Alliance for European Integration
ARF	ASEAN Regional Forum
ARGP	ArmRosGazprom
BSF	Black Sea Fleet
BTC	Baku-Tbilisi-Ceyhan
BTE	Baku-Tbilisi-Erzurum
CACO	Central Asian Cooperation Organisation
CAF	Collective Aviation Forces
CAR	Central African Republic
CBR	Central Bank of Russia
CBM	Confidence-Building Measures
CFDP	Council for Foreign and Defence Policy
CU	Customs Union – *Tamozhennyi Soiuz*
CES	Common Economic Space
CET	Common External Tariff/s
CFE	Conventional Forces in Europe
CIS	Commonwealth of Independent States *Sodruzhestvo Nezavisimykh Gosudarstv*
CPRF	Communist Party of the Russian Federation
CRDF	Collective Rapid Deployment Forces
CRO	Congress of Russian Communities
CSCE/OSCE	Conference on (subsequently Organisation for) Security and Co-operation in Europe
CSS	Community of Sovereign States
CST/CSTO	Collective Security Treaty (subsequently) Organisation – *Organizatsiya Dogovora o Kollektivnoi Bezopasnosti*
CUC	Customs Union Commission
DCFTA	Deep and Comprehensive Free Trade Agreement
DNR	Donetsk People's Republic *Donetskaya Narodnaya Respublika*
EAEU	Eurasian Economic Union *Evraziiskii Ekonomicheskii Soiuz*
EaP	Eastern Partnership

ECU	Eurasian Customs Union *Evraziiskii Tamozhennyi Soiuz*
ECT	Energy Community Treaty
EEC	Eurasian Economic Commission
ENP	European Neighbourhood Policy
ETG	EuralTransGas
EU	European Union
EUMM	EU Monitoring Mission
EuU	Eurasian Union – *Evraziiskii Soiuz*
EvrAzES	Eurasian Economic Community – *Evraziiskoe ekonomicheskoe soobshchestvo*
FSB	Federal Security Service – *Federal'naya Sluzhba Bezopasnosti*
FPC	Foreign Policy Concept
FSS	Former Soviet States
FTA	Free Trade Area
GDP	Gross Domestic Product
GRU	Main Intelligence Directorate – *Glavnoe razvedyvatel'noe upravlenie*
GUAM/GUUAM	Georgia Ukraine (Uzbekistan) Azerbaijan Moldova
IC	Integration Committee
IDP	Internally Displaced People
IEC	Inter-state Economic Committee
IMF	International Monetary Fund
IMU	Islamic Movement of Uzbekistan
INF	Intermediate-Range Nuclear Forces
ISC	Inter-State Council
JAF	Joint Armed Forces
JCC	Joint Control Commission
KGB	Committee for State Security – *Komitet Gosudarstvennoi Bezopasnosti*
KSOR	Collective Rapid Deployment Forces – *Kollektivnye sily operativnogo reagirovaniya*
LDPR	Liberal Democratic Party of Russia
LNR	Lugansk People's Republic – *Luganskaya Narodnaya Respublika*
LoC	Line of Contact
MFA	Ministry of Foreign Affairs
MID	Motorised Infantry Division
MoD	Ministry of Defence
MRD	Motorised Rifle Division
NATO	North Atlantic Treaty Organisation
NBC	Nuclear-Biological-Chemical
NIS	Newly Independent States
NSC	National Security Concept
NTB	Non-tariff barriers
OBOR	One-Belt-One-Road initiative

OGRF	Operational Group of Russian Forces – *Operativnaya gruppa rossiiskikh voisk*
OPEC	Organisation of the Petroleum Exporting Countries
OSCE	Organisation for Security and Co-operation in Europe
PARP	Planning and Review Process
PfP	Partnership for Peace
PJC	Permanent Joint Council
PoR	Party of Regions
PSC	Political-Security Committee
PM	Prime Minister
RATS	Regional Anti-Terrorist Structure
RCGF	Regional Coalition Groups of Forces – *Koalitsionnye regional'nye gruppirovki voisk (sil)*
RDCF	Rapid Deployment Collective Forces – *Kollektivnye sily bistrogo razvertivaniya*
RSCS	Regional Systems of Collective Security - *Regional'nye sistemy kollektivnoi bezopasnosti*
RUE	RosUkrEnergo
RSFSR	Russian Soviet Federative Socialist Republic
SBU	Security Service of Ukraine – *Sluzhba bezpeki Ukraini*
SCMC	Staff for the Co-ordination of Military Co-operation
SES	Single Economic Space – *Edinoe ekonomicheskoe postranstvo*
SCO	Shanghai Cooperation Organisation
SRSG	Special Representative of the Secretary General
SRV	Foreign Intelligence Service – *Sluzhba vneshnei razvedki*
TANAP	Trans- Anatolian Natural Gas Pipeline
TAPI	Turkmenistan-Afghanistan-Pakistan-India
TMD	Theatre Missile Defence
UAF	Ukrainian Armed Forces
UGE	UkrGazEnergo
UN	United Nations
UNGA	United Nations General Assembly
UNOMIG	United Nations Mission in Georgia
UNSC	United Nations Security Council
USA	United States of America
USSR	Union of Soviet Socialist Republics
UTO	United Tajik Opposition
VAT	Value-added tax
WEU	Western European Union
WTO	World Trade Organisation
XUAR	Xinjiang Uighur Autonomous Region

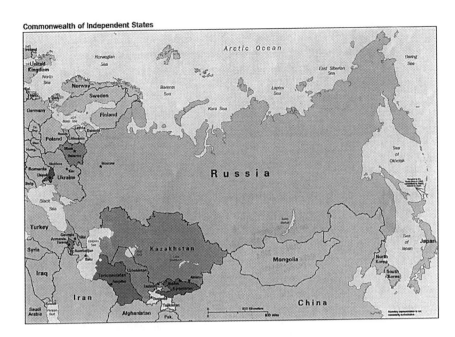

Map 1 Russia and The Commonwealth of Independent States.

Map 2 The Caucasus and Central Asia.

Commonwealth of Independent States - European States

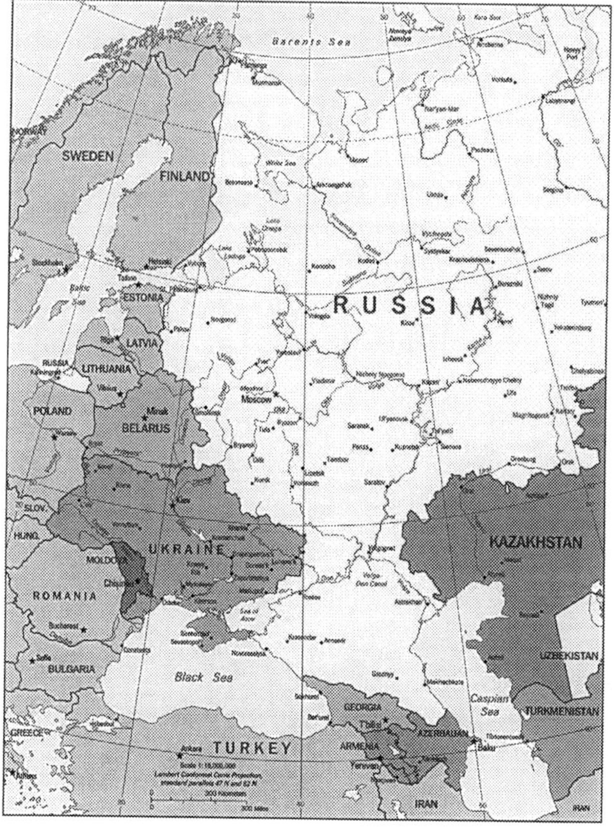

Map 3 The Commonwealth of Independent States – European Russia.

Introduction

The break-up of the Soviet Union in 1991 entailed a profound transformation of the geopolitical landscape in the Eurasian land mass. A truncated Russian state, surrounded by a series of politically and economically fragile newly independent states, emerged in the territory of the former USSR (Union of Soviet Socialist Republics). This created a fundamental problem, namely whether Russia, having lost vast amounts of land and over 25 million ethnic nationals would be able to discard its imperial legacy and consider the new states as independent and entirely sovereign entities of international law, or whether instead, its leaders would attempt to restore Russia's hegemony over the post-Soviet space. This challenge proved to be particularly profound as the Russian SFSR, re-baptised as 'the Russian Federation', was in fact a Bolshevik invention. Its external borders and internal divisions did not correspond to any pre-existing geographical, political or ethnic reality, with the possible exception of mid-seventeenth century Russia before the treaty of Pereyaslav (Trenin, 2009, p. 6). The borders of the Russian empire at the times of the last tsar, Nicholas II, almost totally coincided with the frontiers of the old USSR, if Poland and Finland were excluded, and not with the actual shape of the RSFSR, the Russian Soviet Federative Socialist Republic. The collapse of the Soviet Union thus, produced a serious national identity crisis among the Russian elite and the Russian population at large, namely over 'What was Russia?' This predicament was magnified by the demise of the Communist ideology, which had been for decades the source of legitimacy of both the Communist system and of the Soviet state.

Thus, a heated political debate ensued on what the new Russian state should look like, where its borders ought to lie, and how far its foreign influences should extend. Throughout much of its modern history, Russia and its national identity has been based on an imperial idea of the Russian state. Unlike other overseas empires, the Russian empire and the Russian state had developed simultaneously, on the basis of the acquisition and colonisation of contiguous territory (Kluchevsky, 1911). Consequently, the distinction between the Russian metropolis and the colonies had always been blurred and remained so even during Soviet times. As a result, Russians tended to associate the idea of Russian statehood with the existence of the Russian empire and thereafter, with the Soviet Union. As Vladimir Balakhonov, pointed out 'among Russians the imperial instinct is tremendously strong, and we cannot as yet imagine any form of existence other than our current empire, stretching from Brest to Vladivostok' (Balakhonov, 1989). The vast extent of the Russian territory and above all, the constant expansion of the Russian state throughout the centuries, was seen by many political scientists and historians as the determining feature of Russia's historical development (Polyakov, 1992). This close identification with the vast expanses of Russian land explains the disarray felt by most Russians after the collapse of the Soviet Union, when the Russian state lost such large amounts of territory. As journalist Dmitry Kosyrev noted,

> The point is not just that we are still living in a state that feels uncomfortable within its new borders.... More than that, the psychological adaptation to the fact that Belarus, Ukraine and [other former Soviet republics] are foreign states and that relations with them are, in fact, the realm of foreign policy, has not been easy. If it has occurred at all.
>
> (Kosyrev, 1992)

This predicament was compounded by a concern over the fate of over 25 million ethnic Russians who found themselves living outside the current borders of the Russian Federation after the collapse of the Soviet Union, and who suddenly became 'foreigners' in their own country, prompting the Russian government to engage in an active policy to protect their rights.

The end of Communism and the collapse of the Soviet Union also put into question the 'Great Power' status of the new Russian state in the world arena – an important source of pride for the Russian people. This, together with the severe economic crisis and social disarray endured by Russia in the 1990s, produced a deep sense of national humiliation among Russians. Although the Russian Federation had become in December 1991, to all intents and purposes, the legal successor of the USSR – it retained the Soviet Union's permanent seat at the United Nations Security Council (UNSC), it inherited its nuclear arsenal, and it took charge of its debts and treaty obligations – Russians soon realised that the possession of nuclear weapons and the holding of a permanent seat at the UNSC were not enough to compensate for Russia's loss of global influence and for its reduced economic and military capabilities.[1] Although Russian politicians and intellectuals tended to insist that Russia still remained a great power, regular proclamations by Russian officials that Russia was a great power indicated the existence of serious doubt as to whether these assertions accurately reflected the new Russian geopolitical reality (Kozyrev, 1992a; Adomeit, 1995, p. 35). Whether or not Russia *was* in fact a great power, its politicians and intellectuals tended to agree on the assertion that Russia should strive to become one, and should be respected as such by the world community.

Nostalgia for empire and great-power status notwithstanding, the Russian government did not always translate these feelings of regret into an active neo-imperial project in the former Soviet space. There is hardly any evidence pointing to a clear and coherent project of an informal empire-building in the ex-USSR during the Yeltsin era, although some elements of neo-imperialism can be found in Russia's policies in the Near Abroad in the 1990s. Yet with the advent of Vladimir Putin to the Presidency of Russia in the year 2000, designs of a more assertive, Russia First policy, began to emerge. The Kremlin, however, initially did not use Russia's hegemonic power in a particularly aggressive manner, and in explicit violation of international law, to achieve influence and fulfil its objectives in Russia's 'Near Abroad'. Yet, there were instances when Russia did engage more forcefully in its relations with the former Soviet states (FSS), especially when it felt that its security and well-being came under threat. As the decade progressed, though, Russia's policies in the Commonwealth of Independent States (CIS) space became increasingly assertive, reflecting Russia's hegemonic power and its aspirations to keep the region under an exclusive sphere of influence. In the 2010s, with Putin's return to the Presidency, the neo-imperialist paradigm was reaffirmed even more convincingly, as Russia aspired to become the leader of an economic and military bloc of states which would help transform Russia into one of the leading poles in a multipolar world.

Many Western and several Russian experts have sustained the view that the re-creation of some sort of 'informal empire' has been the objective of Russia's policies in the CIS during the past three decades – as early as the 1990s (Hill and Jewett, 1994; Pipes, 1994), and especially after Putin came to power in 2000, and Russia regained its economic strength (Lucas, 2008; Bugajski, 2010; Sherr, 2013; Kotkin, 2016). This book takes issue with such analysis, and instead argues that Russia's behaviour is a lot more complex and multi-faceted than is often assumed. The evidence obtained as a result of a thorough examination of Russia's policies in the Near Abroad, primarily towards the CIS states, indicates that Russia's policies have combined both assertive actions, conducted sometimes in violation of international law, and more benign activities, which complied with acceptable and legal international practices. While a neo-imperialist design for the former USSR emerged in the mid-2000s – with notions of a Russian *civilisational space* covering the entire CIS space – a neo-imperialist project was only pursued more forcefully and more comprehensively in the 2010s, with the return of Vladimir Putin to the Presidency for a third time in 2012. It must be noted, however, that already in the mid-2000s, Russia began engaging in hegemonic practices, reflected in the use of hard power instruments, which were intended to keep the former Soviet states, in particular the CIS states, within Russia's sphere of influence. On the other hand, it can well be argued that, in many instances, Russia's policies also followed legitimate state concerns, related to the newly emerging threats and security challenges emanating from the region. Moscow's actions also followed the economic needs of Russia and the other former Soviet states, which resulted from the close commercial and industrial ties that brought these countries together. More importantly, Russia's behaviour tended to change according to developments not only in the region, but also in the international arena. Policies were shaped by events inside Russia – including instabilities in the North Caucasus; economic difficulties; economic progress; political dysfunction; increased domestic stabilities – as well as by the actions of external powers – be it the European Union, NATO, the United States or China – in Russia's closest neighbourhood.

Theoretical framework

This book intends to analyse in detail Russia's policies towards the newly independent states, and particularly towards the members of the CIS, since the end of the USSR in 1991 until these days in order to determine the kind of relationship Russia has been trying to establish with the former Soviet space over the past three decades. This book sets out to determine whether over the past 25 years Russian leaders have attempted to restore a sphere of influence or informal empire over the former Soviet republics – similarly to what the French did in sub-Saharan Africa after decolonisation – or whether instead Russia's policies have reflected a genuine desire to establish normal state-to-state relations with the new states. In other words, the book tries to establish whether bilateral and multilateral cooperation between Russia and the FSS has tended to approach the model of 'symmetric' relations, which Hendrik Spruyt (1997) defined as a situation in which privileged ties are established with the former Soviet states, but the new states are not penalised for choosing policies that do not correspond entirely to Russia's interests, and relations are based on voluntary contracting (pp. 316–317). In order properly to assess Russia's policies towards the FSS, this book also examines whether Russia's proactive policies in the area responded to legitimate state interests or whether instead they were motivated by an 'imperial design' and a desire to restore an 'informal empire' or 'neo-empire' over the former Soviet states.[2]

Legitimate state interests are defined as those interests pursued by a country's leadership for the sake of preserving the state's territorial integrity and protecting its own people. These include preventing conflict and instability along the country's external borders, ensuring regional stability, preventing the spread of crime, weapons, drugs and illegal immigrants into the country, maintaining and developing economic links with major trading partners, preserving open trade routes, and protecting citizens or co-ethnics living beyond the borders. In order for these interests to be pursued legitimately, state actions must conducted in accordance with the agreed principles of international law governing inter-state relations. The Helsinki Final Act, to which all former Soviet states abided to when signing the 1990 Conference for Security and Cooperation in Europe (CSCE) Paris *Charter for a New Europe*, defines the following ten principles that should regulate inter-state relations: respect for sovereignty and sovereign equality; refraining from the threat or use of force; inviolability of frontiers; respect for territorial integrity; peaceful settlement of disputes; non-intervention in the internal affairs of states; respect for human rights and fundamental freedoms; equal rights and self-determination of peoples, cooperation among states, and fulfilment in good faith of international obligations (CSCE, 1975, 1990).[3] It is also possible, however, that a state may be pursuing its interests not in accordance with international law, but still its actions are not aimed at establishing a neo-empire. In such case we would rather be talking about assertive action by a hegemonic power and not necessarily about neo-imperial behaviour by a former imperial power, although the distinction between the two may turn out to be a very thin one.

A hegemonic power, or *hegemon*, generally enjoys strong power, in terms of military capabilities and economic resources. But more importantly, it displays an intention, or an ambition, to dominate (Layne, 2006; Deyermond, 2009). It is not just a *primus inter pares* among a group of states, but instead its role and power are qualitatively different from that of other states (Jervis, 2006, p. 14; Deyermond, 2009, p. 153). As noted by Christopher Layne (2006), 'a hegemon acts self-interestedly to safeguard its security, economic, and ideological interests' (p. 11). Moreover, it 'purposefully exercises its overwhelming power to impose order on the international system' (Layne, 2006, p. 11). Robert Keohane and Joseph Nye (1977, p. 44) in this respect have rightly argued that hegemony predominates in the international system when 'one state is powerful enough to maintain the essential rules governing inter-state relations, and is willing to do so'. In such instances, there are often violations of international law, accompanied by efforts to exert great influence in the internal and external affairs of other states. In this book, the author is concerned above all with the *regional* dimension of Russia's hegemonic behaviour, while not ignoring Russia's more recent, and quite explicit, global hegemonic ambitions (Deyermond, 2009). More importantly, this book analyses how Russia, as a potential regional hegemon, may affect not only the external rules of the game, but also how it may influence the internal rules and the domestic behaviour of the weaker states in the post-Soviet system (Deyermond, 2009, p. 153). Furthermore, this book also examines how other hegemonic powers, such as China, the United States, and the EU may or may not 'coexist at different levels of international relations', and act in the former Soviet space (Deyermond, 2009).

Outcomes or results are also extremely relevant. As David Wilkinson clearly noted, hegemony is to be 'understood as a unipolar configuration of politico-military capability with a structure to *influence* [my italics] that matches capability' (Wilkinson, 1999, p. 143, my emphasis). Hegemony is not only about 'strength' but also about 'mastery', namely, obtaining the desired outcome or effect in another state's behaviour (Wilkinson, 1999, p. 143). In such instances, the weaker state loses *autonomy*, meaning that the external actor, in this case Russia, enjoys some form of authority within the borders of the weaker state (Krasner, 1995/1996, p. 117). This may go as far as 'territorial violations' of the Westphalian model of state sovereignty, which entail 'the creation of authority structures that are not coterminous with geographical borders', such as the British Commonwealth or the European Union, and most probably the CIS (Krasner, 1995/1996, p. 116). It must be noted, however, than in the case of the European Union, the transfer of sovereignty is voluntary, and does not result from the exercise of hard power or coercion. The same predicament may also apply to the British Commonwealth, but not necessarily to the CIS or the Eurasian Economic Union (EAEU). In many instances we may notice a clear attempt to exert power and influence *without* obtaining the desired outcome, in which case we would define the hegemon as an *aspiring* one. Wilkinson defines a series of areas where this 'mastery' can be exercised – investiture of governments, adjudication of controversies, maintenance of order, command of collective action, distribution of subsidies, payment of tributes, export of ideology (Wilkinson, 1999, pp. 143–144). Hegemony, however, does not necessarily entail wresting sovereignty over a particular territory. In this respect we can find several levels of influence that a stronger or hegemonic power can exert over a weaker state – from determining the country's foreign policy orientations to affecting its internal political, social, economic and cultural developments. Hegemony may also result in the dominant power exerting 'informal' sovereignty – or *neo-empire* – over the weaker state, and may even lead to the hegemon taking control over territory, in which case we would be talking about imperial behaviour if there is no acquiescence of the subordinate unit.

As far as the concept of *informal empire* or *neo-empire* is concerned, Miles Kahler (1997, p. 289) defines it as a 'looser and more geographically circumscribed system of influence [than the previous empire] over militarily weak and economically dependent societies'. Bruce Parrott (1997, p. 14), in turn, argues that an informal empire entails the domination by the metropolitan state of the external and internal affairs of other nominally independent states. Hendrik Spruyt adds another important element. He notes that hegemonic relations develop when the symmetry of benefits diminishes, and the contracting process becomes less voluntary (1997, p. 317). *Informal empire will therefore be defined as an area, usually composed of former colonies, over which the dominant power – or former mother country – has a substantial capacity to influence both external and internal developments, and over which other countries are denied a hegemonic presence*. This capacity to influence events is usually obtained as a result of an important military and economic presence, or through the development of close military, political and economic ties with the weaker state. It does not involve an effort to wrest formal sovereignty from another country, which is a trait specific of imperialist policies (Dawisha, 1995, p. 341). Informal empire, however, can entail the partial surrender of sovereignty by the former colonies to the former metropolis – for example, by ceding control over external borders, over the economy or the currency, or over foreign policy. This crucial aspect of informal empire is highlighted by David A. Lake (1997), who argues that informal empires differ from their more formal counterparts 'only in the breadth of residual rights of control transferred from the subordinate state' (p. 35)

At the more extreme end of informal empire – which is to be defined as a 'hierarchical' form of rule – one can find the kind of political and economic relationship established between the USSR and its satellite states in Eastern Europe during the Cold War. In this situation, 'formal institutionalised overlapping features' of rule, as explained by Hobson and Sharman (2005, p. 75), were established involving the Soviet Communist Party and several state bodies, such as the police and the military. 'Soviet authority structures were formally imbricated in Eastern European states', and this resulted in the Eastern bloc countries losing significant dimensions of their own state sovereignty (Hobson and Sharman, 2005, p. 76). It must be pointed out that in this case, *hierarchical authority* also meant that this loss of sovereignty, even if partial, was recognised as *legitimate* by the subordinate state's authorities, although not by the general public. In other words, it was enshrined in juridical authority, and it did not rely exclusively on 'pure coercive power' (Hobson and Sharman, 2005, p. 76). The hierarchical form of authority was recognised as legitimate by the leaders of the Eastern European states, who espoused a similar ideology, even though such policies did not have the broad support of the population. Similar features can also be found in certain aspects of the current relationship between Russia and some of the FSS. Yet, one must add that, whereas in formal empires, the metropolis' control over the rights belonging to the subordinate partner is nearly total, in informal empires, the control is substantial, but is less than complete, and is not necessarily always enshrined in judicial authority. Moreover, neo-empire status implies a relationship that develops over time, and which is quite comprehensive. It cannot be ascribed to a single policy or a single series of events confined to a limited period of time. Continuity is essential. Finally, a clear motivation to create systemic dependency must be present for policies to be classified as neo-imperialist (Dawisha, 1995, p. 341). *Informal-empire building* will therefore be defined as the process whereby the former metropolis establishes an informal empire over its former colonies.

Dmitry Trenin (2011) in one of his recent books introduces the notion of *post-Imperium*, which he defines as 'a fairly prolonged exit from the imperial condition', to explain Russia's behaviour in the former USSR region (p. 13). This means according to Trenin that Russia is no longer an empire and will probably not become one in the future. But, it retains many of its past imperial features, both internally and externally, as it tries to transform itself. It is not clear, though, what Russia is transforming into, as there is no 'immediately identifiable end station', he notes (Trenin, 2011, p. 14). Russia, in Trenin's view is a 'rare case of a formal imperial polity having neither disappeared nor reinvented itself as a nation-state, but seeking to reconstitute itself as a great power, with a regional base and global interests' (2011, p. 13). The Russian state 'is at a point where it recognises all former borderland republics as separate countries, even if it does not yet see all of them as foreign states', Trenin notes (2011, p. 14). Moreover, Trenin also rightly points out that Russia was not the only post-imperial state emerging from the collapse of the USSR. Several other ex-Soviet states – the former colonies – also often suffered from an imperial syndrome in reverse. They frequently engaged in clear and deliberate efforts to distance themselves from Russia, the former hegemon, and attempted to create new national myths that highlighted their independence by re-writing history and engaging in similar intolerant or unclear or dubious behaviour against Russia (Trenin, 2011). These views in many instances best reflect this book's findings, especially as far as Russia's actions in the Near Abroad are concerned during the first two decades after the end of the USSR. Russian leaders, in turn, talked of a 'zone of privileged interests', where external influences would be excluded (Trenin, 2009).

This raises the question of *motivation* behind Russia's policies. Was the Russian state following a particular *idea* of 'Russia', and of Russia as an 'empire' when behaving assertively in the former Soviet space, or was the Russian leadership responding to legitimate security concerns? Was Russia responding to legitimate challenges to its own security or was its own sense of insecurity being exaggerated by the Russian leadership? Was Russia, instead, being 'power-greedy'? *Structural realists* believe that the state of anarchy of the international arena makes states feel insecure, and therefore the main task for countries is to search for ways in which to protect their country and ensure their own security. *Offensive structural realists* argue that insecurity drives states to seek security by maximising power, reaching out for hegemony (Kydd, 1997; Mearsheimer, 1994/1995). According to John Mearsheimer (2001), 'the ultimate goal for state powers is to achieve regional hegemony and block the rise of peer competitors in distant areas of the globe' (p. 237.) Although this can lead to conflicts with other states, the seeking of power and regional hegemony, however, is seen by offensive structural realists as instrumental, and aimed at increasing states' own security (Glaser, 2010, p. 18). States, however, often also recognise the constraints imposed by the international system and therefore, they try to avoid always maximising power to prevent other states from balancing against them. *Defensive structural realists*, in that respect, argue that states seek to defend and protect themselves through cooperation and restraint. Aware of the risks posed by the security dilemma, states will try to reduce an adversary's sense of insecurity by engaging in cooperative policies with allies rather than increasing their own power at the expense of others. Taking this course, however, could still lead the adversary to enhance its own military capabilities, which in turn, would leave the original state feeling more insecure (Glaser, 2010, p. 25). On the other hand, *Motivational realists* like Randall Schweller, building on Hans Morgenthau's argument that states' pursuit of power is rooted in human nature's desire for power, argue that many states are not merely interested in their survival but also wish to expand territory, exert influence, and acquire additional wealth and power – as objectives in themselves (Schweller, 1996).

This book will disagree with the latter line of reasoning when applied to Russia in the 'Near Abroad', and will tend to argue that especially in the late 1990s, and 2000s, Russia was reacting, rightly or wrongly, to a perceived sense of insecurity, behaving as an offensive or defensive structural realist depending on the circumstances. In the 2010s, however, Russia increasingly adopted a more hegemonic and neo-imperialist approach, infused by a neo-imperialist ideology, which combined elements of *Eurasianism*, Russian nationalism and Great-Power *etatism*. When analysing Russia's behaviour in the CIS space, this book will therefore find agreement with Social Constructivists who give great relevance to ideas, identity and interaction in the international system. Social constructivists argue that 'security' is a socially constructed notion created by actors in the international arena. The actions, beliefs and interests of states have, therefore, to be put into context and have to be understood as being part of the world that has been created by state actors themselves (Agius, 2010, p. 50).

In other words, the ideas that Russia has about itself, and about its own place in the world have very much shaped its behaviour in the Eurasian landscape. Finally, this book will show that in many instances Russia actually cooperates quite actively with its former Soviet neighbours. As liberal thinkers of international relations would argue, 'international politics is not inherently full of conflict and violence', and instead cooperation is possible to achieve peace, security and socio-economic progress (Morgan, 2010, p. 35). Liberals not only emphasise the positive role that international organisations and international regimes play in fostering cooperation of all kinds, they also give relevance to the domestic input – domestic policies and actions – in shaping foreign policy making. These aspects, and the role of domestic factors, are explored in this book. Yet, this book challenges the realist and neo-liberal institutionalist concepts that take the sovereign and autonomous *Westphalian* state as the unit of analysis. As pointed out by Krasner (1995/1996), and by Hobson and Sharman (2005) there are many instances when sovereignty in the *Westphalian* sense has been eroded – during the era of Western Imperialism, in Eastern Europe during the Cold War, and in arrangements in the European Union, and it is these kinds of situations that this book sets out to explain.

Particularly relevant in this respect is also the way in which this power or influence are exerted – whether through *hard power*, understood as the coercive use of military and economic might, or through *soft power*, which refers to a state's influence through persuasion and the attraction and legitimacy of ideas, culture, and particular economic or social models (Averre, 2009). *Coercive diplomacy*, in turn, is a form of hard power, which entails engaging in credible threats or the limited use of force to influence the adversary's behaviour (Viggo Jakobsen, 2010, p. 279). The adversarial state may or may not acquiesce. *Imposition*, goes a step further, and forces the weaker adversary to comply with the desires of the stronger power. The former is so weak that it has no other option but to acquiesce (Krasner, 1995/1996). In both these latter cases, the Westphalian notion of sovereignty is compromised, and therefore we may be facing a situation of hegemony or neo-empire, depending on the extent to which the weaker state has lost its sovereignty. *Soft power*, instead, has been defined by Joseph Nye as 'the ability to get what you want through attraction' (2004, p. x). Important points in this respect are both the context and 'the preferences' of those states that a stronger country is trying to influence, as Joseph Nye correctly argued (2004, p. 2). 'When we measure power in terms of the changed behaviour of others, we have first to know their preferences', Nye noted (2004, p. 2), otherwise we may be attributing external influence and power to a particular behaviour, when we should not do so. In such case, the weaker actor may have been willing or ready to behave in that particular way, irrespective of the pressure. James Sherr (2013), when analysing Russia's behaviour in the Near Abroad introduces the notion of *soft coercion*, and describes it as 'the influence that is indirectly coercive, resting on covert methods (penetration, bribery, blackmail) and on new forms of power such as energy supply, which are difficult to define as hard or soft' (p. 2). In such instances, the power utilised is harder rather than softer, and therefore actions may be seen as approaching and reflecting the behaviour of a hegemonic power. On the other hand, when states engage in *voluntary contracting* they may agree to compromise the Westphalian notion of sovereignty – understood as the exercise of power autonomously, by the domestic political authorities, over a particular territory – for the sake of obtaining greater benefits (Krasner, 1995/1996). In such a case we cannot talk about hegemony or neo-Empire.

The imperialist argument

So far we have assumed that the Soviet Union was an empire, but if we are to discuss whether Russia is able to discard its '*imperial* legacy', and if we are to compare its post-Soviet behaviour with, for example, the French experiences in post-colonial Africa, we must explain first why we consider the Soviet Union to be an empire. Michael W. Doyle (1986) defines *empire* as a 'relationship, formal or informal, in which one state controls the effective political sovereignty of another political society' (p. 45). Miles Kahler (1997, p. 287), in turn, refers to two fundamental dimensions which distinguish imperial rule from other forms of international relations: *hierarchy* of power, as opposed to devolution of decision-making; and *monopoly* of external ties, as opposed to diversification of external relations. Hierarchy means that 'one society – the metropolis or centre – assumes supreme decision-making authority over internal and external policies' (Lake, 1997, p. 35). On the basis of these definitions, we may conclude that an *empire* entails tight centralised control over the external and internal relations of distinct political communities. In the Soviet Union, Moscow exercised a monopoly of control through the Communist Party, the military and the security structures over the external and internal policies of very distinct political societies, such as the developed and westernised Baltic regions, the more conservative Muslim societies of Central Asia, the various ethnic groups inhabiting the Caucasus mountains and South Caucasus regions, and the Slav republics of Belorussia and Ukraine. These distinctions were deepened by the creation of ethnically defined territorial-administrative units – the union republics, autonomous republics and autonomous *oblasts* – which were usually based on historical ethnic homelands, and helped to sustain or deepen distinct national identities among the principal ethnic minorities. These considerations therefore argue in favour of classifying the USSR as an empire.

Ghita Ionescu (1965, p. 7), in turn, refers to three basic elements, which characterise empires, all of which were present in the Soviet Union: first, a strong political centre, animated by a historical mission of expansion; second, religious or ideological coercion; and third, a 'sense of final purpose' in its elite. In this respect, the USSR's Marxist-Leninist ideology, embedded with a sense of mission, provided a powerful instrument of external expansion and a very effective instrument of coercion. According to Dominic Lieven (1995), *empire* implies possession of widespread territories inhabited by peoples varying widely in their history, ethnicity, religion and culture, as well as a considerable degree of direct administrative supervision. An empire, in his view, must be a great power, play a major role in shaping not just the international relations but also the values and culture of an historical epoch. In this, sense, then, the Soviet Union can also be considered an empire. Mark R. Beissinger (1995) adds a very valuable element to the various definitions of empire listed above – the 'subjective' dimension (p. 155). Beissinger emphasises that the most important aspect of any imperial situation is perception; in other words, whether politics and policies are accepted as 'ours' or rejected as 'theirs'. The latter case implies both a well-developed sense of separate group identity and a recognition of the illegitimacy of the existing polity's authority. In his view, empire should be understood not as a thing, but as a set of practices that give rise to perceptions and claims that the polity represents a fundamentally alien rule, an 'other' (p. 155). Although it is correct to assume that in many areas of the Soviet Union the perception of being ruled by an 'alien' and illegitimate authority was very weak, as for example in Ukraine or Belarus, in other areas of the Soviet Union, in particular in the Baltic States, Georgia, and to a certain extent in Moldova and Azerbaijan, the sense of belonging to a different political and ethnic polity, and of being ruled by 'alien' Russians was very strong. In this sense, therefore, we can also argue that the Soviet Union was, to all intents and purposes, an empire – although a very peculiar one, given the physical proximity of its 'colonies' and the efforts of its leaders to develop a high sense of equality among all ethnic groups, by fostering the emergence of a *Homo Sovieticus*, all of which tended to blur the imperial character of the political entity.

Was the Soviet Union a *Russian* Empire? Russian dissident Aleksandr Solzhenitsyn rejected the idea that the USSR was indeed a Russian Empire, arguing instead that the Soviet Union was a Communist empire (1980). John Dunlop (1993) and Alan Besançon (1986) also refused to consider the USSR a Russian empire. Besançon argued that the Russian people did not enjoy any special privileges, as the French and the British did in their own empires. The 'advantages' enjoyed by Russians, according to Besançon, derived from their support of Communism and not from their being Russian (p. 10–11). In other words, although Russians were seen as the surest allies of communism, they enjoyed a privileged position mainly because of their loyalty to the regime. A similar position was adopted by Paul Kolstoe (1995), who argued that 'the most important dividing line in Soviet society, namely that between the haves and the have-nots, was not related to ethnic criteria but determined by membership or non-membership of the ruling elite' (p. 103). In other words, the privileged came from distinct ethnic origins but all belonged to the *nomenklatura*. It can well be argued that in some respects there was total equality among ethnic groups, given that Soviet citizenship was extended to Russians and non-Russians alike, and Russians, like other nationalities, very much suffered at the hands of Communist leaders, especially, although not only, when they displayed too overt a support for Russian nationalism. Moreover, individual Russians did not enjoy any special privileges when living in the non-Russian republics, and the RSFSR was deprived of such essential symbols of official Soviet recognition as a separate Russian Communist Party, a Russian Academy of Sciences and a Russian Central Committee.

Nevertheless, as Bruce Parrott (1997, pp. 11–12) correctly pointed out, many other considerations do argue in favour of classifying the USSR as a Russian empire. Moscow's policies towards mass education and senior political appointments were based on the assumption that the Russian culture and the Russian language were superior to those of other nationalities. The official status of the Russian language, the dominant position of Russians in republican and national governing structures, as well as in the army and the police, secured the dominant status of the Russian people and ensured the absence of threats to their own ethnicity (Rywkin, 1980). Although there is no doubt that Russian culture did suffer significantly during the Soviet era, and that many Russians did indeed endure pain and ostracism in the USSR, Russians generally dominated and mostly managed the Soviet system. It can well be argued, therefore, on the basis of these assumptions, that the Soviet Union was, to a great extent, a Russian empire. It should be recalled, however, that the status of Russians fluctuated significantly over time. Under Stalin, for example, Russians were clearly more favoured than they had been both before and after. But during the post-Stalinist period, Russian diasporas were still culturally and linguistically privileged in relation to other non-titular ethnic groups (Kolstoe, 1995).

The 'imperial character' of the Soviet Union allows us to make some interesting comparisons with the French experience in its former empire in Africa, given that France devised and successfully implemented a system of influence over its former colonies in sub-Saharan Africa after de-colonisation. Although France *had* an overseas empire, as opposed to the Soviet Union which *was* a contiguous empire, the French still considered the empire to be part of France – they named it *'France d'outre-mer'* – and consequently, experienced a major national identity crisis during the various stages of decolonisation, similar, although probably not as acute, as the crisis experienced by Russia after the disintegration of the Soviet Union. Moreover, as was the case with Russia when the Soviet Union collapsed, France had to deal with the legacies of empire in its African colonies – i.e. a vast number of military garrisons, important economic interests, substantial cultural penetration, as well as the presence of a significant number of French immigrants who had settled in the African continent. This makes the comparison between the disintegration of the Soviet Union and French decolonisation in Africa all the more valuable, and certainly more appropriate than, for example, a comparison with American policies in Central America in the twentieth century or Soviet policies in Finland after the Second World War. In the latter examples, we are not dealing with the setting up of spheres of influence over territories that belonged to an imperial entity, but with contiguous areas that fall under the influence of a major hegemonic neighbouring power.

The French state managed to establish a 'neo-empire' in sub-Saharan Africa after decolonisation, many aspects of which still persist today. In the 1960s and 1970s, a network of bases was established and a system of bilateral defence agreements was set up, which allowed France to keep an important military presence in the area – about 4,000 troops were stationed in Djibouti, and smaller numbers in Senegal, Gabon, Chad, and the Central African Republic (CAR).[4] During the 1960s to 1980s, almost 2,000 African officers were trained regularly in France each year, and in turn, France sent around 1,000 military advisers to 23 African states (Chipman, 1989, p. 109). In the economic field, France established control over the currencies, central banks, fiscal policies, and treasuries of all but two of its former colonies through the Franc Zone, thus tying the colonies' economies very closely to the former mother country (Destanne de Bernis, 1980).[5] The Franc Zone financial system, although modified, still remained in play in the late-2010s, with the CFA franc being pegged to the European currency, the Euro, used by France. France also negotiated preferential trade agreements with its former colonies in the 1960s and 1970s, and paid higher than world prices for African raw materials. French investment and targeted financial aid flowed, as well as large resources devoted to the propagation of French language and culture – key elements necessary to retain elite loyalties to France (Kahler, 1997, p. 301). Intelligence cooperation became the norm between France and its former colonies in Africa, and on several occasions, French troops intervened to preserve friendly governments against internal threats, such as in the CAR, the Congo, Gabon, Niger, Mauritania, Chad. Most recently, its troops have intervened again in several African countries – in the Ivory Coast to help remove President Gbagbo from power, in Mali to prevent the establishment of a terrorist state, and in CAR, to reduce instability after a rebel coalition overthrew the country's government. In the diplomatic sphere, France succeeded in establishing cooperation with its former African colonies at the United Nations and regular high-level encounters reinforced the ties between France and the leaders of francophone Africa (Kahler, 1997, p. 301). This system of tight military, economic and diplomatic cooperation allowed France to maintain a 'neo-imperial' system in its former African colonies for over 40 years. Regular Franco-African summits took place and helped preserve important diplomatic, economic and military ties, despites regular calls for an end to *Françafrique* – France's special relations with its former colonies in Africa.

Testing the imperialist argument

In order properly to assess the nature of Russia's relations with the FSS, particularly with the CIS states, and in order to determine correctly whether Russian policies were aimed at building an informal empire in the Near Abroad, this book first analyses the underlying principles of Russia's foreign policy towards the ex-USSR states and examines the overall debate on Russian foreign policy priorities which characterised the first years of Russia's post-Soviet life. A close look is taken at the official policy concepts and ideas of Russian decision-makers regarding Russia's national interests in the post-Soviet space. What did Russian leaders consider to be the boundaries of the Russian state? What area did Russia regard as its strategic space? Did Russia feel entitled to defend the sovereignty and territorial integrity not only of Russia but of the other CIS countries as well?

What populations did Russian leaders consider as Russian and therefore entitled to protection? What were Russia's national interests and how did they differ from Russia's former imperial interests? What were the threats to the territorial integrity and survivability of Russia? Having clarified Russia's leaders' views on the configuration of the Russian state and its national interests, the research then examines Russia's military, economic and diplomatic policies towards the republics of the former Soviet Union in order to determine to what extent and how Russia was attempting to restore its previous influence in the area.

Withing this context the book analyses the peculiar structure of the CIS and the extent to which Russia used this political framework to achieve hegemony over the former Soviet republics. It then examines the processes of military and economic integration within the CIS in order to determine whether Russia conducted an assertive policy aimed at restoring some sort of renewed union during the Yeltsin, Putin and Medvedev Presidencies. The book also explores in great detail the nature of Putin's integration projects – the Eurasian Economic Community (EvrAzES) and the Eurasian Economic Union (EAEU), as well as the Collective Security Treaty Organisation (CSTO – in order to evaluate their neo-imperial character.

In the economic field, more specifically, the book examines Russia's trade and monetary policies within the CIS, EvrAzES and the EAEU, and the Belarussian–Russian negotiations on monetary and economic integration. In the military field, the book looks at multilateral and bilateral forms of CIS military cooperation, more specifically at the CSTO, and also examines the development of joint border protection and joint air-defence arrangements. The objective is to determine whether these Russian policies were aimed at establishing a military sphere of influence over the CIS states, besides enhancing Russia's own security. The research also looks at Russia's participation in five major military conflicts that erupted as the USSR collapsed – the wars in Transdniestria, Abkhazia, South Ossetia, Nagorno-Karabakh, and Tajikistan – in order to examine whether Russia's involvement followed legitimate state concerns or whether, instead, it represented an attempt to destabilise these states in order to bring them back into Russia's orbit. The book also analyses the energy trade – gas in particular – by looking first at Russia's policies towards those states that depended on its resources, such as Ukraine, Belarus, Moldova, Georgia and Armenia, in order to determine whether Russia used their energy dependence to exercise control over political and economic developments. The book then looks at Russia's policies towards the energy-rich Caspian states, to determine whether Russia's attempted to control the flow of Caspian and Central Asian gas were aimed at bringing these states under Russia's sway.

The book reaches the conclusion that after the collapse of the Soviet Union and in the 1990s Russia's policies only partially reflected an attempt by Russia to reassert its influence over the states of the former Soviet Union and to create an informal empire in the post-Soviet space. Russia's behaviour was particularly assertive in the military field as well as in its attempts to build a Russian-dominated CIS military infrastructure. Russia's policies, however, were less aggressive in the economic sphere, except probably as far as energy policy is concerned. Russia's assertive behaviour was largely due to the difficulties that Russia was experiencing when trying to discard its imperial legacy. Russian leaders found it difficult to come to terms with the fact that the former Soviet states no longer belonged to the Russian state and were to be treated as third countries. The lack of a clear idea among the Russian elites regarding what Russia was, where its boundaries ought to lie, and therefore, what its national interests were, seems largely to account for Russia's neo-imperialist actions. Yet, motives that could be interpreted as legitimate state concerns – legitimate in that they were derived from Russian leaders' perceptions of the basic requirements of security, and economic and social well-being of the Russian state – also played an important part in determining Russia's actions. The pursuit of what were perceived as legitimate state interests demanded that Russia either conduct an active policy in the 'Near Abroad' for the sake of its own stability and survival, or conversely, that it limit its actions when imperial overstretch was perceived as detrimental to Russia's domestic economic development. In other words, both the dimension of national interests and of imperial legacies combined to shape Russia's policies towards the former Soviet states, and this explains why policies were sometimes more restrained than is usually assumed. More often than not, though, Russia's policies followed an ambivalent and incoherent pattern, a result of the weak and fragmented character of the Russian state. Conflicting bureaucratic agendas, strongly divergent views among the various Russian ministries involved in devising policies with the FSS, and the struggle for power between the executive and the legislature, accounted for highly contradictory and counter-productive policies towards the CIS and the Baltic states. The absence of a clear foreign policy project determined that policies were most often reactive, rather than proactive, to events in the area. These three elements of imperial legacy, national interest, and incoherence, which were always present in Russia's policies towards the Near Abroad, elucidate to a great extent the complexities of Russia's behaviour in the former Soviet space, and explain why Russia's policies resulted in what may be called 'restrained assertiveness' – an assertive behaviour which rarely went beyond what Russia's leaders considered to be the country's interests.

In the 2000s, however, the Kremlin increasingly engaged in attempts to create a sphere of influence around its neighbouring states, although its policies were not necessarily characterised by an extremely assertive behaviour in all the spheres of policy-making. As the decade progressed, though, Moscow's actions in the 'Near Abroad' became clearly more forceful, were increasingly characterised by the use of *hard power*, and were often conducted in direct violation of international law. In the mid-2000s, and especially during Putin's second Presidency, the Kremlin made growing use of Russia's hegemonic power, which resulted from its renewed economic and military strength, to bring the former USSR region under its sphere of influence. Russian leaders began defining the former Soviet territory not only as an area of 'special interests', but also as a common 'civilisational space' – an area that brought together the peoples of the former space, untied by a common history, culture and tradition – where Russia's influence was expected to remain predominant. Concerned over the growing penetration of the West its 'Near Abroad', and worried over China's rise in Central Asia, the Russian leadership tried in the mid- to late 2000s, to create an alternative, Russian-led, geopolitical bloc, which would align most of the former Soviet states closely to Russia, and in this way, allow Russia to become one of the leading centres of a new 'multipolar world'. Furthermore, in the late 2000s and during 2010s, the promotion of the 'Russian world' concept – understood as a supranational community of people who associated themselves closely with Russia, with its values and its culture – became the guiding principle of a Russian foreign policy, which was increasingly endowed with a Messianic mission – Russia as the global leader of a 'Conservative' world.

When analysing Russia's policies towards the FSS two additional important points must be taken into consideration. First, there is the impact of the legacies of empire, which compelled Russia and the former Soviet states to interact amongst each other long after the collapse of the Soviet Union. Tight economic, military and political ties, which bound all the republics in a single whole, remained in place well after the collapse of the Soviet Union. Moreover, the disintegration of the Soviet Union left about 25 million ethnic Russians living beyond the borders of the Russian Federation. The main question to be asked in this respect, therefore, is whether Russia, as the dominant military, demographic, geographic and economic power in the region, faced a realistic alternative of disengagement or whether instead, it was bound to seek regional integration given that, at least geographically, 'Russia continued to reside in their midst' (Dawisha, 1997, p. 358). Karen Dawisha raised an important point in this respect. According to her, Russia's continuing pre-eminence in Eurasia as the dominant geographic colossus and economic power gave it an enormous advantage. To conclude from this alone, however, that Russia would 'naturally' exercise imperial ambitions over the other new states was, according to Dawisha (1997), to be too geographically deterministic (p. 342), a position also sustained by this book. A second point to be taken into account is the fact that the distinction between the legitimate pursuit of state interests and informal empire-building is usually, although not always, entirely nebulous. There is probably no other region in the world where empire-building and state-building have been subject to such ambivalence. As Mark Beissinger (1995) correctly pointed out,

> whereas Russian elites seemed incapable of recognising the essential ambiguity that surrounded state-building and empire-building in the Eurasian context and the dilemmas that this present[ed], nationalising elites among the non-Russian states [were] obsessed with this ambiguity, reading imperial intent into actions that, in other contexts, would be unlikely to be understood in that fashion.
>
> (p. 180)

The new Russian state that emerged from the disintegration of the Soviet Union, was as weak and fragmented as most of the other newly independent states. Like them, Russia also went through a transitional phase of state-building, resulting in policies often being incoherent and ambivalent, thus making the distinction between informal empire-building and state-building all the more difficult.

This book focuses on the CIS states, given that Russia's policies towards those states were particularly assertive, especially in the 2000s. During the 1990s, the Baltic states remained of great significance to Russia, primarily because of the presence of a large Russian-speaking community, and the existence of important military installations, such as the Skrunda early-warning radar station. Moreover, the Baltic states hosted port facilities and transit routes which allowed Russia to access the Russian enclave of Kaliningrad, and Western markets. Nevertheless, there seemed to be an acknowledgement, broadly shared among members of the Russian elite, that Russia 'had lost' this traditionally significant region, as indicated by the readiness to withdraw all Russian troops, and the lack of pressure exercised over these countries so that they join the CIS and its military, political and economic institutions (Lipitsky, 1992).

Notes

1 Kozyrev preferred to call Russia not the successor but the 'continuer' state of the USSR, knowing that this would reduce tensions with those newly independent states that had raised objections to Russia's position, such as Ukraine (Kozyrev, 1992b).
2 Throughout this work, the concept of informal empire and neo-empire will be used interchangeably.
3 These principles are in agreement with, and complement, those upheld by UN member states in the UN Charter (art.2 and art. 51).
4 By the time of writing, France still kept military deployments in Mali, CAR, Chad, Djibouti, Gabon and Ivory Coast.
5 The common currency, the CFA franc, was pegged to the French franc at a rate of 50:1. Members of the franc zone enjoyed a number of advantages, such as a freely convertible currency guaranteed by France, access to pooled reserves to deal with external shocks, and low inflation rates, since monetary policy was effectively removed from national control.

Bibliography

Adomeit, H. (1995). Russia as a 'Great Power' in World Affairs: Images and Reality, *International Affairs*, 71(3), 35–68.
Agius, Ch. (2010). Social Constructivism. In: A. Collins, ed., *Contemporary Security Studies*, second edition. Oxford: Oxford University Press, pp. 49–68.
Averre, D. (2009). Competing Rationalities: Russia, the EU and the 'Shared Neighbourhood', *Europe-Asia Studies*, 61(10), 1689–1713.
Balakhonov, V. (1989). *Russkaya mysl'*, 23 June, p. 7.
Beissinger, M.R. (1995). The Persisting Ambiguity of Empire, *Post-Soviet Affairs*, 11(2), 149–184.
Besançon, A. (1986). Nationalism and Bolshevism in the USSR. In: R. Conquest. *The Last Empire: Nationality and the Soviet Future*. Stanford: Hoover Institution Press.
Bugajski, J. (2010). Georgian Lessons: Conflicting Russian and Western Interests in the Wider Europe. *CSIS*, October 31. Available at: www.csis.org/analysis/georgian-lessons [accessed 10 August, 2019].

CSCE (1990). *Charter of Paris for a New Europe*, Paris: CSCE, 19–21 November. Available at: www.osce.org/mc/39516?download=true [accessed 10 October 2017].

CSCE (1975). *Conference on Security and Co-operation in Europe Final Act*, Helsinki. Available at: www.osce.org/helsinki-final-act?download=true [accessed 10 October 2017].

Chipman, J. (1989). *French Power in Africa*. Oxford: Basil Blackwell.

Dawisha, K. (1997). Constructing and Deconstructing Empire in the Post-Soviet Space. In: K. Dawisha and B. Parrott, eds. *The End of Empire? The Transformation of the USSR in Comparative Perspective*. Armonk, New York and London: M.E. Sharpe, pp. 338–362.

Dawisha, K. (1995). Conclusion. In: A. Dawisha and K. Dawisha, eds. *The Making of Foreign Policy in Russia and the New States of Eurasia, The International Politics of Eurasia*, 4, New York and London: M.E Sharpe, 1995, pp. 340–346.

Destanne de Bernis, G. (1980). Some Aspects of the Economic Relationship between France and its Ex-colonies. In: W.H. Morris-Jones, and G. Fischer, eds. *Decolonisation and After: the British and French Experience*. Abingdon, Oxon, New York: Frank Cass and Co., pp. 107–127.

Deyermond, R. (2009). Matrioshka Hegemony? Multi-levelled Hegemonic Competition and Security in Post-Soviet Central Asia, *Review of International Studies*, 35(1), 151–173.

Doyle, M.W. (1986). *Empires*. Ithaca and London: Cornell University Press.

Dunlop, J. (1993). Russia: Confronting the Loss of Empire. In: I. Bremmer and R. Taras, eds. *Nations and Politics in the Soviet Successor States*. Cambridge: Cambridge University Press, pp. 45–46.

Glaser, Ch. L. (2010). Realism. In: A. Collins, ed., *Contemporary Security Studies*, second edition. Oxford: Oxford University Press, pp. 15–33.

Hill, F. and P. Jewett (1994). *'Back to the USSR': Russia's Intervention in the Internal Affairs of the Former Soviet Republics and the Implications for the United States Policy towards Russia*. Ethnic Conflict Project, John F. Kennedy School of Government. Cambridge Mass.: Harvard University, January.

Hobson, J.M. and J.C. Sharman (2005). The Enduring Place of Hierarchy in World Politics: Tracing the Social Logics of Hierarchy and Political Change, *European Journal of International Relations*, 11(1), 63–98.

Ionescu, Gh. (1965). *The Break-up of the Soviet Empire in Eastern Europe*. Harmondsworth: Penguin Books.

Jervis, R. (2006). The Remaking of a Unipolar World. *The Washington Quarterly*, 29(3), 7–19.

Kahler, M. (1997). Empires, Neo-empires, and Political Change: The French and British Experience. In: K. Dawisha and B. Parrott, eds. *The End of Empire? The Transformation of the USSR in Comparative Perspective*. Armonk, New York and London: M.E. Sharpe, pp. 286–312.

Keohane, R.O. and Nye, J.S. (1977). *Power and Interdependence: World Politics in Transition*. Boston: Little, Brown.

Kluchevsky, V.O. (1911). *A History of Russia*, tr. C.J. Hogarth. London: J.M.Dent & Sons; New York: E.P.Dutton & Co.

Kolstoe, P. (1995). *Russians in the Former Soviet Republics*. Bloomington and Indianapolis: Indiana University Press.

Kosyrev, D. (1992). *Rossiiskaya gazeta*, 1 December, p. 6.

Kotkin, S. (2016). Russia's Perpetual Geopolitics: Putin Returns to the Historical Pattern, *Foreign Affairs*, May/June. Available at: www.foreignaffairs.com/articles/ukraine/2016-04-18/russias-perpetual-geopolitics [accessed 18 June 2017].

Kozyrev, A. (1992a). *New Times*, 3, p. 21.
Kozyrev, A. (1992b) *Nezavisimaya gazeta*, 1 April 1992, p. 3.
Krasner, S.D. (1995/1996). Compromising Westphalia?, *International Security*, 20(3), 115–151.
Kydd, A. (1997). Sheep in Sheep's Clothing: Why Security Seekers Do Not Fight Each Other, *Security Studies*, 7(1), 114–154.
Lake, D.A. (1997). The Rise and Fall of the Russian Empire: A Theoretical Interpretation. In: K. Dawisha and B. Parrott, eds. *The End of Empire? The Transformation of the USSR in Comparative Perspective*. Armonk, New York and London: M.E. Sharpe. pp. 30–62.
Layne, Ch. (2006). The Unipolar Illusion Revisited: The Coming End of the United States' Unipolar Moment, *International Security*, 31(2), 7–41.
Lieven, D. (1995). The Russian Empire and the Soviet Union as Imperial Polities, *Journal of Contemporary History*, 30, 608–609.
Lipitsky, V. (1992). *Rossiiskaya Gazeta*, 26 June, p. 1.
Lucas, E. (2008) *The New Cold War: How the Kremlin Menaces Both Russia and the West*. London: Bloomsbury.
Mearsheimer, J. (2001). *The Tragedy of Great Power Politics*. New York, London: W.W. Norton & Co.
Mearsheimer, J. (1994/1995). The False Promise of International Institutions, *International Security*, 19(3), 5–49.
Morgan, P. (2010). Liberalism. In: A. Collins, ed. *Contemporary Security Studies*, second edition. Oxford: Oxford University Press, pp. 34–48.
Nye Jr, J.S. (2004). *Soft Power: The Means to Success in World Politics*. New York: Public Affairs.
Parrott, B. (1997). Analysing the Transformation of the Soviet Union in Comparative Perspective. In: K. Dawisha and B. Parrott, eds. *The End of Empire? The Transformation of the USSR in Comparative Perspective*. Armonk, New York and London: M.E. Sharpe, pp. 3–39.
Pipes, R. (1994). Imperial Russian Foreign Policy, *Times Literary Supplement*, 20 May, pp. 3–5.
Polyakov, Y. (1992). Rossiiskie prostory: blago ili proklyatie? *Svobodnaya mysl'*, 12, pp. 17–22.
Rywkin, M. (1980). The Russia-Wide Soviet Federated Socialist Republic (RSFSR): Privileged or Underprivileged? In: E. Allworth, ed. *Ethnic Russia in the USSR: The Dilemma of Dominance*. New York and Oxford, pp. 180–187.
Schweller, R.L. (1996). Neorealism's Status Quo Bias: What Security Dilemma?, *Security Studies*, 5(3), 90–121.
Sherr, J. (2013). *Hard Diplomacy and Soft Coercion: Russia's Influence Abroad*. London: Chatham House.
Shevtsova, L. (2007) *Russia Lost in Transition: The Yeltsin and Putin Legacies*. Brookings Institution Press.
Solzhenitsyn, A. (1980). Misconceptions about Russia are a Threat to America, *Foreign Affairs*, 58 (4), 797–834.
Spruyt, H. (1997). The Prospects for Neo-Imperial and Non-Imperial Outcomes in the Former Soviet Space. In: K. Dawisha and B. Parrott, eds. *The End of Empire? The Transformation of the USSR in Comparative Perspective*. Armonk, New York and London: M.E. Sharpe, pp. 315–337.
Trenin, D. (2011). *Post-Imperium: A Eurasian Story*. Washington DC, Moscow: Carnegie Endowment for International Peace.

Trenin, D. (2009). Russia's Spheres of Interest, Not Influence, *The Washington Quarterly*, 32 (4), 3–22.
Viggo Jakobsen, P. (2010). Coercive Diplomacy. In: A. Collins ed., *Contemporary Security Studies*, second edition. Oxford: Oxford University Press, pp. 277–298.
Wilkinson, D. (1999). Unipolarity Without Hegemony. *International Studies Review*, 1 (2), 141–172.

1 What is Russia? Russia's foreign policy orientation under Yeltsin

The collapse of the Soviet Union produced a serious national identity crisis among the Russian elite and the Russian population at large, namely over 'What is Russia?' As pointed out in the introduction, the Russian Soviet Federation Socialist Republic (RSFSR), re-baptised as 'the Russian Federation', lacked any historical legitimacy, as it was in fact a Bolshevik invention. Its external borders and internal divisions did not correspond to any pre-existing geographical, political or ethnic reality, maybe with the single exception of mid-seventeenth century Russia. This predicament was magnified by the demise of the Communist ideology, which had been for decades the source of legitimacy of both the Communist system and of the Soviet state. Thus, a heated political debate ensued on what the new Russian state should look like, where its borders ought to lie, and how far its foreign influences should extend. This chapter examines how ideas, identities and beliefs about Russia, and about its place in the world shaped and influenced the country's foreign policy behaviour in the former Soviet states (FSS). Several prominent thinkers refused to admit the possibility of a Russian state within the frame of the RSFSR and instead stressed the artificial nature of its existing borders. Political Scientist Aleksandr Tsipko, for example, argued that the RSFSR had neither a historical nor an ethnic legitimacy. 'It is essentially a vestige of the division of old Russia into separate Soviet socialist republics', Tsipko noted and added, 'this division was done in an off-hand way. No one, neither Lenin nor Stalin took a serious attitude towards the borders of these semi-state formations. As a result, the borders of the RSFSR are purely random in nature' (Tsipko, 1991a). Consequently, he pointed out, some age-old Russian areas which were colonised by people originally from Central Russia ended up as parts of Ukraine and Kazakhstan. At the same time, many purely imperial conquests carried out by Tsarist Russia, for example in the Northern Caucasus, remained within the RSFSR, as part of what Tsipko called 'lesser Russia' (Tsipko, 1991a). Moreover, like many Russians, Tsipko feared that the breakdown of the Union of Soviet Socialist Republics (USSR) would eventually lead to the disintegration of RSFSR along similar lines. 'If all the republics become sovereign states', Tsipko (1991b) argued, 'the centre will die, and along with it, the state that for centuries has been called Russia'.

Old and new ideas on 'What is Russia?'

This predicament led to new proposals by Russian thinkers which envisaged different models of reintegration of the former Soviet lands. Tsipko proposed turning the existing Commonwealth of Independent States (CIS) into an asymmetrical confederation including those countries most eager to keep close ties with Russia, namely Belarus, Georgia, Armenia, Moldova, Tajikistan and Kazakhstan (Tsipko, 1994, p. 447). Russian writer and dissident Aleksandr Solzhenitsyn in his renowned article '*Rebuilding Russia*' instead placed emphasis on the Slavic nature of Russia by advocating that Russia, Ukraine, Belarus and Northern Kazakhstan remain united in what he called a 'Russian [*Rossiisky*] Union' (Solzhenitsyn, 1990). Similarly, Konstantin Zatulin, chairman of the Russian Duma CIS Committee from 1993 to 1995 and founder of the Congress of Russian Communities (CRO), also expressed support for a union between Russia, Belarus, Ukraine and Kazakhstan, eventually to be joined by Tajikistan and Georgia.[1] Academician Aleksei Arbatov, however, taking a more pragmatic line, held the view that only an economic union with a selected group of states, particularly Ukraine and Belarus, because of their similar socio-economic developments, proved desirable.[2]

The future of 'Russia' was also closely tied to the fate of the 25 million ethnic Russians who lived outside the borders of the Russian Federation after the collapse of the Soviet Union. These Russians suddenly became 'foreigners' in their own country, and also suffered from the severing of their personal ties with family and friends living in Russia. After the collapse of the USSR, the Russian government felt responsible for the protection of their rights. Presidential advisor Sergei Stankevich stated that Russia had both the moral obligation and the political responsibility to protect the fate of Russians living in the Near Abroad, while Academician Andranik Migranyan stressed Russia's special role as the protector of Russians inhabiting the newly independent republics. 'Russia cannot be indifferent to the fate of Russians in Kazakhstan and Ukraine, or to the fate of the minorities in the autonomous entities of the seceding republics in general', he wrote (Migranyan, 1991). More radical voices, such as that of Ksenia Myalo, expressed the view that the Russian people had become a 'divided nation' as the Germans, the Jews and the Armenians had been divided in the past. Reintegration of the former Soviet republics, in one sort or another, was considered the best way to overcome such a tragedy (Myalo, 1993, p. 8).[3]

The idea of 'Russia' was also closely linked to the place that Russia, it was believed, had to occupy in the international system as well as to the country's foreign policy orientation. Should it become part of the West, should it remain part of a 'Eurasian' civilisation, or instead should Russia concentrate on its own internal development and remain isolated from the world arena? A heated debate among political scientists took place in 1992 which had a significant impact on the developments of Russian foreign policy. This debate on the overall orientation of Russian foreign policy was closely intertwined with a similar discussion on the various models of domestic transformation. It began well before the collapse of the USSR and was, to some extent, the result of a revival of Russian national sentiments. During the years of perestroika, nationalism in the RSFSR developed into two contrasting ideologies which envisioned two radically different developments of the Russian nation. On the one hand, patriotic nationalists insisted on the distinctiveness of Russian development and the specific mission of the Russian people, whereas liberal nationalists emphasised the unifying features of world civilisation and preferred to see Russians as 'normal people living in a normal country' (Chuprinin, 1990, p. 211). As Viktor Zaslavsky rightly explained, this reflected an earlier clash between the liberal-democratic, Europe-oriented anti-Communist nationalism and the xenophobic, authoritarian and anti-Western nationalism that had already occurred in the Soviet Union in the late 1960s. It took the form of an ideological struggle between Russian intellectuals connected with the more liberal journal *Novy mir*, and those grouped around the journals *Molodaya gvardiya* and *Nash sovremennik*, who took up the banner of Russian patriotism (Zaslavsky, 1992, p. 80). The latter combined a genuine concern for the destruction of Russian culture and peasantry, the Russian Orthodox Church and Russian traditions, with a defence of Stalinism as the legitimate continuation of Russian imperial traditions. This movement suffered from an internal contradiction, since its supporters could never decide between either a 'Russian revival' or 'the preservation of the empire' (Streliany, 1990).

During the late 1980s, the imperial idea slowly lost ground, in view of the growing influence of liberals and the dissemination of nationalist ideas among the Russian liberal-democratic intelligentsia. General perceptions about the economic costs of the empire on the Russian population increased the desire of 'seceding' from the rest of the Soviet republics. For the first time, an anti-imperial Russian nationalism, which aspired toward the creation of a 'national' Russian state, emerged, as noted by Zaslavsky (1992). Liberal nationalists called on the Russian people to cast off the backward, non-European, non-Christian component of the Soviet Union and to return to the home of European culture. They supported 'the opening of Russia to the influences of the industrially developed countries', and Russia's 'transition to a market economy and [its] integration into the world market system' (Zaslavsky, 1992, p. 88). Yet, as imperialist nationalism lost ground, a more conservative group of Russian national patriots adopted a 'Russia first' isolationist posture, 'understood not only as a separation from all non-Slavic or even non-Russian republics, but even more crucially as a repudiation of the West and a search for a specifically Russian way of life and Russian spiritual values' (Zaslavsky, 1992, p. 88).

The failed August 1991 coup dealt a major blow to the Russian imperial nationalist idea. The autumn of 1991 saw the progressive implementation of liberal nationalist ideas, which resulted in the disintegration of the Soviet Union in December 1991 and the emergence of a new Russian state. The new geopolitical reality confronted liberal nationalists with a series of new problems. On the one hand, many Soviet republics, usually the most economically dependent on Russia, proved reluctant to secede from Russia. On the other, Russia was forced to handle a series of delicate issues, such as the presence of large Russian minorities living in the newly independent states, various border disputes, and the existence of several dozen nationalities and ethno-territorial units within the Russian Federation, which were expected to press their claims for independence from Russia. In view of these difficulties, imperialist nationalist ideas in support of the restoration of the Soviet Union, albeit in a new form, again made themselves heard. Among the Russian population deep nostalgia for the Soviet Union gained ground as people found it hard to come to terms with the existence of the Russian state within its new boundaries and the development of the former Soviet republics, particularly Ukraine and Belarus, as independent states. However, the longing for empire did not immediately translate into an active and consistent strategy aimed at the restoration of the USSR. Neither did it lead to the effective creation of an informal empire, despite the fact that certain aspects of Russia's policies towards the FSS, particularly towards states belonging to the Russian-led CIS, did acquire a neo-imperialist character in the early to mid-1990s, as will be shown in the next chapters.

The foreign policy of the new Russian state

Russia's pro-Western orientation (1991–1992)

The collapse of the USSR opened up a new era in the foreign policy of the Russian Federation, no longer a republic of the defunct Soviet Union but now an independent sovereign state. Following on the lines of the Russian national liberal programme, Foreign Minister Andrei Kozyrev adopted a distinctly pro-Western orientation and a clearly anti-imperialist approach, based on the recognition of the former Soviet republics as sovereign and independent states. This also entailed the rejection of any forcible change of borders among the FSS.[4] 'We simply have to learn to live as independent states and to view each other as equal partners', Kozyrev wrote in an article on *Izvestiya* in January 1992 (Kozyrev, 1992a). The newly independent states were encouraged freely to join a new organisation with Russia, the CIS. The latter was seen by Russian leaders as a way of preserving a common economic and politico-military space in the former Soviet territory and as a means of further deepening integration. This project was promoted on a voluntary, non-coercive fashion. Kozyrev sustained that only natural, voluntary ties among the CIS, and not forceful integration, would create a viable and solid institution (Kozyrev, 1992a). He called for the creation of 'belt of good-neighbourliness' along the entire perimeter of the Russian Federation, and the withdrawal of Russia's military presence from abroad (Leonov, 1992). Similar views were shared by Galina Starovoitova, Yeltsin's advisor on nationality issues, who claimed that Russians had to discard their imperial legacy once and for all, and abandon a significant part of responsibility for developments in the former 'colonies of the empire' (Starovoitova, 1992). She believed that the Soviet Union was the last disintegrating empire and saw decolonisation as 'the basic meaning of [Russia's] present history' (Inform-TV, 1991). She supported a Western-oriented foreign policy because, according to her, 'the Russian people, by their mentality, are oriented to European values' and stressed that Russia could not be divided by the Ural mountains between Europe and Asia, East and West (Inform-TV, 1991).

These views were reflected in Russia's policies not only towards the CIS but also in Russia's approaches to the world as a whole. During the early 1990s, Russia's foreign policy was aimed above all at creating a favourable domestic and international environment which would facilitate the economic and political transformation of Russia. Kozyrev repeatedly stressed Russia's desire to join the club of the more dynamically democratic states in the world, and Moscow's wishes to transform its old enemies in the West into partners and eventually allies (Kozyrev, 1992b). President Yeltsin also several times expressed Russia's intentions to cooperate with the United States in order to bring a long era of Cold War confrontation to an end. 'We will no longer consider ourselves potential opponents, but allies', he said in the spring of 1992 (*Izvestiya*, 1992). In a speech at the United Nations Security Council (UNSC) in February 1992, Yeltsin went as far as proposing the creation of a global defence system in cooperation with the United States, based on the establishment of a joint global anti-missile project (*Rossiiskaya gazeta*, 1992). The Russian Ministry of Foreign Affairs (MFA) in turn envisaged the fulfilment of the country's national interests through Russia's participation in various global and regional security systems, such as the United Nations (UN), the Conference on Security and Co-operation in Europe (CSCE) and even NATO, and through the development of multilateral agreements and international cooperation – espousing a clear liberal-internationalist view (Leonov, 1992).

An active foreign policy debate begins (1992)

This pro-Western stance immediately provoked a negative reaction from influential academics and members of Russia's political elite, and a heated discussion on Russia's national identity and the orientation of its foreign policy soon ensued. The old nineteenth-century debate between *Slavophiles* and *Westerners* resurfaced, although with some noticeable differences due to the new Russian internal circumstances and the changed international environment. *Liberal Westernisers*, following directly on Gorbachev's *New Political Thinking*, stressed the link between Russia's domestic political configuration and its foreign policy orientation. Scholar Nikolai Kosopalov, insisted that the primary concern of Russia's foreign policy had to be the establishment and the consolidation of a democratic and liberal domestic political system. Only by transforming its internal structure, Kosopalov argued, would Russia be able to discard its old imperial legacy and its assertive foreign policy traditions (Kosopalov, 1993). *Liberal Westernisers* cast off pre-existing Soviet foreign policy traditions of a realist nature which tended to perceive the world as a struggle for power among states. Instead, they supported the development of an international system based on the primacy of international law and cooperation through international organisations. These views, which were adopted by the Russian MFA, received very harsh criticisms from Russian *Imperial Nationalists*, and from their new variant, the *Neo-Eurasianists*, all of whom could not resign themselves to the loss of the Soviet Empire.

Russian *Imperial Nationalists*, such as the writer Aleksandr Prokhanov; Eduard Limonov, founder of the National Bolshevik Party; and Sergei Baburin, leader of the Russian nationalist opposition in the Supreme Soviet, all regretted the collapse of the Soviet Union, and refused to consider such developments as irreversible. They believed that the Russian empire had to be recreated in one form or another. Limonov advocated the re-creation of a single powerful state 'within the limits of Russian civilisation' (1992). Russian borders should, as a minimum, include those areas inhabited by Russians, and as maximum cover those regions resided by people who regarded themselves as belonging to the Russian civilisation (Limonov, 1992). Baburin questioned the new borders of Russia, arguing that the Russian Federation was 'an offspring of Bolshevik experiments ... an unnatural formation' (Todres, 1992). Similar views were shared by high-ranking officials in the Russian government, such as Vice-President Aleksandr Rutskoi, who refused to equate the Russian Federation with the true borders of Russia, and saw the CIS as 'a transitional form between the former Soviet Union and a new unitary state to be created by the former Union republics' (Rutskoi, 1992a). Rutskoi called for the restoration of a single democratic state in the territory of the Eurasian landmass. If the Union could not be revived, Russia had to become a strong power and discontinue its economic assistance to other CIS states, he argued (Rutskoi, 1992b). *Imperialist Nationalists* were endowed with strong anti-Western sentiments, and as such they rejected Russia's membership of the International Monetary Fund (IMF) and other Western-dominated organisations. In sharp contrast to Liberal-Western thinking, they tended to interpret the world as an arena of perennial struggle between two global forces, one maritime – or Atlanticist – and the other continental – or Eurasianist – which had only one predetermined outcome. 'The future belongs to the East not to the West', Yury Borodai wrote (Borodai, 1991, p. 147).

These views very much coincided with the ideas of *Neo-Eurasianists*, like Konstantin Pleshakov and Brontoi Bediurov. Digging in the sources of the Eurasian movement of the 1920s–1930s, *Eurasianists* stressed the unique cultural and geopolitical character of the Eurasian space, going as far as bestowing Russia with a special mission in Eurasia. 'Living together within common borders for decades or centuries has formed a common space of civilisation', Pleshakov argued, and added,

> in a sense, Russia does not end on the border of the Baltic states or on the foothills of the Great Caucasian Range, any more than it does on the steppe-lands of northern Kazakhstan. The empire is gone. But its geopolitical, political, military, economic, cultural and intellectual space is not. Russia is closely integrated in the affairs of all the new independent regions of the former Soviet Union.
>
> (Pleshakov, 1993, p. 20)

Pleshakov foresaw total chaos in continental Eurasia, and a redrawing of frontiers and war, unless Russia dominated the region militarily, and deterred conflicts and potential aggressors (Pleshakov, 1993, p. 20). In a similar tone, Brontoi Bediurov repeated the earlier Eurasianist view that Eurasia constituted a unique continent. 'We are indeed an integral state-political and cultural-historical continent, a distinctive Eurasian cosmos. We are neither Europe nor Asia; we are both of them together' he wrote, and stressed the need for all the FSS to live together (Bediurov 1993). Although *Eurasianists* advocated the restoration of the Soviet Union, their views remained at a theoretical level, given that they neither put forward clear foreign policy proposals on how to achieve the desired goals, nor did they examine more practical issues such as the resolution of ethnic conflicts or the protection of Russian minorities in the near abroad.

More moderate *Eurasianists*, such as Sergei Goncharov and Professor Aleksei Vasilev limited themselves to stressing Russia's links with the Islamic world and emphasised the need to develop close relations with predominantly Muslim former Soviet states (Goncharov, 1992).

> The Eurasian space that used to be occupied by the Soviet Union and the largest part of which is now occupied by Russia, has traditionally been a zone of cohabitation, interpretation and interaction between the Slavic (primarily Russian) and Turkic ethnic groups, between Orthodox and Moslems.
>
> (Vasilev, 1992)

Therefore, he added 'it is in the interests [of both Islam and Russia] to use all conceivable means to convert inevitable conflicts between them into a non-violent form and work to resolve them' (Vasilev, 1992). These views were challenged by leading democrats, such as Yury Afanasev, who argued that Russians had to repudiate their pretence 'to originality, uniqueness, and a special predestination'. Russia, in Afanasev's view, represented an exhausted form of 'Eurasian civilisation which combined Buddhist and Byzantine Christian elements, and which had to be rejected in favour of the contemporary Western model'.

Kozyrev's pro-Western, 'anti-imperialist' foreign policy approach received also more moderate, though certainly more influential critics from Russian scholars and from other members of the political elite during the course of 1992 and 1993. *Moderate Liberals* such as Russian Ambassador Vladimir Lukin, and Academician Aleksei Arbatov neither questioned the collapse of the Soviet Union nor challenged the independence of the other former Soviet republics. They argued instead that the Helsinki principle of the inviolability of borders should form the basis of relations among the former Soviet republics (Arbatov, 1993, p. 27). Although their views were not significantly different from those of the *Liberal Westernisers*, they emphasised the need for a distinctly Russian foreign and security policy based on the specifics of Russia's geopolitical reality. Consequently they placed highest priority on Russia's relations with the newly independent states. 'Relations with its closer neighbours have always been a priority for Russia', Lukin wrote in the autumn of 1992, 'but the break-up of the Soviet Union, having turned Russia's former territories into new and independent neighbours, has transformed traditional interests into something much more complex and vital' (Lukin, 1992, pp. 66–67). Lukin believed that Russia had a special role to play in the Eurasian heartland, 'Russia cannot just passively observe threatening developments taking place within the zone of its vital interests, especially in areas inhabited by millions of Russians' (Lukin, 1992, pp. 66–67). Arbatov argued, however, that Russia had to be extremely cautious as far as intervention in the internal affairs of other republics was concerned, even when invited by local governments. Peacekeeping or peace-enforcement operations, if conducted, had to be carried out on the basis of multilateral decisions and actions. Russia's main role should be that of an impartial mediator. Arbatov supported the use of sanctions, including the use of military force, only as an instrument of last resort, in order to protect the rights of minorities, especially of Russian-speakers living beyond the Russian Federation (Arbatov, 1992).

Moderate Nationalists such as Academician Andranik Migranyan, and Evgeny Ambartsumov, Supreme Soviet Chairman of the Committee on International Affairs and Foreign Economic Relations, on the other hand, could not reconcile themselves to the demise of the Soviet Union. Although they did not advocate the reunification of the former USSR by military force, they adopted a very assertive stance as far as the former Soviet space was concerned, and vehemently criticised Russia's pro-Western foreign policy orientation. According to them, Russia's specific role in the former Soviet space resulted from the presence of over 30 million Russian-speakers in those states, and the arbitrary character of the borders of the former USSR, which had given rise to inter-ethnic conflicts and clashes between nationalities. According to Migranyan, 'many of these territories, such as South Ossetia, Karabakh, Crimea and Transdniestria, were part of the Russian Empire long before they were incorporated into the newly formed independent states', and therefore they had to be protected by Russia (Migranyan, 1992). Ambartsumov was particularly emphatic on the need to call the entire geopolitical space of the former USSR a *sphere of Russia's vital interests*, and of having such interests recognised by the world community. In his view, Russian leaders had to make sure that the international community recognised Russia's role as 'the political and military guarantor of stability in the post-Soviet space' (Eggert, 1992). Ambartsumov believed that the dismantling of the USSR was a completely irresponsible and not properly considered step. Only through cooperation with the former Soviet republics could Russia overcome the current crisis. 'The fusion of the CIS states is inevitable', he thought, 'because it is impossible to draw geographic and even family borders' (Ambartsumov, 1992).

Russian leaders adopt a more assertive policy (1993)

Faced with harsh criticism from influential academic circles, and under strong pressure from the powerful centrist groups in the Supreme Soviet, Yeltsin and

Kozyrev began progressively to adopt a more assertive stance regarding the post-Soviet-space in the autumn of 1992.[5] In a speech at the Foreign Ministry Collegium on 27 October 1992, Yeltsin stressed the need to take national interests into account when formulating foreign policy and criticised the 'excessive timidity' with which the Russian MFA was behaving in the world community, especially in the near abroad. In his view, this resulted from what he called an 'inverted imperial syndrome' (*Krasnaya zvezda*, 1992). 'We are hesitant to speak about our Russian national interests', Yeltsin said, 'we are constantly afraid that we will be accused of great-power chauvinism ... worst of all is the fact that we are not countering attempts by some of the former USSR republics to resolve their problems at Russia's expense' (*Krasnaya zvezda*, 1992).

In an attempt to reach broader consensus, Kozyrev presented to parliament, in December 1992, a new *Draft Foreign Policy Outline*, which gave clear priority to relations with Russia's neighbours in the former Soviet space. Russia would aim at establishing a 'belt of good-neighbourliness' along its borders and would work towards the development of multilateral forms of cooperation with the CIS states, the document stated (Kozyrev, 1992c). Particular attention was devoted to the settlement of conflicts in the CIS, the defence of the CIS external borders, and the protection of the rights of Russian minorities. Regarding the latter, Kozyrev proposed protecting 'the rights, lives and dignity of Russians above all by political means and diplomatic methods, and using the mechanisms of international organisations', and not by force (Kozyrev, 1992c). If these methods failed, however, 'the carefully considered application of economic and military force, not in the Yugoslav version, needless to say, but within the framework of the law', had to be envisaged (Kozyrev, 1992c). Despite the growing focus of Russia's foreign policy on the former Soviet space as opposed to the West, the document still contained elements of Kozyrev's pro-Western stance and clearly reflected an anti-imperialist approach. The promotion of Russian democracy, the creation of favourable conditions for the development of a market economy, and the integration of Russia into the world community 'in a manner befitting its status as a great power', were considered fundamental national interests. Foreign and domestic policies were strongly connected, and priority was given to individual, human and minority rights. In its relations with other states, Russia committed itself to use diplomatic methods. Force would be used only in a carefully considered manner, and strictly within the framework of international law. Moreover, Russia would try to transform the previous relations of global confrontation with the West into a system of global cooperation. More importantly, it would aim at partnership and allied relations with the West (Kozyrev, 1992c).

Although Russia's policies in 1992 cannot be characterised as either neo-imperialist or hegemonic, the Russian leadership did pay growing attention to events in the former Soviet states. Particular efforts were devoted by the President and the Foreign Minister to mediate in the military conflicts that erupted in former Soviet territories, as Russian troops became involved in peacekeeping operations in Transdniestria and South Ossetia. Despite the disintegration of the post-Soviet economic and military spaces, the Russian government attempted to preserve a certain degree of military and economic cooperation among CIS states. Russian diplomats moreover, conducted various efforts aimed at settling the thorny issue of discrimination against Russian minorities in the Baltic states. The adoption of a more active policy and a more assertive rhetoric were determined by a series of key factors. First and foremost, the failure of economic reforms led to a deterioration of the economic and social environment in Russia and to a growing dissatisfaction among the population at large. As a result, the Russian political leadership became more vulnerable to pressure from nationalist circles and from increasingly powerful and uncompromising factions within the Supreme Soviet, and began giving in to their demands. In May 1992, Yeltsin set up the Security Council under the leadership of its Secretary, Yury Skokov, a promoter of *Moderate Nationalist* ideas. The Ministry of Defence (MoD) in turn, became more directly involved in policy formulation and policy-making, openly rivalling the MFA.

Second, the economic interdependence of all republics and the difficulties of 'going it alone' soon became apparent. The potential collapse of neighbouring economies meant that Russia could not simply stand idly by. Deep economic recession in the former Soviet states was bound to have direct negative repercussions on Russia's own industrial and agricultural production. This explained the leadership's efforts to strengthen economic and political cooperation within the CIS framework. Third, the eruption of ethnic conflicts along Russia's borders, which created casualties among the local Russian population and among the Russian troops located in the areas of tension, and resulted in widespread instability, prompted the Russian government to react. Moreover, Russian minorities became victims of discrimination, especially in the Baltic states and in certain Central Asian countries. Last but not least, disappointment over Western behaviour led to the partial discard of pro-Western views. The rather limited financial support provided by Western governments and by international financial institutions, and the unfulfilled expectations, as far as international cooperation with Europe, the US and NATO was concerned, led to a general disenchantment with the West and Western ideas.

During the early spring of 1993, as pressure from the opposition increased in the domestic front, Russia's foreign policy discourse became much more self-confident. Speaking at the Civic Union Forum in late February 1993, Yeltsin stressed the need for closer integration among the CIS states and clearly stated Russia's special role in the territory of the former USSR,

> Stopping all armed conflicts on the territory of the former USSR is in Russia's vital interest. The world community sees more and more clearly Russia's special responsibility in this difficult undertaking. I believe the time has come for distinguished international organisations, including the UN, to grant Russia special powers as a guarantor of peace and stability in the regions of the former USSR.
>
> (Russian Television, 1993)

In mid-March, Yeltsin directly appealed to the leaders of the CIS states, calling for deeper military and economic cooperation. Yeltsin expressed Russia's eagerness to cooperate with the CIS states, 'on the basis of equality, in order to achieve further economic and social development, and so as to provide the necessary stability and security in the entire CIS space' (*Nezavisimaya gazeta*, 1993). Although these speeches were intended primarily for internal consumption and CIS support, they also pointed to a new direction in Russia's foreign policy in favour of closer ties with the FSS. Above all, they indicated Yeltsin's readiness to compromise with the opposition on foreign policy issues, in order to preserve the upper hand in the Russian domestic agenda. As a result, during 1993, Russian foreign policy became significantly more assertive and the political discourse took a more nationalist tone, focusing increasingly on developments in the Near Abroad, particularly on the need to deepen CIS integration and settle military conflicts.

The *Basic Provisions of the Russian Federation Foreign Policy Concept* (hereafter *Basic Provisions*) approved by Yeltsin in April 1993, provided the best indication of this change in course. Primarily the work of Yury Skokov, but approved by all the major Russian ministries involved in foreign policy, the document significantly diverged from the Foreign Ministry Draft both in terms of tone and content. It proposed a firmer policy by Moscow towards the West and a more active engagement by Russia in the FSS (Chernov, 1993). Top priority was given to relations with the former Soviet republics and to the deepening of integration among the states of the former Soviet Union – integration which had to be based, however, on principles of strictly voluntary participation and reciprocity. Russia was entrusted with the responsibility of strengthening stability and security on the territory of the former Soviet Union, and this explained the inclusion in the document of provisions on the development of CIS military and political cooperation. These included the creation of an effective collective security system, the protection by Russia of the CIS' external borders, and the preservation of Russian military infrastructure in the former Soviet states, as part of an integral CIS military-security system. Human rights' violations, armed conflicts along Russia's periphery, and any actions intended to weaken or undermine Russia's international prestige, its territorial integrity, and its efforts at CIS integration, were seen as potential threats to Russia's security (Chernov, 1993).

A broad consensus is reached (1994–1995)

The approval of the *Basic Provisions* reflected the emergence of a broad consensus among the various sections of the Russian political elite over Russia's role in the world and its relations with the FSS. The tenets endowed in the Concept reflected the views of *Moderate Nationalists* and, to a great extent, indicated a readiness by Moscow actively to engage in the former Soviet space in order to fulfil Russia's national interests. Such views continued to permeate Russian foreign policy thinking throughout 1993–1995, despite the military victory of

President Yeltsin over conservative forces in his clash with the Russian Supreme Soviet in October 1993. In the autumn of 1993, the Russian President, and in particular Foreign Minister Kozyrev adopted an increasingly assertive tone. Between September and November 1993, Kozyrev issued a series of statements which not only stressed Russia's unique role as the guarantor of stability in the post-Soviet space, but also clearly expressed Russia's willingness to remain the dominant power in the region, ascribing to Russia a clear hegemonic role in the FSS. In an article in *Nezavisimaya gazeta* on 22 September 1993 Kozyrev mentioned Russia's historical duty to provide stability to the areas of the former Soviet Union. 'This is not a "neo-imperialistic" space, he wrote, but a unique geopolitical one in which no one is going to keep the peace for Russia' (Kozyrev, 1993b). In a subsequent article on 13 October 1993, Kozyrev's words became even firmer, as he maintained that 'no international organisation or group of states is able to replace Russia's peace-keeping efforts in the specific post-Soviet space' and added, that

> either [Russia starts] carrying out military actions for the support and restoration of peace in the areas of our traditional geopolitical interests, or [we] will lose our influence there, and the vacuum will be filled by others, including unfriendly forces or even forces competing against us.
>
> (Kozyrev, 1993b)

Similarly, at a Foreign Ministry's conference on 18 January 1994, Kozyrev characterised the protection of the rights of Russians in the former Soviet state as one of Russia's main strategic aims, and stressed the need to maintain a military presence in all former Soviet states, an area where 'Russia's vital strategic interests' lay (Portnikov, 1994). Kozyrev feared that if Russian troops withdrew, the security vacuum would be filled by forces which might be hostile and unfriendly to Russia (Portnikov, 1994).

Thereafter, Russian foreign policy paid increasing attention to the strengthening of CIS economic and military integration, although emphasis was also placed on the notion that integration had to be cost-effective and not detrimental to Russia's interests (Kozyrev, 1994; Ostankino TV, 1994). Renewed importance was also given to the idea that that Russia had to become a strong economic and political state first, before CIS integration could move ahead. It was assumed that a strong and economically successful Russia would act as a magnet of deeper CIS integration. Following along those lines, the *Strategic Course of the Russian Federation towards the member-states of the CIS*, was approved by Yeltsin in September 1995. The document stated that Russia's main aim was to create an economic and political association of states, 'capable of occupying a fitting place in the world' (*Strategicheskii Kurs*, 1995). Integration was considered essential for the sake of containing centrifugal tendencies inside Russia and for ensuring lasting stability within the CIS states. Russia was to become the leading force behind the formation of a new system of inter-state political and economic relations in the post-Soviet space, while its policies in the area would take strict account of Russia's national interests (*Strategicheskii Kurs*, 1995).

During 1993–1995, therefore, overall agreement was reached among the government and most members of the Russian political elite on Russia's foreign policy priorities. Russia's foreign policy was to focus on deepening economic, military and political integration within the CIS framework, on keeping the peace in the post-Soviet space, and on protecting the rights of Russian minorities living beyond Russia's borders. Agreement was also reached on the notion that Russia had to strive to remain a Great Power, and this was to be reflected in Russia's hegemonic position in the Near Abroad. The reaching of an overall consensus on foreign policy reflected a change in foreign policy focus by Yeltsin and Kozyrev, and clearly indicated that *Moderate Liberal* and *Moderate Nationalist* views had managed to reach the higher echelons of power. *Liberal Westernisers* in turn became increasingly marginalised from power and their views lost popularity among the elite. They either abandoned the government – Gennady Burbulis, Yegor Gaidar and Boris Fyodorov had all left by early 1994 – or adopted more conservative views – Kozyrev and Yeltsin. Moreover, the MoD, supportive of an active involvement in the former Soviet space, played a growing role in foreign policy formulation and implementation, given that military issues remained high on the agenda. In addition, the security and defence agencies – the MoD, the Foreign Intelligence Service, and the Federal Security Service (FSB) – gained major influence in policy-making and Yeltsin increasingly relied on his old team of subordinates from his time as Secretary of the Sverdlovsk Communist Party Organisation for advice – Yury Petrov, Viktor Iliushin and Oleg Lobov – most of whom had quite authoritarian credentials. Furthermore, representatives of *Moderate Nationalist* thinking became part of Yeltsin's team of advisors, such as the Academician Andranik Migranyan.

The change in the foreign policy approach of both Yeltsin and Kozyrev reflected, to a great extent, their own political weaknesses. Yeltsin's growing dependence on the military and security services to keep his hold on power after the October 1993 storming of the Russian parliament, and the gains of the ultra-nationalist politician Vladimir Zhirinovsky and his Liberal Democratic Party of Russia (LDPR) in the 1993 Duma elections, compelled the President to adopt a more assertive stance, in order to retain their support. But this mood of national accord was brought at a price. Lack of clarity in policy and disarray in decision-making were to characterise Russian foreign policy-making during 1993–1995. Foreign policy tended to reflect attempts to reach a broad compromise and satisfy domestic constituencies, rather than consistently follow Russia's national interest (Malcolm, 1996, p. 139). It is important to note however, that the increasingly forceful discourse adopted by the Russian leadership was not always reflected in policy-making in the former Soviet space. Some of Russia's actions in the ex-USSR region were indeed quite assertive. During 1993, all FSS, except for the Baltic states, were brought into the CIS, and Russia became deeply involved in the military conflicts that flared up beyond its borders – by providing military support to the warring factions, by introducing peacekeeping forces, and establishing military bases. Yet, in the economic field, Russia behaved much less assertively. The CIS economic space underwent further disintegration, as Russia seemed increasingly unwilling and also incapable of paying for the high price of integration. Although major economic integration treaties were signed in 1995–1996, they were never fully implemented. This was due, to a great extent, to the unwillingness of Russia's leaders to cover the high costs involved and to force integration upon CIS states. Russian energy prices to CIS states progressively approached world levels, and Russian subsidies to CIS states were significantly curtailed – although Russia tried to obtain control over the Caspian oil transportation routes and to participate in major oil and gas deals in the area. As far as military integration was concerned, the year 1993 saw a further disintegration of the common military space as CIS states moved ahead with creating their own armed forces. Yet, in 1994 and 1995 Russia began progressively to restore parts of the former joint military infrastructure by reaching bilateral military agreements with most CIS states. Thus, by the end of 1996, many elements of the previous military system were partly restored. Russia defended more assertively the rights of Russian minorities in the Baltic states but refrained from adopting radical measures, such as the imposition of an economic blockade or the prolonged suspension of troops withdrawals. Russia's policies in this field remained restricted to diplomatic initiatives, as by 1994 Russia had withdrawn all its troops from the region.

Despite Russia's more assertive behaviour in various aspects of its relations with the FSS, and the overall consensus reached in foreign policy, differences of opinion remained and debates over foreign policy did not stop. Throughout 1994 and 1995, the debate continued, albeit in a less passionate manner. The growing assertiveness of Russian foreign policy led to growing criticisms, on the one hand, from *Liberal Westernisers* and *Moderate Liberals* who became alarmed about the radical shifts in Russian foreign policy. Professor Vyacheslav Dashichev and Aleksei Arbatov expressed great concern over the Russian leadership's apparent efforts to transform the former Soviet Union into a sphere of Russia's special influence. Dashichev (1994) saw Russia's policies towards the Near Abroad as a return to Great-Power expansionism, and insisted that only a concept of interdependence could serve as the basis of CIS integration. Arbatov (1994) recognised that Russia had special interests in the near abroad but considered the claiming of 'special responsibilities' as counter-productive. Similarly, the *Council for Foreign and Defence Policy* (CFDP), an organ which brought defence and foreign policy experts together, produced a document, *Strategy for Russia (2)*, which expressed regret over the deterioration of relations with the West, and stated concern over Russia's increasing isolation in the world arena, while worrying about a possible revival of the Cold War. Russian leadership's Great-Power rhetoric was creating suspicions that Russia was aiming at 'imperial revanche' (*Nezavisimaya gazeta*, 1994, p. 4).

On the other hand, *Moderate Nationalists* and *Imperialist Nationalist*, also criticised Russia's foreign policy behaviour, but from the opposite angle. They believed Kozyrev's new policies reflected only cosmetic changes and expressed great worries over Russia's growing isolation in the world arena, made more evident by NATO's enlargement plans (Migranyan, 1994; Deikin, 1995). Russia's inability to counter NATO's enlargement and to influence effectively Western policy in Bosnia during the September–December of 1995 Dayton negotiations, made Russia's isolation and its loss of Great Power status all the more evident (Karpov, 1995). Communist Party leader Gennady Zyuganov made it clear that his party would fight for the restoration of Russia's Great Power and prestige if he won the Presidential elections. Zyuganov argued that he would restore Russia's role as the unique guarantor of security and stability in Eurasia, if he came to power, and would work towards the restoration of the Soviet Union – thus attesting to a clearly neo-imperialist mindset (Zyuganov, 1996). Zyuganov based his arguments on the assertion that Russia belonged to a different, 'communal' type of civilisation, which was prevalent in Asia, and which was in opposition to Western individualist approaches to politics.[6] Vladimir Zhirinovsky, in turn, called for the creation of a powerful new Russian state within the old Soviet Union borders, to be divided into tsarist-like provinces rather than ethnically based republics (LDPR, 1995). He also called for drastic action against the discrimination of Russian minorities in the Baltic states, Kazakhstan and Moldova (Zyuganov, 1992). *Conservative Nationalists*, moreover, saw Western, and in particular American, increased involvement in the FSS with great concern (Migranyan, 1994). These were, however, extreme views. Although criticism of the Foreign Ministry's policies on 'near' and 'far abroad' issues continued to be voiced during 1994–1995, the Russian Duma, however, took a less hostile stance than the Supreme Soviet had in the past and proved more ready to engage in negotiation and persuasion (Ostapchuk, 1994; Pravda, 1996, p. 209).

Yevgeny Primakov and the doctrine of 'multipolarity'

With the appointment of Yevgeny Primakov at the head of the Russian Foreign Ministry in January 1996, the country's foreign policy became more articulate, better organised, and no longer the object of fierce debate among political parties and interest groups. The focus turned to top priority issues, such as managing relations with the West, responding to NATO's enlargement, resolving ethno-territorial conflicts along Russia's southern and western periphery, and deepening CIS integration, primarily with those countries most willing to cooperate with Russia. A Statist-realist at heart, Primakov placed great emphasis on the need to strengthen the Russian state – understood in Russia as *gosudarstvennichestvo* – and on the necessity to enhance the country's position and influence in the international arena – defined as *derzhavnost'*. His views resembled, to a certain extent, those of Russian *Moderate Conservatives*, although he did not entirely share their strong anti-Western stance. Despite the country's economic and military weaknesses, Primakov held the view that Russia remained a Great Power, which had to be respected and recognised as such by other major international players (Chigrin, 1998). Although there was a clear understanding that Russia's influence in the international arena had significantly diminished over the past five to six years, the consensus persisted among the Russian elite that Russia was destined to become a Great Power again. To this end, Moscow had to conduct an active foreign policy aimed at 'consolidating Russia's positions as a great power', and directed at making Russia 'one of the influential centres of the developing multi-polar world', the *National Security Strategy* read (*Rossiiskaya gazeta*, 1997). This required the formation of a fully integrated, voluntary association of CIS states, which together could play a relevant role in the international arena (*Rossiiskaya gazeta*, 1997). In other words, Russia's Great-Power status was closely linked to the place it occupied and the influence it exerted in the former Soviet space. The main objective, in Primakov's view, was to 'achieve a situation in which the CIS [became] an important centre of global economic growth and international stability', as he noted in a speech to the UN General Assembly, in September 1996 (*Rossiiskaya gazeta*, 1996). The deepening and development of relations with CIS member states was also seen as essential to ensure socio-political stability along Russia's borders, and ultimately to 'prevent centrifugal phenomena [from occurring] within Russia itself' (*Rossiiskaya gazeta*, 1997).

Relations with the West in general and with the United States in particular, had to be conducted on the basis of equality and mutual respect. Rather than creating a strategic alliance with Washington, where Moscow would invariably take a subordinate role, Primakov advocated establishing a mutually advantageous partnership with the United States, which would take the interests of both sides into account (Kondrashov, 1996a). In Primakov's view, the bipolar configuration of the international system which had characterised much of the Cold War was slowly being replaced by a *unipolar* world organisation, which was dominated by the United States. Moreover, Russian leaders believed that the West was trying to take advantage of Russia's current fragility and was attempting to weaken Russia's global positions, by preventing the further integration of countries within the CIS framework (*Rossiikaya gazeta*, 1997). Such a predicament had to be avoided, and instead, a *multipolar* world, where Russia played a leading role had to be established (Chigrin, 1998). 'The bipolar world of the previously rival superpowers and blocs must evolve not into a *unipolar* world under the command of the United States, but into a *multipolar* world where Russia has more latitude to protect its national interests', Primakov noted (Kondrashov, 1996b). This could be achieved, by diversifying foreign relations away from the United States, and by establishing closer ties not only with Russia's European partners but also with countries in Asia and the Middle East, and in particular, by developing a strategic partnership with India and China, in order to counter-balance the United States' world hegemony (Tsygankov, 2010, pp. 110–112).

This doctrine of *multipolarity*, which reflected a structural realist line of thinking did not, however, exclude the possibility of fruitful cooperation with the United States and its allies in certain areas of common interests, such as counter-proliferation, disarmament, counter-terrorism, and European security. This indicated a readiness also to embrace cooperative internationalist behaviour whenever it was considered necessary. Despite serious disagreement over key security issues, such as NATO enlargement, and Russia's sense of vulnerability vis-à-vis the West, Moscow proved ready, under Primakov, to engage in fruitful cooperation with the West. Until the Kosovo crisis in 1999, Primakov actually avoided any unnecessary confrontation with Europe and the United States (*Rossiiskaya gazeta*, 1997).[7] Instead, during his tenure as Foreign Minister, Russia signed the first all-encompassing cooperation agreement with NATO, the *Founding Act on Mutual Relations, Cooperation and Security*, which set up the Permanent Joint Council (PJC), a standing body that brought NATO and Russian officials together on a regular basis. Moreover, in December 1997, the 1994 EU–Russia *Partnership and Cooperation Agreement*, which created the basis for deeper economic ties between the two entities, came into force.

NATO's war in Kosovo in the spring of 1999, however, significantly altered Russia's perceptions of NATO and the West. It created great concern in Russia that the West was trying to replace key tenets of international law such as the respect for the sovereignty and the territorial integrity of states with new notions of 'limited sovereignty' and 'humanitarian intervention' (Ivanov, 2000). Moscow proved particularly worried over the possibility that the same military actions that had been conducted by NATO against Yugoslavia in Kosovo could eventually be carried out against Russia – in Chechnya – or against countries or regions in its immediate neighbourhood – in Nagorno-Karabakh for example (Baranovsky, 2000, p. 258). This would have been further facilitated by the enlargement of NATO into eastern Europe – in March 1999, NATO admitted three new members, Poland, the Czech Republic and Hungary – and the deployment of the Alliance's military infrastructure closer to Russia's borders, which would result from such an enlargement. Furthermore, in April 1999, NATO adopted a new *Strategic Concept* that envisioned 'out-of-area' military operations. Even though these operations were to take place within the framework of international law, the Concept provided the basis for NATO's military actions beyond its borders, potentially close to Russian territory. These key developments were all seen as threatening Russia's national security directly. Similarly, American plans to amend the Anti-Ballistic Missile (ABM) treaty and deploy a National Missile Defence system in Europe, as well as American and British military operations in Iraq in 1998, which took place without a renewed and explicit UNSC mandate, were all perceived as undermining strategic stability and challenging key principles of international law.

These new negative predicaments, required, in Primakov's view, a more forceful reaction from the Kremlin, in order to better protect the interests of Russia. This involved efforts to strengthen the Russian state, the pursuit of global multipolarity, and pressures on the West to ensure it abided by the rules of international law. Primakov and his successor at the Foreign Ministry in 1998, Igor Ivanov, insisted on the need to establish an international system based on the supremacy of the United Nations and the respect for international law, rather than a world order based on the indiscriminate and unsanctioned use of force (Ivanov, 2000). In their view, a central place had to be reserved for the United Nations, as the key mechanism responsible for regulating the entire system of international relations. The authority of the UN and of its Security

Council had to be reinforced, and their supremacy in international affairs had to be reinstated (Ivanov, 2000). Russian leaders, however, also saw the UNSC as an institution which reflected Russia's Great-Power status, and as arena which allowed Russia to exercise its global power, through its permanent seat and its right to use its veto on proposed UNSC resolutions. The readiness by Russian leaders to operate within the international legal framework often reflected a concern over Russia's own international vulnerability rather than a profound belief in the superiority and benefits of international law, even though Primakov himself proved keen to ensure that Russia abided by the agreed principles of international law.

Primakov's views found broad support throughout Russian society and among the Russian political elite at large, and this allowed him to conduct a more effective foreign and security policy. His world outlook was also embraced by Igor Ivanov, his successor at the Foreign Ministry, who took over when Primakov became Prime Minister of Russia in 1998. Yet, Primakov's doctrine of multipolarity, power-balancing and advantageous cooperation with the West, was not devoid of critics. *Eurasianists-Civilisationalists*, while supporting the change of course introduced by Primakov, saw Russia as a unique civilisation which had to compete rather than cooperate with the West. *Liberal-Westernisers* on the other hand, objected to Primakov's Great-Power balancing, and instead, insisted that Russia's future lay in the development of a vibrant economy and in cooperating with, rather than confronting, the West (Tsygankov, 2010, pp. 100–101). They generally proved less supportive of prioritising Russia's reintegration with the other CIS states, and instead favoured closer economic ties with developed economies in Europe and elsewhere. Still, Primakov's *doctrine of multipolarity* proved very attractive to the vast majority of the Russian elites, and thus, it remained predominant in Russian politics well after Primakov abandoned the political scene. In particular, Primakov's efforts to establish Russia and the CIS as important centres of economic development and global power, proved remarkably persuasive. Such a predicament determined his attempts, and those of his successors, to establish 'ever closer' ties between Russia and its former Soviet neighbours.

Conclusions

As clearly shown, most members of the Russian leadership, and the Russian political elite at large had serious difficulties in accepting the disintegration of the Soviet Union and the emergence of a new Russian state within the administrative borders of the old RSFSR. Their idea of 'Russia' remained closely linked with the former Soviet Union and the Russian Empire, both in terms of territorial dimension and population composition. Moreover, Russians were at great pains to accept the new reality that their country no longer fitted entirely with the qualities of a 'Great Power' in the world arena. Russian national consciousness was shattered by the psychological effects of Russia's loss of empire and status. Nevertheless, despite the longing for empire, the Russian leadership,

President Yeltsin and Foreign Minister Kozyrev in particular, did not adopt a neo-imperialist attitude towards the FSS when the USSR collapsed. On the contrary, endowed with a strong anti-imperialist approach, Yeltsin and Kozyrev attempted to bring Russia into the 'civilised group of Western nations'. More importantly, they treated the former Soviet states as independent and sovereign entities of international law, and embraced a liberal-internationalist view of global affairs, as shown by their desire to join and strengthen international organisations. Harsh criticisms from both Moderate and Imperialist Nationalists groups, however, as well as new realities in the former Soviet states, such as the eruption of military conflicts and the partial discrimination against Russian minorities, as well as the deep economic interdependence among the FSS, compelled Kozyrev to adopt a more assertive stance towards the Near Abroad. The arrival of Primakov at the Foreign Ministry not only crystallised Russia's more active behaviour not only in the Near Abroad, but also internationally. Russia abandoned its 'liberal-internationalist' outlook and fully embraced a *realist* view of international relations, which translated into efforts to emerge as one of the dominant centres of global power. While the change in policy represented a reaction to the West's increased influence in the Eastern European security scene, it also reflected a long-standing view that saw Russia as one of the Great Powers that should be reckoned with in the international arena. It, therefore, combined both *defensive* and *offensive realist* understandings of international affairs, although Russia's new foreign policy paradigm did not go as far as embracing more extreme 'motivational realist' views.

Nevertheless, despite the more forceful tone adopted by Russian foreign policy-makers, the foreign policy record in the former Soviet space during the two Yeltsin's Presidencies was not as neo-imperialist as indicated by Russian official discourse, except for certain areas, and primarily in relation to Russia's involvement in the military conflicts that erupted along Russia's borders in the CIS space. And here again, Russia's policies often followed legitimate state interests, such as the restoration of stability along Russia's borders, the prevention of the spread of weapons, conflict, and instability into Russia. Furthermore, Russia's actions in this area regularly underwent significant modifications. More often than not though, Russia's policies were characterised by a lack of clarity and disarray, rather than by the systematic pursuit of national interest, a result of Yeltsin's attempt to establish a broad domestic consensus to counter-balance his own domestic political weakness. Still, Russia remained highly involved in events in the former Soviet Union, and this was determined by various factors. First, deep economic and military links tied all former Soviet states together making it extremely difficult for Russia to adopt an isolationist policy. Second, the presence of a large Russian and Russian-speaking community in the Near Abroad, whose civil rights were often infringed upon, particularly in the Baltic states, meant that Russian leaders could not just stand idly by. Third, Russian leaders considered the Near Abroad a source of constant instability and conflict, and feared the spread of weapons, refugees, drugs and criminals into Russia. No borders existed between the former Soviet states, and as a result, events in the former Soviet space had a direct impact on Russia's internal developments. Fourth, Russian leaders were very much concerned about the potential disintegration of Russia and the effects that events in the Near Abroad could have on Russia's own fragile territorial integrity. Fifth, Russians feared the spread of Islamic fundamentalism in Russia, as well as the overall spread of instability. As a result, Russians tended to view the former Soviet space as a sphere of Russia's vital interests, if not exclusive influence, and as such were particularly worried about other states potentially acquiring a predominant influence in the region. Although, as is shown in this book, Moscow welcomed the participation of the UN and the CSCE/OSCE in the mediation of conflicts in the ex-USSR, it refused to grant these organisations a predominant role in the post-Soviet space. Russian also refused to allow foreign military forces play the role of peacekeepers, thus indicating a reluctance by Russian elites totally to discard Russia's imperial legacy.[8]

Yeltsin's second term as president was characterised by great disarray and chaos in decision-making. As his health severely deteriorated, Yeltsin proved incapable of running the country in an effective and coherent fashion. The political system became completely dysfunctional as key decisions were relegated to a small clique of close advisors with direct access to the President, which included Yeltsin's daughter, Tatyana Dyachenko, and her husband and head of the Presidential Administration, Valentin Yumashev, as well as Russian oligarch Boris Berezovsky. A small group of five or six oligarchs, who controlled large sectors of the economy, became increasingly influential. Despite a slight recovery of the economy during 1996 and 1997, the financial system collapsed in 1998 under the heavy burden of a massive public debt. The Russian state lost its capacity to conduct even its most basic functions such as raising taxes and imposing law and order. Within the Russian Federation, the process of decentralisation continued to gather speed. Regional leaders ruled their regions as personal fiefdoms, almost totally independently from the Kremlin, and often in violation of Russian laws and the Russian Constitution. In the Caucasus, the Chechen republic plunged into anarchy and disarray after the withdrawal of Russian troops in the summer of 1996. Its new leader, President Aslan Maskhadov proved incapable of bringing Chechen warlords under his fore. By the end of the decade, Chechnya had turned into a hotbed of crime, Islamist radicalism, and violent extremism which threatened to engulf the entire region. In August 1999 a group of *jihadist* fighters invaded neighbouring Dagestan, threatening the very existence of Russia's authority over the eastern North Caucasus. These inherent weaknesses had a major impact on Russia's ability to operate internationally and project its power onto the former Soviet space. They significantly reduced Russia's ability to behave assertively within the CIS, and to a great extent reinforced Russia's moderate behaviour. Russia's policies in the Near Abroad, nevertheless, followed a relatively coherent and consistent path during Yeltsin's second term in office, contrary to developments taking place inside Russia, thanks to Primakov's clear strategies. Efforts at integration continued to gather speed, even though the results were far from satisfactory from Russia's point of view. Significant engagement by the Foreign Ministry in the resolution of the various violent conflicts that had erupted in the CIS space in the early 1990s, produced some positive results – the end of the Tajik civil war in 1997 being a good example – while tensions were reduced around South Ossetia, Nagorno-Karabakh and Transdniestria. To conclude, despite the Great-Power rhetoric, during Yeltsin's second term in office, Russia's policies in the former Soviet space were not as assertive as usually assumed and were not characterised by the use of *hard power* instruments. Instead, Russia's behaviour very much fitted Trenin's *post-Imperium* paradigm, characterised by attempts to exit the previous imperial condition and transform Russia into a 'normal' country, albeit with key interests in the Near Abroad which Moscow intended to uphold.

Notes

1 Personal interview with Konstantin Zatulin, Moscow, November 1996.
2 Personal interview with Aleskei Arbatov, Moscow, November 1995.
3 Personal Interview, Moscow, October 1995.
4 Although in late August 1991, President Yeltsin questioned the legitimacy of the new republic's borders, the CIS agreements adopted in December 1991, which put an end to the Soviet Union, explicitly proclaimed the inviolability of the existing borders among the new states (CIS, 1991).
5 In July 1992, the Supreme Soviet proposed the creation of a separate Ministry for Commonwealth affairs, in order to strengthen cooperation with the FSS (Golub, 1992). In December 1992, the Russian Congress of People's Deputies appealed for the creation of a confederation joining together the states of the former USSR (Moscow Radio Rossii, 1992).
6 The Communist Party of the Russian Federation (CPRF) Programme stipulated that once in power the party would 'do everything within [its] power to promote the economic and political integration of the republics of the ... dismembered Soviet Union' (*Sovetskaya Rossiya*, 1995).
7 The 1997 National Security Strategy read,

> there has been an expansion in the commonality of Russia's interests with many states on problems of international security such as countering the proliferation of weapons of mass destruction, settling and preventing regional conflicts, countering international terrorism and the drugs business.
> (*Rossiiskaya gazeta*, 1997, p. 4)

8 In 1994, the CSCE became the Organisation for Security and Cooperation in Europe (OSCE).

Bibliography

Ambartsumov, E. (1992). *Rossiiskaya gazeta*, 13 April, p. 7.
Arbatov, A. (1994). Russian National Interests. In: R. Blackwill and S. Karaganov, eds., *Damage Limitation or Crisis: Russia and the Outside World*. Washington: CSIA Studies in International Security, pp. 60–67.

Arbatov, A. (1993). Russia's Foreign Policy Alternatives', *International Security*, 18 (2), 5–43.
Arbatov, A. (1992). 'Imperiya ili velikaya derzhava?', *Novoe Vremya*, 49, 16–18.
Baranovsky, V. (2015). The Kosovo Factor in Russia' Foreign Policy, *International Spectator*, 50(4), 256–274.
Bediurov, B. (1993). *Den*, 9–15 May, p. 5.
Borodai, Yu. (1991). Trety Put', *Nash sovremennik*, September, pp. 130–147.
Chernov, V. (1993). *Nezavisimaya gazeta*, 29 April, p. 1 and 3.
Chigrin, A. (1998). *Trud*, 29 April, p. 4.
Chuprinin, S. (1990). Situatsiia: bor'ba idei v sovremennoi literature, *Znamia*, 1, pp. 201–219.
CIS (1991). Agreement on the Creation of a Commonwealth of Independent States, 8 December 1991, art. 5, Tass, 9 December 1991.
Dashichev, V. (1994). *Nezavisimaya gazeta*, 23 April, p. 4.
Deikin, A. (1995). *New Times*, October, p. 42.
Golub, P. (1992). *Izvestiya*, 24 July, p. 2.
Goncharov, S. (1992). *Izvestiya*, 25 February, p. 6.
Eggert, K. (1992). *Izvestiya*, 7 August, p. 6.
Inform-TV (1991). 16 November.
Ivanov, I. (2000). *Nezavisimaya gazeta*, 20 January, p. 9.
Izvestiya (1992). Vera, nadezhda, i terpenie, spasut svobodnuiu Rossiiu, 11 June, p. 1.
Karpov, M. (1995). *Nezavisimaya gazeta*, 14 March, pp. 1–2.
Kondrashov, S. (1996a). *Izvestiya*, 6 March, p. 3.
Kondrashov, S. (1996b). *Izvestiya*, 9 August, p. 3.
Kosopalov, N. (1993). Vneshnyaya politika Rossii: Problemy stanovleniya i politiko-formiruiushchie factory. *Mirovaya ekonomika i mezhdunarodnye otnosheniya*, 2, 5–20.
Kosyrev, D. (1992). *Rossiiskaya gazeta*, 1 December, p. 6.
Kozyrev, A. (1992a). *Izvestiya*, 2 January, p. 3.
Kozyrev, A. (1992b). *Nezavisimaya gazeta*, 1 April, p. 1.
Kozyrev, A. (1992c). *Rossiiskie vesti*, 3 December, p. 2.
Kozyrev, A. (1993a). *Nezavisimaya gazeta*, 22 September, p. 1.
Kozyrev, A. (1993b). *Nezavisimaya gazeta*, 13 October, p. 1.
Kozyrev, A. (1994). *Rossiiskaya gazeta*, 2 February, p. 1.
Krasnaya zvezda (1992). 28 October, p. 2.
LDPR (1995). *Izvestnyi-neizvestnyi Zhirinovskii i ego partiya posle oktyabrya 1994 goda (dokumenty i materialy)*. Moscow, pp. 50–58.
Leonov, Y. (1992). *Nezavisimaya gazeta*, 20 February, p. 4.
Limonov, E. (1992). *Sovetskaya Rossiya*, 12 July, p. 1.
Lukin, V. (1992). Our Security Predicament, *Foreign Policy*, 88, pp. 57–75.
Malcolm, N. (1996). Foreign Policy Making. In: R. Allison, M. Light, N. Malcolm, A. Pravda, *Internal Factors in Russian Foreign Policy*. Oxford: The Royal Institute of International Affairs, pp. 101–168.
Migranyan, A. (1991). *Moskovskie novosti*, 6 October. p. 9.
Migranyan, A. (1992). *Rossiiskaya gazeta*, 4 August, p. 4.
Migranyan, A. (1994). *Nezavisimaya gazeta*, 10 December, p. 1.
Moscow Radio Rossii (1992), 14 December, in *FBIS-SOV-92–241-S*, 15 December 1992, p. 3.
Myalo, Ks. (1993). Russkie idut?, *Etnologicheskii Vestnik Rossii*, p. 2.
Nezavisimaya gazeta (1993). El'tsin obratilsya k lideram SNG, 18 March, p. 1.
Nezavisimaya gazeta (1994). Strategiya dlya Rossii – Tezysy Soveta po Vneshnei i Oboronnoi Politike', 27 May, pp. 4–5.
Ostankino TV (1994). Yeltsin's speech to Federation Council, Moscow, 24 February.

Ostapchuk, A. (1994). *Nezavisimaya gazeta*, 3 August, p. 1.
Pleshakov, K. (1993). Russia's Mission: The Third Epoch, *International Affairs* (Moscow), 1 January.
Portnikov, V. (1994). *Nezavisimaya gazeta*, 20 January, p. 1.
Pravda, A. (1996). The Public Politics of Foreign Policy. In: R. Allison, M. Light, N. Malcolm, A. Pravda, *Internal Factors in Russian Foreign Policy*. Oxford: The Royal Institute of International Affairs, pp. 169–229.
Rossiiskaya gazeta (1992). 3 February, p. 3.
Rossiiskaia gazeta (1996). 26 September, p. 7.
Rossiiskaya gazeta (1997). Russian National Security Strategy, 26 December, pp. 4–5. In: FBIS-SOV-97-364, 30 December, p. 4–5.
Russian Television (1993). 28 February, in *FBIS-SOV-93-038*, 1 March, p. 21.
Rutskoi, A. (1992a). *Pravda*, 30 January, p. 1.
Rutskoi, A. (1992b). *Nezavisimaya gazeta*, 13 February, p. 2.
Solzhenitsyn, A. (1990). Kak nam obustroit Rossiyu? *Literaturnaya gazeta*, 18 September, pp. 3–6.
Sovetskaya Rossiya (1995). 2 February 1995, pp. 1–2.
Starovoitova, G. (1992). *Moskovskie novosti*, 5 April, p. 2.
Strategicheskii Kurs Rossii s Gosudarstvami-Uchastnikami Sodruzhestva Nezavisimykh Gosudarstv (1995), 14 September, p. 1, unpublished manuscript.
Streliany, A. (1990). *Literaturnaya gazeta*, 8 August, p. 3.
Todres, V. (1992). *Nezavisimaya gazeta*, 9 January, p. 2.
Tsipko, A. (1991a). *Rossiia*, 6–12 July, p. 6.
Tsipko, A. (1991b). *Izvestiya*, 1 October 1991, p. 5.
Tsipko, A. (1994). A New Russian Identity or Old Russia's Reintegration?, *Security Dialogue*, 25(4), 443–455.
Tsygankov, A. (2010), *Russia's Foreign Policy: Change and Continuity in National Identity*. 2nd edn. New York and Toronto: Rowman & Littlefield Publishers.
Vasilev, A. (1992). *Izvestiya*, 10 March, p. 6.
Zaslavsky, V. (1992). The Evolution of Separatism in Soviet Society Under Gorbachev, In: G.W. Lapidus, V. Zaslavsky, and Ph. Goldman, eds. *From Union to Commonwealth: Nationalism and Separatism in the Soviet Republics*. Cambridge, Cambridge University Press, pp. 71–97.
Zyuganov, G. (1992). *Den*, 27 September–3 October, p. 1.
Zyuganov, G. (1996). *La Repubblica*, 8 February, p. 11.

2 Russia and the Commonwealth of Independent States

On 8 December 1991, the leaders of the Ukrainian, Belorussian and Russian Soviet Federative Socialist Republic (SFSR) put an end to the 70-year-old Soviet state and created the Commonwealth of Independent States (CIS) *or Sodruzhestvo Nezavisimykh Gosudarstv*, out of its remains. They were joined on 21 December 1991 by most of the former USSR (Union of Soviet Socialist Republics) with the exception of the Baltic states, which had achieved internationally recognised independence after the August 1991 coup, and Georgia, which at the time was entrapped in a fierce civil war between supporters and opponents of President Zviad Gamsakhurdia. Conceived as an association of independent states, the CIS was initially aimed at putting an end to the Soviet Union as a subject of international law, at dismantling the old state structures of the USSR and at establishing a new type of relations among its members – relations which were to be based on mutual recognition and respect for state sovereignty, equality and non-interference in internal affairs.[1] However, the CIS was also envisaged as an instrument for the preservation of a common economic and military-strategic space and for the promotion of cooperation in the fields of security, the economy and foreign policy (Tass, 1991a). Cooperation was expected to be particularly deep in the field of economic policy due to the legacy of close economic interdependence amongst the former USSR republics. The new states pledged to conduct coordinated economic reforms, and to construct economic relations and carry out settlements on the basis of the existing monetary unit – the rouble. The CIS states also agreed to coordinate their foreign policies and to preserve, under joint command, a common military-strategic space. This also included single control over nuclear weapons, so as to ensure international stability and guarantee the security of CIS member states (*Pravda*, 1991).

Russia and the end of the USSR

What led to the dismantling of the USSR and what were the objectives pursued by the Russian leadership when establishing the CIS? The leadership of the RSFSR has often been accused of having greatly contributed to the dismantling of the Soviet Union, indeed of being the main promoter of the collapse of the Soviet state (Grachev, 1995). Although there is hardly any doubt that many of the policies conducted by RSFSR President Yeltsin during 1991, and especially after the August 1991 coup, dealt a severe blow to the preservation of central union structures, many of the non-Russian republics also played a major role in the process of disintegration of the USSR. Many of their actions, such as establishing national military forces and taking control over resources on their territories, made the preservation of the Union an almost impossible task. Moreover, it would be a mistake to assume that the ultimate objective of Yeltsin's policies was to dismantle the Union. Most of his actions were aimed above all at tearing down the totalitarian system of the Soviet state and introducing market reforms in the economy. However, in view of the fierce opposition to radical economic reforms that he encountered at Union level, Yeltsin decided to use Russian governmental structures instead, to pursue his reformist policies. Interviewed in 1990, Yeltsin explained that when he became USSR People's Deputy in 1989, he soon understood that there would be no radical reforms at the union level 'and so I thought to myself: If the reforms cannot be carried out at that level, why not try Russia?' (*Soyuz*, 1990). In fact, during 1990, the Russian parliament under Yeltsin acted much more radically in support of transforming the Soviet economy than the all-Union legislature, by voting in favour, for example, of an immediate switch to a market system in Russia – a drastic move that the USSR Supreme Soviet immediately overturned (Rahr, 1991, p. 1). In his book, *The View from the Kremlin*, Yeltsin explained that his disagreements with USSR President Gorbachev during the winter of 1990–1991 had resulted, among other things from Gorbachev's decision to bury the 500-day economic programme which was being sponsored by economist Grigory Yavlinsky, and which proposed radical economic reforms. 'It had been our only economic hope at the time,' Yeltsin wrote in his memoirs (1994, pp. 23–24).

Yeltsin, however, seemed most willing to conduct the necessary economic reforms within the Union state, if renewed structures granted Russia the necessary powers to do so. This was clearly shown by his support for the *Treaty on the Union of Sovereign States* which USSR republican leaders were expected to sign on 20 August 1991, but which was derailed by the August coup. The treaty was intended to transform quite considerably the USSR's internal federal structures by conferring significant powers to the Union republics. While the treaty left all matters of foreign policy, defence and a large part of the financial system under Soviet control, it granted USSR republics, including Russia, the right to conduct their own economic programmes independently. As Yeltsin noted,

> It will create the conditions for transferring to the Russian republic's jurisdiction all enterprises and organisations operating on Russian territory and, in turn, will make it possible to accomplish what is perhaps the most important task – immediately granting the republics the right to choose for themselves the form of ownership and terms of economic management.
>
> (*Nezavisimaya gazeta*, 1991)

However, the August 1991 coup dealt a severe blow not only to the negotiations on the Union treaty but to the Union itself. The Russian SFSR and most of the other USSR Union republics proceeded hastily towards gaining control over the resources on their respective territories. Immediately after the coup, many Union republics – but not Russia – declared their independence from the USSR and placed Communist Party property under their own republican jurisdictions. Some even started forming their own armed forces. Russia, in turn, seized control over many Union structures, and especially over those bodies responsible for running the economy, and placed them under its own jurisdiction. The other Union republics, in turn, began demanding increasing powers from the centre. As a result, executive power was transferred to a State Council, which was composed of the Presidents of the Union republics, and which in early November 1991 abolished 36 Union ministries and 37 departments, including the Ministry of Foreign Economic Relations, the Ministry of Justice, the Ministry of Finance and the Ministry of Agriculture (Alimov, 1991). There is little doubt that many republican leaders also moved fast, either consciously or unconsciously, towards the demise of the USSR.

However, all efforts to carry out a coordinated policy of economic reforms within a Common Economic Space (CES) as envisaged by the 1991 Union Treaty failed to produce any significant results. Many republics saw keeping the Union as a means of preserving the economic subsidies that they were receiving from the centre in the form of budget transfers and low prices. Russian leaders, instead, were anxious to start economic reforms by freeing internal prices and reducing subsidies to companies and republics. In mid-November 1991, when the Russian leadership decided to launch a package of radical economic reforms, which introduced market mechanism into the Russian economy, Moscow was not followed by any other single USSR republic, and this produced severe havoc in the overall Union economy. Another blow to the union was dealt by Ukraine's decisions to set up its own armed forces, to distance itself from the economic treaty, and, last but not least, to conduct a referendum on the republic's independence. Russia could hardly have accepted a union that excluded Ukraine. As commentator Vladimir Kuznechevsky wrote 'it would be very difficult for Russia to be part of the Union without Ukraine, its own blood sister', and added, 'this is difficult to imagine even genetically and psychologically. Russia began in Kiev after all' (Kyzhnechevsky, 1991).

In view of these developments, on 8 December 1991, Yeltsin together with the Ukrainian and Belarusian republican leaders decided to put an end to the USSR and create the CIS in its place. Russia's decision was determined by various factors. First, the Commonwealth appeared as a means of overcoming the impasse that had been reached in the negotiations on a new Union Treaty during the autumn of 1991 (Tass, 1991c). In the words of RSFSR State Secretary and first Deputy Chairman of the government, Gennady Burbulis '[the CIS] is a constructive way out of the long negotiating process. Hopefully a full-blooded and fully viable union of independent states will be created out of the ruins of the totalitarian communist system' (Moscow Radio, 1991). Russian leaders had become aware that the secession of the republics from the USSR, and the formation of independent states as a result of it, had become an irreversible process. According to Russian State Counsellor Sergei Shakhrai, 'the actual inactivity of the union bodies is obvious. Therefore, at issue is not the dismantling of the union, not the legal decision to eliminate it, but a medical diagnosis, the establishment of a fact' (Moscow Radio, 1991). Thus, an association of independent states appeared as the only possible solution to overcome the existing deadlock.[2]

Second, Russian leaders were particularly concerned over the reluctance shown by Ukraine to sign any kind of Union Treaty within the USSR framework. They were also aware of the dangers that a reckless dismemberment of the USSR could pose to regional security. In his speech to the Supreme Soviet on 12th December 1991, Yeltsin explained,

> ... the people of Ukraine voted for independence in a referendum. Ukraine has refused to sign the treaty and the consequences of this are obvious: serious disruptions in the geopolitical equilibrium in the world, and an escalation of the conflicts within the former Soviet Union. Under these conditions, it would have been criminal to conclude a treaty on a Union of seven republics, without Ukraine, to remain calm, wait for the next co-ordination meetings and do nothing.
> (*Rossiiskaya gazeta*, 1991)

In other words, an association agreement with Ukraine was seen as essential to prevent a disruptive and bloody end to the Union, and as the only way to keep Russia and Ukraine closely together in some form. As noted by Yeltsin in an interview with newspaper *Trud*,

> without the Ukraine we do not represent the Union. First, it is a state with a colossal population – 52 million people. Second, 11 million of these are Russians. Third, we are linked by a millennium of history and by thousands of economic, political and social threads to this day.
> (Lepskii and Potapov, 1991)

The presence of over 25 million Russians in the new independent republics also determined the creation of an organisation which could deal with the problems resulting from the potential discrimination and violation of their human and civil rights (Lepskii and Potapov, 1991).

Finally, the reform-minded and democratic politicians of the RSFSR saw the CIS as a way of finally getting rid of the centre, and gaining control over the Russian economy, its enterprises and natural resources, in order to carry out the long-awaited radical economic transformations. As Sergei Shakhrai noted 'the Commonwealth has opened the way for economic reform in the Russian Federation', and added that from now on, the Russian government and parliament will not have to fight on three fronts, against the old Union structures, against the lack of agreement among the positions of republics having different social and economic conditions, and against the crisis in the economy.

(Katanyan, 1992)

The CIS agreements actually stipulated that members should conduct radical economic reforms, within the CES (Tass, 1991b). The CIS, however, was not conceived by Russian leaders simply as an instrument of 'civilised divorce'. Russian leaders saw it as a new mechanism aimed at coordinating the relations of the republics that had been part of a single unified state, and as a means of peacefully dividing the USSR assets and property among its member states.

Russia's policy orientations towards the CIS

Russia's policy towards the CIS underwent significant evolution in 1992. Whereas in the autumn of 1991, the view had prevailed that only by significantly reducing the power of the Union structures, and eventually abolishing the centre altogether, Russia would quickly and effectively pursue economic and political reforms, already in early 1992, preserving a high degree of integration within the post-Soviet space became a main foreign policy priority. As early as February 1992, Foreign Minister Kozyrev noted that Russia's foreign policy attached particular importance to the establishment of a viable CIS. In his view, 'the forming of the CIS involves our vital interests and [it relates to] fundamental issues connected with Russia's [desire to] join the civilised world' (*Interfax*, 1992). Russia's interests in the CIS lay in preserving a single army, an integrated economy, a unique cultural space and a common language (*Interfax*, 1992). Kozyrev, however, made it clear that the CIS would be formed on a strictly voluntary basis. In his view, 'the viability of the emerging CIS lies in the fact that natural ties will be much stronger than the shackles of a totalitarian system', clearly attesting to a non-imperialist outlook (Kozyrev, 1992). Forcible restoration of the USSR was considered counter-productive. Instead, patient and persistent talks with CIS partners was seen as the only realistic path towards strengthening the CIS, however complex the process might become. Kozyrev made clear that Russia would seek coordination of joint work 'every time our Commonwealth partners are ready for it' (Kozyrev, 1992).

This strategy of cooperation on a strictly voluntary basis reflected an understanding and an awareness of the close ties that brought all former Soviet states together. The deep integration of all CIS economies, the heavy reliance of all new independent states on supplies and subsidies from Russia, the sharing of a common currency, as well as the bad shape of all republican economies – all these elements argued in favour of cooperation and economic integration between the former Soviet states. The former Soviet republics were part of a highly integrated and centralised economic command system, where planning was largely carried out by sector. The emphasis on economies of scale through the operation of large enterprises resulted in the concentration of production in a limited number of enterprises and high levels of republican specialisation. As a result, the level of inter-republican trade remained extremely high, even when compared to other trading blocs. Seventy-five per cent of the Soviet trade prior to independence was conducted at intra-republican level (Christensen, 1994, p. 6). Moreover, not only were the republics highly integrated, but they were all, to a great extent, dependent on trade with Russia, both in terms of exports as well as imports (Smith, 1994, p. 37).[3] Russia was also their main industrial partner. In 1991, Russian industries produced about two-thirds of the machinery and a preponderant share of the R&D output and military potential (Sagers, 1992, p. 342). This high level of integration argued in favour of a concerted effort to overcome the deep economic crisis that all former Soviet republics faced. Economic cooperation and support for intra-CIS trade, moreover, could provide a temporary respite for Russian industry and, eventually, open the way for the creation of a big economic market tied to Russia.

In the military field, the unexpected collapse of the Soviet Union and the emergence, in its place, of 15 newly independent states created an entirely new geopolitical situation. The new Russian state, although still representing a significant portion of the earth surface, lost an important part of its territory in the strategically vital areas of Eastern Europe and the South Caucasus, with the end of the USSR. During the Cold War, Soviet military planners had based the defence of the Russian heartland on the forward deployment of high-readiness units in the western and southern fringes of the Soviet territory, on an air-defence network located mostly in the non-Russian republics, and on the assumption that the nations neighbouring Russia would not align themselves against it (Falkenrath, 1995, p. 177). The loss of Eastern Europe dealt a severe blow to the implementation of such a forward-based strategy, but the disintegration of the USSR completely eviscerated Russia's traditional defence strategy. As pointed out by Russian Defence Minister Pavel Grachev in the spring of 1992, 'We have found ourselves faced with a truly unprecedented situation. The Moscow military district has essentially become a frontier district' (Burbyga and Plutnik, 1992). The Moscow district, moreover, had almost no combat worthy troops, whereas the largest, best equipped, and best trained forces were located along Russia's western borders, especially in Ukraine and Belarus (Garthoff, 1994, p. 10). In addition, the collapse of the Soviet Union severely disrupted the existing air defence and early-warning systems, significantly eroding the defensive capabilities of the new Russian state. The non-Russian CIS states were left without proper air cover, and without effective armed forces, whereas gaps opened up in Russia's own air defences (Simakov, 1995). All these factors argued in favour of the preservation of a common military space. At the 31 December 1991 CIS Minsk Summit, Russia managed to convince all CIS states to put nuclear weapons under single control and to place the former Soviet 'strategic forces' under joint command. The strategic forces were sufficiently broadly defined so as to include the strategic missile forces, the air force, the navy, the air-defence forces, the space forces and the paratroopers (Tass, 1991c).

Russia also succeeded in obtaining the support of Belarus, Armenia and the five Central Asian states to keep joint 'general-purpose forces' and joint border troops under joint CIS command (Tass, 1991b). However, the CIS states were granted the right to create their own armed forces, which opened the way to further disintegration (*Rossiiskaya gazeta*, 1992).

Russia's policies towards the CIS in the early 1990s

Kozyrev's strategy of cooperation on a strictly voluntary basis was based on the assumption that the new states would be unable to resist the gravitational pull of Russia's military and economic might, and would thus eventually re-orient themselves back to Moscow. In other words, the *soft power* of Russia's attraction would bring them towards tight cooperation. Such an approach reflected an intention to abandon Russia's previous imperialist policies, and a readiness to conduct relations with the former Soviet states (FSS) on an equal basis. But contrary to Russia's expectations, the 1990s witnessed the rapid disintegration of the post-Soviet military and economic spaces. In the early spring of 1992, most CIS states began setting up their own armed forces, and at the CIS summit in Minsk on 14 February 1992, it was agreed that the list of 'strategic forces' was to be 'defined by each state in agreement with the Strategic Forces Command, to be approved by the Council of Heads of State' (*Krasnaya zvezda*, 1992). This meant that their size would be much smaller than initially envisaged, given that the composition of the forces would be the result of negotiations. Moreover, the new national armed forces of the newly independent states, which were part of the general-purpose forces, remained subordinated to the national Defence Ministries. However, the latter were allowed to participate, together with the CIS command, in the development of operational planning, training and direct combat control (*Sodruzhestvo*, 1992a, pp. 26–30). More significantly, in May 1992, Russia itself decided to go ahead with the creation of its own military structures, thus burying any hopes that a united, albeit smaller, CIS army could be preserved.[4] There was a clear perception in Moscow that Russia's security interests would hardly be fulfilled by an undefined CIS military organisation, whose composition, structure, subordination and allegiance remained extremely blurred. The establishment of national armies tied by a collective security pact, with joint force structures, was seen as a better option to satisfy Russia's interests (Rogov, 1992, p. 12). Moreover, there was growing concern among Russian political circles that the army, deprived of a state and of civilian supervision, was getting out of control. Furthermore, the question of loyalty among individual soldiers was becoming an increasingly complicated matter. Only by creating its own MoD and other relevant military structures, could the Russian leadership ensure political control over the military (Gross, 1992, p. 257).

Russia, however, decided to retain the CIS Joint Armed Forces (JAF), which included the strategic nuclear forces, air-defence structures, and navy forces, in order to ensure continued central control over the entire former Soviet nuclear arsenal. The Russian leadership also viewed the CIS defence structures as useful instruments for the promotion of Moscow's security interests throughout the CIS. The new organisational structure of the JAF placed Russian officers in key positions, thus ensuring Russia's control over such relevant formations as the CIS air-defence system, the air force system, and the navy, many parts of which still remained under joint command (*Sodruzhesvto*,1992c, pp. 69–70). To boost CIS military cooperation further, Russia also decided to create a system of collective security by signing the *Collective Security Treaty* (CST) in May 1992 with five CIS states – Kazakhstan, Tajikistan, Kyrgyzstan, Uzbekistan and Armenia. The treaty was seen by Russia as an instrument of collective security and as a means to maintain a united military-strategic space through the preservation of joint armed forces (*MNB*, 1992a).[5] Moscow also saw the treaty as a way of preserving under joint control those elements of the former Soviet army that had not been already nationalised, or at least as a means of delaying the complete disintegration of the former Soviet army (Plotnikov, 1994; Volkov, 1994).

The CST, however, failed to satisfy Russia's expectations. First, as the CIS states proceeded with the creation of their own armed forces, CIS military agreements reflected the increasing trend towards a nationally based CIS defence. The October 1992 *CIS military doctrine*, for example, foresaw the fulfilment of collective defence on the basis of both CIS JAF and individual armed forces, but the latter were to be placed only *voluntarily* under CIS command. Second, although the *CIS military doctrine* had provided the basis for the creation of an integrated military system of joint forces and common operational planning, very little of this was developed in practice (*MNB*, 1992b). By the end of 1992, the CIS JAF included only the nuclear forces which were located in Russia, Ukraine, Belarus and Kazakhstan. Collective security remained very much in the early stages of policy coordination. Also, very little was achieved in terms of joint operational planning or the development of integrated military structures. Third, the July 1992 agreement on a united air-defence system under CIS command failed to materialise. As far as border protection was concerned, although all five Central Asian states, Russia, Armenia and Belarus agreed jointly to protect the external CIS borders, with common CIS border troops and national border forces (*Sodruzhestvo*, 1992b, pp. 36–39), Georgia, Azerbaijan and Ukraine, instead, decided to patrol their external borders on their own, leaving Russia's borders partly open and unprotected (*Komsomol'skaya Pravda*, 1992). This prompted Russia to go ahead in June 1992, with the creation of its own border troops in order to start protecting its own borders. However, between 1992 and 1995, Moscow reached bilateral agreements with various CIS states – Georgia, Armenia, Kazakhstan, Turkmenistan, Kyrgyzstan, Tajikistan and Belarus – to assist them in jointly or individually patrolling their external CIS borders, and this allowed Russia partially to retain control over the former USSR borders.

In the economic sphere, intra-republican trade suffered quite significantly in 1992–1993, as tariff barriers were erected, Russia took control over the rouble, republics introduced parallel currencies, and CIS states conducted completely uncoordinated economic policies (Michalopoulos, 1996, p. 6).[6] Russia tried in mid-1992 to avert the total collapse of intra-CIS trade by providing substantial amounts of *technical credits* on very easy terms and without restrictions to the new republics. It also sold oil and gas to CIS states at highly subsidised prices and signed several bilateral trade agreements to foster intra-CIS trade. However, Russia's actions did not prove very successful. Trade within the CIS contracted quite significantly, and the CIS space became an area where exchanges were conducted mainly on a bilateral basis, at state level. Yet, trade did not break down entirely. Russian credits and subsidies allowed for the preservation of some form of trade, albeit at a significantly reduced level. But this proved to be a very expensive undertaking – over 1.5 trillion roubles or $7 billion dollars were given to the CIS republics in the form of technical credits during 1992 mid-1993, amounting to 9.5 per cent of Russian's Gross Domestic Product (GDP) (Illarionov, 1993; Odling-Smee and Wolf, 1994, p. 10). CIS states proved unable to cover these credits, and thus, by the end of 1993, their debts to Russia reached U$5.2 billion, increasing Russia's leverage over them (Michalopoulos, 1996, p. 20).[7]

CIS states also failed to reach agreement on the creation of a supranational bank responsible for regulating the amount of cash emissions and in charge of implementing common credit and monetary policies. Instead, at the end of December 1991, Russia dissolved the Soviet Central Bank (Gosbank) and transferred its facilities to the Russian state (Zhagel, 1991). The move was dictated by Russia's desire to keep control over currency emissions and by the wish of CIS states such as Ukraine to introduce their own currencies. The absence of a supranational banking agency, however, resulted in a total lack of coordination of CIS monetary and credit policies and led to major disruptions in the proper-functioning of the rouble zone, eventually contributing to its final demise (Granville, 1994).[8] The issuing of soft credits by CIS states to obtain cash led to the rapid devaluation of the rouble and the erection of inter-state trade barriers, leading to the collapse of the single economic space. It was becoming increasingly clear that Russia's policies of voluntary reintegration in the economic, as well as in the military field, were not working.

The CIS space disintegrates further

These rapid processes of CIS disintegration led to strong criticism of government policy from members of the opposition in parliament and from prominent figures in the Russian elite, such as deputy Evgeny Ambartsumov and Andranik Migranyan (Golub, 1992; Ambartsumov, 1992). They argued that the Yeltsin government's actions were harming Russia's interests, and instead called on Russia to play a leading role in a future confederation of states, integrated by all the CIS states. More specifically, they recommended that Russia consider the entire geopolitical space of the former Union a 'sphere of vital interests', an area where it was called upon to play an active role (Ambartsumov, 1992; Migranyan, 1992). The Seventh Congress of People's Deputies, held in December 1992, in turn, appealed to the parliaments of the newly independent states (NIS) to create a new confederation involving all the former Soviet states

(*Itar-Tass*, 1992). Similarly, the Civic Union's January 1993 programme insisted on the need to create a new confederation on the territory of the former USSR, which would replace the CIS, as the latter was seen as a non-viable organisation in the longer term (Rahr, 1993).

In view of the mounting centrifugal tendencies and in order to counter the ever-increasing domestic political pressure, the Russian MFA adopted a more assertive policy towards the CIS, especially at the rhetoric level. Russian leaders began talking with greater insistence about the need to deepen military and economic integration among the CIS states and about the necessity to strengthen CIS institutions. The *Draft Concept of the Foreign Policy of the Russian Federation*, approved in November 1992, referred to 'relations with the near abroad' as a priority of Russia's foreign policy and insisted on the need to strengthen cooperation within the CIS (*International Affairs*, 1993, p. 15). In February 1993, speaking at the Civic Union Forum, Yeltsin also stressed the need for closer integration among the states of the Commonwealth. He noted that 'our countries, which until recently constituted one country, perceive especially strongly today, how great their mutual independence is' (Russian Television, 1993). He also stated clearly Russia's special role in the territory of the former USSR, that of being the main guarantor of peace and stability in the post-Soviet space (Russian Television, 1993). This was reflected in the *Basic Provisions of the Russian Federation Foreign Policy Concept* approved by Yeltsin in April 1993, which stressed Russia's special responsibility 'for the creation of a new system of positive relations among the former Soviet states, Russia being the guarantor of the stability of those relations' (Chernov, 1993). Top priority was given, in the document, to relations with the former Soviet republics and to the desire to achieve the greatest possible degree of integration among the states of the former Soviet Union. Moreover, actions aimed at undermining the integrationist process within the CIS were considered a fundamental threat to Russia's security (Chernov, 1993).

In spite of all these vehement calls for deeper CIS integration, the record on CIS integration for 1993 remained mixed. In the institutional field, a CIS Charter outlining the main objectives and the structures of the organisation was adopted, and Russian pressure helped to bring new members – Azerbaijan, Georgia and Moldova – back into the organisation in the autumn.[9] However, no supranational or enforcing bodies were created and most of the agreements signed were never implemented. In the economic field, the process of disintegration gathered speed, as trade continued to decline, Russia reduced its CIS subsidies and increased its energy prices, the rouble zone was brought to an end, and the integration projects adopted turned out to be too ambitious to be properly implemented. In July 1993, Russia transformed its easy-term credits to the CIS states into state-to-state credits, denominated in US$ dollars at LIBOR-linked interest rates. Furthermore, the total amounts were significantly reduced (Michalopoulos, 1996, p. 19).[10] Moreover, Russia's CIS energy prices increasingly approached world market levels. Previous efforts to preserve within the CIS a Russian-subsidised trading-zone were replaced in 1993 by efforts to create a more economically efficient and viable union, based on free market principles. Moscow progressively liberalised its CIS trading regime and reached various economic agreements with its CIS partners, which were aimed at bringing down trade barriers and increasing economic policy coordination among CIS states. On 24 September 1993, Russia and other eight CIS states signed an *Economic Union Treaty*, which envisaged the progressive creation of an economic union – through the establishment of a free trade area (FTA), a customs union (CU) or *tamozhennyi soiuz*, and a common market of goods, services, capital and labour, and eventually also a monetary union – based on a highly homogenous economic, free market space (RIA-Novosti, 1993b).[11] The Economic Union project, however, failed to materialise, given the different levels of economic development among the various CIS economies, the lack of substantial market transformation in the majority of them, and the unwillingness of most CIS states, including Russia, partially to surrender their economic sovereignty to supranational institutions (Bekker, 1993). The establishment of the Inter-state Economic Committee (IEC) in October 1994 created the hope that some sort of economic coordination could be achieved among the CIS states. The IEC was made responsible for developing joint CIS economic programmes and monitoring the progress of economic reform. A wide range of IEC decisions would be adopted by an 80 per cent majority, with 50 per cent of the votes belonging to Russia. However, because the CIS states were allowed to decide exactly what powers they wanted to delegate to the IEC, the latter failed to develop into a truly effective structure, and instead simply remained an auxiliary agency (Portnikov, 1994b).

More significantly, on 24 July 1993, the rouble zone was brought to an end quite abruptly, when the Central Bank of Russia (CBR) announced that pre-1993 rouble bank notes would no longer be legal tender in Russia (*Rossiiskaya gazeta*, 1993). The main impact of this measure was to 'Russify' the rouble and therefore de-link the cash component of the money supply of the rouble zone states from that of Russia (Odling-Smee and Wolf, 1994, p. 44). The CBR's decision effectively forced republics to choose between keeping the Russian rouble or introducing their own currencies. Between July and November 1993, Moldova, Georgia, Azerbaijan and Turkmenistan proceeded with the introduction of their national currencies. Kazakhstan, Uzbekistan, Tajikistan, Belarus and Armenia, instead, engaged in long negotiations with Russia aimed at setting up a 'new-type' rouble zone, where the monetary rules were, to all intents and purposes, determined entirely by Russia. The CBR would keep total control over the money supply while countries would be obliged to coordinate with Russia the basic parameters of their monetary, credit, financial, foreign-exchange and customs policies, as well as their consolidated budget deficits (Kolokol'tseva, 1993). Although preliminary agreements were reached during September 1993 on the procedures of monetary coordination and unification, the whole deal collapsed in November 1993, when Russia asked the relevant CIS countries to collateralise, with gold or foreign exchange, some 50 per cent of any new bank notes delivered, with full compensation to be made if a country exceeded monetary ceilings. Although these tough measures may seem 'neo-imperialist', they actually reflected Russia's genuine concerns and legitimate economic interests, as well as its attempts to curb inflation and ensure macro-economic stability in Russia. However, to Kazakhstan, Uzbekistan, and Armenia, all these conditions proved unacceptable and they thus decided to introduce their own national currencies in 1993–1994.

Belarus announced in November 1993 its intention to make the Belarusian *rubel'*, the sole legal tender in the country, but in early January 1994, as its economic situation became very precarious, it entered into negotiations with Moscow on a monetary union with Russia. Belarus' decision in 1992 to pursue a gradual approach to structural change and to favour the maintenance of traditional Communist economic management methods had extremely negative consequences for the Belarusian economy, as the country became increasingly dependent on credits and cheap energy from Russia (IMF, 1993, p. 2). The impact of the terms of trade shock, in particular Russia's higher energy prices, meant that Belarus needed two to three times its current budget to cope with such increased expenses. In view of this situation, Belarus' leaders signed all the appropriate agreements aimed at merging Belarus' monetary system with Russia's, in the autumn of 1993 (Tsygankov, 1993). Tajikistan, the only state of the CIS that had not moved to differentiate its currency, reached a preliminary agreement on the provision of 100 billion new Russian roubles from the CBR in the autumn of 1993 (Odling-Smee and Wolf, 1994). For almost a year and a half, Tajikistan lived both with old and new Russian roubles. But serious difficulties in keeping the adequate amounts of cash in circulation forced the Tajik authorities, under Russian pressure, to introduce Tajikistan's own currency in May 1995 (Grigorev, 1995).

In the military sphere, very little was achieved at multilateral level during 1993, as most CIS states proceeded with the creation of their own armed forces. The CST failed to develop into a multilateral instrument for regional security, and no supranational air-defence and border protection systems were set up. The Russian military began increasingly to focus on bilateral forms of military cooperation with each individual CIS state, and worked towards the creation of coalition forces no longer subordinated to the CIS High Command, but to the Russian Ministry of Defence (MoD) instead.[12] Russia along with Uzbekistan put forward a proposal based on the old Warsaw Pact command structure that made the CIS commander a Russian deputy Defence Minister subordinate to the Russian Defence Minister (Falichev, 1993). The other signatories to the CST, as well as the CIS command, instead proposed a structure that would follow the NATO model, maintaining a permanent CIS command subordinated to a collective security council, composed of the leaders the six member states (Falichev, 1993; Zhilin, 1993).[13] The Russian MoD, however, openly rejected the creation of permanent unified CIS armed forces, and instead supported the formation of such forces only during wartime (Baev, 1996, p. 111). Russia's proposal was in fact heading in the opposite direction, having all CIS structures subordinated to the Russian MoD. To this end, Russia went ahead with abolishing the CIS JAF Command in June 1993, and replaced it with a coordinating body, the *Staff for the Co-ordination of Military Co-operation* or SCMC.

With the elimination of the CIS JAF Command, however, central control over the CIS air-defence system was lost, and any hopes of setting up joint CIS forces, in the foreseeable future, were dashed. Instead, in December 1993, Moscow managed to get the approval for a less ambitious collective security project, which instead envisaged the defence of the CIS space on the basis of national armed forces of minimal strength.[14] Collective security was to be achieved through mutual voluntary cooperation and coordination of operational planning in case of attack, as well as joint training and technical support (Litovkin, 1993). In view of these new realities, Russia tried to achieve integration outside the CIS structures, through a dense network of bilateral agreements it signed with several CIS states. These agreements allowed Russia to increase its military presence in the CIS area, in the form of peace-keeping operations, military bases, military assistance, technical cooperation, air defence and border protection, and eventually formed the basis of the multilateral integration projects agreed upon in 1995–1996. The goal of creating a united military-strategic space in the CIS was not abandoned, but the Russian military preferred to pursue military integration independently from the existing supranational CIS structures.

Renewed efforts at deeper integration

In view of this predicament, the idea that integration had to be pursued strictly in accordance with Russia's own interests began to gain ground in the mid-1990s and slowly turned into a core tenet of Russia's CIS policy. Although during 1994–1995, the goal of achieving deep CIS military and economic integration remained, emphasis was placed on its cost-effectiveness. In his speech to the Federation Council in 1994, Yeltsin spelled out Russia's aim of closer CIS integration, but added that 'integration should not damage Russia itself, nor should it be conducted at the cost of our forces and resources, material and financial alike, being stretched to breaking point' (Ostankino TV, 1994). Similarly, Kozyrev stressed in 1994 that integration had to benefit both sides, and made it clear that Russia would reject those proposals put forward by some CIS states, which were clearly motivated by the bid to get more help from Russia (*International Affairs*, 1994, p. 14). Renewed emphasis was also placed on the idea that Russia had to become a strong economic and political state first, before CIS integration could go ahead. It was assumed that only a strong and economically successful Russia would act as a magnet for further and deeper CIS integration (Ostankino TV, 1994). Russia's CIS integration record during 1994 and early 1995, thus reflected this combination of assertiveness and cost-effectiveness.

In the economic sphere, the Belarus-Russian monetary union project was abandoned despite the support it had among several members of the Duma, because it was considered too expensive and not capable of entirely satisfying Russia's economic interests. Although the April 1994 draft treaty on Belarusian–Russian monetary union kept the CBR as the only monetary-emission centre and Russia in control of overall monetary policy, Belarus retained oversight over its own state budget (Selyaninov and Smirnov, 1994). If implemented, this project was bound to lead to possible disagreements, and most probably, to Russia and the CBR ending up financing the Belarusian state budget. The overall cost of monetary integration was estimated at approximately $2.5 billion (Selyaninov and Smirnov, 1994). This, together with disagreements on the final Russian rouble-Belarusian *rubel'* exchange rate, as well as Minsk's unwillingness to adjust to Russia's financial, credit, customs and tax policies, eventually buried the project and all efforts to establish a Belarusian–Russian monetary union in 1994 (Zhdanko, 1994a). In the words of Prime Minister (PM) Chernomyrdin, 'Right now unification would mean that Russia would take on the additional burden of a neighbouring state's problems', and added, 'we cannot afford that' (Zhdanko, 1994b). This was a clear sign of a non-imperialist approach towards one of Russia's closest CIS neighbours, especially if we consider the significant strategic benefits that could potentially be obtained by Russia from deeper integration with Belarus – free transit of goods through Belarusian territory and free leasing of Belarus' military facilities (Zhdanko, 1994b). Russia's rejection of the deal indicated that it was not ready to pay any price for the sake of keeping a close monetary union with Belarus.

Instead, Moscow engaged in efforts to develop mutually advantageous economic relations with its CIS partners. On 15 April 1994, an agreement on the creation of a FTA was finally reached by all CIS states, within the framework of the 1993 *Economic Union Treaty* (*Ekonomika i zhizn'*, 1994). CIS states pledged gradually to abolish customs duties, taxes, fees and quantitative restrictions on mutual trade.[15] The free transit for goods within the area was guaranteed, while countries also committed themselves not to allow the unsanctioned re-export of commodities. However, while during 1994–1996 some CIS states, Russia in particular, began liberalising their trading regimes, they did so only partially. Russia progressively abolished export quotas and export taxes on most of its exported products but it introduced a new system of tariffs on imported goods, including an excise tax on products imported from Ukraine and other CIS countries, leading to major disruptions in intra-CIS trade (*RET*, 1995b, pp. 77–78, 1996a, pp. 82–84, 1996b, pp. 92–93; Bardin and Levin, 1996). The other CIS states also conducted little trade liberalisation, with the exception of smaller countries, such as Kyrgyzstan, Armenia, Georgia and Moldova, and then again, in some cases, the main exporting items remained subjected to tariffs.

In January 1995, Russia reached an agreement with two of its major CIS trading partners, Belarus and Kazakhstan on the establishment of a CU (Rybak, 1995). The treaty envisaged the abolition of customs duties and quantitative trade restrictions, as well as the introduction of common external schedules with regard to third countries. The treaty also foresaw the coordination of economic reforms and uniform regulatory mechanisms (Rybak, 1995). Moreover, a memorandum was signed stipulating for the standardisation of foreign trade, customs, monetary and price laws. Russia had a particular stake in the CU, as it granted duty free transit to its goods, especially natural gas shipments, through the territories of Belarus and Kazakhstan. Russia also hoped that the treaty would allow it better to control the illegal re-export of Russian goods (RET, 1994, p. 83). Belarus and Kazakhstan, in turn, hoped to benefit from the purchase of Russian goods, especially energy products, free of tax (RET, 1995a, p. 72). Despite these common advantages, the three states proved unwilling to coordinate their economic and financial policies, and this made implementation of the treaty quite difficult. However, some initial successes in trade liberalisation were nevertheless achieved. The customs borders between Russia and Belarus were eliminated in May 1995 and the customs border with Kazakhstan was lifted during the first half of 1996. In 1996, all three countries negotiated common external tariffs (CET), based mostly on Russian tariffs. Yet, during 1996 all three members unilaterally introduced modifications to their new external tariffs (Michalopoulos and Tarr, 1997, p. 3). As a result, the so-called 'Belarusian corridor' opened up as a lucrative channel for the smuggling of goods on a massive scale. Western and other CIS goods were registered as Belarusian goods and imported into Russia with zero tariffs (Michalopoulos and Tarr, 1997, p. 3).

In the military field, assertiveness seems to have dominated over caution, as new emphasis was placed by Russia on restoring a unified CIS military-strategic space. Although all CIS states were reluctant to re-establish highly centralised military structures, they were also aware that a certain degree of military cooperation with Russia was indeed necessary (Volkov, 1994). Most CIS states were experiencing enormous difficulties when trying to set up their own armed forces and needed Russia's financial support and technical expertise to proceed in their endeavour. Russia, in turn, proved eager to keep the CIS states within a military-strategic alliance that would bind their security tightly to Russia. By the end of 1993, support for deeper multilateral cooperation had gained strength among Russia's political and military circles, especially after Russia succeeded in bringing three additional CIS states – Azerbaijan, Georgia and Belarus – into the CST, and this facilitated the Kremlin's actions. Deeper military cooperation also reflected Russia's worries that a neglect over CIS military integration during 1992–1993 had undermined the ex-Soviet integrated structures upon which Russian security relied (Mironov, 1995). In addition, the prospects of NATO enlargement towards Eastern Europe, heightened concerns over Russia's increased vulnerability vis-à-vis the Western alliance, and this galvanised support for tighter military integration with the CIS states, especially in Russia but also in Belarus, on the western CIS front. Furthermore, military integration was seen as the best way to counter the new potential threats to Russia's security, which the *Foreign Intelligence Service* in 1994 identified as inter-ethnic conflicts and Islamist extremism (*Rossiiskaya gazeta*, 1994). During 1994–1995, therefore, Russia conducted renewed efforts aimed at restoring the unity of the former Soviet military-strategic space to be achieved by the materialisation of the principle of collective security, the restoration of the ex-Soviet air-defence system, joint CIS border protection, the legalisation of military bases in the CIS states, and the creation under Russia's aegis, of coalition, and in future united CIS armed forces (Trenin, 1994). Furthermore, bilateral ties were expected to complement developments at multilateral level.

Russia's renewed support for CIS multilateral cooperation resulted in the adoption by CST member states of a *Collective Security Concept* in February 1995. The concept represented a less ambitious version of the plans for military cooperation proposed by the CIS SCMC, which if implemented would have come close to restoring the old united Soviet armed forces within a single military-strategic space. The SCMC project, as presented by Lt.-Gen. Leonid Ivashov, Secretary of the CIS Defence Ministers' Council, envisaged the creation of permanent political and military bodies, common or joint military structures, *joint armed forces*, and coordinated operational planning and training. In the longer term, the CST 'military-political alliance' was expected to develop into a highly integrated military structure, with supranational powers whose decisions would be binding on all member states. States would share a common defence budget, in addition to the national defence budgets, as well as single armed forces under single command (Plotnikov, 1994). The approved Concept, instead, envisaged the creation of a collective security system based on *regional coalition forces* as well as on the armed forces of individual member states, and on a joint air defence system and joint border protection (*MNB*, 1995c). The formation of *joint armed forces*, as had been suggested by Lt.-Gen. Leonid Ivashov, was however left to a later stage. No supranational organs were set up, and the main CST organ – the Collective Security Council – retained purely coordinating functions. This showed that although Russia was eager to deepen military integration, it proved either reluctant or incapable of creating new military organs with supranational functions within the CIS/CST framework.

Still, in March 1996, a Committee of Chiefs of Staff of the CIS Armed Forces responsible for joint military planning and operations was set up, made up of the General Chiefs of Staff of the national armies, and led by Russian General Chief of Staff, Mikhail Kolesnikov. This meant that the operational actions and combat training activities of national armies would be conducted under Russian leadership.[16] However, despite these renewed efforts regional coalition forces were not fully established. Many CIS states proved reluctant to subordinate their armed forces to supranational structures, as they were trying to develop their own statehood and establish their own national institutions. Many rightly feared that these structures would be fully controlled by Russia, the dominant military power. Most of those CIS states willing to develop tight military cooperation with Russia, with the possible exception of Armenia and Tajikistan, were generally motivated in their decisions by the desire to obtain Russian financial support and technical expertise for their military development, rather than by the conviction that their country's security was best safeguarded through cooperation with Russia. Others, such as Georgia and Azerbaijan, which had been to a great extent compelled to join the CST against their will, felt that only through CST membership would they succeed in retaking control over their separatist regions.

Despite these shortcomings, significant efforts were conducted by Russia to restore a unified air-defence system, through a series of *bilateral* deals on the joint use of air-defence capabilities that were reached with most CIS states – Armenia, Georgia, Azerbaijan, Kazakhstan, Kyrgyzstan, Tajikistan, Turkmenistan, Belarus, and Ukraine. Furthermore, in February 1995, all CIS states except for Azerbaijan and Moldova agreed to establish a *joint* air-defence system based on the forces and installations of individual CIS states, and responsible for joint monitoring, early warning, and attack repelling (Webber, 1997, pp. 40–41). The forces were to be controlled by individual states, but their actions would be coordinated from the Central Command of Russia's Air Defence Forces (*MNB*, 1995b).[17] In May 1995, Russia also managed to obtain the agreement of Armenia, Belarus, Georgia, Kazakhstan, Kyrgyzstan and Tajikistan for the development of a multilateral joint border protection system (Abarinov, 1995). President Yeltsin considered that the reliable protection of borders along the CIS external perimeter corresponded with Russia's national security and the overall interests of all other CIS member states, a clear sign that Russia still viewed most former Soviet states as belonging to a common security space. However, hardly any cooperation on border protection developed at CIS multilateral level; most joint border protection instead occurred at bilateral level between Russia and the individual CIS states just mentioned, as well as, with Ukraine, Moldova, Azerbaijan, Uzbekistan and Turkmenistan.

Moscow also signed several agreements on bilateral military cooperation with several CIS states – Belarus, Kazakhstan, Tajikistan, Uzbekistan, Kyrgyzstan, Georgia and Armenia – which envisaged Russia's assistance in the formation of individual armed forces, both in terms of training, equipment and military expertise. Of particular relevance were the December 1995 and May 1996 agreements reached with Belarus, which foresaw joint defence policy planning and the development of Russian and Belarusian armed forces on the basis of common principles. Similarly, the March 1994 agreement between Russia and Kazakhstan also envisaged the formation of integrated military units, which would operate under joint command, and would be assigned to joint defensive missions. In a subsequent January 1995 agreement, Russia and Kazakhstan agreed to work towards the formation of united armed forces based on the principles of joint planning and training, and to use military installations located in each other's territories in the interest of mutual security (*MNB*, 1995a). On the other hand, strategically vital countries such as Ukraine, Azerbaijan, as well as Uzbekistan and Moldova refused to develop tight military cooperation with Russia. Moscow, nevertheless, managed to keep an important military presence in Ukraine and Moldova. Russia delayed the withdrawal of the 14th Army located in Transdniestria (Moldova), and succeeded in keeping a big share of the Black Sea Fleet (BSF) in the Crimean peninsula of Ukraine.[18] In addition, Russia retained two military bases in Armenia, at Gyumri and Yerevan, and three military facilities in Georgia at Batumi, Alkhalkalaki and Viziani, as well as the naval bases of Poti and Ochamchira (Bulavinov, 1995a, 1995b).

During the rest of 1995 the main traits of Russia's policy orientation towards the CIS, as it had developed in the previous year, therefore became crystallised. CIS integration remained a top priority of Russia's foreign policy and all efforts were devoted to establishing a CES and a joint collective security system. However, the notion that integration should not harm Russia's interests and that benefits had to be obtained from CIS integration remained a priority (*Rossiiskie vesti*, 1996a). Emphasis was placed on the idea that Russia had to profit from free access to CIS markets and CIS resources, as well as from the free transit of its products through the CIS space (Kondrashov, 1996). Moreover, CIS states were expected to reach a similar level of economic development for integration to proceed (*Rossiiskie vesti*, 1996a). However, in view of the upcoming 1996 presidential and parliamentary elections, Yeltsin undertook several initiatives that had a direct bearing on the integration issue. Authoritative documents which defined Russia's CIS policy were published. Of particular relevance was the above-mentioned *Strategic Course of Russia Towards the Member States of the CIS*, a highly comprehensive document, which spelled out in a systematic form the main objectives of Russia's CIS policy. Russia's main aim in the area was 'to create an economic and political integration of states, capable of occupying a fitting place in the world' (MID, 1995). Integration was considered essential for the sake of containing centrifugal tendencies inside Russia and for ensuring lasting stability within the CIS states as well. However, CIS cooperation had to be conducted only if it did not impair Russia's national interest. Russian leaders considered that the most effective way to achieve this goal was to allow each country to choose its own mode of rapprochement. Bilateral ties, which took into account the specific peculiarities of each state, were to be developed as a complement to multilateral forms of cooperation (Filipov and Shchipanov, 1995; *Rossiiskaya gazeta*, 1995). On the other hand, an 'integrated core' of states within the CIS was identified, with which integration would move forward at a faster pace. This was exemplified in the signing of two fairly ambitious economic agreements in 1996 – the Russian–Belarusian treaty on the creation of a *Community of Sovereign States* (April 1996) and the agreement on *Deepening Integration in the Economic and Humanitarian Fields among Russia, Belarus, Kazakhstan and Kyrgyzstan* (March 1996), discussed in greater detail in Chapter 3.

These treaties envisaged, among others, the establishment of common energy and transport systems. Gazprom, in particular, had a strong interest in acquiring ownership of the gas facilities that it had lost as a result of the collapse of the Soviet Union, in order to restore, in some way, the former Soviet energy complex. It also wished to put an end to the siphoning of gas destined to Europe, which was regularly carried out by Ukraine and Belarus. Unable to pay for increased gas prices, and faced with regular cutbacks in their supplies, Minsk and Kiev very often siphoned Russian gas transiting through their territories to Europe, in order to fulfil their own energy needs. Disruptions in gas supplies to Europe convinced Moscow of the need to obtain ownership of the pipeline networks transiting through CIS consumer countries, and, if possible, to diversify export routes. Gazprom also tried to gain control over local distribution networks inside the CIS states themselves in order to increase revenues. In this respect, Gazprom's aims fully coincided with those of the Russian government which saw the energy industry as an adequate instrument for the reintegration of the CIS states. The December 1994 government document *Energy Strategy of Russia* promoted 'the use [of] energy systems as the most important means of integration of the regions of Russia and countries of the CIS' (IEA, 1995, p. 278). Russia's energy policy, according to the document, was aimed at developing CIS integration in the energy sector, which was understood as the joint exploitation of energy production systems and joint control over energy export routes (IEA, 1995, p. 305).[19] Yeltsin's May 1995 decree on *The Main Lines of Development of Energy Policy until 2010* also stated that Russia's energy policies were intended to promote 'mutual co-operation of the Russian Federation and the CIS states' (IEA, 1995, p. 266). In other words, integration of the former Soviet energy sector around Russia was seen as an instrument of further CIS integration under Russia's lead. It can therefore be argued that both elements – the internationalisation and expansion of the energy sector – as well as the desire to achieve deeper CIS integration played a role in Russia's attempts to acquire energy assets in Ukraine, Belarus and Moldova.

Assessment of the CIS

In the early and mid-1990s, the CIS did not develop into a robust and performing organisation, similar to the European Union (EU), NATO or the former Warsaw Treaty Organisation. Instead, the CIS remained an amorphous entity because of the unwillingness and inability of Russia and the CIS states to develop political institutions and coordinating instruments at supranational level, capable of ensuring the effective functioning of the organisation. Neither did the founding documents nor did the CIS Charter envisage the creation of any supranational bodies enjoying the power to impose decisions on member states (RIA-Novosti, 1993a; Tass, 1991a). Moreover, the highest bodies of the CIS, the Council of Heads of State and the Council of Heads of Government, which enjoyed executive power, adopted all decisions by consensus. In addition, the Charter stated that 'any state could declare non-interest in a given question, which should not be regarded as an obstacle to making a decision' (RIA-Novosti, 1993a). This condition, which allowed a CIS state to *opt out* of provisions with which it disagreed, and which was aimed at avoiding the veto, was extensively used by the CIS states in the 1990s.[20] As a result, support for most of the CIS documents was far from unanimous, leading to a differentiated membership within the CIS. A first group of states, comprising Armenia, Belarus, Kazakhstan, Kyrgyzstan, Russia, Tajikistan and initially also Uzbekistan, usually favoured close cooperation within the CIS and signed most CIS agreements. A second group, consisting of Azerbaijan, Moldova, Turkmenistan, Ukraine, and after 1994 Uzbekistan, only signed a minority of CIS agreements, and either opposed the creation of coordinating structures or entered into them half-heartedly.

A further obstacle to effective coordination within the CIS was the lack of any real mechanism for enforcing compliance with the signed agreements. Decisions taken within the institutions of the Commonwealth were not legally binding even upon those members that had agreed to them. In such cases as the IEC, where executive functions were mooted, they were to little effect (Webber, 1996, pp. 91–94). Some agreements had legal standing by virtue of them being international treaties requiring ratification by national parliaments, such as the founding CIS agreements, the CST and the Economic Union Treaty. However, once signed and subsequently ratified, there was no guarantee that their provisions would be carried out and no machinery for punishing non-compliance (Shinkarenko, 1993).[21] Moreover, from the very beginning of the creation of the CIS, differences of opinion emerged on the introduction and the pace of economic reform, as well as on the establishment of a common military-strategic space. This resulted in violations of provisions previously signed, leading to a total lack of coordination in economic and military policy. This inconsistent behaviour resulted from the contradictory visions of the various CIS states regarding the aims and purposes of the organisation. From the very beginning, Ukraine made it clear that it viewed the CIS as an association of independent states, where decisions could not be imposed on its members (Lugovskaya, 1993). Ukraine's sceptical views on the CIS were shared by Azerbaijan, Moldova and Georgia, all of which were brought back into the organisation as a result of either military pressure (Georgia and Azerbaijan) or economic coercion (Moldova) in late 1993–early 1994. Three Central Asian states – Kazakhstan, Kyrgyzstan and Tajikistan – instead, became the most active supporters of close CIS integration, partly a result of their high level of economic dependence on Russia. Moreover, the presence of large Russian minorities in their territories, as in Kazakhstan, or internal political instabilities, as occurred in Tajikistan and Kyrgyzstan, also argued in favour of closer ties with Russia. These countries were joined in their support for close integration by Belarus and Armenia (Portnikov, 1993; Gagua, 1992). Uzbekistan, instead, had significant regional ambitions, and therefore adopted a more independent line in 1995–1996, although in the early 2000s it tilted back into the CIS orbit. Turkmenistan, instead, preferred to conduct an entirely independent and officially 'neutral' foreign policy.

This predicament, however, does not mean that Russian leaders entirely relinquished efforts aimed at deepening political, military and economic integration among the CIS states. As noted in this chapter, Russia managed to develop very tight bilateral cooperation with several CIS states in the military sphere – it provided significant assistance to CIS states for the formation of their own armed forces, and succeeded in jointly patrolling most of the external CIS borders. Russia was also able partially to restore the old Soviet air-defence system, and to impose the peace in most of the 'hot-spots' of the former Soviet space with its own troops. In the economic sphere, Russia conducted major efforts aimed at developing trade among the CIS states and preserving a single currency during 1992–1993. Although the single market eventually disintegrated and the rouble zone collapsed in the autumn of 1993, Russia managed to set up a CU with a restricted group of CIS states in January 1995 (Belarus and Kazakhstan, later joined by Kyrgyzstan and Tajikistan). Very ambitious integration projects were signed with Belarus, and the other partners of the CU in 1996, but diverse economic developments and reduced financial resources made their proper implementation almost impossible.

Russia's dominant economic position as the main trading partner, however, kept these states often economically heavily dependent on Russia.

Conclusions

Although this record might suggest that Russia attempted and managed, to a certain extent, to restore a 'sphere of influence' or 'informal empire' in the CIS, a close examination reveals a different picture. First, Russian leaders did not pursue a coherent and coordinated strategy of empire-building in the CIS during the early and mid-1990s, although the Kremlin's rhetoric could at times suggest otherwise. On the contrary, Russia's CIS policies varied depending on domestic political developments and on Russia's financial capabilities. Second, Russia's policies were much more restrained than is frequently assumed, especially in the economic sphere, and often reflected Russia's legitimate concerns, namely the need to preserve existing intra-CIS commercial ties while at the same time ensuring that Russia successfully implemented much needed structural economic reforms. In the energy sphere, in particular, Russia's actions clearly reflected a financial logic, with the Russian state and private energy companies following the understandable rationale of making profits. Even if pressure may have been exerted by the Kremlin to acquire industrial or energy assets in the CIS gas-consuming states, Russia had a powerful argument, as many of these countries failed to pay on time for Russian energy resources and, as a result, accumulated significant arrears vis-à-vis Russia. Energy price rises were rarely utilised as 'hard power' instruments to exert political influence and advance specific policies, as occurred in the mid-2000s under President Putin. Third, deeper cooperation was reached in the military sphere (particularly at bilateral level), and this resulted in Russia partially restoring its military influence over the CIS states. However, Russia's successes were often offset by the lack of implementation of the various agreements reached due to limited funding. Furthermore, Russia's policies were often curbed by the CIS states themselves, and by Russia's inability and unwillingness to impose its will on the CIS states, and prevent the CIS states from diversifying their foreign policies. While there is little doubt that Russia used its *hard power* to bring countries such as Georgia or Azerbaijan into the CIS, it generally relied on *soft power* instruments in relation to other CIS countries.

Moreover, it can be argued that Russia *itself* proved reluctant to accept the creation of supranational organs which might have resulted in other CIS states dictating policies to Russia. Kazakhstan's initiatives to create a *Eurasian Union* with those CIS states in favour of deeper economic, military and political integration, did not enjoy Moscow's support (Nazarbaev, 1992). If implemented, Kazakhstan's proposals would have radically altered the nature of the existing CIS organisation, transforming its ailing structures into an entity similar to that of the EU. Nazarbayev's Eurasian Union project envisaged the delegation of some state powers to inter-state coordinating bodies, the creation of common executive organs enjoying substantial supranational powers, above all in the economic sphere, as well as the introduction of citizens' freedom of movement

(Portnikov, 1994a). Russian leaders, instead, preferred to develop bilateral forms of cooperation, which best took Russia's interests into account, and allowed the country to keep its predominance and hegemonic role in the CIS space. This was particularly reflected in the broad web of bilateral and multilateral military agreements which tied CIS' state security to Russia. This network allowed Russia potentially to exert influence over the CIS/CST states, and more importantly, theoretically prevent other external actors to display a military presence in the CIS states and penetrate the ex-USSR region. However, in the 1990s, Russia failed effectively to exercise this hegemony, due to the lack of real capabilities and because to the absence of a clearly neo-imperialist agenda.

In the economic field, agreements were less the result of attempts to establish an economic dependency by the CIS on Russia, and were, instead, primarily dictated by the logic of ensuring mutual trade and economic profits. Moreover, Russian leaders accepted, albeit reluctantly, that other CIS states disagreed over the speed and development of the CIS, while also allowing for the cohabitation of very contrasting views within the organisation. This indicated that Russian leaders both lacked the willingness and the financial capabilities to create a neo-empire in the CIS space. It had become clear to Moscow's leaders that the only way to dominate supranational political CIS organs would have been through the recreation of a political entity akin to the former USSR state, something both Russian and other CIS leaders refused to contemplate.

More importantly, it must be noted that Russia's attempts at pursuing deeper integration in the mid-1990s were dovetailed by the increasing desire of many – if not most – CIS states to develop closer ties with Russia, a result of their bad economic performances and of their awareness that links with Russia were stronger and more difficult to destroy than initially envisaged. In this respect, it is not possible to describe the relationship between Russia and those CIS states willing to develop closer bilateral and multilateral ties with Russia within the CIS framework as reflecting a purely *neo-imperialist* model. Instead, in many instances, aspects of the Russian–CIS relationship can be better characterised as approaching the model of *voluntary contracting*. Furthermore, even if Russia's motivations may have reflected a desire to exert influence over these countries, Russia did not always succeed. Furthermore, Moscow's actions also followed legitimate state interests – namely the need to develop close mutually beneficial economic and military ties with neighbouring states, which had previously been part of a same political entity. Although nostalgia for the Soviet Union remained deeply embedded in Russian political thinking, especially among members of the parliamentary opposition and nationalist groups, and was reflected in the government rhetoric after 1993, the actual policies of the government tended to be much more cautious. Many of the most ambitious integration projects were never implemented, because of Russia's own financial constraints – a reflection of Russia's poor economic performance – and because of the absence of a strong political will to pursue such undertakings. It can therefore well be argued that Russian leaders neither fully tried nor did they succeed in imposing the Kremlin's views on other CIS states, and thus Moscow's policies did not entirely fit into the neo-imperialist paradigm.

Notes

1 The CIS states also recognised and respected the territorial integrity of one another and the inviolability of existing borders within the Commonwealth. (Tass, 1991a)
2 This view was shared by President Yeltsin. See his interview in *Rossiiskie vesti*, 1996b.
3 Russia was, still in 1995, the largest destination of CIS states' exports, and in the majority of cases accounted for more than half of the individual republics' 'intra-Soviet' trade.
4 The Russian Armed forces were set up on the basis of the senior echelons located on Russian territory, the former Soviet forces deployed outside the former USSR, and those located in the Baltic states, Armenia, Georgia, Azerbaijan and Moldova.
5 The CST states saw aggression against one member state as an aggression against them all, with states expected to render the necessary assistance including military aid. Participants were barred from joining other military alliances, or taking part in actions aimed against another member state.
6 Between late 1991 and 1993 trade among FSS contracted quite significantly. Exports declined by an overall 56.3 per cent and imports by 47.9 per cent (Michalopoulos, 1996, p. 6).
7 Ukraine was the highest debtor with a U$2.5 billion liability, followed by Kazakhstan (U$1.25 billion), Belarus (U$385 million) and Uzbekistan (U$418 million).
8 Fifteen independent central banks emerged and a network of correspondent accounts was established in early 1992. But, the system became clogged as it took up to two to three months to clear an inter-state payments order (Konovalov, 1994, pp. 34–35; Michalopoulos, 1993, p. 6).
9 Azerbaijan re-joined the CIS in September 1993, Georgia joined in December 1993, and Moldova ratified its membership in April 1994.
10 Russia's total credits to the CIS during 1993–1995 amounted to US$702 million, compared to US$5.2 billion during 1992 to mid-1993 (Michalopoulos, 1996, p. 20).
11 The treaty was signed by Russia, Belarus, Moldova, Armenia, Azerbaijan, Kazakhstan, Kyrgyzstan, Uzbekistan and Tajikistan. Turkmenistan joined the union as a full member on 24 December 1993, and Ukraine became an associate member on 15 April 1994.
12 Personal Interview with Andrei Zagorsky, Moscow, November 1996.
13 Marshal Shaposhnikov, Commander-in-Chief of the JAF also hoped to create mixed-troop formations of CIS national armies at regional level (Zhilin, 1993).
14 The Russian Military Doctrine adopted in November 1993 envisaged cooperation among CIS states 'in solving collective defence and security problems', but no reference was made to integration of CIS armed forces under joint command (*Izvestiya*,1993).
15 They also agreed to coordinate their trade policy with respect to third countries.
16 Although the specific functions of the committee were not spelled out, the idea behind the committee's creation was to unite the potential of the general staffs.
17 The operations of early-warning facilities deployed beyond Russia's borders were supervised by the Russian MoD through the office of the Air Defence Forces of the Russian Federation (Korotchenko, 1996).
18 Final agreement on the fate of the BSF vessels, infrastructure and basing facilities was only reached in May 1997.
19 This was understood as 'the exploitation of the objective benefits of the joint work of energy production systems', and 'the improvement of the reliability of transport systems linking Russia with Europe and crossing the CIS and the Baltic States' (IEA, 1995).
20 The Tashkent summit of CIS Heads of State on 15 May 1992 adopted the formula of 'consensus minus one', and simple majority voting for procedural issues, but still any state could declare that it was not interested in a particular decision and was thus exempted (Sakwa, 1993, p. 325).
21 The CIS states' leaders were in fact never able to agree on a mechanism for the implementation of joint decisions.

Bibliography

Alimov, G. (1991). *Izvestiya*, 5 November, p. 1.
Abarinov, V. (1995). *Segodnya*, 30 May, p. 3.
Ambartsumov, E. (1992). *Rossiiskaya gazeta*, 13 April, p. 7.
Baev, P. (1996). *The Russian Army in a Time of Troubles*. London: PRIO.
Bardin, V. and K. Levin (1996). *Kommersant-daily*, 13 April, p. 2.
Bekker, A. (1993). *Segodnya*, 28 September, p. 2.
Bulavinov, I. (1995a). *Kommersant-daily*, 17 March, p. 1.
Bulavinov, I. (1995b). *Kommersant-daily*, 25 March, p. 4.
Burbyga, N. and A. Plutnik (1992). *Izvestiya*, 1 June, p. 1.
Chernov, V. (1993). *Nezavisimaya gazeta*, 29 April, p. 1.
Christensen, B.V. (1994). *The Russian Federation in Transition*, Occasional Paper 11, Washington DC: The International Monetary Fund.
Ekonomika i Zhizn' (1994). 19 May, p. 16.
Falichev, O. (1993). *Krasnaya zvezda*, 2 March, p. 1.
Falkenrath, R.A. (1995). *Shaping Europe's Military Order: The Origins and Consequences of the CFE Treaty*. Cambridge Massachusetts: MIT, Centre for Science and International Affairs.
Filipov, B. and M. Shchipanov (1995). *Rossiiskaya gazeta*, 18 August, p. 9.
Gagua, A. (1992), *Nezavisimaya gazeta*, 30 July, p. 5.
Garthoff, R. (1994). *Russian Military Doctrine and Developments*, Russian Littoral Project, University of Maryland and John Hopkins University.
Golub, P. (1992). *Izvestiya*, 24 July, p. 7.
Grachev, A. (1995). *Final Days: The Inside Story of the Collapse of the Soviet Union*, Boulder, Co: Westview Press.
Granville, B. (1994). *Farewell Ruble Zone*, Stockholm: Stockholm Institute of East European Economics, Working Paper. 95, November.
Grigorev, A. (1995). *Segodnya*, 11 May, p. 4.
Gross, N. (1992). Russia's Strategy: East or West?, *Jane's Intelligence Review*, June.
IEA (1995). *Energy Policies of the Russian Federation, 1995 Survey*. Paris.
Illarionov, A. (1993). *Izvestiya*, 16 September, p. 4.
Interfax (1992). 26 February.
International Affairs (1992). A Transformed Russia in a New World, Moscow, 4–5.
International Affairs (1993). Russia's Foreign Policy Concept, Moscow, 1.
International Affairs (1994). Russian Interests in the CIS, Moscow, 11.
International Energy Agency (IEA) (1995). *Energy Policies of the Russian Federation, 1995 Survey*. Paris.
International Monetary Fund (IMF) (1993). Belarus, *IMF Economic Review*, 11.
Itar-Tass (1992). 14 December.
Izvestiya (1993). 18 November 1993, p. 4.
Katanyan, K. (1992). *Kuranty*, 6 January, p. 4.
Kolokol'tseva, E. (1993). *Segodnya*, 9 September, p. 1.
Komsomol'skaya Pravda (1992). 27 May, p. 2.
Kondrashov, S. (1996). *Izvestiya*, 6 March, p. 3.
Konovalov, V. (1994). 'Russian Trade Policy'. In: C. Michalopoulos and D.G. Tarr, eds. *Trade in the New Independent States*, eds., *Studies of Economies in Transformation*, 13. Washington DC: The World Bank.
Korotchenko, I. (1996). *Nezavisimoe voennoe obozrenie*, 13 January, p. 4.
Kozyrev, A. (1992). *Izvestiya*, 2 January, p. 3.

Krasnaya zvezda (1992). 20 February, pp. 1–3.
Kyzhnechevsky, V. (1991). *Rossiiskaya gazeta*, 28 November, p. 1.
Lepskii, Y. and A. Potapov (1991). *Trud*, 16 December, p. 1.
Litokvin, V. (1993). *Izvestiya*, 26 August, p. 2.
Lugovskaya, A. (1993). *Izvestiya*, 6 January, p. 3.
Michalopoulos, C. (1993). *Trade Issues in the New Independent States*, Studies of Economies in Transformation, Washington DC: The World Bank, 7.
Michalopoulos, C. (1996). *Payments and Finance Problems in the CIS*, Policy Research Working Paper. Washington DC: The World Bank, 1587.
Michalopoulos, C. and D. Tarr (1997). The Economics of Customs Unions in the Commonwealth of Independent States, *Policy Research Working Paper*, 1786, Washington DC: The World Bank.
MID (1995). *Strategicheskii Kurs Rossii s Gosudarstvami-Uchastnikami Sodruzhestva Nezavisimykh Gosudarstv*, 14 September, p. 1. Available at: www.mid.ru/foreign_policy/official_documents/-/asset_publisher/CptICkB6BZ29/content/id/427752
Migranyan, A. (1992). *Rossiiskaya gazeta*, 4 August, p. 4.
Military News Bulletin (MNB) (1992a). Treaty on Collective Security, 5, May, pp. 1–2.
Military News Bulletin (MNB) (1992b). Concept of Military Security of the Member-States of the CIS, 12, December, p. 9.
Military News Bulletin (MNB) (1995a). Stages of Military Cooperation, 2, February, p. 6.
Military News Bulletin (MNB) (1995b). Agreement on the Creation of a Joint Air Defence System of the CIS, 2, February, pp. 6–7.
Military News Bulletin (MNB) (1995c). Collective Security Concept of States, Parties to the Collective Security Treaty, March, p. 8.
Mironov, V. (1995). *Segodnya*, 20 July, p. 5.
Moscow Radio (1991). 10 December. In: FBIS-SOV-91-238, 11 December, pp. 36–37.
Moscow Radio (1992). 18 April.
Nazarbaev, N. (1992). *Literaturnaya gazeta*, 19 August, p. 1.
Nezavisimaya gazeta (1991). August 13, p. 1.
Odling-Smee, J. and T.A. Wolf (1994). *Financial Relations Among Countries of the Former Soviet Union*. Washington DC: International Monetary Fund.
Ostankino TV (1994). Moscow, 24 February.
Plotnikov, N. (1994). *Nezavisimaya gazeta*, 6 July, p. 1.
Portnikov, V. (1993). *Nezavisimaya gazeta*, 18 May, p. 1.
Portnikov, V. (1994a). *Nezavisimaya gazeta*, 31 March, p. 1.
Portnikov, V. (1994b). *Nezavisimaya gazeta*, 22 October, p. 1.
Pravda (1991). 23 December, p. 1.
Rahr, A. (1991). Gorbachev and El'tsin in a Deadlock. *RFE/RL Report on the USSR*, 15 February, pp. 1–5.
Rahr, A. (1993). Russia: The Struggle for Power Continues, *RFE/RL Research Report*, p. 3.
RIA-Novosti (1993a). *Charter of the Commonwealth of Independent States*, 22 January.
RIA-Novosti (1993b). *Treaty on the Formation of the Economic Union*, 24 September.
Rogov, S. (1992). Commonwealth Defence Arrangements and International Security, *CNA Occasional Paper*, Centre for Naval Analysis.
Rossiiskaya gazeta (1991). 13 December, p. 1.
Rossiiskaya gazeta (1992). 21 February, p. 1.
Rossiiskaya gazeta (1993). 27 July, p. 1.
Rossiiskaya gazeta (1994). 22 September, pp. 1 and 6.
Rossiiskaya gazeta (1995). 17 February, p. 1.

Rossiiskie vesti (1996a). 20 January, p. 4.
Rossiiskie vesti (1996b). 30 April, p. 1.
Russian Economic Trends (RET) (1994). 3(4).
Russian Economic Trends (RET) (1995a). 4 (3).
Russian Economic Trends (RET) (1995b). 4(4).
Russian Economic Trends (RET) (1996a). 5(1).
Russian Economic Trends (RET) (1996b). 5(2).
Russian Television (1993). 28 February.
Rybak, S. (1995). *Nezavisimaya gazeta*, 31 January, p. 1.
Sagers, M. (1992). Review of Energy Industries in the Former USSR in 1991, *Post-Soviet Geography*, 33(4), 340–365.
Sakwa, R. (1993). *Russian Politics and Society*. London: Routledge.
Selyaninov, G. and K. Smirnov (1994). *Kommersant-daily*, 15 April, p. 1.
Shinkarenko, P. (1993). *Rossiikie vesti*, 18 May, p. 2.
Simakov, V. (1995). Air Space Defence in CIS Common Space, *Military News Bulletin*, July, p. 3.
Smith, A. (1994). *International Trade and Payments in the Former Soviet/CMEA Area: Reorientation or Reintegration?* London: The Royal Institute of International Affairs.
Sodruzhestvo (1992a). O statuse sil obshchego naznacheniya Ob'edinennykh Vooruzhennykh Sil na perekhodnyi period, 4, 20 March.
Sodruzhestvo (1992b). Soglashenie o statuse Pogranichnykh Voisk Sodruzhestva Nezavisimykh Gosudarstv, 4, March 20.
Sodruzhesvto (1992c). Soglashenie ob organizatsii deyatel'nosti Glavnogo Komandovaniya Ob'edinennykh Vooruzhennykh Sil Sodruzhestva Nezavisimykh Gosudarstv na perekhodnyi period, 6, July.
Soyuz (1990). September, 38, pp. 6–7. In: J. Dunlop, *The Rise of Russia and the Fall of the Soviet Empire*, Princeton, New Jersey: Princeton University Press.
Tass (1991a). Agreement on the Creation of a Commonwealth of Independent States, 8 December 1991. In: RIA-Novosti, January 1992, p. 2 (pp. 1–5).
Tass (1991b). Agreement between Commonwealth Heads of State on Armed Forces and Border Troops. 31 December.
Tass (1991c). Agreement between the Members of the Commonwealth of Independent States on Strategic Forces, 31 December.
Trenin, D. (1994). *Nezavisimaya gazeta*, 4 November, p. 3.
Tsygankov, V. (1993). *Nezavisimaya gazeta*, 20 November, p. 3.
Volkov, V. (1994). *Nezavisimaya gazeta*, 2 March, p. 3.
Webber, M. (1996). *The International Politics of Russia and the Successor States*. Manchester: Manchester University Press.
Webber, M. (1997). *CIS Integration Trends: Russia and the Former Soviet South*. London: The Royal Institute of International Affairs.
Yeltsin, B. (1994). *The View from the Kremlin*. London: Harper Collins.
Zhagel, I. (1991). *Izvestiya*, 26 December, p. 2.
Zhdanko, V. (1994a). *Segodnya*, 4 August, p. 1.
Zhdanko, V. (1994b). *Segodnya*, 16 September, p. 5.
Zhilin, A. (1993). *Moskovskie novosti*, 30 May, pp. 8–9.

3 CIS integration under Yevgeny Primakov
Russia's post-Imperial model

During his term in office as Foreign and Prime Minister, Primakov actively encouraged further integration among the former Soviet states, although he insisted this had to occur on a voluntary and cooperative basis, to a great extent reflecting a non-imperialist attitude (*Rossiiskaya gazeta*, 1996). In Primakov's view, the independence that had been achieved by the former Soviet republics had become irreversible (Isayev, 1995). As he noted in his first statement as Foreign Minister,

> the strengthening of centripetal tendencies ... does not and cannot mean the rebirth of the Soviet Union in the form in which it used to exist. The sovereignty obtained by the republics is irreversible, but this does not negate the need for reintegration processes, first of all in the economic field.
> (*Moskovksie novosti*, 1996)

In Primakov's view, the vast array of military, economic, cultural, and personal ties that had developed during the Soviet era brought these countries together – establishing an objective basis for integration (Yusin, 1996). Primakov envisaged the creation of a varied-speed organisation, involving a group of leading states supportive of deeper ties, such as Belarus, Kazakhstan, Kyrgyzstan and Armenia, moving faster along the path of integration. These countries would join their economies and establish common supranational structures, to which they would delegate some of their sovereignty, similarly to the EU model of pooled-sovereignty, while remaining independent states (Kondrashov, 1996). The other former Soviet states could then decide whether or not they wanted to join the process of deeper integration (Kondrashov, 1996). Following a soft-power approach, it was hoped that the Commonwealth of Independent States (CIS) would 'serve as a catalyst for prosperity and cooperation throughout the post-Soviet space', and contribute to the resolution of conflicts along Russia's southern and western periphery (Eggert, 1998).

Renewed attempts at CIS economic integration

When Primakov became Foreign Minister in 1996, he sponsored two highly ambitious integration treaties – the *Treaty on the Deepening of Integration in the*

Economic and Humanitarian Fields (29 March 1996) among Russia, Belarus, Kazakhstan, and Kyrgyzstan and the agreement on the creation of a *Community of Sovereign States* (CSS) between Russia and Belarus (2 April 1996). These agreements established the basis for future integration projects established in the 2000s/2010s, such as EvrAzES (Eurasian Economic Community) and the Eurasian Economic Union (EAEU). *The Treaty on Deepening Integration*, which was joined by Tajikistan in April 1998, was aimed at creating a 'community of integrated states' through the establishment of a single market, a single currency and common energy and transport systems (Kalashnikova, 1996). In order to achieve such goals, signatory states agreed to coordinate tightly their monetary and credit policies, and to harmonise their industrial and agrarian strategies. In an initial stage, the four CIS states were expected to establish a Customs Union (CU) and create an efficient payments union, as a precondition for the creation of a CES, at a later stage. The treaty also envisaged that the parties would coordinate their foreign and security policy, as well as their social and education policies, thus creating a powerful and well-integrated block.

Moreover, signatory states also agreed to create joint administrative bodies to help implement the integration policies – an *Inter-State Council* (ISC), the supreme administrative body of the organisation, with a capacity to adopt binding decisions; an *Integration Committee* (IC), the permanent executive body responsible for ensuring compliance and helping implement decisions taken by the ISC; and an *Inter-parliamentary Committee*, responsible for inter-parliamentary cooperation among member states (Kalashnikova, 1996). It should be noted, however, that the ISC, which was composed of the heads of state and government, the foreign ministers, and the head of the IC, was formed on a parity basis and could only take decision on the basis of unanimity (EvrAzES, 1996).[1] This meant that no decisions could be imposed on member states. In February 1999, a new agreement was signed, on the formation of a CU and a CES (Common Economic Space), within the framework of the *Treaty on Deepening Integration*. These agreements essentially fleshed out the details for the establishment of a CU and a CES, involving the free movement of goods, services, capital and labour; coordinated trade, monetary, economic and fiscal policies; harmonised legislation, as well as the establishment of a single transport infrastructure (EvrAzES, 1999). The agreement also envisaged the implementation of a full-scale FTA in goods, 'without exceptions or restrictions' among its members (art. 8).

Despite these ambitious commitments, the *Treaty on Deepening Integration* remained only in an embryonic form at the end of 1999. Belarus, Russia and Kazakhstan had, by then, only harmonised 55 per cent of their Common External Tariffs (CET), and if Kyrgyzstan is included, the four countries had standardised only 25 per cent of their CET (IMF, 1999a, p. 113). Tajikistan began slowly harmonising its external tariffs with the rest of the CU-states only after it joined in 1998. Even though better CET harmonisation was achieved between Russia and Belarus – 95 per cent of their CET had been harmonised by 1999 – Minsk granted a large number of tariff exemptions to non-CU members. These were then applied to other members of the CU, thereby reducing the efficiency of the CU. Furthermore, all five members had failed by the late 1990s effectively to coordinate their external trade legislation, as they all engaged separately in membership negotiations on external tariffs and trade with the World Trade Organization (IMF, 1999a, p. 11).[2]

More significantly, the five CU member states failed to move actively towards the establishment of a fully functioning FTA *within* the CU (IMF, 1999a, p. 113). Although some progress was indeed made towards removing trade restrictions within the CU, import tariffs were not lowered in any significant way (IMF, 1999a, p. 113). Paradoxically, movement towards deeper economic integration was being held back primarily by Russia, the only country in the CU which had failed to ratify both the 1994 CIS Free Trade Area (FTA) agreement, as well as its 1999 amended version. Russia feared that if the FTA was implemented, it would lose millions in revenue obtained from taxing the export of its energy resources. This rendered the whole treaty on integration, from a legal point of view, inoperative (Chubchenko, 2000a). Instead, during the late 1990s, trade between CU member states, as well as among all CIS states, was mostly regulated by a vast web of bilateral free trade agreements which had been reached among CIS states during the early to mid-1990s. Moreover, even within the CU-framework itself, CU member states were not fully covered by free trade agreements. Whereas Russia, Kyrgyzstan and Tajikistan had signed free trade accords with all other four CU member states, Belarus had failed by 1999 to reach a free trade agreement with Kazakhstan, one of the major economies of the CU.

Furthermore, these free trade accords within the CU-zone and the CIS as a whole, were not always properly implemented, and, more importantly, they often included a series of taxes and exemptions on specific goods, which made their functioning cumbersome and unpredictable. Interestingly, the driving force behind many of these measures were often the bigger CIS countries, such as Russia, Ukraine and Kazakhstan, which introduced many of these exclusions in their mutual trade (Freinkman *et al*., 2004, p. 45). Moreover, many of the free trade agreements envisaged the introduction of temporary protective measures, anti-dumping recourses and safeguard instruments, intended to shield their domestic markets from unfair competition, hampering the promotion of intra-CIS free trade (Freinkman *et al*., 2004, p. 47). Contingent protective measures were most pronounced in the bilateral Russian–Ukrainian trade, and as a result, disputes and retaliatory actions plagued trade relations for many years (Freinkman *et al*., 2004, p. 46). Furthermore, the CIS lacked proper institutional mechanisms to enforce contracts between trading partners, and as a result, the effectiveness of these free trade agreements remained very limited. No system, akin to the one established by the World Trade Organization (WTO), was put in place to impose penalties on parties that deviated from the system (Tumbarello, 2005, p. 8). The agreements had to be self-enforcing and this weakened implementation. (Tumbarello, 2005, p. 8)

In an effort to resolve this unfavourable situation, CIS Executive Secretary Boris Berezovsky succeeded, in the autumn of 1998, in negotiating a Protocol which amended the 1994 FTA agreement, and which stipulated for the gradual elimination of the existing exemptions to free trade within the CIS area (Dragneva and de Kort, 2007, p. 251). The Protocol was approved by all CIS states in April 1999, opening the way for further trade liberalisation (CIS, 1999; Sinyakevich, 1999). Berezovsky also managed get the approval of all CIS states for the creation of a new CIS body – the Executive Committee – intended to ensure implementation of the free trade agreements signed (Makhovsky, 1999). Yet, the Russian Duma refused to ratify the agreement, convinced that it would only benefit the interests of big private business (Mikhailov, 1999; Tregubova and Novoprudsky, 1999). As a result, and in part, because of Russia's actions, the 1999 Protocol was never fully implemented and, instead, most of the intra-CIS trade continued to be based on the existing bilateral agreements. The biggest blow to intra-CIS trade, however, was dealt by the financial crisis, which hit Russia in August 1998. The crisis led to a sharp contraction of the Russian economy – Gross Domestic Product (GDP) fell by 6 per cent – and this resulted in a significant fall in local demand, including demand for CIS goods. In addition, the sharp devaluation of the Russian rouble, which in one month lost two-thirds of its value, also contributed to a significant decrease in the demand for CIS products inside Russia itself. In turn, countries like Kazakhstan and Uzbekistan set up barriers on imports from Russia in order to protect their own markets from cheaper Russian goods (Pastor and Damjanovic, 2001, p. 19). More significantly, after the crisis, trade between Russia and the CIS became increasingly market-based, and settled in US dollars rather than in local currencies or barter. As a result, Russia re-oriented its exports, the majority of which consisted of energy products, away from the CIS, in order to obtain payments in hard currency (Westin, 1999, p. 48). Although Russian foreign trade began to pick up in 1999 as energy prices began to rise, Russia's trade continued to be directed towards Europe and away from its trading partners in the CIS.

The Russian financial crisis, in fact, very much accelerated the process of geographical diversification of CIS trade away from the region. By 2001, only Belarus and Moldova continued to export primarily to the CIS, which accounted for about 60 per cent of their exports. For Azerbaijan and Russia, instead only 10 per cent of their exports went to the CIS, while for the majority of CIS states, exports to other CIS states represented between 20 and 30 per cent of their total exports (Freinkman *et al.*, 2004, p. 11). In terms of imports, however, CIS states still relied more heavily on products coming from within the CIS markets, than from outside the CIS. In 2001, over 50 per cent of Belarus', Kazakhstan's, Kyrgyzstan's, Tajikistan's and Ukraine's imports originated within the CIS. Only Armenia and Russia received less than 20 per cent of their imports from other CIS states (Freinkman *et al.*, 2004, p. 11). It could therefore be argued that some basis for deeper intra-CIS trade remained in place. But despite the existing potential, not much progress towards further economic integration was made, even among those states which had signed the *Treaty on Deepening Integration*. Between 1997 and 2000 trade among CU members, initially increased, but eventually declined (Freinkman *et al.*, 2004, p. 7). Kazakhstan and Kyrgyzstan, and especially Russia, continued to diversify their trade away from the CU and from the CIS as a whole, and towards the developed countries of Europe, the US and Canada, and partly to Asia (Freinkman *et al.*, 2004, p. 13). The only exception in this respect was to be found in Belarus' trade with Russia – Belarus' imports from Russia actually increased in the late 1990s, and while exports to Russia declined, they did so only mildly.

Russia–Belarus efforts at deeper integration

As pointed out above, on 2 April 1996, Russia and Belarus signed the CSS treaty. Even more ambitious than the *Treaty on Deepening Integration*, this new treaty was aimed at uniting 'the material and intellectual potentials of the two countries', and at developing very tight economic and military integration between Russia and Belarus, by setting out clear deadlines (Shinkarenko, 1996). The treaty envisaged the *synchronisation* of Russia's and Belarus' economic reforms by the end of 1997, as well as the introduction of uniform laws and regulations in order to create a FTA. The treaty also stipulated for the creation of a CU between Belarus and Russia in 1997, as well as the introduction of similar anti-monopoly legislation, analogous levels of taxation, similar state support for production, and the same rules of investment (Bovt and Kalashnikova, 1996). The objective was to create a common market in goods, capital, services and labour between Russia and Belarus by the end of the decade (Shinkarenko, 1996). Moreover, the treaty also envisaged that by the end of 1997, the monetary, credit and budget systems of both countries would become standardised, in order to establish the conditions for the introduction of a common currency (Bovt and Kalashnikova, 1996). The treaty also stipulated for the formation of a common transportation system, and a unified energy system (Latsis, 1996). In addition, the agreement also envisaged that both countries would work together in ensuring security, protecting their common borders, and jointly combating crime. More importantly, the treaty envisaged the joint use of 'elements of military infrastructure' by both countries (Latsis, 1996).

In order to fulfil these highly ambitious objectives, a Union budget was established, responsible for financing joint programmes. Furthermore, for the first time, joint supranational structures were created to manage the integration process. Highest authority within the community was entrusted to a *Supreme Council* (art.9), which was composed of the two countries' Presidents, PMs, and Speakers of Parliaments, and whose decisions were adopted on the basis of unanimity, thus ensuring that no decisions could be imposed on either side. The treaty also envisaged the establishment of an *Executive Committee*, as a permanent executive body, and a *Parliamentary Assembly*, made up of an equal number of parliamentarians from each side, whose objective was to submit proposals to the Russian and Belarusian parliaments and to adopt model legislative acts (art. 10) (Bovt and Kalashnikova, 1996). However, it was also made clear that no decisions could be introduced contrary to the countries' Constitutions.

On 2 April 1997, the CSS treaty was superseded by a new bilateral agreement signed by the two Presidents – the *Treaty on the Union of Russia and Belarus* – which took integration a step further and transformed the CSS into a *Union*. The objective of this new treaty was to strengthen bilateral ties between the two countries further in a variety of fields – political, economic, military, scientific and cultural – and to work 'towards the voluntary unification of the two states, on the basis of the free will of the peoples', but 'observing the Constitutions of member states, and proceeding on the basis of the sovereign equality of its members' (*Rossiiskaya gazeta*, 1997a). This meant that the two states retained their sovereignty, independence and territorial integrity, as well as their Constitution, and other key attributes of statehood, but became very closely integrated.

The treaty also envisaged, for the first time, the introduction of Union citizenship, for all citizens of Russia and Belarus, so that citizens could work and travel unhindered in both countries. The agreement also placed emphasis on the promotion of democracy and the respect for human rights and individual freedoms (*Rossiiskie vesti*, 1997). This aspect was of especial relevance to the Russian leadership. The liberal entourage of President Yeltsin was very concerned about the authoritarian tendencies of President Lukashenko, and about the prospect of creating a Union with such a dictatorial leadership. In the economic field, the new treaty resembled very much the previous CSS treaty, as it envisaged the creation of a CES, a common customs policy, the implementation of coordinated market reforms, and the introduction of a single currency unit (*Rossiiskie vesti*, 1997). However, as in prior agreements, no details were provided on the currency-emission centre, and thus it remained unclear how monetary integration would be implemented (*Segodnya*, 1997). On the other hand, the supranational organs established in the 1996 treaty were retained, and similar decision-making procedures were kept. On 23 May 1997, a *Charter* of the Union was signed and on 25 December 1998 a new series of additional bilateral agreements were reached, which called for the rapid formation of the Union (*Rossiiskaya gazeta*, 1997b; IMF, 1999b, p. 24).

However, as had occurred previously, the *Union* treaty proved difficult to implement because of sharp differences in the economic systems of both countries. The Belarusian economy remained mostly in state hands while the Russia economy, instead, underwent further economic liberalisation and industrial restructuring (Gulde *et al.*, 2004, p. 27).[3] This made the 'synchronization of reforms' between Russia and Belarus an almost impossible task. These difficulties were compounded by Russia's reluctance to continue subsidising the Belarusian economy. Lukashenko, in fact, hoped that by joining the Union, Moscow would cancel Belarus' $270 million debt, and would grant Belarus preferential access to its goods in the Russian market, and more importantly, would sell energy to Belarus at Russian domestic prices (Anisko, 1999). But Russia proved reluctant to acquiesce, as it had already written off a Belarusian gas debt of $1.3 billion in 1996, and was already selling gas to Belarus at reduced prices – $40–50/mcm between 1996 and 2002 (Balmaceda, 2009, p. 82). These prices were almost half the price paid by European consumers – $80/mcm (Stern, 2005, p. 45).[4]

In the area of trade, some progress was indeed made towards aligning CETs between Russia and Belarus. By 2000, CETs applied to imports from third countries were almost totally unified (IMF, 2000a, p. 41). However, there were some notable exceptions, such as food products, where different external tariff rates were still kept in place. Furthermore, quantitative restrictions on trade with third countries also often differed between Russia and Belarus (IMF, 2000a, p. 41). With the Russian financial crisis, Belarus introduced quantitative restrictions on the export of foodstuffs (IMF, 1999b, p. 19) while in January 1999, Russia reintroduced export taxes on crude oil, natural gas and a variety of ferrous metals, to bolster revenues (IMF, 1999a, p. 113). Furthermore, Russia once again enhanced border controls with Belarus in 1997, in order to restrict the import of goods that had import exemptions in neighbouring Belarus, such as tobacco, alcohol, automobiles, and which were carried into Russia without paying the necessary customs duties, through the so-called 'Belarusian corridor' (Murtazayev, 1997). Furthermore, in March 2000, Russia imposed tariffs on goods imported from third countries transiting through Belarus. In response, Belarus introduced in August 2000 a similar regulation for Belarusian imports transiting through Russia (IMF, 2000a, p. 41).

Important progress was instead made towards liberalising internal trade between Russia and Belarus. Tariffs and quantitative restrictions between the two countries were mostly removed by the late 1990s, although Belarus maintained controls on the export prices of those goods that were subjected to domestic price regulations (IMF, 2000a, p. 41). Thus, trade between Belarus and Russia increased quite substantially during the late 1990s, especially across the neighbouring regions of Russia. By the 2000s, Belarus became Russia's second trading partner behind Germany (Rontoyanni, 2005, p. 60). Bilateral trade, however, was also fostered by the implicit subsidies that Russia provided to the Belarusian economy, estimated at around $2 billion annually, in the form of low energy prices, debt cancellations, low-interest loans, and purchases of Belarusian goods at inflated prices (Rontoyanni, 2005, p. 60; Zlotnikov, 2009, p. 69). These subsidies could be seen as an attempt to keep Belarus within Russia's sphere of influence. But they were conducted to the benefit of Belarus, and to sustain both Russian and Belarusian industries, which in many respects remained strongly inter-connected. Yet, trade disputes between the two countries persisted – for example, in the late 1990s Belarus and Russia virtually waged an all-out war over access to the Russian trucking market (Novoprudsky, 1999).

The more ambitious programme of a single currency, instead, remained a distant dream. Russia supported the introduction of a single currency, yet it wanted Belarus to adopt the Russian rouble as its currency, because it opposed surrendering its own currency to a new supranational common currency (*Kommersant-daily*, 1997a). Only if the Union of Russia and Belarus became a real federal state, and all economic indicators were unified would the Central Bank of Russia (CBR) be ready to create a unified monetary system (*Kommersant-daily*, 1997a). The Belarusian leadership, in turn, refused to hand over its own monetary sovereignty and over its currency-emission rights entirely to Russia. Thus, it remained unclear how a single currency could be implemented if two money-emitting centres were to be retained. Furthermore, although, Lukashenko supported the introduction of a single currency in principle, he never implemented the necessary measures required to make monetary unification possible. The Belarusian government retained control over the foreign currency market, failed to free the exchange rate and refused to shift from a multiple to a single exchange-rate for the Belarusian *rubel'* (Sitnikova, 1997; Kulakova, 1997). Moreover, Belarus' monetary policy remained far too lax to allow for proper monetary integration with Russia to proceed (IMF, 1999b, p. 25).[5]

More importantly, though, the Russian and Belarusian leaderships fundamentally disagreed on the overall strategy to be pursued jointly in order to achieve further integration at the institutional level. Whereas Russia argued that legal harmonisation and economic integration had to be achieved first before institutional integration could go ahead, Lukashenko instead favoured the pursuit of political unification first (Sayenko, 1997). In a way, he favoured the restoration of the old Soviet system of administration, and the re-establishment of the pre-existing economic ties, which had been severed with the end of the Soviet command economy (Feduta, 1999). More importantly, Lukashenko and the Russian leadership fundamentally diverged over the kind of internal structure that the future Union State should adopt. Lukashenko remained adamant in his refusal to see Belarus become the 90th province of Russia, as this would have resulted in Belarus' total loss of state sovereignty. Instead, he supported the establishment of a Union state, in which both Russia and Belarus would share the same rights and enjoy equal weight. At the same time, he favoured a strictly vertical chain of command within the supranational Union bodies (Sayenko, 1997; Vaganov, 1999). His aim was to grant the new Union institutions real clout, by ensuring that the decisions adopted by the Union's Supreme Council would become binding on the national governments of Russia and Belarus (Polezhayev, 1997).

Such proposals were unacceptable to Russian leaders, who wanted either to create a single Federal state, in which the various provinces of Belarus would become attached to Russia, or establish a 'loose federation', in which case, executive decisions would have been taken collectively by both sides (Galko, 1997; Pletnyov, 1999; Vaganov, 1999). In a way, Yeltsin wanted to gain the political dividends from having re-established a union with Belarus, but seemed unwilling to implement any of the measures that would have made that possible and would have allowed for the Union fully to materialise. As journalist Otto Latsis pointed out, these treaties had more of a geopolitical significance than an economic long-term impact. They represented a trade-off between a reduction or a cancellation of Belarus' large debts to Russia and the sale of subsidised Russian energy to Belarus, in exchange for allowing Russia the possibility to use the military bases located in Belarus (Latsis, 1996). The treaties were also intended for internal domestic consumption, in view of the forthcoming Presidential elections to be held in Russia. As pointed out by Georgy Bovt, 'The man in the street, who is yearning for Russia's Great-Power past, will believe that a Union is being created and that this is the beginning of a long and shining path' (Bovt, 1996). However, at the time, nothing proved to be more distant from the truth, as limited integration in the economic field, followed. It must be noted, however, that if implemented these treaties would have resulted in partial losses of sovereignty by both Russia and Belarus, in favour of jointly controlled supranational structures. But because these agreements resulted from *voluntary contracting*, they cannot be entirely considered neo-imperialist projects, even though they would have given Russia, as the dominant economic and military power, a stronger say in Belarusian affairs. This was not a union of equals, and if implemented, these agreements would have enhanced Russia's hegemonic ascendancy over Belarus.

CIS military cooperation: limited achievements

During Yeltsin's second term in office, Moscow also continued with its efforts to strengthen bilateral and multilateral military cooperation within the CIS/CST frameworks, in the face of newly emerging security challenges along its borders. On the CIS southern rim, Russia and the Central Asian states were confronted with a series of new serious threats to their security, which tested their military capabilities and the ability of the CST to act effectively – the advance of the radical Islamist Taliban movement in Afghanistan, the smuggling of illegal narcotics, the civil war in Tajikistan, and an upsurge of Islamist extremism and *jihadism* in Central Asia. In early October 1996, just a few weeks after having taken control of the Afghan capital Kabul, the Taliban movement launched an offensive north against the Afghan *Mujahideen* warlord Ahmad Shah Massoud, raising the prospect of conflict spilling across the border into neighbouring Tajikistan – still engulfed in a civil war. The CST states responded by holding several emergency meetings between 1996 and 2000, involving primarily Russia and Central Asian states. Moreover, the Treaty itself, which stipulated for a collective response in the event of external armed aggression, was invoked numerous times. In May 1997, when Mazar-i Sharif was first captured by the Taliban, the Russian government clearly stated that 'if the borders of the CIS states [were] violated, the CIS Collective Security Treaty mechanism [would] be activated immediately' (*Kommersant-daily*, 1997b). CST states also agreed to provide covert military support both to Massoud and to General Abdul Rashid Dostum, the Uzbek warlord who ruled over several northern provinces of Afghanistan (Abarinov and Velekhov, 1996). In addition, CST states decided to strengthen defences along the Tajik–Afghan border by moving army units from the 201st Motorised Rifle Division (MRD), equipped with heavy weaponry to the border area (Abarinov and Velekhov, 1996).[6] Moreover, at the margins of the Collective Security Treaty (CST), successful efforts were also conducted by Russia, Iran and Pakistan, to resolve the inter-Tajik conflict, in order to enhance security along the Tajik frontline.

All these measures seemed to indicate that, for the first time the CST was able, at least theoretically, under Russia's leadership, to address common threats, in an effective and coordinated manner. However, success remained elusive. Despite the covert military help provided to Dostum, Mazar-i-Sharif and neighbouring areas fell to the Taliban in May 1998. Similarly, Massoud was compelled during 1999–2000 to relinquish a significant amount of territory and to withdraw to the north-eastern area of Badakhshan, close to the Tajik border. More worryingly, the Tajik–Afghan border remained vulnerable to attacks by Islamist fighters, as Russia's reinforcements proved to be only temporary. In October 1998, the two separate air squadrons that had been providing air cover for Russia's border detachments in Tajikistan were disbanded, and several of the artillery systems that had been deployed near the border areas, were dismantled. Moreover, the strength of Russian border troops in Tajikistan was reduced quite significantly, from 16,500 men in 1996 to 11,000 in mid-1999, primarily because of Russia's limited financial resources (Jonson, 2000; Golotyuk, 1998). The small number of Uzbek, Kyrgyz and Kazakh border troops which had been patrolling the Tajik–Afghan border, was also withdrawn between 1997 and 2001, placing the burden of controlling the frontier entirely on Russia's and Tajikistan's shoulders. To offset the reduction in border troops, Russia put highly-mobile reserves at the disposal of the Tajik government. Although based on Russian territory, they could be moved immediately to the Tajik–Afghan border in case of need (Golotyuk, 1998). In turn, the Tajik component of both the Russian border troops and of the 201st MRD was increased, and assistance was provided by Russia to the Tajik government to build the country's security forces (Jonson, 2004, p. 54).

While this represented a reduction of Russia's direct involvement in Tajikistan, Russia did not completely withdraw its military forces from that country. In April 1999, Moscow reached agreement with the Tajik leadership on the establishment of a permanent Russian military base in Tajikistan for its 201st MRD, outside the Tajik capital, Dushanbe (Lachowski, 2007, p. 54).[7] A treaty on *Friendship and Military Cooperation* was also signed with Tajikistan, which stipulated for Russia's help and assistance to bolster Tajikistan's security, including joint protection of the Tajik–Afghan border (Chubchenko, 1999). Russia also signed a Friendship treaty with Kazakhstan, which envisaged mutual assistance in case of aggression and established the basis for deeper military cooperation between the defence establishments of the two countries (Paramonov and Stolpovski, 2008). However, these CIS/CST military efforts in Central Asia were hampered by the lack of participation in the CST of Turkmenistan, a country which shared an 800 km long border with Afghanistan (Vinogradov, 1996).[8] Furthermore, in April 1999, Uzbekistan withdrew from the CST and openly condemned Russia's anti-Taliban policies in the region, arguing that they were aimed primarily at enhancing Russia's grip of Central Asia, thus further undermining the CST ability to operate effectively in the area.[9] Tajikistan, in turn, remained highly unstable, despite the political settlement reached in 1997 that put an end to the civil war. More significantly, Tajik warlords continued to provide shelter to many Islamist fighters belonging to the jihadist *Islamic Movement of Uzbekistan* (IMU). Thus, the Russian-led system of collective security in Central Asia remained deficient, especially when confronted with the newly emerging terrorist threats, as was clearly shown in the summers of 1999 and 2000 when the IMU launched a series of attack on Kyrgyzstan and Uzbekistan from its bases in Tajikistan and Afghanistan.

The IMU incursions represented a direct threat to the security of the CIS Central Asian states, but the immediate responses once again showed the shortcomings of the CST alliance, and the inability of Central Asian states and Russia to act effectively, and in concert. Right after the first IMU raid in 1999, Uzbek Air Force units attacked guerrilla positions inside Kyrgyzstan and Tajikistan, straining relations between Uzbekistan and its two neighbours, both of which were signatories to the CST. While official Dushanbe responded with a diplomatic protest note, the Kyrgyz Air Defence Forces returned fire with artillery attacks (Golotyuk, 1999). Relations were further damaged by regular violations of the Tajik airspace by Uzbek aircraft during the summer of 1999 and 2000, and the decision of Uzbekistan to mine most sections of the Uzbek–Tajik and Uzbek–Kyrgyz borders in 1999 (Korbut, 2000). Russia responded to the various IMU attacks and to the various requests for help by providing military assistance to Kyrgyzstan and Uzbekistan, in the form of weaponry and ammunition (Chernogayev and Mikhailov, 2000). However, Moscow refused to send in ground troops for fear of getting entangled in a long and bloody counter-insurgency war. Russian Defence Minister Igor Sergeyev clearly stated that the main task of subduing the armed guerrillas was to be conducted by the Central Asian states themselves (Panin *et al.*, 1999). Although Uzbek armed forces and Kyrgyz special troops eventually managed to quell the insurgents after several months of fighting, the weakness and unpreparedness of the Kyrgyz and Uzbek forces, and the lack of adequate training and proper equipment of the CST troops as a whole, became clear. The flaws in CIS' regional security cooperation were further exposed and the need for better coordination among Central Asian military and security forces became imperative. This prompted President Putin to enhance military cooperation when he took office in 2000, leading to the formation of the CST *Organisation* or CSTO in 2002. However, to Moscow's great concern, Russia's weaknesses opened the door to foreign support in Central Asia, as countries as diverse as China, France, Japan and the US poured in military assistance to Kyrgyzstan and Tajikistan.

On Russia's western flank, the contours of the post-Cold War European security framework slowly started to take shape. Several developments that occurred in this region during the second half of the 1990s were seen with great suspicion and concern in Moscow – NATO's enlargement into Eastern Europe, which was accompanied by the movement of NATO military infrastructure closer to Russia's borders, together with the adoption by NATO of a new Strategic Doctrine, which envisaged the use of force 'out-of-area' (i.e. out of its area of responsibility). Although NATO's actions were to be conducted within the framework of international law, the decision by NATO to use force in Kosovo in 1999, occurred without UN Security Council approval, and this created great apprehension in Moscow. The signing in 1997 of the *Founding Act* with NATO, which led to the creation of the Permanent Joint Council (PJC), did ease some of Russia's concerns, as these instruments granted Russia a special consultative role in European security affairs.[10] But they failed to dispel Russia's overall sense of weakness and vulnerability vis-à-vis the West. Although Russian leaders were aware that 'the threat of large-scale aggression against Russia [was] virtually absent', the presence of 'powerful groupings of armed forces (understood as NATO forces) in regions adjacent to Russia's territory, [was seen as] a constant threat to Russia's national security', as stated in the 1997 National Security Concept (*Rossiiskaya gazeta*, 1997c). NATO's 'transformation into the dominant military-political force in Europe' elicited great worries in Russia, because the Atlantic alliance was seen as being directed against Russia, and because such alterations created a new division in the European continent around security arrangements, with some countries inside NATO and others left out of the Alliance. This predicament was seen as extremely dangerous given the preservation in Europe of mobile strike groupings of troops and the inadequacy of existing multilateral mechanisms, such as the Organisation for Security and Cooperation in Europe (OSCE), for maintaining peace and security in Europe. These worries were compounded by the emergence of GUAM – a new strategic organisation in the former Soviet space, which was sponsored by the United States (USA), and which involved Georgia, Ukraine, Azerbaijan and Moldova. It not only excluded Russia, but was, on the contrary, purposefully intended to reduce the Kremlin's influence in the CIS region.

This new paradigm, therefore, gave further impetus to the establishment of close bilateral military ties between Russia and Belarus, Moscow's most loyal ally on its western borders (Bohdan, 2013). In the autumn of 1995, the Russian General Staff for the first time articulated its designs to deploy a large Russian military force in Belarus, on the borders with Poland and Lithuania, to counter NATO's potential enlargement eastwards (Bohdan, 2013). After Poland, Hungary and the Czech Republic were invited to NATO in July 1997, Belarus was identified as the forward line of defence of the Russian–Belarusian Union against NATO, and the Russian MoD and its General Staff began regarding the Belarusian army as the Belarusian Military District of the Russian Armed Forces – a view which also gained support in Minsk (Bulavinov, 1998). In the event of a military conflict with NATO, it was expected that the Belarusian armed forces would automatically become part of a combined Russian–Belarusian army and operate as part of a single group of forces (Bulavinov, 1998). Joint collegial sessions of the two countries' Ministries of Defence (MoDs) were initiated in 1998, in order to design a common defence policy, establish integrated armed forces, and develop shared weapons' procurement systems (Rontoyanni, 2000). Progress was also made towards the development of a common defence doctrine with the adoption of the 'Concept of Common Defence' and the 'Security Concept of the Union of Russia and Belarus'. Agreements were also signed on the joint use by Russia and Belarus of military infrastructure objects in their border regions (Rontoyanni, 2000).[11] Belarus and Russia also conducted a series of large-scale bilateral exercises involving their air-defence and air force units during 1996 and 1999 (Korotchenko, 1999).[12]

In the sensitive region of the South Caucasus, Russia signed a *Treaty of Friendship, Cooperation and Mutual Assistance* with Armenia in August 1997, which reinforced their military-strategic partnership. Armenia retained strong relevance to Russia because of its strategic location in the turbulent South Caucasus, and on the borders of another NATO country – Turkey. Russia and Armenia pledged to cooperate in matters of defence and to 'consult immediately' on the joint use of military facilities and mutual assistance, in case of foreign aggression. Russia also agreed to sell weaponry to Armenia at lower prices and to provide free training for Armenian officers at Russian military academies (Eaton, 2001, p. 89). To enhance this alliance, Russia deployed a squadron of MIG-29 fighters and various S-300V surface-to-air missiles in its military bases in Armenia in late 1998. The objective was to protect its forces and those of Armenia from aircraft and missile attacks, within the framework of the CIS air defence system (Sokut, 1999). Russia also continued in its efforts to develop close military ties with Georgia and tried to keep a permanent military presence on its territory – in Abkhazia, South Ossetia, and along the Georgian Black Sea Coast. But as pressure from both Georgia and the West mounted, Moscow agreed, at the OSCE Istanbul summit in November 1999, to close two of its military bases in Georgia – Gudauta, in Abkhazia, and Vaziani near Tbilisi; while also committing itself to negotiating the fate of the other two Russian bases at Batumi and Akhalkalaki.

In May 1997, Russia also reached an accord with Ukraine on the final division of the ex-Soviet Black Sea Fleet (BSF) and on the lease by Russia of a naval base at Sevastopol. With this agreement, Moscow succeeded in stationing its BSF at the strategic naval base at Sevastopol in Crimea for 20 years, allowing Russia to project its power and better defend itself in the Black Sea region (Bulavinov, 1997).[13] However, as part of the agreement, Moscow was forced to relinquish 18.3 per cent of its vessels to Ukraine, and also had to acquiesce to the stationing of the Ukrainian Navy next to the Russian BSF at Sevastopol's Streletskaya Bay (Golubev, 1997; Koretsky et al., 1997). More significantly, the agreement recognised Sevastopol as a Ukrainian city, while an additional bilateral agreement also acknowledged Crimea as part of Ukraine. In this way, Russia renounced any territorial claim over Crimea, an area of high national symbolic value for Russia, and this seemed to indicate a readiness by Moscow partly to discard its imperial legacy. But the presence of the BSF in Crimea occurred against Kiev's wishes, primarily because of Ukraine's inability – due to its economic weakness and energy dependency on Russia – to stand up to Russia's pressures. In this respect, therefore, it can be argued that Russia's policies regarding the basing of the BSF in Crimea, reflected to a certain extent, a neo-imperialist behaviour, even if also motivated by clear security concerns. For example, in 1997, right after the BSF agreements were signed, NATO conducted a series of naval exercise with Ukrainian naval forces, very close to the Crimean peninsula.[14]

Assessment of Russia's actions in the CIS military realm

As shown, in the late 1990s, Moscow continued with its efforts to strengthen bilateral and multilateral military cooperation within the CIS/CST frameworks, but primarily with those CIS states which proved eager to strengthen their military ties with Russia, and only with partial success – a clear sign that despite Russia's rhetoric and desires, it had neither the capacity nor the willingness to create a neo-empire in the CIS space. In the mid- to late-1990s, Russia actually proved unable to transform the CST into an effective collective security organisation, endowed with a supranational structure and bestowed with well-coordinated and effective coalition forces capable of addressing newly emerging threats, in particular those related to Islamist-*jihadist* terrorism (Golotyuk, 2002). Effective CIS military cooperation was to a great extent impaired by Russia's own domestic weaknesses – its limited financial capabilities, its economic disarray, and its dysfunctional system of governance – all of which were exacerbated by the Kremlin's failures in Chechnya and by the subsequent difficulties the Russian government was facing when trying to modernise its own armed forces. This made sustaining the CST security system and implementing the agreements reached all the more challenging. The effectiveness of the CST/CIS was further hampered by the lack of a common enemy that could naturally bring the CST states together, and by the absence of a unifying concept shared by all CST members. Different views on the nature of the CST and on the objectives of the military alliance coexisted within the security system. While Armenia remained eager to get military support and security guarantees against its main adversaries – Turkey and Azerbaijan – Tajikistan instead sought to get help to fight local rebels and Islamist extremists. Belarus, in turn, was keen to ensure Russia's continued financial support to sustain its economy, as well as Russia's protection against a potential NATO attack, while Kazakhstan remained interested primarily in getting Russian military assistance to build its own armed forces. Moreover, Russia failed to develop a clear and coherent policy towards its main geo-strategic adversary, NATO – hesitating between partnership and confrontation. As a result, the CST alliance remained a hybrid undertaking, which did not allow Russia effectively to extend its influence over the CST states.

Furthermore, Russia increasingly lost its influence over the rest of the CIS states. When the CST was renewed for another five years in April 1999, Uzbekistan, Azerbaijan and Georgia withdrew entirely from the treaty, preferring instead either to remain neutral (Uzbekistan) or to develop closer military ties with Western countries (Azerbaijan and Georgia). Azerbaijan remained disappointed over Russia's failures to resolve the Nagorno-Karabakh conflict in its favour, while Georgia proved very concerned over Russia's military presence on its territory, and anxious over the Kremlin's intentions in Abkhazia and South Ossetia. Uzbekistan, in turn, proved eager to emerge as Central Asia's hegemon, and therefore challenged Russia's presence in the region. It accused the Kremlin of exploiting the Taliban threat to further expand its influence in Central Asia (Weinstein, 2007, p. 171). As they moved away from Russia's orbit, Georgia and Azerbaijan, and to a lesser extent Uzbekistan, started to develop closer ties with Western countries, both on a bilateral basis, and through multilateral frameworks, such as NATO and its Partnership for Peace programme (PfP). They were followed in their steps by Moldova and Ukraine, whose leaders also remained eager to move their countries away from the Russian orbit and towards closer ties with the West. All these countries joined their forces and participated in the establishment of the US-sponsored organisation GUAM/GUUAM, which was composed of Georgia, Ukraine, Azerbaijan and Moldova, with Uzbekistan becoming a member in 1999, but withdrawing again in 2005. First established in 1997, GUAM was intended to become a political, economic and strategic alliance, aimed at strengthening the independence and sovereignty of its members and balancing Russia's influence in the region. It looked at enhancing regional economic cooperation through the development of a Europe-Caucasus-Asia energy and transport corridor. Although it never became more than a loose grouping of countries, it was rightly seen by Moscow as a clear attempt by the USA to challenge its hegemony in the former Soviet space.

Despite the emergence of alternative geopolitical projects and the progression of centrifugal forces, Russia remained, nevertheless, the main provider of security assistance and military support to most countries within the CIS/CST space. Moscow helped its CST allies to develop their own armed forces, with officers from CST states undergoing military training at Russian military academies at discounted rates. This was intended to allow CST military forces to operate jointly, under Russian command, in the event of an attack. Russia also succeeded in partially restoring the former Soviet air-defence system with all CIS states, except for Moldova and Azerbaijan.[15] Within this framework, in the spring of 1996, Russia started undertaking bilateral joint patrols with Kazakhstan and Belarus, and 1999 it merged its air-defence efforts with those of Armenia (Webber, 1997, p. 41).[16] In 1998, after the USA conducted air strikes in Sudan and Afghanistan, the first-ever joint air-defence exercises involving Russia, Belarus, Kazakhstan and Kyrgyzstan were held near Astrakhan. This evidenced the great concern felt by several CIS, first and foremost Russia, over the use by the United States of its air power abroad, without proper United Nations' sanctioning. Worries over the United States use of force grew with NATO's military actions in Yugoslavia in 1999, thus spearheading plans to establish a fully *integrated* CIS air-defence system. In the wake of NATO's bombings, it was reported that Russia for the 'first time began thinking seriously about how to finance the integrated air defence system' (Yadukha, 1999). Russian Air Force Commander, Anatoly Kornukov, noted that the establishment of a CIS integrated air-defence system was the only way 'to avoid ending up in the shoes of Iraq or Yugoslavia' (Yadukha, 1999).

The CIS air-defence system became one of the most effective mechanisms of CIS military cooperation, allowing Russia to maintain a system of forward defence to the west and south of the country, and in this way better protect Russia – and the CIS – from potential foreign attacks (Sokut, 1998; Bulivanov, 2000). In early 1995, Belarus granted Russia rent-free use of the Baranovichi missile warning station and the Vileika submarine communications facility for 25 years (Rontoyanni, 2000). Russia also rented out the use of the Balkhash radar station in Kazakhstan, and the Gabala radar station in Azerbaijan (Kassianova, 2005, p. 88). Ukraine appropriated the radars on its territory for its own military use but shared the data and maintained inter-operability with the

Russian system. Russia was thus, able, partially to restore the former Soviet air-defence system, and, as a result, partly to re-establish its hegemonic presence in the CIS space. Yet, legitimate and pragmatic concerns also dictated Russia's actions. All the existing early warning stations, which were essential for the protection of Russian skies from an aerial attack, were located in the territory of the FSS, and thus, reaching agreement on the joint use of these facilities proved more reasonable than recreating an entire air-defence system inside Russia (Golotyuk, 1996a).

This more restricted, albeit meaningful, military cooperation within the CIS/CST remit allowed Russia to keep a certain degree of influence and hegemony over most CIS states, as they all remained to greater or lesser extent dependent on Russia for their defence and security. However, Russia's influence was primarily residual, and of a 'post-imperial' nature, as CIS states pressed ahead with their own nation- and state-building – developing their own security structures, establishing their own armed forces and engaging in more independent foreign policies. Although Russia kept a military presence in Georgia (Gudauta, Tbilisi, Batumi and Akhalkalaki) and Moldova (Transdniestria) against the wishes of the states concerned, Russia committed itself at the OSCE Istanbul Summit 1999 to withdraw its troops and close these bases. There is little doubt that the initial agreements that were signed on the deployment of Russia's military forces (including peacekeeping forces) in Georgia, Moldova and in Ukraine (Crimea) were reached without the express support of the CIS states concerned, and in many instances, they were the product of outright coercion. As such, they were the product of a neo-imperialist policy. Yet, they also reflected the actions of a 'post-imperial' power in retreat, rather than an 'imperial power' in advance. While Russia's actions in and of themselves can rightly be considered as neo-imperial, they must be seen within the broader context of a country that was in the late 1990s slowly moving away from its assertive behaviour in the former Soviet space – a trend which also characterised Russia's policies in Georgia and Moldova in the later part of the decade. As shown in Chapter 5, Russia's neo-imperialist behaviour in relation to Abkhazia, South Ossetia, and Transdniestria was partly reversed in the late 1990s. It followed the overall trend towards imperial disengagement from the former USSR region, which characterised Russia's polices in the latter half of the decade.

In this respect, it is particularly interesting to note that in the late 1990s, Russia proved ready to share the Central Asian geopolitical space with China, within the remit of the *Shanghai Five*, a forum which also included Kazakhstan, Kyrgyzstan and Tajikistan. Initially conceived as a 'conflict-management' and 'confidence-building' mechanism intended to address security issues along their mutual borders, the forum soon turned into an instrument of multilateral cooperation, aimed at discussing and countering regional security challenges – radical extremism, separatism and organised crime – and strengthening regional cooperation (Maksutov, 2006). Such transformation of the Shanghai platform into a more formal arrangement reflected a recognition by the five Asian states, including Russia, of the need to adopt a more coherent and collective response to the security threats faced by the region (Maksutov, 2006). The emergence of the Shanghai Five, nevertheless, challenged Russia's regional predominance in Central Asia, as Moscow was now addressing sensitive security issues within its traditional 'sphere of influence' with a new external power, China, whose weight in the region was bound slowly but steadily to increase. Russia was compelled to allow Chinese increased presence – and growing economic penetration – of the region, if only because it did not have the means or the capability to challenge it. The fall of the USSR and the end of the Communist system opened up new opportunities for cross-border trade and investment between China and the Central Asian states. Beijing seized the opportunity and became a strong promoter of deeper Chinese economic cooperation with Central Asian countries, within the Shanghai framework. Given the complementarity of the Chinese and Central Asian economies, Beijing hoped that bilateral and multilateral trade could spur regional growth, especially in the more remote and unstable Chinese Xinjiang Uighur Autonomous Region (XUAR). Central Asia could become a market for Chinese consumer products while, at the same time, it could become a source of energy, given the region's vast oil and gas resources (Yuan, 2010, p. 859). At the same time, Central Asia could provide a land route for the export of Chinese products to Western markets. The Central Asian states, in turn, could benefit from diversifying their export markets away from the former USSR, and in this way, become less dependent on trade with and transit through Russia. Moscow, however, remained sceptical about the opening of the Central Asian markets to Chinese trade, concerned about the competitive pressures that Chinese products could exert on Russian manufactured goods, not only in Central Asia, but also within Russia itself. It therefore discouraged efforts aimed at further trade liberalisation within the Shanghai framework. Nevertheless, China's increased presence in Central Asia significantly reduced Russia's relative economic power in the region, and partly contributed to the loss of Russia's economic hegemony in Central Asia, even though Moscow remained for a while the key provider of security to Central Asian states.

Conclusions

By the end of Yeltsin's second term in office, Russia had failed to establish an effective CIS organisation around its distinct leadership. Despite Russia's efforts to create a powerful economic bloc with those CIS countries most eager to expand cooperation with Russia, the record on CIS integration at the end of the decade was not particularly satisfactory. The CIS economies remained uncoordinated, intra-CIS barriers to trade persisted, and an effective CU failed to materialise. Similarly, despite the significant political and financial investments made by the Kremlin to establish a *Union State* with Belarus, implementation progressed sluggishly. While some advancement was made in the area of trade alignment, obstacles still remained in the realm of trade liberalisation. Monetary integration between Russia and Belarus, in turn, remained a distant dream. Disagreements also persisted over the contours and the institutional arrangements around which the future political union between the two countries would be established. More importantly, Russia seemed no longer ready to pursue integration at any cost. As the decade progressed, and the Russian economy faltered, a 'Russia First' policy progressively began to impose itself. The Kremlin increasingly insisted that CIS integration had to reflect, first and foremost, Russia's interests and be a conduit for the economic and political well-being of Russia. Russia proved no longer willing to pay for 'neo-empire' in the Near Abroad, unless it obtained substantial advantages in return. Such an approach can be interpreted as an attempt to strengthen Russia hegemonic position in the CIS space, yet the existing evidence does not seem to support such an argument in its entirety. Russia's cautious approach seems to attest to a post-imperial mindset among its leadership. This is especially true if we consider that Russia no longer forced CIS integration upon its recalcitrant former Soviet neighbours, as it had done in the early 1990s, with Georgia, Moldova and Azerbaijan. Instead, it allowed CIS states – albeit reluctantly – to pursue alternative foreign policy paths. Furthermore, the various economic integration agreements signed with the CIS states were the product of *voluntary contracting*, rather than of outright coercion, and as such, they indicate an absence of a neo-imperialist policy. Yet, it can well be argued that if properly implemented many of these economic agreements would have granted Russia a predominant role within the CIS space, if only because of its sheer economic weight in relation to the other CIS states. However, there is no evidence that indicates that this was the primary objective pursued.

In the security field, Russia also failed to establish an effective security organisation, endowed with supranational structures and powerful forces capable of addressing the newly emerging threats, despite the significant efforts conducted by the Kremlin to enhance bilateral and multilateral ties, especially within the CST framework. Limited funding and lack of support among many CIS states precluded much advancement in this field. Nevertheless, Russia did remain the main provider of security and military assistance to many CIS/CST states, and this gave it a certain degree of influence over the affairs of these states. Yet, as noted above, this influence was primarily of a residual and 'post-imperial' nature, as all CST states moved ahead with the setting up of their own security structures and pursuing increasingly independent foreign and security policies. Furthermore, in the late 1990s, a group of CIS states – Georgia, Moldova, Azerbaijan, Ukraine and to a lesser extent Uzbekistan – moved away from the CIS/CST security arrangements altogether and instead began nurturing military ties with Western and NATO states, in order to counter what they perceived was Moscow's hegemonic weight in the region. On the other hand, it must be noted that Russia's military assistance within the CST framework was often welcomed by the CST member states themselves. The latter benefited quite significantly from Russia's financial and military support, as it helped them to enhance their own military security and defence establishments. Russia's actions, thus, cannot be described as reflecting a strictly neo-imperialist behaviour, even though Russia remained the dominant military power in the CIS/CST realm – instead, Russia's behaviour can again best be defined as fitting the pattern of post-imperial engagement, characterised by normalisation and *voluntary contracting*. CIS/CST military cooperation responded not only to Russia's own legitimate security concerns but also to the worries of the CIS states themselves, which faced severe challenges related to the rise of Islamist extremism, the spread of organised crime, and the outbreak of conflict in their vicinity. These security concerns were shared by Russia as well. As noted in the 1997 Russian *National Security Strategy*, 'Hotbeds of local wars and armed conflicts close to Russia's state border' were perceived as real and constant threats to Russia's own security (*Rossiiskaya Gazeta*, 1997c). CIS military cooperation was therefore seen by the Kremlin as essential to enhance Russia's own security, and necessary to address many of the newly emerging threats, especially along the country's southern rim (*Rossiiskaya gazeta*, 1997c).

The *Shanghai Five* Forum, in turn, was expected to become a successful cooperative framework, which would allow Russia, China and the Central Asian states themselves effectively to address issues of regional border security in a multilateral fashion. Through its participation and sponsorship of the *Shanghai Five* Framework, China became a novel and quite powerful regional actor in the Central Asian security space. Yet, Russia did not perceive China's presence as directly challenging Russia's security hegemony in the region, if only because it saw in Beijing an actor which shared Russia's security concerns and adopted similar approaches when addressing the challenges faced. This turned out to be a quite novel paradigm, and it contrasted quite sharply with Russia's worries over NATO's enlargement eastwards and the Kremlin's growing concerns over the Atlantic Alliance's military ties with several western and southern CIS states. Only very reluctantly, had Russia relinquished its military influence over those CIS states which had proven eager to develop closer ties with the West – Georgia, Moldova, Ukraine and to a lesser extent Azerbaijan and Uzbekistan, and it had done so only because in three of these states – Ukraine, Georgia and Moldova – Russia had managed to keep an important military presence. Russia had kept a naval base in Ukraine's Crimea peninsula, and military bases and peacekeeping forces in Georgia and Moldova, in order to acquire additional strategic depth and better protect itself from what it perceived were NATO's challenges to its own security. While such actions partly attested to a neo-imperialist mindset, they also reflected Russia's legitimate concerns over its own security.

If we examine the CIS overall framework, multilateral cooperation also remained quite modest. No supranational CIS structures were established, and all key decisions continued to be taken at inter-governmental level by the CIS highest bodies – the Council of Heads of State and the Council of Heads of Government. Participation in agreements remained uneven, as states continued to be able to opt out of them. More significantly, non-implementation of signed agreements remained widespread, reducing the effectiveness and nullifying the validity of any joint decisions taken (Webber, 2002, p. 170). In addition, hardly any coordination developed in the realm of foreign policy, a trait which would have transformed the CIS into an effective global player. Only a few exceptions can be mentioned, such as the common stance taken by CIS states against the abrogation of the ABM Treaty at the June 2000 CIS Summit (Grigoryeva, 2000).

Furthermore, within the framework of the *Treaty of Deepening Integration*, which was signed by Russia, Belarus, Kazakhstan, Kyrgyzstan and Tajikistan, the Executive Committee, failed to turn into an effective institution of the CIS, even though at times it did produce valid projects aimed at better coordination. The other various organs – the Inter-state Economic Committee, the Economic Court, and the Inter-Parliamentary Assembly, while potentially capable of fostering closer integration, also proved unable to achieve any significant results, because of the reluctance of various CIS states, including Russia, to push further ahead with deeper integration (Webber, 2002, p. 170). Furthermore, in June 2000, at Russia's instance, the CIS visa-free travel regime was abolished, thereby reducing the freedom of movement of people within the CIS space. While this was done primarily in the interest of national security, in order better to monitor the entrance of illegal immigrants, organised crime, and terrorist fighters, it further weakened the CIS space (Chubchenko, 2000b).[17] Although Russia eventually kept a visa-free regime with its CU/EvrAzES partners, and with other CIS states with whom it enjoyed close relations (Armenia and Uzbekistan), the Kremlin proved particularly keen to introduce a visa regime with Georgia after the outbreak of war in Chechnya (Chubchenko, 2000c).[18] As a result, the CIS space disintegrated further, with Primakov's efforts to create an effective bloc around Russia, to develop his vision of global *multipolarity*, failing to match the expectations.

Notes

1 These organs were formed on a parity basis, and only the Inter-State Council, could take compulsory decisions. However, the latter operated on the basis of unanimity.
2 For example, when Kyrgyzstan joined the WTO in 1998, it accepted obligations on tariffs which in many instances were at variance with already agreed CU tariffs.
3 When he first took office in 1994, Lukashenko actually went back in the process of economic reform. He stepped-up state intervention in the economy, nationalised banks, placed restrictions on currency markets, and put a break on the privatisation of state-owned companies.
4 The launch of the bilateral negotiation process was accompanied by progressive reductions in the gas prices charged to Belarus, until they became equal to the rate paid by neighbouring Russian regions (Rontoyanni, 2005, p. 59).
5 As a result, the inflation rate in Belarus remained very high – 64 per cent in 1997, 73 per cent in 1998 and 294 per cent in 1999 – as opposed to the Russian rate, which had been brought down close to 21 per cent in 1996 and 11 per cent in 1997.
6 Forces were placed under the operational command of the Russian border troops, in support of the lightly armed Russian border troops (Golotyuk, 1996c).
7 The treaty entered into force on 16 October 2004.
8 Turkmenistan chose not to attend CIS meetings and disregarded CIS joint efforts to counter the Taliban threat. Instead, it opened a line of communication with the Taliban and tried to broker a political settlement between the Taliban and the Northern Alliance in Ashgabat (Vinogradov, 1996).
9 In February 1999, after a series of bomb attacks in Tashkent, the Uzbek leader entered into talks with the Taliban, and openly condemned Russia's anti-Taliban policies in the region, before withdrawing from the CST.
10 Some minor concessions were granted to Russia – no nuclear weapons or supporting infrastructure would be placed in the new member states, and the CFE treaty was adapted so as to take into account Russia's new strategic environment.

11 The Russian and Belarusian militaries could use all kinds of military installations in the two countries' border regions for military training or on a temporary basis.
12 Particularly significant, in this respect, were the massive *Zapad-99* exercises held in June 1999, which involved land, sea and air elements, and covered five military districts embracing all of European Russia and Belarus. The exercises were jointly planned and directed by Russian and Belarusian officers and took into account the new situation on Russia's western strategic front after NATO launched its operation in Kosovo (Korotchenko, 1999)
13 It must be noted that Russia had insisted that the entire BSF belonged to Russia. Russia was also forced to agree to a 20-year lease as opposed to a 99-year lease as it had originally wished (*Kommersant-daily*, 1997b).
14 The agreement resulted in a compromise, as Russia succeeded in paying a much lower rent fee ($97.75 million per year) for lease of the base at Sevastopol, than Ukraine had initially requested ($423 million per year) and it also obtained a 31.7 per cent share of Ukraine's BSF (Sherr, 1997, p. 43).
15 The system involved the joint monitoring of CIS air traffic and the introduction of similar procedures for the use of the CIS airspace.
16 Russia also assisted Tajikistan in setting up its own air-defence system (Paramonov and Stolpovski, 2008, p. 10).
17 The first country to withdraw however, was not Russia, but Turkmenistan, in 1999.
18 Additional measures were also introduced in 2002 which made it harder to obtain Russian citizenship, although stateless citizens in the separatist regions were granted an accelerated path to acquire it.

Bibliography

Abarinov, V. and L. Velekhov (1996). *Segodnya*, 8 October, p. 2.

Anisko, S. (1999). *Segodnya*, 2 October, p. 2.

Balmaceda, M.M. (2009). At a Crossroads: The Belarusian–Russian Energy-political Model in Crisis. In: S. Fischer, ed. *Back from the Cold? The EU and Belarus in 2009*. Chaillot Paper, Paris: EUISS, pp. 79–91.

Bohdan, S. (2013). Russia Refuses To Supply Weapons to Belarus, Belarus Digest, 6 September. Available at: http://belarusdigest.com/story/russia-refuses-supply-weapons-belarus-15366 [accessed 9 November 2017].

Bovt, G. and N. Kalashnikova (1996). *Kommersant-daily*, 3 April, p. 1.

Bulavinov, I. (1997). *Kommersant-daily*, 29 May, p. 1.

Bulavinov, I. (1998). *Kommersant-daily*, 17 October, p. 3

Bulivanov, I. (2000). *Kommersant*, 10 February, p. 11.

Chernogayev, Yu. and V. Mikhailov (2000). *Kommersant*, 31 August, p. 2.

Chubchenko, Yu. (1999). *Kommersant*, 17 April, p. 2.

Chubchenko, Yu. (2000a). *Kommersant*, 24 May, p. 11.

Chubchenko, Yu. (2000b). *Kommersant*, 9 June, p. 3.

Chubchenko, Yu. (2000c). *Kommersant*, 31 August, p. 2.

CIS (1999). Protocol On Amendment and Supplements to the Agreement on the Creation of a Free-Trade Area of 15 April 1994, 2 April. Available at: https://wits.worldbank.org/GPTAD/PDF/archive/CIS.pdf [accessed 8 October 2016].

CNPC (2003). Overseas Oil and Gas Operations. 2003 Annual Report. Available at: www.cnpc.com.cn/en/2003en/201407/10f816cf5e004e0088175e54177369d0/files/4073256ee0f1481e83b9586201f58f5c.pdf [accessed 9 October 2016].

Dragneva, R. and J. de Kort (2007). The Legal Regime for Free Trade in the Commonwealth of Independent States, *International and Comparative Law Quarterly*, 56, April.

Eaton, M. (2001). Major Trends in Military Expenditure and Arms Acquisitions by States of the Caspian Region. In: G. Chufrin, ed. *The Security of the Caspian Sea Region*. Oxford, Oxford University Press, pp. 83–118.
Elborgh-Woytek, K. (2003). *Of Openness and Distance: Trade Developments in the Commonwealth of Independent States, 1993–2002*. Washington DC: International Monetary Fund, October.
Eggert, K. (1998). *Izvestiya*, 28 October, p. 1.
EvrAzEs (1996). *Treaty between the Russian Federation, the Republic of Belarus, the Republic of Kazakhstan and the Kyrgyz Republic on Increased Integration in Economic and Humanitarian Fields*. 29 March. Available at http://evrazes.com/docs/view/120 [accessed 10 April 2018].
EvrAzEs (1999). *Treaty on the Customs Union and the Common Economic Space of 26 February*, 26 February. Available at http://evrazes.com/docs/view/128 [accessed 11 April 2018].
Feduta, A. (1999). *Moskovskie novosti*, 5–11 October, p. 6.
Freinkman, L., E. Polyakov, and C. Revenco (2004). *Trade Performance and Regional Integration of the CIS Countries*. Washington DC: IBRD/World Bank.
Galko, N. (1997). *Nezavisimaya gazeta*. 22 May, p. 3.
George, K. (1999). Russia Resumes Big Military Exercises, *EIR News Service*, 26 (27), July 2, available at www.larouchepub.com/eiw/public/1999/eirv26n27-19990702/eirv26n27-19990702_070-russia_resumes_big_military_exer.pdf [accessed 8 July 2017].
Golotyuk, Yu. (1996a). *Segodnya*, 2 April, 1996.
Golotyuk, Yu. (1996b). *Segodnya*, 21 September, p. 2.
Golotyuk, Yu. (1996c). *Segodnya*, 31 October, p. 2.
Golotyuk, Yu. (1998). *Izvestiya*, 23 October, p. 2.
Golotyuk, Yu. (1999). *Izvestiya*, 3 September, p. 2.
Golotyuk, Yu. (2002). *Vremya novostei*, 18 June, p. 2.
Golubev, V. (1997). *Rossiiskiye vesti*, 30 May, p. 1.
Gornostayev, D. (1999). *Nezavisimaya gazeta*, 12 October, p. 1.
Grigoryeva, Y. (2000). Vremya MN, 22 June, p. 1.
Gulde, A-M., E. Jafarov, and V. Prokopenko (2004). *A Common Currency for Belarus and Russia?*, IMF Working Paper, December, Washington DC: International Monetary Fund.
IMF (1999a). *Russian Federation: Recent Economic Developments*. Washington DC: International Monetary Fund. September. Available at: www.imf.org/external/pubs/ft/scr/1999/cr99100.pdf [accessed 9 April 2016].
IMF (1999b). *Belarus: Recent Economic Developments*. Washington DC: International Monetary Fund, December.
IMF (2000a). *Republic of Belarus: Recent Economic Developments and Selected Issues*. Washington DC: International Monetary Fund, November. Available at: www.imf.org/en/Publications/CR/Issues/2016/12/30/Belarus-Recent-Economic-Developments-and-Selected-Issues-3841 [accessed 10 June 2016].
IMF (2000b). *Russian Federation: Selected Issues*, November. Washington DC: International Monetary Fund. Available at www.imf.org/external/pubs/ft/scr/2000/cr00150.pdf [accessed 11 June 2016].
Isayev, M. (1995). *Nezavisimaya gazeta*, 22 December, 1995.
Ivanov, I. (2000). *Nezavisimaya gazeta*, 20 January, p. 9.
Jonson, L. (2000). Russia, NATO and the Handling of Conflicts at Russia's Southern Periphery: At a Crossroads? *European Security*, Winter, 9 (4), 45–72.

Jonson, L. (2004). *Vladimir Putin and Central Asia: The Shaping of Russian Foreign Policy*. I.B. Tauris.
Kalashnikova, N. (1996). *Kommersant-daily*, 30 March, p. 1.
Kassianova, A. (2005). Roads Not (Yet) Taken, Russian Approaches to Cooperation in Missile Defence. In: S. Rynning and B. Heurlin, eds. *Missile Defence, International, Regional and National Implications*. New York: Routledge, pp. 84–110.
Kondrashov, S. (1996). *Izvestiya*, 6 March, p. 3.
Kommersant-daily (1997a). 10 April, p. 5.
Kommersant-daily (1997b). 27 May, p. 1.
Kommersant-daily (1997c). 29 May, p. 2.
Korbut, A. (2000). *Nezavisimaya gazeta*, 13 October, p. 5.
Koretsky, A., V. Yadukha, and V. Skachko (1997). *Segodnya*, 30 May, p. 1.
Korotchenko, I. (1999). *Nezavisimaya gazeta*, 23 June, p. 2.
Kulakova, N. (1997). *Kommersant*, 2 August, p. 4.
Lachowski, Z. (2007). *Foreign Military Bases in Eurasia*, Stockholm: SIPRI Policy Paper, 18, June.
Latsis, O. (1996). *Izvestiya*, 3 April, p. 2.
Makhovsky, A. (1999). *Vremya MN*, 19 February, p. 1.
Maksutov, R. (2006). *Shanghai Cooperation Organisation: A Central Asian Perspective*. Stockholm: SIPRI, August. Available at: www.sipri.org/contents/worldsec/eurosec.html, [accessed 27 August, 2017.]
Mikhailov, Yu. (1999). *Kommersant*, 20 February, p. 3.
Mikhailov, V. and G. Smolnikov (1999). *Nezavisimaya gazeta*, 7 May, p. 5.
Moskovskie novosti (1996). 14–21 January, p. 13.
Murtazayev, E. (1997). *Sevodnya*, 14 January, p. 1.
Nezavisimaya gazeta (1996). 23 May, p. 4.
Novoprudsky, S. (1999). *Izvestiya*, 27 February, p. 1.
Panin, L., Yu. Stepanov, and I. Shestakov (1999). *Kommersant*, 2 September, p. 4
Paramonov V. and O. Stolpovski (2008). *Russia and Central Asia: Bilateral Cooperation in the Defence Sector*, Defence Academy of the United Kingdom, Central Asian Series 8/15, May. Available at: www.files.ethz.ch/isn/92591/08_May.pdf [accessed 8 June 2016].
Pastor G. and T. Damjanovic (2001). *The Russian Financial Crisis and its Consequences for Central Asia*, IMF Working Paper, Washington DC: International Monetary Fund. October.
Pletnyov, S. (1999). *Nezavisimaya gazeta*, 29 April, p. 1.
Polezhayev, M. (1997). *Kommerant-daily*, 30 April, p. 3.
Qi, R. (2017). Energy ties further boosted in Central Asia. China Daily. 6 September. Available at: www.chinadaily.com.cn/business/2017-06/09/content_29678580.htm [accessed 9 November 2017].
Rigzone (2003). CNPC Takes Another Stake in North Buzachi Field. 23 September. Available at: www.rigzone.com/news/oil_gas/a/8543/cnpc_takes_another_stake_in_north_buzachi_field/ [accessed 10 November 2017].
Rontoyanni, C. (2000). *Russia-Belarus Union: The Role of NATO and the EU*, Conflict Studies Research Centre, December.
Rontoyanni, C. (2005). Belarusian Foreign Policy. In: D. Lynch, ed. *Changing Belarus*, Chaillot Paper, 85, Paris: EU Institute for Security Studies, November, pp. 47–66.
Rossiiskaya gazeta (1996). 26 September, p. 7.
Rossiiskaya gazeta (1997a). 3 April, p. 1.

Rossiiskaya gazeta (1997b). 24 May, p. 1.
Rossiiskaya gazeta (1997c). 26 December, pp. 4–5.
Rossiiskiye vesti (1997). 9 April. pp. 1 and 3.
Sayenko, L. (1997). *Moskovskie novosti*, 19–26 January, p. 1.
Segodnya (1997). 24 May, p. 1.
Sherr, J. (1997). Russia-Ukraine Rapprochement? The Black Sea Fleet Accords, *Survival* (Autumn), 39(3), 33–50.
Sinyakevich, I. (1999). *Noviye Izvestia*, 3 April, 1999, p. 2.
Shinkarenko, P. (1996). *Rossiiskie vesti*, 3 April, p. 1.
Sitnikova, Y. (1997). *Segodnya*, 12 March, p. 5.
Sokut, S. (1998). *Nezavisimaya gazeta*, 1 September, p. 2.
Sokut, S. (1999). *Nezavisimaya gazeta*, 19 January, p. 1.
Swanstrom, N. (2005). China and Central Asia: A New Great Game or Traditional Vassal Relations?, *Journal of Contemporary China*, 14 (45), 569–584.
Tregubova Y. and S. Novoprudsky (1999). *Izvestia*, 6 March.
Tumbarello, P. (2005). *Regional Trade Integration and WTO Accession: Which Is the Right Sequencing? An Application to the CIS*, IMF Working Paper, Washington DC: International Monetary Fund, May.
Vaganov, S. (1999). *Trud*, 26 May, p. 5.
Vinogradov, B. (1996). *Izvestiya*, 5 October, p. 3.
Webber, M. (1997). *CIS Integration Trends*. London: The Royal Institute of International Affairs.
Webber, M. (2002). A Confederation in the Making? Means, Ends and Prospects of the Commonwealth of Independent states. In: A. Heinemann-Grueder (ed.) *Federalism Doomed: European Federalism between Integration and Separation*, New York, Oxford, Berghahn Books, pp. 167–193.
Westin, P. (1999). The Domino Effect of the Russian Crisis, *Russian Economic Trends*, 8, 4. December. pp. 46–54.
Weinstein, A. (2007). Russian Phoenix: The Collective Security Treaty Organisation. *The Whitehead Journal of Diplomacy and International Relations*. Winter/Spring.
Wu, H-L. and Chen, Ch-H. (2004). The Prospects for Regional Economic Integration between China and the Five Central Asian Countries. *Europe-Asia Studies*, 56 (7), 1059–1080.
Yadukha, V. (1999). *Segodnya*, 14 October, p. 4.
Yevplanov, A. (1997). *Finansoviye izvestiya*, 30 September, p. 2.
Yuan, J.D. (2010). China's Role in Establishing and Building the Shanghai Cooperation Organization (SCO), *Journal of Contemporary China*, 19(67), 855–869.
Yusin, M. (1996). *Izvestiya*.10 February, p. 3.
Zlotnikov, L. (2009). The Belarusian 'Economic Miracle' – Illusions and Reality. In: S. Fischer, ed. *Back from the Cold? The EU and Belarus in 2009*, Paris: EUISS, Chaillot Paper, pp. 65–78.

4 Russia's CIS gas trade during Yeltsin's Presidencies

Towards market-based relations?

At the time of the collapse of the USSR, Russia was the biggest producer and the main supplier of gas to those Commonwealth Independent States (CIS) states with insufficient energy reserves, in particular Moldova, Ukraine, Belarus, Armenia and Georgia. It also controlled the export lines of those ex-USSR states with abundant energy resources such as Kazakhstan, Azerbaijan and Turkmenistan, which wished to export their energy supplies to other CIS states and to world markets. The energy trade – gas in particular – became, therefore, a key aspect of Russia's relations with the CIS states, because of Russia's disproportionately high share of oil and gas exports in intra-CIS trade, and because as this and other chapters show, energy increasingly became an instrument of Russia's foreign policy and hegemony in the former Soviet space. The energy trade is particularly relevant in Russia's relations with the former Soviet states also because of the significance of energy inputs in a country's economy in general, and in the Soviet economy in particular, given the high energy intensity of Soviet industry. Finally, the energy sector played, since the end of the USSR, a dominant role within the Russian economy itself. During the 1990s, tax revenues from the energy complex covered more than half of the Russian state budget, while the energy industry accounted for more than 70 per cent of Russia's total export earnings (Bekker, 1993). Such high dependence on the energy complex implied that its interest could hardly be ignored. In fact, very close links soon developed between Russian energy companies and the government, as reflected in both the appointment of Viktor Chernomyrdin, previously head of the Soviet gas conglomerate, as Russian Prime Minister, and of Yury Shafranik, formerly director of a major oil-production association, as Minister of Fuel and Energy. The gas conglomerate Gazprom, which dominated the gas sector, and was under the control of Chernomyrdin, remained mostly in state hands, and thus was increasingly turned by the Kremlin into an instrument of state policy. The oil sector, instead, progressively fell into private hands, and thus operated in a much more independent fashion. As a result, the relations between the government and the energy industry remained, during the 1990s, extremely complex. Certain decisions followed primarily the interests of the energy companies, whereas others tended to reflect the predominance of state interests over those of the energy conglomerates. This chapter focuses on the Russian gas trade with its CIS partners, because, as noted above, it became one of the most relevant and controversial aspects of the Russian–CIS overall relationship.

Russia's gas trade with Ukraine

Ukraine depended quite heavily on Russia's energy supplies when the Soviet Union collapsed in 1991. It bought 60 per cent of its gas and almost 90 per cent of its oil from Russia, although it produced some 20 per cent of its own gas needs, and obtained another 20 per cent from Turkmenistan (*Petroleum Economist*, 1992; Gorst, 1993a). Its five nuclear power stations produced about one-third of Ukraine's electricity, and the country also had a large coal mining industry in the Donbass. In all, Ukraine was able to cover approximately one-third of its own energy needs, yet it depended on Russia for the rest of its requirements (Markus, 1996, p. 14). At the same time, 90 per cent of the oil and most of the gas that Russia exported to Europe was transported on pipelines passing through Ukraine.[1] This created a system of mutual dependency, albeit asymmetrically in Russia's favour, which was nevertheless at several opportunities exploited by Ukraine to obtain better price conditions. On many occasions Ukraine siphoned Russian gas destined to Europe, jeopardising the Russian-European gas relationship. Nevertheless, as the main provider of gas to Ukraine – a big gas consumer given the high energy intensity of the Ukrainian economy – Russia ultimately held the upper hand.

When the USSR disintegrated, and the Soviet command economy collapsed, Russia progressively increased the prices of gas it charged to Ukraine, until they almost reached world prices in 1996 (Whitlock, 1993; Markus, 1995a, 1995b; EIU, 1994, p. 36, 1995, p. 13). Although the rises occurred incrementally, they proved to be very significant for the energy-intensive Ukrainian industries, hitting the local economy very hard. In 1993 Russia agreed to supply Ukraine with 69 Bcm at $40/mcm, a fivefold increase from the previous price, while in 1994, prices increased again, reaching $60/mcm, making it very hard for Ukraine to cancel its debts. (Markus, 1995b, p. 15). Ukraine's inability to pay for the agreed deliveries on time, prompted Russia to reduce gas supplies on several occasions – in October 1992, in late August 1993 and in November 1994 (Moscow Radio, 1992; Womack, 1993; IEA, 1996, p. 155). As a result of delays in payment, Ukraine accumulated significant debts towards Russia, prompting the Russian leadership in 1993–1994 to propose the acquisition by Russian companies of shares in Ukraine's industrial production and gas transport facilities. While several preliminary *debt-for-equity* swaps agreements were reached with Ukraine in 1993–1996, they were not fully implemented due to internal opposition in Kiev to these transfers (Markus, 1995b, 1996; Narzikulov, 1994; Balmaceda, 2013). In 1993, the energy situation in Ukraine had become so critical that at the September Russian–Ukrainian summit in Massandra, Ukrainian President Kravchuk seemed almost ready to transfer half of the entire BSF to Russia as payment for Ukraine's outstanding debts (Womack, 1993).[2] Ukraine's potential 'economic capitulation' to Russia, was not only related to an increase in Russian energy prices, it was also the result of the high energy intensity of

Ukrainian industry, and more importantly, Ukraine's economic underperformance. The total absence of macro-economic stabilisation in Ukraine, the lack of fundamental structural reforms, and the external terms-of-trade shock that resulted from the collapse of the USSR, all provoked a sharp fall in Ukrainian industrial output and an upsurge in hyperinflation (Le Gall, 1994, p. 66).[3] By the end of the summer of 1993, the Ukrainian economy was in shambles. The 1993 preliminary Black Sea Fleet (BSF) deal was, however, scrapped at the last moment, because of strong opposition inside Ukraine. Nevertheless, Russia continued to subsidise the Ukrainian economy through low interest loans, and lower-than-world energy prices during 1992 and 1995 (Krasnov and Brada, 1997, p. 828). Ukraine, in turn, managed to cover its energy debts with foreign loans and with financial support from the IMF.

In 1996–1997 Russia's gas prices to Ukraine were raised to world levels reaching $80/mcm, continuing a trend that had begun in the mid-1990s. Ukraine, in turn, charged world market prices for the transit of Russian gas through its pipeline system, setting the gas relationship on a clear business footing (Emerenko, 1996). Gazprom also committed itself to allow 25 Bcm of Turkmen gas in destination to Ukraine to transit through its pipeline systems in 1997. Kiev, however, proved unable to pay in full for Russian – and Turkmen – gas deliveries, leading once again to the accumulation of arrears. To address this issue, a major debt cancellation agreement was reached between Ukraine and Russia in May 1997, which this time granted Russia the possibility to obtain a major share of the BSF. The deal also foresaw the 20-year lease of the Ukrainian naval base at the Crimean port of Sevastopol to Russia for the stationing of its fleet. Russia agreed to pay a total of $2.5 billion for the acquisition of 31.7 per cent of the BSF out of Ukraine's 50 per cent share, and for the lease of the Sevastopol base during a 20-year time frame. This almost cancelled out Ukraine's overall state debt towards Russia, which by then totalled $3 billion (Sherr, 1997, p. 43). While this can rightly be interpreted as a successful attempt by Russia to use its 'hard power' in order to obtain significant strategic benefits at the expense of Ukraine, it must also be noted that the agreement reflected the vulnerabilities of the Ukrainian economy, its energy intensity and its inability effectively to transform and grow, and last but not least, its energy dependency on Russia. It should be noted also, that in a separate Friendship Agreement, Russia recognised the territorial integrity of Ukraine and its sovereignty over Crimea and Sevastopol, in a major victory for Kiev.

In December 1997, a new agreement was reached between Kiev and Moscow for the delivery of Russian gas to Ukraine for 1998, which established a clear link between the price of gas supplied by Russia and the transit tariffs charged by Ukraine (Stern, 2005, p. 88). Contrary to previous agreements, Gazprom committed itself this time to supplying Ukraine with 52 Bcm in 1998, at the considerably lower price of $50/mcm as opposed to the previous fare of $80/mcm it had charged in 1996–1997 (Stern, 2005, p. 88). In turn, Ukraine agreed to reduce its fees for the transit of Russian gas through its pipeline system by 75 per cent. Because the amount of gas that Russia was expected to provide Ukraine exceeded the corresponding amount of Russian gas transported through Ukrainian pipelines to Europe, Russia was effectively subsidising the Ukrainian economy (*FT Energy Newsletters*, 1998). Russia's readiness partly to bankroll Ukraine's energy purchases must be seen within the context of the severe financial crisis that hit Ukraine in October 1997, when the country endured the fallout of the Asian financial crisis. Facing the prospect of total financial collapse, Ukrainian President Kuchma signed with Russian President Yeltsin a bilateral *Treaty on Economic Co-operation* on 27 February 1998, which envisaged common trade and economic policies between Ukraine and Russia, as well as the opening of Ukrainian markets to Russian companies eager to invest in Ukraine (Sinyakevich, 1998).

Despite the mutual promises, the bilateral treaty, however, was never properly implemented. Neither did Russia and Ukraine move ahead down the path of deeper economic integration, nor were Russian companies able to acquire significant shares in the major Ukrainian state enterprises that were privatised in 1998–1999 (Aslund, 2009, p. 140). Energy relations between Russia and Ukraine became further strained in the second half of 1998, when the global financial crisis hit the Russian economy hard and depleted Russia's state coffers. The situation for Russia's energy companies was made worse by the ongoing problems of non-payment in the domestic Russian energy sector and the sharp drop in oil and gas prices in the international market ($11–$12/barrel in 1998). This forced Gazprom to collect the maximum possible revenues from its CIS customers (Stern, 2005, p. 88). As in previous opportunities, however, Ukraine again proved unable to pay on time, prompting Russia to reduce its supplies of gas to Ukraine, and compelling it to provide deliveries only in exchange for the transit of Russian gas through Ukraine's pipeline systems – 30.5 Bcm in 1998 (Stern, 2005, p. 69). Ukraine in turn, siphoned substantial amounts of Russian gas transiting through its pipelines destined to Europe, significantly jeopardising Russia's export deliveries to hard currency markets (*Financial Times*, 1999; Kuzmichov, 1998). Furthermore, Ukraine re-exported Russian gas to Europe in violation of previous agreements (Shiryayev, 2000). In response, Gazprom proposed the construction of a pipeline, which would bypass 25 per cent of Ukraine's transit capacity, by carrying 30 Bcm of Russian gas directly from Belarus to Poland and south to Slovakia, and from there to the rest of Europe (Stern, 2005, p. 89).

Ukraine's inability to pay and Russia's incapacity to continue subsidising Ukraine's energy consumption significantly strained the bilateral relationship. Russia, however, continued its deliveries to Ukraine. Because of its dependency on the transit of its gas through Ukraine, Moscow was unable to interrupt supplies to Ukraine without undermining its credibility as a reliable gas supplier to Europe. Russia also could not risk the entire collapse of the Ukrainian economy – a certainty if Russia cut gas supplies and increased gas prices further – and this explains why Gazprom also continued to sell gas to Ukraine at relatively favourable prices. However, in view of the difficulties that Gazprom was facing in Ukraine, and in other CIS states, the company decided partly to abandon the Ukrainian and other CIS markets in the mid-1990s. The trade was handed over, instead, to the intermediary company *Itera*, which had emerged originally as go-between in Turkmenistan's CIS gas trade.[4] While Russia tried to use its dominant position as the energy provider to acquire shares in lucrative Ukrainian companies, in exchange for debt cancellations, it generally failed in its endeavour, as Ukraine's privatised companies remained off-limits to Russia. Moscow only succeeded in acquiring a big share of the BSF and obtaining a 20-year lease for the BSF naval base at Sevastopol. This was not a minor achievement, but it came at the high price, from Russia's point of view, of abandoning any claims to Crimea and to the port of Sevastopol.

Russia's gas trade with Belarus

Belarus depended even more heavily on Russia's energy supplies than Ukraine. It drew all of its gas supplies from Russia and imported most of its electricity from both neighbouring Lithuania and Russia. It only produced 10 per cent of its oil consumption, while importing the rest of its oil needs from Russia (Markus, 1995a). However, Belarus hosted the *Northern Lights* gas pipeline, and since 1997 a section of the *Yamal-Europe* line, which together carried significant amounts of gas to Europe – 18.4 Bcm in 2007, with a capacity theoretically to carry 46–48 Bcm (Yafimava, 2009, p. 142). Belarus also hosted the northern and part of the southern branches of the oil *Druzhba* pipeline, which together carried about 37 per cent of Russia's oil to Central and Southern Europe. This also created a system of mutual dependency which nevertheless was tilted very much in Russia's favour, given the high reliance of Belarus on cheap Russian oil and gas. As with Ukraine, Russia also progressively increased gas prices to Belarus in the early 1990s, although fares generally remained lower-than-world energy price levels. Nevertheless, these increases hit the Belarusian economy quite hard and made it difficult for Minsk to pay back its energy debts on time, leading to severe oil and gas shortages in the summer of 1993. In August 1993, Russian supplier Gazprom cut off natural gas deliveries for nine days paralysing much of Belarusian industry, which was already suffering from chronic oil shortages (Shimansky, 1993). To resolve the crisis, Minsk committed itself to signing over to Gazprom shares in Beltransgaz, the company which operated Belarus' gas transport facilities, in order to settle part of its debts. The agreement on Beltransgaz, however, fell through as it failed to win the support of the more nationalist members of the Belarusian parliament. Yet, Belarus used a $98 million IMF credit it received in 1993 to cancel part of its energy debt, and the crisis was temporarily resolved.

The situation deteriorated again in early March 1994, when strikes by Russian gas workers in Siberia over unpaid wages led Gazprom to cut off supplies to both Ukraine and Belarus. Part of Belarus' bill was cancelled, by granting Gazprom shares in authorised funds of Belarusian private businesses and joint-stock companies. Minsk also managed to negotiate a significant reduction in Russian gas prices – down to $50/mcm from $80/mcm (Itar-tass, 1994). Yet, these proved to be only temporary measures. Belarus' economy, remained heavily under-reformed and this significantly limited the country's ability promptly to pay for its energy supplies, to the extent that in the spring of 1994, Minsk opted for economic and monetary integration with Russia to address its energy needs. The April 1994 preliminary agreement on monetary union with Russia envisaged reduced Russian oil and gas prices for Belarus in exchange for the free transit of Russian goods and Russian energy products across Belarus. Yet, monetary union never saw the light of day, and therefore energy prices continued to rise, reaching approximately 70 per cent of world prices in 1994 (EIU, 1994, p. 36). In an effort to clear Belarus' energy bill, Lukashenko signed a 'zero option' deal with Russia in February 1996, whereby Moscow cancelled Minsk's overall debt to Gazprom. In exchange Belarus agreed not to claim compensation for the plutonium contained in Belarus' nuclear missiles removed to Russia, and not to charge for the presence of Russian servicemen in Belarus (Sukhova, 1996). A few months later Minsk signed two integration agreements with Russia, the *Treaty on Deepening Economic Integration* and the treaty on a *Community of Sovereign States*, which foresaw the establishment of common energy and transport systems, but which did not envisage any special energy price discounts for Belarus. By mid-1996, therefore, Belarus had failed to find a lasting solution to its chronic energy dependence on Russia. Swapping assets for debts remained the only available and realistic short-term option to cover energy debts. While preliminary agreements were reached on the handing of control over the Novopolotosk oil refinery to Russian companies Lukoil and Yukos (EIU, 1996, p. 12), the deals eventually fell through (Balmaceda, 2013).

During the second half of 1990s, disruptions once again plagued the Russian–Belarus gas relationship as Belarus debts towards Russia continued to accumulate and Minsk proved incapable of paying them off. As a result, Gazprom several times reduced gas deliveries to Belarus – by 50 per cent in December 1996 and in July 1997, and by 40 per cent in June 1998 (Karmanov, 1996; Karpekova, 1998; Bruce, 2005, p. 11). Despite these challenges, Russia continued to sell gas to Belarus at discounted prices between 1996 and 2002, in the range of $40–50/mcm (Balmaceda, 2009a, p. 82). Although these prices were higher than Russian domestic prices, which in 1998–2000 hovered around $12–15/mcm, they were almost half the price paid by European consumers at the time (Stern, 2005, p. 45).[5] In exchange, Russia expected to acquire ownership of several valuable Belarusian energy assets. Yet, at each opportunity, Belarusian President Aleksandr Lukashenko refused, and instead demanded domestic Russian gas prices by appealing to 'the brotherly relationship between the two countries' (Bruce, 2005, p. 13). The rationale behind Moscow's and Gazprom's decision neither to cut supplies to Belarus for a prolonged length of time, nor to increase substantially its gas prices to Belarus was partly related to the dependency that Russia had established over the export of its gas through Belarus. Although the amounts of Russian gas transiting through Belarus' *Northern Lights* Pipeline system were significantly smaller when compared to those transiting through Ukraine's *Brotherhood* or *Druzhba* and Southern pipelines, Gazprom still depended on Belarus for the transit of part of its gas to Europe, primarily for the gas destined to Poland. Furthermore, in 1997 small quantities of gas were starting to reach Germany through the new *Yamal-Europe* gas pipeline, which transited Belarus on its way to Poland and Western Europe, increasing Belarus' relevance as a transit country for Russian gas exports (Stern, 2005, p. 119).[6] This argued in favour of positive energy relations and against disruptions in supplies. Moreover, the strategic value of Belarus to Russia had, by then, been clearly established by the Kremlin, in view of NATO's enlargement into Eastern Europe, and the growing ties of several CIS states with the European Union, the United States and its military. Moscow had every incentive to keep a friendly and pro-Russian regime in Minsk, even if this entailed selling gas at significant loss, especially as the amounts sold to Belarus were not substantial.

Russia's gas relations with other CIS gas consumers: Moldova, Armenia and Georgia

During the 1990s, Gazprom delivered between 2 Bcm and 3 Bcm gas to Moldova despite the difficulties that it faced with non-payments, as it also depended on Moldova's territory for the transport of its gas to south-eastern Europe (Stern, 2005, p. 69). However, Gazprom did so only in exchange for a corresponding amount of gas transiting through Moldova, with additional demand being covered by the intermediary company Itera. Gazprom charged Moldova $80/mcm, for its gas, the highest gas price in the CIS at the time, and equal to world market prices, although Russia also paid a high transit fee for the transport of its gas through Moldova. On several occasions, Gazprom significantly reduced its gas supplies because of severe delays in payments – a 50 per cent reduction in the summer of 1999, and a 40 per cent drop in November 1999). In February 2000, Gazprom went as far as completely cutting-off supplies to Moldova, when Chisinau siphoned off gas destined for Europe (Bruce and Yafimava, 2009, p. 179). Supplies were quickly restored, however, not only because of Russia's dependency on Moldova for gas transit to Europe, but also because one-third of Russia's total deliveries were consumed by the Transdniestrian separatist region, which was closely allied to Moscow (Bruce and Yafimava, 2009, p. 177). Furthermore, in a debt-for-equity swap in October 1998, Gazprom had succeeded in acquiring a 50 per cent ownership of *MoldovaGaz*, the joint venture which controlled Moldova's gas transportation and distribution systems, thus granting the Russian gas conglomerate a hold in Moldova's pipeline system and distribution markets (Stern, 2005, p. 101). As Gazprom held in trust management the 13.44 per cent of MoldovaGaz shares owned by the Transdniestrian administration, it effectively held a much bigger share of the company, allowing it to gain significant control over the Moldovan transport system.

Those CIS states which were not transit routes for Russian gas to European hard currency, such as Georgia and Armenia, instead relied increasingly on Itera, for their supplies, as Gazprom partly abandoned these markets in the mid-1990s, due to the challenges it faced in ensuring prompt payment for its supplies. Yet, Gazprom succeeded in 1997, together with Itera and the Armenian state, in establishing *ArmRosGazprom* (ARGP), a joint venture intended to import, deliver and distribute gas inside Armenia, as well as building pipelines and underground storage facilities (Yeghiazaryan, 2009, p. 244).[7] This operation, which was part of an debt-for-equity swap, increased Gazprom's presence in the Armenian gas market. In Georgia, instead, Itera – the main provider of gas – succeeded in running a profitable business because it conducted a tough payments policy. This permitted it to acquire assets, such as the Azot nitrogen plant, in exchange for debt cancellations (Stern, 2005, p. 84).

Central Asia: the gas triangle involving Ukraine, Turkmenistan and Russia

The complexities of the Russian–Ukrainian gas trade described above were further exacerbated by the fact that Ukraine also bought gas from Turkmenistan – about 25 Bcm yearly between 1991 and 1996. During the Soviet era, Turkmenistan had become an important supplier of gas to Russia and to the other republics. However, when the Soviet Union collapsed, the intra-republican trade faced severe strains, as Turkmenistan began demanding high gas prices to its CIS customers, including Russia, to be paid in 'hard currency' (Stern, 2005, p. 72). This proved particularly challenging for Ukraine, and as a result, the Turkmen-Ukrainian gas trade suffered from several disruptions and severe disputes over non-payment. Furthermore, Turkmen gas had to transit through the Russian pipeline system on its way to Ukraine. This gave Moscow strong leverage in the bilateral Ukrainian–Turkmen energy trade, which nevertheless continued until early 1997. In March 1997, the Turkmen leadership, however, decided unilaterally to dissolve *Turkmenrosgaz*, the joint venture established between Gazprom, Turkmenneftegaz and the Russian intermediary Itera, to streamline the gas trading relationship between Ukraine and Turkmenistan, leading to a halt in the Ukrainian–Turkmen gas trade (Mikhailov and Smolnikov, 1997a). This was done due to non-payments by Ukraine, and also because of the lack of substantive investment by Gazprom into the Turkmen gas sector as had been previously agreed (Gafarly, 1997). In retaliation, Gazprom cut Turkmen gas access to Russian pipelines, thereby shutting Turkmenistan off the European and CIS markets, including Ukraine (Bragov, 1997). To remedy the situation, Turkmenistan began exporting small amounts of gas to Iran through the Korpeje-Kurtkui line, which opened in December 1997.

In August 1997, under pressure from President Yeltsin, Gazprom allowed Turkmen gas destined to Ukraine once again to transit through the Russian pipeline system (Bragov, 1997). However, Moscow barred the transportation of Turkmen gas destined to Europe through its pipeline system for another two years (between 1997 and 1999), thus preventing Turkmenistan from earning hard currency from its gas sales in European markets (*FT Energy Newsletters*, 1997). This decision not only displayed Russia's hegemonic power, it also violated an accord reached between the two countries in 1996, which allowed Turkmenistan to export 20 billion cubic metres of natural gas per year to

Western Europe through Russia. Yeltsin was actually supporting Gazprom's objective of taking over Turkmenistan's share of gas exports to the lucrative Western European markets (*FT Energy Newsletters*, 1997).[8] Moreover, during 1997–1998, Turkmenistan also proved unable to sell gas to Ukraine because Moscow and Ashgabat could not agree on the price at which Gazprom would buy Turkmen gas at the border. An agreement on gas sales among the three countries, Russia, Ukraine and Turkmenistan was finally reached in December 1998, at a price favourable to Gazprom at the Turkmen-Uzbek border. The flow of Turkmen gas to Ukraine through the Russian pipeline lasted for only a few months, however, because of Ukraine's inability to pay.

A major turning point in the Ukrainian–Russian–Turkmen energy relationship took place in December 1999, when Gazprom's CEO Rem Vyakhirev, under instructions from Prime Minister Vladimir Putin, signed an agreement with the Turkmen President Saparmurat Niyazov, which envisaged the purchase of a substantial amount of Turkmen gas by Russia in the year 2000. Russia was to acquire 20 Bcm of Turkmen gas in 2000 – more than 90 per cent of Turkmenistan's annual production at the time – at the relatively low price of $36/mcm (Novoprudsky, 1999).[9] With this agreement, Russia succeeded in obtaining cheap Turkmen gas partly to satisfy its own domestic energy needs (Stern, 2005, p. 74). Due to a decline in gas output in Russia during the late 1990s, there was a risk that Gazprom would not be able to meet its foreign export commitments while also fulfilling agreed deliveries to Russian domestic consumers (Dubnov and Annageldiyev, 1999). The Russian–Turkmen deal helped remedy this situation. At the same time, with this deal Russia effectively denied Ukraine a chance to diversify its gas imports by acquiring gas directly from Turkmenistan, and this sharply increased Ukraine's dependence on Russian gas supplies. It should be noted, however, that Turkmenistan was no longer willing to sell its gas to Ukraine, at the time, in view of the latter's inability to pay (Novoprudsky, 1999). Instead, Ashgabat preferred to sell its gas to Russia rather than to Kiev, albeit at a lower price, because there was a higher certainty of payment being received (Dubnov and Annageldiyev, 1999). By agreeing to sell large quantities of its gas to Russia, Turkmenistan also indicated that it was ready to give up the Turkish gas market to Russia, while at the same time it remained willing to collaborate with Gazprom in their share of the Eurasian gas market. Turkmenistan was compelled to take such a stance as it still depended on Russia for the transport and sale of its gas products (Novoprudsky, 1999). Turkmenistan had begun in the late 1990s to work on the *Transcaspian* gas pipeline project, intended to transport 16 Bcm of gas to Turkey, through a line under the Caspian Sea, but Russia, as a riparian state, was blocking the line, allegedly on 'environmental grounds', but effectively in order to prevent Turkmen gas from reaching the Turkish and European markets. Russia, on its side, had started working on the *Blue Stream* project, a gas pipeline which crossed the Black Sea in order to ship Russian gas to Turkey. Aware of its dependency on Russia for transit, Turkmenistan began considering two alternative export routes, one to China and another one to India and Pakistan potentially breaking Russia's export monopoly control.

Russia's gas trade with other Central Asian and Caspian producers

In Central Asia, the energy-importing countries, Kyrgyzstan and Tajikistan, purchased very limited gas during the 1990s, and then, primarily from Uzbekistan, and therefore they remained beyond Gazprom's reach. The energy-producing countries Kazakhstan, Uzbekistan and Azerbaijan, instead, did purchase some Russian gas, but only in small amounts, and then primarily from the intermediary company Itera. Yet, they mostly remained dependent on the sale of their gas through the Russian pipeline system and this reduced their freedom of action. In 1995, Gazprom joined the BG and Agip consortium to develop the big Karachaganak gas field in northern Kazakhstan. However, Gazprom withdrew from the project in 1997, selling its shares to Lukoil, 'on the grounds that the non-Russian partners were not ready to recognise the financial investments conducted by the gas giant during the Soviet era to develop the gas field' (Stern, 2005, p. 79). Furthermore, Kazakhstan's gas exports became subjected to transit problems, as Kazakhstan, like all other CIS Central Asian gas producers, still depended on the Russian pipeline system for gas deliveries to potential CIS and non-CIS customers in Europe. When Gazprom pulled out from the Karachaganak joint venture, it openly threatened 'never' to authorise the export of Karachaganak gas to international markets through the Russian network, in a clear display of hegemonic power (*Agence France Presse*, 1997). Gazprom's CEO, Vyakhirev agreed to accept a certain amount of Kazakh gas transiting through the Russian system, as long as it was processed at Russia's Orenburg plant in the Urals (*Agence France Presse*, 1997). This was eventually agreed in 2002, when the KazRosGaz joint venture was set up to buy and process gas from Kazakhstan's Karachaganak field, in a sign of Russia's hegemonic sway over Kazakhstan. Uzbekistan, in turn, began selling small volumes of gas to Ukraine, with Itera as the shipper, in 1998, and, was able to transport its gas through the Russian gas pipeline system – thus remaining within the framework of Russia's energy structures (Stern, 2005, pp. 81–82). Azerbaijan, instead, decided to sell most of its gas through the Baku-Tbilisi-Erzurum (BTE) system to Turkey, bypassing Russia – once gas was discovered at Shah Deniz in the early 2000s. The Central Asian gas-producing states Kazakhstan, Uzbekistan and Turkmenistan, thus mostly remained within the Russian sphere of influence, with the exception of Azerbaijan.

Assessment and concluding thoughts

In early to mid-1990s, both Ukraine and Belarus remained very much dependent on energy supplies from Russia. Gazprom progressively increased its energy prices up to world level, severely straining their economies. Both countries faced a substantial reduction in supplies and regular disruptions in deliveries from Russia, due to non-payments. Energy price increases, however, were not aimed at strangling the neighbouring economies, but instead reflected Russia's own efforts to correct the unfavourable terms of trade inherited from the Soviet Union. Russia's reduction in energy supplies to these two countries seems to have been linked above all to a fall in production at home, rather than being connected to an attempt to bring both countries under Russia's influence. Moreover, as far as Ukraine was concerned, Russia lacked clear political incentives to reduce energy prices. Ukraine had from the start adopted quite a negative attitude towards the Russian-led CIS, while at the same time, various issues of contention tainted relations between both countries – sovereignty over Crimea, the division of the BSF, the fate of Ukraine's nuclear weapons. This weakened Russia's desires to grant Ukraine special treatment. Still, while Russian prices slowly reached world markets, barter payments were accepted in the commercial exchange. Moreover, despite the accumulation of arrears by Kiev, Russia never completely cut off gas supplies to Ukraine. More importantly, despite Russia's own shortage of funding, the Kremlin, nevertheless, decided to continue subsidising both Belarus' and Ukraine's energy imports. Very close economic links existed between the Russian, the Belarussian and Ukrainian industries. It was clear that any severe and prolonged disruption in supplies would have had a negative impact on the Russian economy.

Russia was eager to avoid the total collapse of the already fragile neighbouring economies, given the presence of large Russian minorities, and the major political instabilities that such actions might have provoked. Both countries hosted major transportation routes which carried Russian energy to the lucrative markets of the West. Such a strategic position strongly discouraged Russia from behaving too assertively. In addition, Belarus became a key strategic ally on Russia's western borders – it joined the CST, it allowed for the joint protection of its western borders, and it consented to the joint operation of its air-defence system together with Russia. Belarus also became a more important gas transit route for Russia, given the difficulties that Moscow was experiencing in the Russian–Ukrainian gas relationship, and this explains why Russia proved more accommodating with regards to subsidising energy supplies to Minsk. The Kremlin, however, did not refrain from applying strong pressure on both countries in order to ensure payment for oil and gas purchases from Russia. Several disruptions characterised the bilateral energy trade in the 1990s, mostly related to the accumulation of arrears by the two countries. Cuts were often used by Russia as leverage in the negotiations over prices and volumes. More significantly, Russia also made use of the 'energy weapon' in order to achieve specific objectives, namely to obtain shares in the coveted Ukrainian and Belarusian industrial and energy facilities, so as to guarantee the unhindered flow of Russia's energy resources to European hard currency markets. Furthermore, Russia did not hesitate to use energy supplies as instruments of pressure to wrest control over Ukraine's share of the BSF, and over the various naval installations located in Crimea's Sevastopol port. A week before the 1993 summit where the fate of the BSF was to be discussed, Gazprom reduced gas supplies to Ukraine by 25 per cent, citing non-payments as a reason (*Platts Oligram News*, 1993). President Yeltsin also noted in June 1993, that progress on the resolution of the BSF dispute had been achieved 'after Russia [had] slightly turned off the oil tap'

(Shchipanov, 1993). This clearly indicated that the Kremlin was ready to use 'energy' as a *hard power* instrument in order to obtain major concessions, including better energy prices from Ukraine, in a clear display of Russia's hegemonic power.

Russia's CIS gas trade in the second half of the 1990s was determined, to a great extent, by the country's negative domestic economic outlook. Although in 1997, the Russian economy finally began to grow after six years of contraction, the Russian government nevertheless faced a severe budgetary crisis, which was exacerbated by the difficulties that the country was facing when trying to raise taxes. This adverse predicament put increased pressure on Gazprom – a major provider of tax revenues to the state – not only to raise gas prices, but also to collect debts and demand swift payment for gas deliveries, including from its CIS customers. Such policies could be interpreted as reflecting a neo-imperialist design, as they could have resulted in countries such as Ukraine, Belarus or Moldova falling under Russia's sphere of influence. Yet, Russia's actions followed, to a great extent, legitimate commercial imperatives. They revealed an eagerness by Moscow to establish energy relations with these countries on a market footing and obtain prompt payment for its gas sales. Similarly, efforts conducted by the Kremlin to obtain shares in coveted Ukrainian companies were intended above all to cancel Ukraine's debts and recover assets, at a time of financial strain. Yet, Russia's efforts at acquiring control over Ukraine's strategic energy assets, such as refineries, storage facilities or pipelines, also followed a neo-imperialist design, namely to re-establish control over the former Soviet energy complex and, in this way integrate the CIS energy space. Similarly, the acquisition by Russia of a significant share of the BSF from Ukraine in exchange for debt cancellations also fitted a clear hegemonic project, and cannot be seen purely as a commercial activity –as a simple debt-for-equity swap. Through this transaction, Russia succeeded in achieving a key strategic objective – it retained control over most of the BSF and obtained a long-term lease for the stationing of its fleet at Crimea's Sevastopol naval base, thus ensuring the semi-permanent deployment of major naval forces in the Crimean Peninsula on the Black Sea. Yet, as part of this agreement, Russia also recognised the territorial integrity of Ukraine and the inclusion of Crimea in Ukraine. The record of neo-imperialism is, therefore, a mixed one, with Russia's actions reflecting the behaviour of a hegemonic power rather than those of a neo-imperialist state.

As far as Belarus is concerned, Russia's readiness to introduce lower gas prices in the second half of the 1990s was not only related to the establishment of a Union State between the two countries. Low energy prices were also made conditional upon the acquisition by Gazprom of several Belarusian energy assets, such as *Slavneft* and *Beltransgaz*, reflecting once again a willingness by Russia to extract tangible benefits in exchange for subsidised gas prices. However, despite several commitments made by the Belarusian leaderships, Minsk refused to sell its strategic companies to Russia, and instead, continued to accumulate unpaid debts. President Lukashenko tried to resolve his country's energy dependency on Russia by joining Belarus in a Union State, in the hope that this would result in cheaper Russian oil and gas supplies. As such, he proved ready to surrender part of the country's sovereignty to Russia for the sake of Belarus' economic – and most possibly his own personal political – survival. Ukraine, on the other hand, refused to sell its major industrial assets to Russia to cancel its massive debts, in an effort to preserve its newly acquired sovereignty. Instead, it resorted to the siphoning of gas and the re-export of its gas to Europe, at the cost of severely disrupting the bilateral relationship with Russia.[10] The Kremlin responded by threatening to stop energy deliveries to Ukraine, and planning to develop bypass transit options through Belarus and Poland.

These difficulties explain why, during the second half of the 1990s, Gazprom lost interest and decided partly to abandon some of the unprofitable CIS markets, where payment was not always forthcoming, and prices were low. While Gazprom continued to deliver gas to Belarus, Moldova and Ukraine, it did so only in exchange for a corresponding amount of gas transiting through their respective territories. The additional gas demanded by these three countries was covered by the intermediary company Itera, which also took over the sale of Central Asian gas to countries such as Georgia and Armenia. In Georgia, Itera succeeded in running a profitable business, while in Armenia, Itera and Gazprom managed to acquire shares in the ARGP joint venture, in exchange for debts. In Moldova, Gazprom also acquired a 50 per cent stake in the local gas distributor *MoldovaGas* in exchange for the cancellation of gas debts. All this clearly indicated that Russia and Gazprom were increasingly turning the gas trade from a subsidised enterprise to a profitable business. Furthermore, as the hegemonic energy power, Russia was able to set prices and determine conditions. It did not always succeed in reaching its objectives, though, as shown by Gazprom's inability to acquire shares in several Ukrainian and Belarusian energy and industrial assets.

Similarly, Gazprom tried to control and profit from the gas trade between Ukraine and Turkmenistan, and to take over Turkmenistan's share of gas exports to the lucrative Western European markets. When in 1997, Ashgabat disbanded the intermediary TurkmenRosGaz, where Gazprom had a significant stake, the Russian gas conglomerate cut Turkmen gas access to Russian pipelines, thereby suspending gas supplies to Ukraine and blocking Turkmenistan's gas exports from European markets. While gas sales to Ukraine were resumed in 1998 – after arduous negotiations on prices – Moscow barred the transit of Turkmen gas to Europe for another two years, exploiting its dominant position in the area and its control over export pipelines. Furthermore, in December 1999, Turkmenistan agreed to sell a significant amount of its gas directly to Russia's Gazprom at a relative low price. Russia could in this way, purchase cheap Turkmen gas for its own domestic consumption, and sell gas more expensively to its customers in European markets – taking advantage of its geographical location. At the same time, with these purchases, Gazprom won control over deliveries to the domestic Turkish gas market, a business which Ashgabat had coveted but could not supply because of the absence of a transit route. Besides holding the only existing major pipeline route, Russia also obstructed the construction of an alternative *TransCaspian* pipeline. Russia was, therefore, effectively making use of its hegemonic position to reduce the ability of Turkmenistan to sell to other CIS, Turkish or European markets. Furthermore, with the 1999 Turkmen–Russian gas deal, Russia also denied Ukraine the possibility of diversifying its gas imports by acquiring gas from Turkmenistan. This sharply increased Ukraine's dependence on Russian gas supplies – even though Turkmenistan was by then no longer willing to sell its gas to Ukraine because of the difficulties that Kiev was having in paying promptly for its gas. In other words, Russia took advantage of its hegemonic status and used its *hard power* to curtail the access of Turkmen gas to Europe, and to limit the ability of Ukraine to diversify its energy sources. As such it succeeded, albeit temporarily, in keeping Turkmenistan and Ukraine partly under its sphere of influence.

Russia, nevertheless, remained dependent on Ukraine's pipeline system for the transport of its energy exports to Europe. Energy exports remained extremely valuable for Russia, as they accounted for almost half of all the country's export earnings and between 45 and 50 per cent of its revenues in the late 1990s (Hill, 2002). Ninety per cent of the oil and most of the gas that Russia exported to Europe was transported on pipelines passing through Ukraine, thus creating a system of mutual dependency. However, as the supplier of the energy and the host of the pipeline carrying Turkmen gas to Ukraine, Russia often retained the upper hand. This allowed it to set prices and determine the conditions of payment. It is therefore more appropriate to talk of 'asymmetrical dependency' (Balmaceda, 2009b, p. 10), rather than equal mutual dependency between the two equal countries. It was only in 2015 that Ukraine finally managed to break this dependency on Russia by no longer acquiring gas directly from either Russia or the CIS and relying on European support instead. In Central Asia, Gazprom also used its dominant transit position to limit the access of Kazakh gas to Europe, as it had done with Turkmenistan, as these businesses were seen by Gazprom as 'surrendering one's market' to a major competitor. As a result, Kazakhstan remained under Russia's energy sphere of influence – the country had difficulties in diversifying its gas exports, and continued during most of the 2000s to sell a large share of its gas to Russia. It was only in the late 2000s, after gas and oil pipelines were opened in the direction of China that Kazakhstan proved able to diversify its gas (and oil) exports away from Russia by selling part of its gas (and oil) production to China. Azerbaijan, instead, was able to diversify its gas export route away from Russia slightly earlier – it began selling its own gas directly to Georgia and Turkey, through the BTE pipeline, once its production at Shah Deniz was ready to sell and the pipeline became operational in December 2006. As such, Azerbaijan succeeded, to a certain extent, in remaining outside Russia's sphere of influence, although it continued to sell some amount of its oil through the Russian pipeline system linking Baku to Novorossiysk, besides using the new Baku-Tbilisi-Ceyhan line.

Notes

1 Ukraine's pipelines included the Soyuz system, which transported gas from the Urals region to Europe, the Urengoi-Uzhgood system, which carried gas from Siberia to Ukraine, and the southern branch of the Druzhba oil pipeline which carried oil to Europe.

2 Under the terms of the agreement, Ukraine would nominally receive 50 per cent of the fleet but would then exchange it for energy debt forgiveness from Russia (Deyermond, 2008, p. 108).
3 In 1993, real GDP fell by 15 per cent, bringing the cumulative fall in output since 1989 to 40 per cent (Mikheev, 1992).
4 Itera was owned partly by Russian businessman Igor Makarov (26 percent, through various organisations). Other individuals owned 13 per cent of the shares, but the remaining 61 per cent were held in two trusts for unnamed top managers and employees (Global Witness, 2006).
5 Negotiations were launched in 1996–1997 which resulted in progressive reductions in the gas price charged to Belarus, until the latter reached the rate paid by neighbouring Russian regions in 2002 (Rontoyanni, 2005, p.59).
6 The first significant gas flow through the Belarusian leg of the Yamal gas pipeline, bringing Russian Siberian gas to Europe occurred in 1999 (Bruce, 2005, p. 13).
7 Gazprom and the Armenian Ministry of Energy each had a 45 per cent stake in the company, and the remaining 10 per cent was owned by Itera.
8 President Niyazov had proposed to the Russian leadership that they become partners, rather than competitors, in the world gas market. But while Yeltsin and Chernomyrdin agreed, Gazprom's CEO Vyakhirev apparently did not (Mikhailov and Smolnikov, 1997b).
9 According to Stern (2005), it later transpired that there had been no agreement on prices.
10 It must be noted that in the 1990s, Ukraine was the largest gas importer in the world, acquiring an average of 53 Bcm per year from abroad, primarily from Russia (Balmaceda, 1998 p. 258). Its high level of energy intensity made its economy highly uncompetitive, and increased its dependency on Russia as a provider of gas.

Bibliography

Agence France Presse (1997). Russia's Gazprom Rules Out Access for Kazakh Gas Exports. 7 August.

Aslund, A. (2009). *How Ukraine Became a Market Economy and Democracy.* Washington DC: Peterson Institute for International Economics.

Balmaceda, M.M. (1998). Gas, Oil and the Linkages between Domestic and Foreign Policies: The Case of Ukraine. *Europe-Asia Studies*, 50 (2), 257–286.

Balmaceda, M.M. (2009a). At a Crossroads: the Belarusian-Russian Energy-political Model in Crisis. In: S. Fischer, ed. *Back from the Cold? The EU and Belarus in 2009.* Chaillot Paper, 119. November, pp. 79–91.

Balmaceda, M.M. (2009b). *Energy Dependency, Politics and Corruption in the Former Soviet Union: Russia's Power, Oligarchs' Profit, and Ukraine's Missing Energy Policy, 1995–2006,* Milton Park, Abingdon and New York: Routledge.

Balmaceda, M.M. (2013). *Politics of Energy Dependency: Ukraine, Belarus, and Lithuania between Domestic Oligarchs and Russian Pressure.* Toronto, London: University of Toronto Press, Studies in Comparative Political Economy and Public Policy.

Bekker, A. (1993). *Segodnya*, 21 January, p. 2.

Bragov, A. (1997). *Kommersant-daily*, 8 August, p. 4.

Bruce, Ch. (2005). *Fraternal Friction or Fraternal Fiction? The Gas Factor in Russian-Belarusian Relations*, Oxford Institute for Energy Studies. March. Available at: www.oxfordenergy.org/wpcms/wp-content/uploads/2010/11/NG8-FraternalFrictionOrFraternalfictionTheGasFactorInRussianBelarusianRelations-ChloeBruce-2005.pdf [accessed 3 September 2018].

Bruce, Ch. and K. Yafimava (2009). Moldova's Gas Sector. In: S. Pirani, ed. *Russian and CIS Gas Markets and their Impact on Europe*. Oxford: Oxford University Press, Oxford Institute of Energy Studies, pp. 170–202.
Deyermond, R. (2008) *Security and Sovereignty in the Former Soviet Union*. Boulder and London: Lynne Reinner.
Dubnov A. and Annageldiyev, K. (1999). *Vremya MN*, 20 December, p. 5.
Economist Intelligence Unit (EIU) (1994). *Belarus: Country Report*. 3rd Quarter.
Economist Intelligence Unit (EIU) (1995). *Belarus: Country Report*. 3rd Quarter.
Economist Intelligence Unit (EIU) (1996). *Belarus: Country Report*. 1st Quarter.
Emerenko, A. (1996). *Zerkalo nedeli*. 7–13, December. In: M.M. Balmaceda (1998). 'Gas, Oil and the Linkages between Domestic and Foreign Policies: The Case of Ukraine', *Europe-Asia Studies*, 50 (2), 257–286.
Financial Times (1999). 10 June, p. 1.
FT Energy Newsletters (1997). East European Energy Report, August 1.
FT Energy Newsletters (1998). Ukraine and Russia Iron Out New Transit Fees. 1 January.
Gafarly, M. (1997). *Nezavisimaya gazeta*, 7 August, p. 4.
Global Witness (2006). *It's a Gas—Funny Business in the Turkmen-Ukraine Gas Trade*. April. Available at: www.globalwitness.org/en/reports/its-gas/ [accessed 3 September 2018].
Gorst, I. (1993a). Neighbours Tussle over Energy Matters, *Petroleum Economist*, April, p. 16.
Hill, F. (2002). *Russia: The 21st Century Energy Superpower?* Brookings Institution. Spring. Available at www.brookings.edu/research/articles/2002/03/spring-russia-hill [accessed 20 September 2018].
IEA (1996). *Energy Policies of Ukraine: 1996 Survey*. Paris: IEA.
International Herald Tribune (IHT) (1992). British Gas and Agip in Kazakhstan Deal, 2 July, p. 2.
Itar-tass (1994). 4 March.
Karmanov, Yu. (1996). *Nezavisimaya gazeta*, 16 December, p. 3
Karpekova, S. (1998). *Izvestiya*, 17 June, p. 1.
Kuzmichov, V. (1998). *Nezavisimaya gazeta*, 7 March, p. 4.
Krasnov, G.V. and J.C. Brada (1997). Implicit Subsidies in Russian-Ukrainian Energy Trade, *Europa-Asia Studies*, 49 (50), 825–843.
Le Gall, F. (1994). Ukraine: A Trade and Exchange System Still Seeking Direction, In: C. Michalopoulos and D.G. Tarr, *Trade in the New Independent States*, Washington DC: International Monetary Fund.
Markus, U. (1995a). Belarus: Heading off an Energy Disaster, *Transition*, 1 (5), 10–13. 14 April.
Markus, U. (1995b). Ukraine: Debt and Desperation, *Transition*, 1(5), 14–19. 14 April.
Markus, U. (1996). Energy Crisis Spurs Ukraine and Belarus to Seek Help Abroad. *Transition*, 2(9), 14–18. 3 May.
Mikhailov, V. and G. Smolnikov (1997a). *Nezavisimaya gazeta*, 6 August, p. 3.
Mikhailov V. and G. Smolnikov (1997b). *Nezavisimaya gazeta*, 6 December, p. 3.
Mikheev, V. (1992). *Izvestiya*, 11 February, p. 5.
Moscow Radio (1992). 21 October.
Narzikulov, R. (1994). *Segodnya*, 11 March, p. 1.
Novoprudsky, S. (1999). *Izvestiya*, 21 December, p. 4.
Petroleum Economist (1992). 'Ukraine: Deal with Iran Poses Market-sharing Questions', March, p. 55.
Platt's Oilgram News (1993). 27 August.

Rontoyanni, C. (2005). Belarusian Foreign Policy. In: D. Lynch ed. *Changing Belarus*. Chaillot Paper. 85. Paris: Institute for Security Studies. November, pp. 47–66.

Shchipanov, M. (1993). *Kuranty*, 16 June, p. 1.

Sherr, J. (1997). *Russia and Ukraine: Towards Compromise or Convergence?*, Conflict Studies Research Centre, August.

Shimansky, M. (1993). *Izvestiya*, 27 August, p. 2.

Sinyakevich, I. (1998). *Noviye Izvestiya*, 28 February, p. 1.

Shiryayev, S. (2000). *Noviye Izvestiya*, 19 April, p. 1.

Stern, J. (2005). *The Future of Russian Gas and Gazprom*. Oxford: Oxford University Press.

Sukhova. S. (1996). *Kommersant-Daily*, 28 February, p. 3.

Whitlock, E. (1993). Ukrainian-Russian Trade: The Economics of Dependency. *RFE/RL Research Report*, 29 October, 38–42.

Womack, H. (1993). Storm Brews on Black Sea Deal, *Independent*, 5 September.

Yafimava, K. (2009). Belarus: The Domestic Gas Market and Relations with Russia. In: S. Pirani, ed. *Russian and CIS Gas Markets and their Impact on Europe*. Oxford: Oxford University Press, pp. 133–169.

Yeghiazaryan, A. (2009). Natural Gas Markets in Armenia. In: S. Pirani, ed. *Russian and CIS Gas Markets and their Impact on Europe*. Oxford: Oxford University Press, Oxford Institute of Energy Studies. pp. 235–255.

5 The outbreak of military conflicts
Russia's difficulties in discarding its Imperial legacy

The end of the USSR saw the outbreak of a series of wars along Russia's periphery. Violence engulfed the two separatist regions of Georgia – South Ossetia (1991–1992) and Abkhazia (1992–1994) – over their status inside the new Georgian state. Violent conflict also erupted over the destinies of Transdniestria in 1991–1992, a primarily Russian-speaking region of Moldova, whose leaders wished to separate from the new Moldovan state, if the latter joined up with Romania. With the collapse of the USSR, war also escalated in and around Nagorno-Karabakh, a province inside Azerbaijan, whose Armenian majority wished for the region to join neighbouring Armenia, and whose inhabitants had experienced conflict since 1988. Violence also broke out in the Central Asian republic of Tajikistan in the spring and summer of 1992, as several political factions and armed militias vied for control of the leavers of power and struggled over the future direction of the country. All these wars witnessed a significant involvement of Russia, both in terms of military support to the warring parties, and mediation efforts among the sides, leading many to argue that Russia intended to use these conflicts to bring the affected former Soviet countries under its 'sphere of influence'. Its peacekeeping activities were seen as a mantle for Russia's neo-imperialist aspirations (Allison, 1994, p. 15; Baev, 1996, p. 113; Ehrhart *et al.*, 1996, p. 162). The nature of Russia's involvement is, however, far more complex than is often assumed, and the evidence available seems to indicate that in the first months of the Yeltsin presidency, which is when most of these conflicts first erupted, the Kremlin adopted a policy of military disengagement, focusing its efforts instead on finding a peaceful resolution of the dispute through diplomatic means. Yet, as violence escalated, the Kremlin became increasingly involved, by providing military aid to one of the warring parties, usually the separatist regions, either directly, as occurred in Abkhazia and Transdniestria, or indirectly through Armenia, as was the case in the Karabakh war. While Russia's military engagement undoubtedly followed legitimate state concerns, namely to put an end to the growing violence along its borders, its actions actually resulted in Russia keeping a prolonged military presence in these former Soviet states. Furthermore, in many instances, Moscow exerted great pressure on the 'mother countries', especially on Georgia and Azerbaijan, to ensure that Moscow would keep a military presence on their soil, in a clear sign of neo-imperialist behaviour. In the case of Tajikistan, Russia decided to throw in its lot with the former Communist forces, whose leaders reproduced the old Soviet alliances and embraced a clearly pro-Russian foreign policy vector.

Russia's involvement: a neo-imperial paradigm?

After the Soviet Union formally collapsed in December 1991, most of the Soviet Interior and Army troops stationed in areas of conflict were initially placed under Commonwealth of Independent States (CIS) command, leaving them, to a certain extent, in a legal limbo. It was only once the Russian Armed Forces were established in May 1992, that most of these forces were transferred to Russia's jurisdiction. Furthermore, in the spring of 1992, a substantial number of the ex-Soviet troops were withdrawn to Russia, while those forces still deployed in conflict zones were ordered by the Kremlin to stay neutral and away from the fight (Aklaev, 1996; Felgengauer, 1992b), in a clear sign that Russia seemed ready to disengage from the ex-USSR. Moreover, a significant amount of equipment was legally handed over by the Russian Defence Ministry to the new states – Georgia, Armenia, Azerbaijan and Moldova – in the spring and summer of 1992, as part of the division of the ex-Soviet armed forces, in accordance with the Conventional Forces in Europe (CFE) Treaty (*Nezavisimaya gazeta*, 1992b; Memorial 1992). In many cases, the weaponry belonging to the ex-Soviet forces was seized directly by the national authorities of the new states (Mukhin, 1992), while in other opportunities armament was either sold by officers or stolen by the new armed militias that emerged when the USSR collapsed (Trenin and Makarenko, 1992; Shevelev, 1992). Much of this equipment was then utilised by the leadership of these states to restore control forcefully over their respective separatist regions, as occurred in Georgia during the incursions of the Defence Ministry's troops into Abkhazia in August 1992, and in Moldova during Chisinau's attack on the town Bendery in June 1992. Similarly, the Azerbaijani armed forces also used equipment that had belonged to the ex-Soviet 4th Army stationed in Azerbaijan, to conduct their successful advances into Nagorno-Karabakh in June–July 1992.[1] The 'mother countries' were, therefore, partly responsible for the outbreak of violence that occurred in their territories with the end of the USSR, although the separatist pressures in all instances were very strong. On the other hand, there is little doubt that several ex-Soviet troops located in these turbulent regions decided to get involved in the fight on the side of the separatist forces once violence escalated, as occurred, for example, with the 366th Motorised Infantry Division (MID) deployed in Nagorno-Karabakh in February 1992 or with the 14th Army based in Transdniestria during the winter of 1991/1992. Yet, their initial involvement seems to have been carried out independently from the line of command, challenging the orders of neutrality that were being issued by the Kremlin and the CIS leadership at the time. In many cases, those ex-Soviet servicemen involved in the fight sympathised with the separatist cause, as occurred in Transdniestria and in Nagorno-Karabakh, while in other instances, the involvement was intended primarily to put an end to the violence, as happened in Tajikistan (Panfilov, 1992). In many opportunities, as was the case in South Ossetia, Soviet Interior Ministry troops stationed in the region also became important buffers between the various fighting groups. In this case, Soviet troops stood between the Georgian gunmen and the Ossetian armed formations when violence erupted in January 1991. Under regular attack from Georgian gunmen, the ex-Soviet troops, however, found it difficult to keep neutrality and often retaliated to the strikes, yet they generally avoided being fully dragged into the conflict (Russian TV, 1991)

As the fighting in these post-Soviet regions intensified in the spring of 1992, however, the policies of the Russian government changed. The Russian leadership became fully engaged in negotiations to stop the fighting, while it also began providing military support to one of the warring sides, usually the separatist regions, either to ensure their victory or to bring the violence to an end, or both. In South Ossetia, Russian combat helicopters launched an assault on units of the Georgian National Guard after a temporary ceasefire was violated by Georgian militias in June 1992, while ex-Soviet armed formations began an attack in support of Tskhinvali, using tanks and armoured personnel carriers (Urigashvili, 1992b). Furthermore, Moscow also introduced a partial economic blockade on Georgia – the gas pipeline and the Georgian military highway which linked Georgia to North Ossetia were closed off – while it also mobilised armed forces on the Georgian–Russian border. The Kremlin also threatened to impose further sanctions and to dispatch additional Russian Interior Ministry troops to South Ossetia, if fighting did not stop (Shevelev, 1992). This compelled the Georgian government to agree to a ceasefire agreement in June 1992, which also resulted in the deployment of a Russian-led tripartite peacekeeping force, and the setting up of a Joint Control Commission (JCC), composed of Georgian, Russian, North Ossetian and South Ossetian representatives, to monitor the implementation of the agreements. The CSCE/OSCE (Conference on (subsequently Organisation for) Security and Co-operation in Europe) was also called to participate as an observer of the ceasefire agreement and a facilitator of the fulfilment of the accords.

In Abkhazia, Russia initially kept a semblance of neutrality when violence escalated after the Georgian National Guard, supported by armoured cars and battle aircraft, entered Abkhazia in mid-August 1992 (Broladze, 1992). The Russian Defence Ministry just sent an airborne division to its military base in Gudauta to protect the Russian Army units stationed in Abkhazia and to help evacuate Russian citizens trapped in the area (*Interfax*, 1992b). Russian paratroopers, however, made it clear that any attempt by Georgian forces to advance further onto Gudauta would have been perceived by Russia as a hostile attack (Baev, 1997, p. 45). An important turning point occurred in October 1992, when Abkhaz military formations launched a successful offensive in northern Abkhazia, and the Russian (Ministry of Defence) MoD decided to support their attack, by providing them with both covert and overt military assistance, in the form of heavy armoury, tanks and rocket launchers (Urigashvili, 1992c, 1992d). By then, the Russian MoD had clearly identified Abkhazia as a key Russian ally in the region – through Abkhazia Russia could keep a military foothold in Georgia, a country of major strategic significance to Russia on the shores of the Black Sea, in a clear display of neo-imperialist behaviour. In the winter of 1992–1993, the Russian military got further involved in the conflict, and as the violence escalated, it began providing direct military support to the Abkhaz war effort. In response to Georgia's bombing campaign against Abkhaz positions in northern Abkhazia, the Russian MoD sent fighter planes in February–March 1993 to bomb Georgian positions in the capital Sukhumi and in the Ochamchira region near the sea (Taranov and Urigashvili, 1993; *Interfax*, 1993). In early March 1993, as the Russian/Abkhaz bombings on Sukhumi intensified, the Abkhaz side received also large amounts of fuel from Russia as well as state-of-the-art T-72 tanks to ensure a complete Abkhaz victory over Georgian forces. Moreover, Russian military specialists arrived in Gudauta to advise the Abkhaz side on how to retake control over the entire region (*Interfax*, 1993). Furthermore, soldiers from a Russian army landing-force battalion stationed in Nizhnyaya Eshera outside Sukhumi allegedly also became directly involved in combat operations on the Abkhaz side (Urigashvili, 1993). Apparently, the Russian airborne assault unit at the Bombora airfield in Abkhazia also took a direct part in the various assaults on Sukhumi, in March, July and September 1993 (Tbilisi 7 DGHE, 1995). The Russian-supported Abkhaz military victories forced Georgian President Eduard Shevardnadze to sign an agreement in 1994 which brought the fighting to an end and resulted in the deployment of Russian peacekeeping forces along the cease-fire line. Russian forces received a CIS mandate while a UN observation mission, UNOMIG, was deployed to monitor its activities.[2] By its actions, Russia had clearly succeeded, at least temporarily, in forcing Georgia out of Abkhazia and brining it back under Russia's sphere of influence. Russia's military presence in Georgia was legalised in a *Friendship and Co-operation Treaty* signed on 3 February 1994 which sanctioned the presence of three Russian military bases in Georgia and the joint border protection of the Georgian-Turkish border.

When the Nagorno-Karabakh conflict escalated in the autumn and winter of 1991/1992, Russia initially did not get involved militarily in the region, and instead withdrew many of its troops from Armenia and Azerbaijan. Yet, the ex-Soviet 366th MID deployed in Nagorno-Karabakh, many of whose officers and soldiers were ethnic Armenians, became fully engaged in the fight on the Karabakh Armenian side, most probably without the Kremlin's support. On 25 February 1992, Karabakh Armenians launched a bloody assault on the strategic town of Khodjali with the support of the 366th MID, which resulted in a high number of Azerbaijani casualties (de Waal, 2003, p. 172; Memorial, 1992). As a result, the 366th division was fully withdrawn to Russia, and thereafter, the Russian government tried to keep a semblance of neutrality as fighting ravaged in and around Nagorno-Karabakh between Karabakh Armenian forces and Azerbaijani troops. Yet, during the spring of 1992, as violence escalated, neighbouring Armenia became increasingly involved in the fight. Furthermore, both sides hired Russian and Ukrainian former servicemen to assist them in their war effort. These mercenaries drove tanks and flew military planes to bomb enemy positions, but they did not respond to Russian orders and instead seemed to have been acting independently (Glotz, 1993; de Waal, 2003, p. 167, 195). In the summer of 1992, however, Russia became more directly involved in the conflict after Azerbaijan conducted a series of successful Azerbaijani counter-offensives against Armenian advances. Fearful of an imminent Karabakh Armenian collapse, Moscow sent Russian attack helicopters to carry out strikes against Azerbaijani positions (de Waal, 2003, p. 196). Moreover, a mechanised division deployed in Yerevan was transferred to Armenian jurisdiction following a confidential agreement between Yeltsin Armenian President Levon and Ter-Petrosian (Felgengauer, 1992a). Russia apparently also helped Armenia to set up an anti-aircraft system in the fall of 1992, to defend Karabakh from Azerbaijani air attacks.

Russia's support for Armenia only increased as the war progressed, especially as Moscow identified Armenia as its key strategic ally in the South Caucasus region. Between August 1992 and June 1994, massive amounts of Russian ammunition, as well as spare parts, fuel and military weaponry were delivered by Russia to Armenia, with the full approval of Russian President Yeltsin (de Waal, 2003). During the entire war, damaged military equipment belonging to the Akhalkalaki division and to the Armenian armed forces was also regularly brought by train to the Russian MoD tank repair factory in Tbilisi. Moreover, when Azerbaijan began conducting a major offensive in December 1993, Moscow put great pressure on the Azerbaijani leadership to stop its advances, in a clear effort to protect its Armenian ally (Mekhtiev, 1994).[3] In its attempts to reach a ceasefire agreement, the Russian Foreign Ministry also introduced its own parallel mediation effort, which was led by Russian diplomat Vladimir Kazimirov, and which competed vehemently with the CSCE/OSCE Minsk negotiating format. These Russian-led diplomatic efforts which also involved the Russian Defence Ministry, eventually succeeded in the spring of 1994 in brokering a lasting ceasefire, which however solidified Karabakh's territorial gains. Furthermore, during the negotiations held in 1993 and 1994, the Russian leadership and the Russian MoD regularly tried to convince Baku to accept the deployment of a Russian peacekeeping force in Nagorno-Karabakh, in a clear sign that Moscow also wished to keep Azerbaijan under its military sphere of influence. However, Baku resisted all of Russia's endeavours in this respect. The final agreement reached between Armenia and Azerbaijan on 27 July 1994 foresaw the introduction of a multi-national peacekeeping force – and not a Russian-led force – as well as the deployment of CSCE observers, and this showed the limits of Russia's hegemonic reach. While OSCE observers were soon deployed to the ceasefire line in Nagorno-Karabakh, the multi-national peacekeeping force, however, never materialised, due to disagreements among the sides over the composition of its troops. The ceasefire, nevertheless, did hold without any major incidents for over two decades, until violence erupted once again in April 2016. On the other hand, the close military cooperation established between Moscow and Yerevan resulted in agreements being reached on the stationing of two Russian military bases in Armenia – at Gyumri and Yerevan – in April 1995, and on the joint protection of Armenia's borders with Turkey in March 1994 (Felgengauer, 1994). This clearly allowed Russia to keep Armenia fully under Russia's sphere of influence.

As far as Moldova is concerned, when the Soviet Union collapsed, the Soviet 14th Army located on the *left bank* of the Dniester, in Transdniestria, was initially placed under CIS command, while the former Soviet troops stationed on the *right bank* of the Dniester were transferred to Moldovan jurisdiction in March 1992 (Radio Romania, 1992). Officially, the 14th Army deployed in Transdniestria was ordered by the leadership of the Odessa Military District, to remain neutral when fighting erupted around Transdniestria (Mulyar, 1991). But its neutrality was systematically violated, as the 14th Army provided significant covert support to Transdniestria's separatists in the form of weapons, equipment, training and personnel during the autumn of 1991 (Radio Chisinau, 1992). At that time, a split had actually occurred among the 14th Army's officer corps, with some detachments actively participating in the conflict, some units even switching to the jurisdiction of the Transdniestrian leadership, while others attempting to stay neutral (Moscow Radio, 1991; Durnov, 1992). As violence in the Dniester region escalated in the spring of 1992, Yeltsin decided to put all military facilities and army units in Transdniestria under Russia's jurisdiction (*Interfax*, 1992a). Yet, despite the orders of neutrality, forces belonging to the 14th Army became increasingly involved in the conflict on the Transdniestrian side – they provided assistance to the Transdniestrian militia and openly supported the separatist cause (Tass, 1991). In early April 1992, as conditions on the ground deteriorated, the 14th Army began mobilising and occupying key positions in the town of Bendery, before establishing a ceasefire line between the Moldovan and Dniester armed formations, not without getting involved in the fight on the Transdniestrian side (Russian TV, 1992a). On 20 May 1992, the 14th Army extended its occupation of the left-bank districts. Its tanks and infantry vehicles appeared in the city of Dubossary, which was being subjected to mortar attack by Moldovan artillery forces (*Nezavisimaya gazeta*, 1992a; Prikhodko, 1993). On 19 June 1992, Moldova conducted a massive attack on the right-bank city of Bendery which resulted in a high number of dead and wounded, compelling the Russian leadership to become more deeply engaged in the war. Russia immediately dispatched Major-General Aleksandr Lebed to Transdniestria to bring the situation under control. Lebed took command of the 14th Army and conducted a series of exercises with his troops, which managed to put an end to Moldova's attacks on Transdniestria, and helped pacify the region (Kakotkin, 1992). In order to enhance security, Lebed also conducted joint peacekeeping activities with Moldovan forces in the town of Bendery (Russian TV, 1992b). Moreover, he successfully confiscated the weapons that had been distributed among the Transdniestrian militia, and properly safeguarded the vast amounts of military equipment belonging to the 14th Army (Radio Rosii, 1992). Russia also succeeded in brokering a ceasefire agreement in July 1992, which foresaw the deployment of a Russian-led peacekeeping force to Transdniestria, not unlike the one established in South Ossetia, made up of contingents belonging to Russia and to the two other sides of the conflict. The role of the 14th Army as a peacekeeping force, however, was ruled out and negotiations on its future status and withdrawal to Russia began (Radio Chisinau, 1992).

When violence first erupted in Tajikistan's capital Dushanbe in the spring of 1992 between supporters and opponents of President Rakhmon Nabiev, the ex-Soviet 201st Motorised Rifle Division (MRD) stationed in Tajikistan did not take any direct military action, as the Russian leadership had instructed all armed forces deployed in Tajikistan to stay neutral. However, former Soviet Ministry of Interior troops under Tajik command did initially help to guarantee security in the streets of Dushanbe (Lugovskaya, 1992). When hostilities intensified in mid-May 1992, Russian forces belonging to the 201st MRD became more involved – they protected refugees and guarded key sites at the request of the Tajik authorities, although they did not become engaged in large-scale fighting (Orr, 1998, p. 152). In the early summer of 1992, as violence throughout the country escalated, Russia took over the direct protection of the Tajik–Afghan border (Rotar and Abrashitov, 1992). The 201st MRD, however, did not become engaged in the war and instead limited itself to protecting strategic sites in the country. In September 1992, the situation deteriorated further as President Nabiev was forced to resign, under pressure from the Islamist/Democratic forces, and power passed to the chairman of the Supreme Soviet, Akbarsho Iskandarov. This plunged the country into complete anarchy, and prompted the Russian 201st MRD, which had so far kept at least some semblance of neutrality, openly to help the new Iskandarov regime to impose order throughout the country. In November 1992, as the situation in Tajikistan continued to worsen, Russia succeeded in obtaining the support of the Tajik authorities to grant the 201st MRD peace-enforcement functions, including assisting the Tajik government to restore peace and order throughout the country (Rotar, 1992). However, the 201st MRD did not intervene when a series of forces loyal to Nabiev began their attack on Dushanbe, with Uzbek military assistance, in early December 1992 (Orr, 1998). Yet, once Dushanbe fell into the hands of these new forces, the 201st MRD did help patrol the streets of the capital city, and soon became the main guarantor of security in key strategic areas of the country (Putovsky, 1992).

As the Islamist/Democratic opposition forces fled to Afghanistan, Russia increased its support for the pro-Russian government led by Imomali Rakhmon, a Kulyabi who had been elected Chairman of the Supreme Soviet in mid-November 1992, and who had been confirmed as Tajikistan's leader in Dushanbe in December 1992. As government forces advanced against opposition strongholds, a significant number of rebel fighters fled to neighbouring Afghanistan, where they began training for a major offensive, with the support of the Afghan *Mujahideen*. In February 1993, they conducted their first attacks against posts along the Tajik–Afghan border, which were being patrolled by Russian border guards. A major Tajik opposition offensive occurred in July 1993 in which as many as 30 Russian border guards were killed. This triggered a sharp reaction from the Russian government which decided to become actively involved in the conflict. The Kremlin enhanced the protection of the Tajik–Afghan border, provided increased military support to the Tajik authorities in Dushanbe, while also fostering a dialogue among the two factions in order to bring about a lasting settlement of the war. On 25 May 1993, Presidents Yeltsin and Rakhmon signed a series of documents on assistance and military cooperation, officially sealing Russia's alliance with the Tajik regime and laying the grounds for Russia's further military involvement in the region (Kuznetsova, 1993). In September 1993 it was agreed that joint CIS peacekeeping forces (*mirotvorcheskie sily*) would be formally established on the basis of Russian, Kazakh, Uzbek, Kyrgyz and Tajik military forces, with a relatively broad peace-making mandate (*Sodruzhestvo*, 1993). Kyrgyzstan, Uzbekistan and Kazakhstan eventually sent battalions to reinforce Russia's forces in 1994, but their small numbers – each national contingent did not surpass 350 men – resulted in Russia carrying the bulk of the peacekeeping operation (Allison, 1994, p. 15).

Assessment: were Russia's actions neo-imperial?

Russia's active military and diplomatic engagement in all these five conflicts resulted in the deployment of Russian-dominated peacekeeping forces in Tajikistan, in Moldova's Transdniestria, and in Georgia's separatist regions of South Ossetia and Abkhazia. These primarily Russian military forces, besides ensuring peace and preventing a resumption of violence in the area, ended up also fulfilling a major strategic role for Russia – strengthening security along Russia's borders and enhancing Russia's defences by providing the country with further strategic depth. In the case of Georgia, the Kremlin also ensured that Tbilisi joined the Russian-led Collective Security Treaty in 1993 and accepted the stationing of Russian military forces on its territory, in the shape of four military bases, for a 25-year period, in 1995. The Kremlin also succeeded in deploying its peacekeeping forces in Moldova's Transdniestria, although Moscow committed itself in October 1994 to withdrawing the 14th Army deployed in Transdniestria back to Russia within a three-year time frame (Feliksova, 1994). Yet, the withdrawal of the army was *synchronised* with the reaching of a political settlement over Transdniestria, thus complicating its realisation (Gamova, 1994; *Interfax*, 1994). Russia also managed to guarantee for itself a military presence in Tajikistan, as the 201st MRD forces deployed in that country were granted a rather broad CIS peace-keeping mandate, while Russia's border troops were entrusted with the protection of the volatile Tajik–Afghan border. Russia also established a close military-strategic partnership with Armenia, which was sealed in the 1997 *Treaty of Friendship, Cooperation and Mutual Assistance*. This allowed Moscow to keep two military bases in Armenia and remain in charge of patrolling the external borders of Armenia with Turkey. The Kremlin, however, failed to guarantee for itself a military presence in Nagorno-Karabakh, despite exerting significant pressure on Baku in 1992–1994, although it did succeed in compelling Azerbaijan to join the Collective Security Treaty in September 1993. More significantly, Russia's involvement in these conflicts allowed Russia to establish 'protectorates' over the break-away regions of South Ossetia, Abkhazia and Transdniestria, and as a result, to extend its influence over Georgia, Moldova, Tajikistan, Armenia, and to a lesser extent Azerbaijan.

Russia's actions in many respects, therefore, clearly fitted the neo-imperialist pattern. There is little doubt that Russia considered these areas as strategically vital for its own security, and therefore saw these CIS states as falling within its own sphere of influence. In this sense, its leaders proved determined to ensure that no country other than Russia exercise a predominant military and diplomatic role in the former Soviet region, although the United Nations (in Abkhazia and Tajikistan), and the CSCE/OSCE (in South Ossetia and Nagorno-Karabakh) were also allowed to engage in the negotiations, albeit in a subordinate role. Yet, the Kremlin also had a legitimate interest in finding a peaceful resolution to these conflicts, and this weakens, to a certain extent, the neo-imperialist argument. Instabilities along Russia's southern borders, however far these regions may have been from Russia proper, were perceived as having a direct negative impact on the country's security, in terms of refugee flows, threats to Russian minorities living in these areas, illegal arms smuggling and the risk of spill over, as no proper Russian border protection system had been established yet. Moreover, Russia was most probably the country best placed – because of its proximity, its historical legacy, and its substantial resources – to persuade the warring factions to reach a ceasefire agreement. It was also the state most willing to take effective action and send in its own military forces into combat in order to bring violence to a halt. Its actions therefore also fulfilled a legitimate defensive purpose, namely ensuring security along Russia's borders. Furthermore, there is hardly any evidence indicating that the *new* Russian leadership under President Yeltsin exacerbated these violent conflicts in order to intervene militarily and preserve a troop deployment in these CIS regions. More often than not, Russia's involvement resulted from an escalation of the situation on the ground, provoked by the leaderships of the 'mother countries' themselves.

However, once violence escalated and the initial diplomatic efforts by the Kremlin did not produce the desired results, Russia became further involved in these conflicts. As the Defence Ministry took the upper hand over the Ministry of Foreign Affairs, it increased its military support to one of the warring factions, generally the separatist regions, as these remained keen to establish close ties with (or even integrate into) Russia. Furthermore, in many opportunities, Russian forces deployed in these areas engaged in robust 'peace-making' activities – for example, the 14th Army in Transdniestria and the 201st MRD in Tajikistan – which resembled military combat. There is little doubt that Russia's more assertive military engagement, the involvement of its 'peace-making' troops, and its active diplomatic efforts, helped to bring the violence of these conflicts to an end. Yet, they also reflected Russia's hegemonic influence. A fine line divided Russia's security efforts from its neo-imperial building, and most often, Russian leaders found themselves conducting assertive actions which very much fitted the neo-imperialist paradigm. More importantly, as a result of Moscow's actions, Russia was able to keep a military presence, either in the form of peacekeeping forces and/or military bases, in all of these former Soviet states, with the exception of Azerbaijan, thus reinforcing its neo-imperialist project and its hegemonic agenda. Furthermore, most often than not, this military presence prolonged itself over time and, more importantly, it occurred against the explicit wishes of the countries concerned (as was the case with the Russian military forces and peace-keeping troops deployed in Georgia and Moldova). As a result, Russia ended up establishing a neo-empire over these Near Abroad states. However, the nature of Russia's engagement in all these states suffering from war and internal conflict is rather more complex than it appears at first hand, as, for example, the Armenian and the Tajikistani leaderships did welcome Russia's military involvement in their respective countries. Technically, therefore, one cannot talk of Russia establishing a neo-empire over these two CIS states. In the case of Tajikistan in particular, Moscow was responding to the requests of the government in Dushanbe, and as such, its actions were not an infringement of international law. Furthermore, Russia complemented its military involvement in Tajikistan with an active diplomatic campaign intended to find a resolution to the conflict, which involved the participation of other key regional players. A series of six rounds of talks were held between April 1994 and May 1997, between the Tajik government and the opposition under UN aegis, which eventually led to a final peace agreement, and which saw Russia working hand in hand with other regional players. Although Russia played a key role in starting the intra-Tajik talks, from the very beginning, it showed a readiness to involve not only the UN, but also other regional actors, such as Afghanistan, Iran, Pakistan, Turkmenistan and Kazakhstan in the negotiations, in a clear sign that it was ready to discard, at least partly, its imperialist ambitions (Rigacci-Hay, 2001, pp. 38–40). Yet, it must be noted that Russia was able thereafter to exert strong influence over Tajikistan – and Armenia – as a result of its military presence and economic support.

When discussing Russia's neo-imperialist behaviour in the former Soviet space, account must also be taken of the fact that Russia's actions were often very much the result of improvisation, rather than cautious planning, and therefore, in many occasions, chaos reigned supreme. Furthermore, strong disagreements emerged between the MoD and the Ministry of Foreign Affairs (MFA) over how to approach the resolution of these wars, and this complicated matters further. The Russian military and most members of the Russian parliament found it very difficult totally to discard Russia's imperial legacy and accept as fixed the new borders of Russia and recognise the independence of the former Soviet states (FSS). They tended to believe that the map of Russia could easily be changed, and therefore were eager to take and protect as many territories loyal to Russia as possible.[4] They favoured the right of self-determination of those entities eager to join Russia, to the detriment of the territorial integrity of the newly independent states. Yet, President Yeltsin and Foreign Minister Kozyrev supported the new countries' territorial integrity and inviolability of borders, in a clear discard of Russia's imperial legacy. They wished to ensure that Russia upheld the principles of international law as enshrined in the UN Charter and the CSCE Paris Declaration of 1990. While they managed, at least officially, to impose their views – Russia upheld the territorial integrity of all the new states – the MoD still succeeded in conducting its independent assertive actions in the CIS space. It is therefore difficult not to consider Russia's actions as partly fitting a neo-imperialist paradigm.

Civil wars and conflict under Primakov: an era of disengagement?

During Primakov's tenure as Foreign Minister and Prime Minister, the Kremlin instead adopted a much more conciliatory stance towards the various separatist conflicts and civil wars that had erupted in the CIS region in the early 1990s, in what seemed to be a readiness by Russia to discard its imperialist legacy. Its policies reflected the negative experiences of Russia's war in Chechnya, and the lack of appetite among the Russian public more generally for continued military engagement either in the North Caucasus or in the Near Abroad. Worried over the spread of secessionist movements inside Russia and beyond its closest border, in view of its defeat in Chechnya in 1996, the Kremlin no longer sided openly with the 'separatist' entities in the former Soviet space. Instead, it engaged in active negotiations in order to reach political settlements, which in the case of the separatist conflicts of Abkhazia, South Ossetia, and Transdniestria, preserved the territorial integrity of the 'mother' countries, while also granting the break-away regions broad autonomous status (Antonenko, 2005, p. 233; ICG, 2003, p. 7, Botan, 2009, p. 120). Options which included awarding the separatist regions 'equal' legal status to the 'mother' countries in a 'common state' were also proposed (OSCE, 1997a; ICG, 2007, p. 8). In Nagorno-Karabakh, a variety of alternatives also were explored, which generally preserved the Armenian-populated region inside Azerbaijan, but which also left the question of status open (OSCE, 1997b, 1997c). In Tajikistan, efforts were made to find a compromise which ensured that the pro-Russian Rakhmon regime was kept in power, although Rakhmon was asked to share government positions with members of the United Tajik Opposition (UTO) (Velekhov, 1996). In contrast to previous years, the Kremlin also began cooperating quite effectively with other international actors, be it the OSCE in Nagorno-Karabakh and South Ossetia; Ukraine and the OSCE in Transdniestria; or the UN and Iran in Tajikistan, in order to try to find a negotiated solution to these disputes (OSCE, 1996; EDM, 1997). Even in Abkhazia, Russia eventually found common ground with the so-called 'Western' Group of Friends of Georgia – the United States, France, the United Kingdom and Germany – and accepted in 2001 the proposals introduced by the UN Special Representative of the Secretary General (SRSG), Dieter Boden (ICG, 2007; Whitfield, 2007, pp. 151–154).

Furthermore, in several instances, Russia went as far as putting strong pressure on the separatist regions – as it did with Abkhazia in 1996 – to reach a negotiated outcome that preserved the 'mother countries' as unified states (Barakhova, 1996; Globachev, 1996). In Tajikistan, Moscow succeeded in moderating the stance of the Rakhmon leadership, forcing it to accept the presence of UTO leaders in the governing structures, and paving the way for a resolution of the conflict (Rotar, 1996). More significantly, the Kremlin ruled out the military involvement of the 201st MRD in the war in support of the Rakhmon regime, and issued orders for it to stay neutral, worried that its servicemen would suffer if the division got involved in the Tajik civil war (Vinogradov, 1996). Instead, Russia engaged in active mediation efforts, conducted in coordination with Iran, several Central Asian states, and the United Nations, which succeeded in putting an end to the war in Tajikistan in 1997. A series of political, military and humanitarian agreements were adopted by the two conflicting sides which brought the high levels of violence to an end and facilitated the return of Tajik refugees (Rigacci Hay, 2001, pp. 38–40). Moscow's negotiations on the future status of the separatist regions located in Georgia, Azerbaijan and Moldova, however, proved less successful. While large-scale violence in all these three areas of conflict was avoided and the agreed ceasefires generally held, the warring sides, nevertheless, found it hard to agree on a compromised solution, which kept the separatist regions as autonomous regions within the 'mother countries'.[5] Primakov, therefore, proposed the creation of 'common states' emulating the ethno-territorial arrangements that had been introduced by the United States in the Bosnian Dayton peace accords (ICG, 2007, p. 8: OSCE, 1997a, 1998). These initiatives, however, also failed to receive the full support of the sides, and as a result, Russia's negotiating efforts floundered. In the case of Nagorno-Karabakh, the proposal was rejected by Azerbaijan on the grounds that, in their view, it violated the country's territorial integrity, while in the case of Abkhazia, Georgia pulled out of the 'common state' project concerned that it would leave open the possibility of Abkhazia's secession from Georgia (ICG, 2007, p. 8). In Moldova, Primakov initially succeeded in reaching a preliminary agreement between the conflicting sides in May 1997 – the *Memorandum on Normalisation of Relations* – which stated that the sides would build their relations 'in the framework of a common state', inside the Republic of Moldova (OSCE, 1997a), but disagreements soon emerged due to different interpretations given to the document by the two sides, thus precluding any advancement on the resolution of the conflict (Timoshenko, 1997; Vinogradov, 1998). Russia, nevertheless, showed a readiness to engage in constructive diplomacy intended to bring these conflicts to an end, and as such its actions no longer fitted the neo-imperialist paradigm.

On the other hand, most of the resolution proposals put forward by Moscow foresaw the role of Russia as the *main* guarantor of the conflict, albeit in collaboration with other actors such as the OSCE in Nagorno-Karabakh and in Transdniestria, or the UN in Abkhazia and Tajikistan (OSCE, 1997a; UN, 1997a and 1997b). Russia also hoped to ensure the continued deployment of its peacekeeping forces in the conflict zones once final agreements were reached, either on their own, or in collaboration with other troops – be it CIS forces in Tajikistan, or OSCE contingents in Nagorno-Karabakh – in the expectation that these additional forces would be placed under Russia's command (ICG, 2005, p. 10). This showed that while Russia may have seemed ready to discard its imperial legacy and consider, at least officially, these countries as independent and sovereign states, it still felt that a forward military presence in these CIS areas was necessary for its own security. As such, Russia's actions can, therefore, be seen as fitting the neo-imperialist paradigm, even though a Russian military presence in these regions may have also fulfilled a legitimate security purpose, namely guaranteeing regional peace and preventing a resumption of violence.

Russia considered the forward basing of its troops and the stationing of forces in the CIS space as essential to gain strategic depth, and in this way, enhance its own security.

While Russia acquiesced at the 1999 OSCE Istanbul summit to the full withdrawal of the 14th Army from Moldova and agreed to close its military bases in Georgia, Moscow also succeeded in obtaining some concessions (OSCE, 1999; Dvali and Sysoyev, 1999). Russia's commitments came hand in hand with the signing of an agreement with NATO on a modified version of the CFE Treaty, which granted Russia a more robust military presence in the North Caucasus and in the north-western regions of Russia (Vladykin, 1999). Furthermore, within the framework of the Istanbul agreement, Russia hoped to keep two of its military bases in Georgia – at Batumi and Akhalkalaki – for an indefinite period of time, even though this could occur only with the consent of Tbilisi (Dvali, 2000). In addition, while Moscow agreed in 1994 to pull out its 14th Army from Transdniestria and began slowly to withdraw its troops and equipment from Moldova (Hill, 2002, p. 135), it made the full withdrawal conditional upon a final resolution of the conflict, insisting on a policy of 'synchronisation' (Prikhodko and Gornostayev, 1997; Gamova, 1998). Furthermore, the Kremlin began staffing its peacekeeping forces in Transdniestria with troops from the OGRF (Operational Group of Russian Forces), the former 14th Army (ICG, 2003, p. 21), while it also contributed to the strengthening of the Transdniestrian armed forces with training, manning and support (Hill, 2012; Waters, 2003, p. 147). In this respect, therefore, Russia's actions can be seen as fitting a neo-imperialist pattern, especially if we consider that both Georgia and Moldova had only reluctantly acquiesced to the presence of Russian military and peacekeeping forces on their territories, and as time progressed they became increasingly opposed to their deployment. These two countries had to accept a Russian military presence – even if temporary – on their territory against their will. However, in other instances, as was the case in Tajikistan and Armenia, Russia's military presence was welcomed by the existing regimes, which saw Russia's troops and its security commitments as guarantors of peace and regional stability. These forces also accomplished additional, but also very important, functions to the benefit of the recipient states – in the case of Tajikistan, Russian forces provided support to the fragile Rakhmon leadership, and in Armenia, Russia's military deployments helped to uphold the country's security vis-à-vis Turkey while also strengthening Armenia's positions in Nagorno-Karabakh. Therefore, Russia's actions, in this respect, did not necessarily reflect a neo-imperialist paradigm, even though it must be noted that Russia succeeded, as a result of its military presence and support, to keep these two countries within its sphere of influence.

On the other hand, as the resolution of the separatist conflicts proved difficult to achieve, the leaders of Georgia and Azerbaijan became increasingly frustrated with Russia, and therefore decided to turn to the West for support. Tbilisi and Baku agreed to transport Azerbaijan's newly extracted Caspian oil and gas through the US-sponsored Baku-Tbilisi-Ceyhan (BTC) (oil) and the Baku-Tbilisi-Erzurum (BTE) (gas) pipelines respectively, both of which carried the energy directly to

Turkey through Georgia, rather than through the existing Russian transport systems. More significantly, Azerbaijan and Georgia moved ahead with establishing closer ties with NATO as they deepened military cooperation between their countries' defence structures and those of NATO's member states (Korbut, 1998; Eaton, 2001, p. 95; Akhundova, 1999). This was facilitated by the inclusion in October 1998 of the South Caucasus republics, into the zone of responsibility of NATO's Allied Command Europe. Georgia and Azerbaijan had by then been identified by the West as key transit countries for the various Western-sponsored projects transporting Caspian oil and gas to Europe and to world markets, and this increased their strategic relevance in the eyes of the United States and Europe (Dvali, 1996). Within this framework, in October 1999, Georgian President Shevardnadze for the first time stated that Georgia would be prepared to apply for NATO membership in 2005, in the hope that this would help Georgia resolve the Abkhaz and South Ossetian conflicts in its favour (Dvali and Sysoyev, 1999). Shevardnadze argued that his attempts at bringing the Abkhaz conflict to an end by making geopolitical concessions to Russia – allowing Russia a military presence in Georgia – had failed (Dvali, 1996). Azerbaijan's Defence Minister Safar Abiev, in turn, openly discussed Azerbaijan's desire to establish a special relationship with the North Atlantic Alliance (Akhundova, 1999) while Azerbaijan's Foreign Advisor Vafa Guluzade, in turn, expressed Baku's wish to open a NATO base in Azerbaijan. Furthermore, in 1999 Georgia and Azerbaijan abandoned the Russian-led CIS military alliance – the Collective Security Treaty – thereby weakening Russia's geo-strategic reach over these countries. In the case of Georgia and Moldova, its leaders went as far as demanding the full withdrawal of Russian military forces from their territories (Dvali and Chubchenko, 2000; Darchiashvili, 2005, p. 132). This created great concern in Russia and led to worries that its presence in these regions of the South Caucasus and south-eastern Europe would be significantly eroded, with the risk that Russia's influence over events in these areas would be lost forever. As NATO enlarged eastwards into central and eastern Europe, and expanded ties with countries of the former USSR, Russia's anxiety increased. This explains why Russia's policies towards the separatist regions of Georgia and Moldova were reversed with the advent of Putin to the Russian Presidency in 2000, while efforts were made to reinforce Russia's military and economic presence in Armenia and Tajikistan, and emphasis was placed on establishing much closer military and economic ties with Azerbaijan.

Conclusions

The years of Primakov at the Foreign Ministry introduced a significant change in Russia's policies towards the various conflicts that had erupted along Russia's borders and in the ex-USSR region in the early 1990s. Primakov adopted a much more conciliatory stance and showed a readiness to engage effectively with the warring sides in order to reach a lasting settlement and enhance regional stability. More significantly, the Kremlin proved ready to exert significant pressure on the separatist regions, which were de facto Russia's 'allies', in order to ensure that the territorial integrity of the newly independent states remained intact. Even Primakov's proposals for the creation of *common states* also stipulated that the original 'mother countries' would retain a certain level of control over these 'separatist' territories. Furthermore, Russia worked much more closely, and collaborated actively, with other international actors in the mediation process – with OSCE in Nagorno-Karabakh and Transdniestria, and with the UN in Abkhazia and Tajikistan – than it had done in the mid-1990s. This seems to suggest that, under Primakov, Russia proved ready to discard its imperial legacy and to consider, at least officially, these former USSR countries as independent and sovereign states. Yet, many of the proposals brought forward by the Kremlin also endowed Russia with the role of 'main guarantor' of the conflict, granting Russia a right of involvement in these regions. Furthermore, Moscow also hoped, and worked hard towards, keeping a military presence in these countries of its Near Abroad. In other words, Russia still felt that a forward military presence in these ex-USSR territories was necessary for the sake of its own security and stability. This again indicated that residues of neo-imperialism remained in Russia's actions vis-à-vis the former Soviet space. In other words, Russia's 'post-imperial' trajectory clearly had some limits. On the other hand, Primakov's efforts to resolve peacefully violent conflicts in the Near Abroad also reflected legitimate state concerns related not only to the possible spill over of violence into Russia, but also to the potential domino effect that events in the separatist regions of the former Soviet space could have on Russia itself. In this respect, developments in Chechnya were of utmost concern to the Kremlin, given that in Grozny a separatist leadership was preparing the ground for the region's independence from Russia.

The record of Russia's neo-imperialism during the late 1990s, in this area of policy, is therefore a mixed one, with elements of neo-imperialism, hegemony and legitimate state interests inter-mingling and co-existing. Yet, Russia's actions in the Near Abroad in the Primakov era are a distant call from the more assertive policies conducted by the Kremlin in the early- to mid-1990s, when the Ministry of Defence engaged in forceful actions in the Near Abroad, which had strong neo-imperial undertones. More significantly, Russia's policy towards these regions benefited from increased coherence and improved planning under the leadership of Yevgeny Primakov, even though the Kremlin's effectiveness was curtailed by the absence of substantial economic and financial resources. Yet, Primakov's active mediation efforts intended to reach a long-standing resolution of the various separatist conflicts did not produce any significant results, with only one exception, the civil war in Tajikistan, which was brought to an end in 1997. Moscow's engagement in the conflict-resolution process in Tajikistan, showed that Russia was able, when it wanted, to work closely with allies and partners in order to bring peace and achieve stability in the fringes of the former USSR space. This did not prove to be the case as far as the other military conflicts in the CIS were concerned. Although large-scale violence did not reignite in Abkhazia, South

Ossetia and Transdniestria, and Russia succeeded in prolonging its military presence in these separatist regions, the situation remained unstable, and highly unsatisfactory for the 'mother countries' – Moldova, Georgia and Azerbaijan. As the resolution of the separatist conflicts proved difficult to achieve, leaders in Tbilisi, Baku and Chisinau became increasingly frustrated with Russia, and in the case of Georgia and Azerbaijan more particularly, they decided to turn to the West for support. This, in turn, significantly diminished Russia's influence over these countries, clearly showing the limits of Moscow's neo-imperialist and hegemonic ambitions in its Near Abroad.

Notes

1 Azerbaijanis succeeded in taking control over a vast amount of the weaponry and ammunition belonging to the 23rd Division of the 4th Army, which had been based in Ganje, before it was finally withdrawn to Russia in June 1993 (Shevelev, 1992).
2 UNOMIG stands for United Nations Mission in Georgia.
3 Russian weapons, however, also reached Azerbaijan during the last two years of the war. Throughout 1993 and 1994, a lucrative, seemingly illegal, arms trade developed with Russia, which supplied both sides with weapons (Corley, 1994).
4 Personal interview with Galina Starovoitova, Moscow, November 1996.
5 Abkhazia saw a flare of violence in 1998. After an attack by Georgian paramilitaries on Abkhaz officials in the Gali district in May 1998, the Abkhaz militias retaliated quite strongly, driving out a high number of Georgian internally displaced people (IDPs) who resided in the area.

Bibliography

Akiner, Sh. (2001). *Tajikistan: Disintegration or Reconciliation*. London: Royal Institute of International Affairs.
Aklaev, A.R. (1996). Dynamics of the Moldova Trans-Dniester Ethnic Conflict (Late 1980s to early 1990s.). In: K. Rupesinghe and V.A. Tishkov, *Ethnicity and Power in the Contemporary World*. Tokyo, New York, Paris: United Nations University Press, pp. 83–115.
Akhundova, E. (1999). *Obshchaya gazeta*, 11–17 February 1999, pp. 1 and 5.
Allison, R. (1994). *Peacekeeping in the Soviet Successor States*. Chaillot Paper, 18, Paris: Institute for Security Studies, Western European Union.
Antonenko, O. (2005). Frozen Uncertainty: Russia and the Conflict Over Abkhazia. In: B. Coppieters and R. Legvold, eds., *Statehood and Security: Georgia after the Rose Revolution*, Cambridge, Mass: MIT Press, pp. 205–270.
Baev, P. (1996). *The Russian Army in a Time of Troubles*. Oslo: Peace Research Institute, Sage Publishing.
Baev, P. (1997). *Russia's Policies in the Caucasus*. London: The Royal Institute of International Affairs.
Barakhova, A. (1996). *Nezavisimaya gazeta*, 11 January, p. 3.
Botan, I. (2009). The Negotiation Process as a Way to Postpone the Solution. In: D. Matveev, G. Selari, E. Bobkova and B. Cseke, eds. *Moldova–Transdniestria: Working Together for a Prosperous Future. Negotiation Process*. Chisinau: Cu drag Publishing House, pp. 116–134.

Broladze, N. (1992). *Nezavisimaya gazeta*, 15 August, p. 1.
Coppieters, B. (2004). The Georgian-Abkhaz Conflict. In: B. Coppieters, M. Emerson, M. Husseune, T. Kovziridze, G. Noutcheva, N. Tocci, and M. Vahl, *Europeanization and Conflict Resolution: Case Studies from the European Periphery*. Gent: Academia Press.
Corley, F. (1994). Nagorno-Karabakh: An Eyewitness Account, *Jane's Intelligence Review*, 4, 6 April, pp. 164–165.
Darchiashvili, D. (2005). Georgian Defence Policy and Military Reform. In: B. Coppieters and R. Legvold, eds., *Statehood and Security: Georgia after the Rose Revolution*. Cambridge, Mass: MIT Press.
Dvali, G. (1996). *Kommersant-daily*, 22 May, p. 4.
Dvali, G. (2000). *Kommersant-daily*, 20 October, p. 3.
Dvali G. and G. Sysoyev (1999). *Kommersant*, 27 October, p. 11.
Dvali G. and Y. Chubchenko (2000). *Kommersant*, 21 April, p. 11.
Durnov, V. (1992). *Izvestiya*, 12 June. p. 5.
Eaton, M. (2001). Major Trends in Military Expenditure and Arms Acquisitions by States of the Caspian Region. In: G. Chufrin, ed. *The Security of the Caspian Sea Region*. Oxford: Oxford University Press, pp. 83–118.
Ehrhart, H.-G., A. Kreikemeyer and A. Zagorsky (1996). The Commonwealth of Independent States (CIS). In: L. Jonson and C. Archer, eds. *Peacekeeping and the Role of Russia in Eurasia*. Boulder Co.: Westview Press.
Eurasia Daily Monitor (EDM) (1997). Russian-hosted Transdniester Negotiations Fail in the Run-up to CIS Summit, 3 (198) 23 October, Jamestown Foundation. Available at: https://jamestown.org/program/russian-hosted-transdniester-negotiations-fail-in-runup-to-cis-summit/#.VPi7cPmsXTo [accessed 8 October 2017].
Felgengauer, P. (1992a). *Nezavisimaya gazeta*, 18 July, p. 1.
Felgengauer, P. (1992b). *Nezavisimaya gazeta*, 11 August 1992, p. 2.
Felgengauer, P. (1994). *Segodnya*, 21 October, p. 2.
Feliksova, L. (1994). *Rossiiskaya gazeta*, 27 October, p. 7.
Gamova, S. (1994). *Izvestiya*, 12 August, p. 2.
Gamova, S. (1998). *Segodnya*, 4 July, p. 3.
Globachev, M. (1996). *Nezavisimaya gazeta*, 24 January, p. 3.
Goltz, T. (1993). Letter from Eurasia: The Hidden Russian Hand, *Foreign Policy*, 92, Autumn, 92–116.
Hill, W.H. (2002). Making Istanbul a Reality: Moldova, Russia, and Withdrawal from Transdniestria, *Helsinki Monitor*, 2, pp. 129–145.
Hill, W.H. (2012). *Russia, the Near Abroad, and the West: Lessons from the Moldova-Transdniestria Conflict*. Washington DC: Woodrow Wilson Center Press.
Interfax (1992a). 10 April.
Interfax (1992b). 17 August.
Interfax (1993). 13 March.
Interfax (1994). 12 August.
International Crisis Group (ICG) (2003). *Moldova: No Quick Fix*, 12 August. Brussels.
International Crisis Group (ICG) (2005). *Nagorno-Karabakh: A Plan for Peace*, 11 October, Brussels.
International Crisis Group (ICG) (2007). *Abkhazia: Ways Forward*, 18 January. Brussels.
Jacoby, V. (2005), The Role of the OSCE: An Assessment of International Mediation Efforts. In: L. Broers, ed. *The Limits of Leadership: Elites and Societies in the Nagorny Karabakh Peace Process*, Accord 17. London Conciliation Resources, pp. 30–33.
Kakotkin, A. (1992). *Moskovskie novosti*, 5 July, p. 4.

Korbut, A. (1998). *Nezavisimaya gazeta*, 13 January, p. 5.
Kuznetsova, V. (1993). *Nezavisimaya gazeta*, 26 May, p. 2.
Libaridian, G. (2005). The Elusive 'Right Formula' at the 'Right Time': A Historical Analysis of the Official Peace Process. In: L. Broers ed., *The Limits of Leadership: Elites and Societies in the Nagorny Karabakh Peace Process*, Accord 17. London: Conciliation Resources, pp. 34–37.
Lugovskaya, A. (1992). *Izvestiya*, 8 May, p. 1.
Maresca, M. (1996). Resolving the Conflict over Nagorno-Karabakh: Lost Opportunities for International Conflict Resolution. In: C.A. Crocker, F.O. Hampson and P. Aall, eds. *Managing Global Chaos* (1st edn). Washington DC: USIP, pp. 255–274.
Mekhtiev, A. (1994). *Nezavisimaya gazeta*, 29 January, p. 1.
Memorial (1992). Doklad pravozashchitnogo tsentra 'Memorial' o massovykh narusheniyakh prav cheloveka, svyazannykh s zanyatiem naselennogo puncta Khodzhali v noch' s 25 na 26 fevralya 1992 g. Available at: www.kavkaz-uzel.eu/system/uploads/article_attachment/attach/0004/42676/Doklad_PTS_Memorial_o_massovyh_narusheniyah_prav_cheloveka__svyazannyh_s_zanyatiem_naselennogo_punkta_Hodzhaly_v_noch_s_25_na_26_fevralya_1992.pdf [accessed 9 September 2016].
Moscow Radio (1991). 27 September, in *FBIS-SOV-91-189*, 30 September, p. 73.
Moskovskie novosti (1992). 17–26 April.
Mukhin, V. (1992). *Nezavisimaya gazeta*, 26 June, p. 2.
Mulyar, N. (1991). *Krasnaya zvezda*, 28 September, p. 2.
Neukirch, C. (2001). Transdniestria and Moldova: Cold Peace at the Dniester. *Helsinki Monitor*, 2, pp. 122–135.
Neukirch, C. (2011). From Confidence Building to Conflict Settlement in Moldova? In: Institute for Peace Research and Security Policy at the University of Hamburg/IFSH. ed. *OSCE Yearbook 2011*. Baden-Baden, 2012, pp. 137–150.
Nezavisimaya gazeta (1992a). 21 May, p. 1.
Nezavisimaya gazeta (1992b), 29 July, p. 1 and 3.
Orr, M. (1998). The Russian Army and the War in Tajikistan. In: M.-R. Djalili, F. Grare and Sh. Akiner, eds. *Tajikistan: The Trials of Independence*. Abingdon, and New York: Routledge, pp. 151–160.
OSCE (1993). *Report No. 13 by the CSCE Mission to Moldova*, 13 November. Available at: www.osce.org/moldova/42307?download=true [accessed 20 July 2018].
OSCE (1996). *Lisbon Document 1996*, 3 December. Available at: www.osce.org/mc/39539?download=true [accessed 20 July 2018].
OSCE (1997a). *Memorandum on the Bases for Normalization of Relations Between the Republic of Moldova and Transdniestria*, 8 May. Available at www.osce.org/moldova/42309 [accessed 20 July 2018].
OSCE (1997b). Comprehensive Agreement on the Resolution of the Nagorno-Karabakh Conflict, July 1997. In: L. Broers, ed. *The Limits of Leadership: Elites and Societies in the Nagorny Karabakh Peace Process*, Accord. London: Conciliation Resources, p. 76.
OSCE (1997c). Agreement on the End of the Nagorny Karabakh Armed Conflict Minsk Group, December 1997. In: L. Broers, ed. *The Limits of Leadership: Elites and Societies in the Nagorny Karabakh Peace Process*. Accord, London: Conciliation Resources, pp. 79–80.
OSCE (1998). On the Principles for a Comprehensive Settlement of the Armed Conflict Over Nagorny Karabakh, Minsk Group, 7 November 1998. In: L. Broers, ed. *The Limits of Leadership: Elites and Societies in the Nagorny Karabakh Peace Process*, Accord. London: Conciliation Resources, p. 82.

OSCE (1999). Istanbul summit, November 1999, Official appendix to the Treaty on Conventional Armed Forces in Europe. Available at: www.osce.org/documents/mcs/1999/11/4050_en.pdf [accessed 9 March 2018].
Panfilov, O. (1992). *Nezavisimaya gazeta*, 22 August, p. 3.
Prikhodko, N. (1993). *Nezavisimaya gazeta*, 21 May, p. 1.
Prikhodko N. and D. Gornostayev (1997). *Nezavisimaya gazeta*, 12 April, p. 1
Putovsky, Ch. (1992). *Nezavisimaya gazeta*, 16 December, p. 1 and 3.
Radio Chisinau (1992). 21 July.
Radio Romania (1992). 17 February.
Radio Rossii (1992). 17 July.
Rigacci Hay, E. (2001). Methodology of the Inter-Tajik Negotiation Process. In: K. Abdullaev and C. Barnes, eds. *Politics of Compromise: The Tajikistan Peace Process*, Accord, London: Conciliation Resources, pp. 38–43.
Rotar, I. (1992). *Nezavisimaya gazeta*, 6 November, p. 3.
Rotar, I. (1996). *Nezavisimaya gazeta*, 25 December, p. 3.
Rotar, I. and A. Abrashitov (1992). *Nezavisimaya gazeta*, 15 August, p. 3.
Russian TV (1991). 28 October.
Russian TV (1992a). 11 March.
Russian TV (1992b). 24 July.
Shevelev, M. (1992). *Moskovskiye novosti*, 21 June, p. 4.
Sodruzhestvo (1993). Soglashenie o kollekitvnykh mirotvorcheskyikh silakh i sovmestnikh merakh po ikh materialno-technicheskomu obespecheniiu, 4, 24 September, pp. 54–65.
Taranov, S. and B. Urigashvili (1993). *Izvestiya*, 23 February, p. 1.
Tass (1991). 23 September.
Tbilisi 7 DGHE (1995). 22–28 September.
Timoshenko, V. (1997). *Nezavisimaya gazeta*, 12 May, p. 3.
Trenin, D. and V. Makarenko (1992). Chto delat' armii, kogda krugom idet voina. *Novoe vremya*, 21, p. 21.
United Nations (UN) (1997a). Tehran Declaration, 28 May 1997. In: K. Abdullaev and C. Barnes. (2001). eds. *Politics of Compromise: The Tajikistan Peace Process*, Accord. London: Conciliation Resources, p. 77.
United Nations (UN) (1997b). General Agreement on the Establishment of Peace and National Accord, 27 June, 1997. In: K. Abdullaev and C. Barnes. (2001). eds. *Politics of Compromise: The Tajikistan Peace Process*, Accord. London: Conciliation Resources, p. 78.
Urigashvili, B. (1992a). 'Georgia is Forming its Own Army', *Izvestiya*, 30 April 1992 p. 2.
Urigashvili, B. (1992b). *Izvestiya*, 20 June, p. 1.
Urigashvili, B. (1992c). *Izvestiya*, 2 October, p. 2.
Urigashvili, B. (1992d). 5 October, pp. 1–2.
Urigashvili, B. (1993). 17 March, p. 1.
Vahl, M. and M. Emerson (2004). Moldova and the Transnistrian Conflict. In: B. Coppieters, M. Emerson, M. Husseune, T. Kovziridze, G. Noutcheva, N. Tocci, M. Vahl, *Europeanization and Conflict Resolution: Case Studies from the European Periphery*. Gent: Academia Press.
Velekhov, L. (1996). *Segodnya*, 12 July, p. 9.
Vinogradov, B. (1996). *Izvestiya*, 24 May, p. 3.
Vinogradov, B. (1998). *Izvestiya*, 19 February, p. 3.
Vladykin, O. (1999). *Obshchaya gazeta*, 23–29 December, p. 5.

de Waal, T. (2003). *Black Garden: Armenia and Azerbaijan Through Peace and War*. New York and London: New York University Press.

Waters, T. (2003). Russian Peacekeeping in Moldova: Source of Stability or Neo-imperialist Threat? In: J. Mackinlay and P. Cross, eds. *Regional Peacekeepers: The Paradox of Russian Peacekeeping*, New York: United States University Press.

Whitfield, T. (2007). *Friends Indeed? The United Nations, Group of Friends, and the Resolution of Conflict*, Washington DC: United States Institute of Peace.

Zulfuqarov, T. (2005). Obstacles to Resolution. In: L. Broers, ed. *The Limits of Leadership: Elites and Societies in the Nagorny Karabakh Peace Process*, Accord (17). London: Conciliation Resources, pp. 38–41.

6 Vladimir Putin at the helm of Russia
A return of Russia's hegemony?

The arrival of Vladimir Putin to the Russian Presidency in May 2000 fundamentally altered the Russian political scene. As soon as he took office, Putin engaged in efforts to streamline the highly dysfunctional administration of the Russian state. He restored control over the various republics and regions of the Russian Federation, ensured the unification of the Russian legal system throughout the Russian territory, and reigned in the powerful oligarchs.[1] However, many of the measures introduced came at the expense of Russians' democratic rights. A direct chain of hierarchical subordination to the President, known as 'vertical of power', was established, and limits were progressively introduced on the freedom of the Russian media. Moreover, restrictions were imposed on the registration of political parties and limits were placed on the autonomy of the upper chamber of parliament (Duncan, 2007, pp. 139–158). These developments, together with a working majority in the State Duma allowed Putin to run the Russian state more effectively and reduce political unpredictability (Duncan, 2007). Against this background, the Russian economy grew quite substantially during Putin's first years in Presidency, at an average rate of 6.2 per cent between 1999 and 2003. This was facilitated by a significant increase in energy prices and a strong value of the dollar vis-à-vis the rouble, which helped to increase state revenues. Russia's economic growth was also spearheaded by the sound management of the state's public finances, and the creation of a relatively benevolent business climate. This allowed Russians to enjoy substantial rises in real incomes, which, in turn, translated into significant increases in consumption and a major reduction in overall poverty (Sagramoso, 2004, p. 123).[2] All these positive socio-economic indicators produced strong support for Vladimir Putin and his administration. By the mid-2000s, Putin's approval ratings had reached very high levels, exceeding 70 per cent, even though many of the changes that he introduced came at a high price – a significant limitation of basic freedoms and severe restrictions in political liberties. Foreign and security policy-making became increasingly concentrated in the hands of the President, who took an active and special interest in the topic. Although Putin listened to advice and received information from a range of sources, including from his closest advisors, such as Sergei Ivanov, Aleksander Voloshin and Anatoly Chubais, as well as from the Foreign Ministry, the economic ministries, and the security apparatus, he remained fully in control of foreign policy decision-making (Lo, 2003, pp. 31–50).

Putin's views on Russia and its place in the world

When Putin reached the Presidency, he initially remained opposed to advancing or enforcing a specific 'state ideology'. He, nevertheless, proved eager to promote what he called 'Russians' (*Rossiyan*) traditional values' (1999).[3] These he identified as patriotism, social solidarity, and a belief in the greatness of Russia (*Derzhavnost'*), as well as support for a strong Russian state (*Gosudarstvennichesto*), following on the lines of former Prime Minister Yevgeny Primakov (Putin, 1999). More importantly, patriotism was understood as a feeling of pride in one's country and a desire to turn Russia into a better place and make its people happier. It was not to be interpreted as a sentiment imbued with nationalist ideologies and imperialist ambitions (Putin, 1999). Similarly, 'Statism' or a strong state was not to be equated with totalitarianism, but instead it was to be identified with a 'democratic, law-based, workable federative state' (Putin, 1999). In Putin's view, the state had to play an important role in the life of the country and its people, as had happened throughout Russian history. Putin saw the state as a guarantor of order and as the driver of change (Putin, 1999). In this respect, he distanced himself from Western European liberalism, which placed its emphasis on the rights of the individual over the state (Putin, 1999; Laruelle, 2009a, p. 143). These traditional Russian values of patriotism, solidarity and strong statehood had to be merged with more universal humanitarian ideals to create a new *Russian idea* [*Rossiiskaya ideya*]. This new *Russian idea* would come about as an 'organic unification of universal, common-to-all-humanity, humanitarian values with traditional Russian [*rossiiskimi*] values which have stood the test of the times' (Putin, 1999). The Russian idea would encompass the ideals around which the country would be organised, which in turn, would establish the foundations of how the country should perceive itself.

The Russian nationalism promoted by the Kremlin in the form of 'patriotism' purposefully placed its emphasis on the 'Russian state', rather than on the 'Russian nation' (*Russkaya natsia*) or on Russian (*Rossiiskie*) citizens, although Russians clearly occupied a special place inside the state. This Russo-centric *etatism* (Brandenbuger, 1999) acquired, in the words of Luke March, an almost 'spiritual, sacred quality, as the distillation of Russia's 'collective will' (2012, p. 407). A strong state was seen by Putin as the true essence of the Russian notion of statehood. As he noted in 1999,

> Our state and its institutes and structures have always played an exceptionally important role in the life of the country and its people. For Russians a strong state is not an anomaly which should be got rid of. Quite the contrary, they see it as a source and guarantor of order and the initiator and main driving force of any change.
>
> (Putin, 1999)

Putin went even further and argued that Russia could only exist as a strong state. 'Our entire historical experience shows that a country like Russia can live and develop within its existing borders *only if it is a strong nation*', he stated in his 2003 Annual Address and added, 'All of the periods during which Russia has been weakened, whether politically or economically, have always inexorably brought to the fore the threat of the country's collapse' (Putin, 2003). The *strong state* paradigm helped to provide the ideological underpinning for the consolidation of a semi-authoritarian regime in Russia, which was established around Vladimir Putin.

The notion of a strong state was closely tied to the understanding of Russia as a Great Power. As his predecessors, Putin actively championed the notion of Russia's greatness and strove to restore the country's Great-Power status, reflecting a realist view of international affairs. As he explained in his December 1999 manifesto, *Russia at the Turn of the Millennium*, 'Russia was and will remain a Great Power. It is preconditioned by the inseparable characteristics of its geopolitical, economic and cultural existence' to become one (Putin, 1999). However, contrary to what is usually assumed, Putin also believed that the greatness and might of Russia could no longer depend primarily on the country's military strength, as it had occurred during the Soviet era. Instead, it had to be achieved through the development of a successful economy, the pursuit of the socio-economic well-being of its people, and the strengthening of the country's internal and external security. In Putin's own words,

> In the present world, the might of a country as a great power is manifested not so much in its military might, but rather in its ability to be a leader in creating and using advanced technologies, ensuring a high level of its people's well-being, reliably protecting its security and upholding its national interests in the international arena.
>
> (Putin, 1999)

Putin showed great concern over the dramatic socio-economic situation and the severe demographic crisis that Russia was facing at the time. In his view, this resulted from the difficulties that Russia had endured during the transition to a market economy in the 1990s, and also from the negative economic legacies left by the Soviet Command-economy system (Putin, 2000a; Putin, 1999). Putin's main objective when he became President was, therefore, to overcome Russia's deep socio-economic and political crisis, achieve fast and stable economic growth, and guarantee social progress (Putin, 2000a). 'Russia needs an economic system which is competitive, effective and socially just, which ensures stable political development', Putin noted, and added 'A stable economy is the main guarantor of a democratic society, and the very foundation of a strong nation that is respected in the world' (Putin, 2000a). Only once Russia had developed internally could the country once again become a respected partner globally, and make its views heard. 'The independence of our foreign policy is in no doubt', Putin stated during this first address to the Federal Assembly in

July 2000, but added that 'the foundation of this policy is pragmatism, economic effectiveness, and the priority of *national* tasks ... we still need to work on making these principles the norm of state life' (Putin, 2000a). The only real choice for Russia was to become 'a country that is strong and confident of itself' (Putin, 2000a). However, in Putin's view, Russia had to be 'strong not in defiance of the international community, not against other strong nations, but together with them' (Putin, 2000a) – a sign that his realist approach to international affairs was tempered by a conviction that fruitful cooperation with other countries, primarily in the West, was also possible. In this respect, Putin proved eager to integrate Russia into the world economy and make it part of the ongoing processes of economic globalisation (MFA, 2000).

However, the Russian President also shared a deep-seated conviction that Western states were eager to weaken Russia, as they considered themselves victorious in the Cold War. As his predecessor Primakov, Putin remained very worried over America's world predominance and its attempts to create an international relations system based only on 'Western values and American leadership', as was made clear in Russia's 2000 *National Security Concept* (MID, 2000).[4] The new Russian leader strongly disliked the tendency of Western countries to engage in unilateral behaviour, including the use of military force, in order to address key problems in world politics, often 'in circumvention of the fundamental rules of international law' (MFA, 2000). Attempts to introduce into the international discourse concepts such as 'humanitarian intervention' and 'limited sovereignty' to justify unilateral actions which bypassed the United Nations Security Council (UNSC) were considered unacceptable also by the new Russian leadership (MFA, 2000). In order to counter-balance such trends, Putin's Russia embraced many of the key principles in the realm of foreign and security policy that had been previously upheld by Primakov – strengthening the sovereignty and territorial integrity of Russia, supporting the creation of a *multipolar* world order with Russia as one of its most influential centres, and ensuring Russia's strong position in the world arena. This would guarantee 'the growth of Russia's political, economic, intellectual and spiritual potential' (MFA, 2000; MID, 2000). But the main objective of Russia's foreign policy remained ensuring the fulfilment of Russia's national and domestic priorities, and these included developing the Russian economy, strengthening the state's capacity to administer the country, and guaranteeing its security (Putin, 2000a).

Despite his quest for global multipolarity, Putin did not see Russia in antagonism to the West. When Putin first became President in 2000, he embraced a clearly articulated vision of Russia as belonging to the West and to Western civilisation. In particular, he emphasised the European dimension of Russia's identity. 'Of course, Russia is a very diverse country', he wrote in his book, *First Person: An Astonishingly Frank Self-portrait by Russia's President*, 'but we are part of Western European culture. No matter where our people live, in the Far East or in the South, we are Europeans' (Putin, 2000b, p. 169). In his Address to the Russian Parliament in 2003, Putin described Russia's European orientation as Russia's 'historical choice', even though he was aware that Russia's integration into Europe would have involved a lengthy and complex process (Putin, 2003; Ambrosio and Vandrovec, 2013). Russia's integration into Europe, although not necessarily accompanied with full EU membership, remained one of the country's top foreign policy objectives. However, Putin's European choice was not based on the full sharing of the European Union's (EU) liberal-democratic values and post-modern notions of sovereignty-sharing.[5] Furthermore, cooperation between Russia and Europe also played, for Putin, an *instrumental* role – it contributed to the strengthening of Russia's role in global affairs. Russia and Europe could together establish a new independent pole of global politics and, in this way, reinforce their mutual strength. As Putin stated in his speech to the German Bundestag on 25 September 2001,

> Europe will reinforce its reputation of a strong and truly independent centre of world politics soundly and for a long time if it succeeds in bringing together its own potential and that of Russia, including its human, territorial and natural resources and its economic, cultural and defence potential.
>
> (Putin, 2001)

While not questioning the 'great value of Europe's relations with the United State', Putin was promoting a deepening of the ties between Russia and Europe to reinforce his country's own strength internationally. Furthermore, in the mid-2000s, as disappointment with the West grew – and frustration increased over Russia's limited 'integration' with Europe in general and the EU in particular – Putin, began promoting, an alternative, more conservative, vision of Europe, which placed emphasis on traditional state sovereignty. These ideas fully crystallised during his third term in the Presidency, as Russia moved further away from the Western/European 'pole' of international affairs.

Putin also gave relevance to Russia's Asian dimension. 'Russia has always felt like a Euro-Asian country' (*Evroaziatskaya strana*), Putin wrote in an article in November 2000, 'We never forgot that the bulk of Russian territory is located in Asia' (Putin, 2000c). He, therefore, promoted Russia's cooperation with countries in the Asian continent, 'it is time that we, together with the countries in the Asia-Pacific region, move from words to actions, and develop closer economic, political and other ties' (Putin, 2000c). But Russia's Asian dimension was understood primarily in a geographical sense – Russia as a country whose territory straddled both into Europe and Asia and whose interests therefore extended into both these directions. Putin made no reference to *Eurasianism* as an ideological construct, nor to Russia as a 'Eurasian state' – *Evraziiskaya strana*, when he assumed office. In the early 2000s, and especially after 9/11, Putin's foreign policy priorities combined improved relations with the West, close rapprochement with Europe, with renewed efforts at integration within the Commonwealth of Independent States (CIS), although primarily on a pragmatic self-interested basis.

The former Soviet space more generally, and the CIS in particular, continued to play a pivotal role within Russia's domestic and international policy orientations.

Developing 'equal and equitable relations with all countries and integrative associations and in particular with the members of the Commonwealth of Independent States and Russia's traditional partners', was considered a key national priority (MID, 2000). As his predecessors, Putin gave primacy to the deepening of integration processes within the former Soviet space. During his first tenure as President, he devoted great efforts to the establishment of strong bilateral and multilateral cooperation with the other CIS states, both within the Collective Security Treaty (CST/CSTO) and the *Eurasian Economic Community* (EvrAzES) remits, as well as within the *Union State of Belarus and Russia*. Yet, the Russian leadership also made it clear, and showed it in its behaviour, that practical relations with the CIS states had to 'be structured with due regard for reciprocal openness to cooperation' and, more importantly, they had to be based on 'a readiness [by the CIS states] to take into account in a due manner *the interests of the Russian Federation*' (MFA, 2000, my emphasis).[6] While eager to expand cooperative ties with the CIS states, Putin, however, did not advocate the restoration of the USSR in any new shape or form. When Putin became President, discussions on the reach of Russia's geographical frontiers subsided as most agreed that Russia's borders could not be forcefully modified or expanded. To compensate for Russia's territorial losses, instead, it was hoped that Russia would remain influential in the former Soviet space, and would, if possible, push ahead with deeper integration within the CIS framework. As stated in the *Foreign Policy Concept*, the objectives and priorities of Russia's policies in the former Soviet space were to develop 'good-neighbourly relations and strategic partnership with all CIS member states' (MFA, 2000). Emphasis was placed in the document on CIS military and economic integration, on preventing the emergence of tension and conflicts in regions adjacent to the Russian Federation, and on protecting the rights of Russian citizens abroad (MFA, 2000).

Putin's views managed to appeal to a broad spectrum of the Russian political landscape – his ideas were embraced by both *Liberal-Westernisers* and *Nationalist-Statist* thinkers and politicians alike. The first group of individuals, whose adherents were found among the liberal elite and among Russian business circles, welcomed his support for capitalism and economic reform. However, there were those to the centre-right of the liberal political spectrum – the Union of Rightist Force, for example – who insisted that Russia had to discard any notion of 'balance of power' and 'state interests', and instead had to focus its efforts on developing the country's economy, ensuring the Russian people's individual well-being, and making sure Russia became part of the globalised world (URF, 2001). *Nationalist-Statist* thinkers instead, liked Putin's emphasis on a strong state and his restoration of patriotic symbols such as the Soviet anthem's music, and the Soviet and Imperial emblems, as well as Putin's stress on military education. More importantly, Putin's views also found support among members of the security forces and the army, and among some prominent *Imperialist Nationalists*, such as Aleksander Prokhanov, who cherished a return to Russia's Great-Power status (Tsygankov, 2010, pp. 132–133). Putin's views were also endorsed by influential *Eurasianists*, and in particular, by the renowned thinker, Aleksandr Dugin, who believed that Putin was embracing many of the Eurasianists views that he had been advocating for long. These argued that Russia and the former Soviet space belonged to a unique 'civilisation' which was distinct from both Asia and the West (Nekhoroshev, 2001).[7] However, Putin only started to embrace civilisational views a few years later, in the mid-2000s, as disappointment with the West grew – Russia failed to establish a true partnership-of-equals with the United States – and the possibilities of developing an effective model of cooperation with Europe started to fade.

Putin's pro-Western turn after 9/11

During the first two years of his Presidency, Putin essentially conducted a multi-vector foreign policy and a far-reaching global diplomacy. On the one hand, the new President actively promoted Russia's rapprochement with Europe, and tried to smooth relations with the United States. On the other, he engaged in building a *multipolar* world system by developing a partnership with China and with India, and by nurturing ties with Iraq, Iran, Syria and North Korea, all identified by the United States as 'rogue-states'. This seemingly inconsistent foreign policy was seen by many as obscuring Russia's priorities and preventing the effective pursuit of Russia's national interests (Trenin, 2001). However, when the 9/11 terrorist attacks in the United States occurred in 2001, Putin immediately revealed his foreign policy preferences. He unequivocally supported the United States in its fight against *Al-Qaeda*, and gave immediate practical assistance to the USA-led coalition fighting in Afghanistan. Russia shared intelligence with the United States, allowed humanitarian cargoes belonging to USA-coalition forces operating in Afghanistan to transit through Russian airspace and territory, and continued to provide arms and ammunition to the Afghan Northern Alliance (*Kommersant*, 2001). More significantly, Putin acquiesced to the United States' military presence in Central Asia, against the objections of many of his supporters and closest advisors, including Russian Defence Minister Sergei Ivanov – a clear sign that he proved ready to discard, at least temporarily, Russia's imperial legacy in the Central Asian area (Vinogradov, 2004).[8] Putin saw the 9/11 attacks as a vindication of his long-held view that Islamist extremism and international terrorism represented a serious threat to international security. He believed that Russia's security interests would best be served by America's successful military operations against *Al-Qaeda* and the Taliban in Afghanistan (Zakatnova, 2001). More importantly, Putin hoped that the formation of a broad-based anti-terrorist coalition would change Western perceptions of Russia's actions in the Chechen war and would result in Western support for Russia's counter-terrorism operations in the North Caucasus (*Kommersant*, 2001).[9] In proclaiming Russia's alliance with the West, Putin also strove to overcome the legacies of the Cold War, and achieve the maximum favourable conditions for Russia's entry into Western institutions and organisations, an essential condition for Russia's economic progress.

Putin's pro-Western choice after 9/11 proved to be a major turning point in Russia's foreign policy orientation. Establishing a strategic partnership with the United States to fight international terrorism and jointly address regional and global security challenges became the country's number one priority (Grigoryev, 2002). However, such an enlightened and cooperative policy with the West did not last long. As the months passed, a sense of disappointment with Western behaviour developed, which soon grew stronger, and turned into outright confrontation by the mid-2000s. As early as December 2001, the United States announced its decision unilaterally to withdraw from the ABM (Anti-Ballistic Missile) treaty, significantly undermining global security and international stability. Moreover, Western criticism of Russia's actions in Chechnya, albeit milder, did not disappear entirely; Russia's foreign debts were not cancelled; and Moscow failed to obtain fast-track World Trade Organization (WTO) membership. More significantly, concern grew in Russia that the American presence in Central Asia risked prolonging itself well beyond the initial period of American victory over the Taliban, thus directly challenging Russia's influence in the region. Furthermore, American military and counter-terrorism cooperation with Azerbaijan and to a lesser extent with Armenia, as well as its support to 'Train and Equip' Georgia's Armed Forces to fight Islamists in the Pankisi Gorge (initiated in 2002), were perceived by many as negatively affecting Russia's interests in the South Caucasus region.

Although renewed cooperation with NATO developed in May 2002, through the newly established *NATO-Russian Council*, the new partnership fell short of Russia's expectations. Many in Russia continued to regard NATO as the enemy, a view that was broadly shared by the Russian military, and by a wide spectrum of the Russian political elite. Hostility towards NATO grew after the Alliance decided to invite new east European members – Bulgaria, Romania, Slovakia, Slovenia – and the three Baltic states, into its fore at the Prague Summit held in November 2002. The Baltic states not only hosted significant Russian communities, but their inclusion into the Western Alliance, brought NATO very close to Russia's borders – only a few kilometres away from St Petersburg. With the accession of Romania and Slovakia to NATO, the latter reached the CIS western borders of Ukraine and Moldova, and this increased Russia's perception of being encircled by the Atlantic Alliance, which was led by the United States. Russia's partnership with the West received a further blow in the spring of 2003, when the USA decided unilaterally to attack Iraq without UN Security Council approval, shattering any hopes that Russia and the USA could work together to address pressing global security issues. It broke the trust that had been established between Russia and the USA after 9/11, and marked the beginning of the end of Russia's rapprochement with the West. Putin placed increased emphasis on the strengthening of the Russian state, and on ensuring the country's international independence and its increased influence in global affairs. As he noted during his 2003 Annual Address,

> We must now take the next step and focus all our decisions and all our actions on ensuring that in a not too far off future, *Russia will take its recognised*

place among the ranks of the truly strong, economically advanced and influential nations. Russia will be a *strong country* with modern, well-equipped and mobile Armed Forces able to defend our nation and its allies and protect the national interests of our state and citizens.

(Putin, 2003)

Putin's second presidency: 'Russia First' and assertiveness in foreign policy

In the mid-2000s, as disappointment with the United States increased, Moscow slowly abandoned its earlier attempts to become a strategic partner of the West, and instead developed a much more assertive and independent *Russia-first* approach in international affairs. As accurately described by Russian scholar Dmitry Trenin (2006), '[Up] Until recently, Russia saw itself as Pluto in the Western solar system, very far from the centre but still fundamentally a part of it. Now [in 2006] it has left that orbit entirely' (p. 87). Russia's leaders had 'given up on becoming part of the West and have started creating their own Moscow-centred system' (Trenin, 2006). Russia's perception that the West, and in particular the United States, did not want a strong Russia, which could challenge their behaviour and their influence in the international arena, was reinforced. Moscow became persuaded that the West desired 'a weak Russia that it could exploit and manipulate' (Trenin, 2006). Russia considered itself 'friendless'. There was a strong belief that Russia had no allies in the international arena and therefore had to safeguard its own security by relying only on its own strength and capacity. Russia remained open to cooperation with the West and proved eager to conduct 'positive joint action [with other partners] to ensure common interests on the basis of equality', Foreign Minister Lavrov noted (2007). But the Kremlin wanted to ensure that it retained freedom of operation in the international arena (Lavrov, 2007). As clearly stated by Putin during his now famous speech in February 2007 at the Munich Conference on Security,

> Russia is a country with a history that spans more than a thousand years and has practically always used the privilege to carry out an independent foreign policy. We are not going to change this tradition today. At the same time, we are well aware of how the world has changed and we have a realistic sense of our own opportunities and potential.
>
> (Putin, 2007)

Russia's increasingly assertive foreign policy approach manifested itself in a series of foreign policy actions which raised serious concerns in the West. Russia enhanced its military cooperation with China, with whom it conducted massive joint military exercises for the first time in 2005. Together with Beijing and its other allies in the Shanghai Cooperation Organisation (SCO), Moscow called for the closure of American bases in Central Asia, in an effort to reduce America's influence in an area perceived as falling within Russia's sphere of 'special interest'. Russia also continued to sell arms and cooperate in the nuclear-energy sphere with Iran, while refusing to place Tehran under sanctions for the pursuit of its uranium-enrichment programme. In addition, Putin welcomed Hamas leaders to Moscow in March 2006 after the United States and Europe had imposed an embargo on the Palestinian organisation for its actions in Gaza, while Russia also sold *Igla* air defence missile systems to Syria, challenging the fragile geopolitical balance of the Middle East. Within the European framework, Moscow announced in February 2007 its possible withdrawal from the *Intermediate-Range Nuclear Forces* (INF) Treaty in response to the United State's intentions to deploy parts of its ground-based missile defence system in Poland and the Czech Republic; and also suspended implementation of the Conventional Forces in Europe (CFE) Treaty at the end of 2007. Russia also resumed strategic bomber patrols close to NATO's borders and increased its naval activity well beyond its frontiers, in order to project its global power. At the same time, the Kremlin enhanced quite significantly its economic and military ties with the CIS states, blatantly interfered in the elections of neighbouring Ukraine in 2004, and acquired lucrative energy assets and business interests in the FSS. The Kremlin also substantially raised energy prices to its weaker CIS neighbours, besides behaving quite assertively towards Georgia and Moldova. All this indicated that Russia was ready to act quite forcefully, not only globally, but also within the former Soviet arena.

Putin's more forceful foreign policy was underpinned by significant improvements in the country's economic performance. Record-high energy prices, which rose from $25/barrel in 2003 to $109/barrel in March 2008, helped the Russian economy to grow at an average of 6.6 per cent between 2004 and 2008 (BBC, 2008).[10] This translated into improved living standards, increased salaries, and a progressive reduction of poverty. All of this produced an overall sense of well-being among the Russian population, which, generated very high approval ratings for President Putin, surpassing 80 per cent in 2007.[11] Furthermore, a marginalised opposition and greater political stability gave Putin more confidence, and pushed him to behave much more assertively, both globally and within the former Soviet space. The second half of the 2000s, thus, witnessed increased efforts carried out by the Kremlin to deepen integration with a group of like-minded states within the CIS space, and more specifically within the framework of the Eurasian Economic Community or EvrAzES, and the Collective Security Treaty Organisation or CSTO. Russia adopted a much more confrontational approach towards the 'mother countries', especially vis-à-vis Georgia and Moldova, in relation to the various separatist conflicts that had erupted in their territories in the early 1990s. Moscow expanded ties with the 'separatist regions', de facto challenging the territorial integrity of countries such as Georgia and Moldova. Putin also proved ready to employ hard power instruments – for example, increases in energy prices – to obtain economic concessions or political benefits. Putin's self-assured behaviour was accompanied by attempts to modernise and strengthen the country's armed forces, through the acquisition of new modern weapons and equipment, and the introduction of a modernising military reform programme (Baev, 2008, p. 10). The objective was to utilise the armed forces to project power and enforce foreign policy goals more effectively.

However, despite Russia's differences with the West, its leaders did not wish to engage in any direct confrontation with the United States or Europe, nor did they desire to put an end to any form of cooperation with Moscow's Western partners (Arbatov, 2007). As Putin himself stated in his Munich speech, Russia still wanted to engage in global cooperation (with Western countries) whenever possible, in order to establish a 'fair and democratic world', that would ensure security and cooperation for all involved (Putin, 2007). What Russia actually desired, as rightly stated by Aleksei Arbatov (2007) was 'to be recognised as a great power among other great powers'. It wanted 'its legitimate rights to be respected, and its views on major issues to be reckoned with – even if these views differed from those of the US and its allies' (Arbatov, 2007). More importantly, if differences emerged, 'they [had to] be resolved on the basis of mutual compromises, rather than by "pushing" American policy' (Arbatov, 2007). Russia's more assertive and independent foreign policy course resulted from a perception that Russia had overcome 'the consequences of the systemic political and socio-economic crisis' of the 1990s (MID, 2009) and was now a strong power capable to 'defend national interests as a subject of multipolar international relations' (Tsygankov, 2009, p. 352). It also reflected Russia's disenchantment with the West, in particular with the USA, and its global behaviour.

The Kremlin became increasingly disappointed with the West once the partnership-of-equals between Russia and the USA, which Putin had hoped would develop after 9/11, failed to materialise. Not only did Russia feel it was being kept at arms-length within the Euro-Atlantic structures, even within the NATO–Russia Council, but it also sensed, rightly or wrongly, that it was being increasingly encircled by NATO. The enlargement of the Atlantic Alliance eastwards, although not accompanied with the increased deployment of NATO troops in Eastern Europe, led nevertheless to the movement of NATO's military infrastructure nearer to Russia's borders. Despite NATO's assurances that the Alliance was not directed against Russia, the Kremlin felt that Russia was increasingly under threat from NATO. From Russia's perspective, NATO countries not only encircled the Russian enclave of Kaliningrad, they also came very close to Russia's borders in the Baltic region.[12] To this had to be added Georgia's and Ukraine's potential membership in NATO, an issue which caused great alarm in Moscow given the close ties that existed with Ukraine, and the strategic relevance that both these two countries had for Russia (Zygar, 2006).[13] As stated by Foreign Minister Lavrov (2007), 'Now we are confronted with what can only be interpreted as the restoration of a sanitary cordon to the west of Russia's borders'. Russia also worried over NATO's readiness to operate far beyond its original 'area' of activities, initially restricted to protecting its member states, but now engaged militarily as far away as Afghanistan. These developments prompted Lavrov to ask, 'How can democracy be promoted by a military-political alliance that, within the framework of its transformation, has been consistently increasing the number of scenarios for the possible use of force?' (Lavrov, 2007). Although the irreconcilable ideological rivalry between the two sides had been relegated to the past, there was a clear sense, according to Lavrov, that the West was again trying to 'contain' Russia (Lavrov, 2007).

This negative security predicament was made worse, from Russia's point of view, by the United State's plans to deploy elements of its anti-ballistic missile system in Poland and the Czech Republic – in contravention to the spirit of the 2002 Russia–USA *Joint Declaration on the New Strategic Relationship*, which envisaged cooperation in the development of anti-ballistic missile defence systems (Arbatov, 2007).[14] Furthermore, Moscow worried that NATO members refused to ratify the CFE Treaty as long as Russia delayed the withdrawal of its troops from Georgia and Moldova. Although NATO states respected the CFE quotas, the non-ratification of the treaty was seen by the Kremlin as threatening the very foundation of European security upon which Russia's security relied. It challenged Russia's understanding of European security, which in Moscow's view, had to be based on equality and mutual benefit (Lavrov, 2007). Similarly, the decision to grant Kosovo unilateral independence, in contravention to past agreements was also seen as undermining one of the pillars of European security – the territorial integrity of states – further exacerbating regional instability. Moreover, NATO's decision at the 2006 Riga Summit to explore the possibility of considering the *energy security* of its members as one of its key areas of responsibility, was perceived by Moscow as an attempt by NATO members to aim the Alliance directly against Russia (Zyagar, 2006).[15]

Moreover, a growing 'values-gap' between Russia and its Western partners developed during the 2000s, as the Russian leadership became subjected to strong criticism from its Western partners over its trampling on democracy – and this brought Russia and the West further apart. In the mid-2000s, the US leadership became very critical of Russia's internal developments, condemning the derailment of the rule of law, while also denouncing in very strong terms Russia's military policies in Chechnya and the North Caucasus (Sidorov and Belov, 2004).[16] Condemnation of Russia became harsher after the Russian Presidential election of March 2004, which granted Putin a second term in office, and especially after the introduction by the Kremlin of a series of internal reforms, following the school siege at Beslan by Chechen rebels, which significantly centralised administrative power in Russia. The direct appointment of Russia's governors and the elimination of single-seat districts in the Russian lower house of the parliament, were interpreted as a 'pulling back' of democracy inside Russia (Sidorov and Belov, 2004). In an article published in the Russian daily *Kommersant* in February 2005, newly appointed USA Secretary of State Condoleezza Rice went as far as 'looking for ways in which [the USA] could support and develop civil society in Russia', to Putin's great concern (Korzun, 2005).[17] Furthermore, in 2006, the USA Administration added Putin's assertive energy policies in the former USSR region to its list of concerns over Russia's foreign policy behaviour, while strongly condemning the Kremlin's 'use of energy levers to exert pressure' over its neighbours.

Within this framework, the Russian leadership became increasingly worried over Western support for and American engagement with 'democratic' forces in the newly independent states, especially during the 'coloured revolutions' in Georgia in 2003 and Ukraine in 2004 (*Time Magazine* and V.V. Putin, 2007). Such actions were seen as intended to challenge Russia's influence and presence in the former Soviet space and as preludes to future attempts aimed at undermining the Russian political system itself (Trenin, 2009). Putin feared that the same methods used by the United States in Ukraine and Georgia would eventually be also employed in Russia, in order to overthrow his regime. His concerns were heightened when the United States and many European countries decided to enhance their support and provide encouragement to civil society groups in Russia in the mid-2000s (Korzun, 2005). This strongly influenced Putin's decision to distance itself and Russia from the West and enhance its grip on power domestically. As pointed out by Vladimir Shlapentokh (2007) 'during his second term, Putin's foreign policy was strongly influenced by his belief that the West's hostility toward Russia could help the opposition change the regime [in the Kremlin], as seen in Ukraine and Georgia'.

The Kremlin responded to Western challenges to his regime by introducing the notion of 'sovereign democracy' as articulated by Putin's advisor and ideologue Vladislav Surkov (Ambrosio and Vendrovec, 2013). In Surkov's view, Russia had to build its own democratic system, slowly, and at its own pace, without external interference, and through the development of its own institutions, if it wanted to avoid falling back again into the 'oligarchic' system of the Yeltsin years (Surkov, 2006). More importantly, Russia had to remain sovereign and independent, and not a member of European institutions, even though Russia, in Surkov's view, remained a European country, by its nature and vocation (Surkov, 2005). This clearly reflected Putin's views, who in 2005 had made reference to the unique nature of Russia's political development,

> Russia is a country that has chosen democracy through the will of its own people. It chose this road of its own accord and it will decide itself how best to ensure that the principles of freedom and democracy are realised here, taking into account our historic, geopolitical and other particularities and respecting all fundamental democratic norms. As a sovereign nation, Russia can and will decide for itself the timeframe and conditions for its progress along this road.
>
> (Putin, 2005)

Another very significant issue of contention with the West which emerged in the mid-2000s was related to Europe's deeper engagement with countries that belonged to the former Soviet space, and the CIS more specifically. As a result of EU's enlargement into Eastern Europe in 2004, the EU's and Russia's *Near Abroads* started to overlap. The EU's new *European Neighbourhood Policy* (ENP), launched in 2004, and designed to enhance EU ties with countries in the EU periphery, including the three South Caucasus states, Belarus, Ukraine and

Moldova, was seen as encroaching directly on Russia's traditional 'sphere of interests'. Even though Russia had been given the opportunity to take part in the EU's ENP, the Kremlin refused to join the project. By the mid-2000s, Russia was less interested in integrating into Europe, and more concerned about enhancing its own sovereignty, strengthening its ties with the CIS states within the framework of EvrAzEs and the CSTO, and playing an independent role in international affairs. Countries within the former Soviet space continued to occupy a special place in Russia's foreign policy priorities. Efforts at both economic and military integration with the FSS were sped up, although the focus centred around a selective group of CIS countries, which remaining willing to develop closer ties with Russia. Cooperation within the CIS framework was seen as essential for Russia's own economic development and its own military security, as well as to ensure regional stability.

Russia's civilising mission in Eurasia

More significantly, starting in 2005, Putin began speaking of Russia's *Civilising Mission* in the Eurasian Continent which entailed making sure that 'democratic values, combined with national interests, enrich and strengthen our historic community' (Putin, 2005).[18] This historic community was understood as encompassing the entire former Soviet space. In other words, Putin increasingly adopted, in his rhetoric and also partly in his actions, a vision of Russia as the leader of a Eurasian civilisation, integrating elements of Russian *Eurasianist* thought. In his 2005 Address to Parliament, Putin stated that Russia was 'bound to the former Soviet republics – now independent countries – through a common history, through the Russian language and the great culture that we share' (Putin, 2005). Russia had to work together with these independent countries in order to 'open up broad possibilities for personal and collective success, [and] achieve for ourselves *the standards of civilisation* we have worked hard for – standards that would emerge as a result of a common economic, humanitarian and legal space' (Putin, 2005). In other words, it was believed that the progress and development of Russia *and* of the other FSS would best be fulfilled through the reintegration of the FSS and Russia into a common socio-economic, cultural and humanitarian space. The Kremlin was essentially promoting a shared *civilisational* project that involved all the FSS, under its undisputed leadership.

In his 2005 address to the Federal Assembly, Putin also famously admitted 'that the collapse of the Soviet Union was a major geopolitical disaster of the century', in a clear reminder that he remained nostalgic of the USSR's glorious past and an admirer of Russia's *grandeur* (Putin, 2005). However, Putin's words were not followed by calls to restore the USSR. No reference was made by Putin to the loss of any specific region or territory of the USSR which Russia should strive to reclaim. Instead, Putin argued that Russians had made a clear choice in favour of building a democratic state, selecting a new vector of development in their 1,000-year-old history (Putin, 2005). During the 1990s, Russians had found their 'own path to building a democratic, free and just society and state', Putin noted. Furthermore, immediately after the above-mentioned quote, the Russian President talked primarily about the internal socio-economic upheaval that had been endured by the Russian state in the 1990s, as a result of the end of the USSR. While this indicated that Putin was not willing to re-create the USSR in any new shape or form, he nevertheless proposed, in this same speech, a new form of organisation for the ex-USSR region – its integration around a new common Russian-led 'civilisational' project. This was reinforced in 2006, when Putin once again called for 'strengthening our common humanitarian space' within the CIS area, which shared not only a 'rich historical and human dimension' but also offered new social and economic opportunities (Putin, 2006).[19] It was clear that Putin increasingly saw the former Soviet space as an area of Russia's exclusive influence, formed by countries sharing a common view of civilisation.

Furthermore, international relations also started to be interpreted by Putin through the prism of Huntington's 'clash of civilisations'. Whereas in his speech to the German Parliament in 2001, Putin had considered talking about a 'war between civilisations', in reference to a possible confrontation with the Muslim world, as 'inadmissible' (Putin, 2001), in the late 2000s, a potential conflict of civilisations, this time with the West, was seen as a likely possibility due to American and Western behaviour. The *Foreign Policy Concept* adopted in 2008 noted that for the first time in contemporary history, 'global competition [was acquiring] a *civilisational dimension*, which [suggested] competition between different value systems and development models, within the framework of universal democratic and market economy principles' (PRF, 2008). As the constraints of the bipolar confrontation were being overcome, 'the cultural and *civilisational* diversity of the modern world [came] increasingly into evidence' (PRF, 2008). Russia had tried to 'prevent a division of the world along civilizational lines' especially in Europe, the 2007 *Foreign Policy Review* stated (MFA, 2008). But the West's unilateral actions were leading to 'destabilization', 'provoking tensions, exacerbating interstate differences, stirring up ethnic and religious strife, endangering the security of other States, and fuelling tensions in *inter-civilizational relations*' (MFA, 2008).

Russia hoped that the UN would play a fundamental role in reducing global tensions by establishing an inter-civilisational dialogue which would help reach agreement between representatives of the various religions, confessions and cultures (PRF, 2008). More importantly, within this new heterogeneous world, Russia's civilisation, its language and culture were seen as providing a 'unique contribution to the cultural and civilisational diversity of the contemporary world' (PRF, 2008). The European Union remained Russia's biggest partner, and there was still hope of establishing 'mutually-beneficial economic ties' as well as cultural, scientific and educational exchanges, through the development of 'common spaces' with Europe (Putin, 2006). But there was no longer talk of deep integration with Europe. The EU was not recognised as the sole representative of Europe, nor was it accepted as the organisation responsible for determining Russia's 'Europeanness' (Trenin, 2007). Instead, Russia proposed itself as the potential leader of an alternative vision of Europe – a 'Greater Europe' – whose members would include those European states most eager to defend and protect their newly acquired sovereignty (Krastev, 2005).[20] In his 2005 Address to Parliament Putin made extended references to Russia's European heritage, its ties to European political and intellectual developments since the 18th century, and to Russia's role as a European Great Power since the times of Catherine the Great (Putin, 2005). This Russia's 'Europeanness', as described by Putin, entitled Russia to become an alternative pole to the EU around which European integration, involving above all CIS states, could occur.

In the mid-2000s, President Putin also began officially to promote the 'Russian World' or *Russkii Mir* concept, as part of his efforts to reach out to Russia's own 'shared civilisational space'. The 'Russian World' notion extended far beyond the territory of the Russian Federation and its 143 million people living within its borders. It involved 'millions of ethnic Russians, native Russian speakers, their families and descendants, scattered across the globe' making up 'the largest diaspora population in the world' (*Russkii Mir*, n.d.). The 'Russian World' also included 'the millions of people worldwide' who had chosen the Russian language as their subject of study, and 'those who have developed an appreciation for Russia and its rich cultural heritage' (*Russkii Mir*, n.d.). More specifically, it involved all those who were 'sincerely interested in Russia and who are concerned about its future' (*Russkii Mir*, n.d.). What united all those belonging to the Russian World, was therefore a desire to be closely connected to Russia and to help in its successful development. Although an ethnic Russian and Christian Orthodox notion of Russia lay at the heart of the Russian World concept, much broader identifications with *Russianness* were welcomed, whether through language, culture, history, religion or territory (Laruelle, 2009b, p. 53). Within this framework, the Russian World project was launched in 2006 with the aim of 'supporting, enhancing and encouraging the appreciation of Russian language, heritage and culture' in the world and to 'reconnect the Russian diaspora with its homeland' through cultural and social programmes, exchanges and assistance in relocation (*Russkii mir*, n.d.). The project also involved supporting Russian associations and the Orthodox Church abroad, and promoting economic investments by the diaspora inside Russia.

The promotion of a positive image of Russia abroad developed in response to the reverses suffered by the Kremlin in Ukraine during the 2004 Orange revolution. When Russia's preferred and openly supported candidate, Viktor Yanukovych, failed to triumph in the 2004 Ukrainian presidential elections, Moscow decided to invest quite significantly in its own soft power and image-making (Laruelle, 2015). Konstantin Kosachev, Chairman of the Foreign Affairs Committee of the Russian Duma, argued that the Kremlin had to provide a credible 'ideological alternative' to the West's democratic agenda – a project that would be appealing to these states, and would instead focus on 'growth, modernisation and independence' (Kosachev, 2004). As clearly explained by Ivan Krastev (2005), Russia's objective when launching the *Russkii mir* project was to develop 'an efficient infrastructure of ideas, institutions, networks and media outlets' which could be used when the new orange-type regimes went into crisis, in order to 'regain influence not simply at the level of government but also at the level of society'. In Krastev's view, Russia would not fight for Western democracy but it would 'fight for democracy – *its* kind of democracy' (Krastev, 2005; Popescu, 2006). Within the CIS context, this translated into the promotion by the Kremlin of democratic or pseudo-democratic regimes that would become closely aligned to Russia. Many political projects were therefore attached to the Russian World Programme, intended primarily to promote these key Russian foreign policy objectives in the Near Abroad. This line of policy was again reinforced in the 2013 *Foreign Policy Concept*, which noted that '*Soft power*, a comprehensive toolkit for achieving foreign policy objectives building on civil society potential, information, cultural and other methods and technologies alternative to traditional diplomacy, is becoming an indispensable component of modern international relations' (MID, 2013).

Conclusion

During the mid-2000s, therefore, Moscow slowly abandoned its earlier attempts to become a strategic partner of the West, and instead developed a much more independent, *Russia-first* approach, in international affairs. This came hand in hand with a more assertive behaviour in the former Soviet space, which was clearly identified by the Kremlin as an area of Russia's 'special interests'. Russia's actions reflected above all its disappointment with Western rhetoric and its behaviour both globally and regionally, closer to Russia's borders. The United States' reckless military intervention in Iraq and its abandonment of the ABM treaty were perceived as direct challenges to the existing normative and strategic international order. NATO's enlargement and its plans to deploy an anti-missile defence system in eastern Europe, in turn, were seen as undermining the strategic stability of the Cold War, and directly impacting Russia's security in a negative way. These last actions, in particular, were interpreted as a reflecting a complete disregard for Russia's legitimate state interests and for its genuine concerns over developments in the Near Abroad. Furthermore, because of the EU's enlargement into Eastern Europe in 2004, the EU's and Russia's *Near Abroads* started to overlap and, as a result, a new geo-strategic contest developed, with Russia and Europe adopting contrasting and conflicting policies. In this respect, the Russian leadership became particularly worried over Western support for 'democratic' forces during the 'coloured revolutions' in Georgia in 2003 and Ukraine in 2004. These actions were seen not only as challenging directly Russia-friendly regimes in the former Soviet space, but also as potentially representing a threat to the Putin regime itself. As the Russian leadership became subjected to strong criticism from its Western partners, the worry that 'regime change' would be instigated in Russia by the West, increased. Developments inside Russia and in the former Soviet space became increasingly inter-linked.

To address these challenges, Russia increasingly saw the need to reinforce its military and economic presence in the CIS, and to strengthen its political influence, in its Near Abroad. To that end, it pushed for deeper military and economic integration within the CIS/CSTO/EvrAzEs frameworks; it expanded its ties with the separatist regions of Georgia and Moldova, while also trying to keep a prolonged military presence in several strategic CIS states – Ukraine, Moldova, Georgia, Armenia and Belarus, as well as in Kyrgyzstan and Tajikistan. More significantly, it also proved ready to utilise 'energy as weapon' in order to obtain political and economic concessions and influence the behaviour of those CIS countries which relied on Russian gas supplies. Last but not least, Russia expanded its 'soft power' instruments in the former Soviet space, by creating a network of partners loyal to Russia, to its citizens, and to its geo-strategic destiny. In other words, by the end of the 2000s decade, Russia's increasingly put in place and actively developed a neo-imperialist project. In order to achieve its aims, the Kremlin did not hesitate to employ hard power instruments vis-à-vis its neighbours, and this policy was facilitated by the increased economic and military strength of the Russian state, which allowed Moscow to behave more assertively. More importantly, Putin and his entourage increasingly adopted a neo-imperialist discourse to explain and justify the Kremlin's actions. In the mid-2000s, as disappointment over integration into Europe and the West increased, Russia started promoting the notion of the former Soviet region as a 'common civilisational space'. This concept was intended to describe an area – the former USSR – which a shared a common history, a similar culture, and a same language, and was therefore destined to share a common future, under Russia's undisputed leadership. It was argued that the overall development and the unbound progress of Russia *and* of the other FSS were deeply intertwined. Such a predicament could best be fulfilled through the reintegration of the FSS and Russia into a common socio-economic, cultural and humanitarian space. But, more importantly, Russia's actions in the Near Abroad were above all intended to transform Russia into a *Great Power*, capable of exercising its influence not only in its immediate neighbourhood but also globally on a par with other global powers such as the United States. In this respect, Putin fully endorsed and embraced Primakov's realist understanding of international affairs – while the Kremlin proved ready to cooperate with the West on issues of strategic relevance, Moscow nevertheless promoted the emergence of a *multipolar world* with Russia as one of its leading 'poles'.

Notes

1 Putin created seven federal districts in Russia directed by special plenipotentiary envoys, to ensure the unification of a legal system throughout Russia.
2 The number of Russians living below the poverty line fell from 64 million in 1998 after the financial crash to 35 million in 2002 (Sakwa, 2008, p. 247).
3 He purposefully used the word *Rossiyan* to emphasise the values of the Russian people and not those of ethnic Russians (*Russkie*).
4 The Concept had been elaborated under Putin's guidance while secretary of the Security Council and prime minister, and was approved soon after he became President.
5 For details on Putin's 'illiberal democratic' project for Russia as soon as he became President in the year 2000 see Dawisha (2014), specifically pp. 251–256.

6 Particular emphasis was placed on the consolidation of the Union of Belarus and Russia, and on the strengthening of the Customs Union (CU) which had been agreed with Belarus, Kazakhstan, Kyrgyzstan and Tajikistan.
7 'We support the president absolutely and radically', Dugin argued at the founding congress of the Eurasian Political Movement in April 2001 (Nekhoroshev, 2001).
8 Ivanov strongly opposed the deployment of NATO forces in the Central Asian states, seen as 'falling within the zone of responsibility of the CIS Collective Security Treaty' (*Rossiiskaya gazeta*, 2001).
9 Putin made 'the extent and nature of this co-operation' directly dependent on 'the overall level and quality of our relations with these countries, and on mutual understanding in combating international terrorism' and this included events in Chechnya (*Kommersant*, 2001).
10 Russia grew by 7.2 per cent in 2004, 5.5 per cent in 2005, 8.2 per cent in 2006, 8.5 per cent in 2007, and 5.2 per cent in 2008.
11 Absolute poverty fell from 29 per cent in 2000 to 13.4 per cent in 2007 (OECD, 2009, p. 21)
12 NATO made it clear that in order to 'carry out its collective defence and other missions' it would 'rely on adequate infrastructure commensurate' to its needs, rather than on permanent military deployments. Reinforcement would take place, 'when necessary, in the event of defence against a threat of aggression and missions in support of peace, consistent with international law, OSCE principles and the adapted CFE Treaty' (NATO, 1997).
13 Speaking in Riga before the start of the NATO summit in November 2006, President Bush affirmed his desire to see Georgia, and eventually also Ukraine as members of NATO (Zygar, 2006).
14 Putin proposed to Washington that Russia and the USA jointly operate the radar facility based at Gabala in Azerbaijan, and that they create a regional monitoring and early-warning system, as way out of the current situation and as means to build trust among the parties.
15 At the Bucharest Summit in 2008, NATO was given a dedicated mandate to work in the field of energy security (NATO, 2008).
16 In January 2004, the US State Secretary Colin Powell, made progress in the relationship between Russia and the USA contingent upon the state of democracy in Russia (Verlin, 2004; Volkhonsky, 2004).
17 Rice, however, ruled out excluding Russia from the G8 or preventing it from joining the WTO (Korzun, 2005). For Rice, Russia remained, nevertheless, a 'strategic partner' of the USA.
18 It is only in the mid-2000s that elements of Eurasianism and references to Russia's civilising mission in Eurasia appeared in Putin's declarations.
19 Cooperation through a common humanitarian and socio-economic project offered opportunities and benefits to all the FSS, all of which belonged a common civilisational space.
20 As conspicuously noted by Krastev (2005), 'At the heart of the current crisis is not the clash between democracy and authoritarianism … but the clash between the post-modern state embodied by the EU and the traditional modern states embodied by Russia'.

Bibliography

Ambrosio, Th. and G. Vandrovec (2013). Mapping the Geopolitics of the Russian Federation: The Federal Assembly Addresses of Putin and Medvedev. *Geopolitics*, 18(2), 435–466.

Arbatov, A. (2007). Is a New Cold War Imminent? *Russia in Global Affairs*, 2, July–September, p. 5. Available at: http://eng.globalaffairs.ru/number/n_9127 [accessed 7 August 2017].

Baev, P.K. (2008). *Russian Energy Policy and Military Power: Putin's Quest for Greatness*. London and New York: Routledge.
BBC News (2008). Oil Sets Fresh Record Above $109. 11 March. Available at: http://news.bbc.co.uk/1/hi/business/7289070.stm [accessed 8 September 2017].
Brandenburger, D. (1999). Proletarian Internationalism, 'Soviet Patriotism' and the rise of Russocentric Etatism during the Stalinist 1930s, *Left History*, 6(2), 80–100.
Dawisha, K. (2014). *Putin's Kleptocracy: Who Owns Russia?* New York: Simon and Schuster.
Duncan, P. (2007). Regime and Ideology in Putin's Russia. In: P. Duncan, ed. *Convergence and Divergence: Russia and Eastern Europe into the Twenty-First Century*, London: UCL/SEES, pp. 139–158.
Grigoryev, Ye. (2002). *Nezavisimaya gazeta*, 15 July, p. 2.
Kommersant (2001). 25 September, p. 2.
Korzun, A. (2005). *Kommersant*, 11 February, p. 1.
Kosachev, K. (2004). *Nezavisimaya gazeta*, 28 December.
Krastev, I. (2005). Russia's Post-Orange Empire. *Open Democracy*, 19 October. Available at: www.opendemocracy.net/democracy-europe_constitution/postorange_2947.jsp [accessed 10 November 2017].
Laruelle, M. (2009a). *In the Name of the Nation: Nationalism and Politics in Contemporary Russia*. New York: Palgrave Macmillan.
Laruelle, M. (2009b). *Inside and Around the Kremlin's Black Box: The New Nationalist Think Tanks in Russia*. Stockholm Paper, Institute for Security and Development Policy. October. Available at: http://isdp.eu/content/uploads/images/stories/isdp-main-pdf/2009_laruelle_inside-and-around-the-kremlins-black-box.pdf [accessed 18 October 2018].
Laruelle, M. (2015). *The Russian World: Russia's Soft Power and Geopolitical Imagination*. Washington: The Center on Global Interests. Available at: http://globalinterests.org/wp-content/uploads/2015/05/FINAL-CGI_Russian-World_Marlene-Laruelle.pdf [accessed 18 November 2018].
Lavrov, S. (2007). Containing Russia: Back to the Future?, *Russia in Global Affairs*, 4,October–December 2007. Available at: http://eng.globalaffairs.ru/number/n_9792 [accessed 12 November 2017].
Lo, B. (2003). *Vladimir Putin and the Evolution of Russian Foreign Policy*. The Royal Institute of International Affairs. Melbourne, Malden, Oxford: Blackwell Publishing, pp. 31–50.
March, L. (2012). Nationalism for Export? The Domestic and Foreign-Policy Implications of the New 'Russian Idea'. *Europe-Asia Studies*, 64 (3), 401–425.
Ministry of Foreign Affairs (MFA) (2000). *Foreign Policy Concept of the Russian Federation*. 28 June. Available at: https://fas.org/nuke/guide/russia/doctrine/econcept.htm [accessed 9 July 2018].
Ministry of Foreign Affairs (MFA) (2008). Foreign Policy and Diplomatic Activities of The Russian Federation In 2007 Overview of The Russian Foreign Ministry. Moscow, March.
MID (2000). Kontseptsiya natsional'noi bezopasnosti Rossiiskoi Federatsii. 10 January. Available at: www.mid.ru/en/foreign_policy/official_documents/-/asset_publisher/CptICkB6BZ29/content/id/589768 [accessed 27 September 2018].
MID (2009). Strategiya natsional'noi bezopasnosti Rossiiskoi Federatsii do 2020 goda. 12 May. Available at: www.mid.ru/foreign_policy/official_documents/-/asset_publisher/CptICkB6BZ29/content/id/294430 [accessed 8 June 2018].

MID (2013). Kontseptsiya vneshnei politiki Rossiiskoi Federatsii, 18 February. Available at: www.mid.ru/en/foreign_policy/official_documents/-/asset_publisher/CptICkB6BZ29/content/id/122186?p_p_id=101_INSTANCE_CptICkB6BZ29&_101_INSTANCE_CptICkB6BZ29_languageId=ru_RU [accessed 6 June 2018].

NATO (1997). Founding Act on Mutual Relations, Cooperation and Security between NATO and the Russian Federation. 27 May. Available at: www.nato.int/cps/en/natolive/official_texts_25468.htm?selectedLocale=en [accessed 23 June 2019].

NATO (2008). *NATO's Energy Security Agenda*. Available at: www.nato.int/docu/review/2014/NATO-Energy-security-running-on-empty/NATO-energy-security-agenda/EN/index.htm [accessed 6 June 2018].

Nekhoroshev, G. (2001). *Nezavisimaya gazeta*, 24 April, p. 2.

OECD (2009). *Economic Surveys: Russian Federation*, Paris.

Popescu, N. (2006). *Russia's Soft Power Ambitions*. CEPS Policy Brief, 115. October. Available: http://aei.pitt.edu/11715/1/1388.pdf [accessed 10 June 2018].

President of Russian Federation (PRF) (2008). The Foreign Policy Concept of The Russian Federation, 12 January. Available at: http://en.kremlin.ru/supplement/4116 [accessed 6 June 2018].

Putin, V.V. (1999). Rossiya na rubezhe tysyacheletii. *Nezavisimaya gazeta*. 30 December. Available at: www.ng.ru/politics/1999-12-30/4_millenium.html [accessed 7 June 2018].

Putin, V.V. (2000a). Annual Address to the Federal Assembly of the Russian Federation. 8 July. Available at: http://en.kremlin.ru/events/president/transcripts/21480 [accessed 10 June 2018].

Putin, V.V. (2000b). *First Person: An Astonishingly Frank Self-portrait by Russia's President Vladimir Putin*. New York, Public Affairs.

Putin, V.V. (2000c). 'Rossiya vsegda oshchushchala sebya evroazyatskoi stranoi …' Strana.ru. 13 November. Available at: http://evrazia.org/modules.php?file=article&name=News&sid=106 [accessed 8 June 2018].

Putin, V.V. (2001). Speech in the Bundestag of the Federal Republic of Germany. Berlin. 25 September. Available at: http://en.kremlin.ru/events/president/transcripts/21340 [accessed 8 June 2018].

Putin, V.V. (2003). Annual Address to the Federal Assembly of the Russian Federation, 16 May. Available at: http://en.kremlin.ru/events/president/transcripts/21998 [accessed 10 June 2018].

Putin, V.V. (2005). Annual Address to the Federal Assembly of the Russian Federation. 25 April, The Kremlin. Available at: http://en.kremlin.ru/events/president/transcripts/22931 [accessed 10 June 2018]

Putin, V.V. (2006). Annual Address to the Federal Assembly. Moscow. 10 May. Moscow, Available at: http://en.kremlin.ru/events/president/transcripts/23577 [accessed 10 June 2018].

Putin, V.V. (2007). Speech and the Following Discussion at the Munich Conference on Security Policy, 10 February. Available at: http://en.kremlin.ru/events/president/transcripts/24034 [accessed 10 June 2018].

Rossiiskaya gazeta (2001). 15 September, p. 7.

Russkii Mir (n.d.) Fond Russkii Mir. Available at: https://russkiymir.ru/fund/ [accessed 20 June 2018].

Sagramoso, D. (2004). L'economie russe sous Vladimir Poutine. *Politique Etrangère*, 1/2004, 123–135.

Sakwa, R. (2008). *Putin: Russia's Choice*. 2nd Edition, Milton Park and New York: Routledge.

Shlapentokh, V. (2007). Perceptions of a Threat to the Regime as a Major Factor of Russian Foreign Policy: From Lenin to Putin. *Johnson's Russia List.* 2007–199 (28), 18 September. Available at: www.russialist.org/archives/2007-199-28.php [accessed 10 July 2018].

Sidorov, D. and P. Belov (2004). *Kommersant*, 17 September, pp. 1 and 9.

Solovyev, V. (2008). *Kommersant*, December 25. In: A. Tsygankov (2009). Russia in the post-Western World: The End of the Normalisation Paradigm? *Post Soviet Affairs*, 25 (4), pp. 347–369 (p. 352).

Surkov, V. (2006). Suverenitet – eto politicheskii sinonim konkurentosposobnosti. Central-Asia.ru, 7 February. Available at: www.centrasia.ru/newsA.php?st=1141973460. [accessed 10 July 2018].

Surkov, V. (2005). Vladislav Surkov's Secret Speech: How Russia Should Fight International Conspiracies. 12 July. Available at: www.network54.com/Forum/155335/thread/1164815166/last-1164815166/Vladislav+Surkov%C2%92s+Secret+Speech-+How+Russia+Should+Fight+International+Conspiracies [accessed 11 April 2018].

Time Magazine, and V.V. Putin (2007). Putin Q&A: Full Transcript, 19 December. Available at: http://content.time.com/time/specials/2007/personoftheyear/article/0,28804,1690753_1690757_1695787-1,00.html [accessed 11 April 2018].

Trenin, V. (2001). *Vladimir Putin's Autumn Marathon: Towards the Birth of a Russian Foreign Policy Strategy.* Carnegie Endowment Briefing, 11. November.

Trenin, D. (2006). Russia Leaves the West. *Foreign Affairs*, July/August, p. 87. Available at: www.foreignaffairs.com/articles/russia-fsu/2006-07-01/russia-leaves-west [accessed 10 May 2018].

Trenin, D. (2007). *Getting Russia Right.* Washington: Carnegie Endowment for International Peace. August.

Trenin, D. (2009). Russia's Spheres of Interest, not *Influence. The Washington Quarterly*, 32 (4), 3–22.

Tsygankov, A. (2009). Russia in the post-Western World: The End of the Normalisation Paradigm? *Post Soviet Affairs.* 25 (4), 347–369.

Tsygankov, A.P. (2010) *Russia's Foreign Policy: Change and Continuity in National Identity.* 2nd edition, Lanham, Boulder, New York, Toronto, Plymouth: Rowman and Littlefield Publishers.

Union of Rightist Forces (URF) (2001). *Nezavisimaya gazeta*, 29 May, p. 8.

Verlin, Ye. (2004). *Nezavisimaya gazeta*, 27 January, p. 1.

Vinogradov, B. (2004). *Noviye Izvestiya*, 8 April, p. 4.

Volkhonsky, B. (2004). *Kommersant*, 16 September, p. 1.

Zakatnova, A. (2001). *Nezavisimaya gazeta*, 3 October, p. 2

Zygar, M. (2006). *Kommersant*, 29 November, pp. 1 and 9.

7 CIS economic integration gathers speed

The arrival of Putin to the Presidency of Russia saw a clear and determined attempt by the Kremlin to establish a properly functioning economic bloc within the CIS space with those countries most eager to align themselves economically with Russia – Belarus, Kazakhstan, Kyrgyzstan and Tajikistan, and to a lesser extent Uzbekistan and Armenia. The new organisation adopted a new name – *Eurasian Economic Community* or EvrAzES – to distance itself from the failing CIS enterprise and to portray itself as a more attractive integration project. At the end of the 1990s, it had become clear that the CIS had turned out to be none other than a forum for discussion and for carrying out a 'civilised divorce', and this forced Russia to rethink its views and priorities towards the organisation (Malashenko, 2000). In February 2001, at the Munich Security Conference, Russian Defence Minister Sergei Ivanov acknowledged that Russia's policy towards the CIS had undergone significant rethinking. Russian leaders had become aware that 'the rapid development of the Commonwealth into a full-fledged integrative association in the near future [was] impossible' (Kasayev, 2001). Rather than continue regarding integration in the post-Soviet space as an absolute value to be pursued at almost any cost, Russian leaders decided, instead, to adopt a pragmatic policy, and to focus their efforts on pursuing integration with those countries most eager to move ahead down the path of economic cooperation. Any economic interaction had to be, above all, mutually beneficial, in the Kremlin's view, and not jeopardise Russia's interests.

Economic integration moves ahead

Economic integration, therefore, received a major boost in October 2000, when the five members of the Customs Union (CU) agreed to establish a full-fledged regional organisation, the *Eurasian Economic Community (Evraziiskoe ekonomicheskoe soobshchestvo* or EvrAzES), in order to implement the various CES agreements reached in 1999 and 2000, and in this way give birth to the CU and the Single Economic Space (SES). This process occurred at the initiative of Russia, but it also had the strong backing of Kazakhstan (Dubnov, 2000). Ever since he had first launched the *Eurasian Union* project in 1994, President Nursultan Nazarbayev had remained a supporter of deeper economic integration within a Eurasian framework (Nazarbaev, 1996), and he therefore backed Russia's renewed cooperative efforts. What proved to be significant about the new organisation, however, was the introduction of new decision-making mechanisms, within existing structures of the CU, which paved the way for the creation of supranational structures. Whereas within the organisation's *Inter-State Council* (ISC) decisions remained unanimous, and based on the principle one-country one-vote, within EvrAzES' *Integration Committee* (IC) decisions were to be taken by a two-thirds majority, with the number of votes of each country being weighed according to its financial contribution to the common budget. Given Russia's economic significance, it was granted 40 per cent of the votes, while Belarus and Kazakhstan were given 20 per cent each, and Kyrgyzstan and Tajikistan, 10 per cent each. This meant that Russia could block any decisions it did not like, and easily pass resolutions if it managed to garner the support of just two countries, one with 20 per cent of the vote (Dubnov, 2001). Theoretically, the bases were thus established for the creation of a tight economic organisation within the CIS space, which would promote internal free trade among its members and provide guarantees of protection against strong external competition. Importantly, Russia potentially ensured for itself a predominant voice inside the organisation as the dominant economic power.

EvrAzES, however, was not to become a supranational organisation of the EU-type, where countries jointly pooled their sovereignty. The *Integration Committee*, where decisions were taken by a two-thirds majority, was primarily responsible for implementing decisions taken by the ISC. The latter remained the principal executive organ of the EvrAzES, and its decisions remained unanimous, based on the principle one-country, one-vote. It was the ISC which defined strategy and took decisions on further integration and on the implementation of EvrAzES goals (EvrAzES, 2000b), whereas the IC, was made responsible only for examining and approving draft proposals and preparing suggestions for the Committee. The implementation of decisions taken by the *Inter-State Council* occurred at national level, and the IC was in practice unable to conduct strict monitoring (Kaveshnikov, 2011, pp. 107–109). Therefore, although Russia remained the dominant economic power within EvrAzES, its influence within the organisation was curtailed by the structure and the functioning of EvrAzES' organs. Moreover, EvrAzES founding agreements also allowed for a multi-speed integration process. Integration was expected to move ahead first amongst those members most eager to move forward with the implementation of common rules, while others were allowed to move ahead more slowly. In other words, member countries were not required to make the necessary changes to national legislation at the same time, and this delayed overall implementation, showing the limits of the EvrAzES integration project (Torjeson, 2009, p. 156).

Nevertheless, the creation of the EvrAzES did represent a significant step forward in terms of legal harmonisation and common regulation within the EvrAzES space. The adoption of the EvrAzES Founding Treaty and other EvrAzES agreements reached by the ISC remained mandatory for any country acceding to the Community. In other words, all member states had to adopt these inter-state treaties, without reservations, when becoming members of EvrAzES (EvrAzES, 2000b). In this way, a unified legal space within EvrAzES was being created, analogous to the EU *acquis communautaire*, although functioning in a much more imperfect fashion (Kaveshnikov, 2011, p. 109). Furthermore, a Community Court of Justice, whose decisions were to be adopted by two-thirds of the judges, was made responsible for providing a uniform interpretation of EvrAzES law and for settling disputes on economic issues (Kaveshnikov, 2011, p. 109). In addition, an EvrAzES Inter-Parliamentary Assembly was placed in charge of parliamentary cooperation, and also made responsible for helping to bring national legislation into line with the treaties concluded within the EvrAzES framework (EvrAzES, 2000b).

Furthermore, as soon as President Putin reached the Presidency, efforts to implement a CU also gathered speed. In February 2000, the five signatory states of the February 1999 CU/CES (Common Economic Space) accord, agreed various procedures for the gradual introduction of Common External Tariffs (CET) for a list of items entering and exiting the CU.[1] The initial CET base list reflected the tariff lines that were common to Russia, Belarus and Kazakhstan. These CET were then to be adopted by the two other members of the CU – Kyrgyzstan and Tajikistan (EvrAzES, 2000a; Shadikhodjaev, 2009, p. 562.). The base list was also expected to be gradually expanded through the harmonisation of the customs duties of the remaining commodities which were not part of the initial CET base list (EvrAzES, 2000a; Shadikhodjaev, 2009, p. 562). For Kyrgyzstan and Kazakhstan, adopting CET generally implied an *increase* in their average CET. For Russia and Belarus, instead, the adoption of the CU's CET schedules resulted in a small *decrease* in their average external tariffs (Tumbarello, 2005, p. 13), thus establishing a CU built primarily around Russia's external tariffs.[2] This was intended to address the concerns of Russia over the growing pressures of economic globalisation and world trade liberalisations (Torjeson, 2009, p. 156). Russia was hoping to establish a protectionist economic bloc where it could sell its less competitive products unhindered and also shield its own industry from external competition. This approach, however, was also shared by the other members of the bloc – especially by Belarus and to a lesser extent by Kazakhstan, which also feared severe external competitive pressures (Torjeson, 2009, p. 156). The February 2000 agreement, in this respect, stipulated for the creation of a list of sensitive imported goods, which would be exempt from CET, allowing each state to set its own tariffs freely (EvrAzES, 2000a). This included goods which were produced locally but had to be protected from external competition. At the same time, though, Russia and the other CU states engaged in separate negotiations on World Trade Organization (WTO) accession. This process, instead, entailed commitments to further trade liberalisation, and therefore contradicted EvrAzES' CU obligations which generally moved in the opposite direction – towards raising tariffs upwards. This seemingly incoherent policy reflected Russia's desire to ensure that other CU/CES member states signed up to Russia's tariffs systems first, before engaging in negotiations on WTO accession, and ideally negotiated jointly, as a unified Russian-dominated bloc (Torjeson, 2009, pp. 156–158). Kyrgyzstan, however, was already a WTO member, and this made its accession to the CU somewhat problematic, especially as the latter entailed raising some of its external tariffs in contravention of its WTO commitments. Therefore, despite commitments by all EvrAzES members to negotiate WTO accession jointly, CU countries eventually opted to negotiate WTO accession separately, as joint talks proved too difficult to pursue (Torjeson, 2009, p. 158).

Towards a single economic space with Ukraine

A significant development regarding CIS economic cooperation occurred on 19 September 2003 at Yalta in Crimea, when three EvrAzES members, Russia, Belarus, Kazakhstan, reached a preliminary agreement with Ukraine on the creation of a *Single Economic Space* (SES), or *Edinoe ekonomicheskoe postranstvo* (Grigoryeva, 2003). The SES agreements entailed first and foremost the creation of a free trade area (FTA) among its signatory states, to be followed by the establishment of a CU. Once a CU was established, a single market for goods, services, labour and capital would follow. Customs frontiers would be completely abolished, and a SES Commission would be put in charge of regulating natural monopolies (Rublyova and Frumkin, 2003). The SES in many ways duplicated the functions of EvrAzES, and therefore its creation responded primarily to political imperatives rather than to economic needs. The only significant new element of the SES initiative, besides Ukrainian membership, was the creation of a supranational body responsible for regulating economic policy – *the Commission* – to which all parties were expected to delegate some of their powers (Vasilyeva, 2003). Decisions within this institution would be made by 'judicious voting' (*vzveshennym golosovaniem*), and the number of votes would be weighed on the basis of each party's economic potential (The Kremlin, 2003). If fully implemented, this agreement would have entailed a significant transfer of sovereignty from the signatory states to the newly established SES institutions, which in practice meant into Russia's hands as the biggest economic power in the association (Bukkvoll, 2004, p. 17).

The SES initiative, as pointed by Bukkvoll (2004), came from the Ukrainian leadership, rather than from Russia itself. Ukrainian President Leonid Kuchma realised that tighter economic integration with Russia was the price to pay in order to obtain Moscow's economic and political support, in order to succeed in the 2004 presidential elections (Bukkvoll, 2004, p. 13). As rightly pointed out by Kazakh expert Dosym Satpayev, 'For Leonid Kuchma to save political face, he had to be seen as the architect of the new regional initiative' (Vasilyeva, 2003).[3] Ukraine, however, portrayed the SES as a pragmatic and purely economic project, which could under no circumstances contradict Ukraine's Euro-Atlantic aspirations and impair Ukraine's future membership of the WTO. Kiev insisted, above all, on the establishment of a FTA, rather than on the formation of a CU/SES with its closest SES trading partners (Bukkvoll, 2004, p. 13).[4] The Russian leadership instead, saw the SES as the beginning of a process of full CIS reintegration. In this respect, Russian Deputy Prime Minister Viktor Khristenko declared in August 2003, 'the Four are prepared to sign their own *Treaty of Rome*, which began the history of the European Union' (Rublyova and Frumkin, 2003). President Putin noted that the SES could become 'a powerful engine for economic progress throughout Eurasia', which could tie the economies of several former Soviet states closely to the Russian economy (Frumkin, 2004). The SES project fulfilled Russia's ambitions of recreating a tight-knit union of the eastern Slavic states and Kazakhstan around its undisputed leadership. As the strongest economic power of all four, Russia would carry the greatest weight within the SES and would hold a predominant voice within the new organisation's structures where votes were weighed according to each country's economic potential. Pragmatic economic objectives also supported the establishment of a SES with Russia's major CIS economic partners. All four countries accounted for over 85 per cent of the economy of the former USSR, and therefore, a vast Eurasian market involving over 230 million consumers could potentially be created, to Russia's benefit and to the benefit of the other SES states. Furthermore, the SES permitted Russia to ensure the proper-functioning of the oil and gas transport networks transitioning through Ukraine and Belarus, which carried Russia's energy exports to its European clients, besides promoting the further development of intra-SES trade, including with Ukraine, Russia's main trading partner (Nikonov, 2004).[5]

However, despite the initial enthusiasm, the project failed to materialise. The disparate views held by Ukraine and the rest of the SES states made implementation of the SES initiative rather difficult, and this explains why the entire project foundered a year later, with the advent of a new leadership in Kiev in November 2004. In the aftermath of the Orange Revolution, the country's Euro-Atlantic aspirations were reinforced and, as a result, Ukraine's priorities changed. Ukraine's new President, Viktor Yushchenko agreed in principle to the creation of a FTA within the framework of the SES (Masterov, 2005). Yet, any common customs or monetary policies which could harm Ukraine's EU membership aspirations were ruled out, and this included any movement towards the creation of a CU with its SES partners (Stepanenko, 2005). Under Yushchenko's leadership, therefore, progress towards the establishment of a FTA moved rather slowly, whereas advancement towards the establishment of a CU hardly occurred. When Viktor Yanukovych became, once again, Prime Minister of Ukraine in August 2006, the SES project was again revived (Solovyov and Zygar, 2006; Yusin, 2006). However, as before, Ukraine accepted belonging to the now Russia-sponsored SES only on the condition that it established a free trade regime and that it did not proceed further down the road of deeper economic integration (Aslund, 2009, p. 216). European aspirations remained strong in Ukraine, even though Yanukovych proposed 'a more evolutionary and less impetuous stride towards European integration' (Makarkin, 2006). Thus, by mid-2006, the SES project lost steam, and instead all efforts were placed by Russia and its closest partners, Belarus and Kazakhstan, into developing a CU within the EvrAzES framework.

EvrAzES makes progress

During 2004 and 2005, as progress towards the establishment of the SES faltered, Russia and its partners instead focused their efforts on establishing a free trade regime within the EvrAzES format. In August 2004, Russia eliminated VAT (value-added tax) charges on its energy exports to all CIS states, thus easing the path towards the establishment of a proper-functioning FTA (Netreba, 2004a).[6] Although the measure was intended primarily to develop the SES and give a boost to Ukraine's pro-Kremlin candidate Viktor Yanukovych in the 2004 presidential elections, it was also applied to all other CIS states, including all EvrAzES states (Netreba, 2004a). Furthermore, within the EvrAzES framework, common rules for the licensing of imports and exports were adopted in September 2004 (Netreba, 2004b) and between June 2004 and January 2006, several agreements were reached in the financial services and insurance sectors to facilitate cross-border investments and financial transactions. EvrAzES states also agreed on the establishment of an integrated foreign exchange market (Kaveshnikov, 2011, p. 113; Lashkina, 2004). More significantly, common measures were also implemented to protect and monitor trade at EvrAzES' external borders, and cooperation among EvrAzES members was advanced in the field of justice – both necessary measures for the establishment of a well-functioning CU (Kaveshnikov, 2011, p. 113). In October 2005, Uzbekistan joined EvrAzES as a full member, allowing for the Central Asian Co-operation Organisation (CACO), which had been established initially in 1994, to be merged into EvrAzES (Kolesnikov, 2005). With the admission of a series of new CIS states as observers – Armenia, Moldova and Ukraine – by the end of 2005, EvrAzES started to look like a much more dynamic organisation than the SES (Gordiyenko, 2005). In January 2006, the Eurasian Development Bank was set up to finance joint development projects within EvrAzES, with a starting capital of $1.5 billion, two-thirds of which were provided by Kazakhstan and the rest by Russia (Dubnov, 2006). EvrAzES members also tried during 2003–2004, to implement a uniform policy line with regards to their negotiations on WTO membership (Lashkina, 2004).[7]

The running of EvrAzES was, however, not always smooth. Although some positive steps towards the creation of a well-functioning CU were made, they remained insufficient. By the end of 2003, CET had been harmonised on 95 per cent of Belarus' and Russia's tariff lines, on 85 per cent of the tariff lines between Russia and Kazakhstan, and on 60 per cent of the tariff lines between Russia and Tajikistan (Michalopoulos, 2004, p. 271). However, these tariff schedules covered only 6,156 tariff lines out of the 11,086 lines identified in the original EvrAzES classification system (Torjeson, 2009, p. 156). The remaining tariffs were not bound yet and were instead set independently by each member state (Tumbarello, 2005, p. 9). For Russia and Kyrgyzstan, tariff harmonisation remained quite low – it only reached 32 per cent, if all the 6,156 tariff lines are considered (Tumbarello, 2005, p. 9). This resulted from the fact that Kyrgyzstan had already joined the WTO and thus, its external tariffs were significantly lower

Table 7.1 Intra-EvrAzES growth in trade, in percentages, between 2000 and 2003, and average GDP growth between 2000 and 2003

EvrAzES member state	Imports from EvrAzES	Exports to EvrAzES	Average GDP Growth
Belarus	34	32	5
Kazakhstan	36.5	16.6	9
Kyrgyzstan	31	–3.6	4.2
Russia	16	41	6.2
Tajikistan	–35	15.4	11

Source for trade figures: EvrAzES, 2010, pp. 37–38. Source for GDP growth: World Bank.

than those of Russia. Furthermore, inside the CU, numerous exemptions to free trade remained, which were not consistent with a FTA, such as quotas, export duties, and import tariffs. It was only in 2008 that serious efforts were conducted to create a proper-functioning CU.

Despite these shortcomings, intra-EvrAzES trade did indeed increase between 2000 and 2008, if we look at the official statistics, as indicated in Tables 7.1 and 7.2.

These increases in intra-EvrAzES trade during 2000 and 2008 look quite significant. However, these surges in trade resulted primarily from substantial increases in the GDP of EvrAzES members states, rather than from the improved functioning of the organisation and the CU/FTA. They partly reflected the significant rises that had occurred in the energy and commodity export prices of EvrAzES countries such as Russia and Kazakhstan, and did not necessarily result from further trade liberalisation within the bloc.[8] By the mid- to late-2000s EvrAzES member states had not yet managed to establish a meaningful FTA, as shown by the variety of bilateral free trade agreements that were still signed amongst its members (Torjeson, 2009, p. 157). In a way, trade grew despite the lack of a

Table 7.2 Intra-EvrAzES growth in trade, in percentages, between 2003 and 2008, and average GDP growth between 2003 and 2008

EvrAzES member state	Imports from EvrAzES	Exports to EvrAzES	GDP Growth 2004–2007**
Belarus	210	120	9.85
Kazakhstan	306	20	9.72
Kyrgyzstan	284	175	4.6
Russia	64	127	7.57
Tajikistan	225	4	7.1
Uzbekistan*	84	53	7.87

Source for trade figures: EvrAzES, 2010, pp. 36–37. Source for GDP growth: World Bank.
*For Uzbekistan trade data is from 2006, when it joined EvrAzES, to 2008.
**GDP in 2008 is not included because of the significant slump resulting from the financial crisis.

proper-functioning FTA. Instead, obstacles to intra-EvrAzES trade remained – in the form of tariffs and regulations – and exchanges were still primarily organised around bilateral trade agreements. Nevertheless, these figures do indicate increased economic interaction among members of EvrAzES in the 2000s, before the region was hit by the 2008/09 financial crisis, and this reinforced the argument in favour of further and deeper CIS/EvrAzES integration (Kuzmin, 2006).[9]

On the other hand, as shown in Table 7.3 and 7.4, most EvrAzES countries continued to diversify their trade away from the CU, especially as far as countries' exports were concerned. This was especially the case for Russia and Kazakhstan, whose exports to the CU in 2003 represented only 8.7 per cent and 18 per cent respectively of their total exports. Belarus remained the exception, given that 50 per cent of its exports went to the CU and 66 per cent of its imports came from the CU in 2003. In 2008, Russia's exports to the EvrAzES represented only 8.3 per cent of Russia's total foreign exports, while its imports from the bloc totalled only 5.6 per cent (Table 7.2). The same applied to Kazakhstan, which in 2008 exported only 10 per cent of its products to EvrAzES countries, even though it remained more dependent on EvrAzES imports than Russia did (Table 7.2). The economies of all other EvrAzES states, however, remained more highly integrated, and this was especially the case for Belarus, which traded heavily with its main EvrAzES partner, Russia. This predicament argued in favour of closer economic ties between some, if not all of the EvrAzES states (Table 7.2). Furthermore, it must be noted that the trade diversification away from EvrAzES, for countries such as Russia and Kazakhstan, did not mean, however, that in absolute terms trade within EvrAzES did not increase – intra-EvrAzES trade did increase, as is shown in Tables 7.1 and 7.2, and this also included Russia's EvrAzES trade. The figures simply indicate that Russia's CIS/EvrAzES/CES trade increased *less* than Russia's trade with Europe and China. This again showed that there was deeper economic interaction between the EvrAzES member states than assumed by the figures, and potentially a solid basis for closer economic ties.

Nevertheless, problems in intra-EvrAzES – and intra-CIS trade as a whole – persisted. In many instances, as noted above, trade was still based primarily on bilateral free trade agreements rather than on multilateral FTA arrangements.

Table 7.3 Percentage of Exports and Imports of EvrAzES members to the CU, as a percentage of EvraAzES members' total trade

EvrAzES member states	Exports to CU as percentage of total exports in 2003	Imports from CU as percentage of total imports in 2003
Belarus	50	66
Kazakhstan	18	41
Kyrgyzstan	32.8	55
Russia	8.7	14
Tajikistan	16	50

Source: EvrAzES, Moscow 2010, pp. 37–38.

Table 7.4 Percentage of Exports and Imports of EvrAzES members to the CU, as percentage of EvraAzES members' total trade

EvrAzES member-states	Exports to CU as percentage of total exports in 2008	Imports from CU as percentage of total imports in 2008
Belarus	33.7	60
Kazakhstan	10	37.8
Kyrgyzstan	28.3	46.9
Russia	8.3	6.5
Tajikistan	10.3	44
Uzbekistan*	38.6	40

Source: EvrAzES, 2010, pp. 36–37.

Note
* For Uzbekistan data is from 2006, when it joined EvrAzES, to 2008.

Many of these bilateral agreements included several exemptions on tariffs, quotas and export duties, with few efforts made to eliminate them (Freinkman et al., 2004, pp. 45–46). Russia, for example, kept trade restrictions on the import of alcohol and tobacco from other CIS states (Netreba, 2004b). It also imposed restrictions on the import of Ukrainian large-diameter pipes, and banned the import of Ukrainian meat and dairy products in 2007 (Bryl, 2006). The Kremlin also continued to limit the imports of sugar from Belarus by imposing restrictive quotas, on the grounds that Belarus was 'dumping' cheap sugar made from the Cuban sugar cane on the Russian market (Netreba, 2004b). Moreover, Russia often used trade as an instrument of pressure over its neighbours. In 2006, for example, Moscow banned the import of Georgian mineral water, as well as Georgian and Moldovan wine, in retaliation for Tbilisi's and Chisinau's obstructions to Russia's WTO membership, and in response to their actions in their respective separatist regions – Abkhazia and South Ossetia in Georgia, and Transdniestria in Moldova (Naumov, 2008). Belarus, in turn, imposed quotas on fish imports from Russia, and introduced transit fees on Russian trucks transiting through Belarus (Vorobyov, 2007).[10] The Belarusian government also compelled its agricultural producers to buy equipment only in Belarus, thus limiting purchases from Russia, or from other EvrAzES member states (Vorobyov, 2007). Kazakhstan, in turn, faced problems with the transit of its oil and gas, as well as grain, through Russian territory. Russia refused to increase the quotas for Kazakh oil transiting through its pipeline system, as it feared the competition of Kazakh oil in traditional and new global markets (Dubnov, 2006). Furthermore, in January 2007, Russia imposed an export duty on oil supplied to Belarus, which it did not levy on oil sent to Kazakhstan, and which was in violation of the free trade and CU agreements previously reached within the EvrAzES framework (Bekker and Ivanitskaya, 2007). Trade wars in the EvrAzES/CIS region, therefore, remained frequent because nobody trusted the letter of the law. Instead of resorting to courts or arbitration, governments and corporations in the post-Soviet space tended to use whatever coercion tools they had at their disposal, such as turning off the gas or shutting down borders, to achieve their goals (Michalopoulos, 2004). Trade was also hampered by slow customs procedures, regulations, and the challenges of implementing the rules of origin for imported and traded products (Michalopoulos, 2004, p. 267). On the other hand, by 2003, four CIS countries – Moldova, Georgia, Armenia and Kyrgyzstan – had become WTO members, and were therefore moving ahead with reducing their trade barriers. Therefore, despite all the rhetoric and all the efforts conducted by Russia to turn the CIS into a powerful economic bloc, EvrAzEs and the CIS remained anything but proper-functioning free trading arrangements (Netreba, 2006).

Towards a new customs union?

A significant turn point occurred in October 2007, when after much discussion, EvrAzES members agreed to establish a fully functioning CU in 2011. Initially only Russia, Belarus and Kazakhstan were expected join the CU, while Kyrgyzstan and Uzbekistan were required to link up later, as these countries were lagging behind in the preparations on the establishment of the necessary regulatory and legal frameworks. Tajikistan, although ahead in the standardisation of legislative acts, remained geographically isolated from the big three – Russia, Kazakhstan and Belarus – as it lacked a common frontier with these EvrAzES countries. It was therefore expected to join at a later date, together with Uzbekistan and Kyrgyzstan (Glanin and Dubnov, 2006). What proved unique about this new CU initiative was the fact that for the first time, members agreed to transfer some of their powers to a supranational body – a newly formed EvrAzES *Customs Union Commission* (CUC) – whose decisions would be binding and would be taken by a two-thirds majority vote (EvrAzES, 2007a; Dubnov, 2007b).[11] Furthermore, within the CUC, votes were allocated on the basis of the countries' levels of economic development and GDP. Russia's economy at the time was over ten times bigger than that of Kazakhstan, and over 25 times bigger than Belarus economy'. It was therefore allocated 57 per cent of the votes, while Kazakhstan and Belarus received only 21.5 per cent of the votes each.

There was a caveat, however, as the CUC was made responsible only for implementing decisions already taken by the signatory states (EvrAzES, 2007a). In other words, the CUC was supposed to act primarily as regulatory body and not as decision-making body, even though it could also provide recommendations on the operation of the CU (EvrAzES, 2007a; Kaveshnikov, 2011, p. 116). Furthermore, while the CUC-weighted system was designed in such a way as to prevent any decisions being imposed on Russia, Moscow could also not enforce decisions upon the other CU member states. If one of the parties, in this case either Belarus or Kazakhstan, was not satisfied with decisions taken by the CUC, it could still appeal to the CU's Supreme Body, the EvrAzES *Inter-state Council*. In that instance, decisions were taken by consensus, by all Heads of State (EvrAzES, 2007b). Moreover, it was agreed that decisions on 'sensitive' issues would be reached by consensus and would be stipulated in advance (EvrAzES, 2007b). Kazakhstan had favoured a one-vote-per-country system with decisions taken by simple majority, except on some predetermined 'sensitive' issues. Moscow, instead, had supported a weighed-voting system, although only on 'non-sensitive' issues, as this would have given it a greater say. Eventually, it was agreed that CUC decisions on 'sensitive' issues would be reached by consensus and would be stipulated in advance, while 'non-sensitive' issues would be decided by a two-thirds majority (EvrAzES, 2007b). Despite these caveats, the bases seemed to be set for the establishment of a proper-functioning CU, within the EvrAzES framework, between those countries most eager to tighten their economic relations.

Russian–Belarusian integration: the challenges of implementation

When Putin came to power, unification with Belarus received a renewed boost, and negotiations started to be conducted on a more serious and pragmatic basis. In December 1999, while Putin was still Prime Minister, President Yeltsin signed a new agreement with the Belarusian President Lukashenko – the *Treaty on the Creation of a Union State*, which followed on the 'Declaration on Further Unification of Russia and Belarus' signed in December 1998. The treaty envisaged the creation of a *Union State* between Russia and Belarus, moving beyond the *Union* established in the 1997 agreement. The new Union state would have common borders, joint citizenship, a single currency, and shared bodies of power and symbols of statehood. Both countries were expected to conduct a single trade and customs policy in relation to third countries, and gradually introduce a single currency, with a single emission centre. It was agreed that the Russian rouble would become the common monetary unit of the two countries on 1 January 2005, while in January 2008, the Russian rouble would be transformed into the *Union rouble* (Pismennaya, 2000). In the Autumn of 2000, Minsk and Moscow also decided that the Central Bank of Russia (CBR) would be the common emission centre between 2005 to 2008 (*Kommersant*, 2000). However, within the Union State, both countries retained their national sovereignty, independence and territorial integrity, and both Russia and Belarus remained subjects of international law. It therefore remained unclear how authority in the new state would be exercised. Moreover, the Union was based on the principle of sovereign equality between the two states, and the respect of the two countries' constitutions (Chubchenko, 1999).

The Union State treaty, however, did modify and enhance some of the powers of the existing bodies that had been set up under previous agreements, and also established more directly representative institutions. It set up a bicameral parliament consisting of an upper chamber or House of the Union and a lower chamber or House of Representatives (*Rossiiskaya gazeta*, 1999). The upper house was formed by an equal number of deputies delegated by the parliaments of each member state, while the lower house, was directly elected every four years by the citizens of the two member states. It contained 75 deputies from Russia and 28 from Belarus, reflecting the unequal size of the two countries' populations. The parliament was given enhanced powers, including the right to pass legislation on topics related to the Union State, which would become immediately valid. The Supreme Council was renamed *Supreme State Council*, and was also given additional powers, as its decisions were granted the status of decrees (*Rossiiskaya gazeta*, 1999). As in previous treaties, however, each country was given one vote, and member states retained the right to veto decisions. A Council of Ministers was set up as the new Union government responsible for proposing legislation, preparing the Union budget, and ensuring the fulfilment of the Union treaty. The treaty also envisaged the creation of a Supreme Court, to ensure 'the uniform interpretation and application of the treaty's stipulations' (Rontoyanni, 2000, p. 83).

Putin strongly supported this latest Union treaty, and as Prime Minister, he pushed for its quick ratification by the Russian parliament in December 1999. Yet, when addressing the members of the Federation Council, he also made it clear that the treaty would not entail the merger of Russia and Belarus into a new single state. Instead, he explained that the treaty would lead towards the establishment of a *Union* between both states, which would share common supranational bodies. He insisted that integration with Belarus would be pursued in a gradual and consistent fashion, but 'without imperialist ambitions' (Barakhova, 1999). Emphasis was therefore placed on the need to achieve economic integration first, before any other form of integration could go ahead. Putin, however, had no desire to rush integration through, as opposed to his Belarusian counterpart, Lukashenko, who was eager to achieve integration quickly in order to benefit from Russia's economic subsidies, such as cheap energy prices and preferential loans, to address Belarus' persistent economic difficulties. Putin instead, proved very cautious as noted in his comments at a meeting of the Supreme State Council in November 2000,

> We are moving along the process of granting power to the various bodies of the Union state, and that will require the surrender of some sovereignty. This is a very delicate process, [and thus] we need to look at the decisions we are making a hundred times, perhaps even a thousand times,' and added, 'but we should not drag them either.
>
> (*Kommersant*, 2000)

More importantly, Putin remained opposed to recreating 'something akin to the USSR', in which decisions could be imposed on Russia, and over which Russia would have no veto power. In his speech at the Bakulev Institute in June 2002, Putin made it very clear that integration should not come at the expense of Russia's economic interests, which was what, in his view, Belarus was trying to achieve (Volkhonsky and Sysoyev, 2002). Yet, in a sign of goodwill towards Belarus, Moscow agreed to sell gas to its western neighbour at the reduced price of $30/mcm in 1999–2001. In 2002, Gazprom lowered its gas prices to Belarus even further, down to $28/mcm – which equalled Russian prices in the Smolensk region (Bruce, 2005 p. 14; Andreyev, 2002b).[12] In return, Russia hoped to acquire a 50 per cent stake in *Beltransgaz*, the Belarusian state entity responsible for running the Northern Lights pipeline and for distributing gas inside Belarus, as stipulated in the 2002 gas agreement (Andreyev, 2002b). In August 2002, as progress towards integration stalled, Putin proposed to Lukashenko that Belarus unite with Russia in a single federal state, under a new federal Russian Constitution. Yet, such a union, according to Putin, had to be conducted on a voluntary basis and carried out only with the support of the Belarusian and Russian peoples, who were expected to approve the absorption of Belarus into Russia in a joint referendum. A second option was also put forward by Moscow – integration of both countries into a Union along EU lines, in which a common parliament would pass laws, which then, would have to be confirmed by national laws. Putin also proposed that the Russian rouble be introduced in Belarus, as a common monetary unit, a year earlier than planned, on 1 January 2004 (Plugataryov, 2002). The rationale behind such proposals was more pragmatic than ideological – it was driven not so much by a desire to restore the USSR in a new fashion, as by a willingness to develop proper-functioning unification projects, which would work effectively and benefit Russia. It was becoming increasingly clear that Lukashenko's suggestions of creating two sovereign states in one, was proving unfeasible (Latsis, 2002). As expected, Lukashenko stringently rejected the first option, and instead seemed more favourable to the creation of a Union State based on the same principles as those of the EU. At the same time, though, he called for the intact preservation of the existing Union treaty. Moreover, although Lukashenko supported the introduction of a single currency, based on the Russian rouble, he refused to hand over the emission rights of the National Bank of Belarus to the CBR, thus thwarting any effective integration efforts in the monetary sphere (Stroganov, 2002).

In view of these disagreements, proper unification between Russia and Belarus was not achieved. In a way, the very same obstacles that had hindered unification during the previous decade again prevented any progress towards further integration. The Belarusian and Russian economic systems remained significantly disparate, as Belarus kept a considerable part of its industry in state hands (Gulde *et al.*, 2004, p. 27). Belarus and Russia did not share similar tax regimes, analogous commercial laws, or common monetary policies (Zotov, 2000). Inflation remained high in Belarus despite the government's efforts in 2002–2003 to conduct a tighter monetary policy. In addition, as noted, Lukashenko remained categorically opposed to surrendering Belarus' right of currency emission entirely to the CBR, despite Russia's efforts to entice Belarus with cash (Andreyev, 2002a; Rublyova and Frumkin, 2003). Lukashenko proved happy to receive stabilisation tranches from Russia to back up the common currency, but opposed establishing a single money-emission centre and introducing stricter controls on inflation (Grigoryeva and Daneiko, 2003). Instead, he insisted on establishing an interbank currency council on a parity basis, which would become the common monetary-emission centre, in replacement of the

CBR. This common emission centre would have to remain independent, and be accountable only to the Union State's Supreme State Council (Smirnov, 2003). Such proposals proved unacceptable to Russia, whose leaders worried that the activities of an independent currency council could lead to the unchecked spiralling of inflation not only in Belarus, but also in Russia (Smirnov, 2003). The Belarusian authorities had grown accustomed to subsidising the economy through credit emissions. Moreover, disagreements remained over the price of Beltransgaz – in July 2003, Belarus upped the value of Beltransgaz to almost $5 billion (Kuznetsova and Grivach, 2004) – and over Belarus' wishes to keep a controlling block of shares in the new venture (Grigoryeva and Daneiko, 2003).

By the autumn of 2003, it was becoming increasingly clear that Belarus would introduce the Russian rouble only on the condition that Russia vastly subsidised the Belarusian state-led economy, by providing it with cheap energy and easy credits. In September 2003, Lukashenko asked that Russia meet Belarus' entire needs of oil, natural gas and electricity at Russian domestic prices (Kuznetsova et al., 2003). Furthermore, in October 2003, the Belarusian Prime Minister Sergei Sidorsky suggested that Russia provide over $2 billion in compensation for what he saw, would be 'the losses to the Belarusian economy which would result from the introduction of the Russian rouble' (Netreba, 2003). In December 2003, Belarus added the request that Russia redeem all Belarus' domestic bonds (Smirnov, 2003). All these demands were difficult for Russia to fulfil. Although the Russian leadership was willing to invest substantial efforts and money into monetary integration, it was not prepared to go ahead with the introduction of a single currency, unless the necessary economic measures were implemented by Belarus and unless Russia managed to retain full control over the single currency's emission centre. The Belarusian president instead, wanted to ensure that political integration came first, before both sides moved ahead with monetary integration. He was hoping to play a key political role in the new Union. This explains his insistence on introducing a Constitutional Act, which would have granted the Union State's governing bodies' greater powers than their national counterparts, such as raising taxes and establishing the Union budget. Furthermore, the new Constitution would have installed the post of Union president, a position Lukashenko so much coveted, but which the Russian leadership refused to agree to (Farizova and Kamyshev, 2003).[13] But by late 2003, the Kremlin had lost enthusiasm and patience, and instead proved more inclined to support a looser form of integration, an association along the lines of the early EU projects, rather than unification of the two countries on equal terms (Grivach and Dubnov, 2003). There was great frustration with Belarus' behaviour, which was seen as unprofessional and lacking in seriousness (Kuznetsova et al., 2003).

These obstacles were compounded by the very negative relationship that existed between the two leaders on a personal level. Putin very much disliked Lukashenko's constant lashing out against Russia, his criticism of Russia's limited advancement towards unification, as well as his tendency to blackmail Russia, by threatening to turn to the West and to NATO for help, if he did not get enough economic and political support from Russia. Russia's frustration with Belarus' behaviour was perhaps best exemplified by a comment provided by a Kremlin official who noted that

> in making preparations for a monetary union, dozens of Russian government officials, acting in good faith, have done everything in their power to prevent a collapse of the Belarusian economy, as a result of unification with the Russian economy, but they have become convinced of just one thing – for the Belarusian President, the topic of a Union makes sense only as political demagoguery.
>
> (Kuznetsova *et al.*, 2003)

It was clear that despite Minsk's efforts to pursue monetary and political integration with Russia, Belarus was not preparing seriously to make it happen. Russia, in turn, was not ready to sacrifice its economic and political sovereignty for the sake of a 'fraternal Union' with Belarus. More importantly, there is no evidence indicating that Russia exerted strong economic pressure on Belarus to push Lukashenko to agree to a monetary or political union with Russia, thus discarding any effective attempt by Moscow to restore a neo-empire in Belarus in the early 2000s.

Russian–Belarusian integration falters

Negotiations between the Russian and Belarusian governments on monetary unification continued during 2004, despite the various obstacles encountered, in the hope that an agreement could be reached that saw the introduction of the Russian rouble in Belarus on 1 January 2005. Yet, reaching agreement on a monetary union between Minsk and Moscow, did not prove to be an easy task, as Belarus continued to place high demands, which were very difficult for the Russian government to accept. Nevertheless, in early 2004, Moscow agreed to end customs controls along the Belarusian border, and to change the way VAT was collected on exports, with the exception of oil and gas (Bagrov, 2004). Furthermore, in February 2004, Russia also offered to grant Belarus a two billion-rouble credit, to facilitate the introduction of the Russian currency in Belarus. In return, Belarus was expected to end strict government regulation of its economy, and allow Russia to acquire stakes in key Belarusian enterprises identified for privatisation (Grigoyeva, 2005). But Belarus refused to accept several of these conditions and instead demanded gas prices equal to those in Russia's domestic market. Minsk continued to see the Belarus' currency union with Russia as an opportunity to obtain both subsidies from Russia to finance its budget deficit and lower Russian energy prices to ensure its economic system could still function profitably. Russia instead hoped to introduce the Russian rouble in Belarus on market terms, and at a reasonable cost. As no compromise solution could be found, in early April 2004, the introduction of the Russian rouble in Belarus was postponed once again (Vorobyov and Tomashevskaya, 2004).

Support for a union with Belarus started to dwindle in 2004, to a great extent because of the difficulties that were encountered as negotiations progressed. The situation was made worse by the emergence of significant disagreements over the price of Russia's gas for Belarus (Antonov, 2004). In December 2003, Putin had instructed Gazprom to increase gas prices to Belarus from $28–30/mcm to $50/mcm, frustrated over the difficulties that Russia was encountering when trying to acquire a 50 per cent stake in Beltransgaz. Furthermore, delays in gas payments prompted Gazprom several times to suspend its gas deliveries to Belarus – on 24 January 2004, and again on 12 and 18 February 2004 (Kuznetsova and Grivach, 2004; Ivzhenko and Mazayeva, 2004). A final agreement on Russian deliveries was eventually reached on 5 June 2004, which stipulated that Gazprom would supply gas to Belarus during the second half of 2004 at the price of $46.68/mcm (Stern, 2005, p. 100). While this new fare was higher than the price Belarus was paying for at the time ($28–30/mcm), Russia was nevertheless heavily subsidising the Belarusian economy (Butrin, 2004). Energy prices in Europe were hovering at $100/mcm – Belarus was therefore receiving a major subvention even if one takes into account the fact that Gazprom was paying low fees for the transit of its gas through Belarus (Mitrova *et al.*, 2009, p. 396). As part of this price agreement Belarus agreed once again to sell half of its shares in Beltransgaz to Gazprom (Butrin, 2004). Russia, in turn, committed itself to meeting all of Belarus' gas supply needs for 2005 either through Gazprom or through Russian independent suppliers (*Interfax*, 2004).[14]

In late 2004, the Kremlin's approach to Belarus became a lot more lenient, in view of developments in neighbouring Ukraine, where an 'Orange Revolution' had replaced the Kremlin's preferred candidate Viktor Yanukovych with a staunchly pro-Western figure, Viktor Yushchenko. Despite the existing differences, ever since Lukashenko had come to power, Belarus had remained a staunch and valuable strategic ally of Russia on its western fringes. Putin therefore, wanted to make sure that Lukashenko was not topped in a 'coloured revolution' and replaced by a pro-Western government in the 2006 presidential elections. In December 2004, Gazprom therefore agreed to supply Belarus with almost double the amount of gas in 2005 than it had previously delivered, and at the unchanged price of $46.68/mcm (Shakhinoglu *et al.*, 2005). These prices were the lowest that Russia was charging to any CIS state at the time, and they were only $6/mcm higher than the average rate in Russia (Naumova and Grivach, 2006). At the time, Russia was increasing prices to all its other CIS customers, as European prices were reaching $140/mcm in 2005 and approached $192/mcm in 2006 (Mitrova *et al.* 2009, p. 395). Yet, Russia was also making it clear that these gas prices were tied to the joint ownership of Beltranzsgas and of Beltopgaz – the supplier of natural gas to Belarusian domestic customers (Naumova and Grivach, 2006). Furthermore, in an additional sign of support for Lukashenko, full agreement was reached on a draft Constitutional Act for the *Union State* in October 2005, to be approved by a referendum in the spring of 2006 (Mazayeva and Panfilova, 2005). Moreover, in December, Belarus was extended a Russian sovereign credit of $175 million, at relatively good terms, to help pay for the purchases of Russian gas (Interfax Business Report, 2004).

Russia's benevolent policies towards Belarus changed in the spring of 2006, once Lukashenko succeeded in winning a third Presidential term in March 2006, despite clear indications of vote rigging on his side (Panyushkin, 2006). With the risk of a 'coloured revolution' in Belarus fading, Putin proved less inclined to make additional concessions to Minsk, unless Lukashenko granted Russia a significant stake in Beltransgaz and, ideally, agreed to implement political and monetary union with Russia, on Moscow's terms (Khodasevich, 2006). This meant that Russia remained fully in charge of monetary policy and partially in control of Belarus' state institutions. As Lukashenko refused, in April 2006 Moscow threatened Minsk with a fivefold increase in gas prices in 2007, from $46.68/mcm to $230/mcm, reflecting European fares (Grib, 2006). By then, a clear link had been established between Russian gas prices to Belarus, the acquisition of Beltransgaz by Gazprom, and the introduction of the Russian rouble in Belarus. Belarus had been allowed to pay much lower gas prices than Ukraine on the expectation that once Belarus introduced the Russian rouble as its currency the positive economic effects of such measures would have been felt (Grib, 2006). However, Belarus continued to insist that only once a single economic and customs space was fully established with Russia would the Russian rouble be introduced in Belarus, and not the other way around, as Russia had wished. At the same time, Minsk was also demanding huge financial compensation for monetary integration (Grivach, 2006).

In view of Lukashenko's inflexibility, the Russian leadership decided at the end of 2006 to bring Russian subsidies to an end, and to start putting relations with Belarus on a market footing (Dubnov *et al.*, 2006). In December 2006, Moscow imposed export duties on Russian oil deliveries to Belarus, the same export duties levied on Russia's oil exports to non-CU CIS countries (Bekker and Ivanitskayay, 2007).[15] This was intended, it was argued, to close the 'Belarusian offshore oil zone' that had come about under the 1995 Russian–Belarusian agreement, which had eliminated customs borders between the two countries (Netreba and Dovnar, 2006).[16] Furthermore, in November 2006, Gazprom once again started talking about significantly raising its gas price to Belarus in 2007, from $46/mcm to $200/mcm, partly in response to the big price differential that existed between Belarusian and European netback gas prices, as the latter reached $210/mcm on average in 2006 (Zygar and Grib, 2006). The change in policy also reflected Russia's frustrations over the failure to acquire control over Beltransgaz at a reasonable price – Belarus continued to demand that Russia pay $2.5 billion for the company (Dubnov *et al.*, 2006). In response to these threats, the Belarusian leader started to demand rent payments for the land located under the pipelines transiting through Belarus. He also threatened to seek closer relations with the West, and with the EU in particular, while forsaking Belarus' closer union with Russia (Tomashevskaya *et al.*, 2007). Lukashenko also launched virulent verbal attacks against Russia and its leadership, accusing Moscow of neo-imperialism, while vowing to present Russia with his own $5 billion bill for 'transit, military cooperation, Kaliningrad, a 1,500-kilometer customs frontier and the defence of our borders' (Tomashevskaya *et al.*, 2007).

A five-year contract was finally signed between Gazprom and Beltransgaz in late December 2006, which foresaw the delivery of 21.2 Bcm of gas for a five-year period, at a price of $100/mcm in 2007. This price was higher than what Belarus had expected but it was still half of the original price that Russia had been asking for (Ritchie, 2007). Starting in 2008, however, prices were expected to rise gradually, until they reached Gazprom's European gas fares in 2011 (Yafimava, 2009, p. 157).[17] In exchange for these concessions, Belarus finally agreed to sell half of Beltransgaz to Gazprom (although at the highly overvalued price of $2.5 billion) and waived its special right to exercise control over the company (Ritchie, 2007). The Beltransgaz contract represented a victory for Gazprom as the Russian conglomerate finally managed to gain access to the coveted Belarusian gas transportation and distribution networks. Also, a gradual increase in wholesale gas prices to end users in Belarus in 2008–2010 was envisaged, adding to the benefits accrued (Yafimava, 2009, p. 158; Gazprom, 2007). As a result of this deal, Belarus, lost exclusive control over its transit network, and more importantly, it faced the risk of losing its entire leverage over Russia in terms of gas transit, as in 2005, construction on the North Stream pipeline connecting Russian Siberian fields directly to Greifswald in Germany was started. Furthermore, in 2007, plans went ahead on the construction of a new *South Stream* gas pipeline (Yafimava, 2009, p. 159). This line was expected to carry Russian gas to south-eastern and central Europe across the Black Sea floor, bypassing Ukraine, thus lessening Russia's dependence on Ukraine, and also Belarus, as transit countries (Gridneva, 2007).

Overall trade relations between Russia and Belarus were also slowly placed on a market footing. In March 2007, an agreement was signed between the two countries on *Measures to Promote Trade and Economic Co-operation*, which essentially put an end to many of the existing obstacles to bilateral trade and investment that had existed between the two countries (Gorelov *et al.*, 2007).[18] The agreement was part of an effort to liberalise trade and establish a genuine single economic space between Russia and Belarus. To a great extent, these deals reflected Russia's ability to enforce changes in the Belarusian economy to its own advantage, as they granted Russian goods and investment full access to the Belarusian market. Theoretically, Belarus could also benefit from full access to the vast Russian market as a result of this agreement. At the time, Belarus held a positive trade balance with Russia on several key products, such as machinery, equipment, textiles, and food products (Romanchuk, 2007). Yet, the Belarusian economy, which was primarily state-led, and heavily reliant on Russian subsidies, lost its competitiveness once Russian support was progressively withdrawn (Romanchuk, 2007). Several sectors of the Belarusian economy therefore suffered greatly in the face of strong competition from Russian products (Romanchuk, 2007). In fact, Belarus witnessed a sharp deterioration of its trade balance with Russia after the agreements entered into force. The negative trade balance increased from $390 million in 2006 to $2 billion in the first half of 2007 (Netreba, 2007). This, however, cannot be entirely blamed on Russia, as Belarus' inability to withstand Russia's competition, very much reflected the weaknesses of the Belarusian economy and its state-led management model (Romanchuk, 2007). In December 2007, Russia decided to extend a $1.5 billion stabilisation loan to Belarus to help it cope with the losses, and to sustain bilateral trade (Dubnov, 2007b). It was also agreed that the price Belarus would pay for Russian gas for the first quarter of 2008, would be $119/mcm – this was higher than the previous price, but still a fraction of European prices (which averaged $327/mcm in 2008), and an indication that Russia was still ready partially to subsidise the Belarusian economy (Dubnov, 2007b). Russia hoped, in exchange, to acquire a stake in the future privatisation of Belarusian enterprises, primarily in the energy sector (oil refineries and petrochemical plants), but Lukashenko proved reluctant to acquiesce.

Assessment and concluding thoughts

The first two terms of Putin at the Russian Presidency witnessed a renewed, and in many ways, a much more successful attempt by Moscow to deepen economic integration with a selected group of CIS states, within the EvrAzES framework. Launched by the Kremlin, the EvrAzES project was intended to create an economic union which would permit Russia to expand its export markets and sell its goods unhindered within the Eurasian Community, while also shield its industry from tougher external competition. More importantly, the new Russian leadership proved eager to re-establish the economic ties that had once existed during the Soviet era, under a different, and more efficient, market footing, which would, however, also benefit the Russian economy. Interestingly, within this new EvrAzES organisation, Russia, proved ready to transfer some of its sovereign powers to an inter-state institution, the *Integration Committee*, in order to build a more efficient organisation, although it was clear that Russia retained a predominant role. However, the IC was endowed primarily with an implementing role. Decision-making prerogatives still remained at the level of the ISC, where Russia, like other members, could exert its veto, thus weakening the supranational nature of the institution. Moreover, decisions taken by the IC were not always enacted in practice, and as a result, the organisation remained imperfect. More importantly, Russia retained a predominant voice within the organisation, as reflected by its ability to impose its own CET over the other members, in order to protect its industry from external competition. In this respect, therefore, it can be argued that Russia succeeded in establishing an economic organisation, fashioned very much to its liking, by exercising its hegemonic power within the CIS/EvrAzES space.

Russia was, nevertheless, not alone in favouring closer economic ties with its neighbours, as other CIS states also saw advantages in collaborating with Russia. Kazakhstan's leader Nursultan Nazarbayev, in particular, had been a keen promoter of deeper economic integration within the former Soviet space. In the mid-1990s, he had proposed his own Eurasian integration project, conscious of the risks that economic disintegration posed to his land-locked country, and aware of the benefits that close economic ties could bring to his country's development. He therefore supported the Kremlin's new integration initiatives, as did his Belarusian counterpart, Aleksandr Lukashenko. Yet, Minsk hoped, above all, to guarantee for itself the systematic provision of cheap credits and subsidised energy resources from Russia as a result of its participation in the project. The EvrAzES initiative, therefore, cannot be seen entirely as neo-imperial project in the strictest sense of the word. Its member states voluntarily agreed to join the organisation, although it was clear that Russia carried the strongest economic weight within its institutions. Yet, as the decade progressed, Russia increasingly saw the Eurasian integration project as an instrument of Russian hegemony and influence in the CIS space. Both EvrAzES and the SES, which included Ukraine, were seen as projects which could help Russia restore its greatness in the former Soviet space, bring back to a certain degree, its 'informal empire' in the ex-USSR, and help Russia project its power both regionally and globally.

Nevertheless, a variety of legitimate factors also argued in favour of regional economic cooperation – above all, the boosting CIS bilateral and multilateral trade – and this explains why the EvrAzES and the SES received support from all other member states, besides Russia. A vast Eurasian market involving over 230 million consumers could potentially be created within the SES, giving a great boost to economic growth. Furthermore, the SES could also ensure the proper-functioning of the various internal oil and gas transport networks that existed within the space, to the advantage of all its members. Such a predicament proved particularly important for Kazakhstan, whose leaders hoped that by joining the SES, the transit fees for Kazakh oil and freight crossing Russian territory would be significantly reduced (Frumkin, 2004). Russia, and to a lesser extent Belarus, in turn, hoped that membership of the EvrAzES' CU would help their respective countries boost their exports within the common customs zone, while at the same time protect the weaker sectors of their economies from external competition. Ukraine, instead, while seeing great benefits in establishing a FTA with its closest CIS neighbours, rejected any further attempts at deepening economic integration with its SES partners, if these efforts hindered its EU membership plans, and if they entailed surrendering sovereignty to a supranational entity (Stepanenko, 2004a; Frumkin, 2004). EU membership remained Ukraine's top economic priority, especially after the Orange coalition came to power in late 2004, and this precluded the possibility of Ukraine ever joining the SES' CU, as no country could be a member of two CU simultaneously. It also explains why the project was abandoned in 2006, as Kiev continued to push for EU association even under Prime Minister Viktor Yanukovych.

When in it became clear that the SES project would not soon materialise, Russia moved ahead with establishing a properly functioning CU within the EvrAzES framework. The 2000s had shown that the basis for closer economic cooperation within EvrAzES remained strong – absolute trade inside the bloc increased quite significantly during the 2000s, even though Russia and Kazakhstan continued to diversify their trade away from the bloc. Close economic ties existed between Russia and Belarus, and these could be developed further within the CU/SES, while the potential of Russia's economic expansion into Kazakhstan remained high. Yet, both within EvrAzES and within the CIS as a whole, full trade liberalisation progressed only slowly during the 2000s. Russia, in particular, imposed restrictive quotas on certain imported products, it limited the access of Kazakhstan's oil and gas through its territory, and it utilised trade bans as instruments of policy, whenever it considered it necessary. Belarus, in turn, restricted the access of fish imports from Russia and imposed fees on Russian trucks and buses transiting through its territory. More importantly, the pace of economic reform remained quite unequal inside the bloc and this hindered further economic coordination. While Russia moved ahead with deeper structural reforms in the early 2000s, it reversed many of these advances in the mid-2000s by re-nationalising key sectors of Russian industry. Kazakhstan, in turn, made uneven progress in its path towards further economic reform and continued to rely primarily on its energy resources to sustain growth, while Belarus kept most of its economy unreformed. This clearly indicated that the economic transformations necessary for the establishment of a proper-functioning economic bloc were still not present. More importantly, it showed that while Russia proved eager to create a strong trading bloc, it wished to establish an economic organisation that reflected its own interests. While theoretically ready to hand over some power to an inter-governmental structure, Moscow remained keen to retain its freedom of action, in order behave in an un-restricted fashion whenever it deemed necessary. Furthermore, on several occasions, Russia pursued its own goals in the former Soviet space through coercive economic methods, or *hard power*, such as economic sanctions, embargoes, restrictions and quotas, in a clear display of its hegemonic power.

On the other hand, unification with Belarus received a significant boost when Putin first reached the Presidency in 2000. Joint projects on establishing an economic union between the two countries – with single trade and customs policies, and a common currency – were agreed. More importantly, the bases were set for the creation of a political Union State between Russia and Belarus, which would see representative institutions, and potentially supranational organs of power, being established. However, during the first years of his Presidency, President Putin remained cautious about the creation of supranational bodies which could limit Russia's independency in decision-making. The Kremlin made sure that Russia's economic and political interests were not jeopardised in any future union state, and that the financial costs of such a Union did not exceed its benefits. This explains why Moscow insisted that economic integration had to be pursued first, before institutional integration could move ahead. Russia also made it clear that monetary integration could not be pursued if Moscow lost control over monetary policy and if the financial costs became too high. While Russia's actions may be interpreted as following a neo-imperialist logic, they actually reflected legitimate state concerns. Russia's actions made perfect economic sense, as the risks of keeping two independent monetary centres within a single currency were too high to take – the experiences of sharing a common rouble with other CIS states in the 1990s had produced a devasting effect on the Russian economy, resulting in high levels of inflation, if not hyperinflation.

Belarusian President Lukashenko, instead, proved eager to achieve political unification first, before economic integration would move ahead, as this would ensure Belarus' influence over a future Union state. It would also guarantee the provision of Russian subsidises to the benefit of the Belarusian economy. When discussing monetary integration, Lukashenko rejected any form of submission of the Belarusian Central Bank to a Russian monetary institution. Instead, the Belarusian leader proved ready to move ahead with monetary integration only if Russia committed itself significantly to subsidise the Belarusian economy with cheap credits and low energy prices. This, however, remained unacceptable to the Kremlin, for perfectly understandable economic reasons, and showed that Putin had not fully embraced a neo-imperialist project vis-à-vis Belarus. Yet, Russia's behaviour towards Belarus changed as the decade progressed. As movement towards economic integration stalled, and the Kremlin's frustrations grew, Russia increasingly used economic pressure – in the form of increased energy prices – to draw Belarus into a Union with Russia, in order to access markets and strengthen its own geo-strategic position in Europe. Russia behaved quite assertively, utilising energy as a '*hard* power' instrument to reach its objectives, and thus, its policies increasingly acquired a neo-imperialist tone. At the same time, though, Russia remained aware that it could not allow the Belarusian economy fully to implode – the economic, political and human ties that existed between the two countries remained very strong, and Belarus had become a key military-strategic ally on Russia's western borders. This explains why, despite the costs involved, Russia continued partly to subsidise the Belarusian economy and its regime by continuing to provide cheap energy and credits.

Notes

1 There was no reference to capital or services.
2 Belarus had already agreed many of its CET with Russia.
3 The new organisation was to be headquartered in Kiev.
4 Kuchma only agreed to sign the SES initiative, after Russia agreed first to implement a FTA, and only after overcoming strong internal opposition (Bukkvoll, 2004, p. 13).
5 Liberal pro-Western politicians, such as Lilia Shevtsova (2003), instead worried that such a union would replace Russia's EU integration to the detriment of Russia.
6 To compensate for the loss in revenues Moscow began raising energy prices (Netreba, 2004a).
7 WTO coordination was urged by Prime Minster Mikhail Fradkov – and supported by Kazakh President Nazarbayev. Russian Trade Minister German Gref, instead, supported achieving WTO membership first (Netreba, 2004b).
8 Oil prices increased from $11.91/barrel in 1998 to $27.69/barrel in 2003.
9 EvrAzES accounted for up to 80 per cent of all foreign trade transactions in the CIS space (Kuzmin, 2006).
10 Belarusian customs officers also regularly confiscated Russian goods in transit to Europe (Vorobyov, 2004).
11 The CUC was expected to start functioning only once the CU had become operational.
12 In exchange, Moscow paid very low gas transit fees through Belarus, three times less than what it paid to Ukraine and Moldova. However, Russia still heavily subsidised the Belarusian economy with its lower energy prices and easy credits.
13 Instead it was agreed that the head of the Union State would be the Supreme State Council (Farizova and Kamyshev, 2003).

14 Putin also agreed to allow Belarusian gas companies to work in the Russian oil and gas sector on the same condition as Russian ones.
15 Belarus retaliated by imposing duties for the transit of oil through Belarus to Europe.
16 In response, Lukashenko decided to siphon oil from the pipeline transiting Belarus to Europe, prompting Moscow to cut off supplies to the pipeline, affecting not only Belarus but also Russia's European customers (Shevtsova, 2007, p. 193).
17 Gazprom, in turn, agreed to increase transit payments to Belarus from 0.75/mcm/100 km to $1.45/mcm/100 km.
18 The deal also opened the Russian market to Belarusian goods as import duties were removed.

Bibliography

Andreyev, Yu. (2002a). *Vremya novostei*, 14 February, p. 5.
Andreyev, Yu. (2002b). *Vremya novostei*, 15 April, p. 3.
Antonov, V. (2004). *Noviye Izvestia*, April 7, pp. 1, 4.
Aslund, A. (2009). *How Ukraine Became a Market Economy and Democracy*. Washington DC: Peterson Institute for International Economics.
Bagrov, A. (2004). *Kommersant*, 11 February, pp. 1–2.
Barakhova, A. (1999). *Kommersant*, 23 December, p. 2.
Bekker, A. and N. Ivanitskaya (2007). *Vedomosti*, 15 January, p. 3.
Bruce, Ch. (2005). *Fraternal Friction or Fraternal Fiction? The Gas Factor in Russian-Belarusian Relations*, Oxford Institute for Energy Studies, March. Available at: www.oxfordenergy.org/wpcms/wp-content/uploads/2010/11/NG8-FraternalFrictionOrFraternalfictionTheGasFactorInRussianBelarusianRelations-ChloeBruce-2005.pdf [accessed 22 June 2018].
Bukkvoll, T. (2004). Private Interests, Public Policy: Ukraine and the Common Economic Space Agreement. *Problems of Post-Communism*, 51 (4), pp. 11–22.
Butrin, D. (2004). *Kommersant*, 9 June, p. 13.
Bryl, R. (2006). After Gas Dispute Ukraine, Russia Start Trade War. Long Live WTO? *IntelliNews – Ukraine This Week*. 6 February. In: A. Szeptycki, *Trade Relations between the Russian Federation and Ukraine*, PISM Research Papers. 8. January 2008. The Polish Institute of International Affairs, p. 40.
Cooper, J. (2009). Russia's Trade Relations within the Commonwealth of Independent States. In: E.W. Rowe and S. Torjesen, *The Multilateral Dimension in Russian Foreign Policy*. Abingdon, Oxon: Routledge, pp. 163–180.
Chubchenko, Yu. (1999). *Kommersant*, 9 December, p. 1.
Dubnov, A. (2000). *Vremya novostei*, 10 October, p. 1.
Dubnov, A. (2001). *Vremya novostei*, 1 June 2001, p. 3.
Dubnov, A. (2006). *Vremya novostei*, 13 January, p. 2.
Dubnov, A. (2007a). *Vremya novostei*, 8 October, p. 1.
Dubnov, A. (2007b). *Vremya novostei*, 17 December, p. 1.
Dubnov, A., A. Grivach and O. Tomashevskaya (2006). *Vremya novostei*, 18 December, p. 1.
EvrAzES (1999). Treaty on a Customs Union and a Common Economic Space, 26 February. Available at: http://evrazes.com/docs/view/128 [accessed 30 June 2018].
EvrAzES (2000a). Soglashenie ob Obshchem tamozhennom tarife gosudarstv-uchasnikov tamozhennogo soiuza. 17 February. Available at: www.lawmix.ru/abrolaw/8518 [accessed 30 June 2018].

EvrAzES (2000b). Dogovor ob uchrezhdenii Evraziiskogo ekonomicheskogo soobshchestva. 10 October. Available at: http://evrazes.com/docs/view/3 [accessed 30 June 2018].
EvrAzES (2003). Agreement on the Establishment of a Common Economic Zone. 19 September. Available at: https://wits.worldbank.org/GPTAD/PDF/archive/Common_Economic_Zone.pdf [accessed 12 September 2019].
EvrAzES (2007a). Dogovor o Komissii tamozhennogo soiuza ot 6 oktyabrya 2007 goda. 6 October. Available at: http://evrazes.com/docs/view/74 [accessed 30 June 2018].
EvrAzES (2007b). Doklad o formirovanii pravovoi bazy tamozhennogo soiuza. 6 October. Available at: http://evrazes.com/docs/view/71 [accessed 30 June 2018].
EvrAzES (2010). *Evraziiskoe Ekonomicheskoe Soobshchestvo. Spravochnik*, Sekretariat Integratsionnogo Komiteta EES, Moscow, pp. 36–38.
Farizova, S. and D. Kamyshev (2003). *Kommersant*, 1 April, p. 2.
Freinkman, L., E. Polyakov and C. Revenco (2004). *Trade Performance and Regional Integration of the CIS Countries*. Washington DC: IBRD/World Bank.
Frumkin, K. (2004). *Russky kuryer*, 25 May, p. 6.
Gazprom (2007). Gazprom and Republic of Belarus Sign Purchase and Sale Agreement for Beltransgaz Shares. 18 May. Available at www.gazprom.com/press/news/2007/may/article63814/ [accessed on 28 June 2018].
Glanin, I. and I. Dubnov (2006). *Vremya novostei*, 17 August, p. 1.
Grib, N. (2006). *Kommersant*, 29 April, p. 2.
Gridneva, N. (2007). *Izvestiya*, 22 May, p. 8.
Grigoyeva, Ye. (2005). *Izvestiya*, 5 April, p. 1.
Gordiyenko, A. (2005). *Nezavisimaya gazeta*, 10 October, p. 2.
Gorelov N., A. Gorshkova and O. Tomashevskaya, O. (2007). *Vremya novostei*, 11 January, pp. 1–2.
Grigoryeva, Ye. (2003). *Izvestiya*, 20 September.
Grigoryeva, Ye. and Daneiko, Ye. (2003). *Izvestiya*, 21 January, p. 2.
Grivach, A. (2006). *Vremya novostei*, 4 May, p. 7.
Grivach, A. and Dubnov, A. (2003). *Vremya novostei*, 15 October, p. 1.
Gulde, A-M., E. Jafarov, and V. Prokopenko (2004). *A Common Currency for Belarus and Russia?*, IMF Working Paper, WP/04/228, December, Washington DC: International Monetary Fund.
Interfax (2004). 23 August.
Interfax Business Report (2004). 31 December.
Ivzhenko, T. and O. Mazayeva (2004). *Nezavisimaya gazeta*, 28 January, p. 5.
Kasayev, A. (2001). *Nezavisimaya gazeta*, 7 February, p. 5.
Kaveshnikov, N. (2011). Developing the Institutional Structure of the Eurasian Economic Community, In: *EBD Eurasian Integration Yearbook*. Chapter 6, pp. 106–123.
Khodasevich, A. (2006). Lukashenko Demands Equal Conditions. *Nezavisimaya gazeta*, 19 April, p. 5.
Kolesnikov, A. (2005). Vladimir Putin Gets Organization as A Gift. *Kommersant*, 7 October, p. 1.
Kommersant (2000). It's A Very Delicate Process, 1 December, p. 1.
Kuzmin, V. (2006). *Rossiiskaya gazeta*, 24 June, p. 1.
Kuznetsova V. and A. Grivach (2004). *Vremya novostei*, 19 January, p. 2.
Kuznetsova, V., N. Viktorova and A. Grivach (2003). *Vremya novostei*, 8 September, p. 1.
Lashkina, Ye. (2004). *Rossiiskaya gazeta*, 19 June, p. 1.
Latsis, O. (2002). *Noviye Izvestiya*, 16 August, p. 1.
Malashenko, A. (2000). *Moskovskie novosti*, 5–11 September, p. 5.

Makarkin, A. (2006). *Nezavisimaya gazeta*, 21 November, p. 3.
Masterov, V. (2005). *Vremya novostei*, 13 April 2005, p. 5.
Mazayeva, O. and V. Panfilova (2005). *Nezavisamaya gazeta*, 24 October, p. 3.
Michalopoulos, C. (2004). The Integration of Low Income CIS-7 into the World Trading System. In: C.R. Shiells and S. Sattar, eds. *The Low Income Countries of the Commonwealth of Independent States: Progress and Challenges in Transition.* Washington DC: IMF/World Bank.
Mitrova, T., S. Pirani and J. Stern (2009). Russia, the CIS and Europe: Gas Trade and Transit. In: S. Pirani, ed., *Russian and CIS Gas Markets and their Impact on Europe.* Oxford: Oxford University Press, Oxford Institute of Energy Studies, pp. 395–441.
Naumov, I. (2008). *Nezavisimaya gazeta*, 29 April, p. 5.
Naumova A. and A. Grivach (2006). *Vremya novostei*, 31 March, p. 1.
Nazarbaev, N. (1996). V poiske novoi integratsii. In: *Pyat' let nezavisimosti*, Almaty: Ilim., pp. 233–242.
Netreba, P. (2003). *Kommersant*, 2 October, p. 1.
Netreba, P. (2004a). *Kommersant*, 19 August, p. 1.
Netreba, P. (2004b). *Kommersant*, 22 September, p. 2.
Netreba, P. (2006). *Kommersant*, 20 May, p. 2.
Netreba, P. (2007). *Kommersant*, 2 July, p. 2.
Netreba P. and V. Dovnar (2006). *Kommersant*, 13 December, p. 1.
Nikonov, V. (2004). *Trud*, 22 May, p. 2.
Panyushkin, V. (2006). *Kommersant*, 21 March, 2006, p. 1.
Pismennaya, Ye. (2000). *Vremya MN*, 31 August, p. 3.
Plugataryov, I. (2002). *Nezavisimaya gazeta*, 15 August, p. 1.
Ritchie, M. (2007). Russia-Belarus Deal Averts Gas Crisis. 2 January. In: *European Spot Gas Markets*, London. 3 January.
Romanchuk, Ya. (2007). *Nezavisimaya gazeta*, 17 September, p. 3.
Rontoyanni, C. (2000). *Russia-Belarus Union: The Role of NATO and the EU*, Conflict Studies Research Centre, December.
Rossiiskaya gazeta (1999). 8 December, p. 1.
Rublyova T. and K. Frumkin, K. (2003). *Nezavisimaya gazeta*, 29 August, p. 1.
Shadikhodjaev, S. (2009). Trade Integration in the CIS Region: A Thorny Path Towards a Customs Union, *Journal of International Economic Law*, 12 (3), 555–578.
Shakhinoglu, E., O. Mazayeva and A. Skornyakova (2005). *Nezavisimaya gazeta*, 13 January, pp. 1 and 3.
Shevtsova, L. (2003). *Noviye Izvestiya*, 10 September, p. 1.
Shevtsova, L. (2007). *Russia: Lost in Transition.* Washington DC: Carnegie Endowment for International Peace.
Smirnov, K. (2003). *Kommersant*, 3 December, p. 2.
Solovyov, V. and M. Zygar (2006). *Kommersant*, 4 August, p. 1.
Stepanenko, S. (2004a). *Vremya novostei*, 21 April, p. 1.
Stepanenko, S. (2004b). *Vremya novostei*. 23 December, p. 2.
Stepanenko, S. (2005). *Vremya novostei*, 14 January, p. 5.
Stern, J.P. (2005), *The Future of Russian Gas and Gazprom*, Oxford: Oxford Institute for Energy Studies.
Stroganov, Y. (2002). *Trud*, 16 August, p. 1.
The Kremlin (2003). Soglashenie o formirovanii Edinogo ekonomicheskogo prostranstva. 19 September. Available at: www.kremlin.ru/supplement/1715 [accessed 10 September 2018].

Tomashevskaya, O., A. Naumova and I. Gordeyev (2007). *Vremya novostei*, 15 January, pp. 1–2.

Torjeson, S. (2009). Russia, the CIS and the EEC: Finally getting it right? In: E.W. Rowe and S. Torjesen, *The Multilateral Dimension in Russian Foreign Policy*. Abingdon, Oxon: Routledge, pp. 153–162.

Tumbarello, P. (2005). *Regional Trade Integration and WTO Accession: Which Is the Right Sequencing? An Application to the CIS*, IMF Working Paper, WP/05/94, Washington DC: International Monetary Fund, May, p. 9. Available at www.imf.org/external/pubs/ft/wp/2005/wp0594.pdf [accessed 8 September 2018].

Vasilyeva, V. (2003). *Nezavisimaya gazeta*, 28 February, p. 5.

Volkhonsky, B. and G. Sysoyev (2002). *Kommersant*, 14 June, p. 1.

Vorobyov, M. (2004). *Vremya novostei*, 22 December, p. 4.

Vorobyov, M. (2007). *Vremya novostei*, 26 March, p. 7.

Vorobyov, M. and O. Tomashevskaya (2004). *Vremya novostei*, 1 April, p. 2.

Yafimava, K. (2009). Belarus: The Domestic Gas Market and Relations with Russia. In: S. Pirani, ed. *Russian and CIS Gas Markets and their Impact on Europe*. Oxford: Oxford University Press, pp. 133–169.

Yusin, M. (2006). *Izvestiya*, 8 August, p. 2.

Zotov, V. (2000). *Vremya MN*, 5 September, p. 5.

Zygar, M., V. Solovyov, N. Asadova and N. Grib (2005). *Kommersant*, 16 December, p. 1.

Zygar, M. and N. Grib (2006). *Kommersant*, 30 September, p. 1.

8 Vladimir Putin strengthens CIS military integration

A new military bloc emerges

When Putin became President of Russia in the year 2000, he gave top priority to the enhancement of military cooperation within the framework of the Collective Security Treaty (CST). On 7 August 1999, a group of about a hundred Chechen and Arab Islamist-*Jihadist* insurgents had conducted a military incursion into the neighbouring Russian republic of Dagestan and had declared an 'Islamic State' (Chernyak and Raskin, 1999). Almost simultaneously, in late July 1999 a group of IMU (Islamic Movement of Uzbekistan) fighters had penetrated the Batken region of Kyrgyzstan, from their bases in Tajikistan, and had captured several villages and taken citizens hostage. These events created great anxiety in Russia and very much shaped the Kremlin's threat perceptions, as reflected in the new *Military Doctrine*, adopted in April 2000, which expressed great concern over 'the strengthening of national, ethnic, and religious extremism', inside and around Russia, and 'the spread of local wars and armed conflicts', in the vicinity of its territory (ACA, 2000). More specifically, the doctrine raised attention to the threat posed by the training and equipping of armed formations in other states 'with the view of transferring them for operations on the territory of the Russian Federation and its allies' (ACA, 2000). In order to address these pressing threats to Russian and regional security, strengthening the CIS/CST collective security system, and enhancing bilateral and multilateral military ties with its CIS/CST allies became essential (MID, 2000).[1] For Putin, CIS military integration, constituted 'one of the most important strategic tasks as far as achieving military security for the Russian Federation [was] concerned', as he noted in January 2000 immediately after he assumed the acting presidency (Spildsboel-Hansen, 2000, p. 92).

Military integration moves ahead

At the May 2000 Minsk CST summit, the first steps were taken to transform the CST alliance into a properly functioning military-security organisation. Member states committed themselves to conducting regular consultations and exchanging information on regional security issues (ODKB, 2000a). More importantly, they agreed to allow for the joint use of CST forces and equipment in the event of direct threats to regional security, and to permit the deployment of CST troops on the territories of other CST states (Dubnov, 2000). These last provisions proved crucial, as they authorised Moscow to deploy its military forces and establish military bases on the territory of CIS/CST states, in order to enhance its own security and gain strategic depth (MID, 2000). At the summit, CST states also decided to start working towards the formation of Rapid Deployment Collective Peace-making Forces or *Kollektivnye Mirotvorcheskie Sily Bystrogo Razvertyvaniya* intended to address these newly emerging terrorist and insurgency threats (ODKB, 2000a). Russia and its CST allies also agreed to develop privileged relations in the field of military-technical cooperation, which in effect meant the sale of Russian military equipment to CST states at reduced prices. This helped to enhance the military capabilities of CST states and also ensured that CST states would use standardised equipment in combat operations. In a further attempt to enhance military inter-operability, for the first time a series of massive joint military exercises involving large numbers of troops (10,000) from Russia, Kyrgyzstan, Kazakhstan, Tajikistan and Uzbekistan – *CIS Southern Shield 1999* and *CIS Southern Shield 2000* – were held under Russian command in the Central Asian region, in October 1999 and March 2000 (Mashin, 2000).[2]

These initial attempts at enhancing CST cooperation set the basis for the establishment of a more effective Russian-led military-security organisation. However, they proved insufficient to deter and properly repulse a second raid launched by the IMU into Kyrgyzstan's and Uzbekistan's southern districts, which occurred in August 2000, and which also coincided with a new Taliban offensive in northern Afghanistan. In response to these attacks, renewed efforts were conducted within the CST framework to give member states more effective military capabilities, and this included establishing the basis for better integrated CST armed forces. At their October 2000 Bishkek, CST states agreed to create joint rapid deployment Regional Coalition Group of Forces (RCGF) or *koalitsionnye regional'nye gruppirovki voisk (sil)*, within regional systems of collective security (RSCS) or *regional'nye sistemy kollektivnoi bezopasnosti* (ODKB, 2000c; Guly, 2000). These CST rapid-deployment forces were expected to repel jointly an external military aggressor and to conduct joint counter-terrorist operations wherever considered necessary (Odnokolenko, 2000). CST states once again agreed that parties to the treaty could send troops to the territory of other CST signatory states for the conduct of joint operations, thus solidifying further the legal deployment of CST national military units on the territory of other CST member states (Golotyuk, 2001).[3] However, troops could only be sent with the consent of the hosting party. Each party to the CST reserved the right to ask the other parties for military assistance on an individual and case-by-case basis, whenever the need arose (Guly, 2000; Odnokolenko, 2000). At the May 2001 CST Yerevan Summit, the contours of the Central Asian Rapid Deployment Collective Forces (RDCF) or *Kollektivnyie sily bistrogo razvertivaniya*, within the Central Asian RSCS took further shape. CST states committed themselves to establish a Central Asian RDCF force totalling 1,600 men, made up of military subdivisions from Russia, Kazakhstan, Kyrgyzstan and Tajikistan. However, rather than being deployed in a single place, the various force battalions were expected to be based in their respective countries of origin – with the exception of Russia's 201st (Motorised Rifle Division) MRD, which would be permanently based in Tajikistan – and activated in case of aggression (Mukhin, 2001; Dubnov, 2001).[4] The coordinating Staff of the force was to be located in Bishkek, as the main source of threats was expected to come from the southern Central Asian region. In April 2001, Russia also reinforced the Tajik–Afghan border with additional border troop and special force units to protect the CST southern borders, in view of the growing instabilities inside Afghanistan as the Taliban gained increased strength (Golotyuk, 2001).

On Russia's suggestion, CST states also agreed at their May 2001 summit to establish two additional regional components of the RCGF – an East European group, with Russian and Belarusian forces; and a Caucasian one, with Russian and Armenian troops – in addition to the Central Asian regional group, thus expanding the geographical remit of CST combined forces' operations further (ODKB, 2000b, 2001). During peacetime, each national component was to be based in its original territories, unless specific agreements on permanent military deployments were reached. In case of aggression, regional groupings would become activated and deployed to the theatre of operations, with national components becoming subordinated to a regional command, most certainly led by Russia. These CST collective security arrangements also involved combined systems of air defence, intelligence, command and communications. These developments reflected Russia's efforts to strengthen the western and southern flanks of the CST through further military integration, ideally leading to the establishment of unified forces under Russian command. As the dominant military power, Russia participated in all the three military groupings, and was expected to take the leading role in case of aggression or war. However, no specific agreement was reached among the CST states on a single mechanism for the management and operational direction of these three regional groups of forces. Instead an inter-governmental system of coordination was established. This weakened the possibilities of setting up effective joint CST forces, while also limiting the efforts by Russia to establish a Russian-led CST combined force (Romanova and Karapetyan, 2001).

In order to reinforce the South Caucasian and East European RCGF, Russia respectively strengthened its military cooperation with Armenia and Belarus (Mukhin, 2001). In March 2000, the lease by Russia of the Armenian military base at Gyumri, for a 25-year period, was officially codified in a bilateral treaty, and in September 2000 various military cooperation agreements were signed on joint Russian–Armenian military planning, which further reinforced bilateral military ties. This helped further to develop the South Caucasus RCGF, while also solidifying Russia's military presence in Armenia (Eaton, 2001, p. 89). Russia was also allowed to keep a military presence at the Erebuni airfield, near Yerevan, where it deployed a squadron of MiG-29 and Mi-24 attack helicopters, to protect the Armenian airspace. Russia and Armenia also agreed to permit their military aircraft to fly into each other's airspace, effectively integrating their national air-defence systems (Eaton, 2001, p. 89; Koryunov, 2000).[5]

182 A new military bloc emerges

In December 2001, an agreement on establishing a common security and defence space between Russia and Armenia also entered into force. It prohibited the military use of Armenia's territory by third countries for purposes that could be detrimental to Russia's interests in the region, thereby precluding any Western military operation in Armenia if disapproved by Moscow (Varlamov, 2001). Moreover, Russia continued jointly to guard Armenia's borders with Iran and Turkey, strengthening in this way its military engagement in Armenia further (Koryunov, 2000).

Russia also tightened its military cooperation with Belarus, within the framework of the Union treaty signed in 1999. The latter foresaw the development of common Russian–Belarusian defence policies, the joint use of military infrastructure, and the coordination of joint military activities. Russia also committed itself, in the treaty, to assist in the development of Belarus' armed forces, 'in support of the defence of the Union state'.[6] To that end, in April 2000, the Russian–Belarusian Group of Forces was established, by combining the entire 100,000-strong Belarusian armed forces and Russia's Western Military District forces into a single 300,000-strong force group. During peacetime, these forces would remain under national command, each deployed on their respective territories. In time of crisis, the forces were expected to be placed under an assigned joint command, with the Russian contingent authorised to operate also in Belarus, in case of attack (Trenin, 2005, p. 71; Shimanskaya and Neverovsky, 2000). In 2001, a joint military doctrine was formally adopted, and thereafter, periodic bilateral military exercises involving Russian and Belarusian forces were held. Moreover, in April 2001, a unified regional air-defence system of the two countries was officially established. Russia saw the Belarusian borders on NATO as the de facto strategic borders of Russia with the West, and as a result, military integration intensified against the background of successive waves of NATO's enlargement.

Military cooperation also developed within the CIS framework but outside the CST. In December 2000, on Putin's initiative, a *CIS* anti-terrorist centre was set up in Moscow, involving all CIS states except for Turkmenistan, to coordinate counter-terrorism efforts among national security structures, by exchanging information, conducting joint training and carrying out joint threat assessments (Socor, 2006; Mylnikov, n.d.). Russia also succeeded in partially recreating the former Soviet air-defence system, and this became one of the most effective mechanisms of the entire CIS military system. By early 2000, all CIS states, with the exception of Moldova and Azerbaijan had agreed to establish a unified air-defence system to monitor jointly the skies over the Baltic Sea, the Black Sea, the Caspian Sea and the Central Asian regions. Russia provided most parties to the agreement with material assistance and technical support to run their national air defence systems (Bulavinov, 1998). Furthermore, Russia also extended its nuclear umbrella to all its CIS allies. The 2000 Military Doctrine noted in this respect that Russia 'reserved the right' to use nuclear weapons in response to all 'weapons of mass destruction attacks', against its territories or against its allies (ACA, 2000).

While such efforts aimed at strengthening CST military cooperation were motivated by clear and legitimate security concerns, and were supported by the CST/CIS states themselves, there is little doubt that, if successful, they would have resulted in the establishment of a Russian sphere of influence over the CIS/CST states. However, it should be noted that Moscow clearly perceived the rise of Islamist extremism in the North Caucasus and Central Asia, and NATO's enlargement eastwards, as real challenges to its own security. In this last respect, the April 2000 *Military Doctrine*, clearly described the deployment of foreign troops, in violation of the UN Charter, near Russia, and the build-up of forces close to Russia's borders and the borders of its allies, as direct threats to the country's security – as these violated 'the existing balance of forces' (ACA, 2000). Similarly,

> actions aimed at undermining global and regional stability, not least by hampering the work of Russian systems of state and military rule, or by disrupting the functioning of [Russia's] strategic nuclear forces, its missile-attack early warning systems, anti-missile defence, and space monitoring systems

were also identified as threats to Russia's national security (ACA, 2000). While it is most probable that the Russian government under Putin would have pursued CST/CIS military integration with great vigour irrespective of NATO's enlargement eastwards, there is little doubt that this factor together with the rise of Islamist extremism, accelerated the processes of military integration. More importantly, these two security challenges gave stronger justification to any attempts by the Kremlin to restore some kind of 'sphere of influence' or informal empire over countries in the former Soviet space.

The CSTO is born

At the May 2002 CST Moscow Summit, member states agreed to transform the alliance into a full-fledged politico-military bloc, the Collective Security Treaty *Organisation* (CSTO), in order to enhance its overall military capabilities (Panfilova and Georgiev, 2002). To that end, CSTO states decided to establish a single military command, a fully functioning rapid reaction force (RDCF), RCGF involving the three different regional components, and a common air-defence system to cover the entire CIS/CSTO area. Member states also agreed to coordinate their foreign, security and defence policies, and to enhance their military-technical cooperation through the standardisation of all new military equipment. Russia also committed itself to selling its military equipment to other CSTO states at domestic prices (Safronov, 2002). In October 2002, member states also adopted a CSTO Charter, which defined the aims and objectives, as well as the organs, of the organisation, and established the legal basis for the deployment of military forces and infrastructure in the countries that were members of the CSTO, further strengthening the organisation. The Charter

184 A new military bloc emerges

stipulated that the CSTO was aimed at strengthening international peace and regional security, and ensuring 'the collective defence of the independence, territorial integrity and sovereignty of the member States' (ODKB, 2002). The bases were thus set for the creation of a significantly more effective and well-coordinated military force within the CSTO remit.

The strengthening of the CST was dictated primarily by concerns over the continued threat posed by Islamist-*jihadist* groups in Central Asia and the North Caucasus, a menace that increased exponentially after the 9/11 attacks. This predicament prompted Russia to boost the CST's collective security system further, and to enhance and solidify its military presence in the Central Asian region (Kulagin, 2002). In the spring of 2002 and in April 2003, the Central Asian Collective Rapid Deployment Forces (CRDF) carried out a series of exercises – *CIS Southern Shield* – involving battalions from Kazakhstan, Kyrgyzstan, Tajikistan and Russia, intended to strengthen military effectiveness and enhance CSTO combat forces' inter-operability (IISS, 2002/03, p. 87; 2003/04, p. 127).[7] These exercises proved to be the start of more effective CIS military cooperation at regional level, even though doubts persisted among experts over the force's ability successfully to counter-terrorist threats given the lack of adequate training and equipment among many of the Central Asian forces (McDermott, 2004a, p. 14). The Central Asian RDCF received a further boost in December 2003, when Russia, Kazakhstan, Kyrgyzstan and Tajikistan all agreed to assign two reinforced battalions each to the force (three in the case of Tajikistan), in permanent combat readiness (Torjesen, 2009, p. 186). Furthermore, in September 2003, Kyrgyzstan acquiesced to the opening of a Russian military air base at Kant, which was intended to provide reliable air cover for the entire Central Asian CRDF (Vorobyov, 2003).

These developments were underpinned by the establishment of tight military cooperation between Russia and all CSTO states at bilateral level. Moscow assisted other CSTO militaries with training and education, provided them with military equipment, either free of charge or at special discount prices, and gave them the necessary repair and maintenance support (Plater-Zyberk, 2004, p. 6). Russia also jointly patrolled the external CSTO/CIS borders of Armenia and Tajikistan, although in the latter case gradual transfer and responsibility was passed onto the Tajik border guards in 2004 (IISS, 2004/05, p. 143).[8] Russia also cooperated closely with Belarus in the protection of its external borders with Poland and the Baltic states (Plotnikov, 1997).[9] By the end of Putin's first term in office, therefore, Moscow had set the basis for the transformation of the CST/CSTO into a more effective collective security organisation, potentially endowed with coordinated commanding structures, coalition forces, and a rapid reaction force, intended to address the various threats to security surfacing in former Soviet space.

While the strengthening of the CST/CSTO followed quite legitimate security concerns, there is little doubt that neo-imperialist designs, namely establishing a strong Russian-led politico-military alliance in the CIS space, also underlay the Russian initiative. With the establishment of the CSTO, not only were members planning to enhance their military cooperation, coordinate their security and foreign policies, and establish a unified air-defence system, they were also intending to develop three regional coalition groups of forces – in the west with Belarus, in the Caucasus with Armenia, and in Central Asia. If properly implemented, all these initiatives would have led eventually to the restoration of unified CSTO forces around a Russian-led military bloc, thus recreating a Russian 'neo-empire' in the CSTO space as well as enhancing Russia's security through the acquisition of strategic depth. CSTO states also agreed to establish more effective rapid deployment forces, which the Kremlin hoped, would be placed under its command. More significantly, Russia expected that this single command, which would replace the amorphous CIS SCMC (Staff for the Co-ordination of Military Co-operation), would be located in Moscow and would be integrated into the Russian General Staff, strengthening in this way Russia's control over the CSTO military structures. However, the Kremlin failed to get the support of other CIS states, for this last initiative, and instead, in April 2003, it was forced to agree with the other CSTO states on establishing a CSTO Joint Staff with representatives from all CSTO states. The Joint Staff was expected to command all three RCGF only in times of crisis (Strugovets, 2004). This predicament showed that there were limits to CSTO integration, and that restraints could be placed by the CSTO states on Russia's hegemonic ambitions.

Furthermore, it must also be recalled that the CST states themselves often welcomed and benefited from Russia's military support and, therefore, the CSTO integration project cannot be seen entirely as a neo-imperialist enterprise. Furthermore, it must also be noted that when the CSTO was set up, President Putin did not envisage the organisation as a counter-balance to NATO's presence in Eastern Europe and Central Asia, as the Belarusian leader had hoped for (Safronov, 2002). Putin made it clear during the May 2002 CST/CSTO summit, and again at the CSTO April 2003 summit, that the CSTO was not aimed at NATO, but instead was intended to address more effectively the new threats challenging the security of Central Asia and the Caucasus. 'The CST countries are allying and cooperating not against anyone in particular, but against the threats that we encounter', Putin explained in 2002 (Safronov, 2002). He also noted in 2003, that 'one of the main tasks will be to fight terrorism and the threat of narcotics' (Glikin, 2003). Nor had the CSTO been established to send a signal to the US to leave Central Asia immediately. According to Valery Nikolaenko, the Secretary General of the CST Council, NATO's presence in the CIS raised no objections, given that the USA and the CST member states were working together in the Central Asian region within the framework of the same anti-terrorist coalition against *Al-Qaeda* (Panfilova and Georgiev, 2002). At the time, Russia's relations with NATO were experiencing a renewal, and this was reflected in the establishment on 28 May 2002, of the new NATO–Russia Council, just two weeks after the CST was officially transformed into an organisation. The October 2003 *Ivanov Military Doctrine* also revealed a more positive view of Russian–NATO relations – it downplayed NATO's direct threat to Russia and instead recognised the benefits of Russia's cooperation with the

Atlantic Alliance, in areas such as joint peacekeeping and counter-terrorism (Brannon, 2009, p. 43; Baran, 2007). As stated by Russian Foreign Minister Igor Ivanov, Russia hoped to address the regional threats through the CSTO framework, but also *in cooperation with NATO*. At the same time, though, CSTO states also agreed that the main responsibility for ensuring peace and stability in Central Asia rested primarily with countries in the region – namely Russia and the Central Asian states (Safronov, 2002). Although Putin had acquiesced after 9/11 to the deployment of American troops in Central Asia (US bases had been established in Uzbekistan and Kyrgyzstan) to help Russia in its fight against Islamist extremism, he objected to a long-term US presence in the Central Asian and Caucasus regions. There was little doubt that Russia saw the CIS space as an area of exclusive Russia's influence as far as NATO was concerned.

Putin's second presidency: the CSTO is strengthened further

In the mid-2000s, Russia redoubled its efforts to create an effective CSTO organisation, with well-coordinated and fully integrated structures, interoperable forces and a rapid deployment force capable of operating also beyond the CSTO borders. In the Central Asian theatre, particular emphasis was placed on the strengthening of the Central Asian CRDF, which had been tasked primarily with counter-terrorism and counter-insurgency operations in the turbulent South Asian and Central Asian regions (AP, 2004; Sysoyev, 2006). Another key objective of the new military formation, which however was never made explicit, was to prevent 'coloured revolutions' from taking place in Central Asia and to combat the growing influence and military presence of the US in the area, which was seen increasingly with great apprehension in Moscow, and also in other Central Asian capitals such as Tashkent (Gafarly, 2005). To that end, the Central Asian CRDF was reinforced with additional troops, which by 2007 totalled about 4,000 men grouped in 10 battalions – Russia and Tajikistan provided three battalions each, while Kyrgyzstan and Kazakhstan provided two each (AP, 2004). Furthermore, in June 2004, Moscow reached agreement with Dushanbe on the establishment of a permanent Russian military base in Tajikistan, to host Russia's 5,000-strong 201st MRD, one of whose battalions was to be assigned to the CRDFs (Panfilova, 2004, Lachowski, 2007, p. 55).[10] In 2007, the Russian base also receive an air component of five Su-25 and several helicopters (IISS, 2009, p. 227). Russia also bolstered the CRDF's aviation force at its Kant air base in Kyrgyzstan, by adding personnel and aircraft, which by 2007 totalled 20 Mi-8 helicopters, five Su-25s, and a few Su-24 and Su-27 fighter planes (IISS, 2008, p. 222, 2009, p. 227).

Furthermore, at their October 2007 Dushanbe summit, CSTO leaders agreed significantly to upgrade the Central Asian CRDF, by providing it with advanced weapons and special equipment. Initiatives were also put forward by Russia in 2006 and 2007 to integrate further the military structures of the Central Asian CRDF through the formation of a single logistic support system and a common training programme (IISS, 2005, p. 153). In 2006, the CSTO Joint Staff, which had been set up in Bishkek with primarily an administrative role, was finally awarded a commanding role, and placed in charge of the CRDF, under the orders of Russian Army General Yury Baluyevsky (Socor, 2006).[11] In addition, a series of military exercises – code-named *Rubezh* – were held yearly during 2004–2007 in Central Asia intended to enhance the effectiveness of the Central Asian CRDF and achieve greater inter-operability (Saat, 2005, p. 1; McDermott, 2004b). The exercises generally involved Russian battalions from the 201st MRD, Russian special forces from the Volga-Urals military district, as well as special forces from Kyrgyzstan and Tajikistan (McDermott, 2004b). The *Rubezh 2006* exercise in particular, which was held in the Caspian Sea and Kazakhstan, involved the armed forces of all four countries, as well as the navies and the air forces of both Russia and Kazakhstan (Weitz, 2006).

In the Western theatre, Russia reinforced the CIS/CSTO air defences by deploying four SAM units equipped with S-300 surface-to-air missiles on Belarusian territory. It also conducted large-scale military exercises involving combined Russian and Belarusian forces – *Allied Security* in 2005 and *Union-Shield* in 2006, the latter involving about 8,800 servicemen (IISS, 2008, p. 222; Belapan News Agency, 2006). The massive military exercise *Stability 2008*, held on Belarusian territory in the summer of 2008, was particularly relevant. It involved Russia's nuclear forces, the Russian air force, and most of the battle-ready navy, as well as Belarusian military formations. In a clear display of Russia's power projection, the exercise also saw the participation of Russian ships armed with nuclear missiles docking on Syrian ports, and strategic bombers conducting manoeuvres as far away as Venezuela. Russia also deployed an air-defence squadron with 18 MiG-29 fighters, two SAM batteries with S-300V surface-to-air missiles, and one SAM battery with SA-6 Gainful missiles, at its Gyumri military air base in Armenia, in order to protect its South Caucasus ally from any sudden attack (IISS, 2008, p. 221).[12] Joint military exercises were also held in Armenia in September 2005, involving Russian and Armenian ground and air forces near the Turkish–Armenian border, while Armenia also participated in the various CSTO joint exercises *Rubezh 2005* and *Rubezh 2008* (de Haas, 2005, p. 22).

Under Russia's leadership, efforts were also made to enhance cooperation and reinforce combat inter-operability among *all* CSTO armed forces, through a series of bilateral and multilateral CSTO military training exercises held in 2005 to 2007. In 2005, the training exercises *Combat Commonwealth, Phases 1, 2* and *3* were carried out at different CSTO locations, involving all Central Asian CSTO states, as well as Russia, Armenia and Belarus. In July–August 2005, the massive counter-terrorism exercise *Kaspiy Antiterror* involving several CSTO states was held in the Caspian Sea region to send a clear message to the USA and its allies to stay away from the region (IISS, 2005, p. 155). Moscow also fostered better technical CSTO inter-operability and tighter military-technical cooperation between Russia and all other CSTO member states, by agreeing to provide them with long-term military assistance on advantageous terms, including state-of-the-art weaponry at reduced prices, as well as free training for military personnel (Kolesnikov, 2004). CSTO states, in turn, agreed to adopt a single standard of military training, and to equip their forces with armaments and military equipment provided primarily by Russia (Saat, 2005). Furthermore, in June 2005, an Inter-Governmental Commission on Military-Economic Co-operation was set up to stimulate cooperation among CSTO defence industries. Moreover, at the CSTO summit held in June 2005, the decision was also taken to create a *united CSTO* Air Defence system, out of the existing CIS Joint Air Defence System, to protect the CSTO air space as a single whole. Within this framework, it was agreed that national CSTO air forces would be placed under a single Russian-led planning and command system to ensure the air defence of the CSTO as a unified air space (Socor, 2005a). In turn, in order to enhance *CIS* air and air-defence cooperation, CIS military exercises involving all the CSTO states, plus Uzbekistan and Ukraine, were held in April 2005.

More significantly, at the June 2005 CSTO summit, Russia put forward proposals to create a *joint standing conventional army* for Central Asia, to protect the region and member states from potential external, as well as internal, military threats (Gafarly, 2005; Socor 2005a). A large military grouping, this standing army would consist of sizeable combined units and formations (as opposed to simply armed battalions), from Russia, Kazakhstan, Kyrgyzstan and Tajikistan (Gafarly, 2005). In case of large-scale war, it was envisaged that all four countries would make their forces ready for the grouping and fight jointly under Russian command. Uzbekistan was also expected to participate in this joint army, as Tashkent had re-applied for CSTO membership in the summer of 2005 (Gafarly, 2005). If implemented, such a force would have resulted in the recreation of armed forces along the lines of the old Warsaw Treaty Organisation, allowing Russia fully to re-establish a 'neo-empire' over the CSTO states. However, several CSTO states, including Kazakhstan, did not prove very supportive of this 'common army' initiative. On the eve of the summit, Kazakh Defence Minister noted that 'creating a cumbersome force for permanent stationing would be worthless', and therefore, the project failed to gain ground (Socor, 2005a). At the 2006 CSTO Minsk Summit, member states, instead, agreed to explore the possibility of strengthening the CRDF and expanding its zone of operations beyond the CSTO area into adjacent areas or *prilegayushchie rayony*. This was proposed by Russia, with a view to deploying the combined CSTO CRDF in Afghanistan, in order to address the Taliban resurgence in Afghanistan, the rise in *Jihadist* terrorism and the increase in drug trafficking in the Central Asian region (Sysoyev, 2006). With the signing of the *Treaty of Allied Relations* between Uzbekistan and Russia in November 2005, and the return of Uzbekistan to the CSTO in 2006, the deployment of the CRDP in Afghanistan became a more likely possibility (Kolesnikov, 2006).[13]

Member states also approved a series of measures in 2006 designed to transform the CSTO into a broader *security* organisation, by moving beyond the purely military remit, and extending cooperation to the areas of internal security and intelligence. At Putin's and Lukashenko's initiative, CSTO states agreed to develop joint internal security capabilities to deal with domestic security threats, such as 'coloured' revolutions, internal upheavals, and civil unrest, as well as to address transnational threats such as illegal migration and narcotics trafficking. To that end, joint structures of multilateral and bilateral cooperation between intelligence and law enforcement agencies, as well as between Internal Ministry structures were established (Socor, 2005b). Putin, in turn, committed Russia to sell equipment and support material to the CIS security services at lower Russian domestic prices. More importantly, in October 2007, the former head of Russia's Foreign Intelligence Service (SRV), Sergei Lebedev, was chosen as executive secretary of the CIS, with the clear objective of countering American activity in the CIS, which in Russia's view was behind the rise of 'coloured revolutions' in the region (Gabuyev and Solovyov, 2007). Concern over the spread of 'Western-sponsored' 'coloured revolutions' was not limited to the Russian leadership. Worries were also particularly acute among Central Asian leaders, who saw these upheavals as directly challenging the security and the stability of their regimes in the Central Asian region– a view which was shared by Moscow. At the July 2005 Shanghai Cooperation Organisation (SCO) Summit, Putin had clearly stated that the United States should not try to impress upon Central Asian states a particular model of political development. It was impossible, in his view, and more importantly, futile, to try to impose templates and standards on the Central Asian countries through the use of force (Kolesnikov, 2005). Joint efforts were therefore conducted by all SCO members to expel the United States' military presence from the region, and to prevent violent changes of regime. As noted, these concerns over the involvement of 'Western forces' in the domestic affairs of states, were not limited to the Central Asian region, as the leaderships in Russia and Belarus also worried over such challenging developments. The CSTO, therefore, increasingly expanded cooperation in the internal security realm in order to address these challenges more effectively. The military organisation, thus became an instrument for the preservation and the protection of the existing regimes from 'revolutionary' upheavals.

Concerns over 'coloured revolutions' also drove the CSTO's decision at the 2007 CSTO summit held in Dushanbe to create *collective peace-keeping forces* that would operate both outside the CSTO area and inside the areas of the alliance. To that effect, a full-fledged Concept for *CSTO peacekeeping operations*, which was sponsored by Russia, was also adopted at the summit. It spelled out the parameters of CSTO peacekeeping force in the CSTO area and further afield. The objective of the force was to 'resolve violent disputes, stabilise volatile situations, and in this way, maintain international peace and security' (Gabuyev and Solovyov, 2007). 'Any hot spot anywhere in the world can become a zone of peacekeeping operations', Nikolai Bordyuzha, CSTO Secretary General stated at the summit (Gabuyev and Solovyov, 2007).[14] However, while it was made clear that when operating outside the CSTO area, the bloc required a UN mandate (ODKB, 2007), when acting within the CSTO, the organisation was able to carry out peacekeeping operations absolutely independently, even without UN approval. This was a clear indication that CSTO peacekeeping troops could be employed to counter any kind of internal rebellion or local instability, which was perceived as a threat to the security of CSTO's regimes, without the explicit support of international legal mechanisms (Gabuyev and Solovyov, 2007). In this respect, it must be noted that the peacekeeping forces could involve not only military forces, but also police and civilian contingents, if considered necessary. However, some caveats were introduced to the CSTO agreements which limited the leeway of such operations and prevented the conduct of military interventions in CSTO states without their explicit approval. It was specifically stipulated that in the event of internal destabilisation, a decision to carry out peacekeeping activities on the territory of a CSTO member states required the approval of the CSTO Council on Collective Security. The Council operated on the basis of consensus, upon an official request by the CSTO country concerned, and this ruled out any operations within a CSTO state without its leadership's approval (Bordyuzha, 2010, p. 343).[15]

CSTOs in the 2000s: assessment

By the end of Putin's second term in office, the Kremlin had succeeded in further reinforcing the CSTO, by strengthening the Central Asian CRDF, enhancing Russia's military cooperation with Armenia and Belarus, increasing the number of CSTO military exercises, and establishing a single CSTO air-defence system. In addition, CSTO collective peacekeeping forces had been set up, and deeper cooperation had been established among CSTO states in the sensitive area of intelligence and domestic security. Furthermore, Russia had managed to establish semi-permanent military bases in Tajikistan, Kyrgyzstan and Armenia, and to develop a similar system of training, equipment and support among all national CSTO military structures. More significantly, Russian military support and equipment was provided on the understanding that the recipient countries would take Russia's strategic interests fully into account (Saat, 2005). All these developments made of the CSTO a potential instrument of Russia's hegemony in the CIS space. Yet, it must be noted that several countries welcomed Russia's military assistance and support. The armed forces of several CSTO countries, such as Kyrgyzstan and Tajikistan, were generally weak, underfunded and not adequately trained to address the serious security challenges that they faced, and therefore they benefited from Russian assistance. Kyrgyz Defence Minister Esen Topoyev, for example, stated in September 2003, in relation to the opening of a Russian military base on Kyrgyz territory, 'Once Russia's military personnel are stationed in Kant, Kyrgyzstan's security will be enhanced considerably, and it will be less likely that gangs of international terrorists [will be able to] mount incursions into the country' (Vorobyov, 2003). Countries like Armenia and Belarus also strongly supported Russia's commitment to secure their defence and protection – Armenia faced challenges from Azerbaijan over Nagorno-Karabakh, while Belarus worried over Western-sponsored 'coloured' revolutions and the enlargement of NATO. They thus welcomed Russian military support, although Minsk remained wary of a Russia military presence on its territory. It is not possible, therefore, to talk of Russia establishing a 'neo-empire' in the CSTO space, in the strict meaning of the word.

Moreover, while Russia remained the predominant military power, it could not always exert its influence inside the CSTO to the full extent, and this showed the limits of its geo-strategic reach. Despite the Kremlin's efforts to establish a single command-and-control body for the CSTO Rapid Reaction Forces, directly subordinated to the Russian General Staff, Russia did not succeed in its endeavour (Vladkin, 2002, Panfilova and Georgiev, 2002). Instead, an inter-state agency – a Joint Staff – consisting of representatives of all the CST countries, was established in 2003 to command the CRDF, albeit with a preponderant Russian presence, and under Russian command (Saat, 2005, p. 7). Although in 2006 the Joint Staff was given a commanding role under the leadership of a Russian general, it still operated in a collegiate fashion. In addition, doubts remained as to the capacity of the CRDF forces to operate jointly and successfully when tested against a real and present danger (McDermott, 2004a). Russia also had to abandon its project for a *joint standing conventional army*, which if implemented, would have placed the armed forces of the Central Asian states directly under Russian command (Gafarly, 2005). Furthermore, limits were established, at least in theory, with regards to the temporary and permanent deployment of CSTO – i.e. Russian – troops to territory of other the CSTO states, as it was made clear that each party reserved the right both to ask for or to reject military support if it so desired (Guly, 2000; Golotyuk, 2001).[16] Similarly, the Collective peacekeeping forces could operate inside the CSTO area only with the consent of the CSTO Council, which involved all member states and operated on the basis of consensus. Russia could not interfere militarily in the CSTO states without their consent, thus restricting – at least theoretically – its room for manoeuvre. It must be noted however, that despite these legal caveats, Russia did exert pressure on countries like as Kyrgyzstan and Tajikistan to allow for a more permanent military presence on their territories in a clear display of its hegemonic power.

On the other hand, in the 2000s, and especially after 9/11, CST member-states began developing much closer military ties with non-CIS states, challenging in this way, Russia's military supremacy in the former Soviet space. While in the year 2000, CST states had adopted a statement which stipulated that relations between members of the CST had to take priority over military relations with third countries (Dubnov, 2000), they also agreed that CST member states could develop cooperative military ties with other countries, as long as they kept other CST members informed of the details (ODKB, 2000a). In the 2000s, therefore, many CST states engaged in military cooperation programmes with NATO and with several of its member states, while Central Asian CSTO states developed military ties with China within the SCO framework. The United States, in particular, became deeply engaged in Central Asia after 9/11 in view of its military operations in Afghanistan, by providing Tajikistan and Kyrgyzstan with substantial assistance in the areas of military training, security and law enforcement. An American military base was opened at Manas airport in Kyrgyzstan, while Tajikistan allowed the United States to establish a military transit centre to facilitate its actions in Afghanistan. Particularly close military ties were also developed with Uzbekistan, which was not at the time a member of the CSTO – the United States provided Tashkent with special guarantees to its security because Uzbekistan was perceived as extremely relevant strategically for the United States' security in the now volatile Central Asian region. To that end, America established an air base at Karshi-Khanabad in Uzbekistan, which became an important command centre for US operations in Afghanistan, as well as a launching pad for its special forces and air strikes (MacFarlane, 2004, p. 454).

Kazakhstan also reached an agreement with the US after the 9/11 attacks, which allowed American aircraft to use the Almaty airport in case of emergencies (IISS, 2002–03, p. 124). Astana also signed up to NATO's Planning and Review Process or PARP in 2002, a review and assessment programme aimed at advancing inter-operability and increasing transparency between NATO members and its partners. The PARP agreement permitted Kazakhstan to enhance its military ties with NATO, in the realms of training assistance, support for the modernisation of its armed forces and improved defence planning. Kazakhstan also participated in several NATO PfP (Partnership for Peace) peacekeeping exercises, as long as they did not display any overt anti-Russian undertones (Legvold, 2003, p. 95). Russia's key strategic ally in the South Caucasus, Armenia, also joined NATO's PARP in 2002, and in June 2003 it hosted NATO's PfP exercise 'Cooperative Best Effort 2003'. Even Belarus, Russia's staunchest ally, developed an Individual Partnership Programme with NATO in 2002–2003, which involved cooperation in emergency situations, crisis management, mine clearing, as well as collaboration in the areas of NBC non-proliferation and defence reform. However, interaction and practical cooperation between Belarus and NATO remained limited, because of the democratic deficiencies of the Lukashenko regime.

All these developments seemed to indicate that Russia was being partly displaced from the region by NATO and the United States. Yet, despite Russia's disagreements over NATO's engagement in the CIS/CSTO space, Russia did propose collaborating with the Alliance in the fight against international terrorism both globally and regionally in Central Asia (Socor, 2005a).[17] The idea, in Putin's mind, was to develop a bilateral NATO–CSTO relationship, which would involve both organisations working jointly to address transnational threats in Eurasia. The Russian leadership, however, expected that Russia and CSTO would be guaranteed a leading role in ensuring security in Central Asia while NATO's actions would instead remain secondary in Eurasia. What Russian leaders actually wished was that NATO and CSTO jointly addressed issues of international security, by establishing 'a clear division of spheres of responsibility', as stated by Sergei Ivanov in December 2006, with Russia keeping a predominant role in Central Asia (Mukhin, 2006). But NATO proved reluctant to acquiesce. It preferred instead to build its relations with each CSTO countries on a bilateral basis, bypassing the Russian-led organisation (Sysoyev, 2006). In view of such a predicament, Russia (and also China) pushed for the withdrawal of Russian forces from the Central Asian region. At the SCO July

2005 summit in Astana, a declaration was issued by Russia and its SCO partners, requesting the United States to set a well-defined deadline for the closure of its military bases in Kyrgyzstan and Uzbekistan (Kolesnikov, 2006). Russia perceived Western military presence as directly challenging Russia's hegemonic geo-strategic position in Central Asia, while China worried over the efforts by the United States to 'contain' China militarily and promote 'coloured revolutions' in Central Asia that further destabilised the region. Pressure was therefore exerted on the Central Asian states to put an end to American military presence on their territories (Sysoyev, 2006). While Uzbekistan asked the United States to close its base at Karshi-Khanabad, Kyrgyzstan, instead, renegotiated a prolongation of the American military presence at its base at Manas, overcoming significant Russian pressure (Orozaliyev and Safronov, 2005). In late July 2005, only three weeks after the SCO Astana summit, Kyrgyz President Kurmanbek Bakiyev acquiesced to a continued US military presence at Manas, after the USA agreed to increase the rent payment to about $20 million a year (Panfilova, 2006; Saidazimova, 2005). Uzbekistan, instead, pressed ahead with calls for US withdrawal, to a great extent in response to the strong criticism that was being voiced by the Bush administration over the Uzbek authorities' violent handling of the May 2005 protests in Andijan.

CSTO and the Shanghai Cooperation Organisation

CSTO states also began forging closer military ties with China, within the remit of the SCO, which had been established by the Shanghai Five at their 2001 Shanghai summit. In its first years, the SCO focused its activities on fighting trans-border crime and countering internal threats to security, as had been stipulated in the 2001 'Covenant on the Suppression of Terrorism, Separatism and Religious extremism'. More specifically, within the SCO area, these threats referred to the challenges posed by *jihadist* groups such as the IMU in Central Asia, and to the risks presented by Muslim Uyghur separatist groups in China's Xinjiang province to the country's territorial integrity. To address these threats, SCO member states agreed to take coordinated measures in the realm of security, to exchange relevant information and intelligence, and to curtail any kind of assistance provided to extremist organisations – such as funding, weaponry, ammunition or ideological support (Sigov and Guly, 2001). In 2003, a SCO Regional Anti-Terrorist Structure (RATS) was set up in Tashkent, with the task of coordinating anti-terrorist activity and exchanging relevant information among the security services in a rapid and effective manner (Suponina, 2005). Collaboration was also established among SCO states' judiciary institutions, law-enforcement ministries, state security councils, and military forces, as an additional platform for security cooperation (Zhao, 2013, p. 440). Furthermore, at China's instance, closer anti-terrorist cooperation between SCO member states was promoted through the holding of joint military exercises (Yuan, 2010, p. 861). In October 2002, China and Kyrgyzstan held bilateral military counter-terrorism manoeuvres in their mutual border zones – these were the SCO's first military exercise and China's first joint military manoeuvres with a foreign army. In August 2003, *Co-operation 2003*, a SCO joint-command-post exercise, which combined joint field manoeuvres was held in Kazakhstan and in China's Xinjiang province, with the participation of China, Russia and all three other SCO states.

Despite these achievements, the development of military cooperation within the SCO framework occurred rather slowly, and was not followed by any plans to create collective military structures within the organisation. Neither China nor Russia supported, at the time, the transformation of the SCO into a new military block. Common military capabilities already existed within the CSTO framework, and Russia preferred to rely on its own CIS security organisation for defence in Central Asia. Moscow, in particular, worried that the SCO would replace the CSTO as the main provider of regional security in Central Asia if military cooperation was enhanced further (Suponina, 2005). Moscow's participation in the first SCO multilateral anti-terrorism exercises in 2003 was therefore rather low key. Russia also proved reluctant to support the further institutionalisation of the SCO and remained rather unenthusiastic about China's wishes to foster economic integration and trade liberalisation within the SCO remit. On the other hand, after 9/11, the United States temporarily replaced Russia as the key provider of security to the Central Asian region, as a number of states in the area reached bilateral security arrangements with the USA, which granted Washington access to local military bases in exchange for economic and military assistance (Yuan, 2010, p. 863). This new security predicament in Central Asia cast a doubt over the SCO's ability to provide security to the region and to address effectively the looming terrorist and separatist threats. Nevertheless, efforts were conducted within the SCO framework to enhance military operability and jointly address common military and terrorist threats, as indicated by the establishment of RATS and the holding of various multilateral and bilateral SCO military training exercises.

The transformation of the Shanghai Forum into the SCO proved to be very significant – it was the first organisation that emerged in the CIS space, which included a non-former Soviet state – China – among its members, and which also comprised Russia. By acquiescing to the establishment of the SCO, Russia opened the way to China's growing influence and involvement in the affairs of the former Soviet Central Asian states – traditionally a remit of Russia's exclusive influence. Whereas in the early 1990s, China had remained quite suspicious of multilateral security organisations in Asia, such as the ASEAN Regional Forum (ARF), in the late 1990s and early 2000s, it began not only to endorse multilateral security dialogues, it also started 'actively to promote such mechanism as alternatives to military alliances' (Yuan, 2010 p. 856). Beijing thus took the lead in establishing, nurturing and promoting the SCO. China also hoped that the SCO would facilitate greater regional economic integration in Central Asia, while allowing China to gain access to local markets and energy supplies. The SCO therefore became a forum where China could exercise its leadership in a multilateral organisation, fulfil its regional geo-economic and security objectives and expand its influence in the region, to Russia's great concern (Yuan, 2010, p. 856). In view of this predicament, Russia remained much more cautious initially about the institutionalisation of the SCO, and this forced China to manage carefully its delicate relationship with Russia and the Central Asian states within the SCO framework (Yuan, 2010, p. 856).

In the mid-2000s, however, Russia reassessed the role of the SCO and became much more supportive of the organisation, after the outburst of 'coloured' revolutions in Ukraine and Kyrgyzstan. These developments and the violent upheavals in the Uzbek city of Andijan in 2005 created great concerns in Russia that the internal security and the stability of regimes in the Central Asian region could be easily undermined. Russia therefore began cooperating more actively with China in order to strengthen the organisation, and together with the other SCO member states, it engaged in efforts to develop a more effective SCO political and military structure. SCO permanent representatives were sent to all member states, and in 2004, a Secretariat was established in Beijing to coordinate activities and provide technical support.[18] In the mid-2000s, military cooperation within the SCO remit was expanded further, spearheaded by the development of closer military ties between Russia and China. In August 2005, both countries conducted a massive joint military exercise within the SCO framework – *Peace Mission 2005* – on China's Shandong peninsula, and near the eastern Russian city of Vladivostok, on the Chinese border, involving 10,000 troops, dozens of surface warships, submarines and aircraft (Myasnikov, 2006). The exercise was seen by Russia as laying the groundwork for the creation of military formations or force components which could jointly and effectively address regional threats in Central Asia (Poroskov, 2005). Russia clearly saw the potential of a stronger Russian–Chinese military partnership, which could head the transformation of the SCO into a more cohesive military organisation.

In the summer of 2007, another major joint anti-terrorism exercise – *Peace Mission-2007* – was held, involving, for the first time, all six full SCO member states (China, Russia, Kazakhstan, Kyrgyzstan, Tajikistan and Uzbekistan). The exercise demonstrated the increasing trend towards deepened security cooperation among SCO member states. The event was labelled an 'anti-terrorist exercise', although it was clearly targeted at countering the potential dangers of state collapse or an American invasion of the region (Pannier, 2007). The *Peace Mission-2007* exercise demonstrated the strategic importance that both China and Russia attached to the organisation. Moscow, in particular, saw the manoeuvres as part of an overall attempt to transform the SCO into a politico-military bloc in Central Asia that would defend Russia's interests and counter the growing penetration of the United States in the region (Gabuyev, 2007). In April 2007, Russia proposed, through its Chief of the General Staff, General Yury Baluyevsky, the creation of a military alliance within the SCO remit, in order to counter the USA's drive to global hegemony (Solovyov and Ivanov, 2007). This raised the prospect of the SCO becoming a regional security organ-isation, along the lines of NATO or the CSTO, with mutually binding security obligations among its members and joint commitments. China, however, remained opposed to transforming the SCO into a military bloc. Although it strongly supported and actively promoted greater military and security cooperation among the SCO states, Beijing proved reluctant to create a military alliance which imposed security commitments on itself and which established permanent military engagements. Kazakhstan, in turn, remained worried that a transformation of the SCO into a military bloc could be seen by the USA as being directed against it. Russia's SCO ambitions were thus thwarted, as the organisation failed to become a military alliance in the Eurasian region capable of countering American global hegemony.

Despite these different approaches, both Russia and China supported strengthening the SCO as a regional security actor responsible for maintaining stability and security in Central Asia. As was clearly expressed in the June 2006 SCO Shanghai declaration, the SCO had 'the potential to play an independent role in maintaining stability and security in its zone of responsibility'. More importantly, both China and Russia remained eager to keep the United States away from Central Asia. Its military presence was seen as potentially threatening their own security and challenging their hegemony in the region (Guang, 2005). Many in China were convinced that the American bases that had been established in Central Asia were intended primarily to contain and encircle China rather than to fight the Taliban and destroy *Al-Qaeda*'s bases in Afghanistan (Skosyrev, 2005). Beijing also worried that as a result of the opening of USA military bases in Central Asia, Chinese nuclear test facilities in Xinjiang could become more vulnerable to a military attack. Furthermore, Washington could potentially intervene in the ethnic relations in Xinjiang and the USA government could bring influence to bear on the Central Asian states (Skosyrev, 2005).[19] This congruence of views made Russia feel less worried about Chinese military penetration into the Central Asian region.

The Medvedev and third Putin presidencies: the CSTO is reinforced further

In the aftermath of the Georgian–Russian 2008 war, when Russia found itself on the verge of direct military confrontation with the West, Medvedev launched an accelerated modernisation process of the country's Armed Forces, which involved the acquisition of new weapons systems and equipment, and a major reorganisation of the forces' overall structure and personnel (de Haas, 2011, p. 30). Within this framework, a new 'Law on Amendments to the *Law on Defence*', which expanded the remit of Russian military forces abroad, was approved by the Russian parliament in November 2009. The law allowed the Russian government to deploy Russian troops abroad to counter attacks against the Russian Armed Forces; to counter or prevent attacks against Russian allies, if so requested; and to protect Russian citizens living abroad from an armed attack, as well as to combat piracy (Fedorov, 2009, p. 1). Previous Russian legislation had restricted the government's ability to dispatch armed forces abroad– only in situations of direct military aggression against Russia, or to perform international missions in accordance with Russia's international treaties and international law (i.e. sanctioned by the UN Security Council). The new Law on Defence, therefore, significantly expanded the range of circumstances under which Russia could utilise force. Its vague and ambiguous wording meant that Russia could potentially use force not necessarily in accordance with international law, as had already occurred in Georgia in 2008. As noted by Fedorov (2009), it helped 'close the gap between Moscow's strategic goals, primarily the establishment of its geopolitical dominance over the former Soviet republics, and Russia's legislation, which restricted its ability to deploy armed forces beyond its initial borders' (Fedorov, 2009, p. 1).

Moreover, during the Medvedev and Putin's third Presidencies, Russia further strengthened the CSTO military capabilities by establishing new CRDF or *Kollektivniye sily operativnogo reagirovaniya* (KSOR). Established as a 16,000–20,000-strong force with contingents from all CSTO member states, KSOR was intended to conduct low-intensity operations, including peacekeeping, counter-terrorism, and counter-insurgency operations primarily but not exclusively inside the CSTO/CIS space (Weitz, 2014, p. 2; Mowchan, 2009, p. 2). Soon after their establishment, KSOR multi-national troops engaged in regular exercises, coded *Vzaimodeistviye* (Interaction), which involved multifaceted scenarios, ranging from peacekeeping to counter-terrorism operations, anti-narcotics operations and combined armed warfare (Norberg, 2013, p. 25). From this it became clear that, despite being a lightly armed force, KSOR forces were expected to join any major CSTO military operation – an indication of the further strengthening of the CSTO's military capabilities. CSTO states also agreed in 2009 to establish a 4,000-strong CSTO peacekeeping force, involving, primarily, troops from Russia, Belarus and Kazakhstan. Permanent contingents were allocated to a peacekeeping force, which trained under the same CSTO system, and used compatible weapons and communications systems, in order to be able to operate jointly in peace-support operations (Bordyuzha, 2010, p. 343). Starting in 2012, a series of CSTO peacekeeping exercises were held, which generally involved traditional peacekeeping operations such as separation of forces, protection of humanitarian convoys and patrolling of unsecure areas. However, on several occasions, the exercises went beyond traditional peacekeeping tasks and instead involved practicing more forceful military actions, including fighting 'international extremist and terrorist organizations' (McDermott, 2012; Kucera, 2012). Large-scale military tasks – not unlike the ones exercised by the KSOR – were often combined with humanitarian missions in support of the population, in a clear sign that the force was expected to engage in quite forceful military actions.

In late 2010, CSTO members also agreed to introduce changes into the organisation's Charter in order to allow the organisation to operate inside member states when countries faced serious *internal* challenges to their security. This was in response to the events that had occurred in southern Kyrgyzstan in June 2010, when an eruption of violence, destruction and looting, left many hundreds of people dead and a high number of displaced mostly among the

Uzbek population. At the December 2010 CSTO summit in Moscow, it was therefore agreed that if a CSTO member state found itself in a situation of great *internal* instability or dangerous conflict the decision by the CSTO to provide help could, if necessary, be taken by a limited number of its member states. The decision did not require the explicit consent of all other members of the organisation on condition, however, that no CSTO state categorically opposed such an intervention (Solovyev, 2010b). This gave the organisation 'more freedom of action' – a CSTO country could simply abstain from participating in the decision of the CSTO to intervene militarily at home or abroad, and the operation could still go ahead. Although CSTO states reaffirmed the principle of non-interference in the internal affairs of states, they also agreed on the necessity to respond, not only to armed attacks from the outside, but also to 'other challenges and threats', against one, or more, member states – in reference to internal threats or upheavals (ODKB, 2010). Yet, in September 2011, it was agreed that the CSTO would use 'ordinary' peacekeepers when addressing internal conflicts inside the CSTO states (Bichurina and Telmanov, 2011). These forces would intervene at the request of the leadership of a particular CSTO state which found itself in internal turmoil. Troops would be dispatched only if the situation was critical, namely if the territorial integrity or the constitutional order of a state were in jeopardy, and the situation was fraught with bloodshed (Bichurina and Telmanov, 2011). In case of fierce disagreements and disputes *between* CSTO member states – for example, the mining along the Tajik–Uzbek border – Bordyuzha instead suggested selecting a special envoy to mediate between the parties to help resolve the conflict (Nikolsky and Kostenko, 2011). At the same time, in order to prevent the presence of Western or other external forces on the territory of the CSTO states, member states agreed in December 2011 that foreign military installations could be hosted *only* with the consent of the other CSTO member states.

In 2013, CSTO states also agreed to form Collective Aviation Forces – primarily involving units from Russia, Belarus and Kazakhstan – intended for the transport and deployment of CSTO forces and expected to provide air cover support to CSTO combat troops (Mukhin, 2013). However, at the time of writing, the CAF had not yet been fully developed. Instead, further progress was being made towards the establishment of a well-functioning CSTO air-defence system, by strengthening joint air-defence cooperation between Russia, on the one hand, and Kazakhstan and Belarus on the other (IISS, 2015, p. 167; Bohdan, 2016). In May 2014, a Joint Air-Defence Agreement between Kazakhstan and Russia was reached, which permitted military aircraft from both countries to enter into each other's airspace, and allowed for the joint use of the Kazakh Balkhash Node missile attack early-warning system based at Karaganda. In Belarus, the 2009 agreement on the establishment of a single air-defence system with Russia finally came into force in April 2016. This involved joint standby alert duty arrangements, information exchanges and joint training sessions between both countries' air defences. Despite Moscow's requests, however, the Kremlin failed to secure a Russian airbase at Belarus' Babruysk, to become part of the joint air-defence system (Bohdan, 2015). On the other hand, Russia succeeded, in August 2010, in extending the lease of the Russian 102nd military base at Gyumri, in Armenia, until 2044, and to expand the scope of Russia's potential combat activities in Armenia – its troops, together with the Armenian army, were made responsible for ensuring the security of the Armenian territory in its totality, as opposed to simply Armenia's border with Turkey (Solovyov, 2010a). In Central Asia, Russia managed, in October 2013, to extend the right to keep a military base in Tajikistan for another 30 years, while it also reinforced the Tajik–Afghan border with additional military equipment, although a return of Russian border troops to the region remained off the agenda (Konovalov, 2011; Nurshayeva, 2015). In Kyrgyzstan, Russia strengthened its military presence at its Kant air base, with the deployment of additional aircraft, leading to a total presence of 13 Su-25 and two Mi-8 helicopters in 2015 (IISS, 2016, p. 201).

Furthermore, cooperation was expanded in the areas of counter-terrorism, counter-narcotics and information security, while efforts were also conducted to strengthen military-to-military cooperation though joint exercises and improved combat inter-operability. Russia became, to all intents and purposes, the de facto security guarantor of the security of the CSTO space. Russia remained the main supplier of troops, weapons, equipment and technology to CSTO states, as well as the key provider of overall security guarantees and nuclear protection to its smaller allies. Furthermore, Russia also dominated the organisation's security structures while Russian forces were put in charge of the operational command of the CSTO common forces – the Russian Airborne Forces, for example, were expected to take operational command of KSOR once an operation started, and a similar arrangement was expected to apply to CSTO peacekeeping forces (Norberg, 2013, pp. 19–20). The CSTO also guaranteed the preservation of Russian military bases and facilities in the post-Soviet space – the Gyumri base in Armenia; the Baikonur cosmodrome and the Sary-Shagan polygon in Kazakhstan; the Kant air base and the test base near Karakol in Kyrgyzstan; the 4th Military base and the 'Okno' optical fibre in Tajikistan, and the Baranavichy radar station in Belarus (Malashenko, 2012). Together with Russia's military bases in other CIS states – the Sevastopol Naval Base in Ukraine and the Gabala radar station in Azerbaijan – this military presence allowed Russia to enhance its security and that of the CIS area, and further expand its geo-strategic reach. Furthermore, the Kremlin also succeeded in ensuring that no Western military bases remained in the CSTO region after 2014, allowing Russia to establish, to a certain extent, an 'exclusive sphere of influence' in the CSTO area. The CSTO also permitted Russia, at least in theory, to operate as the leader of a coalition of like-minded states in world affairs, although internal disagreements persisted on crucial issues, such as the independence of Abkhazia and South Ossetia (Panfilova and Yerzhanova, 2008), and the annexation of Crimea (Golts, 2014).

All this seems to indicate that Russia had been able to establish a hegemonic security space in the CSTO space under its undisputed leadership. Yet, the CSTO also suffered from the fact that it was not a congruent or homogenous organisation, and instead encompassed three dissimilar regional security complexes – the East European, the South Caucasus and the Central Asian regions – which did not share a common understanding of threats and similar enemy perceptions (Baev, 2014, p. 42; Arbatov, 2012). While Russia developed a very robust bilateral military alliance with Belarus in eastern Europe, Minsk remained reluctant to send troops anywhere outside its immediate neighbourhood. Belarus' reasons for supporting the CSTO were primarily of an internal nature – to ensure the survival of the regime in the face of growing isolation from the West, although concerns over NATO's enlargement also permeated its geo-strategic choice. In the South Caucasus, Russia established a strong military and strategic partnership with Armenia, but at the same time, it also cultivated friendly relations with Azerbaijan, which nevertheless remained outside the CSTO and was engaged in a confrontation with Armenia over Nagorno-Karabakh. While Russia tried to avoid being dragged militarily into the smouldering Karabakh conflict on the Armenian side, it nevertheless sold significant amounts of weaponry to Azerbaijan, whose leaders seemed prepared to use force in order to retake control over its lost territories. At the same time, Russia also provided military assistance to Armenia, thus spearheading a dangerous arms race in the South Caucasus region (Baev, 2014, p. 43).

In Central Asia, the CSTO proved better positioned to act as a collective security provider, as the region faced a series of common threats shared by all states, ranging from Islamist terrorism to inter-ethnic tensions, drug trafficking and organised crime. Yet, Russia and the CSTO proved reluctant in the 2000s and 2010s to become militarily involved in any of the conflicts that erupted in the region despite the existence of military instruments, such as the CSTO's KSOR force, showing the limits of its efficacy. The CSTO did not intervene in Kyrgyzstan when inter-ethnic violence erupted in its southern regions, and failed to assist the Tajik government when a group of former UTO rebels conducted an ambush in the Rasht Valley in September/October 2010 (Kucera, 2010). The Tajik government, in turn, did not request CSTO assistance when an armed criminal group conducted an incursion into the city of Khorog in July 2012. Furthermore, many CSTO states in Central Asia had antagonistic relations, with countries such as Uzbekistan, Tajikistan and Kyrgyzstan exerting claims over sections of each other's territories (Golts, 2010). Uzbekistan, in turn, remained suspicious of Russia's intentions, hesitating between staying in the CSTO or leaving the bloc. More importantly, for many CSTO members, the main threats to stability were of an internal as opposed to external nature – they reflected a high level of popular dissatisfaction with the socio-economic and political realities (Panfilova, 2015). The CSTO therefore simply became, as rightly noted by Aleksei Arbatov (2012), an umbrella covering a series of bilateral military relations involving Russia and its neighbours. The organisation lacked a clear unifying strategy, and instead involved countries with different strategies, pulling in different directions. Furthermore, the 'preservation of socio-political stability' and regime self-protection increasingly became the main goals and the maximum values of the organisation for CSTO member states (Yurgens, 2011).

Furthermore, despite belonging to the same security alliance, many CSTO states continued to develop military ties with the West and with China, thus curbing Russia's geo-strategic influence and challenging its hegemonic reach. Not only did NATO establish military partnerships with more pro-Western CSTO states such as Kazakhstan, Armenia and Kyrgyzstan, it also developed cooperation with Belarus and Tajikistan, two countries which had remained distant from NATO in the 1990s. Furthermore, in the 2010s, Beijing became more profoundly engaged militarily in the Central Asian region – it increased quite significantly the frequency of its military exercises with its Central Asian partners both within the SCO and outside of it (Breitmaier, 2016), and it also augmented quite substantially its contributing troops to the SCO *Peace Mission* military exercises – from 1,700 in 2007 to 5,000 in 2014 (de Haas, 2016). In August 2016, China also set up an anti-terrorism alliance, the 'Quadrilateral Cooperation and Coordination Mechanism', together with Pakistan, Afghanistan, and Tajikistan in order to boost military and intelligence cooperation and jointly tackle the growing extremist and terrorist threats (Gao, 2017; Kucera, 2016). Within this remit, Beijing offered to finance and build several outposts and other military facilities in Tajikistan, and to strengthen Tajikistan's defences along its southern borders with Afghanistan (Shahbazov, 2017). It also held major bilateral counter-terrorism exercises together with Tajikistan in 2016, which were aimed at deterring a potential Taliban incursion into the country. Furthermore, in early September 2017, China and Tajikistan established a 'Comprehensive Strategic Partnership', which expanded cooperation in the areas defence, security, law enforcement and intelligence sharing (*Reuters*, 2017; Gao, 2017). China also developed closer military ties with Kyrgyzstan and Kazakhstan, in the areas of law enforcement, counter-narcotics and counter-terrorism, concerned over the spread of instability from Central Asia and Afghanistan into China's Xinjiang province. More worryingly from Russia's perspective, was the Chinese decision in 2015 to sell the sophisticated HQ-9 air-defence systems to Turkmenistan and Uzbekistan to protect their air space from a potential attack (Kucera, 2015). Yet, while China's influence in Central Asia undoubtedly increased, its military activities in the region remained a far lower priority than its economic cooperation with the Central Asian states. Beijing made sure it did not antagonise its Russian partner, which remained the military hegemon in the region. China made sure its military cooperation in Central Asia also developed within the SCO framework – and this included Russia. Yet, Moscow's dominant and hegemonic position in Central Asia in the security realm was increasingly being disputed by its stronger Chinese neighbour.

Conclusion

Despite China's growing military presence in Central Asia, Russia remained, nevertheless, the main provider of security to countries in the CSTO/CIS region. As the dominant military power in Eurasia, Russia assisted the CSTO member states with the training of their armed forces at its military academies, provided

CSTO states with military equipment at reduced prices, developed joint training programmes, organised and financed military exercises, and – last but not least – shared its nuclear umbrella to guarantee their security. Furthermore, as noted above, Russia's military support and equipment were granted on the basis that CSTO states took full consideration of Russia's strategic interests (Saat, 2005). All these developments made of the CSTO an instrument of Russian hegemony in the CIS space. Russia's efforts to strengthen the CSTO, and the CIS, more generally, to a certain extent, followed from Moscow's point of view, legitimate state concerns, related to the United States' growing military presence and political engagement in the region. As pointed out by Gabuyev and Solovyov, 'The Kremlin proceeds from the premise that the need to strengthen Russia's influence in the CIS is directly related to the need to counter the greatly increased activity of the US in the region', which was seen as the orchestrator of the so-called 'colour revolutions' in Georgia, Kyrgyzstan and Ukraine (Gabuyev and Solovyov, 2007). Western support for democratic alternatives in Russia and in other CIS states was seen by the Kremlin as directly challenging the existing political regimes of the region, many of which were of a strong authoritarian nature, such as the Islam Karimov leadership in Uzbekistan or the Alexander Lukashenko presidency in Belarus. The West's actions remained an issue of utmost concern not only to the Kremlin, but also to its CSTO allies, whose leaders worried not only about their own fate but also about the potential spread of instability in the Eurasian region resulting from violent changes of regime. On the other hand, in the Western theatre, the Kremlin – and the Russian General Staff – continued to see the Belarusian western borders on NATO as Russia's de facto strategic borders with the West. Military integration with Belarus, therefore, intensified against the background of NATO's several waves of enlargement eastwards (Trenin, 2005, p. 71). NATO's expansion close to Russia's western and southern borders, as well as the United States' military presence in Central Asia and the Caucasus, were clearly perceived by the Kremlin as serious geopolitical threats to Russia's security and as direct challenges to its influence in the region.

Yet, Russia's actions also undoubtedly reflected a Russian neo-imperialist drive. Moscow clearly considered the former Soviet space, and the CSTO in particular, as an area of Russia's 'special interests,' whose control remained essential in order to ensure the country's security. The CSTO provided Russia with additional strategic depth on all its geo-strategic fronts. It allowed Russia to delay a potential attack by NATO on the west, to keep a foothold in the turbulent South Caucasus region and to contain a possible advance of the Taliban or ISIS into Central Asia. Moscow, therefore, tried to revive and re-establish a new military structure, which to a certain extent, replicated the old Warsaw Treaty Organisation's model. In it, all the CSTO armed forces would be subordinated to the Russian General Staff. Its intention was to keep these countries within a Russian-led sphere of influence. Yet, it must be noted, that all those countries which formed part of the CSTO, welcomed Russia's military support, and this factor slightly weakens the neo-imperialist argument in Russia's favour. All CSTO states, and especially the weaker ones – Tajikistan, Kyrgyzstan and Armenia – were consumers rather than providers of security, and as such, remained eager to obtain Russian military support in case of aggression. All CSTO states were keen to obtain Russian financial assistance to develop their own national armed forces, while countries such as Tajikistan and Kyrgyzstan remained eager to receive financial compensation for the deployment of Russian troops on their territories. Furthermore, it must be noted that efforts to strengthen the CSTO also responded to legitimate state concerns of all the states concerned – because of the weaknesses of the CSTO states and the transnational nature of the threats faced, countries felt the need to act *jointly*. Only together could they effectively tackle violent extremism, Islamist terrorism, illicit drug trafficking, organised crime and illegal immigration – challenges which threatened the security and stability of the Central Asian and Caucasus region as a whole (RIA Novosti, 2005).[20] There was a clear understanding among CSTO states that fruitful cooperation was necessary in order properly to address these threats. Furthermore, many countries in Central Asia and the South Caucasus faced several internal security challenges related to insecure borders, inter-ethnic strife and widespread corruption. The CSTO, in this respect, proved to be a fundamental vehicle to ensure Russia's support to address these challenges. Having said that, many CSTO partners, nevertheless, also developed military ties with external actors, in particular with Western countries such as the United States and NATO, as well as with China, with whom they cooperated actively within the SCO framework. This again highlighted the limits of Russia's influence in the Eurasian region. It reduced Moscow's ability to create an effective neo-empire in the CIS/CSTO space, where its dominance would remain undisputed.

Notes

1 The 2000 *National Security Concept* (NSC) also noted that 'one of the vital strategic directions in providing for the Russian Federation's military security [was] the effective collaboration and cooperation with members of the Commonwealth of Independent States.' (MID, 2000).
2 Uzbek forces also took part in the 2,000 exercises.
3 The CST was moving away from conducting only peacekeeping operations to approving the conduct of military operations directly involving the use of force in case of aggression.
4 In April 1999, agreement had been reached between Russia and Tajikistan on the establishment of a permanent military base for Russia's 201st MID based outside the Tajik capital, Dushanbe (Lachowski, 2007, p. 54).
5 Armenia and Russia had instituted joint alert duties by their defence forces in 1999 (Bulavinov, 2000).
6 Agreement on the creation of a Union State, 8 December 1999.
7 The 2002 exercise rehearsed combating terrorist incursions into Kyrgyzstan and Kazakhstan, and also included elements from the security agencies and from the CIS anti-terrorist centre (Glumskov, 2002).
8 The USA promised financial training and support to help the Tajik border troops and in 2001.
9 In 1997, within the Union of Russia and Belarus framework, a joint Border Committee was set up, to coordinate the actions of the two countries' border agencies (Plotnikov, 1997).

10 The 201st MID military personnel was lowered from 7,500 to 5,000.
11 Previously, a standing operational group based in Bishkek had been in charge of the CRDF, under Russian command (Socor, 2006).
12 Russia kept over 3,100 men at the Gyumri air base.
13 The Russian–Uzbek accord foresaw the right by the sides to use military installations on their respective territories (Panfilova *et al.*, 2005).
14 Sergei Lavrov, however, denied that the peace-keeping force would be used to settle conflicts in Abkhazia or South Ossetia – ruling out its involvement in CIS separatist wars.
15 To avoid any involvement in the domestic affairs of CSTO states, the CSTO Charter had made explicit reference to the principle of non-interference of the CSTO in the internal affairs of its members (ODKB, 2002).
16 The RCSF would help repel a potential external aggressor and conduct joint counter-terrorist operations in the CST area (Odnokolenko, 2000).
17 This was discussed by Putin at a meeting with the NATO's Secretary General de Hoop Scheffer in Moscow in late June 2005.
18 The secretariat has a staff of 30 persons and was initially allocated a budget of US$2.6 million (Bailes *et al.*, 2007, p. 1).
19 Furthermore, the American presence in Central Asia potentially allowed Washington to intervene in the ethnic relations in Xinjiang and bring influence to bear on the Central Asian states (Skosyrev, 2005).
20 The CSTO Charter read,

> The Member States shall coordinate and harmonise their efforts in combating international terrorism and extremism, the illicit traffic in narcotic drugs, psychotropic substances and arms, organized transnational crime, illegal migration and other threats to the security of the Member States.
>
> (Art. 8.) (ODKB, 2002)

Bibliography

Arbatov, A. (2012). Odkb kak voennogo soiuza ne sushchestvuet. Russian Council. 18 July. Available at: http://russiancouncil.ru/analytics-and-comments/comments/odkb-kak-voennogo-soyuza-ne-sushchestvuet/?sphrase_id=11141058 [accessed 5 June 2017].

Aris, S. (2009). The Shanghai Cooperation Organisation: 'Tackling the Three Evils'. A Regional Response to Non-Traditional Security Challenges or an Anti-Western Bloc? *Europe-Asia Studies*, 61 (3), 457–482.

Arms Control Association (ACA) (2000). *Russia's Military Doctrine*. 22 April. Available at: www.armscontrol.org/act/2000_05/dc3ma00?print [accessed 10 June 2017].

Associated Press (AP) (2004). Ex-Soviet Republics to Boost Cooperation. 18 June.

Baev, P. (2014). The CSTO: Military Dimensions of the Russian Reintegration Effort. In: S.F. Starr and S.E. Cornell. eds. *Putin's Grand Strategy: The Eurasian Union and Its Discontents*, Central Asia-Caucasus Institute & Silk Road Studies Program, pp. 40–48.

Bailes, A.J.K, P. Dunay, P. Guang and M. Troitskiy (2007). The Shanghai Cooperation Organization. SPRI Policy Paper. 17. May. Available at: www.sipri.org/sites/default/files/files/PP/SIPRIPP17.pdf [accessed 10 June 2017].

Baluyevsky, Yu. (2006). *Krasnaya Zvezda*. 25 January. Available at: www.shakhty.su/world/articles/2006/01/25/baluevski/ [accessed 10 June 2017].

Baran, Z. (2007). *Democratic Breakdown and the Decline of the Russian Military*. Princeton and Oxford: Princeton University Press.

Belapan News Agency (2006). 1 June.

Bichurina, V. and D. Telmanov (2011). *Izvestiya*, 14 September, p. 4.

Brannon, R. (2009). *Russian Civil-Military Relations*. Surrey, England: Ashgate.
Breitmaier, M. (2016). *China's Rise and Central Asia's Security*. Alert Issue. 21. June. European Union Institute for Security Studies. Available at: www.iss.europa.eu/sites/default/files/EUISSFiles/Alert_21_Central_Asia_MB.pdf [accessed 6 June 2018].
Bohdan, S. (2015). Russian Airbase in Belarus: A Long Story with No End in Sight? *Belarus Digest*. 24 September 2015. Available: https://belarusdigest.com/story/russian-airbase-in-belarus-a-long-story-with-no-end-in-sight/ [accessed 6 June 2017].
Bohdan, S. (2016). Does the Single Air Defence System Bring Belarus Closer to Russia? *Belarus Digest*, 12 April. Available: https://belarusdigest.com/story/does-the-single-air-defence-system-bring-belarus-closer-to-russia/ [accessed 6 June 2017].
Bordyuzha, N. (2010). The Collective Security Treaty Organization: A Brief Overview. In: *OSCE Yearbook*, Hamburg. IFSH, pp. 339–350.
Bulavinov, I. (1998). *Kommersant-daily*, 16 April, p. 2.
Bulavinov, I. (2000). *Kommersant*, 10 February, p. 11.
Chernyak, M. and Raskin, A. (1999). *Vremya MN*. 9 August. p. 1.
Dubnov, A. (2000). *Vremya novostei*, 25 May, p. 2.
Dubnov, A. (2001). *Vremya novostei*, 24 May, p. 2.
Eaton, M. (2001). Major Trends in Military Expenditure and Arms Acquisitions by States of the Caspian Region. In: G. Chufrin, ed. *The Security of the Caspian Sea Region*. Oxford, Oxford University Press, pp. 83–118.
Fedorov, Yu. (2009). *Medvedev's Amendments to the Law on Defence*. The Finish Institute of International Affairs, 27 November.
Gabuyev, A. (2007). *Kommersant*, 9 August, p. 7.
Gabuyev A. and V. Solovyov (2007). *Kommersant*, 8 October, p. 9.
Gafarly, M. (2005). *Noviye Izvestiya*, 13 October, p. 4.
Gao, Ch. (2017). China and Tajikistan To Establish Comprehensive Strategic Partnership. *The Diplomat*, 1 September. Available at: https://thediplomat.com/2017/09/china-and-tajikistan-to-establish-comprehensive-strategic-partnership/ [accessed 8 September 2018].
Glikin, M. (2003). *Nezavisimaya gazeta*, 29 April, p. 2.
Glumskov, D. (2002). *Kommersant*, 18 June, p. 10.
Golotuyk, Yu. (2001). *Vremya novostei*, 28 April, p. 3.
Golts, A. (2010). *The Moscow Times*, 31 August. Available at: https://themoscowtimes.com/articles/csto-is-dead-1012 [accessed 6 June 2017].
Golts, A. (2014). *The Moscow Times*, 20 May, p. 8.
Guang, P. (2005). The Chinese Perspective on the Recent Astana Summit', *Jamestown Foundation China Brief*, 5(18), 16 August. Available at: https://jamestown.org/program/the-chinese-perspective-on-the-recent-astana-summit/ [accessed 10 July 2018].
Guly, S. (2000). *Noviye Izvestia*, 12 October, pp. 1–2.
de Haas, M. (2005). Russian-Chinese Military Exercises and their Wider Perspective: Power Play in Central Asia. Conflict Studies Research Centre, 51(5), October.
de Haas, M. (2011). Russia's Military Doctrine Development (2000–10). In: S.J. Blank. Ed. *Russia's Military Politics and Russia's 2010 Defence Doctrine*. Strategic Studies Institute. March, pp. 1–62. Available at: www.clingendael.org/sites/default/files/pdfs/20110300_haas_doctrine.pdf [accessed 6 June 2017].
de Haas, M. (2016). War Games of the Shanghai Cooperation Organization and the Collective Security Treaty Organization: Drills on the Move! *Journal of Slavic Military Studies*, 29(3), 378–406.
IISS (2002/2003). *The Military Balance*. London.

IISS (2003/2004). *The Military Balance*. London.
IISS (2004/2005). *The Military Balance*. London.
IISS (2005). *The Military Balance*. London.
IISS (2006). *The Military Balance*. London.
IISS (2007). *The Military Balance*. London.
IISS (2008). *The Military Balance*. London.
IISS (2009). *The Military Balance*. London.
IISS (2015). *The Military Balance*. London.
IISS (2016). *The Military Balance*. London.
Kolesnikov, A. (2004). *Kommersant*, 19 June, 2004, p. 1.
Kolesnikov, A. (2005). *Kommersant*, 6 July, p. 1.
Kolesnikov, A. (2006). *Kommersant*, 24 June, p. 2.
Konovalov, S. (2011). *Nezavisimaya gazeta*, 5 September, p. 1.
Koryunov, L. (2000). *Kommersant*, March 3, p. 11.
Kulagin, V. (2002). *Nezavisimaya gazeta*, 27 March, p. 2.
Kucera, J. (2010). Violence in Tajikistan. *The Diplomat*, November 30. Available at: https://thediplomat.com/2010/11/violence-in-tajikistan/2/ [accessed 6 June 2017].
Kucera, J. (2012). CSTO Holds First-Ever Peacekeeping Exercises, 8 October. Available at: www.eurasianet.org/node/66023 [accessed 6 June 2017].
Kucera, J. (2015). Has China Made Its First Big Military Sale in Central Asia? 6 February. Available at: https://eurasianet.org/has-china-made-its-first-big-military-sale-in-central-asia [accessed 6 June 2017].
Kucera, J. (2016). Afghanistan, China, Pakistan, Tajikistan Deepen 'Anti-Terror' Ties. 4 August. Available at: https://eurasianet.org/node/80006 [accessed 6 June 2017].
Lachowski, Z. (2007). *Foreign Military Bases in Eurasia*, Stockholm: SIPRI Policy Paper, 18 June.
Legvold, R. (2003). US Policy Towards Kazakhstan. In: R. Legvold (ed.), *Thinking Strategically: The Major Powers, Kazakhstan, and the Central Asian Nexus*. Cambridge, Mass.: The MIT Press, pp. 67–106.
Macfarlane, S. (2004). The United States and Regionalism in Central Asia. *International Affairs*, 80(3), 447–461.
Malashenko, A. (2012). *Tsentral'naya Aziya: na chto rasschityvaet Rossiya?* Moscow: Carnegie Center and Rossiiskaya Politicheskaya Entsiklopediya.
Mashin, Yu. (2000). *Kommersant*, 30 March, p. 11.
McDermott, R. (2004a). *Countering Global Terrorism: Developing the Anti-terrorist Capabilities of the Central Asian Militaries*, Conflict Studies Research Centre. February.
McDermott, R. (2004b). Anti-terrorist Exercises Underway in Central Asia, *Eurasia Daily Monitor*, 1 (67), 4 August.
McDermott, R. (2012). CSTO Stages First Peacekeeping Exercise. *Eurasia Daily Monitor*, 9 (188), 16 October. Available at: https://jamestown.org/program/csto-stages-first-peacekeeping-exercise/ [accessed 6 June 2017].
MID (2000). Kontseptsiya natsional'noi bezopasnosti Rossiiskoi Federatsii. 10 January. Available at: www.mid.ru/en/foreign_policy/official_documents/-/asset_publisher/CptICkB6BZ29/content/id/589768 [accessed 11 June 2018].
Mowchan, J.A. (2009). *The Militarization of the Collective Security Treaty Organisation*. CSL Issue Paper. 6(9) Center for Strategic Leadership, US Army War College. July.
Mukhin, V. (2001). *Nezavisimaya gazeta*, 25 May, p. 1.
Mukhin, V. (2006). *Nezavisimaya gazeta*, 4 December, p. 1.
Mukhin, V. (2013). *Nezavisimaya gazeta*, 17 April, p. 1.

Myasnikov, V. (2006). *Nezavisimaya gazeta*, 27 April, p. 2.

Mylnikov, B. (n.d.) "Predotvrashchenie i presechenie terrorizma: rol' i deistviya regional'nykh i subregional'nikh organizatsii, initsiativ i koordiniruiushchikh struktur", Anti-terrorist Centre website, www.atcsnug.ru/articles.cgi?id=96 [accessed 11 June 2018].

Nikolsky, A. and N. Kostenko (2011). *Vedomosti*, 12 September, p. 2.

Norberg, J. (2013). *High Ambitions, Harsh Realities: Gradually Building the CSTO's Capacity for Military Intervention in Crises*. FOI, Sweden Defence Ministry. May.

Nurshayeva, R. (2015). Russian Border Guards' Return to Tajikistan 'Not on Agenda': Official. 12 November. Available at: www.reuters.com/article/us-russia-tajikistan-border/russian-border-guards-return-to-tajikistan-not-on-agenda-official-idUSKCN0T-10BY20151112 [accessed 6 June 2017].

ODKB (2000a). Memorandum o povyshenii effektivnosti Dogovora o Kollektivnoi Bezopasnosti ot 15 Maya 1992 goda i evo adaptatsii k sovremennoi geopoliticheskoi situatsii, Minsk, 24 May. Available at: http://cons.parus.ua/map/doc/05RXBC3944/Memorandum-o-povyshenii-effektivnosti-Dogovora-o-kollektivnoi-bezopasnosti-ot-15-maya-1992-goda-i-ego-adaptatsii-k-sovremennoi-geopoliticheskoi-situatsii.html [accessed 10 June 2018].

ODKB (2000b). Reshenie Soveta Kollektivnoi bezopasnosti, 'O xode raboty po formirovaniu sistemy kollektivnoi bezopasnosti'. Bishkek, 11 October. Available at: http://cons.parus.ua/map/doc/05U5MF1472/Reshenie-Soveta-kollektivnoi-bezopasnosti-o-khode-raboty-po-formirovaniyu-sistemy-kollektivnoi-bezopasnosti.html [accessed 11 June 2018].

ODKB (2000c). Soglashenie o statuse formirovanii sil i sredstv sistemy kollektivnoi bezopasnosti, Bishkek, 11 October. Available at: www.conventions.ru/view_base.php?id=13089 [accessed 11 June 2018].

ODKB (2001). Protokol o poryadke formirovaniya i funktsionirovaniya sil i sredstv sistemy kollektivnoi bezopasnosti gosudarstv-uchastnikov Dogovora o kollektivnoi bezopasnosti ot 15 maya 1992 goda. Yerevan, 25 May. Available at: http://cbd.minjust.gov.kg/act/view/ru-ru/17412 [accessed 11 June 2018].

ODKB (2002). Charter of The Collective Security Treaty Organization. 7 October, www.odkb-csto.org/documents/detail.php?ELEMENT_ID=1896 [accessed 8 June 2018].

ODKB (2007). Agreement of The Collective Security Treaty Organization About Peacekeeping Activities, 6 October. Available at: http://cis-legislation.com/document.fwx?rgn=19059 [accessed 11 June 2018].

ODKB (2010). Soglashenie o poryadke formirovaniya sil i sredstv sistemy kollektivnoi bezopasnosti Organizatsii Dogovora o Kollektivnoi bezopasnosti, 10 December. Available at: https://base.garant.ru/70166618/ [accessed 18 November 2017].

Odnokolenko, O. (2000). *Segodnya*, 12 October, p. 1.

Orozaliyev, B. and I. Safronov (2005). *Kommersant*, 22 September, p. 10.

Panfilova, V. (2004). *Nezavisimaya gazeta*, 8 June, p. 5.

Panfilova, V. (2006). *Nezavisimaya gazeta*, 20 February, p. 3.

Panfilova, V. (2015). *Nezavisimya gazeta*, 2 September, p. 7.

Panfilova V. and V. Georgiev (2002). *Nezavisimaya gazeta*, 15 May, p. 2.

Panfilova, V. and Z. Yerzhanova (2008). *Nezavisimaya gazeta*, 11 September, p. 8.

Panfilova, V., V. Kiselyov and I. Plugataryov, I. (2005). *Nezavisimaya gazeta*, 15 November 2005, p. 5.

Pannier, B. (2007). Eurasia: U.S. Security Expert Talks About SCO Exercises, Summit. *Radio Free Europe – Radio Liberty*. 9 August. Available at: www.rferl.org/a/1078065.html [accessed 19 October 2019].

Poroskov, N. (2005). *Vremya novostei*, 26 August, p. 2.
Plater-Zyberk, H. (2004). *Tajikistan: Waiting for the Storm*, Conflict Studies Research Centre, Defence Academy United Kingdom.
Plotnikov, N. (1997). *Nezavisimaya gazeta*, 26 July, p. 3.
Reuters (2017). Tajikistan agrees to more intelligence exchanges with China. 1 September. Available at: https://uk.reuters.com/article/uk-china-tajikistan-security/tajikistan-agrees-to-more-intelligence-exchanges-with-china-idUKKCN1BC3N1 [accessed 6 June 2017].
RFE/RL (2006). U.S. To Stay in Kyrgyz Military Base. 21 July. Available at: www.rferl.org/a/1070019.html [accessed 11 June 2018].
RIA Novosti (2005). Eurasian States Set to Build Effective Military Capability for Collective Security. 22 June.
Romanova, L. and R. Karapetyan (2001). *Nezavisimaya gazeta*, 26 May, p. 1.
Rontoyanni, C. (2000). *Russia-Belarus Union: The Role of NATO and the EU*, Conflict Studies Research Centre, December.
Saat, J.H. (2005). *The Collective Security Treaty Organization*. Conflict Studies Research Centre. February, p. 1, p. 7.
Safronov, I. (2002). *Kommersant*, 15 May, p. 2.
Saidazimova, G. (2005). Bishkek Assures Rumsfeld That U.S. Air Base Can Stay. *RFE/RL.org*, July 26. Available at: www.rferl.org/a/1060185.html [accessed 12 June 2018].
Shahbazov, F. (2017). China's Long March into Central Asia: How Beijing Expands Military Influence in Tajikistan. The Central Asia-Caucasus Analyst. 21 February. Available at: https://cacianalyst.org/publications/analytical-articles/item/13429-china%E2%80%99s-long-march-into-central-asia-how-beijing-expands-military-influence-in-tajikistan.html. [accessed 6 June 2017].
Shimanskaya K. and A. Neverovsky (2000). *Kommersant*, 12 April, p. 3.
Sigov, Yu and S. Guly (2001). *Noviye Izvestiya*, 15 June, p. 3.
Skosyrev, V. (2005). *Moskovskie Novosti*, 1–7 April, p. 9.
Socor, V. (2005a). CIS Collective Security Treaty Organization Holds Summit, *Eurasia Daily Monitor*, 2 (123), 24 June. Available at: https://jamestown.org/program/cis-collective-security-treaty-organization-holds-summit/ [accessed 5 June 2019].
Socor, V. (2005b). From CIS to CSTO: Can a "Core" be Preserved? *Eurasia Daily Monitor*, 2 (125), 28 June. Available at: https://jamestown.org/program/from-cis-to-csto-can-a-core-be-preserved/ [accessed 5 June 2019].
Socor, V. (2006). CSTO Summit: Military Bloc Not Yet Cemented. *Eurasia Daily Monitor*, 3 (125), 28 June. Available at: https://jamestown.org/program/csto-summit-military-bloc-not-yet-cemented/ [accessed 6 June 2019].
Solovyov, V. (2010a). *Kommersant*, 21 August, p. 1.
Solovyev, V. (2010b). *Kommersant*, 11 December, p. 1.
Solovyov, V. and V. Ivanov (2007). *Nezavisimaya gazeta*, 10 August, p. 1.
Spildsboel-Hansen, F. (2000). GUUAM and the Future of CIS Military Cooperation. *European Security*, 9(4), 92–110.
Strategic Comments (2006). The Shanghai Cooperation Organisation: Internal Contradictions. 12 (6), 1–2.
Strugovets, V. (2004). *Russky kuryer*, 16 March, p. 2.
Suponina, Ye. (2005). *Vremya novostei*, 6 June, 2005, p. 5
Sysoyev, G. (2006). *Kommersant*, 23 June, p. 9.
Swanstrom, N. (2005). China and Central Asia: A New Great Game or Traditional Vassal Relations? *Journal of Contemporary China*, 14 (45), November, 569–584.

Torjesen, S. (2009). Russia as a Military Great Power: The Uses of the CSTO and the SCO in Central Asia. In: E. Wilson Rowe and S. Torjesen, eds. *The Multilateral Dimension in Russian Foreign Policy*, London: Routledge, pp. 181–192.

Trenin, D. (2005). Moscow's Relations with Belarus: An Awkward Ally. In: D. Lynch, *Changing Belarus*. Chaillot Paper, 85. Paris: Institute For Security Studies. November, pp. 67–78.

Varlamov, A. (2001). *Vremya MN*, 20 December, p. 2.

Vladkin, O. (2002). *Obshchaya gazeta*, 16–22 May, p. 5.

Volkhonsky, B. (2002). *Kommersant*. May 24, p. 2.

Vorobyov, V. (2003). *Rossiiskaya gazeta*, 23 September, p. 1.

Weber, M. (2002). A Confederation in the Making? Means, Ends and Prospects of the Commonwealth of Independent States. In: Heinemann-Grueder, A., ed. *Federalism Doomed? European Federalism between Integration and Separation*. New York, Oxford: Berghahn Books, pp. 167–193.

Weitz, R. (2006). The CSTO Deepens Military Ties. CACI Analyst. Available at: www.cacianalyst.org/publications/analytical-articles/item/11149-analytical-articles-caci-analyst-2006-10-18-art-11149.html?tmpl=component&print=1 [accessed 15 June 2018].

Weitz, R. (2014). The Collective Security Treaty Organization: Past Struggles and Future Prospects. *Russian Analytical Digest*, 152, 21 July, pp. 2–4. Available at: https://css.ethz.ch/content/dam/ethz/special-interest/gess/cis/center-for-securities-studies/pdfs/RAD-152-2-4.pdf [accessed 20 October 2019].

Wu, H-L. and Chen, C-H. (2004) The Prospects for Regional Economic Integration between China and the Five Central Asian Countries, *Europe-Asia Studies*, 56 (7), 1059–1080.

Yuan, J.D. (2010). China's Role in Establishing and Building the Shanghai Cooperation Organization (SCO). *Journal of Contemporary China*, 19 (67), 855–869.

Yurgens, I. Yu. (2011). ODKB: Otvetsvennaya bezopastost'. Moscow. August. Available at: www.insor-russia.ru/files/ODKB.pdf [accessed 6 June 2017].

Zhao, H. (2013). China's View of and Expectations from the Shanghai Cooperation Organization. Asian Survey, 53 (3), 436–460.

Zotov, V. (2000). *Vremya MN*, 5 September, p. 5.

9 Separatist conflicts in Eurasia
Russia's hegemonic power is reinforced

With the arrival of Putin to the Kremlin, Russia adopted a much more assertive policy vis-à-vis the Georgian separatist conflicts of Abkhazia and South Ossetia, reflecting the worsening of relations between Moscow and Tbilisi. Endowed with an increased 'neo-imperialist' outlook and concerned over security developments in the North and South Caucasus, the Kremlin ended up establishing effective protectorates over Georgia's de facto separatist states. Moscow's relations with Moldova, instead, initially took a more positive turn, and by 2003, it seemed as though a resolution of the Transdniestrian conflict, which suited Russia's interests, could be achieved. Yet, as the decade progressed, Russia's actions in both Georgia and Moldova became much more forceful, and increasingly revealed a neo-imperialist paradigm. While Moscow's behaviour may have reflected legitimate state concerns, related to the enlargement of NATO into Romania and Bulgaria, and the possible expansion of NATO into Georgia, they nevertheless showed an eagerness by the Putin leadership to keep Moldova – and Georgia – under a Russian sphere of influence. Russia's behaviour in these two countries contrasted, quite sharply instead, with the positions adopted by the Kremlin in relation to the Nagorno-Karabakh conflict. During Putin's first and second Presidencies, Russia generally took a positive stance in the negotiations and collaborated quite actively with the other OSCE Minsk co-Chairs on the Nagorno-Karabakh dispute, in a sign that it had, at least apparently, discarded its imperial legacy in this region. Although Russia continued to explore the possibility of sending peacekeeping forces to Nagorno-Karabakh, the Kremlin seemed less eager than previously to impose such a military presence on the sides through coercive diplomacy and hard power. Yet, Russia had by the mid-2000s, largely achieved its key objectives in the region – a strong strategic and economic partnership had been established with Armenia, which effectively kept the country under Russia's sphere of influence, while close military and security ties were also being developed with Azerbaijan, and this ensured that Baku did not act entirely against Russia's interests.

The Georgian separatist conflicts

Russia's relations with Georgia deteriorated quite significantly during Putin's first Presidencies as the outbreak of the second Chechen war in 1999 once again turned the South Caucasus into an area of heightened concern for Russia. Tbilisi's refusal to allow Russian military forces to operate in Georgia's border regions and fight against Chechen rebels, and Georgia's demands that Russia rapidly close its military bases and withdraw its troops from Georgia were strongly resented by Moscow (Vignansky et al., 2001; Babichev and Chubchenko, 2000). Furthermore, Georgia's increased military cooperation with NATO and the USA through the 'Train and Equip' programme, created great anxiety in the Kremlin, and led to worries that Georgia could eventually become a member of NATO (Dvali and Sysoyev, 2002). Russia, in turn, established extremely close ties with the separatist regions of Abkhazia and South Ossetia, which effectively turned these areas into Russian 'protectorates', in a clear sign that Moscow viewed these regions as channels of influence over its Georgian neighbour. Russia assisted Georgia's separatist regions militarily and economically (Illarionov, 2009, p. 53; Felgengauer, 2001) fostered bilateral trade relations with Abkhazia and South Ossetia (Dvali, 2002), and facilitated the acquisition of Russian passports by their citizens. While in the winter of 1999–2000 Moscow introduced a visa regime for Georgians wishing to enter Russia, it did not impose the same strict requirements on Abkhaz and South Ossetians, allowing them to enter Russia unhindered (Golotyuk, 2000; Sychova, 2000). The Kremlin also orchestrated the accession to power of a staunchly pro-Russian leader in South Ossetia, who appointed members of the Russian security structures to key government positions, thus placing the separatist region fully under Russian control (Illarionov, 2009, p. 52; Sysoyev, 2001). In Abkhazia a pro-Russian regime, eager to achieve independence for its 'republic', remained in place. Demands for close association with Russia by the Abkhaz were reinforced after a group of Chechen insurgents and Georgian paramilitaries seized various villages in the Gulripsh district of Abkhazia in October 2001 (UNSC, 2001).[1] Yet, while Russia helped the Abkhaz to rebuff the Chechen/Georgian incursion, it refused officially to recognise the separatist regions as independent states. Instead, Moscow engaged in active diplomatic efforts intended to find negotiated settlements to the disputes, which theoretically kept the territorial integrity of Georgia intact (Antonenko, 2005, p. 239). Russia collaborated actively with Western governments and with the United Nations (UN) in Georgia to resolve the conflict in Abkhazia, while it also worked hand in hand with the OSCE mission to South Ossetia to bring an end to the dispute (UNSC, 2002b; ICG, 2007a).

Despite Russia's alleged pressures over the separatist regions, Moscow proved unable to enforce a negotiated solution on either the Abkhaz or the South Ossetians, which kept these regions inside Georgia (Francis, 2011, pp. 148–151). It is difficult to ascertain whether or not Russia played a double game, officially pushing for a resolution of the dispute which kept these regions inside the 'mother country', but secretly asking Sukhumi and Tskhinvali not to acquiesce to the proposed solutions, in order to keep a foothold in the region. While such an outcome of events cannot be entirely excluded, it is nevertheless highly unlikely. Most probably, the Kremlin wished for a settlement of the conflict which granted the separatist regions significant autonomy and relative influence in the internal affairs of the 'mother state', but remained short of independence. This would have allowed Russia an indirect say in the affairs of Georgia and would have guaranteed Moscow that policies which impaired Russia's interests in the North and South Caucasus – such as Georgia's membership of the North Atlantic Alliance – would not be adopted by Tbilisi. Yet, Russia failed in its endeavour, as the Abkhaz categorically refused to accept any resolution of the conflict which did not recognise their independent status. As the UN-led talks on Abkhazia's future failed to make any significant inroads, in February 2003, the UN SRSG (Special Representative of the Secretary General) suggested that the sides restart joint work on three clusters of Confidence-Building Measures (CBMs) as agreed in 1997 – economic cooperation, the return of IDPs (Internally Displaced People) and security guarantees (UNSC, 2002a). Putin, in turn, opened parallel negotiations directly with the Georgian leadership of Eduard Shevardnadze in March 2003, which further strengthened Russia's ties with the separatist region of Abkhazia (Vignansky and Glanin, 2003). The Putin–Shevardnadze talks officially sanctioned Russia's economic activities in Abkhazia, perpetuated Russian peacekeeping operations in the region and allowed Russia officially to represent Sukhumi in the UN-led negotiations, effectively sealing Russia's grip over the 'republic' (Antonenko, 2005, p. 242; Vignansky and Glanin, 2003). In South Ossetia, the new staunchly pro-Russian leadership of Eduard Kokoity abandoned an agreement that had been successfully brokered by the OSCE in 2000 in Baden (Austria), which kept South Ossetia as a region inside Georgia with broad autonomous powers, and instead, Kokoity expressed his clear support for 'closer relations with North Ossetia and broader ties with Russia' (Sysoyev, 2001).[2] It seemed as though both South Ossetia and Abkhazia were falling tightly within Russia's sphere of influence.

During Putin's second term in office, Russia policies towards Georgia hardened as the Kremlin felt that its presence in Georgia was coming increasingly under threat. In 2004, Mikhail Saakashvili became Georgia's President in the aftermath of the Georgian Revolution, and although as soon as he took office he expressed an eagerness to improve ties with Russia, he also enhanced, quite significantly, Georgia's military ties with NATO, and engaged in an unprecedented effort, with Western support, to rearm and revamp the country's armed forces (Transparency International, 2007; SIPRI, 2007, pp. 189–190). This created great worries not only in Russia, but also in the separatist regions, Abkhazia and South Ossetia, that force would be used once again by Tbilisi to restore control over these territories. Furthermore, Saakashvili also demanded the closure of Russia's bases at Batumi and Akhalkalaki, to Russia's great concern as Moscow saw its presence in Georgia, 'an area where it had held sway for centuries', as essential for its own security. Such presence was now being further undermined (ICG, 2004a, p. 9; Novikov and Sysoyev, 2004). In 2000–2001, Russia had already proceeded with the closure of two of its military bases in Georgia – Vaziani and Gudauta – in accordance with the agreements reached with Tbilisi at the OSCE summit in Istanbul in November 1999 (Dvali, 2001; Mukhin, 2001). Moscow had also destroyed and removed all of its excess military hardware from Georgia as required by the Conventional Forces in Europe (CFE) Treaty in the autumn of 2000 (Dvali, 2000). It therefore worried about having to close its two remaining bases in Georgia at Batumi and Akhalkalaki, and opposed such Georgian demands. Instead, it insisted on keeping Russia's military forces in these two sites for a 15-year period (Loria, 2001; Babichev and Chubchenko, 2000).

Furthermore, with the arrival of Saakashvili to the Georgian presidency, Russia's presence in the separatist regions of Abkhazia and South Ossetia was also further challenged. Soon after he became President in 2004, Saakashvili used a combination of soft power measures – humanitarian and economic aid, more inclusive peace proposals – and a series of hard power instruments, including the reinforcement of a maritime blockade in Abkhazia, and the strengthening of police posts along the borders of South Ossetia, to bring Georgia's separatist regions under Tbilisi's fold (Vignansky, 2004; Francis, 2011, p. 153; Civil Georgia, 2003). Saakashvili also attempted to seize South Ossetia by force when violence escalated in the region in August 2004, raising concerns not only in Moscow but also among Georgia's Western partners, that violence could get out of hand and large-scale war could break out again (ICG, 2004a, pp. 11–15; Civil Georgia, 2004). Russia responded to this predicament by further strengthening its ties with the separatist regions, worried that its presence and influence in Abkhazia and South Ossetia, would be seriously undermined if Tbilisi's plans to restore control over these regions and remove Russia's forces proved successful. The Kremlin not only enhanced its economic and military support to South Ossetia and Abkhazia, it also ensured that the political leadership in these republics remained entirely loyal to Russia. In the autumn of 2004, Putin directly interfered in the Abkhaz presidential elections and made sure that his preferred candidate – Raul Khadjimba – ran on a joint ticket with the favourite contender Sergei Bagapsh in order to reach the presidency (Ekho Moskvy Radio, 2004). In South Ossetia, the Kremlin strengthened further the presence of Russian intelligence and military officials in the de facto republic's government structures (Illarionov, 2009, 53). Furthermore, Russia also challenged all attempts by Tbilisi in 2005 and 2006 to change the composition and scope of the peacekeeping forces deployed in both Abkhazia and in South Ossetia. It also countered Georgia's efforts to modify the official South Ossetian and Abkhaz negotiating formats by including Western mediators in the talks, as these initiatives significantly reduced Russia's influence in Georgia (Novikov and Yozh, 2006; Civil Georgia, 2005a, 2005b). Russia had by then already agreed to close its two remaining bases in Georgia (a process to be completed in 2006), in order to ensure its compliance with the 1999 Adapted CFE Treaty and the attached Istanbul agreements. This, it was hoped, would guarantee a similar observance of the treaty by all NATO members. The CFE military agreement was seen by Moscow as a cornerstone of European security and Russia did not wish to be seen in breach of its obligations. Yet, the Kremlin tried to compensate for its undesired retreat from Georgia by significantly enhancing its ties with Abkhazia and South Ossetia.

Moscow increasingly perceived Abkhazia and South Ossetia as buffer zones located between Russia and NATO, and as instruments that could allow Moscow to keep Georgia within its sphere of influence, and away from NATO. The Kremlin, became especially worried after Georgia was granted Intensified Dialogue by NATO in September 2006, as this seemed to pave the way for Georgia's NATO membership. Russia saw the potential enlargement of the Atlantic Alliance into the South Caucasus, as a direct threat to its own security, which was being further undermined by the forced withdrawal of its troops from Georgia. Furthermore, close ties were being established by NATO at the time also with Ukraine, a country which occupied a key strategic location in the Black Sea region and was the seat of Russia's Black Sea Fleet (BSF). Tbilisi, in turn, saw Russia's peacekeeping forces in Abkhazia and South Ossetia as tools utilised by Moscow to annex Georgia's territory, and as key obstacles to the resolution of the separatist conflicts. It therefore increasingly called for their removal and partial replacement (Iashvili, 2005). Concern in Tbilisi grew in 2006, when Russia for the first time officially questioned the territorial integrity of Georgia and Moldova within the context of Kosovo's negotiations with the international community on its future independent status (Parsons, 2006; Blinov et al., 2006). The Georgian leadership responded by promoting new alternative governments in the separatist regions of Abkhazia and South Ossetia to avert their recognition by Russia as independent states – Tbilisi organised the 'election' of an alternative pro-Georgian leadership in South Ossetia in November 2006, and the deployment of the 'Abkhaz-government-in-exile' in the Upper Kodori region of Abkhazia in July 2006 (UNSC, 2006; Solovyov et al., 2006; Novikov, 2007). The objective was to create new governing structures which would have to be considered in any future negotiations on the regions' status.

These outcomes proved unacceptable to Russia, especially as Georgia also promoted the development of a direct dialogue between Tbilisi and the separatist regions, which bypassed Russia, and thus undermined Moscow's influence in the talks. Furthermore, when establishing its loyal government in northern Abkhazia, Tbilisi conducted a police operation in the area which resulted in the increased presence of Georgian Interior Ministry troops in Abkhazia's Upper Kodori region (UNSC, 2006, 2007).[3] This created great concern in Abkhazia, as the Kodori gorge was five minutes away from Sukhumi by helicopter, and offered direct access to the Gagra region and neighbouring areas in northern Abkhazia (Vignansky and Solovyov, 2006). Russia responded by conducting a combined Russian–Abkhaz military operation in Upper Kodori in March 2007 against the pro-Georgian Abkhaz government. The Russian Armed Forces also held massive military exercises in the North Caucasus in the summer 2007 (UNSC, 2007) in order to send a clear message to Tbilisi neither to use force nor to expand its influence over its separatist regions. In South Ossetia, tensions increased as violence became routine and both sides strengthened their military presence inside and around the security zone, setting the stage for the violence to come (ICG, 2007b, pp. 14–17). These developments occurred against the background of a significant worsening of Russia's overall relations with Georgia, as series of explosions occurred on the Mozdok–Tbilisi gas pipeline in North Ossetia in January 2006, which left Georgia and Armenia without gas for a few days. A month later, Russia stopped issuing entry visas to Georgians wishing to travel to Russia, while in March 2006 the Kremlin imposed a ban on the import of Georgian wine and mineral water (Gamova and Simonyan, 2006; Vignansky, 2006). Furthermore, Moscow also closed crucial border crossings between the two countries in July 2006 – effectively sealing Georgia off Russia – in an attempt to increase its pressure on Georgia. Russia not only wished to prevent Georgia's membership of NATO, it was also trying to preclude a Georgian violent take-over of the separatist regions of Abkhazia and South Ossetia. Relations reached an all-time low when in September 2006, President Saakashvili accused Russia of plotting a coup in Georgia after several Main Intelligence Directorate (GRU) officers belonging to Russian military intelligence were arrested in Tbilisi, creating worries in Georgia that the Kremlin would go as far as orchestrating 'regime change' in Tbilisi (Novikov et al., 2006).[4] There was little doubt by then that Russia considered Georgia a sphere of its exclusive influence, as it proved ready to use hard power instruments to ensure it was not evicted from the region, in a clear display of its hegemonic power.

The future of Transdniestria

With the arrival of Putin at the Russian presidency negotiations on the future of Transdniestria acquired renewed impetus. In August 2000, under Putin's instructions, former Russian Prime Minister Yevgeny Primakov presented a draft proposal, which suggested the establishment of a loose federation between Moldova and Transdniestria, resembling a confederation in several important respects. The powers in this federation were defined as shared competencies, which would be regulated by agreements reached between Chisinau and Tiraspol (ICG, 2004b, p. 6). Once a final settlement was reached, it was suggested that Russian military units stationed in the region would be reorganised into a peacekeeping force responsible for promoting peace and stability (Prikhodko and Gornostaev, 2000). The proposal was strongly criticised by Chisinau because it was seen as granting Transdniestria too many sovereign powers, while it was rejected in Tiraspol because it did not confer Transdniestria the status of an independent entity recognised by international law, and therefore the Primakov plan failed to make any serious headway (Neukirch, 2001, p. 129). By then, Tiraspol's position had hardened quite substantially, and this was shown in the refusal of its leaders to participate in the OSCE-led negotiations devoted to the resolution of the Transdniestrian conflict during the year 2000 (Neukirch, 2001, p. 129). Significant pressure exerted by Russia on Transdniestria also failed to overcome Tiraspol's objections to the resolution proposal, and therefore, in the autumn of 2000, Russia attempted to establish an alternative structure of power to the Smirnov regime in Tiraspol, which however failed to materialise (ICG, 2004b, p. 6). Smirnov and the Transdniestrian leadership cracked down on the new Moscow-sponsored party 'Transdniestrian Unity', clearly indicating that Moscow's leverage over Tiraspol was much weaker than had previously been assumed.

Yet, Russian pressure proved crucial in ensuring the destruction and the withdrawal of a significant amount of military equipment belonging to the OGRF (Operational Group of Russian Forces) – previously the 14th Army stationed in Transdniestria – back to Russia. Between 1999 and 2001, despite strong obstructionism from the Transdniestrian leadership, OGRF officials managed to eliminate an enormous stock of heavy weaponry and ammunition belonging to the former 14th Army located in the region – more than 500 pieces of CFE Treaty-limited equipment (Hill, 2012; Gamova, 2001a, 2001b). This permitted Russia to fulfil the first of the two deadlines regarding the withdrawal of the 14th Army from Moldova as agreed at the OSCE Istanbul summit in 1999 and, in this way, abide by the Adapted CFE Treaty (OSCE, 1999). Russia attached great importance to the Adapted CFE Treaty, which limited NATO's and Russia's conventional military forces in Europe. Within this context, Moscow proved particularly eager to ensure that the Baltic States also signed up to the Treaty once they became members of NATO in 2004. Ratification of the new CFE Treaty, however, had been linked by the USA and other OSCE states to the fulfilment by Russia of its obligations (taken at the 1999 Istanbul OSCE summit) regarding the withdrawal of its troops from both Moldova and Georgia. Russia therefore felt compelled to fulfil its commitments in this respect for the sake of upholding the CFE Treaty, even if that implied that it had to withdraw its military forces from Moldova and from Georgia. On the other hand, Russia still kept a significant contingent of peacekeeping forces in Transdniestria, and this allowed it to maintain a military presence in Moldova, and as a result, retain its hegemony over the country. This also explains why the Kremlin resisted all efforts to change the peacekeeping format in Transdniestria.

The election of Communist Vladimir Voronin to the Presidency of Moldova in April 2001 opened up new opportunities for the resolution of the Transdniestrian conflict, as Voronin took a decidedly pro-Russian course, not excluding the possibility of bringing his country into the Russian–Belarusian Union (Sergeyev and Volkhonsky, 2001). In a significant step, he agreed in November 2001 to establish a 'Strategic Partnership' with Russia and to grant Moscow the role of 'co-mediator and guarantor' in any future settlement of the Transdniestrian conflict (MID, 2001). Yet, all efforts conducted jointly by Moldova, Russia, Ukraine and the OSCE in late 2001 and 2002 to find a political resolution to the conflict and achieve a breakthrough in the talks ultimately failed. This was primarily because of Tiraspol's opposition to the various proposals that were presented to it, on the grounds that they did not grant Tiraspol significant autonomous powers (Hill, 2012). Moldova, in turn, rejected the notion of 'building' a state together with Transdniestria, as was being suggested by mediators and proposed in the OSCE-sponsored *Kiev document*. Voronin, however, remained open to establishing a federal state with Transdniestria, even one in which Tiraspol would be awarded a significant say in internal and external decision-making (ICG, 2003, pp. 8–9). Attempts initiated by Chisinau and Tiraspol in July 2003 jointly to draw a Moldovan Constitution also made limited progress. Instead a parallel, secretive channel of negotiations was launched by Russia that same summer, at the initiative of Moldovan President Voronin, which directly involved Chisinau and Tiraspol, and bypassed the OSCE negotiating format (Hill, 2012, pp. 115–116). Led by Deputy Head of the Russian Presidential Administration Dmitry Kozak, the negotiations succeeded in producing an agreement – the Kozak Memorandum – in November 2003, which very much suited Russia's interests. The deal not only foresaw the establishment of an asymmetric federation in Moldova, which granted Transdniestria – and Moldova's Gagauzia – significant powers within a new Moldovan federal state, it also foresaw a prolonged Russian military presence in the country in the form of peacekeeping forces (Prikhodko and Melikova, 2003; Hill, 2012). The project represented a triumph of Russian diplomacy, as it not only solved the dispute, but it also allowed Russia to keep significant influence in Moldova, both through an autonomous Transdniestria and through the deployment of its military forces in the separatist region. This could also ensure that Moldova stayed away from NATO and European Union (EU) membership. Yet, soon after the deal was announced, President Voronin changed his mind and rejected the entire Kozak proposal, under strong pressure from EU and NATO leaders, as well as from the country's right-wing opposition. It was clear that Moldova had been forced to accept a Russian military presence on Chisinau after the Kremlin had exerted strong pressure through the introduction of high energy prices, and this had proven unacceptable to the domestic political opposition (Hill, 2012, p. 95). Furthermore, as noted by the OSCE, the proposed government formula of the Kozak Memorandum made the smooth running of state affairs almost impossible. There were too many shared competencies, and there was strong concern over the ability of Transdniestria to block any initiative brought forward by the federal government, by exerting its veto power in the upper chamber of the legislature (Hill, 2012, p. 145).

The collapse of the Kozak Memorandum produced bitter disappointment in Russia and brought to the surface the growing clash of interests between the Russian and European 'Near Abroads'. The events were interpreted by the Kremlin as an effort by the West and Europe to weaken Russia and curtail its influence in Moldova, more specifically, and in the former Soviet space more generally. This view was reinforced by NATO's second wave of enlargement eastwards in 2004, which brought the Atlantic Alliance to the confines of Moldova with the membership of neighbouring Romania. Furthermore, the accession of several eastern European countries, including Hungary, Poland, the Czech Republic and Slovakia, into the EU in 2004, moved the EU borders much closer to Moldova – Romania was expected join the EU in 2007 – and as result, the EU's and Russia's 'Near Abroads' increasingly overlapped. Moreover, in November 2004 a pro-European government came to power in Ukraine in the wake of the Orange Revolution, eliciting great hopes among Moldovans that their country could also embrace a pro-European course (Gamova, 2005). Last but not least, Traia Băsescu, a supporter of Moldova's unification with Romania, won the Romanian presidential elections in December 2004, creating concerns in Tiraspol – and in Moscow – that Moldova could soon be reunified with Romania (Shestakov, 2005). In Russia, all these events were perceived as being intended to push the country further into geo-strategic isolation, keeping it detached from fundamental developments occurring in the European continent (Hill, 2012, p. 161). They encouraged President Putin to act a lot more forcefully not only in Ukraine but also in Moldova, through the Kremlin's open and active involvement in support of clearly pro-Russian opposition candidates in the February 2005 parliamentary elections (Prikhodko and Dubnov, 2005), and through the introduction of a temporary ban on the export of Moldovan fruit and vegetables to Russia in May 2005, which hit these Moldovan industries particularly hard. Russia proved by then clearly determined to utilise whatever 'hard power' instruments it considered necessary to ensure that Moldova did not join Western institutions and instead remained within its specific sphere of influence.

Russia felt further displaced from the region when in 2004 and 2005, both Moldova and Ukraine came up with conflict resolution proposals which envisaged not only the democratisation of Transdniestria, but also the full demilitarisation of Moldova *and* Transdniestria, and this included the withdrawal of Russian peacekeeping and regular troops from the region (Botan, 2009, pp. 123–124). These projects were accompanied by Kiev's proposals to add a Ukrainian military contingent to the existing peacekeeping forces, which were essentially dominated by Russian troops (Strokan, 2005). The new proposals also foresaw an increased involvement of the EU and the United States in the talks being held at the time on the resolution of the Transdniestrian conflict, to counter-balance Russia's considerable weight in the negotiations, creating worries in Moscow that Russia's special role in Transdniestria was being further 'delegated to the background' (Stepanenko *et al.*, 2005). The proposals were rejected out of hand by Moscow, whose leadership made it clear that any changes in the configuration of the peacekeeping arrangements had to obtain Russia's consent (Strokan, 2005). Russia clearly identified its military presence in Moldova as fulfilling a strategic objective – securing Russian's territory, through the acquisition of additional strategic depth while also, hopefully, preventing the enlargement of NATO into Moldova. By then, Russia undoubtedly viewed the entire CIS space as falling under its unique sphere of influence – an area where it held a predominant military presence, in order better to protect itself, and prevent the potential expansion of the North Atlantic alliance closer to its borders. Russia's worries of being displaced from Moldova were aggravated by the demands made by the Moldovan parliament that Russia withdraw its OGRF troops from Transdniestria by the end of 2005, that the peacekeeping operation be suspended altogether and replaced by civilian observers, and that the Transdniestrian 'army' be disbanded (Solovyov, 2005). Close ties existed between the Russian OGRF and the Transdniestrian military structures, and therefore Russian opposition to the full 'demilitarisation' of the area remained strong (Hill, 2012, p. 70; ICG, 2004b, p. 8).

Despite Russia's objections, the EU and the USA were formally incorporated as observers in the OSCE negotiations in the five-plus-two (5+2) format in September 2005 (Hill, 2012, p. 171). In addition, the EU also deployed in

November a border assistance mission along the Transdniestrian–Ukrainian border to counter local smuggling, further expanding Europe's presence in Moldova. Moreover, in July 2005, following on the Ukrainian proposal, the Moldovan Parliament adopted *a Law on the Special Legal Status of Transdniestria*, which unilaterally translated into Moldovan law many of the crucial details that had long been under negotiation in the talks. The Law envisaged that Transdniestria would become a territorial-administrative entity within the Republic of Moldova, and that it would exercise its powers in accordance with the Constitution of Moldova (Botan, 2009, p. 126). Although Transdniestria would be represented in the Supreme Council, its status was significantly diminished, when compared to the powers that it had been granted in the 'Kozak Memorandum'. Furthermore, the first elections to the Supreme Council were to be supervised by the OSCE and would take place only after the withdrawal of Russian troops from Transdniestria, and after the demilitarisation of the region took place (Botan, 2009, p. 126). This directly challenged the potential influence that Russia could exert inside Moldova though Transdniestria, and therefore, as expected, the policy was rejected out of hand not only by Tiraspol, but also by Moscow (Hill, 2012, p. 170). Russia clearly saw Transdniestria as a channel for influence inside Moldova, which would ensure that Chisinau did not engage in policies that ran counter to Russia's interests in the region. Russia had by then established very close ties with Transdniestria, which had, to all intents and purposes, become a Russian 'protectorate'. Not only did a tight relationship exist between the Russian Armed Forces and Transdniestrian troops, but also strong cooperation had developed between the two sides in the military-industrial sector as well. Russia heavily subsidised the region's purchases of its gas, while close ties were also established in the cultural and educational spheres, to ensure the region remained part of the 'Russian world' (ICG, 2004b, p. 9). More importantly, many Transdniestrians had obtained Russian passports, giving Russia an additional justification to become their protector if they felt aggrieved.

Relations between Russia and Moldova worsened when, in March 2006, Ukraine agreed to enforce Moldovan customs regulations for Transdniestrian goods transiting into Ukraine by enhancing controls along the Ukrainian-Transdniestrian border (Solovyov and Darin, 2006). Tiraspol referred to this as the beginning of a 'full-scale 'economic blockade' by Moldova and Ukraine. However, the blockade was, to a large extent, self-imposed, as those Transdniestrian companies which properly registered in Moldova were allowed nevertheless to operate and trade (Solovyov and Darin, 2006). Yet, Russia responded by imposing a ban on the import of Moldovan agricultural products, and by raising quite significantly gas prices to Moldova in 2006 (Gamova and Simonyan, 2006; Solovyov, 2006). Moscow also supported the Transdniestrian 'referendum' on independence, held in September 2006, in this way abandoning the more cautious approach which had characterised its previous policies as far as Moldova's territorial integrity was concerned (Solovyov, 2006). Russia was by then openly siding with Transdniestria, not hiding its readiness to use to use hard coercive power to achieve its aims in the region. Furthermore, Russia began establishing closer 'official' ties with Transdniestria, in view of developments around Kosovo's future independent status and in response to the West's growing demands that Russia promptly withdraw all of its OGRF troops from Moldova (Solovyov and Novikov, 2006). Russia's policies had by then acquired a clear neo-imperialist character, as far as Moldova was concerned. Under pressure from Russia, Voronin was forced to engage in a rapprochement with Moscow in the summer of 2006, which however, helped diffuse tensions, and lift Russia's economic embargo on Chisinau.

Furthermore, in the autumn of 2006 Russian mediators once again engaged in active negotiations with Chisinau on Transdniestria's status outside the 5+2 OSCE framework, displaying an attempt, once more, to resolve the conflict in ways which primarily suited Russia's and Transdniestria's interests. Moscow continued to insist that previously agreed proposals, such as the 1997 Primakov Memorandum, which had granted the two sides 'equal status' in the negotiations, had to form the basis of the negotiations. Although Moldovan negotiators regularly informed their Western partners and Ukraine, on the course of the talks (Socor, 2007), the risk of a compromise that sacrificed Moldova's pro-Western course still existed. Furthermore, Voronin changed his approach, aware that Chisinau's anti-Russian rhetoric was not the best way to make progress on the negotiations over Transdniestria and on the presence of Russian troops in the separatist region. Whereas previously Chisinau had demanded the immediate withdrawal of Russian troops and had rejected out-of-hand the idea of granting Transdniestria the status of a Republic, in 2006–2007 Voronin proved ready, once again, to incorporate provisions from the Kozak memorandum 'and use them together with other documents pertaining to a Transnistria settlement' (Vyzhutovich, 2007). However, the success of Russia's 'neo-imperialist' policies in Moldova had its limits. Although in 2007 Voronin had seemed once again more willing to compromise on Transdniestria's status, he continued to insist on the complete demilitarisation of the country and the withdrawal of Russian troops from the region, even though he pledged not to ask for the deployment of NATO peacekeeping forces in Transdniestria and also confirmed Moldova's commitment to retain its constitutional state neutrality (*Komsomolskaya Pravda*, 2007; Botan, 2009, p. 132).

Attempts at resolving the Nagorno-Karabakh conflict

During the early 2000s, Russia slightly lost the initiative in the negotiations over the future of the Nagorno-Karabakh separatist region in Azerbaijan, and instead, France and the United States, the other two co-chairs of the Minsk group, took centre stage. In the winter and spring of 2001 they engaged in active diplomatic efforts in Paris and in Key West, Florida, aimed at resolving the ethno-territorial dispute. The new American President George W. Bush had a particular interest in settling the conflict, given that American companies were at the time developing promising oil and gas fields off the Azerbaijani coast. The USA wanted to ensure the safe transport of these resources to world markets through the Baku-Tbilisi-Ceyhan (BTC)/ Baku–Tbilisi–Erzurum (BTE) pipeline systems, which partly traversed the turbulent region, although they avoided Armenia and Nagorno-Karabakh (Peuch, 2001). Contrary to previous experiences, Russia proved ready to accommodate the United States' and France's initiatives, and collaborated quite closely with the other co-Chairs, to create a united front in the talks. Russia's policies vis-à-vis the Nagorno-Karabakh conflict, therefore, differed from its approach towards the separatist regions of Georgia and Moldova, as Russia proved less eager to enforce a diplomatic solution onto the parties. Furthermore, the Paris and Key West talks coincided with a more balanced approach towards Armenia and Azerbaijan taken by the new Russian President, Vladimir Putin. Whereas during 1990s, Moscow had established a close military partnership with Armenia at the expense of fruitful cooperation with Azerbaijan, in 2000 Putin started slowly to mend Russia's relations with Azerbaijan. In the autumn of 1999, Moscow and Baku began cooperating closely in the area of counter-terrorism, in view of the outbreak of war in Chechnya (Eaton, 2001, p. 92). In January 2001, during a visit by President Putin to Baku, a preliminary agreement on the division of the Caspian Sea was signed by the two presidents, and a series of deals were reached on the joint exploitation of energy resources in the Azerbaijani section of the Caspian Sea (Sokolova, 2001). Closer military ties were also established between Russia and Azerbaijan, after a stand-off between Azerbaijan and Iran over the ownership of disputed fields in the Caspian Sea took place in the summer of 2001, and Russia immediately offered Azerbaijan its support. Last, but not least, in January 2002, an agreement was finally reached on the ten-year lease to Russia of the Azerbaijani strategic radar facility Gabala-2, after several years of negotiations (Plotnikov, 2001). At the same time, though, Russia also reinforced its military-strategic partnership with Armenia through the development of joint military planning between the two armed forces, the creation of joint air defences, and the strengthening of Russia's military forces deployed at the Gyumri and Yerevan military bases in Armenia (Hovhannisyan, 2011, p. 69; RFE/RL, 2001). Furthermore, in September 2001, both countries agreed to introduce reciprocal visa-free travel regimes for their citizens, while during a visit by Putin to Yerevan in 2001, various documents were signed which laid the foundations for the expansion of Russian business in key sectors of the Armenian economy (Dzhilavyan, 2001). It rightly seemed in the early 2000s that Armenia remained strongly within Russia's sphere of influence.

On the other hand, little advancement was made on the Nagorno-Karabakh front. Despite the high level of involvement of the United States and France in the Nagorno-Karabakh negotiations and the intensity of the pressure exerted on the two sides, little headway was made. The talks collapsed in the face of strong opposition inside Azerbaijan to any territorial exchanges around Karabakh – as had been envisaged in the projects presented to the sides. Yerevan and Stepanakert, in turn, no longer accepted a solution which foresaw the existence of Nagorno-Karabakh within Azerbaijan, and instead insisted on a settlement which would place Nagorno-Karabakh and Azerbaijan on an equal footing

(Katin and Khanbabyan, 2001). In October 2003, Ilham Aliyev, President Geidar Aliyev's son, came to power and took a much more uncompromising stance on the Karabakh conflict. He rejected any land exchanges, and instead, insisted that Armenia had first to withdraw from the occupied territories before any discussions on the status of Karabakh could go ahead (ICG, 2005, p. 11). Armenians in turn, insisted that Baku had to either recognise Nagorno-Karabakh's independence or accept its attachment to Armenia. Against this complex background, a new round of more intensive negotiations on Nagorno-Karabakh nevertheless began in 2004 under the aegis of the OSCE Minsk group, in what was termed the *Prague process*. The Minsk co-Chairs proposed a new concept for the resolution of the Karabakh conflict, which was based on granting the enclave 'interim status'. What differentiated the more recent suggestions from previous proposals was their long-term incremental approach, as opposed to the 'package' solutions which had been tried previously (ICG, 2007c, p. 2). In an effort to reach an agreement based on these 'Prague proposals', the OSCE brokered a series of high level meetings between Armenia's President Robert Kochariyan and Azerbaijan President Aliyev, first at Rambouillet in February 2006, then in Bucharest in June 2006 and in Minsk in November 2006. However, by the end of 2006, the mood had changed, and this significantly diminished the chances of reaching a negotiated agreement. The Azerbaijani and Armenian presidents proved both incapable and unwilling to make the necessary compromises in order to achieve a breakthrough in the negotiations. Disagreements remained over the future status of Nagorno-Karabakh, with Yerevan and Stepanakert rejecting any solution that entailed the subordination of Nagorno-Karabakh to Azerbaijan, and Baku reverting to its original position, that of granting Nagorno-Karabakh only highest autonomy within Azerbaijan (ICG, 2007c, p. 4). Furthermore, shootings and violations along the 1994 ceasefire line began to occur quite frequently in Karabakh, as the sides engaged in a dangerous arms race, and Azerbaijan, in particular, adopted a more belligerent rhetoric, frustrated over the lack of progress in the resolution of the dispute (Fuller, 2006). Yerevan responded by increasing quite significantly its own military expenditures, while it moved ahead with progressively integrating the economy, the infrastructure and the social system of Nagorno-Karabakh into Armenia.

In late November 2007, the *Madrid Principles*, which revolved around three fundamental elements, the non-use of force, territorial integrity, and self-determination, were officially presented to the parties by the OSCE Minsk co-Chairs (Odinets and Mostafayev, 2007). Both sides accepted the proposals as a framework for discussions, but serious differences remained on the specifics, making it hard to make any progress in the talks, as the negotiations were held on the basis that 'noting is agreed until everything is agreed'. By the time Putin left the Russian Presidency in 2008, therefore, no major advances on the resolution of the Karabakh conflict had been made. The absence of a resolution, despite the great efforts conducted by the OSCE co-Chairs, can be primarily ascribed to the uncompromising stance taken by the warring sides, rather than to the policies carried out by the co-Chairs or the behaviour of regional external actors. Russia generally took a positive, collaborative, stance in the negotiations, and seemingly did not engage in any obstructionist policies. Although Russia continued to explore the possibility of sending peacekeeping troops to Nagorno-Karabakh, the Kremlin seemed less eager than in previous occasions to impose such a force on the parties to the dispute (Litovkin, 2006). Russia accepted that its peacekeepers, if deployed, would have to operate under OSCE aegis, and would most probably function alongside Western – either EU or NATO – troops (*Rossiiskie vesti*, 2006). Yet, deep distrust in the mediating process remained on both sides of the conflict (ICG, 2009, p. 8). Many in Armenia, and especially in Azerbaijan, accused the co-Chairs of not being interested in a resolution of the dispute, and instead, of using the conflict to promote their own geopolitical agendas, although evidence in that respect was hard to come across (ICG, 2009, p. 8). Russia's cooperative policies, instead, reflected a more favourable and positive relationship with the two conflicting sides. Russia had by then established a close military and security partnership with Armenia and had expanded its military cooperation with Azerbaijan, to whom it began selling significant amounts of valuable military equipment in the late 2000s–early 2010s, while it also trained Azerbaijani officers in Russian military academies. Russia also expanded its commercial ties with Baku while its oil companies invested substantially in Azerbaijan's energy resources.

However, there were limits to Russia's influence in Azerbaijan, as Baku concurrently extended its military collaboration with NATO. In February 2000, Azerbaijan for the first time clearly expressed its wishes to join NATO and agreed to hold NATO military exercises on its soil in 2001 (Romanov, 2000). After the 9/11 attacks, Azerbaijan developed closer military ties with the United States and approved the use of Azerbaijani military facilities by American forces in support of their operations in Afghanistan (Nichol, 2013, pp. 25–28). Through its programme of military assistance to Baku, the US Navy began establishing a presence in the Caspian, which not only irritated Iran but also created significant displeasure in Russia (Panfilova and Aliyev, 2004) More worryingly for Moscow, in the spring of 2003, the United States began contemplating the possibility of welcoming Azerbaijan into the Atlantic Alliance (Dzhanashia, 2003). Azerbaijan had by then been identified by the United States as a key strategic ally in the Caspian region – the country remained essential to the USA to fight Al-Qaeda in the Caspian/Central Asian region while it could also provide European and global markets with much needed alternative sources of energy. Therefore, in 2004, the first NATO Individual Partnership Action Plan for Azerbaijan was devised and approved, while at the 2006 NATO Summit in Riga, countries issued a declaration in support for Azerbaijan's territorial integrity. To Russia's great concern, Azerbaijan also supported the USA's plans, presented in 2003, to establish a rapid-response force known as *Caspian Guard* in the Caspian Sea (Sysoyev, 2007).[5] Russia's ability to exert influence over Azerbaijan's geo-strategic orientation was therefore more restrained, as it had to accept NATO increased penetration of the region. However, this did not preclude Azerbaijan from developing good relations with Russia, although the latter viewed such ties with NATO very unfavourably.

Conclusions

With the arrival of Putin to the Russian Presidency, the Kremlin's approach towards the separatist conflicts in Abkhazia, South Ossetia, Transdniestria and Nagorno-Karabakh slightly differed, as Russia's relations with the 'mother countries' evolved in somewhat different directions. Russia's relations with Georgia witnessed a significant deterioration as conflict once again broke out in neighbouring Chechnya, and Tbilisi initially refused to allow Russian military forces to operate in Georgia's border regions. This Georgian approach, which had full American backing, was strongly resented by the Kremlin, which saw the entire Caucasus region as an area of major concern, whose instabilities could potentially spill over into Russia and challenge the entire foundations of the Russian state. Georgia, in turn, worried over the decision by Moscow to establish close economic, political and military ties with the separatist regions of Abkhazia and South Ossetia, de facto challenging in this way, Georgia's territorial integrity. While Russia refused *officially* to recognise the independence of Georgia's separatist regions, and instead supported UN and OSCE proposals which kept the Georgian state's integrity intact, it nevertheless pursued a policy which significantly weakened the links between Georgia and the separatist regions. Forced to close its four military bases in Georgia and concerned over Georgia's strong military cooperation ties with the United States, Russia saw its peacekeeping forces and its close ties with the separatist regions as instruments of influence over Tbilisi, and as ways in which it could prevent the further encroachment of the West and NATO into the region. As such, its actions fitted neatly into a neo-imperialist pattern of behaviour, especially as the Kremlin's actions increasingly turned both South Ossetia and Abkhazia into de facto Russian protectorates.

Russia's actions in Moldova, instead, were initially characterised by a more benevolent approach, and this was facilitated by the positive attitude towards Russia that had been taken by the new President of Moldova, Vladimir Voronin when he reached the presidency in 2001. Voronin looked forward to establishing a strategic partnership with Russia, to a great extent in order to resolve the Transdniestrian conflict in Moldova's favour. Moscow responded by trying to broker a settlement of the territorial dispute which guaranteed the integration of Transdniestria into Moldova, while granting Transdniestria broad autonomy, even within a loose federation. Furthermore, Russia's negotiations were held in conjunction and in cooperation with the OSCE and Ukraine, in what seemed to indicate a readiness by Russia to discard its imperial legacy in Moldova, as long as Chisinau remained closely aligned to Moscow. Russia also moved ahead with the withdrawal of the 14th Army, which was deployed in Transdniestria, back to Russia and carried out the destruction of its military equipment in collaboration with the OSCE, in order to fulfil its obligations to comply with the 1999 OSCE Istanbul Agreements and the revised CFE Treaty.

Yet, in 2003 Russia succeeded in brokering a settlement on Transdniestria, which, if implemented, would have kept Moldova tightly aligned to Moscow, and strictly within Russia's sphere of influence. The Kozak proposal not only granted the separatist region significant powers inside Moldova, but, in its final version, it also allowed Russia to keep a military presence inside Transdniestria at least until 2020. This would ensure that Moldova would neither join NATO nor become a member of the EU in the near future. More importantly, the Kremlin exerted great pressure on Chisinau in order to convince its leadership to accept a Russian peacekeeping force on its territory. To that end, it significantly raised energy prices, in a clear display of its hegemonic might. Moscow's main geo-strategic goal was to keep Moldova tightly aligned to Russia, but its efforts, at least temporarily did not succeed, as Moldova rejected the Kozak Memorandum under strong pressure from the EU and NATO – a clear indication of the emergence of a struggle over influence between the EU and Russia over Moldova's destinies in their respective Near Abroads.

As far as the Nagorno-Karabakh conflict is concerned, Russia decided to accommodate its position and support the conflict resolution initiatives promoted by the other two co-Chairs of the Minsk Group, France and the United States, in 2001, once Putin reached the Russian Presidency in early 2000. Moscow also assisted the Minsk Group in its negotiations within the *Prague Process*, which were launched in 2002 and were intended to find a lasting and satisfactory resolution to the dispute, in what seemed to indicate, at least at first sight, a readiness by the Kremlin to discard Russia's imperial legacy in this region. Yet, there were limits to Russia's policies of accommodation. While working hand in hand with external partners, Russia at the same time, significantly reinforced its cooperative ties both with Armenia and with Azerbaijan, in what could well be interpreted as an attempt by the Kremlin to keep these areas under Russia's influence. Moscow not only strengthened its military and strategic partnership with Armenia, it also enhanced its military and economic ties with Azerbaijan, especially in the energy sector, having identified the Caspian Sea region as an area of key strategic significance to Russia. At Putin's instance, great attention was devoted by the Kremlin to devise a coherent and effective policy which would allow Russia better to exploit the Caspian's energy resources and increase its economic and military presence in the Caspian Sea area (Antonenko, 2004, p. 247). Yet, it must be noted that both Yerevan and Baku supported, and to a certain extent, benefited from the strengthening of closer ties with Moscow, especially in the military and security fields, and therefore, Russia's actions cannot be seen as entirely fitting with a neo-imperialist paradigm. Russia (and the USA), for example, had come to Azerbaijan's support when the latter had almost entered into a direct military confrontation with Iran in August 2001 over a series of disputed fields exploited by Baku in the Caspian Sea, thus highlighting the significance of Russia's security umbrella for Azerbaijan. Armenia, in turn, relied on Russia to enhance its security vis-à-vis Turkey and to strengthen its position in the negotiations on the future of Nagorno-Karabakh. An element of voluntary contracting was therefore also present in Russia's relations with both Azerbaijan and Armenia.

Nevertheless, during Putin's second Presidency, the neo-imperialist paradigm in all these ex-USSR conflict regions was reinforced. Russia's policies towards

Georgia hardened as Moscow felt that its presence in the country was being further undermined by Tbilisi's actions. The Georgian government demanded the immediate closure of Russia's two military bases remaining on Georgian territory while President Saakashvili attempted in 2004 to restore full control over the separatist regions of Abkhazia and South Ossetia through a combination of 'hard' and 'soft' policy instruments. The Kremlin responded to these challenges by further enhancing its ties with the separatist regions and ensuring that the leaderships in these 'republics' remained entirely loyal to Russia. While Russia agreed to close its two bases at Akhalkalaki and Batumi in Georgia in order to comply with the Adapted CFE Treaty, it nevertheless tried to compensate for such a loss by trying to keep a military presence in Abkhazia and South Ossetia, either in the form of peacekeeping forces or in the shape of new military bases. Moscow increasingly viewed its close relations with these two separatist regions as essential for its own security – as instruments which the Kremlin could use to prevent Georgia from joining NATO and the West, and in this way, keep its southern neighbour within Russia's sphere of influence. Under Saakashvili, Georgia had witnessed a significant increase in its defence spending and a strengthening of its military capabilities with the substantial help of Western military training and support. This was viewed with concern not only in Moscow but also in the separatist regions, whose leaders feared that Tbilisi would resort to the use of force to settle the various disputes in Georgia's favour. Russia therefore sent several clear messages to Tbilisi – including holding military exercises in the North Caucasus – in order to dissuade Georgia from using force against the separatist regions. It even threatened to intervene militarily to protect the two separatist entities, in a clear display of its neo-imperialist power. Yet, Georgia's ties with the West only expanded as Russia strengthened its cooperation with Abkhazia and South Ossetia, and this showed the limits of Russia's geo-strategic reach.

As far as Moldova is concerned, the collapse of the Kozak Memorandum produced great disappointment in Moscow, and brought to the surface the growing clash of interests between Russia and the European Union in their respective 'Near Abroads'. Russia felt progressively displaced from the region by NATO and the EU. As NATO and EU enlargement reached the south-western borders of the CIS, Russia felt increasingly encircled by the West. This reinforced the view that the West was intent on weakening Russia, and determined Putin's decision to act much more assertively in the western and southern fringes of the former Soviet space. As was clearly noted by OSCE Ambassador William Hill (2012, p. 161) the aim of Russia was to 'retain its waning influence and to resist growing Western involvement in the heart of the former Soviet empire'. Moscow's concerns over its weakened position in Moldova increased when conflict resolution proposals on Transdniestria were put forward by Ukraine in 2005 which foresaw the full demilitarisation of the country, including also the withdrawal of Russian troops from the separatist region of Transdniestria. Russia clearly saw its presence in Moldova's Transdniestria as fulfilling a major strategic role – that of keeping Moldova tightly aligned to Russia. This would, in turn, strengthen Russian security, through the acquisition of additional strategic depth, while also, hopefully, preventing the enlargement of NATO and the EU into Moldova, closer to Russia's borders. The Kremlin therefore enhanced its military and economic ties with the separatist region, effectively turning Transdniestria into a Russian 'protectorate'. A major turning point, in this respect, occurred when Russia decided in 2006 to question, for the first time, the territorial integrity of Moldova and Georgia, within the context of the UN negotiations on Kosovo's independence. This rightly led to concerns in both Chisinau, and Tbilisi, that Russia would follow a similar path in relation to their respective separatist regions. Although Russia did not move that far against Georgia and Moldova at the time, it nevertheless increasingly brought the respective separatist regions in each of these countries under its influence. Moscow, moreover, did not hesitate to utilise *hard power* instruments, ranging from the imposition of trade embargoes to the revoking of visas and the closing of border crossings, in its relations with either Moldova or Georgia, in order exert pressure on these countries. The aim was clear, namely to keep these countries within its sphere of influence in order to ensure they did not align themselves fully to the West and join the Euro-Atlantic structures, in a clear display of hegemonic power.

In Nagorno-Karabakh, instead, Russia continued to support the efforts of the OSCE mediators to reach a political resolution to the dispute. Yet the opportunities for a breakthrough never materialised. Contrary to what is often assumed, however, the failure to advance in the negotiations towards a final resolution of the dispute was related primarily to the lack of readiness by warring sides – Armenia, Nagorno-Karabakh and Azerbaijan – to make significant compromises. Russia generally took a cooperative stance in the talks and moved away from the more obstructionist policies that it had adopted in the early 1990s. These had been characterised by efforts to dominate the mediation process and deploy a peacekeeping force in Nagorno-Karabakh against Azerbaijan's wishes. Russia's accommodating policies reflected a more favourable and positive relationship between Moscow and the two conflicting sides, Armenia and Azerbaijan. By the mid-2000s, Moscow had established a close security partnership with Yerevan – and this included major investments by Russian companies in key sectors of the Armenian economy – and had also expanded its military cooperation with Azerbaijan, by selling it significant amounts of valuable military equipment. While Russia's presence in Armenia remained overwhelming, there were limits, however, to Russia's influence over Baku. After the 9/11 attacks, Azerbaijan had decided to expand quite significantly its cooperative ties with NATO and the United States, whose military influence in the Caspian and Central Asian region had significantly increased at the time, directly challenging Russia's hegemony in the area. Russia's attempts to establish a sphere of influence in these regions of the Near Abroad, therefore, did not entirely succeed. While Russia managed to strengthen quite substantially its presence and establish a neo-empire over the *separatist regions* of Moldova, Georgia and Azerbaijan, its ability to keep the 'mother countries' under its sway was more restricted, as these countries increasingly pivoted to the West, and tried to enhance ties with either NATO (Azerbaijan) or the EU (Moldova), or both (Georgia).

Notes

1 They were rebuffed with Russian military support (Yanchenkov, 2001; Felgengauer, 2001; Novoprudsky, 2001).
2 The Baden deal established special links between South Ossetia and North Ossetia, and foresaw the introduction of international security guarantees, including the presence of Russian troops, to ensure respect of the agreement.
3 This was in violation of the 1994 ceasefire agreement.
4 GRU stands for Main Intelligence Directorate.
5 The Kremlin responded by suggesting an agreement that would prohibit the presence of warships of 'third countries' in the Caspian Sea, and by proposing instead to create *Casfor* – a naval group based on Caspian Sea littoral states' forces. Moscow, however, failed to gain Azerbaijani support.

Bibliography

Accord (1999). *A Question of Sovereignty: The Georgia–Abkhazia Peace Process*. Conciliation Resources. Available at: www.c-r.org/accord/georgia-abkhazia [accessed 17 November 2018].

Adliba, I. and A. Sborovo (2001). *Kommersant*, 12 October, p. 11.

Antonenko, O. (2004). Russia's Policy in the Caspian Sea Region: Reconciling Economic and Security Agendas. In: S. Akiner, ed. *The Caspian: Politics, Energy and Security*. Milton Park, Abingdon and New York, Routledge/Curzon, pp. 244–262.

Antonenko, O. (2005). Frozen Uncertainty: Russia and the Conflict over Abkhazia. In: B. Coppieters and R. Legvold eds., *Statehood and Security: Georgia after the Rose Revolution*, Cambridge, Mass: MIT Press, pp. 205–269.

Babichev, N. and Y. Chubchenko (2000). *Kommersant*, 26 April, p. 11.

Blinov, A., Yu. Simonyan and S. Gamova, S. (2006). *Nezavisimaya gazeta*, 2 June, p. 1.

Botan, I. (2009). The Negotiation Process as a Way to Postpone the Solution. In: D. Matveev, G. Selari, E. Bobkova and B. Cseke (eds.). *Moldova–Transdniestria: Working Together for a Prosperous Future*. Chisinau: Cu drag Publishing House, pp. 116–134.

Brown J. and K.G. Lowmaster (2013). The Minsk Group Mediation Process from 1992 to the Present. In: P.T. Hopmann and I.W. Zartman, *Nagorno Karabakh: Understanding Conflict 2013*. Johns Hopkins University, School for Advanced International Studies. Available at: www.saisjhu.edu/sites/default/files/CM%20Field%20Trip%20NK%20March%2029%20Final.pdf [accessed 18 November 2018].

Civil Georgia (2003). Georgia Launched Anti-smuggling Operation in South Ossetia. 11 December 2003. Available at: www.civil.ge/eng/article.php?id=5796&search= [accessed 17 November 2018].

Civil Georgia (2004). Fresh Fighting Shatters Short-Lived Ceasefire deal. 18 August. Available at: www.civil.ge/eng/article.php?id=7645 [accessed 17 November 2018].

Civil Georgia (2005a). Saakashvili Presents Peace Plan at the PACE. 26 January. Available at: www.civil.ge/eng/article.php?id=8891&search= [accessed 17 November 2018].

Civil Georgia (2005b). Georgian PM Outlines South Ossetia Action Plan at OSCE. 27 October. Available at: www.civil.ge/eng/article.php?id=11056 [accessed 17 November 2018].

Dvali, G. (2000). *Kommersant*, 20 October, p. 3.
Dvali, G. (2001). *Kommersant*, 25 April, p. 11.
Dvali, G. (2002). *Kommersant*, 14 June, p. 11.
Dvali G. and G. Sysoyev (2002). *Kommersant*, 1 March, p. 11.
Dzhilavyan, A. (2001). *Nezavisimaya gazeta*, 18 September, p. 5.
Dzhanashia, V. (2003). *Kommersant*, 21 April, p. 10.
Eaton, M. (2001). Major Trends in Military Expenditure and Arms Acquisitions by States of the Caspian Region. In: G. Chufrin, ed. *The Security of the Caspian Sea Region*. Oxford: Oxford University Press, pp. 83–118.
Ekho Mosvky Radio (2004). 8 December.
Felgengauer, P. (2001). *Moskovskie Novosti*, 16–22 October, p. 4.
Francis, C. (2011). *Conflict Resolution and Status: The Case of Georgia and Abkhazia (1989–2008)*. Brussels: UBPRES Brussels University Press.
Fuller, L. (2006). Armenia/Azerbaijan: Karabakh Wants to Be in on Settlement Talks, February 21. Available at: www.rferl.org/content/article/1066008.html [accessed 11 November 2018].
Gamova, S. (2005). *Noviye Izvestiya*, 9 February, p. 4.
Gamova, S. (2001a). *Kommersant*, 25 May, p. 11.
Gamova, S. (2001b). *Vremya novostei*, 9 November, p. 6.
Gamova S. and Yu. Simonyan (2006). *Nezavisimaya gazeta*, 29 March, p. 5.
Golotyuk, Yu. (2000). *Vremya novostei*, 9 December, p. 3.
Hill, W.H. (2012). *Russia, the Near Abroad, and the West: Lessons from the Moldova-Transdniestria Conflict*. Washington DC: Woodrow Wilson Center Press.
Hovhannisyan, V. (2011). Major Development Trends of The Russian-Armenian Relations At The Beginning Of The 21st Century. *21st Century: Information and Analytical Journal*, 2 (10), pp. 66–76.
Iashvili, A. (2005). *Izvestiya*, 12 October, p. 5.
Illarionov, A. (2009). The Russian Leadership's Preparation for War, 1999–2008. In: S.E. Cornell and S.F. Starr Ed. *The Guns of August 2008: Russia's War in Georgia*. Armonok: New York and London: M.E. Sharpe, pp. 49–84.
International Crisis Group (ICG) (2003). *Moldova: No Quick Fix*, 12 August. Available at: https://d2071andvip0wj.cloudfront.net/147-moldova-no-quick-fix.pdf [accessed 15 November 2018].
International Crisis Group (ICG) (2004a). *Georgia: Avoiding War in South Ossetia: A Precarious Peace is Back*. Brussels/Tbilisi. 26 November. Available at: https://d2071andvip0wj.cloudfront.net/159-georgia-avoiding-war-in-south-ossetia.pdf [accessed 15 November 2018].
International Crisis Group (ICG) (2004b). *Moldova: Regional Tensions over Transdniestria*, 17 June. Available at: www.crisisgroup.org/europe-central-asia/eastern-europe/moldova/moldova-regional-tensions-over-transdniestria [accessed 17 November 2018].
International Crisis Group (ICG) (2005). *Nagorno-Karabakh: A Plan for Peace*, 11 October. Available at https://d2071andvip0wj.cloudfront.net/167-nagorno-karabakh-a-plan-for-peace.pdf [accessed 16 November 2018].
International Crisis Group (ICG) (2006). *Abkhazia Today*, 176. Brussels/Tbilisi. 16 September. Available at: https://d2071andvip0wj.cloudfront.net/176-abkhazia-today.pdf [accessed 18 November 2018].
International Crisis Group (ICG) (2007a). *Abkhazia: Ways Forward*, 176. Brussels/Tbilisi. 18 January. Available at: https://d2071andvip0wj.cloudfront.net/179-abkhazia-ways-forward.pdf [accessed 17 November 2018].

International Crisis Group (ICG) (2007b). *Georgia's South Ossetia Conflict: Make Haste Slowly*, 183. Brussels/Tbilisi. 7 June. Available at: https://d2071andvip0wj.cloudfront. net/183-georgia-s-south-ossetia-conflict-make-haste-slowly.pdf [accessed 17 November 2018].

International Crisis Group (ICG) (2007c). *Nagorno-Karabakh: Risking War*, International Crisis Group Europe Report, 187. 14 November.

International Crisis Group (ICG) (2009). *Nagorno-Karabakh: Getting to a Breakthrough*. Europe Briefing. 7 October. Available at: https://d2071andvip0wj.cloudfront.net/ b55-nagorno-karabakh-getting-to-a-breakthrough.pdf [accessed 16 November 2018].

Katin, V. and A. Khanbabyan (2001). *Nezavisimaya gazeta*, 27 January, p. 5.

Komsomol'skaya Pravda (2007). 4 October. Available: http://old.kp.md/freshissue/ life/267723/ [accessed 6 June 2016].

Lachowski, Z. (2007). *Foreign Military Bases in Eurasia*. SIPRI Policy Paper. 18. June.

Litovkin, D. (2006). *Izvestiya*, 25 January, p. 2.

Loria, Ye. (2001). *Noviye Izvestiya*, 3 July, p. 2.

MID (2001). Dogovor o druzhbe i sotrudnichestve mezhdu Rossiiskoi Federatsiei i Respublikoi Moldova. Moscow, 19 November. Available at: www.mid.ru/ru/maps/ md/-/asset_publisher/dfOotO3QvCij/content/id/571548 [accessed 17 October 2017].

Mukhin, V. (2001). *Nezavisimaya gazeta*, 27 June, p. 5.

Mumpaey, L. (2008). *Les pyromanes du Caucase: les complicités du réarmement de la Géorgie*. GRIP, Groupe de recherche et d'information sur la paix et la sécurité. 26 September. Available at: http://archive.grip.org/fr/siteweb/images/NOTES_ANALYSE/2008/ NA_2008-09-26_FR_L-MAMPAEY.pdf [accessed 20 November 2018].

Neukirch, C. (2001). Transdniestria and Moldova: Cold Peace at the Dniester. *Helsinki Monitor*, 12 (2), 122–135.

Neukirch, C. (2012). From Confidence Building to Conflict Settlement in Moldova? In: Institute for Peace Research and Security Policy at the University of Hamburg/IFSH. ed. *OSCE Yearbook 2011*. Baden-Baden, pp. 137–150.

Nichol, J. (2013). *Azerbaijan: Recent Developments and U.S.* Congressional Research Service CRS Report for Congress. 22 February. Available at: https://fas.org/sgp/crs/ row/97-522.pdf [accessed 17 October 2017].

Novoprudsky, S. (2001). *Izvestiya*, 10 October, p. 1.

Novikov, V. (2007). *Kommersant*, 6 April, p. 10.

Novikov, V. and G. Sysoyev (2003). *Kommersant*, 27 November, p. 9.

Novikov, V. and G. Sysoyev (2004). *Kommersant*, 13 February, p. 10.

Novikov, V. and P. Yozh (2006). *Kommersant*, 8 February 2006, p. 9.

Novikov, V., V. Solovyov, F. Maksimov and I. Safronov (2006). *Kommersant*, 28 September, p. 1.

Odinets, A. and R. Mostafayev (2007). *Kommersant*, 1 December, p. 4.

OSCE (1999). Official Appendix to the Treaty on Conventional Armed Forces in Europe. Available at: www.osce.org/documents/mcs/1999/11/4050_en.pdf [accessed 22 November 2018].

Panfilova V. and Ya. Aliyev (2004). *Nezavisimaya gazeta*, 29 January, p. 5.

Parsons, R. (2006). Is Putin Looking to Impose Solutions to Frozen Conflicts? 2 February, RFE/RL.org. Available at: www.rferl.org/content/article/1065363.html [accessed 20 November 2018].

Peuch, J-Ch. (2001). Armenia/Azerbaijan: International Mediators Report Progress on Karabakh Dispute. RFE/RL, 10 April. Available at www.rferl.org/content/ article/1096184.html [accessed 20 November 2018].

Peuch. J-Ch. (2002). Georgia: Shevardnadze Officially Requests Invitation to Join NATO. Radio Free Europe/Radio Liberty. 22 November. Available at www.rferl.org/a/1101463.html [accessed 20 November 2018].

Plotnikov, A. (2001). *Noviye Izvestiya*, 11 September, p. 1.

Prikhodko, N. and A. Dubnov (2005). *Vremya novostei*, 21 February, pp. 1–2.

Prikhodko, N. and D. Gornostayev (2000). *Nezavisimaya gazeta*, 20 June, p. 6.

Prikhodko, N. and N. Melikova (2003). *Nezavisimaya gazeta*, 19 November, p. 5.

RFE/RL (2001). RFE/RL Newsline, 17 April. Available at www.rferl.org/a/1142384.html [accessed 20 November 2018].

Romanov, P. (2000). *Nezavisimaya gazeta*, 22 February, p. 5.

Rossiiskie Vesti (2006). 22 June, p. 6.

Sergeyev, I. and B. Volkhonsky (2001). *Kommersant*, 27 February, p. 2.

Shestakov, Ye. (2005). *Rossiiskaya gazeta*, 16 February, p. 8.

SIPRI (2007). *Yearbook: 2007*, Stockholm: Stockholm International Peace Research Institute.

SIPRI (2017). Military expenditure by country as percentage of gross domestic product, 1988–2002. Available at: www.sipri.org/sites/default/files/Milex-share-of-GDP.pdf [accessed 20 November 2018].

Socor, V. (2007). Confidential Russia-Moldova Bilateral Negotiations Fail. *Eurasia Daily Monitor*, 4(23). 1 February. Available at: https://jamestown.org/program/confidential-russia-moldova-bilateral-negotiations-fail/ [accessed 8 November 2018].

Sokolova, V. (2001). *Izvestiya*, 10 January, p. 4.

Solovyov. V. (2005). *Kommersant*, 11 June, pp. 1, 4.

Solovyov, V. (2006). *Kommersant*, 23 March, p. 9.

Solovyov, V. and A. Darin (2006). *Kommersant*, 7 March, p. 9.

Solovyov, V. and V. Novikov (2006). *Kommersant*, 2 June, pp. 1, 10.

Solovyov, V., O. Allenova, V. Novikov and G. Gotua (2006). *Kommersant*, 27 July, p. 1.

Stepanenko, S., P. Lukyanchenko and A. Dubnov (2005). *Vremya novostei*, 16 December, pp. 1–2.

Strokan, S. (2005). *Kommersant*, 20 July, p. 10.

Sysoyev, G. (2001). *Kommersant*, 8 December, p. 8.

Sysoyev, G. (2007). *Kommersant*, 21 June, p. 9.

Sychova, V. (2000). *Segodnya*, 6 December, p. 4.

Transparency International (2007). Reform of Georgia's Defence Sector. January Available at: www.transparency.ge/sites/default/files/Reform%20of%20Georgia's%20Defence%20Sector.pdf [accessed 8 November 2018].

United Nations Security Council (UNSC) (2001). S/2001/1008. *Report of the Secretary-General, Concerning the Situation in Abkhazia, Georgia*. 24 October. New York: United Nations.

United Nations Security Council (UNSC) (2002a). S/2002/469. *Report of the Secretary-General, Concerning the Situation in Abkhazia, Georgia*. 19 April. New York: United Nations.

United Nations Security Council (UNSC) (2002b). S/2002/1141. *Report of the Secretary-General, Concerning the Situation in Abkhazia, Georgia*. 14 October. New York: United Nations.

United Nations Security Council (UNSC) (2006). S/2006/771. *Report of the Secretary-General on the Situation in Abkhazia, Georgia*. 28 September. New York: United Nations.

United Nations Security Council (UNSC) (2007). S/2007/182. *Report of the Secretary-General on the Situation in Abkhazia, Georgia*. 3 April. New York: United Nations.

Vignansky, M. (2004). *Vremya novostei*, 4 March, p. 5.
Vignansky, M. (2006). *Vremya novostei*, 22 February, p. 1.
Vignansky, M., A. Dubnov and I. Maksimov (2001). *Vremya novostei*, 19 September, p. 1.
Vignansky, M, and I. Solovyov (2006). *Vremya novostei*, 28 July, p. 1.
Vignansky, M. and I. Glanin (2003). *Vremya novostei*, 11 March, p. 2
Vyzhutovich, V. (2007). *Rossiiskaya gazeta*, 22 June, p. 3.
Yanchenkov, V. (2001). *Trud*, 6 October, p. 2.

10 From Putin to Medvedev ... and back to Putin
Whither Russia?

In May 2008, a new President took the helm of Russia, Dmitry Medvedev – previously First Deputy Prime Minister and head of the Russian Presidential Administration, as well as a close associate of departing President Vladimir Putin. The Medvedev Presidency from 2008 to 2012 did not really represent an end to Vladimir Putin's presence and influence in the Russian political scene. Putin became the head of government as Prime Minister and, although his position was formally inferior to that of the President, he remained in many respects the dominant actor, of the Medvedev–Putin *tandem*. Nevertheless, it would be a mistake to describe the new governing relationship simply as a Putin presidency 'in disguise'. While one can question the authorship of several of Medvedev's initiatives in the domestic and foreign policy realms, there is little doubt that Medvedev did introduce a significant change of style in politics, which was characterised by a less confrontational approach, especially in the international arena (Medvedev, 2009). Furthermore, in his speeches, Medvedev put greater emphasis on the role of the individual over the state, and embraced a less nationalistic agenda at home than his predecessor. At the same time, it must be noted that Medvedev did take responsibility for several key decisions in the foreign policy realm, including those which reflected a more assertive and 'neo-imperial' policy, such as the use military force in Georgia's separatist regions of South Ossetia and Abkhazia. Furthermore, the Medvedev Presidency did not really represent a break with the policies of the past. With Putin at the Premiership, efforts to deepen cooperation within the CIS framework were enhanced and the bases were set for the establishment of the *Eurasian Economic Union*, which was fully established once Putin returned to the Presidency 2012. Russia also tried to strengthen its position inside the CIS gas market, while continuing to use energy deliveries and gas prices as instruments of policy. In the military field, the Kremlin continued in its attempts further to strengthen the Collective Security Treaty (CSTO), with efforts to create more effective joint forces under Russian command, while it also tried to reduce Western military presence in many countries of Russia's Near Abroad. On the other hand, Russia had to come to terms with an increased Chinese military and economic presence in the Central Asian region, which directly challenged its own clout.

Much of the focus of the Medvedev presidency was devoted to managing the negative impact on Russia of the 2008 global financial crisis. The worldwide financial meltdown brought to light many of the weaknesses of the Russian economy, especially its over-reliance on commodity exports, primarily oil and gas, the existence of an unfavourable business climate and the systemic pervasion of corruption. Renewed efforts were, thus, conducted to *modernise* the economy, through a wide-ranging programme of reforms in several areas of the economy, the rule of law, civil society, the media and the political system, in an attempt to enhance competition, tackle corruption, and make institutions more open (Medvedev, 2009). However, as Kenneth Wilson (2015, p. 145) righty pointed out, the various measures taken, rather than introducing far-reaching transformations, were often of a cosmetic and presentational nature, thus producing scant results. The Duma December 2011 elections are one of the best examples of the lack of any 'transformational' changes in the Russian political system. Elections were marred by irregularities, large-scale use of administrative resources, falsification of results, ballot stuffing and biased media coverage. Perhaps the only reform which proved to be relatively successful was that of the Armed Forces, which produced much more effective and well-equipped professional Russian troops. In the international arena, the Medvedev Presidency was marked by Russia's five-day war with Georgia, which broke out only a few months after Medvedev took office. The war represented a watershed in Russia's foreign policy towards countries in the Near Abroad. For the first time, Russia openly utilised force to protect its interests in the former Soviet space, and unilaterally modified the borders of Georgia, a neighbouring state, by recognising the independence of its separatist regions, South Ossetia and Abkhazia. From Moscow's point of view, the war allowed Russia to reassert its position as a global power capable of defending its interests, by military force, if necessary. Moreover, the conflict also succeeded in putting a halt, at least momentarily, to NATO's continued enlargement into the former Soviet space, and 'served as a as payback for what Russia viewed as the "dangerous precedent" of an independent Kosovo' (IISS, 2012). These feats, however, came at the expense of a quite significant deterioration in Russia's relations with the West. The United States and all European countries stringently condemned Russia's actions in Georgia and denounced its subsequent recognition of Abkhazia's and South Ossetia's independence. NATO momentarily froze most military and political cooperation with Russia, and called on Moscow to withdraw its troops from the areas that it occupied in Georgia (de Haas, 2009). This, in turn, reduced NATO–Russian collaborative efforts in the areas of counter-terrorism, non-proliferation, arms controls and counter-insurgency.

The situation was made worse by sharp disagreements between Moscow and Washington over America's theatre missile defence (TMD) plans in Europe. While the United States saw its future TMD installations in Poland and the Czech Republic as necessary military arrangements to counter Iran's missile and nuclear capabilities, Moscow instead interpreted these deployments as intended to weaken Russia's own strategic defences. When Medvedev took office in May

2008, he therefore decided to suspend Russia's plans to take three nuclear missile regiments off combat duty in Kozelsk, in response to America's TMD projected deployments in Europe. He also threatened to deploy *Iskander* missile systems in Kaliningrad and hinted at using radio jamming against the USA's defence system, if deemed necessary (Medvedev, 2008b). The risk of an arms war loomed on the horizon. Many experts talked about a 'New Cold War' developing between the West and Russia (Lucas, 2008). However, direct confrontation between Russia and the United States was avoided, and less than a year after the outbreak of the Georgian–Russian war, Russia and the United States agreed to 'reset' their relations. Medvedev proved ready to embrace the offer presented by the new USA President Barack Obama to restart Russian–American relations afresh, concerned over Russia's isolation and eager to obtain American support for his programme to modernise the Russian economy (Black, 2015, p. 156). The re-establishment of a dialogue at the highest levels between Obama and Medvedev produced some significant results in the areas of arms control, non-proliferation and counter-insurgency (Deyermond, 2012, p. 501). After Russian–American negotiations on strategic arms reductions resumed in Geneva in November 2009, a new *Strategic Arms Reduction Treaty* between Washington and Moscow was signed in April 2010. Moreover, in a controversial move, President Obama agreed to review the United States' TMD programme, and to suspend, at least temporarily, the deployment of missile defence systems in the Czech Republic and Poland. The USA also decided to slow down Ukraine's and Georgia's accession to NATO, although closer military ties were still established between NATO and these countries, which went short of membership, especially with Georgia. Ukraine, however, exerted a clear geo-strategic turn towards Russia once Viktor Yanukovych became President in 2010. In April 2010, a major treaty was signed between Kiev and Moscow which extended the lease of the Black Sea Fleet's (BSF) naval base at Sevastopol for another 25 years, after 2017; and, more significantly, in June 2010 Yanukovych emphasised Ukraine's neutral status while significantly reducing Ukraine's cooperative engagement with NATO (Sherr, 2010).

Moscow responded to these encouraging moves by ordering a reduction in the number of troops stationed at Kaliningrad, supporting additional sanctions against North Korea and, more significantly, cancelling the planned sale of S-300 air-defence-missile systems to Tehran. Moreover, to Washington's great satisfaction, Moscow also approved an extensive package of UN sanctions against Iran in June 2010. This atmosphere of renewed trust between Russia and the United States permitted NATO–Russian political and military cooperation to resume once again in June 2009. An important aspect of that collaboration regarded NATO's counter-insurgency efforts in Afghanistan – the USA was allowed once again to fly its troops and its lethal equipment over Russian territory on their way to Central Asia. Reflecting this new rapprochement, NATO stated in its 2010 *Strategic Concept* that the Alliance wanted to seek a 'true strategic partnership' with Russia, 'with the expectation of reciprocity', and invited Russia to participate in an all-European missile defence system

(NATO, 2010). President Medvedev, who attended the 2010 NATO Lisbon summit, welcomed the Alliance's new positive stance towards Russia, and even mentioned the possibility of Russia requesting NATO membership, if NATO significantly changed its military outlook (Felgengauer, 2010).

These significant achievements increased mutual confidence and allowed for a change in the tone of the relationship, which, in turn, gave way to cooperation in areas that went beyond the initial specific items present in the bilateral agenda. On 17 March 2011, Russia abstained from voting on UNSC Resolution 1973 at the UN Security Council, a resolution which allowed for the creation of no-fly zones in Libyan areas under attack from Gaddafi's government forces, and authorised the use of all necessary means, short of military invasion, to protect local civilians (UNSC, 2011). President Obama, in turn, showed a readiness to explore Medvedev's proposals on European security, by supporting the establishment of a 'comprehensive dialogue to strengthen Euro-Atlantic and European security' (White House, 2009). In the spring of 2008, Medvedev had proposed the holding of a European summit to draft a new legally binding treaty on European security. This was suggested as an alternative to NATO's further enlargement eastwards, after Georgia and Ukraine were promised membership in 2008 (Shpakov, 2008). The objective was to establish a European security framework which granted an inclusive place to Russia and which ensured that the continent's security remained indivisible by unifying 'the Euro-Atlantic space, from Vancouver to Vladivostok' (Shpakov, 2008). The project, however, was greeted with limited enthusiasm in Europe and across the Atlantic, and was ignored by the majority of OSCE states when they met at the Athens OSCE Ministerial Council in early December 2009, a few days after the Kremlin had published its draft *European Security Treaty* text (Solovyov, 2009). Many Europeans remained sceptical of Medvedev's European security project, and saw it as an attempt by Moscow to change the post-Cold War European security architecture in order to suit Russia's needs, and in such a way that it would grant Russia a power of veto over crucial European security issues (Solovyov, 2009). This approach among primarily eastern Europeans clearly showed the limits of Russian–Western rapprochement.

Medvedev's foreign policy outlook

Medvedev's Presidency was characterised by a growing sense of confidence over Russia's domestic achievements and over its place in the international arena. 'Russia has overcome the consequences of the systemic political and socio-economic crisis of the end of the 20th Century', the 2009 *National Security Strategy* read (MID, 2009). By the late 2000s, the Kremlin had managed to improve the quality of life of Russia's citizens, in 2010 the economy had recovered from the immediate shocks of the 2008/09 financial crisis, and the country had withstood the centrifugal pressures of separatism, although a *jihadist* insurgency still remained strong in the Russian North Caucasus. Moreover, Russia had succeeded in preserving its territorial integrity and had enhanced its role and competitiveness internationally (MID, 2009). The country's successful war against Georgia in August 2008 had re-established renewed confidence in Russia's foreign and military capabilities, despite the weaknesses shown by the Russian armed forces during the military operation. There was a strong perception in the Kremlin that Russia was finally regaining its relevant role in the international arena, 'A new Russia ... has now acquired a full-fledged role in global affairs', due to its renewed internal strength and its capacity to project power externally, the *Foreign Policy Concept* (FPC), adopted in July 2008 read (PRF, 2008). Russia was, therefore, eager to participate more actively in world affairs, and engage in what Andrei Tsygankov (2009) called a strategy of 'Great Power normalisation'.[1] One of the key objectives of Russian foreign policy was 'to achieve strong positions of authority in the world community that best [met] the interests of the Russian Federation, as one of the influential centres in the modern world' (PRF, 2008). In a sign of renewed *Messianism*, Russia also hoped to 'influence global processes to ensure the formation of a just and democratic world order', intended to challenge Western global supremacy. Russia was seen by the Kremlin as potentially capable of exerting 'substantial influence on the formation of a new architecture of international affairs' (PRF, 2008). Pre-eminence was given to the need to find collective solutions to international problems, rather than engaging in unilateral fixes, even though the Kremlin was in practice engaging in similar unilateral actions in its Near Abroad.

Russia continued to worry over the 'inadequacy of the current global and security architecture', especially in the Euro-Atlantic region, where NATO had been allowed to occupy a predominant role. NATO's plans to expand its military infrastructure into Eastern Europe and close to Russia's borders remained unacceptable to Russia. Furthermore, the decision by NATO members to endow the alliance 'with global functions that go counter to the norms of international law', still created great concern in Moscow (MID, 2009). The Kremlin, however, was hopeful that the current transition from American predominance to a 'system of multivector diplomacy' in international affairs, would grant Russia an opportunity to 'reinforce its influence on the world stage' (MID, 2009). While Russia was prepared to develop ties with NATO, it was ready to do so only on the 'basis of equality and in the interest of strengthening the general security of the Euro-Atlantic region' (MID, 2009). Russia hoped to create an 'equitable and valuable strategic partnership with the United States, on the basis of shared interests, and taking into account the key influence of Russian-American relations on the international situation as a whole' (MID, 2009). As noted by Tsygankov (2009), 'Russia [had] not become anti-American' nor was it 'call[ing] for any concerted effort to undermine the US global position'. Instead, 'it defended the notions of collective leadership and multilateral diplomacy as the alternatives to unilateralism and hegemony in international relations' (Tsygankov, 2009). While according to Medvedev, Russia and the West shared many of the same values, they had to ensure that these 'values [were] understood in the same way' (*ITAR-TASS*, 2008).

On the other hand, when Medvedev became President in 2008, he gave less prominence to Russia's unique Eurasianist *civilisational* vocation, and instead re-emphasised Russia's European destiny.² In his June 2008 speech to parliamentary and civic leaders in Berlin, Medvedev reaffirmed the notion that Russia belonged to the European civilisation,

> Having cast aside the Soviet system and any idea of its restoration, Russia has laid the foundations of a state that is completely compatible with the rest of Europe, or to be more precise, with the best of all that makes up the common heritage of European civilisation.
>
> (Medvedev, 2008a)

Medvedev (2008a) believed that Russia and Europe enjoyed a common culture – 'the humanistic ideals and values that are shared by all of Europe and are an integral part of the culture of Russia and unified Germany', he noted while speaking in Berlin. More importantly, according to Medvedev, the end of the Cold War had made it possible 'to build genuinely equal cooperation between Russia, the European Union and North America as three branches of European civilisation' (Medvedev, 2008a). However, Medvedev argued that *Atlanticism* had already seen its day and had lost its previous appeal. In its place, he proposed developing 'unity between the whole Euro-Atlantic area, from Vancouver to Vladivostok' (Medvedev, 2008a). Foreign Minister Lavrov similarly argued in July 2008 that while Russia viewed itself 'as part of a European civilisation with common Christian roots', it did not adhere to the Anglo-Saxon model of development (Lavrov, 2008a). The Anglo-Saxon paradigm, according to Lavrov, had shown its fundamental weaknesses during the 2008 financial crisis. In its place, the experiences of Europe and Russia could best be used, to 'stimulate forthcoming global processes' (Lavrov, 2008a). Lavrov, furthermore, placed great emphasis on Russia's *civilisational mission*, in slight contrast to Medvedev. In his view, competition was becoming 'truly global and was acquiring a civilisational dimension' (Lavrov, 2008a). Rather than the entire globe acquiring Western values, Lavrov proposed that a new world order be established, with Russia, as the representative of a unique civilisation, becoming one of the leading poles. In this new world order, a 'core group of leading' nations, which would be 'truly representative [of the world] both geographically and civilisationally' would ensure world governability and promote successful global development (Lavrov, 2008a).

Furthermore, both Lavrov and Medvedev placed emphasis on Russia's special role in the former Soviet space, with Medvedev famously describing the region as a sphere of Russia's 'privileged interests', in the aftermath of the Georgian/Russian war (Medvedev, 2008c). Medvedev subsequently toned down his comments by noting that all countries had special interests. Thus, it was only natural for Russia to regard the former Soviet states (FSS) as being 'key strategic zones of its interest' (Trenin, 2009, p. 4). Yet, the notion of *privileged interests* entered the Russian political lexicon. In an article in *Diplomaticheskii Ezhegodnik* in December 2008, Foreign Minister Sergei Lavrov stated that the 'mutual privileged relations' between countries in this area could not be defined as a 'sphere of influence'. In his view, not only did Russia have *privileged interests* in its relations with its closest neighbours, but these states also had the same privileged interests in its relations with Russia (Lavrov, 2008b). Lavrov (2008b) also advanced the notion of the CIS space as a *civilisational area*, which is 'common to all peoples living here, [and] which allows us to preserve our historical and spiritual heritage'. Geographical realities, economic interdependence, the civilisational and cultural commonalities, all gave the CIS states 'tangible competitive advantages', which had to be positively exploited and reinforced through deeper cooperation. The CIS space therefore could not become a 'chessboard' where Great Powers played geopolitical games (Lavrov, 2008b). In Lavrov's view, the integration imperatives of globalisation remained as strong in the CIS area as in other regions of the world. In the summer of 2009, Lavrov went as far as using the term 'greater Russian civilisation' in a Latvian-language newspaper, in reference to Russia and the broader Russian world, which in his view had to be further integrated (Zevelev, 2014).

Putin's return to the Presidency: the *civilisational* paradigm is reinforced

When Putin returned to the Presidency in 2012, Russia's civilisational dimension was emphasised further. Putin argued that Russia represented a unique multi-ethnic and multi-cultural *civilisation* with a long and rich history.

> For centuries, Putin noted, Russia developed as a multi-ethnic nation ... as a civilisation-state bonded by the Russian (*Russkie*) people, Russian (*Russkie*) language and Russian (*Russkie*) culture, uniting us and preventing us from dissolving in this diverse world. To the rest of the planet, regardless of our ethnicity, we have been and continue to be one people.
>
> (Putin, 2012b)

There was little doubt in Putin's mind that, within this state-civilisation, Russians occupied a special place as the state-building nation. 'The Russian people and Russian culture are the linchpin, the glue that binds this unique civilisation together', Putin stated, and added,

> The Russian people are state-builders, as evidenced by the existence of Russia. Their great mission is to unite and bind together a *civilisation*. Language, culture and something Fyodor Dostoyevsky defined as 'universal responsiveness' is what unites Russian Armenians, Russian Azeris, Russian Germans, Russian Tatars and others, in a type of state civilisation where there are no ethnicities, but where 'belonging' is determined by a common culture and shared values. This kind of *civilisational* identity is based on preserving the dominance of Russian culture, although this culture is represented not only by ethnic Russians, but by all the holders of this identity, regardless of their ethnicity.
>
> (Putin, 2012b)

Interestingly, this citation by Putin clearly blurred the distinction between ethnicities inside the Russian Federation and titular nationalities in the former Soviet states. For Putin, the inhabitants of both Russia and of the ex-Soviet states were all members of a same Russian-led ethno-cultural civilisation (Putin, 2012b). Russia's civilisational dimension was also highlighted by Putin during his September 2013 Valdai Club speech. He cited philosopher Konstantin Leontyev, who had noted that Russia 'had always evolved in "blossoming complexity", as a state-civilisation, reinforced by the Russian people, Russian language, Russian culture, the Russian Orthodox Church and the country's other traditional religions' (Putin, 2013). Russia, in Putin's view, had always sought to 'accommodate the ethnic and religious specificity of particular territories, ensuring diversity in unity'. In his view 'Christianity, Islam, Buddhism, Judaism and other religions are an integral part of Russia's identity, its historical heritage and the present-day lives of its citizens'. The main task of the state, according to Putin, as enshrined in the Russian Constitution, was 'to ensure equal rights for members of traditional religions and atheists, and the right to freedom of conscience for all citizens' (Putin, 2013).

In his third term, Putin also emphasised the *civilisational* nature of global affairs. As noted in the 2013 *Foreign Policy Concept*,

> For the first time in modern history, global competition is taking place at a civilisational level, whereby various values and models of development based on the universal principles of democracy and market economy are starting to clash and compete against each other.
> (MID, 2013)

Globalisation and its attempt at homogenisation, had given rise to new 'civilisational identit[ies]', and therefore, one of the priorities of world leaders was to prevent 'civilizational fault line clashes'. This was to be achieved by forging 'partnership of cultures, religions and civilisations, in order to ensure a harmonious development of mankind' (MID, 2013). Russia proposed establishing a constructive 'dialogue and a partnership between civilisations', in order to enhance 'accord among the various cultures and confessions and ensure their mutual enrichment' (MID, 2013). More importantly, Russia was proposing that a set of 'common values' be adopted, as a foundation for joint action – 'a common moral denominator', in order to pursue global peace and justice. While Russia was actively developing relations with leading states and alliances, and integrating into the global economic and political systems, it nevertheless remained determined to pursue 'an independent foreign policy guided by its national interests and based on unconditional respect for international law' (MID, 2013).

Putin believed that Russia only gained respect and consideration of other states, 'when it is strong and stands firmly on its feet' (Putin, 2012a). The Kremlin, therefore, continued to promote global *multipolarity* in the international arena through the establishment of regional centres of power 'to ensure sustainable manageability of global development'. This required '*collective leadership by the major states of the world*' (my emphasis). These states, in the Kremlin's view, had to be 'representative in geographical and civilizational terms' and fully respectful of the central role of the United Nations (MID, 2013). Russia clearly perceived of itself as one of the leading world powers, which would collectively manage global affairs. This would create a 'stable and sustainable system of international relations' which would be based on the full respect of 'international law and the principles of equality, mutual respect and non-interference in internal affairs of states' (MID, 2013). When Putin returned to the Russian Presidency in 2012, he also placed renewed emphasis on Russia's Great-Power status, and on the need for Russia not only to 'preserve its geopolitical relevance' but also to 'multiply it' (Putin, 2012b). This implied mobilising Russia's economic, cultural, scientific and diplomatic potential to 'generate demand among our neighbours and partners for our products'. It also foresaw enhancing Russia's military might in order to 'guarantee Russia's security and independence' (Putin, 2012b).

Putin remained extremely concerned over the decision by Western countries to address regional and global crisis through unilateral sanctions and other coercive measures, including armed aggression, without the approval of the UN Security Council. There was a sense that the West was 'blatantly neglecting the principles of international law', and was overthrowing the legitimate authorities of sovereign states 'under the pretext of protecting the civilian population' (MID, 2013). In his 2012 *Moskovskii novosti* article, Putin expressed his worries over the outbreak of war in Libya, Syria and Iraq – conflicts which he argued were started by the West 'under the pretext of humanitarian goals' (Putin, 2012a). In his view, such military actions, rather than reducing tension, only expanded the areas of conflict, provoking instability and aggravating internal strife (MID, 2013). Russia also remained worried over the attempts by Western countries to build up and modernise offensive weapons, which undermined the global security architecture and challenged previously agreed international treaties (MID, 2013). The United States, according to Putin, was 'obsessed with the idea of becoming absolutely invulnerable', and this was 'unfeasible both technologically and geopolitically', as it would have required total vulnerability by others, something which was unacceptable to Russia (Putin, 2012a).

While Putin remained very critical of NATO's decision to expand its military infrastructure and deploy missile-defence systems in Europe, in 'close proximity to Russia's borders' (Putin, 2012a), he still hoped that Russia could create an 'equitable partnership' with NATO. The aim was to establish a 'common space of peace, security and stability', in the Euro-Atlantic area, based on the notion that security was indivisible (MID, 2013). Russia wished to build 'a truly unified region without dividing lines' by establishing a genuine partnership between Russia, the European Union and the United States (MID, 2013). In particular, Putin supported creating a 'harmonious community of economies from Lisbon to Vladivostok, which will, in the future, evolve into a free trade zone and even more advanced forms of economic integration' (Putin, 2012a). However, Russia remained keen to translate political declarations on friendship and cooperation, and on the indivisibility of security, *into legally binding obligations* (MID, 2013). Putin proposed creating a *common economic and human space* from the Atlantic to the Pacific Ocean, commonly referred as 'the Union of Europe'. At the same time, though, Russia was also pivoting towards Asia – 'a fast-developing geopolitical zone toward which the centre of world economy and politics is gradually shifting' (Putin, 2012a). The Kremlin wished to strengthen Russia's presence in the Asia-Pacific region and enhance its participation in regional integration processes, in order to boost the economies in the Russian Far East (MID, 2013). Putin, at least officially, did not see Chinese economic growth as a threat to Russia, but as an opportunity for business cooperation 'a chance to catch the Chinese wind in the sails of our economy' (Putin, 2012a). The technological and productive capabilities of both Russia and China could help develop the economy of Siberia and the Russian Far East. More importantly, Putin welcomed China's growing voice in international affairs, as 'Beijing shares our vision of the emerging equitable world order' (Putin, 2012a).

Concluding thoughts

With the return of Putin to the Presidency in 2012, Russia adopted a significantly more assertive policy both internationally – in Syria and in the Balkans – and regionally – in the former Soviet space, especially in the South Caucasus, and towards Moldova, Ukraine and Belarus. The Kremlin's policies not only responded to new geo-strategic imperatives – the enlargement of the EU and the implementation of the EU's Eastern Partnership programme by several CIS states – they also reflected genuine security and economic concerns, respectively related to the spread of instability and Islamist fundamentalism in the broader Middle East and the potential loss of traditional markets in the CIS space to the benefit of the EU. Yet, Russia's new course of action also followed clear neo-imperialist designs. By the mid-2010s, Putin had fully embraced a 'civilisational' discourse, as the driver and justifier of Russia's actions in Eurasia. Russia and the CIS states were seen as belonging to a unique civilisational whole, which shared a common destiny and a same geo-strategic space. This civilisational entity, which reached as far as Vladivostok in the east and Brest in the west, was bound to revive under Russia's leadership. It was Russia that held it together through its powerful culture and its Russian language, and it was Russia that fostered and strengthened it through its economic power and military might. This civilisational paradigm, which was fully embraced by Putin, was reflected in efforts by the Kremlin in the 2010s to establish a powerful Russian-led economic and military bloc in the former Soviet space which would turn Russia once again into a Great Power in the international arena.

The adoption by the Kremlin of a civilisational narrative to explain not only the nature of international relations but also to justify Russia's internal and regional actions, reflected the revival and the growing popularity within Russia – in the first decades of the twenty-first century – of *civilisational* and neo-imperialist discourses (Tsygankov, 2007; Larulle, 2009). *Civilisationalists* and *Eurasianists*, such as Aleksandr Dugin (2014a, 2014b) and Mikhail Leontyev (2006), understood Russia and its closest neighbours as belonging to a unique cultural, socio-political and ontological civilisation, distinct from both the West and the East. *Neo-Imperialists* such as Stanislav Belkovsky (2004), Roman Karev (Belkovsky and Karev, 2005) and Mikhail Yuriyev (2006, 2007), in turn, took a positive view of Empires. They placed emphasis on Russia's imperial heritage and insisted on the need to restore an imperial entity around Russia, integrated primarily by those countries that belonged to the USSR. The Orthodox variant of these two understandings, as expressed by Natalya Narotchinskaya (2003a, 2003b), promoted the notion of an Orthodox civilisation – Christian Orthodoxy was seen as the historical and spiritual foundation that bound Russia and its closest neighbours together. *Ethno-Nationalists*, such as Ksenia Myalo and Mikhail Remizov (2012), instead, stressed the relevance of Russian ethnicity, the Russian nation and the Russian people as the true builders of the Russian state. These Nationalist and Imperialist ideas, which had remained at the margins of political discourse in the 1990s, increasingly penetrated official circles during the 2000s, influencing policy and directing intellectual debates. They were partly adopted by the Kremlin in an effort to explain and justify Moscow's actions both globally and regionally. The liberal paradigm, instead, which had been predominant during the early 1990s, and seemed to have reappeared under President Medvedev, lost relevance and was pushed to the background (Pain, 2009; Laruelle, 2009).

While Putin did not fully embrace the more extreme Eurasianist and neo-Imperialist views which were being promoted by renowned intellectuals, and which often included a full redrawing of Russia's newly acquired borders, his discourse increasingly echoed an imperialist narrative. His neo-imperialist narrative, moreover, often translated into quite aggressive foreign policy behaviour in the Near Abroad, especially after he returned to power in 2012. Moscow's actions in the CIS region revealed a new understanding of the former Soviet space and of Russia's place in it. While the independence of the CIS states was not officially questioned, the Kremlin nevertheless saw all of these countries as belonging to the same civilisational reality as Russia. After 2012, therefore, Russia's behaviour in the former Soviet space became much more forceful, displaying clear attempts at establishing a sphere of influence or *neo-Empire* in the Near Abroad. In this respect, great efforts were conducted to create a Eurasian Union under the rubble of the USSR, to strengthen the CSTO, and to keep CIS states geo-strategically aligned to Russia. However, this did not necessarily translate into the acquisition of new territory through the redrawing of Russia's external borders, as was being suggested by the more extremist Imperialists.

Yet, in the summer and autumn of 2013, this paradigm began to shift as the Kremlin proved increasingly ready to employ the full array of its *hard power* instruments in order to compel several CIS states to join its newly established Eurasian Economic Union project and abandon their Association agreements with the EU. This was followed by the forceful annexation of Crimea in 2014 and the further integration of South Ossetia and Abkhazia de facto into Russia in 2015. These events were of a vast magnitude – they totally transformed the existing geopolitical realities of Eurasia and showed the full extent of Russia's neo-imperial reach. Russia moved away from its previous stances as a conservative actor in the former USSR-space, which, at least formally, respected the existing former Soviet borders as officially recognised. Instead, Russia turned into a 'revisionist' power, ready to shift and modify the internationally recognised borders of its immediate neighbours by force, in order to suit its own interests and global ambitions. While it could well be argued that these actions reflected legitimate concerns over events inside Ukraine and Georgia, as well as worries over the enlargement of the EU and NATO into areas dear to Russia in the CIS space, such analysis is incomplete at best. Russia's behaviour in the former Soviet space in 2014 brought to light the full embrace by the Kremlin of a neo-imperialist agenda, which put into question the international arrangements that had emerged in 1991. They directly challenged the broader European security order, two decades after the end of the USSR. It must be noted, finally, that Russia's actions in the CIS space also revealed concerns over the possibility of an abrupt 'regime change' in Russia and in the countries of the Near Abroad. The advent of the Arab Spring and the growth of internal opposition against Putin's leadership in 2011–2012, created the spectre of a revolutionary – even if peaceful – change of government in Russia. The 2013/2014 EuroMaidan revolution, which occurred closer to home, only reinforced such worries. Concerns about this new predicament also very much influenced policy, and, as a result, new civilisational and neo-imperialist discourses became predominant.

Notes

1 The Russian Federation possessed 'real capacity to play a well-deserved role globally', the *Foreign Policy Concept*, adopted in July 2008, noted (MID, 2013).
2 There was no mention of Russia's civilisation's mission in Medvedev's various addresses to Parliament.

Bibliography

Belkovsky. S. (2004). *Vedomosti*, 12 May, p. 2.
Belkovsky. S. and R. Karev (2005). Dokumenty: Sodruzhestvo Stran-Soiuznikov Rossii. Lenta.ru. 12 April. Available at: www.balancer.ru/society/2005/04/t32737-novyj-sssr-po-belkovskomu.5704.html [accessed 10 July 2018].
Black, J.L. (2015). *The Russian Presidency of Dmitry Medvedev, 2008–2012: The Next Step Forward or Merely a Time Out?* London and New York: Routledge.
de Haas, M. (2009) NATO-Russia relations after the Georgian Conflict. Clingendael. Available at: www.clingendael.nl/sites/default/files/20090000_cscp_artikel_mhaas.pdf [accessed 10 July 2018].
Deyermond, R. (2012). Assessing the Reset: Successes and Failures in the Obama Administration's Russia Policy – 2009–2012, *European Security*, 22 (4), 500–523.
Dugin, A. (2014a). *Eurasian Mission: An Introduction to Neo-Eurasianism*. London: Arktos Media, p. 9.

Dugin, A. (2014b). *Main Principles of Eurasianist Policy*, 28 June. Available at: https://neweuropeanconservative.wordpress.com/2014/06/28/main-principles-of-eurasist-policy-dugin/ [accessed 10 July 2018].

Evans, A. (2015). Ideological Change under Vladimir Putin in the Perspective of Social Identity Theory. *Demokratizatsiya: The Journal of Post-Soviet Democratization* 23 (4), 401–426.

Felgengauer, P. (2010). *Novaya gazeta*, 24 November, p. 3.

IISS (2012). Assessing Russian Foreign Policy Under Medvedev. *IISS Strategic Comments*, 18 (18), May.

ITAR-TASS (2008). December 5.

Lavrov, S. (2008a). Rossiya i mir v XXI veke, *Russia in Global Affairs*, 20 July. Available at: http://globalaffairs.ru/number/n_11159 [accessed 2 July 2018].

Lavrov, S. (2008b). Vneshnyaya politika Rossii i novoe kachestvo geopoliticheskoi situatsii, 15 December 2008. MID. Available at: http://tiras.ru/v-mire/5685-lavrov-vneshnjaja-politika-rossii-i.html [accessed 10 July 2018].

Leontyev, M. (2006). *Komsomolskaya Pravda*, 26 April.

Lo, B. (2009). *Medvedev and the New European Security Architecture*. Policy Brief. London: Centre for European Reform, July.

Laruelle, M. (2009). *Inside and Around the Kremlin's Black Box: The New Nationalist Think Tanks in Russia*. Stockholm Paper, Institute for Security and Development Policy. October. Available at: http://isdp.eu/content/uploads/images/stories/isdp-main-pdf/2009_laruelle_inside-and-around-the-kremlins-black-box.pdf [accessed 10 July 2018].

Lucas, E. (2008). *The New Cold War: How the Kremlin Menaces both Russia and the West*. London: Bloomsbury.

McDermott, R. (2010). Kremlin Contemplates a Seismic Shift in Russian Foreign Policy, *Eurasia Daily Monitor* 7 (97), 19 May. Available at: https://jamestown.org/program/kremlin-contemplates-a-seismic-shift-in-russian-foreign-policy [accessed 10 July 2018].

Medvedev, D. (2009). *Go Russia!* 10 September. Available at: http://en.kremlin.ru/events/president/news/5413 [accessed 10 July 2018].

Medvedev, D. (2008a). *Speech at Meeting with German Political, Parliamentary and Civic Leaders*, 5 June. Available at: http://en.kremlin.ru/events/president/transcripts/320 [accessed 10 July 2018].

Medvedev, D. (2008b). Address to the Federal Assembly of the Russian Federation, 5 November. Available at: http://en.kremlin.ru/events/president/transcripts/1968 [accessed 10 July 2018].

Medvedev, D. (2008c). Interview Given by Dmitry Medvedev to Television Channels Channel One, Rossiya, NTV. 31 August. Available at: http://en.kremlin.ru/events/president/transcripts/48301 [accessed 10 July 2018].

Ministry of Foreign Affairs of the Russian Federation (MID) (2009). Strategiya national'noi bezopasnosti Rossiiskoi Federatsi do 2020 goda. 12 May. Available at: www.mid.ru/foreign_policy/official_documents/-/asset_publisher/CptICkB6BZ29/content/id/294430 [accessed 10 July 2018].

Ministry of Foreign Affairs of the Russian Federation (MID) (2013). Kontseptsiya vneshnei politiki Rossiiskoi Federatsii, 18 February. Available at: www.mid.ru/en/foreign_policy/official_documents/-/asset_publisher/CptICkB6BZ29/content/id/122186?p_p_id=101_INSTANCE_CptICkB6BZ29&_101_INSTANCE_CptICkB6BZ29_languageId=ru_RU [accessed 10 July 2018].

Narochintskaya, N. (2003a) Rossiya, SNG i zapad. Chast 1. Ideologiya i istoriya kak factory geografii. Pravoslavie.ru. 22 December. Available at: https://web.archive.org/

web/20080429225317/http:/www.pravoslavie.ru/analit/global/russngzapad1.htm [accessed 10 July 2018].

Narochintskaya, N. (2003b) Rossiya, SNG i zapad. Chast 2. Starye geopoliticheskie proekty v novom oblich'i. Pravoslavie.ru. Available at: https://web.archive.org/web/20080429225321/www.pravoslavie.ru/analit/global/russngzapad2.htm [accessed 10 July 2018].

NATO (2010). *Active Engagement, Modern Defence: Strategic Concept for the Defence and Security of the Members of the North Atlantic Treaty Organisation.* Lisbon. Available at: www.nato.int/nato_static_fl2014/assets/pdf/pdf_publications/20120214_strategic-concept-2010-eng.pdf [accessed 10 July 2018].

Novaya gazeta (2009). Obama's Interview with Novaya Gazeta. 6 July. Available at: www.novayagazeta.ru/articles/2009/07/06/42241-obama-interview-with-novaya-gazeta [accessed 10 July 2018].

Pain, E. (2009) Russia Between Empire and Nation. *Russian Politics & Law*, 47 (2), 60–86.

President of Russian Federation (PRF) (2008). The Foreign Policy Concept Of The Russian Federation, 12 January. Available at: http://en.kremlin.ru/supplement/4116 [accessed 10 July 2018].

President of Russian Federation (PRF) (2014). Meeting of the Valdai International Discussion Club. Sochi. 24 October.

Putin, V.V. (2012a). *Moskovskie novosti*, 27 February.

Putin, V.V. (2012b). Address to the Federal Assembly, 12 December. Available at: http://en.kremlin.ru/events/president/news/17118 [accessed 10 July 2018].

Putin, V.V. (2013). *Presidential Address to the Federal Assembly*, 12 December. Available at: http://en.kremlin.ru/events/president/news/19825 [accessed 10 July 2018].

Remizov, M. (2012). Nationalism and Geopolitics: A Case for Russia, Will Russia Follow Turkey's Lead? *Russian in Global Affairs*. 7 October. Available at: http://eng.globalaffairs.ru/number/Nationalism-and-Geopolitics-A-Case-for-Russia-15686 [accessed 10 July 2018].

Sherr, J. (2010). Mortgaging of Ukraine's Independence. Chatham House Briefing Paper. August. Available at: www.chathamhouse.org/sites/default/files/public/Research/Russia%20and%20Eurasia/bp0810_sherr.pdf [accessed 22 July 2018].

Shpakov, Y. (2008). *Vremya novostei*, 6 June, p. 2.

Solovyov, V. (2009). *Kommersant*, 2 December, p. 8.

Trenin, D. (2009). Russia's Spheres of Interest, not Influence, *The Washington Quarterly*, 32 (4), 3–22.

Tsygankov, A.P. (2007). Finding a Civilisational Idea: 'West', 'Eurasia', and 'Euro-East' in Russia's Foreign Policy, *Geopolitics*, 12. pp. 375–399.

Tsygankov, A.P. (2009). Russia in the Post-Western World: The End of the Normalization Paradigm? *Post-Soviet Affairs*, 25 (4), 347–369.

United Nations Security Council (UNSC) (2011). *Resolution 1973 (2011)*, 17 March. Available at: www.un.org/ga/search/view_doc.asp?symbol=S/RES/1973%20%282011%29 [accessed 10 July 2018].

White House (2009). Joint Statement by President Barack Obama of the United States of America and President Dmitry Medvedev of the Russian Federation on Nuclear Cooperation. 6 July. Available at: https://obamawhitehouse.archives.gov/the-press-office/joint-statement-president-barack-obama-united-states-america-and-president-dmitry-m [accessed 10 July 2018].

Wilson, K. (2015). Modernization or More of the Same in Russia: Was There a "Thaw" Under Medvedev?, *Problems of Post-Communism*, 62 (3), 145–158.

Yuryev, M. (2006). 'Estestvennym dlya russkikh variantom gosudarstvennogo ustroistva yavlyaetsya smes' ideokratii i imperskogo paternalizma'. Fond Liberal'naya Missiya. 2 August. Available at: www.liberal.ru/articles/cat/1273 [accessed 10 July 2018].

Yuryev, M. (2007) *Tret'ya Imperiya: Rossiya, kotoraya dolzhna byt'*, St. Petersburg: Limbus Press.

Zevelev, I. (2014). The Russian World Boundaries. *Russian in Global Affairs*, 2. 7 June.

Zygar, M. (2014). *All the Kremlin's Men: Inside the Court of Vladimir Putin*. New York: Public Affairs.

11 The Eurasian Economic Union
A neo-Imperial paradigm?

The late 2000s saw a renewed and much more effective effort by Russia to establish an economic bloc around a Customs Union (CU) and a single economic space in the Commonwealth of Independent States (CIS), which eventually paved the way for the creation of the *Eurasian Economic Union* (EAEU) once Putin returned to the Presidency in 2012. As progress towards the formation of a Single Economic Space (SES) with Ukraine, Belarus, and Kazakhstan dwindled, emphasis was placed on the strengthening of the Eurasian Economic Community (EvrAzES), whose members agreed in October 2007 to create and fully implement a CU by 2011. The CU project received a significant boost from Russia's closest CIS trading partners, Kazakhstan and Belarus, in the aftermath of the 2008 global financial crisis, which saw a sharp fall in commodity and energy prices – Russia's and CIS' main export items. This in turn, produced major contractions in the Gross Domestic Product (GDP) of several CIS countries, particularly in Russia, whose GDP fell by -7.8 per cent. In order to arrest the negative implications of the economic crisis, Russia and Kazakhstan, followed by Belarus, decided to move ahead with the implementation of the *Eurasian Customs Union* (ECU) or *Evraziiskii Tamozhennyi Soiuz*. In early 2009, the Customs Union Commission (CUC), whose founding agreements had been reached in October 2007, was established in Moscow to implement and manage the new ECU. On 9 June 2009, it was announced that that ECU would start functioning on 1 January 2010, while all necessary procedures would be completed by 1 July 2011 (Shapovalov, 2009). This was to be achieved through the adoption of Common External Tariffs (CET) on all traded goods and through the introduction of a common Customs Code, which would replace existing national legislation on foreign trade (ICG, 2016, p. 2). The objective was to establish a unified customs area, in which goods would move freely 'from the Polish-Belarusian border to the Kazakh-Chinese border' (Batyrshin, 2009). The three sides also agreed to withdraw their individual bids to join the World Trade Organization (WTO), and instead decided to engage in negotiations as a single bloc, although a few weeks later, on 10 July, Russia stated that it intended to resume its negotiations on WTO accession individually, considering it an easier enterprise, more likely to be successful (Batyrshin, 2009).

Towards a single economic space

Furthermore, in December 2009, movement towards the formation of a SES within the ECU framework accelerated, with the adoption by Russia, Belarus and Kazakhstan, of a very comprehensive *Plan of Action*, which laid the grounds for the creation of a tight economic union (ICEU, 2009). The Plan of Action involved the harmonisation of macro-economic policy, common rules on competition, a common industrial policy and agreed agricultural subsidies. It also stipulated for the creation of common policies on public procurement, trade of services, and regulation of intellectual property. ECU states also agreed to create the necessary conditions for the free movement of capital and investment within the SES, and to establish a common monetary policy. In addition, a common energy market in oil, petroleum products and gas would be set up, as well as a single telecommunications market. The sides also committed themselves to grant each other access in the electricity, rail-transport and energy sectors, and to implement a common policy in the transport of gas and oil products. To addresses the challenges of non-tariff barriers (NTB) to trade, common principles and rules on technical regulations, standards and veterinary and phytosanitary measures would also be agreed (ICEU, 2009). In the area of labour, the SES also envisaged cooperation in the fight against illegal migration from third countries, and more importantly, common regulations on visas and the status migrant workers. All this indicated a renewed willingness by Russia and its partners finally to create a highly integrated, homogenous economic bloc, akin to the European Union (EU). This was complemented with the adoption of a Treaty on a Free Trade Area (FTA) reached in October 2011 between a series of key CIS member states – Russia, Belarus, Ukraine, Kazakhstan, Moldova, Armenia, Kyrgyzstan and Tajikistan – and intended further to liberalise intra-CIS and intra-ECU trade, through the removal of import and export duties, the elimination of discriminatory practices and the progressive abolition of quantitative restrictions to trade.

Changes were also introduced in the structures of the organisation in preparation for the establishment of the Eurasian Economic Union. At the end of 2011, Eurasian Customs Union (ECU)/SES member states agreed to replace the CUC with a new institution, the *Eurasian Economic Commission* (EEC), which became responsible for implementing and managing the SES. The EEC had a two-tier structure – a *Collegium* and a *Council*. The *Collegium* was the executive body of the Union, consisting of nine members, with each member state providing three Ministers, and made responsible for overseeing 23 departments. Formally, the Collegium adopted decisions by a two-thirds majority, unless they were considered politically sensitive, in which case they were either approved by consensus, or were instead taken at the level of the EEC Council (EEU, 2014). Russian Minister for Industry and Trade, Viktor Khristenko, was initially appointed chair of the Collegium for four years, and the seat of the Commission was established in Moscow. The *Council*, which brought together the deputy Prime Ministers of ECU/SES states, and had a rotating presidency, became the main decision-making body (EEU, 2014). Decisions within the Council were taken by consensus, with each member having an equal voice. This was done in an attempt not to alienate countries like Belarus, Kazakhstan or potentially Ukraine. Although the EEC became a *supranational body* with the capacity to overrule states, its power to enforce decisions was diluted by the elimination of the weighted voting system at the level of the EEC Council, if decisions were politically sensitive. Moreover, the ECU was characterised by the absence of any effective mechanisms of enforcement (ICG, 2016, p. 2). The EvrAzES Court located in Minsk, which started functioning in January 2012, became responsible for addressing issues related to the functioning of the ECU and the SES, and for ensuring compliance with rules and regulations adopted by the Union organs, but it did not have any truly effective enforcement powers (Roberts and Moshes, 2016, p. 548).[1]

Implementation of the ECU and the SES

In January 2010, the ECU was formally declared in existence even though the new common Customs Code did not take effect until 1 July 2010. The delay in the ratification of the ECU's Code was caused by a trade dispute between Russia and Belarus over customs duties on oil products and external tariffs on automobiles. Only after these trade disputes were partly resolved – Belarus was allowed *temporarily* to introduce its own import duties on foreign vehicles purchased by private dealers while Russia promised to eliminate oil export duties imposed on Belarus once the SES was established – was the new Customs Code finally adopted (Kolesnikov, 2010). The creation of a *real* common customs area, however, took a year longer to materialise. Only in 2011, were customs post between Russia, Belarus and Kazakhstan fully removed, and this helped to reduce transaction costs at the border. Moreover, considerable progress was also made in the following two years in standardising trade regulation, sanitary and phytosanitary controls, technical regulations and protective measures, thus further eliminating NTB to trade (Cooper, 2013a, pp. 22–23; EBRD, 2012, p. 65).

Significant progress towards implementing the SES *Plan of Action* was also made in the two years following its approval in 2009. In November 2010, agreements were reached on coordinating macro-economic policy, on introducing uniform competition rules and on cooperation in the fight against illegal migration. Progress was also made in the energy sector, with agreements reached on the access of natural monopolies to the energy sectors of other ECU/SES states, on common energy pricing and on similar tariff policies (Sitnina and Suvarov, 2010). In December 2010, the three Presidents signed 'all the necessary agreements', for the implementation of the SES, although many of the provisions that had caused controversy were removed – for example, the agreement on the trade of services stipulated for only loose commitments on the further privatisation of business and state companies. In an effort to accelerate the integration process, countries were given the right, in several instances, either to provide exemptions on sensitive goods or to apply national laws (Sitnina and Susarov, 2010). This allowed Russia, Belarus and Kazakhstan to declare the official existence of the SES on 1 January 2012, even though not all previously agreed provisions had been put in place and important delays remained in the implementation of regulations relating to the free movement of capital and the harmonisation of economic policy (Cooper, 2013a, p. 25).[2]

Progress towards establishing a well-functioning SES nevertheless continued, and with Russia's accession to the WTO in August 2012, most SES customs duties were brought in line with Moscow's WTO commitments. Furthermore, in September 2012, the CIS FTA agreement came into force, leading at least in theory, to further multilateral trade liberalisation within the SES. Much work was also conducted towards improving customs administration, trade regulation and the removal of NTB to trade (Cooper, 2013a, p. 26). Nevertheless, problems and obstacles to intra-ECU trade still remained. Despite efforts to harmonise standards, governments – Russia in particular – continued to utilise national quality requirements, primarily on foodstuffs, to restrict bilateral trade (Biryukova and Khimshiashvili, 2013). For example, in 2013, Russia limited Belarus' milk imports, allegedly for quality concerns, but in reality, in order to retaliate for the detention by the Belarusian authorities of Vladislav Baumgertner, the CEO of Uralkali, the world largest potash producer (RT.com, 2013). In April 2012, Moscow revoked the licence of the Belarusian national carrier Belavia, for flights to Russia, in an attempt to gain access to the Belarusian aviation market, which was under Belavia's tight control (Bohdan, 2012). Kazakhstan and Belarus, in turn, faced discrimination when wanting to access the Russian energy-transport system (Roberts and Moshes, 2016, p. 549). Russian local authorities also often used double standards and NTB to block the access of Kazakhstan's goods trying to enter the Russian market, while Russian goods instead, generally had full access to the Kazakh market (Kassenova, 2013, p. 152).[3] More significantly, Russia unilaterally, at times, introduced trade bans on products coming from non-ECU partners, either as instruments of its foreign policy or in order to protect its own market. It did so without consulting its partners, and in contravention of the laws regulating the functioning of the ECU. For example, in 2010, Russia banned the import of American chicken on the grounds that it failed to meet new sanitary standards, and in late 2011, Moscow imposed a ban on cheese imports from Ukraine. This was done because Ukraine's products allegedly failed to meet quality standards, but in reality it was done to apply pressure on Ukraine in a dispute over gas prices.[4] It was clear that Russia was exercising its hegemonic economic power to administer the ECU in its favour. Furthermore, in many instances, access into the ECU by non-ECU states became more, and not less difficult, after the establishment of the ECU, as clearance times at external-ECU borders increased.

Rationale behind the establishment of the ECU and the SES

The accelerated pace of the ECU/SES integration process, when compared to previous attempts, clearly indicated a strong determination by its members, and particularly by Russia, to move ahead with the project. The negative impact of the global financial crisis on Eurasian economies had shown not only the vulnerabilities of these countries to the fluctuations in world energy prices, but also their dependence on the global economy and on world financial markets. A consensus had therefore emerged in 2009 among the three ECU/SES states that only through stronger cooperation and deeper integration could their economies fully develop and better protect themselves from similar crisis in the future. Furthermore, the complete elimination of internal barriers to trade within the CES space would potentially allow producers to benefit from increased market size, and this could, in turn, facilitate innovation. The SES could therefore boost mutual trade and expand investment in order to improve these countries' economic competitiveness in a global economy (Roberts and Moshes, 2016, p. 544). On the other hand, the introduction of relatively high CET, which were aligned with Russia's external tariffs, could temporarily protect domestic production from more competitive foreign goods. The high CET were intended by Russia as a tool of industrial policy – they reflected Moscow's attempt to foster import substitution by protecting domestic production from external competition, as well as Russia's efforts to promote the sale of Russian products inside the ECU (EBRD, 2012, p. 66).[5]

The decision to accelerate the formation of the ECU/SES also reflected the difficulties that countries such as Russia and Kazakhstan were experiencing when trying to join the WTO (Susarov, 2010). In June 2009, President Medvedev had expressed Moscow's disappointment with the pace of Russia's WTO accession negotiations. In his own words, 'This process has been dragging on for too long and in recent years it has looked more like feeding us empty promises' (Batyrshin, 2009). While Russia was not prepared to give up WTO membership, the slow progress in the talks convinced Moscow that ECU integration had to be given precedence over the WTO accession. The same was true for Kazakhstan. After the country had been 'swept into the vortex of the global financial crisis, Astana wanted to show [some] immediate, tangible benefits of joining the WTO' and not 'future, theoretical [ones]' (Wikileaks, 2009b). Astana's frustrations with the USA and the EU over their lack of flexibility in Kazakhstan's WTO negotiations compelled the country to turn to Russia for economic cooperation, as noted by Kazakhstan's Trade Minister Zhanar Aitzhanova (Wikileaks, 2009b). Belarus, instead, had generally been less supportive of WTO membership. As Ales Alachnovič (2015) noted, Belarus 'imitated [its] engagement' in the WTO negotiations, and preferred instead to give priority to economic ties with Russia, its main trading partner, and eventually join the WTO together with its eastern neighbour.

From Russia's perspective, progress towards the rapid establishment of the ECU also followed clear geopolitical objectives. In the aftermath of the global financial crisis, the view that regional economic blocs were poised to become more relevant in the face of the United States' dwindling economic power became widespread among decision-makers in Moscow (Belton and Gorst, 2009). 'For Russia, the most important strategic task is now to create an independent centre of power, its own economic bloc. One's own club is now more important than the global club', noted Carnegie Endowment expert, Dmitry Trenin (Belton and Gorst, 2009). Furthermore, in its ambitions to become a full-fledged Great Power of global reach, Russia felt it necessary to develop close allied ties with its neighbouring states, as this was seen as further enhancing the country's strength and its standing in the international arena. As Trenin (2009) explained, 'the former imperial borderlands of Russia are [now] deemed to be both elements of its power center and a cushion to protect Russia itself from undesirable encroachments by other great powers'. In this respect, Moscow felt it necessary to counter the European Union's Eastern Partnership (EaP) project, which was seen as directly challenging Russia's traditional influence and significant presence in the western and southern CIS states. Launched in May 2009, the EaP envisaged greater integration between the EU and six former Soviet states (Ukraine, Belarus, Moldova, Georgia, Armenia and Azerbaijan) in the areas of trade, energy and freedom of movement. More importantly, the Partnership stipulated for *legal approximation* between these countries' laws and EU legislation in order to foster deeper economic integration. Furthermore, it also envisaged the development of 'political associations' between the EU and its partner countries (EU, 2009). Given these far-reaching objectives, the EaP was seen in Moscow as an attempt by the EU 'to penetrate into Russia's [traditional] sphere of interests' (Dymarsky, 2009). Russia decided therefore to promote an alternative 'soft power' option – the Eurasian Union – in order to attract these countries back into the Russian geopolitical orbit (Dymarky, 2009). The Eurasian Union project was accelerated, and the CUC was awarded significant increases in its budget.

The integration of Belarus and Kazakhstan into the ECU/SES, however, was not entirely voluntary, and this clearly showed the limits of this project and its strong neo-imperialist undertones. Russia used coercive measure or *hard power* to achieve such results, especially as far as Belarus was concerned. In June 2009, Russia banned the import of Belarusian dairy products for several weeks, arguing they did not meet Russia's technical standards. While this was also done to get access to the Belarusian dairy industry market, to protect Russian milk producers from cheaper Belarusian imports and to reduce Belarusian subsidies to agriculture (Khodasevich, 2009), a key underlying objective was also to exert pressure on Belarus in order to obtain its full commitment to the Russian-led ECU (Konovalov and Zygar, 2009; Bohdan, 2012). The Kremlin also threatened in June 2010 to introduce duties on the oil products Russia sold to Belarus for domestic consumption, if Belarus did not sign up to the ECU Customs Code (Khodasevich, 2010). In early 2010, Russia had already raised the customs export duty on the oil supplied to Belarus for industrial consumption from 35 per cent to 100 per cent, severely hitting the chemical and petrochemical industries, which heavily relied on cheap Russian oil (Klysinski and Kononczuk, 2010, p. 1; Gabuev *et al.*, 2010). In view of this predicament, the Belarussian president could not face additional price increases without any major disruptions, and this forced him to make the necessary compromises vis-à-vis the Russian-led ECU/SES.

In addition, an information war was launched by the Russian media against Lukashenko at a time when he was facing upcoming presidential elections, seriously endangering his chances to succeed. As political analyst Valery Karbalevich explained, 'The very fact that Belarus joined the CU on Russia's terms looks like a capitulation' (Khodasevich, 2010). Moreover, it was only once Belarus decided to sign all the necessary agreements on the implementation of the SES in December 2010, that Russia finally agreed to scrap the export tariff for oil and petroleum products sold to Belarus (Ioffe and Yarashevich, 2011, p. 753).

Joining the ECU also carried some significant drawbacks for Belarus. Once Russia joined the WTO, Belarus would have been compelled to reduce its CET accordingly – in line with Russia's WTO commitments. Yet, it would not have necessarily enjoyed greater access to foreign markets, as WTO states would have not been compelled, in turn, to reduce their customs rates on Belarusian imports. Furthermore, Belarusian industry would have been automatically exposed to greater competition from non-ECU countries, members of the WTO, as well as from Russia and Kazakhstan (Connolly, 2013, p. 66). Despite these disadvantages, Belarus agreed to join the ECU, primarily because of its dependence on Russia for trade and subsidies. Cheap oil and gas from Russia remained essential for Belarus to keep its economy afloat – it allowed Minsk to avoid conducting the necessary but painful structural reforms that would have made its economy more competitive (Frear, 2013, p. 119). In turn, Belarus helped Russia to enhance its own security. It provided Russia with military-political allegiance and additional strategic depth for Russia's own territorial defence. In view of these significant benefits, Russia agreed to continue subsidising the Belarusian economy. In exchange for Minsk's membership of the ECU/SES Belarus was granted substantial financial support from Russia in late 2011 and 2012, and allowed to pay significantly reduced gas prices – they were reduced from $244/mcm in 2011 to $165/mcm in 2012 (Preiherman, 2011a, 2011b). Minsk, in turn, agreed in November 2011 to sell Belarus' remaining 50 per cent stake in Beltransgaz to Gazprom for the significant sum of $2.5 billion, granting the Russian gas conglomerate increased access to the Belarusian gas distribution market and allowing Moscow to control the main gas pipelines transiting through Belarus.

Russia also put strong pressure on Kazakhstan in the summer of 2009, to accelerate the establishment of the ECU, according to the declarations of Kazakh Trade Minister Aitzhanova (Wikileaks, 2009b). The Kazakh government, however, had generally been a strong supporter of Eurasian integration, aware of the close economic interconnections and human ties that existed between Kazakhstan, Russia and other Central Asian states. Kazakh industries were linked to Soviet production cycles, and its exports products transited through Russian territory to foreign markets. Furthermore, Kazakhstan hosted a big Russian minority as well as other ethnic minorities from Central Asia. It therefore generally supported CIS economic integration products. President Nazarbayev had been the first to launch the Eurasian Union project as early as March 1994, and had also proposed creating a full-fledged SES in 2008. When the ECU was reinvigorated in 2009, President Nazarbayev again became a strong supporter of the project, arguing that joining the ECU would allow his country to become a member of a market of 170 million people, and in this way, make Kazakhstan more attractive to foreign investors. This, in turn, would force Kazakhstan to adopt a business-friendly economic environment and would help prepare Kazakh products to withstand global competition once Kazakhstan entered the WTO. More significantly, President Nazarbayev hoped that the ECU would help the country overcome the negative implications of the global financial crisis, by turning the ECU into a market for Kazakh manufactured and processed goods (KazInform, 2009). 'I am now even more firmly convinced that in the long-term no alternative to the Eurasian integration exists', Nazarbayev (2009) noted in the aftermath of the global financial meltdown. In 2008–2009, Kazakhstan had given priority to joining the WTO, and had agreed with Russia that only after both countries joined the organisation would they together form the ECU (Wikileaks, 2009a). Kazakhstan had apparently been ready even to 'slow down' the process of ECU-formation, if only the United States had sent Astana a clear message in support of rapidly accepting Kazakhstan's WTO membership. However, the West's hesitation and its failure to accelerate Kazakhstan's WTO membership tilted Astana's decision in favour of the ECU.

It must also be noted, however, that once the CU/SES project was implemented, it reflected primarily Russia's economic interests. Moscow succeeded in ensuring that the ECU's CET were based on Russia's external tariffs, and this, in turn, allowed Russia to protect its industry from more competitive foreign products. Furthermore, the establishment of the SES permitted Russia to expand its products into Belarus and Kazakhstan unhindered, and shielded from external competition. Belarus, in particular, suffered quite significantly from the competitive pressures of Russian industrial and agricultural products, although this predicament was also determined, to a great extent, by its own economic weaknesses, and the failure of its state-led economic model. Kazakhstan, in turn, was compelled to raise its external tariffs quite substantially (on average from 4.3 per cent to 12.67 per cent), to its own economic disadvantage (Kassenova, 2013, p. 151). The rise in tariffs led to substantial increases in imports of higher priced or lower quality goods from Russia, and the displacement of cheaper and more competitive goods previously imported from either Europe or China (Tarr, 2012, p. 2). Although Kazakhstan could benefit from the introduction of unified standards and equal transport tariffs for oil and petroleum products inside the ECU, tariffs for Kazakh oil products transiting through Russia, but destined to customers outside of the ECU, still remained two times higher than the fares for energy products intended for Russian producers (Tashimov, 2010). Similarly, Kazakhstan's gas exporters had no full access to the Russian gas pipeline system if the products were destined to third countries, and were instead forced to sell their gas at the Russian border (Rakhmatulina, 2012, pp. 81–82).

When examining the intra-ECU trade figures, it is clear that the only significant improvement in trade patterns since the establishment of the CU/SES was manifested in Russia's trade with Kazakhstan. Its share of exports to Kazakhstan grew from 31.3 per cent in 2009 to 39.4 per cent in 2010, and 41.4 per cent in

2011. Kazakhstan's share of its exports to Russia and Belarus, instead, hardly grew – from 8.3 per cent of total exports in 2009, to 10.1 per cent in 2010, and down to 8.5 per cent in 2011 (Kassenova, 2013, p. 151). Belarusian membership of the ECU did not particularly help Belarus expand the market for its goods beyond the access it already had (Frear, 2013, p. 128). Russia was, therefore, the only country of the three CU member states that benefited from trade *creation* within the CU as a result of increases in CET (EBRD, 2012, p. 70). On the other hand, for both Russia and Kazakhstan, intra-ECU trade represented only a modest share of their total foreign trade (Cooper, 2012). In 2012, intra-ECU trade totalled only 7 per cent of both Russia's exports and imports. For Kazakhstan, intra-ECU trade represented only 9 per cent of its exports and 40 per cent of its imports in 2012. For Belarus, instead, trade with its ECU partners represented quite a substantial share of its total foreign trade in 2012 (35 per cent of exports and 55 per cent of imports) but these exchanges were almost totally dominated by trade with Russia (Cooper, 2012). It can therefore be concluded that Russia succeeded in establishing an economic project first and foremost to its own advantage, in a clear display of its *hegemonic* power.

Putin launches the Eurasian Union project

With his return to the Presidency in 2012, Putin promoted the transformation of the CU/SES into new organisation – the *Eurasian Union*. As stated in his article published in *Izvestiya* on 4 October 2011, the objective of the Eurasian Union (EuU) was to make integration 'a comprehensible, sustainable and long-term project attractive to both individuals and businesses' – a union which would operate independently from fluctuations in the political environment (Putin, 2011). The EuU, in Putin's view, was not intended to lead to the restoration of the USSR in a different form. 'None of this entails any kind of revival of the Soviet Union', Putin argued in his *Izvestiya* article, and added that 'it would be naïve to try to revive or emulate something that has already been consigned to history' (Putin, 2011). In his view, new times called for close integration based on 'new values and a new political and economic foundation' (2011). Putin's project, however, had a clear geopolitical aim – to establish 'a powerful supranational association capable of becoming one of the poles in the modern world', which would serve as an efficient bridge between Europe and the dynamic Asia-Pacific region (Putin, 2011). In his view, the EuU would help 'establish ourselves within the global economy and trade system and play a real role in decision-making, setting the rules and shaping the future' (Putin, 2011).[6] Putin believed that only by collaborating and 'standing together' would countries in Eurasia be able to succeed, prosper and occupy a leading place in world politics (Putin, 2011).

Putin viewed the EuU as an essential part of Greater Europe, which in his view, was united by the shared values of freedom, democracy, and a market economy (Putin, 2011). He actually proposed setting up 'a community of harmonised economies stretching from Lisbon to Vladivostok', based on the CES that was agreed between Russia and the EU in 2003. This community could involve a free trade zone, compatible regulatory economic systems, and deeper integration programmes. Putin even proposed pursuing 'coordinated policies [with the EU] in industry, technology, the energy sector, education, science', and also eventually introducing a visa-free regime with the EU.[7] More importantly, 'a balanced and economically consistent' partnership between the EuU and the EU would, according to Putin, 'prompt changes in the geo-political and geo-economic setup of the continent as a whole with a guaranteed global effect' (2011). The partnership between the EU and Russia's EuU was therefore seen as a way of overcoming the existing divisions within the European continent. The Eurasian Union project also had a clear economic objective. It would allow its members to combine their natural and human resources and place them in 'a strong competitive position in the industrial and technological race, and in the struggle for investors' (2011). This, in turn, would lead to the creation of new jobs and the establishment of cutting-edge facilities. Once the SES became operational in 2012, 'a huge market of over 165 million consumers, with unified legislation, and the free movement of capital, services, goods and labour', would be established (2011). The SES would then lay the foundations for the establishment of a EAEU, along the lines of the EU. Thereafter the EAEU would become a *Eurasian Union* – a political union, potentially involving also other former Soviet states (FSS).

When a draft EuU treaty was first proposed by Moscow in May 2011, all three CU members agreed on the establishment of a SES in goods, services, capital and labour, within the EuU framework. They also agreed on the adoption of common industrial, transport and energy policies, as well as on similar economic policies based on commonly agreed macro-economic indicators. However, Kazakhstan initially did not show great enthusiasm for the transformation of the CU/SES into a *political* Eurasian Union. Nazarbayev was a strong supporter of economic integration, but he remained sceptical about further institutional integration, and therefore, opposed to Russia's attempt to achieve closer political integration. In his view, integration had to be voluntary and based on the principle of equality, respect for state sovereignty, inviolability of borders, and non-interference in the internal affairs of states. (Nazarbayev, 2011). When in 2012, Russian State Duma Speaker Sergei Naryshkin proposed the establishment of a Eurasian parliament, Kazakhstan immediately expressed its reservations, with Yerlan Karin, the Secretary of the ruling Nur Otan Party reacting very negatively, considering it 'in breach of the sovereignty and the Constitution of Kazakhstan' (Kassenova, 2013, p. 156). According to this proposal, Russia would have had an overwhelming representation in the Eurasian parliament to the detriment of Kazakhstan (Guznekova, 2013, pp. 25–26). At the instance of Kazakhstan, therefore, the entity was called *Eurasian Economic Union* and not Eurasian Union, with emphasis being placed on the 'functioning of a single economic space' (International Agreement, 2011).

Belarus' leadership, in turn, showed support for Putin's Eurasian project primarily because Minsk had succeeded, during 2011, in getting substantial financial support from Russia. Lukashenko (2011) considered the EuU a 'qualitatively new integrative formation', which however, had to be equitable and mutually beneficial to all its members. This entailed, in his view, the same economic conditions for all economic actors, and unhindered access to common energy and transportation systems. Lukashenko remained supportive of Russia's integration projects as long as these ensured Russian-subsidised energy prices and they were accompanied by substantial financial support from Moscow. As somebody who very much regretted the end of the USSR, he proved quite favourable of developing the political dimension of the new EuU. He therefore proposed 'creating a solid social and political infrastructure with shared values, legal systems, living standards and benchmarks' (Lukashenko, 2011). Lukashenko, however, insisted that Belarus had to enjoy equal political status within the new union, and enjoy full sovereignty over its own affairs, especially in the field of economic and monetary policy (Zatulin, 2011). Belarus thus proved reluctant to move ahead with monetary integration, despite the benefits that a monetary union with Russia could have brought, primarily because Moscow's proposals limited Minsk's ability to exercise an independent monetary and credit policy. When proposals were put forward by Moscow in 2013 to create a political union, establish a single currency and set up a full-fledged Eurasian parliament, Lukashenko, therefore, showed some hesitation (Podberezkin and Podberezkina, 2015, p. 52) He explained that Belarus would only delegate sovereign rights to a supranational entity, if Minsk had a clear understanding of whom it was delegating these powers to, and what Minsk was getting in return, thus posing limits to Russia's geopolitical ambitions (Lukyanov, 2013).

Despite these competing visions on the future of the Eurasian project, all three ECU/SES member states agreed to advance towards the creation of an economic union, and on 29 May 2014 in Astana, they formally established the EAEU, in replacement of EvrAzES. The EAEU was to become operational on 1 January 2015, after all three national parliaments ratified the EAEU Treaty. As with previous integration projects, the EAEU envisaged the formation of a single market in goods, services, capital and labour, and stipulated for deep cooperation in a variety of areas – economic and monetary policy, transport, energy and industry, competition and taxation – to enhance the competitiveness of the EAEU national economies (EEU, 2014). The new agreement also introduced new decision-making bodies – an *Eurasian Inter-Governmental Council* (previously the EEC Inter-Governmental Council), which brought together the deputy Prime Minister and Prime Ministers of the member states; and the *Supreme Eurasian Economic Council* (or Supreme Council), which gathered only the EAEU Presidents (EEU, 2014; ICG, 2016, p. 9). The establishment of these new bodies, however, did not entail the creation of supranational organs, as in these two new bodies decisions were to be taken by consensus. When the project was launched, Kazakhstan's President Nazarbayev reinforced the premise that decision-making within the EAEU would have to be consensus-based, so that 'each country's vote will be crucial' (Panfilova, 2014). Belarus' President Lukashenko also made it clear that the EAEU was not a 'revival of the Soviet Union', and that Belarus would not lose its sovereignty (Panfilova, 2014).

However, once decisions were approved by the EAEU supreme bodies, they became binding on all members. The basis for a proper-functioning economic bloc seemed to have been set.

The Eurasian Union and the Silk Road

Although the Eurasian Union had been in the makings for several years – a first draft declaration was made public in May 2011 (Cooper, 2013a) – the project was accelerated after Chinese President Xi Jinping launched his ambitious 'One Belt-One Road' (OBOR) initiative in September 2013, during a visit to Kazakhstan. Russia viewed OBOR as a serious competitor, which could challenge Moscow's economic presence in the Central Asian region. The objective of OBOR was to develop a modern version of the Silk Road that would connect China and the Eurasian economies through infrastructure, trade and investment. The 'One Belt' dimension more specifically, entailed a massive investment in on-land infrastructure projects – roads, rail routes, and oil and gas pipelines – that would link Chinese Western regions to Central Asia, and from these areas, through either Russia, or Iran and Turkey, they would run all the way to European ports and markets (Farchy, 2016). A key aspect of the OBOR initiative involved promoting global and regional trade, through the lowering of trade barriers, the elimination of non-tariff barriers to trade and through progressive regulatory harmonisation (*Financial Times*, 2017). This specific dimension of the 'Silk Road' project proved to be of particular concern to Russia, whose leaders worried over the potential negative implications of a deeper Chinese economic penetration into the Central Asian region to the detriment of Russia's own economic interests in the area. In 2013, Chinese trade with the five Central Asian states had reached $50 billion, up from $1.8bn in 2000, turning China into the single largest trading partner of the region, largely surpassing Russia (Farchy, 2015, 2016). Chinese companies had also invested quite significantly in the Central Asian region – acquiring oil refineries, oil companies, and cement plants, and building roads and tunnels in Kyrgyzstan and Tajikistan. China also built oil and gas pipelines running from Turkmenistan and Kazakhstan all the way to China, opening up new markets for Central Asian energy producers (Farchy, 2015).

Chinese leaders, however, insisted that OBOR was an 'inclusive' project, which presented all countries in the region, including Russia, with a 'win-win' opportunity to grow. Russia, however, worried that the OBOR project would eventually reduce its economic presence in the region in favour of China. It feared that it would lead to the merging of the SCO and the Silk Road, further opening Central Asian markets to Chinese products. More importantly, Moscow saw the 'Silk Road' project as a challenge to its own EAEU integration project in Central Asia and this also explains why it accelerated the formation of the Eurasian Economic Union. Yet, Moscow soon realised that it could not successfully compete with China in Central Asia and instead had to accommodate itself to China's new ambitious project. Thus, in May 2015, Putin signed a joint declaration with Chinese president Xi Jinping, which essentially established an 'interface' between the Silk Road project and the EAEU (Lukyanov, 2015). Both sides committed themselves to coordinating their mutual projects in order to avoid the overlap of schemes, while also agreeing to implement joint initiatives, relying on Chinese funds (Lukyanov, 2015; Wilson, 2016, p. 119). Furthermore, China promised to engage with the EAEU as a single entity and not only to talk to member states separately. More importantly, Moscow and Beijing agreed to coordinate the two projects in order eventually to build 'a common economic space' in Eurasia (Gabuyev, 2015). Reference was made to the desire to reach a Free Trade Agreement between the EAEU and China, although the project was eventually declared a distant goal, and put off for a future date. While Russia succeeded in engaging with China within the OBOR framework, it was becoming increasingly clear that the Chinese initiative represented a challenge to its economic predominance and its hegemonic role in Central Asia.

Functioning of the Eurasian Economic Union

Within the ECU, most of the internal trade was liberalised by 2015 (except for certain sectors such as sugar, tobacco, alcohol, pharmaceuticals or rice), while 85 per cent of its import duties were also harmonised. In 2011, border controls between countries largely disappeared and in late 2017 agreement was finally reached on the introduction of a common EAEU Customs Code, to be implemented on 1 January 2018. Furthermore, by 2016, almost all legal barriers for the free movement of labour within the EAEU were eliminated. Employers were able to hire employees from other EAEU states, and EAEU citizens could freely work in other EAEU states (Vinokurov, 2016). The years 2011–2014 indeed saw significant increases in ECU/EAEU-labour migration into Russia and Kazakhstan (Schenk, 2017, p. 168). However, free movement of labour within the EAEU remained problematic, with Russia and Kazakhstan delaying full implementation of the migration commitments undertaken under EAEU law. EAEU policies on a common labour market and on freedom of movement actually ran counter to the migration restrictions being imposed by Russia and Kazakhstan at the time on non-EAEU citizens, including citizens from CIS states (Schenk, 2017, pp. 166–167). Moreover, numerous exemptions and restrictions to trade still remained within the EAEU at the time of writing, especially as far as transport and transit were concerned, as well as alcohol and pharmaceuticals. Kazakhstan and Belarus faced discrimination when accessing the Russian energy-transport system; while Kazakhstan, in turn, negotiated exemptions in the liberalisation of its own transport services (Roberts and Moshes, 2016, p. 549). Furthermore, a common energy market was not fully put in place, and a regime of sanctions on Russia persisted with little sign of change.

The Union also suffered from currency volatility (ICG, 2016, p. 11). Although closer monetary and financial integration had been envisaged by the EAEU treaty, both dimensions remained distant prospects, as countries failed to coordinate their monetary and tax policies. Kazakhstan devalued the *tenge* by 19 per cent in February 2014, in response to the weakening of the Russian *rouble*, while in January 2015, the Belarus Central Bank devalued its currency twice in a week by 7 per cent to protect Belarus from Russia's economic turmoil (*Reuters*, 2015). The free movement of services and capital also failed immediately to materialise (Robert and Moshes, 2016, p. 549). More importantly, the economies of the EAEU states were neither very liberal internally nor very open externally, and in many instances, the state remained a key actor, controlling relevant sectors of the economy.[8] This was the case particularly of Belarus, whose economy relied heavily on government subsidies and state ownership. Cartels and monopolies existed in many of these countries, especially in Belarus and in Armenia but also in Russia, and the EEC proved unable to challenge their existence (Roberts and Moshes, 2016, p. 548). One of the most visible threats to the well-functioning of the EAEU were the various 'trade wars' that erupted occasionally between its members. In the spring of 2016, a dispute flared up between Russia and Belarus over milk, while in January 2017 a row over meat blew up between the two countries, resulting in the unilateral reintroduction of stronger controls by Russia on the borders with Belarus (*Reuters*, 2016; Zelensky and Polivanov, 2017). Similarly, a 'potato war' broke out between Kyrgyzstan and Kazakhstan in 2016, leading to the introduction of exemptions on the free trade of Kyrgyz potatoes into Kazakhstan on alleged violations of food and safety standards (Dragneva and Wolczuk, 2017, p. 20).

Furthermore, Russia also resorted to unilateral trade restrictions in its commercial relations with CIS and non-CIS states, often for political reasons, and often without the support of the other EAEU states concerned. In 2013, Russia imposed a full-blown trade blockade on Ukraine's exports to Russia, in order to deter its western neighbour from signing the EU Association and Free Trade agreements. A year later, it introduced a ban on the import of Ukrainian dairy products and potatoes, and restricted imports of Ukraine's railway equipment – in contravention of the 2011 CIS FTA agreement – as bilateral relations between the two countries severely deteriorated (Dreyer and Popescu, 2014b, p. 3). In August 2014, Russia imposed restrictions on the import of several agricultural products – fruit, vegetables, meat, fish and dairies – from the European Union, the US and Canada, in response to the economic and financial sanctions slashed on Russia, after its annexation of Crimea and the outbreak of war in east Ukraine. But the other EAEU countries did not follow suit, and instead found ways to profit from the introduction of the Russian embargo on EU agricultural products, as many of these products found their way into Russia through Belarus and Kazakhstan (Bondarenko, 2014a). Belarus, in particular, allowed EU imports to enter the Russian market via its territory with forged documentation or by listing Kazakhstan as the country of destination (ICG, 2016, p. 12). This led to a severe trade dispute between Russia and Belarus in December 2014, which effectively involved the reintroduction of customs controls along the common border. Although the issue was gradually resolved, and Russia relaxed its border controls in 2015, tensions between the two countries over the smuggling of EU goods into the EAEU remained. When Russia introduced sanctions against Turkey in December 2015, in retaliation for the shooting down of a

Russian fighter-plane on the Turkish–Syrian border, Kazakhstan and Kyrgyzstan refused to follow. Nor did these countries support Russia's sanctions on Ukraine. In 2016, Russia suspended its recognition of the CIS Free Trade Agreement with Ukraine, after Kiev's Association Agreement (AA) and Deep and Comprehensive Free Trade Agreement (DCFTA) with the EU entered into force – but this decision was neither supported by Belarus nor Kazakhstan.

The functioning of EAEU organs was, also, not always effective. The EEC was made responsible for setting key rules on the functioning of the ECU/SES, including harmonising the bloc's standards to boost internal trade, and handling the bloc's trade relations with third countries (Dreyer and Popescu, 2014a, p. 2). However, as rightly noted in the 2016 ICG report, 'the EEC was often side-lined by national leaders, who continued to manage their economic disputes through political deals rather than through agreed rules and procedures' (ICG, 2016, p. 9). Decisions were usually taken by consensus after long negotiations with national agencies, and when disputes arose they were taken to the Eurasian Inter-Governmental Council or the Supreme Eurasian Economic Council (ICG, 2016, p. 9). As Roberts and Moshes (2016, p. 550) clearly explained, 'the Commission [remained] too weak to effectively push the integration process forward', because 'Leaders in EAEU member states ... continue to be wary of pluralism and sources of independent economic power'. Furthermore, there were few ways in which sanctions could be enforced, and instead countries relied on peer pressure to ensure compliance, as the EAEU Court in Minsk was not utilised by plaintiffs to bring member states into line (ICG, 2016, p. 10). The EEC no longer had the power to bring a country before the EAEU Court in case of non-compliance with Treaty obligations, as had been the case previously when the EEC was first established. It could only notify the sides and plead for a change in the state's course of action (Dragneva and Wolczuk, 2017, p. 15).

Enlargement of the EAEU to new members

When the EAEU was launched, EvrAzES countries such as Kyrgyzstan, immediately showed a willingness to join the new organisation, fearful that staying out of it would negatively affect the country's economy. Kyrgyzstan could face economic isolation if external tariffs were raised by the new organisation, as two of its main trading partners – Russia and Kazakhstan – were members of the EAEU, while Kyrgyz immigrants working in Russia could suffer if migrations laws were tightened for non-EAEU citizens (ICG, 2016, p. 4). Bishkek therefore requested membership of the EAEU soon after the organisation was launched and was admitted into the ECU/EAEU in May 2015. After it joined the EAEU, however, Kyrgyzstan was forced to increase its average import tariff from 5.04 per cent to 9.4 per cent, in contravention of its WTO commitments (Export.gov; 2017). Although CET were expected to fall gradually in line with Russia's WTO obligations, Kyrgyzstan was compelled – as was Kazakhstan after it joined the WTO in 2015 – effectively to establish two sets of tariffs, one for goods destined to the internal market and one for goods destined to the EAEU (Tarr, 2016, p. 8).[9] In addition, imports from China and Turkey on their way to Russia became significantly more expensive – dealing a blow to Kyrgyzstan's local trading industry. Instead, Russian goods (often of lower quality) became cheaper in Kyrgyzstan, largely as a result of a weaker rouble (ICG, 2016, p. 11; Yalovkina, 2015). To counter all these challenges, some transitional arrangements were put in place, which envisaged introducing lower tariffs on many goods, until 2020 (ICG, 2016, p. 11). Yet, Kyrgyz companies still faced obstacles when trying to expand their activities inside the EAEU, as the Kazakh government limited the circulation of Kyrgyz goods to protect its own local industry – leading many to question the positives of joining such an organisation (Galdini and Nematov, 2016).

Tajikistan, also an EvrAzES member, could also potentially gain from EAEU membership through increased EAEU trade and investment in the Tajik economy. Moreover, Russia hosted a large diaspora of Tajik migrant workers, whose remittances accounted for roughly 42.2 per cent of Tajikistan's GDP in 2013 (IWPR, 2016). Tajikistan also had a stake in keeping strategically aligned to Russia, by becoming a member of the EAEU, in view of its reliance on Russia for its own security. Nevertheless, Tajikistan showed cautious support for the ECU and the EAEU when these two institutions were established. While it engaged in preliminary talks with Russia on EAEU membership in 2014, its leaders did not submit any formal admission proposals, and it remained outside the bloc at the time of writing (Eursianet.org, 2017). Tajikistan, instead, engaged in efforts to diversify its economy away from Russia and towards Asia and the Middle East, with China emerging as the country's main investor and its key trading partner.[10] Russia, however, continued to press for Tajikistan's EAEU membership, in a display of its hegemonic power. In early July 2016, Russian Duma deputy Leonid Slutsky stated that Tajikistan would soon announce its intention to join the EAEU, before adding that Tajikistan 'seeks this more than any other CIS nation' (Putz, 2016). Soon thereafter, the head of the Tajik Customs Service, Abdufattoh Ghoib informed Russia that relevant working groups had been preparing 'all the necessary materials' for Tajikistan's EAEU membership (Putz, 2016). In December 2016, massive arrests of Tajik migrants in Russia were carried out, in an effort to increase the pressure on Dushanbe to sign up to the EAEU (Salimzoda, 2016). However, this did not tilt Tajikistan's decision in favour of the EAEU, despite the country's bleak economic prospects.

Armenia, a country traditionally closely allied strategically to Russia, had nevertheless stayed away from the various economic projects developed within the CIS and EvrAzES. Instead, in 2012 Yerevan engaged in negotiations with the EU on a AA/DCFTA package, which was expected to be officially signed in November 2013 at the EU's EaP summit in Vilnius. However, after a meeting with President Putin on 3 September 2013, the Armenian President Serzh Sargsyan announced Armenia's decision to suspend its EU AA/DCFTA arrangements and instead declared Armenia's readiness to join the Russian-led ECU/EAEU (Socor, 2013b). Armenia depended heavily on Russia for militarily protection against two of its main adversaries, Turkey and Azerbaijan, and this forced

Yerevan to bow to Russia's pressures. During a visit to Baku in August 2013, Putin had called Azerbaijan Russia's 'strategic partner', sending a clear signal to Yerevan that Moscow's foreign policy direction could change if Armenia did not embrace Russia's integration projects (Grigoryan, 2014). In addition, several very explicit warnings had been issued by Russian officials in the summer of 2013 to dissuade Yerevan from signing the agreed EU AA/DCFTA treaties. In July 2013, the former Russian Ambassador to Armenia, Vyacheslav Kovalenko, told Armenia that it risked alienating Moscow if it chose the EU over the Russian-led Eurasian project (Danielyan, 2013). In August 2013, Aleksandr Vassiliyev, Russian diplomat at the Embassy in Yerevan was even more blunt when he referred to the economic, mental and psychological problems that awaited Armenia if it signed an AA with the EU and did not join the EAEU. He also hinted at the possibility of a '*hot autumn*' if Yerevan's plans of EU Association were not halted (Grigoryan, 2014, p. 106).

Moscow had several leverages that it could use to exert pressure on Yerevan besides providing military support to Azerbaijan. Armenia remained heavily dependent on Russia for energy imports, while Russian companies had almost full control over key sectors of the Armenian economy – energy, telecommunications, transportation, finance, insurance and mining. Furthermore, Russia remained Armenia's key investor and its main trading partner, while it also hosted a significant Armenian diaspora of labour migrants, whose remittances reached $1.4 billion in 2013 (Vasilyan, 2017, p. 35). These external pressures prompted President Sargsyan to abandon Armenia's EU AA/DCFTA and instead join the EAEU in January 2015. Yet, once it joined the bloc, Armenia was compelled to increase its CET quite significantly in accordance with ECU levels and had to renegotiate its WTO commitments (Minasyan, 2015).[11] These increases in tariffs affected the more dynamic sectors of the Armenian economy, such as the IT industry, which relied heavily on imports, and represented about a third of the country's exports in 2013 (Giragosian, 2015). On the other hand, duties on natural gas, petroleum products delivered from Russia were abolished, allowing Armenia annually to save $200 million (Minasyan, 2015). Russia also reduced its gas prices to Armenian consumers in 2015 to around $190/mcm, well below EU prices, after an increase of $270/mcm in early 2013. However, the entire margin of the price reduction was received by Gazprom's daughter company in Armenia, ArmRosGaz, which in turn kept prices unchanged for domestic customers – questioning the benefits of such a measure (Halatyan, 2016).

In May 2014, Russia also threatened Georgia with possible economic or financial retaliatory measures if Tbilisi signed an AA/DCFTA with the EU, in a clear sign that it wished to keep the country within its economic sphere of influence (Civil Georgia, 2014). Since Russia had lifted its economic embargo on Georgia in 2012, bilateral trade between the two countries had increased quite significantly. In the first quarter of 2014, Russia had become Georgia's third largest trading partner (Civil Georgia, 2014). If Tbilisi signed up to the EU's AA/DCFTA, Russia could potentially retaliate by once again introducing an embargo on Georgian products, inflicting severe damage on its economy. More worryingly, Moscow could make use of the conflicts in Abkhazia and South Ossetia and increase tensions, in order to put additional pressure on Tbilisi. In that respect, in the autumn of 2013, Russian border guards accelerated the so-called process of 'borderisation', which entailed putting up barbed wire fences along the line dividing Georgia from South Ossetia, in an effort to pressure Tbilisi (*Vesti Kavkaza*, 2013). Russia also persisted in its refusal to restore visa-free travel for Georgian citizens wishing to go to Russia. Yet, in July 2014, Georgia went ahead and signed the EU's AA/DCFTA with Brussels, prompting the Russian government to threaten to suspend the 1994 CIS FTA, to which Georgia was also a signatory. The Russian side argued that 'cheap EU products' would easily penetrate the Russian market once Georgia ratified the AA/DCFTA, and this was forcing Moscow 'to take defensive steps' (Menabde, 2014). Had this Russian retaliatory measure been implemented, it would have put Georgian agricultural producers in a very difficult position as large-scale access to the EU common market had not materialised yet (Menabde, 2014). Russia, however, refrained from suspending the Russian–Georgian free trade agreement, and instead, Russian–Georgian trade continued to grow (Ria Novosti, 2014). 'In reality', as David Avalishvili explained, 'Russia [was] much angrier about Georgia's continued military cooperation with NATO' (Menabde, 2015). In June 2015, Georgia had acquired the latest anti-aircraft systems, including radars and medium-range missiles from France, while NATO Secretary General Jens Stoltenberg was expected to arrive in Georgia in late August to open a 'joint military training centre' under the auspices of the North Atlantic Alliance (Menabde, 2015). This explained why on 4 August 2015, Russia's Rospotrebnadzor issued a warning to Georgia about the 'low quality' of Georgian wines being exported to Russia (Menabde, 2015).

As far as Moldova is concerned, the Kremlin threatened Chisinau with economic sanctions and the definitive loss of Transdniestria, if it went ahead and signed the EU AA/DCFTA at the November 2013 EU/EaP Vilnius Summit, in a clear display of its hegemonic power. During a visit to the country in early September 2013, Deputy Prime Minister Dmitry Rogozin very explicitly noted that Russia would 'revise the existing trade agreements with Moldova', hinting at possible restrictions on the access of Moldovan agricultural products to the Russian market, if Chisinau signed the EU AA/DCFTA (Socor, 2013b). Russia's chief sanitary inspector Gennady Onishchenko, in turn, talked about imposing restrictions on the import of Moldova's wines, fruit and vegetables to Russia. While the share of Moldovan wine exported to Russia had already fallen to 10 per cent in 2007 after the introduction of the 2006 wine embargo, the Moldovan economy could suffer even more from such a comprehensive economic blockade. Russia remained one of Moldova's biggest trading partners, it was the largest single foreign investor in the country, and it controlled the Moldovan banking sector – all these elements could be utilised by the Kremlin against Moldova's favour (Beyer and Wolff, 2016, pp. 344–45; Nizhnikau, 2016, p. 209).

In his trip to Moldova, Rogozin also made reference to the 'hundreds of thousands of Moldovans who worked in Russia', implying that significant obstacles could be introduced for Moldovan labour migrants wishing to work in Russia. The Russian government also threatened to repatriate about 190,000 Moldovan migrant workers living in Russia, allegedly on the grounds that they were violating the country's immigration rules (Beyer and Wolff, 2016, p. 345).[12] Rogozin also threatened to disrupt Russia's energy supplies, noting that 'the cold season [was] near', and that Moldovans could 'freeze this winter', if the country signed the EU's AA/DCFTA (Socor, 2013b). Rogozin added that Moldova's pro-European government was 'disregarding its own people' – in reference to the rise of pro-Russian forces and the loss of popularity of pro-EU parties inside Moldova. More significantly, Rogozin very explicitly stated that Moldova 'would lose Transdniestria' if it continued to 'move towards the European Union'. Pressures were also exerted on Chisinau through Moldova's Gagauz minority – in February 2014, a Russia-sponsored referendum on self-determination was held in Moldova's Gagauzia province in which the vast majority of citizens voted in favour of the region joining the Russian-led CU, as opposed to the EU. Furthermore, after the referendum was held, the embargo on agricultural products and wine imposed on Moldova was lifted on the Gagauz region (Nizhnikau, 2016, p. 210). Despite these threats, the pro-European government in Chisinau decided, nevertheless, to sign the AA/DCFA with the EU in July 2014. Russia responded by announcing its intention to cease the import of Moldovan fruits and vegetables, on the grounds that Moldova could become a gateway through which European products entered the Russian market (Minzarari, 2014). New restrictions were also imposed on Moldovan workers in Russia, prohibiting them from sending remittances home and tightening residency rules (Nizhnikau, 2016, p. 209).

Moscow also exerted great pressure on Ukraine to abandon the EU DCFTA/AA and join the ECU/SES, in a clear sign that it intended to keep the country within its 'sphere of influence'. In March 2013, Vladimir Putin threatened Ukrainians with the prospect of losing their rights to work and move freely within the ECU after 2015, if Ukraine did not join the Russian-led bloc (Ivzhenko, 2013a). In April 2013, Russia also started talking about implementing the Yamal-Europe 2 project – a gas pipeline which bypassed Ukraine, and instead transited through Belarus and Poland, thereby reducing Ukraine's revenues and its leverage in negotiations over gas prices with Russia. There were also discussions about building the third and fourth branches of the Nord Stream gas pipeline, which already bypassed both Ukraine and Belarus, thus further challenging Ukraine's status as a key energy transit country (Kulikov, 2013a). Furthermore, in July, 2013, Gazprom decided to halt the prepayment of gas transit fees to Ukraine's energy company *Naftohaz Ukrainy*, and also stopped pumping gas into Ukrainian underground storage facilities in a clear sign that Russia was ready to use all kinds of hard-power instruments to force Ukraine into the ECU/SES and out of the EU's AA/DCFTA project (Kulikov, 2013b). In the summer of 2013, as negotiations on association between Ukraine and the EU accelerated, Russia increased its pressure on Kiev. In early August, Russia blocked the import of Ukrainian chocolates into Russia, after the Ukrainian government had imposed prohibitive import duties on foreign cars, which had severely hit Russia's AvtoVAZ car-making company (Latynina, 2013b). In mid-August 2013, in what amounted to a trade blockade, Russia's customs services introduced tight regulations for the clearance of Ukrainian goods, effectively obstructing all of Ukraine's exports into Russia for over a week (Latynina, 2013a). In early September 2013, in an attempt further to entice Ukraine into the ECU, Moscow offered Kiev reduced gas prices, the elimination of export duties and the removal of other technical barriers to trade – all of which would have resulted in savings of $12 billion per year for Ukraine – if the country joined the Russian-led bloc (Visloguzov, 2013). But this proved to be of no avail as Ukraine's President Viktor Yanukvych refused to renounce to the EU's DFCTA/AA. Instead, on 18 September, the Kiev government approved a draft AA with the EU and submitted the document to President Yanukovych for final signature.

Kiev, however, insisted that rapprochement with the EU did not mean distancing itself from Russia, and proposed instead developing strong economic cooperation with Russia within the ECU/SES framework, short of membership. These Ukrainian proposals failed to satisfy Moscow's ambitions. Russia responded by once again tightening Russia's controls at the border with Ukraine and introducing new customs legislation, which hit Ukrainian producers dependent on inputs from and markets in Russia particularly hard (Kisilyov, 2013). On 28 October 2013, Sergei Lavrov made it clear that while Russia would not impose a ban on Ukraine's exports to Russia if Kiev signed the EU AA/DCFTA, Moscow would still halt Ukraine's free trade access to Russia, although this was in violation of the CIS/FTA agreements that had been signed by both countries, and several other states, in 2011 (Chernenko, 2013). The Kremlin made it clear that while it did not oppose in principle the establishment of a FTA between the EU and Ukraine, it wanted Ukraine to join the ECU first. Once that happened, the ECU *with Ukraine as a member*, would develop closer ties with the EU. In November 2013 Russia went further – it again threatened to introduce visas to Ukrainians wanting to travel to Russia, and more worryingly, it hinted that it might revise the 1998 *Friendship Treaty* with Ukraine, which guaranteed Ukraine's territorial integrity. At the same time, Putin promised Ukraine a $15 billion loan and significantly lower gas prices – $270/mcm instead of $450/mcm – if Ukraine rejected the EU deal (Frolov, 2013). The EU, in turn, continued to insist that for the DFCTA/AA to be signed, opposition politician Yuliya Timoshenko, who had been imprisoned in 2011 allegedly on false charges, had to be allowed to travel to Germany to receive proper health treatment (Musafirova, 2013).

These EU pressures and the various trade reprisals taken by Russia eventually pushed Yanukovych's decision in Russia's favour. On 21 November 2013, the Ukrainian President suspended Ukraine's AA/DCFTA preparatory work with the EU, and instead tasked his government with resuming negotiations with Moscow on enhancing economic ties. The Ukrainian government argued that the decision had been taken to guarantee Ukraine's national security, restore economic ties with Russia and the CIS, and ensure that Ukraine's domestic market reached parity with the EU before the country became associated with the EU

(Frolov, 2013). Many correctly argued that Yanukovych's refusal to sign the EU's DCFTA/AA was also related to the various political obligations that had been placed by the EU on Ukraine, which threatened his own political survival and that of his regime – democratisation of the political system, running free and fair elections, establishing an independent judiciary, and releasing his political rival, Yuliya Timoshenko (Frolov, 2013). However, the Kremlin's pressures also played a key role in tilting Yanukovych's decision in Russia's favour, as Moscow's trade restrictions were placing great strains on an already very fragile Ukrainian economy. There is little doubt that the Ukrainian economy was suffering quite severely from Russia's de facto closure of the border. During August–November 2013 Ukraine lost about 30-to-40 billion hryvnias in trade turnover because of Russia's trade obstructions, and this, in turn, had led to the loss of between 15,000–20,000 jobs a month.

Ukraine, however, did not completely break its ties with the EU, and during the EuroMaidan upheavals which followed Yanukovych's November 2013 decision, Kiev continued its discussions with the EU on future Association (Sidorenko and Chernenko, 2013). The EU, in turn, began devising ways in which it could help Ukraine alleviate the negative economic consequences of potentially signing an AA/DCFTA with the EU in the future. Events around Ukraine clearly showed how EU's policies of further integration with eastern European countries clashed with Russia's concept of building a 'Greater Europe'. The EU's actions in its immediate neighbourhood now directly challenged Putin's wishes of establishing a major geopolitical association around the EAEU which also included Ukraine. This overall competition between opposing trading blocs – the EU and the Russian-led EAEU was compounded by a rivalry over values, with the Russian state having 'refused to follow the West as the mainstream of national development', and instead declaring itself 'the bearer of a specific civilisation rooted in [Russian] Orthodoxy, yet enriched by the centuries-long cohabitation of different ethnic groups within the boundaries of a Eurasian empire' (Trenin, 2014). As result of this, Russia and the West, which now also included central and eastern Europe, were once again clearly divided, 'after trying to overcome historical divisions more than a quarter of a century' (Trenin, 2014). The situation in Ukraine required a level of understanding and cooperation between Moscow and Brussels, which also the EU failed to grasp. Instead competition over 'influence' in the EU's and Russia's Near Abroads ensued and brought the two entities to an imminent clash.

Conclusions

The late 2000s saw the emergence of a much more coherent an effective effort by Russia to pursue economic integration within the EvrAzES framework through a revamped CU and a full-functioning SES. The project reflected Russia's desires to create a powerful economic bloc around its leadership, which could counter the increased presence of the EU on the western fringes of the CIS, and the relentless economic penetration of China in Central Asia.

Clear geo-strategic objectives, therefore, lay at the heart of the project. As noted by Russian commentator Fyodor Lukyanov, 'The only chance for Russia to build its position [globally] is to create its own regional centre of influence', around the CIS and the EAEU. 'This is the multi-polar world Putin has been speaking of for so long', he added (Belton and Gorst, 2009). Yet, there were also obvious economic advantages to be gained from the creation of a big market of 165 million consumers and workers, in terms of increased economic growth and larger investments. The 2008/09 global financial crisis had shown that there existed legitimate economic considerations which argued in favour of closer CIS integration, especially in times of crisis. Tight economic cooperation would allow CIS states to deal more effectively when hit by sudden shocks to their economic and financial systems. As argued by the President of Kazakhstan, Nursultan Nazarbayev in his *Izvestiya* article in March 2009, 'Only together can we ensure the sustainable economic development of our countries. The effects of the current global crisis have broken many hopes. In the current situation we should not expect any help from the outside' (Nazarbayev, 2009). Concerns over the slow speed of WTO membership, as explained above, also pushed towards closer Eurasian economic integration, and they explained why Russia – and Kazakhstan – remained eager to expand their economic ties and create a closer economic union. Legitimate economic imperatives, therefore, also underpinned the CU/SES project.

Furthermore, it must be noted that the CU/SES initiative generally enjoyed the support of Russia's closest partners, and therefore it cannot be seen as entirely fitting into a neo-imperialist model. Yet, despite the backing that the project received from several of its members, Russia nevertheless proved ready to use *hard power* instruments to bring several more hesitant CIS 'countries into the CU/SES fold', attesting to a clear neo-imperialist behaviour. Belarus, in particular, was subjected to coercive methods by the Kremlin – increases in gas prices, reduction in subsidies and the introduction of NTB in bilateral commercial exchanges – to assure its membership of the CU. On the other hand, Russia also utilised *soft power* instruments, such as subsidies and lower energy prices to lure CIS states such as Belarus and Armenia into the CU. More significantly, as the dominant economic power, Russia was able to establish an economic project modelled very much according to its preferences. Moscow made sure that the ECU's CETs were based on Russia's external tariffs, as this allowed Russia to expand its products into Belarus and Kazakhstan, shielded from external competition. Kazakhstan (and later also Kyrgyzstan and Armenia) instead had to raise their external tariffs quite significantly, to their own economic disadvantage and commercial detriment. Belarus, in turn, was faced with the competitive pressures of Russian industrial and agricultural products flooding its less performing markets, even though Belarus' negative economic predicament was determined, to a great extent, by its own economic weaknesses, and its dependency on Russia for subsidised energy products and preferential credits. Furthermore, while Russia, in theory, accepted to engage in a 'legalized forms of integration', which had a *binding* character, it nevertheless behaved in a unilateral fashion when it considered it necessary, to further its own national objectives.[13] Russia restricted the access to its energy-transport network for ECU states in contravention to agreed ECU/SES commitments, and utilised NTB to trade and other measures such as quotas and embargoes against foreign products to either protect its industries or to pursue clear foreign policy objectives, as it did in relation to Ukraine in 2013 and Moldova in 2014. Interestingly, while Russia benefited the most from its expanded penetration of the ECU/SES markets, it also concurrently diversified its trade away from the CIS space, showing the economic limits of the project.

When the Eurasian Economic Union (EAEU) was launched by President Putin in 2014, the Kremlin once again employed both *soft power* instruments and *hard* coercive methods to compel other CIS states to join. Intended as a powerful association of states, capable of becoming one of the leading poles in the contemporary world, the Eurasian Union was primarily set up to counterbalance the growing influence of the EU in Eastern Europe and the South Caucasus which was occurring as a result of the EU's EaP initiatives. The EAEU was also intended to shield Russia's influence in Central Asia from China's growing commercial competition and economic penetration of the region, made all the more evident with the launch of Beijing's One-Belt-One-Road initiative in 2013. Conceived by Russia and presented as a tightly integrated economic project, the EAEU did not real entail a qualitatively new integration project. The new economic union incorporated the existing ECU and the SES projects within its fold – it foresaw the removal of border controls; the free movement of labour, goods, capital and services; and the adoption of common policies in a variety of areas, related to the economy, energy and finance. Russia, however, had hoped to move further down the path of integration by establishing deeper cooperation in the areas of security, defence, border management and monetary policy – creating, in this way, a proper-functioning political union led by Russia, out of the EAEU – and in this way restore a neo-empire over the former Soviet space. Yet, other CIS states, Kazakhstan in particular, refused to acquiesce, worried over the potential dilution of their sovereignty in a new supranational state dominated by Russia. In this respect, Moscow's proposal to create a Eurasian parliament of directly elected members, caused particular concern among Russia's EAEU partners, given that a weighted representation system and the voting-share mechanism proposed by Moscow would have significantly eroded independence of the EAEU smaller members. This explains why such initiatives were subsequently rejected. Nevertheless, the new EAEU project, with its emphasis primarily on economic cooperation, did permit Russia to present itself as the leader of a new geopolitical entity in Eurasia. Furthermore, the way in which the EAEU was conceived, and above all, the methods utilised by Russia to compel hesitant CIS states, such as Ukraine, Moldova and Armenia, to join the organisation, clearly showed that Russia was ready to use a vast array of *hard power* instruments at its disposal in order to establish a sphere of influence or neo-empire in Eurasia. If successful, the Eurasian Union project would have transformed Russia (and its allies) into one of the leading commercial blocs in the world.

Notes

1 The new Eurasian Court consisted of eight judges (two from every member state except momentarily for Kyrgyzstan) who were appointed for nine years.
2 Following Russia's WTO accession in 2012, Belarus and Kazakhstan secured several additional exemptions in a revised code of CET, which were approved in that same year (Frear, 2013, p. 128.)
3 It must be noted that with the full establishment of the ECU, the Russian market had seen a substantial increase in Chinese counter-fait products coming from Kazakhstan (Kassenova, 2013, p. 155).
4 The other ECU states, however, refused to follow suit.
5 It must be noted, however, that this was expected, in theory, to be a temporary phase, as Russia (and Kazakhstan) were expected to join the WTO in the near future, and this required a reduction in external tariffs.
6 Alongside other key players and regional structures, such as the EU, the United States, China and APEC, the Eurasian Union was seen as 'helping ensure global sustainable development'.
7 Putin envisaged the ECU and later the EuU, 'joining in a dialogue with the EU'. In his view membership of the Eurasian Union would 'help countries integrate into Europe sooner and from a stronger position'.
8 Kazakhstan was rated as 'moderately free' on the Heritage 'index of Economic Freedom', and the 69th freest economy out of 178 countries. Russia ranked 143 (unfree) and Belarus 153 (repressed) (Roberts and Moshes, 2016, p. 550).
9 Kazakhstan joined the WTO in 2015 with a bound average tariff of 6.1 per cent – ECU CET exceeded their WTO bound tariff levels on many tariff lines (Tarr, 2016, p. 8).
10 Investments totalled over $1.5 billion in 2016 in the areas of infrastructure, industry, energy and agriculture (Panfilova, 2016).
11 In 2011, Armenia's trade-weighted average was quite low, around 3.6 per cent (Popescu, 2014, p. 12).
12 In April 2014, the number of potential expulsions threatened by Russia was increased to 250,000 migrants.
13 The project envisaged the delegation of certain powers to supranational organs, while also foreseeing the establishment of binding dispute-resolution mechanisms to address controversies (Dragneva and Wolczuk, 2013, p. 34).

Bibliography

Alachnovič, A. (2015). Will Belarus Ever Become a WTO Member? *Belarus Digest*, 27 July 2015. Available at: http://belarusdigest.com/story/will-belarus-ever-become-wto-member-22951 [accessed 17 September 2018].
Barabanov, I. and Ye Chernenko (2014). *Kommersant*, 25 January, p. 1.
Batyrshin, R. (2009). *Izvestiya*, 15 June, p. 6.
Belton, C. and I. Gorst (2009). WTO Tries to Make Sense of Russia's Rethink, *Financial Times*, 13 June. www.ft.com/content/4091fcb8-57a5-11de-8c47-00144feabdc0 [accessed 17 September 2018].
Beyer, J. and S. Wolff (2016). Linkage and Leverage Effects on Moldova's Transdniestria Problem, *East European Politics*, 32 (3), 335–354.
Biryukova, L. and P. Khimshiashvili (2013). *Vedomosti*, 25 October, p. 2
Bohdan, S. (2012). Trade Wars with Russia: From Sugar to Airlines. *Belarus Digest*, 2 April. Available at: https://belarusdigest.com/story/trade-wars-with-russia-from-sugar-to-airlines/ [accessed 17 September 2018].

Bondarenko, M. (2014a). Rossiiya obvinila vlasti ES v podderzhke reeksporta zapreshchennykh produktov. RBC.ru, 16 October. Available at: www.rbc.ru/politics/16/10/20 14/543fe1c9cbb20f429eb17998 [accessed 17 September 2018].

Bondarenko, O. (2014b). *Izvestiya*, 6 February, p. 6.

Breitmaier, M. (2016). *The Eurasian Union: Rising or Shooting Star?* Alert Issue, 27. European Union Institute for Security Studies (EUISS). 23 June.

Chernenko, Ye. (2013). *Kommersant*, 29 October, p. 7.

Civil Georgia (2014). Russian MFA on EU-Georgia Association Agreement, 22 May. Available at: https://civil.ge/archives/123726 [accessed 17 September 2018].

Connolly, R. and P. Hanson (2012) Russia's Accession to the World Trade Organization, *Eurasian Geography and Economics*, 53 (4), 479–501.

Connolly, R. (2013). Russia, the Eurasian Customs Union and the WTO. In: R. Dragneva and K. Wolczuk, eds. *Eurasian Economic Integration: Law, Policy and Politics*. Cheltenham, Glos, and Northampton, Mass.: Edward Elgar Publishing, pp. 61–80.

Cooper, J. (2012). *Prospects for the Eurasian Economic Union*. St Antony's College, Oxford. 21 May. Unpublished paper.

Cooper, J. (2013a). The Development of Eurasian Economic Integration. In: R. Dragneva and K. Wolczuk, eds. *Eurasian Economic Integration: Law, Policy and Politics*. Cheltenham, Glos, and Northampton, Mass.: Edward Elgar Publishing, pp. 15–33.

Cooper, J. (2013b). Russia and the Eurasian Customs Union. In: R. Dragneva and K. Wolczuk eds. *Eurasian Economic Integration: Law, Policy and Politics*. Cheltenham, Glos, and Northampton, Mass.: Edward Elgar Publishing, pp. 81–99.

Danielyan, E. (2013). European Integration Unlikely to End Armenia's Alliance with Russia. RFE/RL. 6 August. Available at: www.rferl.org/a/armenia-russia-european-integration/25068199.html [accessed 17 September 2018].

Dragneva, R. and K. Wolczuk (2012). *Russia, the Eurasian Customs Union and the EU: Cooperation, Stagnation or Rivalry?* Chatham House Briefing Paper, London: Chatham House. August.

Dragneva R. and Wolczuk, K. eds. (2013). *Eurasian Economic Integration: Law, Policy and Politics*. Cheltenham, Glos, and Northampton, Mass.: Edward Elgar Publishing.

Dragneva, R. and K. Wolczuk (2017). *The Eurasian Economic Union Deals, Rules and the Exercise of Power*. Russia and Eurasia Programme Chatham House Research Paper, London: Chatham House. May. Available at: www.chathamhouse.org/sites/default/files/publications/research/2017-05-02-eurasian-economic-union-dragneva-wolczuk.pdf [accessed 17 September 2018].

Dreyer, I. and N. Popescu (2014a). *The Eurasian Customs Union: The Economics and the Politics*. Brief Issue, 11. March. Paris: European Institute for Security Studies.

Dreyer, I. and N. Popescu (2014b). *Trading with Moscow: The Law, the Politics and the Economics*. Brief Issue, 7 November. Paris: European Institute for Security Studies.

Dulman, P. (2013). *Rossiiskaya gazeta*, 27 February, p. 8.

Dymarsky, V. (2009). *Rossiiskaya gazeta*. 14 May, p. 3.

EBRD (2012). *Transition Report 2012: Integration Across Borders*, London, EBRD.

European Union (EU) (2009). Joint Declaration of the Prague Eastern Partnership Summit. Council of the European Union. Prague, 7 May. Available at: www.consilium.europa.eu/media/31797/2009_eap_declaration.pdf [accessed 16 September 2018].

Eurasian Economic Union (EEU) (2014). *Treaty on The Eurasian Economic Union*. Astana, 29 May. Available at: www.un.org/en/ga/sixth/70/docs/treaty_on_eeu.pdf [accessed 5 September 2020].

Evraziiskaya Ekonomicheskaya Komissiya (EEK). Analiticheskie materialy. Available at: www.eurasiancommission.org/ru/act/integr_i_makroec/dep_stat/tradestat/analytics/Pages/default.aspx [accessed 17 September 2018].

Eursianet.org (2017). Tajikistan: Feeling the Eurasian Union's Gravitational Pull, 31 January. Available at: www.eurasianet.org/node/82176 [accessed 17 September 2018].

Export.gov (2017). Kyrgyz Republic Import Tariffs, 28 July. Available at: www.export.gov/article?id=Kyrgyz-Republic-Import-Tariffs [accessed 17 September 2018].

Farchy, J. (2015). China's Great Game: In Russia's backyard. *Financial Times*, 14 October. Available at: www.ft.com/content/d35d34ca-6e70-11e5-aca9-d87542bf8673 [accessed 17 September 2018].

Farchy, J. (2016). China seeking to revive the Silk Road, *Financial Times*, 9 May. Available at: www.ft.com/content/e99ff7a8-0bd8-11e6-9456-444ab5211a2f [accessed 17 September 2018].

Financial Times (2017). One Belt, One Road — and Many Questions. 14 May. Available at: www.ft.com/content/d5c54b8e-37d3-11e7-ac89-b01cc67cfeec [accessed 17 September 2018].

Frear, M. (2013). Belarus: Player and Pawn in the Integration Game. In: R. Dragneva and K. Wolczuk eds. *Eurasian Economic Integration: Law, Policy and Politics*. Cheltenham, Glos, and Northampton, Mass.: Edward Elgar Publishing, pp. 119–138.

Frolov, A. (2013). *Sovetskaya Rossiya*, 23 November, p. 1.

Gabuyev, A. (2015). Eurasian Silk Road Union: Towards a Russia-China Consensus? *The Diplomat*, 5 June. Available at: http://thediplomat.com/2015/06/eurasian-silk-road-union-towards-a-russia-china-consensus/ [accessed 11 September 2018].

Gabuyev, A. and Ye. Chernenko (2012). *Kommersant*. June 6, p. 8.

Gabuyev, A., A. Gudkov and M. Gadzhiyev (2010). *Kommersant*, 11 January, p. 1.

Galdini, F. and E. Nematov (2016). Kyrgyzstan: Putin's Eurasian Economic Union and Its Discontents, *The Diplomat*, 20 May. https://thediplomat.com/2016/05/kyrgyzstan-putins-eurasian-economic-union-and-its-discontents/ [accessed 17 September 2018].

Giragosian, R. (2014). *Armenia's Strategic U-Turn*. Policy Memo. European Council on Foreign Relations. April.

Giragosian, R. (2015). Armenia and the Eurasian Economic Union: The View from Yerevan. European Council on Foreign Relations. 8 January. Available at: www.ecfr.eu/article/commentary_armenia_and_the_eurasian_economic_union_the_view_from_yerevan387 [accessed 17 September 2018].

Grigoryan, A. (2014). Armenia: Joining under the Gun. In: S.F. Starr and S.E. Cornell eds. *Putin's Grand Strategy: The Eurasian Union and Its Discontents*. Central Asia-Caucasus Institute & Silk Road Studies Program, pp. 98–109.

Guznekova, T. (2013). Evraziiskii ekonomicheskii soyuz: otnoshenie k proektu v stranakh SNG, *Problemy natsional'noi strategii*, 1 (16), 7–41 (p. 26). Available at: https://riss.ru/images/pdf/journal/2013/1/04.pdf [accessed 15 September 2018].

Halatyan, A. (2016) Pozitsiya Rossii po Karabakhu ugrozhaet evraziiskoi integratsii – armyanskii ekspert. Evraziya ekspert. 8 August. Available at: http://eurasia.expert/pozitsiya-rossii-po-karabakhu-ugrozhaet-evraziyskoy-integratsii-armyanskiy-ekspert/ [accessed 19 September 2018].

IWPR (2016). Russian Crisis Continues to Bite for Labour Migrants. 10 March. Available at: https://iwpr.net/global-voices/russian-crisis-continues-bite-labour-migrants [accessed 17 September 2018].

Inter-governmental Council of the Eurasian Union (ICEU) (2009). O Plane deistvii po formirovaniyu Edinogo ekonomicheskogo prostranstva Respubliki Belarus', Respubliki

Kazakhstan i Rossiiskoi Federatsii. 19 December. Available at: http://adilet.zan.kz/rus/docs/H09E0000035 [accessed 16 September 2018].

International Agreement (2011). Reshenie Komissii tamozhennogo soiuza ot 23 sentyabrya 2011g. 'O proekte Deklaratsii o formirovanii evraziiskogo ekonomicheskogo soiuza', 23 September. Available at: www.alta.ru/tamdoc/11sr0803/ [accessed 15 September 2018].

International Crisis Group (ICG) (2016). *The Eurasian Economic Union: Power, Politics and Trade*. Europe and Central Asia Report, 240, International Crisis Group. 20 July.

Ioffe, G. and V. Yarashevich (2011). Debating Belarus: An Economy in Comparative Perspective. *Eurasian Geography and Economics*, 52 (6), 750–779.

Ivzhenko, T. (2013a). *Nezavisimaya gazeta*, 6 March, p. 1.

Ivzhenko, T. (2013b). *Nezavisimaya gazeta*, 19 September, p. 1.

Kassenova, N. (2013). Kazakhstan and Eurasian Economic Integration: Quick Start, Mixed Results and Uncertain Future. In: R. Dragneva and K. Wolczuk eds. *Eurasian Economic Integration: Law, Policy and Politics*. Cheltenham, Glos, and Northampton, Mass.: Edward Elgar Publishing, pp. 139–162.

KazInform (2009). Nursultan Nazarbaev schitaet sozdanie Tamozhennogo soiuza vygodnym resheniem. 23 December. Available at: http://online.zakon.kz/Document/?doc_id=30533199#pos=0;18 [accessed 17 September 2018].

Khodasevich. A. (2009). *Nezavisimaya gazeta*, 9 June, p. 6.

Khodasevich, A. (2010). *Nezavisimaya gazeta*, 7 July, p. 6.

Kisilyov, Ye. (2013). *The New Times*, 18 November, p. 18.

Klysinski, K. and W. Kononczuk (2010). *Lukashenka Has to Choose: Reforms or Concessions to Russia*. OSW Commentary. 42. Warsaw: Centre for Eastern Studies, 27 October.

Kolesnikov, A. (2010). *Kommersant*, 29 May, p. 2.

Konovalov, M. and M. Zyagar (2009). *Kommersant*, 1 June, p. 1.

Kulikov, S. (2013a). *Nezavisimaya gazeta*, 5 April, p. 1.

Kulikov, S. (2013b). *Nezavisimaya gazeta*, 1 July, p. 1.

Latynina, Yu. (2013a). *Novaya gazeta*, 16 August, p. 5.

Latynina, Yu. (2013b). *The Moscow Times*, 21 August, p. 61.

Lukashenko, A. (2011). *Izvestiya*, 18 October, p. 1.

Lukin, A. (2015). Shanghai Cooperation Organization: Looking for a New Role. Russia in Global Affairs, 10 July. Available at: http://eng.globalaffairs.ru/valday/Shanghai-Cooperation-Organization-Looking-for-a-New-Role-17576 [accessed 11 September 2018].

Lukyanov, F. (2013). *Rossiiskaya gazeta*, 29 May, p. 8.

Lukyanov, F. (2015). *Rossiiskaya gazeta*, 13 May, p. 3.

Menabde, G. (2014). Is Russia Resuming a Trade War Against Georgia? *Eurasia Daily Monitor*, 11 (144), 6 August. Available at: https://jamestown.org/program/is-russia-resuming-a-trade-war-against-georgia/ [accessed 17 September 2018].

Menabde, G. (2015). Russia Threatens Georgia With Renewed Trade War. *Eurasia Daily Monitor*, 12 (154). 14 August. Available at: https://jamestown.org/program/russia-threatens-georgia-with-renewed-trade-war/ [accessed 17 September 2018].

Minasyan, S. (2015). Armenia Keeps on Balancing: Between the European Union and the Eurasian Economic Union. *Ponars Eurasia. Policy Memos 377*, August. Available at: www.ponarseurasia.org/memo/armenia-keeps-balancing-between-european-union-and-eurasian-economic-union [accessed 17 September 2018].

Minzarari, D. (2014). Russia Likely to Review Its Strategy Toward Moldova. *Eurasia Daily Monitor*, 11 (134), 23 July. Available at: https://jamestown.org/program/russia-likely-to-review-its-strategy-toward-moldova/ [accessed 17 September 2018].

The Moscow Times (2013). 5 August, p. 23.
Musafirova, O. (2013). *Novaya gazeta*, 11 November, p. 12.
Nazarbayev, N. (2009). Evraziiskii ekonomicheskii soiuz: teoriya ili real'nost'. *Izvestiya*, 19 March. Available at: http://personal.akorda.kz/ru/category/stati/evraziiskii-ekonomicheskii-soyuz-teoriya-ili-realnost [accessed 17 September 2018].
Nazarbayev, N. (2011). *Izvestiya*, 26 October, p. 1.
Nechepurenko, I. (2013). *The Moscow Times*, 29 July.
Nizhnikau, R. (2016). When Goliath Meets Goliath: How Russia and the EU Created a Vicious Circle of Instability in Moldova, *Global Affairs*, 2 (2), 203–216.
Panfilova, V. (2014). *Nezavisimaya gazeta*, 30 May, p. 2.
Panfilova, V. (2016). *Nezavisimaya gazeta*, 18 August, p. 1.
Podberezkin, A. and O. Podberezkina (2015). Eurasianism as an Idea, Civilizational Concept and Integration Challenge. In: P. Dutkiewicz and R. Sakwa eds. *Eurasian Integration – The View from Within*. Milton Park, Abingdon: Routledge, pp. 46–60.
Popescu, N. (2014). *Eurasian Union: The Real, the Imaginary and the Likely*. Chaillot Paper. Paris, European Union Institute for Security Studies. September.
Preiherman, Ya. (2011a). Return of Russian Subsidies: What Are the Implications for Belarus' Economy? Belarus Digest, 29 November. http://belarusdigest.com/story/return-russian-subsidies-what-are-implications-belarus-economy-6745 [accessed 17 September 2018].
Preiherman, Ya. (2011b). Belarus the Indebted, *Belarus Digest*. 9 December. Available at: http://belarusdigest.com/story/belarus-indebted-6882 [accessed 17 September 2018].
Putin, V.V. (2011). *Izvestiya*, 4 October.
Putz, K. (2016). Tajikistan: The Eurasian Economic Union's Next Member? *The Diplomat*, 19 July. Available at: http://thediplomat.com/2016/07/tajikistan-the-eurasian-economic-unions-next-member/ [accessed 17 September 2018].
Rakhmatulina, G (2012). Vliyanie Tamozhennogo soiuza na ekonomicheskoe razvitie Kazakhstana. Perspektivy integratsii v neftegazom sektore. *Evraziyskaya Ekonomicheskaya Integratsiya*, March–May, 1 (14), 77–92.
Reuters (2013). Nazarbaev i Lukashenko ostudili Evraziiskii pyl Putina. 24 December, Available at: https://ru.reuters.com/article/topNews/idRUMSE9BN02M20131224 [accessed 17 September 2018].
Reuters (2015). Belarus Devalues Currency Again to Protect Against Russian Economic Fallout, 8 January. Available at: www.reuters.com/article/russia-crisis-belarus-currency/update-1-belarus-devalues-currency-again-to-protect-against-russian-economic-fallout-idUSL6N0UN17L20150108 [accessed 17 September 2018].
Reuters (2016). Russia Plays Down Threat to Ban Belarus Dairy Imports, 22 June. Available at: https://uk.reuters.com/article/russia-belarus-dairy/update-2-russia-plays-down-threat-to-ban-belarus-dairy-imports-idUKL8N19E29Z [accessed 16 September 2018].
Ria Novosti (2014). Rezhim svobodnoi torgovli mezhdu Gruzieii RF prodolzhaet deistvovat'. 10 September. Available: https://ria.ru/world/20140910/1023547655.html [accessed 17 September 2018].
Roberts, P. and A. Moshes (2016). The Eurasian Economic Union: A Case of Reproductive Integration? *Post-Soviet Affairs*, 32 (6), 542–565.
Rukhadze, V. (2014). Russia Warns Georgia Against Signing Association Agreement with European Union. *Eurasia Daily Monitor*, 11 (100), 29 May. Available at: https://jamestown.org/program/russia-warns-georgia-against-signing-association-agreement-with-european-union/ [accessed 17 September 2018].

RT.com (2013). Russia Hints at 'Milk War' after Belarus takes 'Potash War' Hostage, 28 August. Available at: www.rt.com/business/russia-belarus-potash-milk-108/ [accessed 17 September 2018].

Salimzoda, F. (2016). Russia Puts Pressure on Tajikistan for Entry into the EAEC. The Khilafah.com. 27 December. Available at: www.khilafah.com/russia-puts-pressure-on-tajikistan-for-entry-into-the-eaec/ [accessed 17 September 2018].

Samokhvalov, V. (2016). The New Eurasia: Post-Soviet Space between Russia, Europe and China. *European Politics and Society*, 17 (1), 82–96.

Shapovalov, A. (2009). *Kommersant*, 10 June, p. 3.

Sidorenko, S. and Ye. Chernenko (2013). *Kommesant*, 26 November, p. 8.

Sitnina, V. and A. Susarov (2010). *Vremya Novostei*, 10 December 2010, p. 1.

Schenk, C. (2017). Labour Migration in the Eurasian Economic Union. In: A. Pikulicka-Wilczewska and G. Uehling, eds. *Migration and the Ukraine Crisis*, E-International Relations Publishing, pp. 164–177.

Sergeyev, M. (2013). *Nezavisimaya gazeta*, 14 October, p. 1.

Snow, Sh. (2016). Central Asia's Lukewarm Pivot to China. *The Diplomat*, 16 August. https://thediplomat.com/2016/08/central-asias-lukewarm-pivot-to-china/ [accessed 17 September 2018].

Socor, V. (2013a). Putin Courting Azerbaijan While Deep-Freezing the Karabakh Conflict. *Eurasia Daily Monitor*, 10, 151, 14 August. Available at: https://jamestown.org/program/putin-courting-azerbaijan-while-deep-freezing-the-karabakh-conflict/ [accessed 17 September 2018].

Socor, V. (2013b). Rogozin Threatens Moldova with Sanctions over Association Agreement with the European Union, *Eurasia Daily Monitor*, 10, 155, 4 September. Available at: https://jamestown.org/program/rogozin-threatens-moldova-with-sanctions-over-association-agreement-with-the-european-union/ [accessed 17 September 2018].

Susarov, A. (2010). *Vremya Novostei*, 27 May, p. 1.

Tarr, D.G. (2012). *The Eurasian Customs Union among Russia, Belarus and Kazakhstan: Can it Succeed where its Predecessor Failed?*, FREE Policy Brief Series, November (p. 1). Available at: http://freepolicybriefs.org/2012/11/05/the-eurasian-customs-union-among-russia-belarus-and-kazakhstan-can-it-succeed-where-its-predecessor-failed/ [accessed 17 September 2018].

Tarr, D.G. (2016). The Eurasian Economic Union of Russia, Belarus, Kazakhstan, Armenia, and the Kyrgyz Republic: Can It Succeed Where Its Predecessor Failed? *Eastern European Economics*, 54, pp. 1–22.

Tashimov, T. (2010). Diversifikatsiya neftedvizhenii. *Ekspert Kazakhstan*, 13 December. Available at: http://expertonline.kz/a2333/ [accessed 17 September 2018].

Tass (2016). Russian military conduct antiterrorist drills in Tajikistan. 29 February. Available at: http://tass.com/defense/859627?_ga=1.75724885.1338776785.14745540 77- [accessed 17 September 2018].

Trenin, D. (2009). Russia's Spheres of Interest, not *Influence*. *The Washington Quarterly*, 32 (4), 3–22.

Trenin, D. (2014). *Vedomosti*, 29 January, p. 6.

Vasilyan, S. (2017). 'Swinging on a Pendulum': Armenia in the Eurasian Economic Union and With the European Union. *Problems of Post-Communism*, 64, 1, 32–46.

Vesti Kavkaza (2013). Gruzinskie mandariny i yabloki vernutsya v Rossiiyu, 15 October. Available at: www.vestikavkaza.ru/analytics/Gruzinskie-mandariny-i-yabloki-vernutsya-v-Rossiyu.html [accessed 17 September 2018].

Vinokurov, Ye. (2016). *Vedomosti*, 3 August, p. 6.

Visloguzov, V. (2013). *Kommersant*, 3 September, p. 2.
Wikileaks (2009a). Monthly Archives: February 2009. 11 February. Available at: https://wikileakskz.wordpress.com/2009/02/page/3/ [accessed 17 September 2018].
Wikileaks (2009b). Kazakhstan: Customs Union With Russia Trumping WTO Was Long Foreshadowed, 15 June. Available at: https://wikileaks.org/plusd/cables/09ASTANA 1018_a.html [accessed 18 September 2018].
Wilson, J.L. (2016). The Eurasian Economic Union and China's Silk Road: Implications for the Russian–Chinese Relationship. *European Politics and Society*, 17 (1), 113–132.
World Bank (2012). *Assessment of Costs and Benefits of the Customs Union for Kazakhstan, Poverty Reduction and Economic Management Union*. World Bank, Washington DC, 3 January 2012.
Yalovkina, A. (2015). Kyrgyzstan joins the Customs Union, and Business Finds Itself in Stand-by Mode, Open Democracy. 23 June. Available at: www.opendemocracy.net/anna-yalovkina/as-kyrgyzstan-joins-customs-union-business-finds-itself-in-standby-mode [accessed 17 September 2018].
Zatulin, K. (2011). *Izvestia*, 19 October, p. 10.
Zelensky, M. and A. Polivanov (2017). *Meduza.io*, 3 February. Available at: https://meduza.io/en/feature/2017/02/03/russia-is-in-a-quarrel-with-belarus [accessed 18 September 2018].

12 Russia's CIS gas trade

An instrument of Russia's hegemony?

This chapter focuses specifically on the Russian–CIS gas trade during the twenty-first century, in view of the relevance of gas exchanges to the overall relationship between Russia and the CIS states and given the efforts by the Kremlin to re-establish a unified energy space within the CIS. When Putin became President of Russia, he gave the energy sector centre stage in Russia's economic policy. In his view, Russia's rich and abundant energy and mineral resources were expected to become the basis for the effective and sustainable development of the Russian economy. The energy industry was supposed not only to contribute to the improvement of living standards, but it was also expected to help transform the country into a great economic power and allow Russia better to implement an independent foreign policy (Putin, 1999, p. 49). In Putin's view, the energy complex also lay at the basis of the country's military might. Above all, the sector was expected to become an effective *instrument of CIS integration*, as well as tool of Russia's economic expansion worldwide. These CIS 'integration processes in the energy sector' were to be achieved 'through the development ... of joint fuel and energy balances of the CIS', and 'the restoration ... of a single energy system within the CIS', as stated in the 2000 *Main Provisions of the Energy Strategy of Russia for 2002* (GRF, 2000). This involved Russia's participation in the exploitation of CIS oil and gas fields, the construction of electric power facilities, and the development of energy and transport infrastructure within the CIS and beyond (GRF, 2000). It was also clearly stated that Russia's energy strategy would entail relying on the use of hydrocarbon resources, especially natural gas, from the CIS Central Asian state to fulfil Russia's own energy needs (GRF, 2000). In other words, Russia's energy diplomacy was expected to, 'become an instrument for effective cooperation within the CIS and with the world community as whole' (GRF, 2000).

Russia acquires CIS energy infrastructure

In order to establish a single and unified CIS energy complex, Russian energy companies participated actively in the development of CIS oil and gas energy projects and succeeded in many instances in acquiring ownership of CIS national energy-transport infrastructure and distribution systems, especially in the gas sector. In Armenia, Gazprom managed to increase its shares in ArmRosGazprom (ARGP), Armenia's gas distribution company, from the 45 per cent stake it had acquired in 1997, to a 58 per cent share in 2006 and a 72 per cent total in 2008, significantly enhancing its control over Armenia's entire gas transport, storage and distribution system (Yeghiazaryan, 2009, p. 244). Through its shares in ARGP, Gazprom also succeeded in handling, as of 2006, the whole of Armenia's gas-electricity barter trade with Iran, as ARGP controlled the Armenian section of the Iranian–Armenian gas pipeline, and also owned the fifth unit of the Hrazdan thermal power plan (Yeghiazaryan, 2009, p. 244; Panfilova and Melikova, 2004). Gazprom's operation of the Iranian–Armenian pipeline reduced the ability of Yerevan to purchase additional gas from Iran, making it harder for Armenia to diversify its gas sources from new providers and, in this way, reduce its dependency on Russia. Furthermore, ownership of the Iranian–Armenian pipeline allowed Russia to control the potential flow of gas from Iran to the EU besides strengthening its geopolitical influence in the South Caucasus (Yeghiazaryan, 2009, p. 246). Gazprom also held a significant stake in Moldova's national transport and distribution company *Moldovagaz*, through its 50 per cent shares in the company, which it had acquired in 1999, and through its management of the 13.44 per cent shares belonging to Transdniestria. This allowed Gazprom to control most of the local Moldovan distribution and gas transit system. In late 2005 and 2006, Gazprom tried, unsuccessfully, to acquire additional shares in Moldovagaz by increasing gas prices to Moldova quite significantly – from $110/mcm to 160/mcm (Bruce and Yafimava, 2009, p. 183). The Moldovan gas transit network was of particular relevance to Russia, as it carried Russian gas to South-Eastern Europe – Romania, Bulgaria and Western Turkey, and this explains Russia's desire to be in charge of it. However, it was Moldova's Transdniestrian region, which remained Gazprom's main worry as far as non-payments were concerned – it failed regularly to cancel its debts, accumulating large arrears. As a result, Tiraspol and not Chisinau remained the main threat to the security of gas transit via Moldova.[1] Yet, despite the Transdniestria's non-payments, Gazprom continued to ensure uninterrupted deliveries of gas to Romania, Bulgaria and Greece through the Moldovan system.

As far as Belarus was concerned, after prolonged and tortuous negotiations, Gazprom finally succeeded in 2006 in acquiring a 50 per cent ownership of Belarus' transport and distribution system Beltransgaz, the company which carried gas to Europe through the *Northern Lights* pipeline and also managed the internal distribution of gas inside Belarus (Ritchie, 2007). Gazprom also owned the *Yamal* gas pipeline system transiting Belarus, and this allowed the Russian gas conglomerate to control most of Belarus' export pipelines carrying gas to Europe. In 2011, Gazprom managed, after exerting significant pressure on Minsk through major increases in gas prices, to obtain the remaining 50 per cent shares in Beltransgaz, in a debt-for-equity arrangement with Belarus. Russia failed, however, despite repeated efforts in the early and mid-2000s, to acquire ownership over Ukraine's *Druzhba* gas pipeline system, the gas transit network which carried the most significant share of Russian gas to Europe. Attempts were initiated by Putin in 2002 to establish a Russian–Ukrainian 'gas consortium' to run and manage the Ukrainian pipeline system. Yet these efforts also floundered due to lack of funding and because of Kiev's insistence to hold a controlling block of shares in the consortium (Rybalchenko, 2002; Len, 2002). Disagreements also persisted between Kiev and Moscow over the possible access of Central Asian gas into the Ukrainian pipeline system. In 2003, Gazprom made it clear that it would not allow for the participation of Central Asian shareholders in the consortium, as had been desired by Ukraine, as this would have challenged its monopoly over exports to Europe, although this was never openly suggested. Russian leaders also insisted that the consortium would work only along the Ukrainian section of the pipeline, and not on Russia's territory, as Ukraine had wished (Butrin, 2003). These demands diminished support within Ukraine for the consortium, and the project was eventually abandoned when President Viktor Yushchenko reached the Presidency of Ukraine in January 2005 and began to question its rationale.

In 2003 and 2004, Gazprom reached a series of agreements with the Georgian government which gave Gazprom full control not only over gas deliveries to Georgia and over the distribution of gas *inside* the country, but also over the transit of gas further afield into Armenia. Gazprom also obtained full responsibility for the refurbishment of the Georgian gas pipeline system (Sepashvili, 2003; Stern, 2005, p. 84). The 2003 agreement between the Georgian government and Gazprom also involved the use of gas for the production of electricity which would then be jointly sold locally by the Georgian state and Gazprom. This arrangement was assisted by the purchase of the Georgian electricity network and a number of power plants in Georgia by Russia's company RAO UES (Stern, 2005, p. 84). All these deals gave Gazprom a significant foothold in the Georgian internal gas market. More significantly, in 2005, the Georgian government announced its readiness to sell to Gazprom its main gas pipeline running from Russia to Armenia through Georgia, as a way of cancelling its energy debts (Simonyan, 2005). This pipeline retained great significance to Russia as it was the sole route for the transit of Russian gas to Armenia (Tokmazishvili and Bowden, 2009, p. 266). However, under pressure from the United States, Georgia's strategic partner, the Georgian government backtracked on its decision, significantly increasing tensions between Tbilisi and Moscow (Simonyan, 2005). In January 2006, an explosion occurred on the main pipeline carrying Russian gas to Georgia and Armenia, which left the Georgian population without heating for almost ten days in the winter (Tokmazishvili and Bowden, 2009, p. 268). In November 2006, cut offs in gas supplies were announced by Gazprom if Georgia did not increase gas prices and sold its main pipeline to the Russian gas company (Woehrel, 2009, p. 11). This pushed the Georgian government to end the country's dependence on Russian gas, and to start purchasing gas directly from Azerbaijan in 2007. Yet, in 2006, Tbilisi had still to accept price increases of over 100 per cent from Gazprom (Konarzewska, 2015). Azerbaijan also began relying on its own gas resources from the newly operating Shah Deniz field, once its reserves became available in 2007, especially after Russia significantly increased prices at the end of 2006, from $110/mcm to $235/mcm (Useinov and Denisov, 2000; Bowden, 2009, p. 223). Russia, however, failed to ensure that the sale of Azerbaijani gas transited through Russia, and instead a gas pipeline was built from Baku to Turkey through Georgia – the Baku–Tbilisi–Erzurum (BTE) line – opening up the flow of Azerbaijani gas to Turkish and possibly European markets.

The Russian–Central Asian gas trade

President Putin proposed, in January 2002, the establishment of a Eurasian Gas Alliance of Producers – an 'gas OPEC' – together with the major Central Asian gas-producing states, Turkmenistan, Kazakhstan and Uzbekistan, in an effort to control the sale of Central Asian gas to Europe (*AFP*, 2002). The alliance – or cartel – was intended to allow the four Eurasian countries to coordinate the volume and the destination of their gas exports, by using a unified pipeline distribution system. Central Asian gas producers – Turkmenistan in particular because of its fast-growing gas output – represented a threat to Russia's quasi-monopoly seller position in several European markets. Russia saw the risk of a gas price war erupting if no agreement was reached with these Central Asian states on gas exports, given the great difference between market prices and production costs. There was plenty of room for the Central Asian states to offer reduced prices in order to obtain market shares and, in this way, displace Russia from lucrative markets in Europe and possibly Asia (*AFP*, 2002). All these Central Asian gas producers, however, were still dependent at the time on the Russian gas pipeline system to access European markets and CIS consumers such as Ukraine, and this placed Russia in a strong negotiating position. Russia's proposed solution, therefore, was to give them access to Gazprom's gas pipeline network in order to allow them to export their gas to European and CIS states in return for control over their sales. Russia also was interested in buying additional cheap gas from Turkmenistan to satisfy its own domestic needs (Dubnov, 2002). The Central Asian states, particularly Turkmenistan, however, did not prove supportive of the Eurasian Gas Alliance, and the project had to be shelved.

Nevertheless, Russia did manage through a series of bilateral trade deals reached between 2002 and 2007 to secure the transport of most of the gas produced by Central Asian states through its own pipeline system, on its way to CIS and Russian consumers. Furthermore, Gazprom also signed several long-term contracts for the direct purchase of significant amounts of Central Asian gas – from Turkmenistan, Uzbekistan and Kazakhstan – to satisfy Russia's own energy needs and expand its own energy potential. In June 2002, the *KazRosGaz* joint venture was established between Gazprom and KazMunaiGaz, the Kazakh energy company, on a 50–50 parity basis, to process, market and transport gas produced in Kazakhstan, thus giving the Russian gas conglomerate a foothold in the Kazakh gas export business (Netreba, 2002). Additional long-term agreements were reached in 2004 and 2007, which stipulated that KazRosGaz would buy substantial amounts of gas from Kazakhstan's Karachaganak gas field, starting with 7.5–8 Bcm/year and possibly reaching 16 Bcm/year in 2012. The gas would be processed at the Russian Orenburg plant and then would be exported to external markets (Yenikeyeff, 2009, p. 344). Kazakhstan had hoped that the joint venture's principal markets would be in Europe, but during 2002–2003, most of the Kazakh gas processed at Orenburg was sold within the CIS, and after 2006, mostly to Ukraine, thus keeping Kazakhstan outside of the lucrative EU gas markets (Yenikeyeff, 2009, p. 344). Gazprom also reached long-term agreements with Tashkent in 2002 on the acquisition of most of Uzbekistan's gas production for the period 2003–2012 (annual sales to Russia were expected to reach 10 Bcm in 2005), partly to re-export it to Ukraine, and partly to satisfy its own needs, thus keeping Uzbekistan away from European markets (Perovic, 2006, p. 99; Zhukov, 2009, p. 368). The 2002 agreement also included an option for the sale of 44 per cent of the shares in UzTransGaz to Gazprom (Zhukov, 2009, p. 364).

Similarly, and more importantly, Russia also managed to acquire most of Turkmen gas exports, through a long-term agreement reached in April 2003 with Ashgabat, which envisaged that Gazprom purchases of Turkmen gas would increase progressively from 4–6 Bcm in 2006 to 10 Bcm in 2006, before reaching 70–80 Bcm in 2010 to 2028 (Gorst, 2003, Stern, 2005, p. 77). The deal allowed Russia to avoid investing in the development of its more costly northern gas fields. More importantly, it helped to reduce the competitive pressures that Turkmenistan could exert in markets that were of strategic significance to Russia in Europe (GRF, 2003). Furthermore, the agreement reduced the ability of countries such as Ukraine effectively to diversify their sources of gas away from Russia. The significance of this accord, in this respect, cannot be over-estimated as it meant that when the bilateral-gas contract between Turkmenistan and Ukraine expired in 2006, Gazprom would probably become the main supplier of Turkmen gas to Ukraine, further deepening the latter's dependency on Russian gas. The April 2003 gas deal, however, also proved to be to the benefit of Turkmenistan, as Ashgabat was certain to have a market for its gas, with greater guarantees of payment – $200 billion over 25 years – than if it continued to sell all of its gas to Ukraine. Furthermore, the *TransCaspian* gas pipeline project, which would have allowed Turkmenistan to sell its gas to Turkey, was starting to encounter major problems. With the discovery of gas at the Azeri field of Shah Deniz, an important part of the Baku-Tbilisi-Erzurum pipeline was expected to be reserved for Azeri gas, rather than for Turkmen gas, thus limiting the ability of Turkmenistan to use this export line (Stern, 2005, pp. 74–75; Pereplesnin and Yashin, 2000). Moreover, Russia itself was blocking all attempts by the West to build *Transcaspian* pipelines which would have connected Turkmenistan's fields directly to the BTE pipeline in Azerbaijan – in a clear display of its hegemonic power. Gazprom thus became the main operator of Kazakh, Uzbek and Turkmen gas in transit towards Russia and beyond (Perovic, 2006, p. 88; Stern, 2005, pp. 81–82). This also allowed Russia to ensure that Central Asian gas was sold primarily either to Russia, or through Russia, to other CIS markets but not further afield, thus limiting the access of Central Asian gas to traditional Russian customers in Europe and to other non-COS consumers, such as Turkey, for example. It also reduced the possibility of Central Asian gas producers to increase their profits, as they remained dependent on transit primarily *via* Russia.

This predicament prompted these Central Asian countries – and the Caspian gas-producing states – to look for alternative markets and to develop new export routes. In February 2003, Azerbaijan took the decision to construct a gas pipeline from Baku, through Georgia, to Erzurum in Turkey to supply the Turkish market, and potentially also Southern Europe (Roberts, 2004, p. 85; Useinov, 2003). The line was completed in the autumn of 2006, with deliveries to Georgia and Turkey starting in early 2007. Russia had proposed that its *Blue Stream* pipeline, which linked Russia to Turkey across the Black Sea, be utilised to transport Azerbaijani gas from the Shah Deniz to Turkey, but Azerbaijan turned down the proposal, thus reducing the chances of Russia becoming the main conduit of Azerbaijani gas to foreign markets (Gordiyenko and Baikova, 2003). In Central Asia, China successfully financed the construction of the *Central Asia-China* pipeline, intended to carry gas from Turkmenistan, Kazakhstan and Uzbekistan all the way to eastern China. This new line, whose construction began in 2007 and was first completed in 2009, gave the three Central Asian producers further independence in their export routes from Russia. The *Transcaspian* pipeline project, instead, was never able to kick off the ground, as Russia blocked the line allegedly on 'technological, legal, and ecological' grounds, as noted by Russian Energy Minister Viktor Khristenko although the true reasons were clear – to prevent the opening of new pipeline routes which bypassed Russia (RFE/RL, 2007). Yet, by the late 2000s new alternatives for the Central Asian/Caspian states had nevertheless emerged, challenging Russia's predominant position as the hub of the post-Soviet gas pipeline system.

The opening up of a new export line from Central Asia to China allowed Turkmenistan, Kazakhstan and Uzbekistan to negotiate substantial increases in the prices of gas that they charged to Russia – in 2008 Turkmenistan charged Gazprom an average of \$140/mcm (Pirani, 2009, p. 293), while Uzbekistan's prices to Russia averaged \$145/mcm. Kazakhstan's prices to Russia, in turn, reached as high as \$180/mcm in 2008, close to 'European' prices and up from \$140–165/mcm in 2007 (Mitrova *et al.*, 2009, pp. 402–403; Grivach, 2007). These prices, including the original lower prices of \$44/mcm, were much higher than the prices that Gazprom was charging Russian domestic consumers at the time (Gorst, 2003), but initially the arrangement proved cheaper to Gazprom than tackling the new challenging deposits in the Russian Arctic or in East Siberia. Russia increasingly depended on gas imports from Central Asia to satisfy its domestic needs and fulfil export agreements. Faced with declining yields at home and growing domestic demand, Gazprom relied on the import of about 63–65 Bcm/year from Turkmenistan, Uzbekistan and Kazakhstan to meet its internal and external requirements. The purchases also showed that Russia wished to remain at the centre of the Central Asian gas trade, despite the potential losses that such commercial agreements might have entailed, and this explains why in the late 2000s, projects were initiated by Moscow to revamp the

Central Asian-Center gas pipeline to ensure it had a higher transport capacity from the existing level of 42 Bcm/year to 55 Bcm/year. Furthermore, Moscow also agreed, in 2007, with its Central Asian gas partners, Kazakhstan and Turkmenistan, to build a new pipeline along the Caspian Sea coast, through Kazakhstan and Russia, in order to export additional Central Asian gas to Europe (RFE/RL, 2007).

Gazprom raises gas prices

After Gazprom's internal restructuring in 2001–2002, the Russian gas conglomerate slowly began regaining control over its various 'lost' assets, through the acquisition of shares in smaller companies previously linked to Gazprom (Stern, 2005, p. 190). As part of this process it also began taking over most of the delivery of gas to CIS gas-consuming states from the intermediary gas company *Itera*. Gazprom began supplying small amounts of gas to Armenia in 2003, and in 2004, it became the main source of all Armenia's gas needs (1.21 Bcm per year). In April 2006, the Russian gas conglomerate signed a major agreement with the Armenian government for the delivery of Russian gas for a 25-year period (Veletminsky, 2006) with volumes reaching 1.9 Bcm in 2007 (Stern, 2009, p. 78). In Moldova, Gazprom increased its share of gas exports from 74 per cent in the year 2000 to 90 per cent in 2003 and to 100 per cent in 2004 (Bruce and Yafimova, 2009, p. 177; Stern, 2005, p. 69). Gazprom also succeeded in taking full control of the Georgian domestic market, by agreeing with Tbilisi in May 2004, to cover all of Georgia's 1 Bcm/year gas supplies (Stern, 2005, p. 84). The Russian gas conglomerate also took over all deliveries of gas to Belarus after a gas payments crisis in January–June 2004, which resulted in several cuts in supplies, doubling sales volumes from 10 Bcm in 2003 to 20.6 Bcm in 2007 (Stern, 2009, p. 78). In Ukraine, Gazprom's share in the country's external gas purchases increased from 45 per cent in 2003 to 98 per cent in 2007, delivering 59.2 Bcm in 2007, up from 26 Bcm in 2003 (Stern, 2009, p. 78). Much of the gas delivered to Ukraine, especially after the January 2006 crisis, theoretically came from Central Asia, but the gas travelled through the Russian pipeline system, and was delivered by RosUkrEnergo, an intermediary company partly owned by Gazprom, thus ensuring Russia's management of Ukraine's Central Asian gas purchases.

This predicament placed Gazprom in a very strong market position, allowing it substantially to increase its CIS gas prices in the second half of the 2000s. Gazprom progressively raised its gas fares to Azerbaijan from $110/mcm in 2006, to $235/mcm in 2007 – a four-fold increase from the 2005 price of $59/mcm (Bowden, 2009). Gas prices to Georgia doubled from $110/mcm in 2006, to $235/mcm in 2007 (Panfilova and Krashakov, 2006; Tokmazishvili and Bowden, 2009, p. 265), while prices to Moldova were increased from $170/mcm in 2007 to $253/mcm in the third quarter of 2008 (Bruce and Yafimava, 2009, p. 177, 183). Ukraine, in turn, was asked to pay $160–$170/mcm, and eventually $220–$230/mcm in 2006, up from the $50/mcm price it had been charged in

2005, a staggering four-times rise (Butrin and Grib, 2005b; Grivach and Gordeyev, 2005). While these price surges reflected overall increases in energy prices worldwide – oil prices had quadrupled between 2002 and 2008, while European gas prices were reaching $300/mcm in 2010 – they clearly indicated a readiness by Russia no longer to subsidise the gas purchases of CIS states, and instead make substantial profits out of the CIS energy trade. This new policy of increased high prices applied especially to those countries which were seen as not being strategically allied to Russia, such as Ukraine, Georgia, and to a lesser extent, Moldova. Russia no longer proved ready to subsidise the economies of those CIS states which had taken a clearly pro-Western stance and were being 'paid by the Americans directly or behind-the-scenes', in the eyes of the Kremlin (Ivzhenko, 2005). As stated by a high-ranking member of Putin's staff at a 2005 CIS Council of Foreign Ministers' meeting,

> The thrust of the new policy direction is not to restore the influence that Russia supposedly lost as a result of the Orange Revolutions. There was no such influence, instead there were only wasted expenditures and stolen Russian natural gas.
>
> (Ivzhenko, 2005)

Yet, even Moscow's closest allies, such as Armenia and Belarus, were asked to pay higher prices, although the increases were not as high as those applied to other CIS states. Belarus was compelled to pay Gazprom $110/mcm for its gas in 2007, up from a low base $46/mcm in 2005, with prices expected to reach $200/mcm in 2011. Similarly, Gazprom's gas fares to Armenia were also doubled from $54/mcm in 2005 to $110/mcm in April 2006, with prices planned progressively to increase in the coming years, until they reached world prices (Panfilova and Krashakov, 2006). This predicament, unexpectedly, led several CIS states to look for alternative sources of energy away from Russia.

The Kremlin's decision to rise energy prices and exploit its dominant position as the main gas supplier was also intended to obtain specific concessions from the respective CIS states – either to gain access to national gas distribution networks or to acquire ownership of key strategic industrial and energy assets, including pipelines and storage facilities. In 2006 and 2007, Gazprom substantially increased prices in Moldova, to a large extent in order to obtain full control over the gas distribution company *Moldovagaz* and, in this way, gain complete ownership over the gas transit lines carrying Russian gas towards southern Europe (Bruce and Yafimava, 2009, p. 183). The Russian gas company also cut off gas supplies for 16 days in January 2006, as Moldova refused to agree to increased gas prices arguing that Gazprom was already operating under a preferential regime through its partial ownership of *Moldovagaz* (Bruce and Yafimava, 2009, p. 183). Although Gazprom failed to acquire full control of *Moldovagaz*, it succeeded, instead, in obtaining additional shares in the Armenian gas conglomerate ARGP (in exchange for a cancellation of Armenia's energy debts), as a result of significant increases in gas prices to Armenia in

April 2006. As a result, Gazprom acquired full control over the Iran–Armenian pipeline and over the Hrazdan thermal power plant's fifth unit through ARGP. Content with its acquisition, Russian decided to freeze gas prices to Armenia until 1 January 2009, in a clear sign that price rises were linked to the purchase of energy assets (Veletminsky, 2006). Gazprom also increased prices to Georgia in 2006, in an attempt to purchase the main gas pipeline running through Georgia to Armenia, but its efforts did not prove successful. It also imposed quite substantial prices rises on Ukraine in November–December 2005, in order to acquire control over the country's pipeline system and gain access to Ukraine's internal distribution market. Yet it only partially succeeded – while it failed to obtain shares in the Ukrainian pipeline system, Gazprom nevertheless obtained a foothold in Ukraine's domestic distribution network through the trader UkrGazEnergo (UGE), a joint venture between RosUkrEnergo (RUE), a Gazprom subsidiary, and the Ukrainian gas company Naftohaz Ukrainy. Russia also increased prices to Belarus in 2004–2006 in order to get control over the gas distributing company *Beltransgaz* and, in this way manage most of the gas transit across Belarus towards Europe. While Russia did not prove entirely successful in Ukraine and Georgia, Gazprom did manage to acquire half of Beltransgaz's shares in 2006, and eventually full ownership of the Belarusian company, in a debt-for-equity swap in 2011, in what represented a significant achievement for Russia and its energy policies vis-à-vis Belarus.

Furthermore, Russia reinforced the use of Gazprom's gas price increases as a *hard power* instruments intended to achieve major political and geo-strategic objectives in the CIS states. Gazprom's substantial rises in gas prices to Ukraine in the winter of 2005/2006, which were coupled with major gas cuts in early January 2006, were intended primarily to weaken the pro-Western Presidency of Viktor Yushchenko, as Yushchenko was actively pushing for the establishment of close ties between his country and the Euro-Atlantic institutions, the European Union and NATO. In April 2005, Ukraine was invited by NATO to start an *Intensified Dialogue*, paving the way for Ukraine's membership of the Atlantic Alliance (*Kommersant*, 2005), while in the same month, Yushchenko also signed a 'Strategic Partnership' declaration between his country and the United States, after having received pledges of substantial financial support from Washington. Furthermore, in August 2005, Yushchenko and Georgian President Mikhail Saakashvili announced the creation of the 'Commonwealth of Democracies from the Baltic, Black Seas and Caspian region', a new regional grouping intended to promote democracy, resolve separatist conflicts, promote economic growth and ensure the protection of human rights in the ex-USSR states (Ratiani, 2005). This initiative was seen by Russia as a renewed attempt to establish an anti-Russian axis within the CIS space, and therefore proved to be unacceptable to Russia. More significantly, Yushchenko also tried to eliminate intermediaries from the Russian–Ukrainian gas trade, and even explored the possibility of establishing alternative gas pipelines linking Ukraine with Turkmenistan and bypassing Russia – proposals which clearly went against Russia's interests and also explained why Russia resorted such harsh measures against

Ukraine in the winter of 2005–2006 (Butrin and Grib, 2005a; Balmaceda, 2009, p. 120).

In a similar vein, Gazprom also increased gas prices to Belarus in 2004 and 2006 to convince Minsk at each opportunity to join Russia in a common monetary union, and again in 2009/2010 to ensure Belarus' membership of the Russian-led Eurasian Customs Union (ECU). In Moldova, Russia utilised increased gas prices in 2003 as instruments of pressure to secure a long-term military presence in Transdniestria, within the framework of the Kozak Memorandum. Similarly, the significant gas price rises introduced in Georgia in 2006 were also intended to punish Tbilisi for its pro-Western turn. These assertive polices by the Kremlin towards CIS energy-consuming countries differed from Russia's initial actions when Putin first took power in 2000. In the early 2000s, Russia had attempted to regularise its bilateral energy relationship with Ukraine, by slowly raising transit fees and gas prices, and by treating Ukraine as a business partner rather than adversary. This included agreements on debt restructuring which proved to be quite favourable to Ukraine (Gubenko, 2001; Shiryayev, 2000). Similarly, Russia's relationship with Belarus during 2000–2003 was also characterised by low prices and advantages to Belarus, in the expectation that a Union State with Minsk would soon be established. However, as the decade progressed, and as Russia failed to succeed in its key foreign policy objectives – creating a belt of neighbouring CIS states closely allied strategically and commercially to Russia – the methods employed by Russia and Gazprom changed. Exorbitant gas price increases were introduced, which made it increasingly difficult, if not impossible, for CIS states promptly to pay.

Yet, Russia's reliance on gas transit through Ukraine and Belarus to reach its customers in Europe reduced Russia's bargaining power. After a severe energy crisis in January 2006, which involved cuts in gas supplies to Ukraine, Russia was compelled to agree to a reduced price for Ukraine – $95/mcm – because it depended on the latter for the transit of most of its gas to Europe. Although the agreed price was almost double the previous fare ($50/mcm), it was still substantially lower than the price initially demanded by Russia ($160–$170/mcm) (Butrin and Grib, 2005b). Russia nevertheless succeeded in accessing the Ukrainian local gas distribution system and to keep intermediaries in the bilateral-gas relationship in the form of RosUkrEnergo and UkrGazEnergo. A similar energy–trade relationship also applied, to a certain extent, to Russia and Belarus. Transport dependencies forced Russia to continue subsidising the Belarusian economy although Russia's reliance on Belarus for gas transit to Europe was not as significant as it dependency on Ukraine. On the other hand, a close strategic partnership bound the two countries together and this also argued in favour of reduced gas prices. Gazprom several times suspended gas deliveries to Belarus in January and February 2004 because of delays in payments, but at each opportunity it was forced to restore supplies to prevent cuts in deliveries to customers in Europe. Starting in 2006, Russia increased prices to Belarus quite significantly in an attempt not only to acquire control over the gas company Beltransgaz but also in order to persuade Minsk to join Russia in a monetary and customs union (CU), in a clear display of its hegemonic power. While Moscow succeed in establishing a CU with Belarus and Kazakhstan in 2007–2009, it failed, however, to establish a common currency with Minsk. Yet, dependencies on transit compelled Russia to continue subsidising its gas trade with Belarus.

This predicament compelled Russia to look for alternative transit lines to carry its gas to its European clients. In 2005, the *Nord Stream* gas pipeline, which bypassed Belarus and Ukraine, and linked Russian Siberian fields directly to Western Europe, across the Baltic Sea, was initiated, and eventually completed in 2011. A similar project, the *South Stream* pipeline, which bypassed Ukraine and linked Russia to Southern and Central Europe across the Black Sea, the Ionian Sea and the Balkans, was launched in 2007. Within this remit, Gazprom also considered building underground storage facilities in Europe, which would allow the Russian company to suspend transit through Ukraine and Belarus for longer periods, if considered necessary (Kulikov and Sklyarov, 2007). The South Stream project, however, had to be abandoned in 2014, as Bulgaria was forced to stop construction of the pipeline, because of its non-compliance with European rules on energy competition in public procurements. European regulations prohibited gas suppliers from owning transportation systems and controlling deliveries of gas to the same markets simultaneously. Instead, a similar project, the *Turkish Stream pipeline*, expected to carry the same amount of gas – 63 Bcm – to Turkey was launched by Russia in December 2014 (Pirani and Yafimava, 2016). These new gas lines, which bypassed both Belarus and Ukraine, were intended to break Russia's dependency on these two countries, and ensure the safe transit of Russian gas to Europe. Yet, together with the Central Asian/Caspian gas exporting pipelines to China, Turkey and Iran, they reflected the 'disintegration' trends occurring within the CIS, and the failure of Russia effectively to create unified energy complex with its closest neighbours in Central Asia, Ukraine and Belarus.

Russian–CIS gas trade in the twenty-first century: towards disintegration?

The relevance of the energy sector in the Russian economy only increased as the twenty-first century progressed, with the oil and gas sectors representing 70 per cent of Russia's total exports in 2012 (Mitrova, 2014, p. 6). Yet, in the 2010s, Russia's economy was faced with a new predicament, which negatively affected its growth prospects. The global financial crisis hit the world economy hard in 2008/2009, producing a recession in several European countries, Russia's main gas customers. This led to a reduction in the demand for Russian gas in Europe and a temporary fall in oil and gas prices, forcing Russia to look for alternative markets for its energy products both in Asia – particularly in China – and in the CIS states. While energy prices recovered after the 2008 crash, they fell once again in the fourth quarter of 2014 under pressure from alternative sources of energy, with world oil prices plummeting to $45–$50/barrel in early 2015. In view of this predicament, Russia began experiencing severe financial difficulties in 2014–2015, a situation which was made worse by the sanctions imposed by Europe and the United States on several key sectors of its economy in 2014, in retaliation for its military actions in Ukraine (Konarzewska, 2015).

Armenia, Georgia and Moldova

Russia responded to this negative outlook by increasing gas sales and gas prices to CIS-consuming countries, such as Armenia, Moldova, Ukraine and Belarus. As journalist Vasili Rukhadze (2016) noted, 'After losing the dominant role on the European energy markets, Russia [was now] attempting to strengthen and cement its position across the post-Soviet space' until it could expand its trade to other more profitable markets worldwide. In Armenia, Russia was able to exploit its monopolistic position to extract significant increases in gas prices, which more than doubled in five years, reaching $270/mcm in 2013. While this reflected Moscow's efforts to bring Russia's CIS energy fares up to world levels, which in 2013 hovered around $390/mcm, the increases proved to be a real challenge for the fragile Armenian economy (RFE/RL, 2010; Gevorgyan, 2014). They were intended to exert pressure on Yerevan to obtain control over the remaining shares of ARGP. In fact, once Gazprom obtained full control over Armenia's entire natural gas infrastructure in 2014, through the acquisition of the remaining 20 per cent shares of ARGP from the Armenian government, Russia agreed once again to reduce its wholesale gas prices to Armenia, down to $189/mcm (Gevorgyan, 2014). The ARGP deal also involved a commitment by Yerevan to buy gas exclusively from Russia for a 30-year period, thus establishing a strong and long-term energy dependency by Armenia on gas purchases from Russia (Gevorgyan, 2014). Moscow also succeeded in reaching a deal with Tbilisi on 11 January 2017, which allowed for the transit of 2.2 Bcm of Russian natural gas annually through Georgia to Armenia during a two-year period, in this way 'helping Moscow entrench itself as a key energy player in the region' (Rukhadze, 2017). The deal granted Georgia the possibility of buying Russian gas at discounted prices, while committing Russia to pay Georgia high transit fees for the gas destined to Armenia (Rukhadze, 2017). Yet, concerned over restoring a dependency on Russia for gas purchases, the Georgian government decided, in early 2018, to continue relying on the acquisition of gas from Azerbaijan, despite the progressive decline in the latter's gas production.

Russia, instead, remained the main supplier of gas to Moldova, by providing Chisinau with almost 100 per cent of its gas needs during the 2000s and early 2010s (Sobják, 2013). Russia's predominant position, reinforced through its partial ownership of Moldovagaz, allowed Russia to increase its gas prices to Moldova quite significantly, from $170/mcm in 2007 progressively up to $420/mcm in 2014. These increases hit the Moldovan economy very hard, at a time when the country was led by a strongly pro-European alliance which was trying to transform the economy and align Moldova closely to the EU (Puiu, 2014). Furthermore, in 2012, under pressure from Gazprom, Chisinau had been compelled to postpone the full implementation of the EU's Energy Community Treaty's (ECT)

Third Package, which would have prevented Gazprom from dominating both the transit systems and the distribution markets in Moldova (Sobják, 2013; Rodkiewicz, 2012, pp. 2–3).[2] The Third Package required 'non-discriminatory third-party access to the gas transmission networks' as well as the 'separation of suppliers from producers and grids', thereby challenging Gazprom's dominant role not only as a provider of gas to Moldova, but also as an internal gas distributor (Nuțu, 2016). In late August 2014, Moldova, therefore, took the first steps towards breaking its strong gas dependency on Russia, with the inauguration of the 43 km long pipeline linking the Romanian town of Iasi to the Moldovan town of Ungheni. This new pipeline allowed Moldova to import gas directly from Romania or Poland, and therefore reduce gas purchases from Russia. In this way, Moldova was able to rebuff Gazprom's requests to continue postponing the implementation of the ECT's Third Energy Package (Nuțu, 2016). Yet, Russia continued in its efforts to sell its gas to Moldova, as the country remained an important transit route for Russia's gas markets in south-eastern Europe. To that end, in 2015, Gazprom reduced prices to Moldova by 40 per cent in line with the overall fall in global energy prices. However, in 2016–2017 the government in Chisinau persisted in its efforts to increase purchases from Romania and Poland and to become further integrated into the EU energy system by expanding gas purchases from Europe and enhancing its gas pipeline capacity.

Belarus and Ukraine

Belarus, instead, remained heavily dependent on Russia not only for the supply of oil for its industries, but also for the provision of natural gas, and therefore very much exposed to Russia's price hikes and economic pressures. In 2008 and 2009, Russia increased gas prices to Belarus quite significantly, reaching $210/mcm in the first quarter of 2009, up from $125/mcm in 2008. While world energy prices fell considerably in 2009, they once again recovered in 2010, and as a result, Russia adjusted prices accordingly. Minsk, however, continued to stick to its 2009 price of $150/mcm, augmenting its debts vis-à-vis Gazprom even further as a result (Yafimava, 2010, p. 8). Disagreements over prices and delays in gas payments prompted Russia to cut supplies to Belarus at several opportunities in June 2010. Although a preliminary agreement which temporarily settled the dispute was reached in July 2010, Gazprom made no major concessions on prices – an indication that the Kremlin was becoming less tolerant towards Belarus vis-à-vis energy prices, especially given Minsk's reluctance to sign up to the Russian-sponsored ECU (Yafimava, 2010, p. 14). It was only when Gazprom succeeded in obtaining the remaining share in the Belarusian energy company Beltransgaz in 2011 and after Belarus agreed to join to the Russian-led ECU and the Single Economic Space in 2010/2011, that Russia agreed once again to reduce gas prices, introducing fares similar to those applied to the internal Russian Yamal-Nenets region. Yet, it was expected that gas prices would reach European levels by the end of 2014 – following on what had also been agreed for Russian domestic consumers (Pirani and Yafimava, 2014, p. 199).

Problems in the bilateral Russian–Belarusian gas relationship continued, however. Supplies to Belarus were again cut in July 2016 in a dispute over prices. While Belarus limited itself to paying the reduced price of $80–107/mcm, Gazprom instead insisted on a price of $132/mcm (Reuters, 2016; Drakakhrust, 2016). A final agreement was reached in the autumn of 2016, which nevertheless proved to be quite favourable to Belarus. Although the agreed fares were higher than those desired by Belarus – $100/mcm rather than $80/mcm – they were still quite low when compared to European gas prices which at the time reached $200/mcm on average. Furthermore, contrary to previous agreements, there was no mention in the deal of any requirement to set up joint ventures with Belarus' strategic companies, despite Belarus' accumulation of a $300 million bill towards Russia (Drakakhrust, 2016). This reflected a readiness by Russia to continue heavily subsidising the Belarusian economy, aware of its dependency on gas transit through Belarus, and conscious of the relevance of its strategic partnership with Minsk. The Kremlin also worried over the instabilities that could result from a potential Belarusian 'EuroMaidan', if the economy collapsed as a result of increased gas prices, however unlikely such a scenario may have seemed at the time. The risk also existed that the Belarusian–Russian alliance would be severely tested if discounted prices were not offered, especially in view of Minsk's openings towards Ukraine in December 2016 (Drakakhrust, 2016).

In neighbouring Ukraine, Gazprom introduced significant gas price discounts during Viktor Yanukovych's Premiership in 2006–2007, as the new Prime Minister conducted a friendly foreign policy towards Russia. Yanukovych kept energy intermediary companies in place, he promised not to pursue Ukraine's NATO membership, and, more significantly, he renewed the lease of the Crimean naval base at Sevastopol for the Russian Black Sea Fleet (BSF) (Netreba and Gavrish, 2006). When Yuliya Timoshenko became Prime Minister in late 2007, however, relations once again became strained because of her persistent attempts to eliminate gas intermediaries RosUkrEnergo (RUE) and UkrGazEnergo (UGE) from the Turkmen–Russian–Ukrainian gas trade. The removal these companies not only challenged the profits made by shareholders in the bilateral Russian–Ukrainian gas business, it also risked putting an end to Gazprom's 25 per cent share in the Ukrainian domestic gas distribution market, which the Russian gas conglomerate had acquired through its subsidiary UGE, jointly owned by Naftohaz and RUE (Grib and Gavrish, 2008). The continued use of intermediaries indicated that personal profits and murky deals were still very much part of the Russian–Ukrainian trading relationship. This predicament also partly explained why Gazprom decided to cut supplies to Ukraine in March 2008, under the pretext that Kiev had failed to pay its gas debts in full (Mordyushenko, 2008; Grivach, 2008). Gazprom was soon forced to restore gas supplies to Ukraine, however, after Kiev threatened to reduce the transit of Russian gas that was being carried through Ukraine's pipeline system on its way to Europe (Grivach, 2008). A new agreement on gas supplies was soon reached which, for the first time, eliminated intermediaries from the relationship. Although this represented a victory for Ukraine, Kiev was compelled to grant Gazprom *direct* access to the Ukrainian domestic market (Grib *et al.*, 2008).

This arrangement, however, turned out to be only a temporary truce. On 1 January 2009, Russia once again cut supplies to Ukraine over a price dispute, eager to exploit political divisions and economic weaknesses inside Ukraine in order to extract better price conditions (Aslund, 2015). The situation worsened on 7 January, when Russia not only persisted in its gas cuts to Ukraine, but also completely suspended gas supplies to countries in south-eastern Europe for two weeks. This was the first time since the gas system had been built decades earlier that supplies to Europe had been completely halted. It showed that Russia proved ready to risk its market positions in Europe for the sake of undermining a pro-European regime which was seen as taking a stance hostile towards Russia – the government in Kiev supported Ukraine's NATO membership and had shown solidarity with Georgia in its confrontation with Russia over South Ossetia and Abkhazia in August 2008. With these actions, Russia made it clear that it was ready to openly use its 'hard power' capabilities to achieve its foreign policy objectives in the Near Abroad, in a distinct display of its economic might, which to a great extent resulted from its energy potential. Eventually, a 10-year gas deal was reached on 19 January 2009 between Prime Ministers Putin and Timoshenko, which put the relationship in a sound business footing. It fully eliminated intermediaries from the Russian–Ukrainian gas trade relationship and established gas prices and transit tariffs based on European pricing principles, and no longer linked to Central Asian fares (Pirani *et al.*, 2009, pp. 26–28). The 'take-or-pay' clause, however, forced Ukraine to pay for whole volumes of gas even if not consumed. Furthermore, the European base price first agreed was quite high – $450/mcm – even though Timoshenko obtained a substantial discount for 2009. In addition, Gazprom's trading subsidiary, *Gazprom-Sbyt* was awarded the marketing of 25 per cent of the imported gas inside Ukraine. As such, the deal represented a victory for Russia.

Once Yanukovych returned to power in Ukraine in 2010, he adopted a Russia-friendly foreign policy, which was seen very positively by the Kremlin. Yanukovych agreed to extend the lease on the BSF at Sevastopol for another 25 years once the deal expired in 2017. More importantly, in June 2010 Yanukovych emphasised Ukraine's neutral status and significantly reduced Ukraine's cooperative ties with NATO.[3] Russia responded by reducing gas prices to Ukraine and softening some of the more punitive aspects of the 2009 gas deal, in a clear indication, once again, that the Ukrainian–Russian gas trade was being subjected to the political realities that underpinned the bilateral relationship. The stipulated prices, however, still remained quite high despite the discount granted by Russia – they equalled $257/mcm in 2010, $315/mcm in 2011 and $424/mcm in 2012 – prompting Ukraine to begin progressively to diversify its gas supplies away from Russia (Pirani and Yafimava, 2014, pp. 185–186). However, when Yanukovych faced strong internal opposition from pro-EU demonstrators in the autumn of 2013, Russia decided once again to reduce gas prices to Ukraine – from 424/mcm down to $268/mcm – in a clear sign of support for the incumbent Ukrainian

President. Instead, when the Yanukovych regime fell in February 2014, and a new, decidedly anti-Russian government took power in Kiev, Russian gas prices were once again raised quite substantially, in a direct challenge the new Ukrainian authorities (Mazneva, 2014). Furthermore, supplies were cut in June 2014 on the grounds that Ukraine had not fully cancelled its debts, while demands were also being placed on Kiev, for the first time to make upfront payments for the gas to be consumed, before the latter was being received (BBC, 2014a). These measures clearly indicated that Russia was ready to use energy as an instrument of policy to exert pressure on – and possibly undermine – the new regime in Kiev. Ukraine, however, succeeded in obtaining EU and International Monetary Fund (IMF) support for the payment of its gas debts. Kiev also decided, in a quite risky step, to move ahead with the diversification of its energy sources away from Russia (BBC, 2014b; De Micco, 2014). The dynamics of Ukraine's foreign policy had by then substantially changed. After the Kremlin's annexation of Crimea and the outbreak of war in the Ukrainian Donbass, the leadership in Kiev adopted a decidedly pro-European and Atlanticist course. By the end of 2015, Ukraine began relying on 'reverse flow' gas arrangements with its European neighbours, breaking in this way, its full dependency on Russian imports and, therefore, coming out of Russia's energy sphere of influence. Yet, Gazprom still depended on Ukraine for the transit of a large share of its gas to Europe, despite the emergence of alternative Russian gas transit pipelines which partly bypassed Ukraine and Belarus, such as Nord Stream 1, Yamal, and Turkish Stream. This predicament placed Ukraine in a stronger position vis-à-vis Russia, although it perpetuated disputes between the two countries over transit and storage, forcing Russia to reach compromises with Ukraine (de Carbonnel, 2016).

The Central Asian–Russian gas trade

Russia continued in the late 2000s partly to rely on Central Asian gas imports, mostly from Turkmenistan, to fulfil its domestic needs and to meet its CIS gas commitments. In 2007–2008, before the global financial crisis, Gazprom struck deals with Turkmenistan, Kazakhstan and Uzbekistan to ensure long-term gas deliveries from Central Asia at relatively high European netback prices (Grivach, 2007; Kulikov, 2008; Pirani, 2014, p. 347). In 2009, however, as the demand for Russian gas sharply fell in Europe, Russia and Gazprom decided to reduce quite significantly the acquisition of Turkmen gas, while initially keeping the levels of gas purchases from Uzbekistan and Kazakhstan equal. The amounts purchased from these two countries remained the same because they were much smaller when compared to Russia's acquisitions of Turkmen gas – over 40 Bcm (2008), compared to 13.1 Bcm (2009) and 11.4 Bcm (2010) from Uzbekistan, and 10.1 Bcm (2009) and 12.4 Bcm (2010) from Kazakhstan (Pirani, 2014, p. 348 and 356). The Russian–Turkmen gas relationship, instead suffered severely in 2009, especially after an explosion occurred 9 April 2009 in Turkmenistan, near the border with Uzbekistan, on the main *Central Asian-Centre* gas pipeline which carried gas to Russia (Grib *et al.*, 2009). Thereafter, supplies of gas from Turkmenistan were halted, and even though the pipeline was soon repaired, Gazprom announced the suspension of gas purchases from Turkmenistan, in a clear breach of contract (Pirani, 2012, p. 81). The entire episode showed how far Russia seemed ready to go, deliberately using dishonest subterfuge and illegal methods, to ensure that its interests in the energy sector were upheld. Although sales of Turkmen gas to Russia were resumed in early 2010, the volumes of gas purchased were reduced by almost a fourth, from 42.3 Bcm in 2008 to 10.7 Bcm in 2010 (Pirani, 2014, p. 355).

The prices charged by Central Asian producers to Russia in the early 2010s, however, remained quite high – above Gazprom's average sales prices in the former Soviet states (FSS), where most of these volumes were sold, thus resulting in significant losses for the Russian energy budget. These prices were 'more than twice the price at which Russian-produced gas [was] delivered to Russia's main consuming areas' (Pirani, 2014, p. 349). Central Asia could extract high prices because Russia had become locked to these purchases. As noted by Pirani (2014, p. 349), Russia 'continued to buy these volumes', at relatively high prices 'mainly for the sake of Russian political interests in Central Asia', namely to keep the Central Asian regimes satisfied, and to ensure that their gas was not diverted to other non-CIS markets. By 2015–2016, however, Russia almost totally halted all purchases of Central Asian gas from Turkmenistan and Uzbekistan, as it considered these purchases no longer profitable. China, in turn, emerged as a major alternative market for Central Asian gas producers, allowing these countries to break away from the ex-Soviet pipeline system. When the *Central Asia-China* gas pipelines running eastwards to China opened in 2009/2011, exports from Central Asia and the Caspian region to China started to grow, slowly overtaking exports to Russia and the CIS in volume terms in 2013–2014.[4] Interestingly, in 2014, Russia also began selling gas to China – in May of that year, an agreement was reached which committed Russia to supply China with 38 Bcm/y of gas, once the 4,000 km eastern *Power of Siberia* pipeline became operational in 2018. This placed the Central Asian states in competition with Russia over gas deliveries to the Chinese market, to the benefit of Chinese buyers, who could rely on a variety of sources, including long-term LNG (Liquefied Natural Gas) contracts into coastal China, to obtain reduced prices (Sherman, 2015). At the same time, the arrival of Azerbaijani gas from the Shah Deniz field to Turkey and potentially to Europe began to challenge, to a certain extent, Russia's predominance in its traditional European markets. Azerbaijan's sales to Turkey ran at 6.3 Bcm/year of gas in 2012 and were planned to reach 7.2 Bcm in early 2018. There was the expectation that deliveries could increase further once the Shah Deniz 2 became fully operational and the Trans-Anatolian Natural Gas Pipeline (TANAP), linking Turkey to Greece and Albania, was fully completed in 2020 (Pirani, 2014, p. 358). Together with the Trans-Adriatic pipeline, which in turn, linked Greece and Albania to Southern Italy, TANAP was intended to turn Turkey into an energy hub and allow for the diversification of EU gas supplies away from Russia.

Furthermore, in 2015 construction began on the Turkmenistan-Afghanistan–Pakistan–India (TAPI) pipeline, a line which would allow Turkmenistan to export about 33 Bcm/year of gas to South Asia once the line was completed supposedly in 2019 (Tabatska, 2015). Russia, in turn, launched the *Turkish Stream* pipeline, which was intended to carry 63 Bcm/year of gas to Turkey, in replacement of the South Stream project. The initial branch of the pipeline was to cross the Black Sea and reach Turkey before joining the Trans-Balkan pipeline across Bulgaria and Romania, while the other branches would reach the Turkish–Greek border (Pirani and Yafimava, 2016, p. 10). The Turkish Stream project, however, was initially rejected by the EU (European countries were expected to become the main customers of the transiting gas), not only on legal, but also on political grounds. Many EU states did not want to 'undermine Kiev's remaining leverage against Moscow or fortify the EU's dependence on Russian gas' (*WSJ*, 2015). Yet, the project was never abandoned, and after a hiatus of almost a year following the shootdown of a Russian fighter jet by Turkey in November 2015, a final agreement on the project was finally reached in October 2016 between Russian President Vladimir Putin and his Turkish counterpart Recep Tayyip Erdogan, and construction began in May 2017. As the 2010s progressed, therefore, new pipelines emerged which challenged the unity of the former Soviet pipeline system, and reduced Russia's hold over the CIS states.

Assessment and concluding thoughts

With the arrival of Putin to the Presidency, the energy sector took centre stage in Russia's economic policy. In the Kremlin's view, Russia's rich and abundant energy and mineral resources were expected to establish the basis for the sustainable development of the Russian economy. Furthermore, the energy complex was supposed to become an effective instrument of CIS integration, as Russia re-established a single energy system under its leadership. This could help to reverse the CIS disintegration processes in the energy sector that had occurred in the 1990s. Such an ambitious project was to be achieved through the establishment of a common CIS energy-transport infrastructure and an inter-connected energy distribution system. To that end, Russia participated actively in the development of CIS oil and gas energy projects and tried – often quite successfully – to acquire ownership of CIS national energy-transport pipelines and distribution systems. This policy, to a certain extent, followed an entirely reasonable economic and commercial logic, as Russia and the CIS states could benefit quite significantly from common energy systems if properly managed and resourced, while Russia could also profit from the acquisition of market shares in the internal gas distribution businesses of CIS states. Furthermore, control over transit pipeline systems could prevent the siphoning of Russian gas destined to European markets by the CIS transiting states, and this, in turn, could ensure the continued flow of Russian gas to consumers in Europe. This last aspect remained one of Russia's key strategic commercial objectives, as gas sales to Europe represented an essential source of revenue for the Russian state's coffers.

Yet, the instruments utilised by Russia to achieve these objectives – especially with regards to the acquisition of CIS energy assets, gas distribution business and gas pipeline systems – did not always correspond to legitimate international practices. Instead, Russia's policies were often characterised by a reliance on *hard* coercive methods, in contravention of international law, especially during Putin's second term in the Presidency. This included sudden and substantial increases in gas prices, as well as threats to cut gas supplies, usually followed by actual cuts in gas deliveries. In many of these instances, Russia's pressures allowed Gazprom to gain partial or total ownership of coveted energy assets in 'debt-for-equity swaps', as occurred in Moldova and Belarus, for example. This, in turn, permitted Gazprom to dominate the local distribution systems of several CIS states – as was the case in Armenia, Belarus, Georgia and Moldova – and either partly or fully to control gas transit lines, as occurred in Armenia, Belarus and Moldova. Russia's leverage capacity, however, was hampered by Gazprom's dependency on the transit of gas through the CIS countries concerned (Belarus, Ukraine and Moldova). This often prevented, or made it harder, for Russia to acquire full control over coveted CIS energy assets, especially as far as Ukraine was concerned. Nevertheless, Gazprom did manage to acquire in 2006 a 50 per cent ownership of Belarus' Beltransgaz, the company which carried gas to Europe, and to penetrate Ukraine's internal gas distribution market after the January 2006 crisis. Furthermore, Gazprom did succeed in the 2000s in becoming the main provider of gas to CIS-consuming countries such as Georgia, Armenia, Belarus, Ukraine and Moldova, thus placing it in a predominant market position, and eventually allowing it, in the mid-2000s, to increase gas prices quite significantly.

Gazprom's gas price increases, especially in the mid-2000s, were often of an exorbitant nature, making it increasingly hard for CIS states promptly to pay the Russian company for their gas purchases. While these rises reflected and followed the substantial increases in global energy prices that were occurring at the time, with world oil prices quadrupling between 2003 and 2008, the way in which these prices were imposed on Gazprom's CIS customers did not reflect appropriate and desirable commercial practices. More significantly, in many instances, Russia clearly utilised gas prices upsurges as *hard policy* instruments to achieve clearly-defined political objectives – to weaken the Yushchenko presidency in Ukraine; to convince Belarus to join the Russian-led CU within the EvrAzES/Eurasian Union framework, or punish Georgia for its pro-Western turn and for its reluctance to hand over control of its key gas pipeline to Russia. Furthermore, what also transpired from the CIS energy relationship, especially as far as Russian–Ukrainian gas sales were concerned, was the presence – and deep entrenchment – of private interests and personal profits, often involving obscure business schemes, which significantly clouded the CIS gas relationships. The Russian–Ukrainian trade, in particular, became characterised, once Gazprom replaced Itera as a go-between in the Turkmen-Ukrainian trade in 2003, by the use of opaque intermediary companies such as EuralTransGas (ETG), RUE and UGE, whose real beneficiaries often remained unknown to the public, but still reflected major business interests in both Russia and Ukraine.

The 2008/2009 global financial crisis and the challenges posed by the growing investment in shale and oil gas production worldwide, produced a reduction in the European demand for Russian gas and also led to a temporary fall in oil and gas prices, forcing Russia to look for alternative markets for its energy products both in Asia – particularly in China – and in the CIS states. While such actions can be interpreted as following a legitimate commercial logic, once again the way in which these objectives were pursued by Russia in the CIS space did not reflect adequate and respectable international business practices. Russia exploited its monopolistic position in the CIS energy market to extract substantial price increases from Armenia, Moldova and Ukraine, and to a lesser extent in Belarus, in a clear display of its *hegemonic power*. Furthermore, in the case of Armenia, Russia succeeded in 2014 in locking all of the country's gas purchases to Russia in a 30-year-long gas agreement. Even though Armenia continued during 2015–2016 to import small amounts of gas from Iran, the deal sealed the country's complete reliance on Russian gas supplies (RFE/RL, 2016). Russia also proved quite successful in raising gas prices to Ukraine, once a major deal with Kiev was reached in January 2009. The latter introduced European gas pricing principles and forced Ukraine to buy Russian gas even if it did not need it, through the 'take-or-pay' clause. Russia's hegemonic position, therefore, allowed it to keep these CIS gas-consuming countries within its economic sphere of influence, and as such its actions can well be characterised as neo-imperialist. In the case of Belarus, Gazprom finally succeeded in December 2011, in acquiring full control over Beltransgaz.

Russia's hegemonic position in the CIS energy space, however, started to fracture in the mid-2010s. With the arrival of a staunchly anti-Russian and pro-Western government in Kiev in 2014, the 2009 'take-or-pay' deal collapsed and had to be renegotiated. With the political backing and the financial support of the West, Kiev was able to obtain more lenient terms – the October 2014 Russian–Ukrainian gas deal, brokered by the EU, reduced prices and eliminated the unfavourable 'take-or-pay' clause (BBC, 2014b; De Micco, 2014). More significantly, thanks to EU and Western support, Ukraine was able to begin diversifying its sources of energy away from Russia, and in 2017, for the first time, it stopped relying on Russia for gas supplies almost entirely. This represented a major geo-economic loss for Russia, especially if we consider that Moscow still depended on Ukraine for the transit of a significant part of its gas to Europe, and was therefore now at a disadvantage. Moldova also began diversifying its energy sources away from Russia in 2014 by acquiring gas from Romania, and relying on financial support from the European Union to complete its purchases. Georgia, in turn, refused to re-establish a full gas dependency on Russia (even though it facilitated Russia's gas sales to Armenia), and instead agreed to continue purchasing most of its gas from neighbouring Azerbaijan. Belarus, instead, did not prove capable of breaking its dependency on subsidised gas purchases from Gazprom, and this placed it in an extremely vulnerable position both economically and politically. Yet, despite Russia's efforts progressively to increase gas prices to Belarus, Gazprom failed in its endeavour. Russia's continued dependence on Belarus for its gas transit to Europe, as well as Minsk's readiness to join Russia in a Eurasian Economic Union, argued in favour of subsidised prices. Armenia was probably the only CIS gas-consuming country whose gas sector and gas purchases remained fully and entirely in Russia's hands, even though this was partly compensated by relatively lower Russian energy prices.

As far as the CIS gas-producing countries in the Caspian/Central Asian region are concerned, Russia also failed to keep intact its previous predominance as the main purchaser of Central Asian gas and as the key transit route for Central Asian energy exports. Azerbaijan relied on the new BTE gas pipeline, a line which connected its offshore Shah Deniz gas fields to Erzurum in Turkey (through Georgia) and bypassed Russia, in order to reach its Turkish consumers. Moscow also failed to establish a Eurasian Gas Alliance of Producers – a 'gas OPEC' – together with the major Central Asian producers. Although it succeeded in the 2000s in ensuring that most of the Turkmen and Kazakh gas (and part of the Uzbek gas) was sold to Russia (or through Russia to Ukraine), the opening of a new China-Central Asia gas pipeline in 2009 diminished Russia's leverage, and forced it to acquire Central Asian gas at much higher prices than had been initially stipulated. This prompted Russia to reverse its long-held strategy of purchasing Central Asian gas for its domestic market, as it attempted to reduce – if not entirely suspend – gas purchases from Turkmenistan. When trying to implement this new policy, Russia proved ready apparently to use quite dishonest methods, as the suspicions explosions in the Turkmenistan gas pipeline in April 2009 seemed to indicate. This episode showed that Russia no longer wished to abide by international and acceptable commercial practices when pursuing its gas objectives in Central Asia. Instead, the Kremlin proved ready to use any means necessary short of direct confrontation, and to exploit its hegemonic power to the full, in order to protect its energy interests in the CIS/Central Asian space. On the other hand, while Moscow succeeded in preventing Central Asian gas from competing directly with Russian gas in the lucrative European markets, it could not forestall the development of alternative markets for Central Asian gas in Asia, once pipelines were set in place. As a result, China emerged in the 2010s as a significant buyer of Central Asian gas, allowing Turkmenistan, Kazakhstan and Uzbekistan to diversify their exports away from the CIS and break loose from clutches of the Russia-dominated ex-Soviet gas pipeline system. Azerbaijan, in turn, was able to expand its sales to Turkey and potentially to Southern Europe through the newly expanding European Southern Corridor (TANAP/Trans-Adriatic) pipeline system. Russia's attempts to revive the ex-USSR energy system, which seemed to have succeeded in the 2000s, thus started to falter in the mid-2010s, as both CIS gas consumers and producers moved away from the Russian gas market. This new predicament underscored the limits of Russia's neo-imperialist project and showed its inability fully to restore its influence and hegemony over the former Soviet space in the energy field. Yet, its lack of success should not conceal the significant efforts that the Kremlin made when trying to establish a unified CIS energy grid under its control. There is little doubt that Russia proved ready to use all sorts of *hard power* instruments in order to pursue its interests in the CIS energy space, in a clear display of its hegemonic power.

Notes

1 The Transdniestrian region was responsible for most of Moldova's energy debts (Bruce and Yafimava, 2009).
2 Gazprom refused to sign a new gas contract unless Moldova gave up the ECT Third Energy Package (Sobják, 2013; Rodkiewicz, 2012, pp. 2–3).
3 Yanukovych also revoked decrees that had given the controversial figures of Stepan Bandera and Roman Shushkevich the tile of 'Heroes of Ukraine'.
4 Turkmen gas sales to China rose from 3.5 Bcm in 2010 to 20 Bcm in 2012, reaching 25.9 Bcm in 2014 and 31.7 Bcm in 2017 (Tabatska, 2015; Pirani, 2014, p. 355).

Bibliography

Agence France Presse (AFP) (2002). Putin calls for energy alliance with Central Asian gas producers. 21 January.
Aslund, A. (2015). *Ukraine: What Went Wrong and How to Fix it*. Washington DC: Peterson Institute for International Economics.
Baev, P. (2008). *Russian Energy Policy and Military Power: Putin's Quest for Greatness*. London and New York: Routledge.
Balmaceda, M.M. (2009). *Energy Dependency, Politics and Corruption in the Former Soviet Union: Russia's Power, Oligarchs' Profit, and Ukraine's Missing Energy Policy, 1995–2006*. Milton Park, Abingdon and New York: Routledge.
BBC (2014a). Ukraine Crisis: Russia Halts Gas Supplies to Kiev. 16 June. Available at: www.bbc.com/news/av/world-europe-27871910/ukraine-crisis-russia-halts-gas-supplies-to-kiev [accessed 18 June 2018].
BBC (2014b). Russia-Ukraine Gas Deal Secures EU Winter Supply. 31 October. Available at: www.bbc.com/news/business-29842505 [accessed 18 June 2018].
Bowden, J. (2009). Azerbaijan: From Gas Importer to Gas Exporter. In: S. Pirani, ed. *Russian and CIS Gas Markets and their Impact on Europe*, Oxford: Oxford University Press, Oxford Institute of Energy Studies, pp. 203–234.
Bruce, Ch. And K. Yafimava (2009). Moldova's Gas Sector. In: S. Pirani, ed. *Russian and CIS Gas Markets and their Impact on Europe*. Oxford: Oxford University Press, Oxford Institute of Energy Studies, pp. 170–202.
Business Report (2010). Russia rejects merging rival gas pipelines. 16 March. Available at: www.iol.co.za/business-report/economy/russia-rejects-merging-rival-gas-pipelines-813151 [accessed 22 November 2018].
Butrin, D. (2003). *Kommersant*, 27 August, p. 1.
Butrin D. and Grib, N. (2005a). *Kommersant*, 29 March, p. 1.
Butrin, D. and N. Grib (2005b). *Kommersant*, 22 June, p. 1.
de Carbonnel, A. (2016). EU Mediates Russia, Ukraine Gas Dispute Talks. 9 December. www.reuters.com/article/ukraine-crisis-russia-gas/eu-mediates-russia-ukraine-gas-dispute-talks-idUSL5N1E4316 [accessed 18 June 2018].
De Micco P. (2014). The Russian-Ukrainian Gas Deal: Taking the Bite Out of Winter? 14 November. Available at: www.europarl.europa.eu/RegData/etudes/BRIE/2014/536415/EXPO_BRI(2014)536415_EN.pdf [accessed 18 June 2018].

Drakakhrust. Y. (2016). Cheap gas for Belarus — What's the Real Price? 1 September. Available at: www.opendemocracy.net/od-russia/yuri-drakakhrust/cheap-gas-for-belarus-what-s-real-price [accessed 18 June 2018].

Dubien, A. (2007). *The Opacity of Russian-Ukrainian Energy Relations*. Russie.Nei. Visions. Paris: IFRI, 19, May.

Dubnov, A. (2002). *Vremya Novostei*, 22 January, p. 1.

Gevorgyan, T. (2014). Russian Energy Giant Captures Armenian Market. IWPR. 24 January. Available at: https://iwpr.net/global-voices/russian-energy-giant-captures-armenian-market [accessed 18 June 2018].

Gordiyenko, A. and Baikova, Ye. (2003). *Nezavisimaya gazeta*, 9 June, p. 6.

Gorst, I. (2003). *Platt's Oilgram News*, 11 April, 81(70), p. 1.

Government of Russian Federation (GRF) 2000. Osnovnye polozheniya Energeticheskoi strategii Rossii na period do 2020 goda. 23 November. Available at: http://old.nasledie.ru/fin/6_2/6_2_1/article.php?art=21 [accessed 11 November 2017].

Government of Russian Federation (GRF) (2003). Energeticheskaya strategiya Rossii na period do 2020 goda. 28 August. www.minprom.gov.ru/docs/strateg/1 [accessed 12 October 2018].

Grib, N. and O. Gavrish (2008). *Kommersant*, 17 January, p. 1.

Grib, N., O. Gavrish and A. Konstantinov (2008). *Kommersant*, 14 March, p. 1

Grib, N., O. Gavrish and S. Yegikyan (2009). *Kommersant*, 10 April, p. 1.

Grigoryeva Ye. and Ye. Korop (2003). *Izvestiya*, 11 April, p. 3.

Grivach, A. (2007). *Vremya novostei*, 28 November, p. 7.

Grivach, A. (2008). *Vremya novostei*, 5 March, p. 1.

Grivach, A. and I. Gordeyev (2005). *Vremya novostei*, 15 December, p. 1.

Gubenko, O. (2001). *Izvestiya*, 5 October, p. 2.

Interfax (2003). Ukrainian and Turkmen Leaders Agree Long-term Deal to Boost Gas Cooperation. 12 April.

Ivzhenko, T. (2005). *Nezavisimaya gazeta*, 24 August, p. 5.

Kommersant (2005). 22 April, p. 9.

Konarzewska, N. (2015). Russia's Gazprom to Deepen Its Presence in the Georgian Market? The CACI Analyst. 7 December. Available at: www.cacianalyst.org/publications/analytical-articles/item/13311-russias-gazprom-to-deepen-its-presence-in-the-georgian-market?.html [accessed 18 June 2018].

Kulikov, S. (2008). *Nezavisimaya gazeta*, 12 March, p. 6.

Kulikov, S. and S. Sklyarov (2007). *Nezavisimaya gazeta*, 25 June, p. 4.

Len, O. (2002). *Konservator*, 11–17 October, p. 5.

Mazneva, E. (2014). Gazprom Raises Gas Export Price as Ukraine Looks for Cash. *Bloomberg*. April 1. Available at: www.bloomberg.com/news/articles/2014-04-01/gazprom-raises-gas-export-price-as-ukraine-looks-for-cash [accessed 18 June 2018].

Mitrova, T., S. Pirani and J. Stern (2009). Russia, the CIS and the Europe: Gas Trade and Transit. In S. Pirani, ed. *Russian and CIS Gas Markets and their Impact on Europe*, Oxford: Oxford University Press, Oxford Institute of Energy Studies, pp. 395–441.

Mitrova, T. (2014). The Political and Economic Importance of Gas in Russia. In: J. Henderson and S. Pirani, eds. *The Russian Gas Matrix: How Markets are Driving Change*. The Oxford Institute for Energy Studies, Oxford University Press, pp. 6–38.

Mordyushenko, O. (2008). *Kommersant*, 4 March, p. 1.

Netreba, P. (2002). *Kommersant*, 8 June, p. 2.

Netreba, P. and O. Gavrish (2006). *Kommersant*, 25 October, pp. 1, 3.

Nuțu, A.O. (2016). Interconnecting Moldova's Gas Market: The Iasi-Ungheni Case. Chisinau: Expert Group. February. Available at: www.expert-grup.org/ro/biblioteca/item/download/1511_d3527cd3fb892d86a39ec496490692c0 [accessed 18 June 2018].
Panfilova, V. and A. Krashakov (2006). *Nezavisimaya gazeta*, 18 January, p. 3.
Panfilova, V. and N. Melikova (2004). *Nezavisimaya gazeta*, 17 May, p. 6.
Perovic, J. (2006). 'Russian Energy Companies in the Caspian and Central Eurasian region'. In: A. Wenger, J. Perovic and R. Orttung, eds. *Russian Business Power: The Role of Russian Business in Foreign and Security Relations*, London and New York: Routledge, pp. 88–113.
Pereplesnin, M. and Ye. Yashin (2000). *Nezavisimaya gazeta*, 30 March, p. 5.
Perovic, J. (2006). 'Russian Energy Companies in the Caspian and Central Eurasian region'. In: A. Wenger, J. Perovic and R. Orttung, eds. *Russian Business Power: The Role of Russian Business in Foreign and Security Relations*, London and New York: Routledge, pp. 88–113.
Pirani, S. ed. (2009). *Russian and CIS Gas Markets and their Impact on Europe*, Oxford: Oxford University Press, Oxford Institute of Energy Studies.
Pirani, S. (2012). Central Asian and Caspian Gas Production and the Constraints on Export. The Oxford Institute for Energy Studies. December. Available at: www.oxfordenergy.org/wpcms/wp-content/uploads/2012/12/NG_69.pdf [accessed 18 June 2018].
Pirani, S. (2014). Central Asia and Caspian Gas for Russia's Balance. In: J. Henderson and S. Pirani, eds. *The Russian Gas Matrix: How Markets are Driving Change*. The Oxford Institute for Energy Studies, Oxford University Press, pp. 347–367.
Pirani, S. and K. Yafimava (2014). CIS Markets and Transit. In: J. Henderson and S. Pirani, eds. *The Russian Gas Matrix: How Markets are Driving Change*. The Oxford Institute for Energy Studies, Oxford University Press, pp. 181–215.
Pirani, S. and K. Yafimava (2016). *Russian Gas Transit Across Ukraine Post-2019: Pipeline Scenarios, Gas Flow Consequences, and Regulatory Constraints*. The Oxford Institute for Energy Studies. February.
Pirani, S., Stern, J. and K. Yafimava (2009) *The Russo-Ukrainian Gas Dispute of January 2009: A Comprehensive Assessment*. The Oxford Institute for Energy Studies. February.
Puiu, V. (2014). Moldova Struggles to Escape Russian Gas. 25 September. Available at: https://eurasianet.org/s/moldova-struggles-to-escape-russian-gas [accessed 18 June 2018].
Putin, V.V. (1999). 'Mineralno-syrevye resursy v strategii razvitiya Rossiiskoi ekonomiki,' *Zapiski Gornogo Instituta*, 144, 1999, 3–9. In: Harley Blazer, Vladimir Putin's Academic Writings and Russian Natural Resource Policy. *Problems of Post-Communism*, January/February 2006, 53(1), 48–54.
Ratiani, N. (2005). *Izvestiya*, 15 August, p. 2.
Reuters (2016). Russia and Belarus Close to Solving Gas Price Dispute – Minister. 30 November. Available at: www.reuters.com/article/russia-belarus-gas-idUSL8N1DV19D [accessed 18 June 2018].
RFE/RL (2007). Central Asia: Russian, Turkmen, Kazakh Leaders Agree On Caspian Pipeline. 12 May. Available at: www.rferl.org/a/1076429.html [accessed 16 June 2018].
RFE/RL (2010). Armenian Premier Expecting Another Rise In Russian Gas Price. 12 September. Available at: www.rferl.org/a/Armenian_Premier_Expecting_Another_Rise_In_Russian_Gas_Price_/2155348.html [accessed 17 June 2018].
RFE/RL (2016). Armenia, Iran Sign Deal To Increase Gas Imports, Power Flows. 3 November 2016. www.rferl.org/a/armenian-iran-sign-deal-increase-gas-imports-power-flows/28092312.html [accessed 18 June 2018].

Ritchie, M. (2007). Russia-Belarus Deal Averts Gas Crisis. 2 January. In: *European Spot Gas Markets*, London. 3 January.

Roberts, J. (2004). Pipeline Politics. In: S. Akiner, *The Caspian: Politics, Energy and Security*, Abingdon New York, RoutledgeCurzon, pp. 77–89.

Rodkiewicz, W. (2012). Russia's Strategy Towards Moldova: Continuation or Change? OSW Commentary. 74, 19 April. Available at: www.osw.waw.pl/sites/default/files/commentary_74.pdf [accessed 10 June 2018].

Rukhadze, V. (2016) Russia Pushes Hard to Capture South Caucasus' Energy Markets. *Eurasia Daily Monitor*, 13(13), 20 January. https://jamestown.org/program/russia-pushes-hard-to-capture-south-caucasus-energy-markets/ [accessed 18 June 2018].

Rukhadze, V. (2017) Georgia Signs Unfavorable New Natural Gas Transit Deal With Russia. *Eurasia Daily Monitor*, 14(3), 19 January. Available at: https://jamestown.org/program/georgia-signs-unfavorable-new-natural-gas-transit-deal-russia/ [accessed 18 June 2018].

Rybalchenko, I. (2002). *Kommersant*, 23 November, p. 1.

Sepashvili, G. (2003). Georgia-Gazprom Deal Signed: Surprise News to Rebound on the Government. *Civil Georgia*, 25 July. Available at: www.civil.ge/eng/article.php?id=4642 [accessed 12 October 2018].

Simonyan, Yu. (2005). *Nezavisimaya gazeta*, 15 September, p. 5.

Sharip, F. (2018). Faced with Chinese Expansion, Kazakhstan Seeks Alternative Energy Markets. *Eurasia Daily Monitor*, 15, 65. 30 April. https://jamestown.org/program/faced-with-chinese-expansion-kazakhstan-seeks-alternative-energy-markets/ [accessed 18 June 2018].

Sherman, A. (2015). Central Asian Gas Increasingly Reliant on Chinese Market. *Petroleum Economist*. 30 June. Available at: www.petroleum-economist.com/articles/politics-economics/asia-pacific/2015/central-asian-gas-increasingly-reliant-on-chinese-market [accessed 18 June 2018].

Shirin, A. ed. (2004). *The Caspian: Politics, Energy and Security*. Milton Park, Abingdon: RoutledgeCurzon.

Shiryayev, V. (2000). *Noviye Izvestiya*, 19 April, p. 1.

Sobják, A. (2013). The Romania-Moldova Gas Pipeline: Does a Connection to the EU Mean a Disconnect from Russia? PISM, 93(546), 9 September www.pism.pl/files/?id_plik=14567 [accessed 17 June 2018].

Stern, J.P. (2005). *The Future of Russian Gas and Gazprom*, Oxford: Oxford Institute for Energy Studies.

Stern, J. (2006). *The Russian-Ukrainian Gas Crisis of January 2006*. Oxford: Oxford Institute for Energy Studies, p. 4, 6, 7. Available at: www.oxfordenergy.org/wpcms/wp-content/uploads/2011/01/Jan2006-RussiaUkraineGasCrisis-JonathanStern.pdf [accessed 12 October 2018].

Stern, J. (2009). The Russian Gas Balance to 2015: Difficult Years Ahead. In: S. Pirani, ed. *Russian and CIS Gas Markets and their Impact on Europe*, Oxford: Oxford University Press, Oxford Institute of Energy Studies, pp. 54–92.

Tabatska, D. (2015). Turkmenistan: The Diversification of Gas Export Markets, 16 December. www.naturalgasworld.com/turkmenistan-the-diversification-of-gas-export-market-27160#snews [accessed 16 June 2018].

Tokmazishvili, M. and J. Bowden (2009). Georgia's Gas Sector. In S. Pirani, ed. *Russian and CIS Gas Markets and their Impact on Europe*, Oxford: Oxford University Press, Oxford Institute of Energy Studies, pp. 256–270.

Useinov, A. (2003). *Nezavisimaya gazeta*, 28 February, p. 5.

Useinov, A. and A. Denisov (2000). *Vremya MN*, 17 February, p. 1.
Veletminsky, I. (2006). *Rossiiskaya gazeta*, 7 April, p. 2.
Woehrel, S. (2009). Russian Energy Policy Toward Neighbouring Countries. CRS Report for Congress. 2 September. Available at: https://fas.org/sgp/crs/row/RL34261.pdf [accessed 19 September 2018].
Wall Street Journal (*WSJ*) (2015). EU Energy Chief Plays Down Practicality of Proposed Russia-Turkey Pipeline. 22 January. Available at: www.wsj.com/articles/eu-official-plays-down-practicality-of-proposed-russia-turkey-pipeline-1421951735?ns=prod/accounts-wsj [accessed 18 June 2018].
Yafimava (2010). The June 2010 Russian-Belarusian Gas Transit Dispute: A Surprise that Was to be Expected. Oxford Institute for Energy Studies. July. Available at: https://pdfs.semanticscholar.org/7a20/9d9ceec3c7ff77cdf1399484d2642428aa9e.pdf?_ga=2.172153447.53715142.1565812281-504452744.1565812281 [accessed 16 June 2018].
Yeghiazaryan, A. (2009). Natural Gas Markets in Armenia. In S. Pirani, ed. *Russian and CIS Gas Markets and their Impact on Europe*, Oxford: Oxford University Press, Oxford Institute of Energy Studies, pp. 235–255.
Yenikeyeff, Sh. (2009). Kazakhstan's Gas Sector. In S. Pirani, ed. *Russian and CIS Gas Markets and their Impact on Europe*, Oxford: Oxford University Press, Oxford Institute of Energy Studies, pp. 316–354.
Zayets, I. and O. Komotsky (2005). *Noviye Izvestia*, 5 April, p. 4.
Zhukov, S. (2009). Uzbekistan: A Domestically Oriented Producer. In: S. Pirani, ed. *Russian and CIS Gas Markets and their Impact on Europe*, Oxford: Oxford University Press, Oxford Institute of Energy Studies, pp. 355–394.

13 The Russian–Georgian war and its aftermath
Russia's neo-empire

In August 2008, Russia for the first time since the end of the USSR sent its forces beyond its borders into a former Soviet state (FSS). Russia conducted a massive campaign in the Georgian separatist regions of South Ossetia and Abkhazia, in clear violation of international law. The military operation was followed by the recognition of these two regions' independence by Moscow, and by their almost de facto integration into the Russian Federation orbit. The outbreak of war in Georgia also brought a renewed sense of urgency to the Nagorno-Karabakh conflict, located in the South Caucasus neighbourhood. In order to avoid an escalation of violence around Nagorno-Karabakh President Medvedev, engaged in a sustained and tireless effort to find a negotiated outcome to the dispute, which however, did not prove very successful. In April 2016, violence significantly escalated in the separatist region, prompting Russia's immediate diplomatic intervention. While the situation around Transdniestria also became tense in the aftermath of the Georgian war, a new opportunity for a full resolution of the conflict presented itself in 2010 with the Meseberg initiative, which however, failed to see the light of day when Putin returned to the Presidency in 2012. This chapter examines in greater detail the nature of Russia's engagement in these conflicts and the extent to which Russia was able to establish a sphere of influence over Georgia, Moldova, Armenia and Azerbaijan, as a result of its actions.

Russia's War in Georgia

The year 2008 witnessed the first major military engagement by Russian forces beyond the country's borders, in a former Soviet state, since the collapse of the USSR. Russia conducted a massive military campaign in Georgia's separatist regions, South Ossetia and Abkhazia, in August 2008, allegedly to protect the South Ossetian (and the Abkhaz) minorities from a major Georgian onslaught. Hostility and exchanges of fire, however, had been escalating in the separatist region since 2006, and immediate responsibility for the outburst of violence remains difficult to ascertain. Nevertheless, the Kremlin's actions were carried out in open violation of international law, and were undoubtedly intended, to keep Georgia within Russia's sphere of influence. The underlying objective of Russia's military actions soon became clear – to prevent Georgia from turning completely to the West by becoming a member of NATO and emerging as a key strategic ally of the Unites States on Russia's southern flank. As such, Russia's military actions partly succeeded in fulfilling the Kremlin's strategic aims – Georgia's membership of NATO was postponed indefinitely while Russia managed to keep a strong foothold over Georgia's two separatist regions. Right after the conflict, Moscow moved ahead with the recognition of the separatists' regions' independence, as this allowed Russia, at least theoretically, to station its military forces on their territories for an indefinite period of time. Thereafter, Russia initiated a process of almost complete de facto absorption of these regions into Russia, again in clear violation of international law and in contravention of the September 2008 ceasefire agreements. However, while South Ossetia and Abkhazia became to all intents and purposes part of Russia, Georgia instead continued in its turn towards the West, by enhancing its ties with NATO (through the establishment of a NATO–Georgia Commission) and strengthening its cooperation with the EU, as shown by the Association Agreement (AA) it signed with the EU in 2014.

Who started the 2008 August war? While all expert reports seem to agree on the fact that the Georgian army launched a significant attack on South Ossetia at around 23.30 hours on 7 August, it remains unclear what exactly happened between the declaration of a ceasefire by Georgian President Mikhail Saakashvili at around 19.00 hours, and the outbreak of violence at around 23.30 hours (Fawn and Nalbandov, 2012, p. 58.) The evidence available seems to indicate that Georgia was trying to avoid engaging in a direct war with either South Ossetia or Russia. On 7 August, in a televised appearance, Saakashvili appealed to South Ossetians and Russians to engage in talks in any format they wished, 'direct, multilateral, whatever works', and urged them 'to give peace and dialogue a chance', while agreeing on an immediate unilateral ceasefire (Sukhov, 2008). As tensions increased and war seemed imminent, Saakahsvili sent his special envoy, Temuri Yakobashvili, to South Ossetia to talk peace with the South Ossetian leader, and to put end to the violent attacks on Georgian policemen and Georgian civilians. But this proved to be of no avail, as the Ossetians refused to engage in any direct talks, other than through the Joint Control Commission (JCC) format, where Russia, their patron, retained a predominant voice. Although shootings and attacks ceased at around 19.30 hours when a ceasefire was called by Saakashvili, exchanges of fire resumed at around 22.00 hours, and at around 23.30 hours Georgian armed forces launched a large-scale attack.

The Georgian attack was presented by Tbilisi as a counter-offensive against South Ossetian aggression, because, in its view, 'no procrastination, not a single additional trip to Tskhinvali' would have produced any additional positive results (Fawn and Nalbandov, 2012, p. 77). There was a clear sense by then in Tbilisi that all diplomatic efforts to bring the conflict peacefully to an end had been exhausted. Nevertheless, it could also be argued that Georgia took the opportunity to put a definitive end to South Ossetia's relentless attacks against the Georgian population living in South Ossetia, by trying to restore full control over the separatist region once and for all. There is little doubt that Georgia's patience had by then run out and that many in Tbilisi were looking for the right opportunity to re-occupy the separatist region, including Defence Minister Davit Kezerashvili, Tbilisi Mayor Gigi Ugulava, and head of the National Security Council of Georgia Alexander Lomaia.[1] On the evening of 7 August, Georgia mobilised over 11,000 troops and equipment very close to the South Ossetian border, in what appeared to be a clear determination to 'restore constitutional order' over the region (Latynina, 2008a; Percy, 2012). The war in South Ossetia, therefore, did not come as an unexpected surprise to Tbilisi. Since 2004, Georgia had been improving, quite substantially, its military capabilities and its military equipment with NATO's support. Therefore, it cannot be entirely ruled out, that Georgia was planning to engage in a massive attack sometime in August to retake control over the region of South Ossetia, but the outbreak was accelerated by the turn of events in the late evening of 7 August, as noted by Russian journalist Yuliya Latynina (2008b).

Similarly, there is overwhelming evidence showing that Russia was also preparing for war against Georgia. On 29 April 2008, Russia set up additional peacekeeping posts in Abkhazia and increased the number of peacekeepers to 3,000 troops (albeit within the limits of the 1994 agreement) arguing that there had been increased provocations against Russian troops deployed in the area from Georgian paramilitaries. Russia justified its actions on the grounds that Georgia had been building up its forces in direct proximity to the two conflict zones in the towns of Gori and Senaki (Belov, 2008). Russia also argued that Georgia was exceeding the strength of military and police units in the upper part of the Kodori Gorge in Abkhazia, and that spy planes were flying regularly over Abkhazia to inspect the area (UNSC, 2008). In early May 2008, Russia also dispatched over 500 Russian paratroopers armed with infantry fighting vehicles, artillery guns and air-defence systems to Abkhazia to reinforce the Russian peacekeeping contingent, in clear violation of the CIS peacekeeping agreement (Solovyov and Dvali, 2008). On 30 May 2008, Moscow sent an additional 400-men strong military railway unit into Abkhazia to rehabilitate the railroad between Sukhumi and Ochamchira and to repair the bridges over the Kodori and Mokva rivers. In late July 2008, Russia withdrew its military railway troops, once the repairs had been completed, but on 11 July 2008, Moscow took further measures to 'increase the combat readiness' of the Russian peacekeeping forces deployed to Abkhazia, allegedly in response to growing tensions in Abkhazia and to persisting provocations against Russian peacekeepers by Georgian militias (*Civil Georgia*; 2008a). Between 15 July and 2 August 2008, Russian troops once again carried out a large-scale military training exercise in the North Caucasus, near the Georgian border and on the Black Sea, this time involving 10,000 troops from the North Caucasus Military District (Sapir, 2015). The United States and Georgia, in turn, held a USA-led military exercise 'Immediate Response' at the Vaziani base in mid-July 2008, involving approximately 2,000 troops from Georgia, the USA, Armenia, Azerbaijan and Ukraine, with the intent of sending a clear message to the Kremlin and hopefully deterring a Russian military attack on Georgia. which seemed imminent at the time. Russia, in turn, completed the construction of a 'military rehabilitation centre' in Tskhinvali, and also established a military base at Ugardanta in the Java district. The base saw the arrival of Russian advisers and military officers in late July 2008 (EU, 2009, p. 207; ICG, 2008, p. 1, 4). By August 2008, therefore, Russia had deployed the necessary infrastructure and logistical support for an invasion of Russian troops into Georgia's separatist regions (Allison, 2008, p. 1149). An elite paratrooper battalion and Russian special forces arrived in South Ossetia *before* the massive Russian ground invasion, which occurred quite swiftly after 'news' of a Georgian attack reached the Russian top leadership in the early hours of 8 August. The operation involved the equivalent of a motor-rifle division of the 58th Army based in the North Caucasus, as well a Black Sea naval task force, all of which were assembled and deployed with extraordinary rapidity, including the dispatch of elements of the 76th Air Assault Division from the Leningrad Military District (Allison, 2008, p. 1150). All this seems to indicate that Russia already had developed an integrated combat plan for military action, which most probably also involved the cooperation of the South Ossetian militias. However, the existing evidence, so far, does not fully elucidate who 'pulled the trigger' first at around 22.30 hours on 7 August 2008, and therefore it is difficult to determine, with certainty, who took the initiative and who is responsible for the immediate outbreak of the war.

What is certain, nevertheless, is that both Russia and Georgia had contingency plans for military action, and both proved ready to use force when it seemed as though all other diplomatic means had been exhausted, and when resorting to violence remained as the only plausible course of action. Tbilisi's main objective when resorting to the use of force was to restore control over the separatist region of South Ossetia, frustrated over years of unsuccessful negotiations, and concerned over South Ossetia's 'creeping annexation' by Russia. The Georgian government also sincerely worried over the relentless attacks against Georgian civilians by South Ossetian militias (Percy, 2012). Russia, in turn, proved eager not only to protect the local population from a possible Georgian assault, but also to ensure that South Ossetia – and Abkhazia – remained under Russia's direct control, as this allowed Russia to keep a military presence in Georgia and, in this, way extend its influence over the region and prevent Georgia's membership of NATO. This was clearly admitted by President Medvedev in 2011, when he noted that had it not been for the actions of the Russian military 'the geopolitical situation would be very different now... and a number of countries which [NATO] tried deliberately to drag into the alliance, would have most likely already been part of it now' (Dyomkin, 2011). It must be also noted that Russia's military actions in Abkhazia – an area which had not experienced a massive Georgian assault – occurred with Abkhazia's full coordination and support, validating the argument that Russia had a predetermined plan to restore Sukhumi's full control over the region, and anchor these regions closely to the Russian state. This line of reasoning is reinforced by the Kremlin's actions immediately after the assault. Moscow subsequently recognised these regions' independent status and moved ahead with establishing very close military, political and economic ties with both South Ossetia and Abkhazia.

Already in April 2008, after NATO's pledges to invite Georgia and Ukraine into the Alliance at the Bucharest Summit, Foreign Minister Lavrov had noted that Russia would 'do everything in our power to prevent the admission of Ukraine and Georgia into NATO' (Sysoyev, 2008). Putin himself also warned NATO leaders at the time of the 2008 NATO Summit against further expanding the Alliance close to Russia's borders, noting that the invitation of Georgia and Ukraine into NATO would be interpreted as nothing less than a direct threat to Russia's national security (Kuzmin, 2008).

A proper assessment of these events, however, would be flawed and incomplete if the war was not examined within the broader historical context which preceded the attack, and if the more recent developments surrounding the conflict regions were not also properly considered. Russia increased its engagement with Abkhazia and South Ossetia already in the early 2000s, in order to improve its security perimeter around the Northern Caucasus, and in order to gain additional strategic depth and, in this way, enhance its own security. As Georgia increased its military ties with the West, Russia expanded its economic ties with Abkhazia and South Ossetia, influenced these regions' internal political developments and, last but not least, provided the two separatist regions with covert and also overt military assistance. The Kremlin's interference only increased after Saakashvili conducted a series of quite assertive policies in South Ossetia and Abkhazia, which risked seriously undermining Russia's presence in these republics and potentially fully dislodging Russia from the region. In 2004, the new Georgian leadership tried to restore Georgia's unity and to retake control over the separatist regions through a combination of coercive pressures, or *hard power*, and attractive policies, or *soft power*, which were not always conducted in accordance with the existing ceasefire agreements – which had been reached in 1992 in South Ossetia and in 1994 in Abkhazia. In the face of strong Russian opposition and great Western concern, especially after violence escalated around South Ossetia in the summer of 2004, Saakashvili was however forced to retreat from his more assertive policies and instead adopt a more conciliatory tone. Thereafter, he tried to establish a direct dialogue with the conflicting parties, albeit bypassing Russia, and presented the sides with new and more attractive conflict-settlement proposals. He also attempted to enlist Western support and assistance to pursue his 'reintegration' agenda and dislodge Russia from the area. To Saakashvili's benefit and advantage, his more assertive actions coincided with a period of increased interest in the West, especially in the USA, for developments in the South Caucasus region. The United States, in particular, looked carefully at the geo-strategic orientation of the South Caucasus and Caspian Sea regions, given their energy potential and their increased strategic relevance after the 9/11 attacks and the wars in Afghanistan and Iraq. This resulted in an increased American military involvement not only in Georgia but also in neighbouring Azerbaijan. Such a predicament created great concern in Moscow and led to fears that Russia would be further dislodged from the South Caucasus, a region of great strategic significance to its own security, thus leaving its sensitive southern flank rather vulnerable and exposed. It pushed Russia to act more forcefully, actively engaging and protecting the separatist regions, while at the same time trying to deter Georgia from using force against them – in a clear indication that Russia saw the area as falling within its sphere of influence, to the point of possibly pursuing a policy of 'exacerbated tensions' in the separatist regions, in order to prevent Georgia from acquiring NATO membership.

In order to be able to keep a military presence in the area, unchallenged and for an indefinite period of time, Russia ended up unilaterally recognising the independence of Abkhazia and South Ossetia on 26 August 2008 (Izvestiya, 2008). While Russia withdrew its troops from the 'buffer zones' adjacent to South Ossetia and Abkhazia soon after the end of the hostilities on 12 August, it nevertheless kept a significant military presence inside these 'newly-recognised' republics (Dubnov, 2008; ICG, 2011, p. 5). Furthermore, Moscow vetoed the extension of the UN's UNOMIG (United Nations Mission in Georgia) to Abkhazia and the OSCE's mission to South Ossetia, in a clear sign that it now considered these areas as direct 'protectorates' under its undisputed influence and tight control (Civil Georgia, 2008b). An EU Monitoring Mission (EUMM) of military observers was deployed to conduct patrols along the administrative borders of Abkhazia and South Ossetia, but it was not able to operate in those areas that were controlled by Russia and by the de facto authorities, as had been stipulated in its original mandate. More importantly, through a series of bilateral agreements reached with Sukhumi and Tskhinvali in September 2008 and September 2009, Russia guaranteed for itself a long-term – almost indefinite – military presence in both Abkhazia and South Ossetia in the form of military bases, military deployments, joint military contingents, and border patrolling (ICG, 2010a, pp. 3–5, 2010b, pp. 7–9; Gerrits and Bader, 2016, p. 302). To all intents and purposes, these regions, became almost integral parts of Russia. Russia took over the full protection of these regions' external perimeters (RFE/RL, 2009), provided South Ossetia and Abkhazia with massive economic and military support (Sozayev-Guryev, 2015; ICG 2013a, pp. 3–7), and ensured that Russian officials – mostly from the *siloviki* or security structures, occupied key positions in the government institutions of these republics (ICG, 2010a, 2010b, pp. 9–11; Preobrazhensky, 2009). These new realities on the ground, which contravened the Medvedev–Sarkozy September 2008 ceasefire agreements, thwarted any substantial advancement in negotiations on the 'stability and security' of the separatist regions, which were held after the end of the hostilities within a joint UN, OSCE and EU negotiating framework in Geneva. They significantly reduced the ability of the international community to influence events in Georgia's separatist regions, despite the deployment of an EU mission on the ground in Georgia.

Furthermore, Russia succeeded in ensuring the emergence of elites almost entirely loyal to Russia, who proved ready to move their republics further down the path of closer integration with Russia, even though the Kremlin was not always able fully to control political outcomes in these new 'republics', as indicated by the victory of the independent candidate, Alla Dzhioyeva, in the November 2011 South Ossetian Presidential elections (Allenova, 2011). Yet, Moscow succeeded in reaching all-encompassing agreements with Sukhumi in

November 2014 and with Tskhinvali in 2015, which almost *de facto* incorporated these regions, in the economic, cultural, legal and military and security fields, into Russia (Sozayev-Guryev, 2015; The Kremlin, 2014). Any semblance of 'independence' of these republics was purely formal, especially as far as South Ossetia was concerned, whose leaders proved eager to join their ethnic brothers in Russia's North Ossetia and form a single state. The Abkhaz, instead, remained slightly more concerned over being fully subsumed into Russia, and therefore challenged their region's complete absorption into their northern bigger neighbour, jealous of their ancient territory and their rich natural resources. Russia's economic and military penetration of the republic, nevertheless, remained quite high. While Russia did not go as far as officially annexing these republics – as it did with Crimea in 2014 – the far-reaching agreements reached in 2014 and 2015 nevertheless consolidated Russia's presence in these republics. This Russian move was spearheaded by Georgia's further rapprochement with the EU, which was manifested in the signing by Tbilisi of the EU's Association and free trade agreements in 2013–2014. It also responded to Georgia's closer ties with NATO, which further expanded in the aftermath of Russia's annexation of Crimea and the outbreak of war in Donbass in 2014.

Attempt to resolve the Nagorno-Karabakh conflict

When he became President of Russia, Medvedev conducted the 'longest sustained mediation effort' in the history of the Nagorno-Karabakh peace negotiations (Remler, 2016, p. 99). Between 6 June 2008 and 23 January 2012, he hosted 11 of the 15 meetings between the Azerbaijani and Armenian Presidents Ilham Aliyev and Serzh Sargsyan (Remler, 2016, p. 100). Trying to resolve the Nagorno-Karabakh conflict allowed Medvedev to mend Russia's tarnished image after the Russian–Georgian 2008 war, 'by presenting [Russia] as a responsible regional power' (ICG, 2009, p. 4). More importantly, the 2008 Russian–Georgian war brought a renewed sense of urgency to the Nagorno-Karabakh conflict, given the potential of a spill over of conflict to the rest of the South Caucasus. To that end, on 2 November 2008, Medvedev negotiated the signing in Moscow of a declaration by the Armenian and Azerbaijani leaders, which foresaw a commitment by the sides to find a *political* resolution to the conflict on the basis of the OSCE *Prague* and *Madrid Principles* (Fuller, 2008). The value of the declaration also lay in the fact that it was the first agreement in paper signed by Armenia and Azerbaijan since the 1994 ceasefire agreement (*Newsru.com*, 2008). It indicated Russia's commitment to play a positive role in the Karabakh conflict, by promoting peace and stability in the South Caucasus, in the wake of the August war with Georgia.

With the arrival of President Obama to the American Presidency in 2009, and the 'reset' in Russian–American relations, new opportunities for cooperation between Russia and its Western partners over Nagorno-Karabakh once again presented themselves. Both sides agreed to collaborate constructively in the resolution of the Nagorno-Karabakh conflict, within the OSCE Minsk framework. All three co-Chairs shared the vision that the conflict had to be resolved peacefully, through negotiations, and in compliance with the *Madrid Principles*. Therefore, in 2009, French and American co-chairs 'put aside [their] previous suspicions' and accepted a 'subordinate position in what became a Russian-led process'. It soon became clear that the French and American leaders were not ready to devote the same amount of time and effort to the Karabakh conflict as Medvedev was prepared to (Remler, 2016, p. 101). This new predicament was facilitated by the Western perception that Medvedev's main objective in the negotiations was to 'boost Russia's prestige and earn him credentials as a statesman', rather than to expand Russia's sphere of influence in the South Caucasus as was suspected, had been Putin's aims when previously formulating Russia's policy towards the region (Remler, 2016, p. 100). During 2009–2011, the USA, France and Russia, therefore succeeded on several occasions – at the G-8 Summit in L'Aquila (Italy) in 2009, and again at the G-8 Summit in Muskoka (Canada) in 2010 – in presenting a united front, by agreeing on common principles that had to guide the resolution of the dispute, and this helped to push the negotiating process forward (OSCE, 2009, 2010a).

Yet, the various proposals introduced to the sides in 2010 and 2011 – even a watered-down version of the Madrid Principles devised by Russian Foreign Minister Sergei Lavrov in August 2010 and agreed by the OSCE co-Chairs – failed to get the support of the conflicting sides. The leaders – and the populations – of Azerbaijan, Armenia and Nagorno-Karabakh continued to resist any significant adjustments to their original positions. Therefore, little progress was made at the various intensive rounds of talks that were held between the Armenian and Azerbaijani sides during 2009 and 2011, despite great efforts conducted by Medvedev and his foreign policy team led by Sergei Lavrov to try to convince Baku and Yerevan to agree to a compromise. Finding a resolution to the conflict became all the more urgent, as violence intensified along the line of contact, the number of casualties increased, and the rhetoric turned increasingly belligerent in 2010 and 2011. Medvedev and the other Minsk co-chairs made a last effort in the run up to the summit in Kazan on 24 June 2011 to reach agreement 'on those basic principles whose text had supposedly been agreed in previous meetings' (Remler, 2016, p. 109). Yet, they proved unsuccessful. The media characterised the Kazan summit's outcome as a blow to Russia's prestige and to the countless efforts made by President Medvedev to resolve the conflict (de Waal, 2013, p. 302). However, the failure has to be primarily attributed to the continued changes in the positions of the conflicting sides. Russia's countless attempts at reaching a final solution seemed to indicate that the Kremlin was ready to discard previous more assertive Russian policies in the region and abandon its neo-imperial approach vis-a-vis Armenia and Azerbaijan. President Medvedev worked hard to find alternative solutions of compromise and effectively coordinated positions with the other OSCE co-Chairs in order peacefully to resolve the dispute.

A new opportunity for a breakthrough in the negotiations emerged in the autumn of 2009, as a result of the Turkish–Armenian *rapprochement*, which also had strong OSCE backing. On 10 October 2009, Turkish and Armenian leaders signed two protocols normalising their relations, in front of the three Minsk co-Chairs' Foreign Ministers. The two protocols stipulated that mutual borders would be recognised and reopened, and that diplomatic relations between the two countries would be established, two months after the ratification of the protocols by their respective parliaments (de Waal, 2013, pp. 299–300, Remler, 2016, p. 105).[2] An important stumbling block to the implementation of the protocols, however, was related to the Nagorno-Karabakh dispute. The protocols purposefully made no specific mention of the Nagorno-Karabakh conflict, in order to avoid touching upon a very complex and sensitive issue for both Armenia and Turkey, Azerbaijan's historical ally in the region. However, the Nagorno-Karabakh war had been the reason behind the introduction of the Turkish blockade on Armenia in the first place (in 1993), and therefore the Turkish–Armenian normalisation process was bound to become linked to the Karabakh dispute and to any progress being made on that front. Azerbaijan worried that the establishment of diplomatic relations between Armenia and Turkey and the opening of the Armenian–Turkish border would reduce the pressures on Yerevan to make the necessary compromises over Nagorno-Karabakh. Immediately after the protocols were signed, President Aliyev therefore began exerting great pressure on Ankara to ensure that the Nagorno-Karabakh dispute became part of the normalisation process, and this included full consideration of Azerbaijan's position (Alekeperova, 2009). Aliyev's efforts to derail the process unless Azerbaijan's interests were taken into account, forced Ankara to change its position and insist that the border with Armenia could not be reopened until Armenians withdrew from some of the territories they occupied in Azerbaijan (Remler, 2016, p. 105). However, the Armenian side refused to move on the Nagorno-Karabakh front and to make any significant concessions without Stepanakert's approval. More importantly, it declined to make the Karabakh dispute part of the 'normalisation' process and this delayed Turkey's ratification of the protocols, and Turkey's ability to become an active mediator in the dispute.

By the time Putin returned to the Presidency in 2012, the Nagorno-Karabakh settlement process had reached a deadlock, and there was little evidence that a peaceful outcome of the dispute could be achieved soon. Strong and coordinated international pressure was lacking, and there was great disappointment and fatigue among the Minsk co-Chairs. Limited progress in the negotiations prompted the sides to look for alternative ways in which they could achieve their political objectives. Both Armenia and Azerbaijan built their militaries, enhanced their rhetoric, and fell back on nationalist positions. While Azerbaijan considered taking the occupied territories by force, Armenia contemplated conducting a pre-emptive strike to prevent Azerbaijan from attacking Karabakh. Russia, in turn, continued to sell substantial amounts of weaponry to both Armenia and Azerbaijan, further heightening tensions. Efforts by the OSCE co-Chairs to engage with the sides produced little of significance besides keeping the dialogue between the two sides open (*Nezavisimaya gazeta*, 2013). However, when exchanges of fire escalated dramatically along the ceasefire line in late July 2014, Putin for the first time in his third Presidency, intervened directly in the dispute. His active mediation efforts and his pressures on both

Armenia and Azerbaijan succeeded in stopping the violence and convincing the two sides to reaffirm their commitment to a peaceful resolution of the Karabakh dispute (RFE/RL, 2014). Russia's particularly close relations with the sides, and Putin's ability to exert strong pressure over Armenia and Azerbaijan gave Russia an edge in the negotiating process.

During 2015, the Kremlin decided to revive bilateral negotiations between the two sides worried over the constant escalation of tensions along the ceasefire line and concerned over the threat of instability spreading to the entire South Caucasus region. Russia's military engagement in Syria, which had begun in September 2015, and the persistence of violence in the Donbass region of Ukraine made the search for a peaceful outcome of the Karabakh dispute all the more pressing. Foreign Minister Lavrov became once again fully engaged in the diplomatic efforts aimed at reaching a peaceful settlement of the simmering conflict. France and the United States gave their support to Lavrov's initiatives, even though doubts remained regarding Russia's intentions, and its adequate consideration of other Minsk co-Chairs in the negotiations (ICG, 2016, pp. 7–8). However, Moscow did pay lip service to the Minsk Group format to ensure that its proposals gained increased legitimacy and obtained respectability internationally (ICG, 2016, p. 8). Nevertheless, there was little coordination by the Kremlin with the other Minsk co-Chairs, if only because of the sharp worsening of relations between Russia and the West after the annexation of Crimea and the outbreak of war in east Ukraine. The Russian *Lavrov Plan*, however, revolved around the partial implementation of the OSCE Madrid Principles, although it also proposed the deployment of a Russian-led peacekeeping force (ICG, 2016, p. 8). The possibility was also discussed of deploying Collective Security Treaty (CSTO) peacekeeping forces in Nagorno-Karabakh (Mukhin, 2015), suggesting a return to the Russian policies of the early 1990s, which had been characterised by efforts to deploy a Russian force in the separatist region. However, Lavrov's proposals failed to succeed. Disagreement remained between the warring sides, primarily over the final status of Nagorno-Karabakh, the timing and sequencing of the implementation of the *Madrid Principles*, and in particular, the schedule for the withdrawal of Armenian troops from the occupied lands (Broers, 2016, p. 9).

The first day of April 2016 saw a significant escalation of violence along the entire line of control in Nagorno-Karabakh, as exchanges of fire quickly erupted into an all-out military confrontation between the two sides, when Azerbaijan conducted a carefully prepared offensive which took Armenians in Nagorno-Karabakh by surprise. While the EU and the OSCE issued statements condemning the violence and the OSCE Minsk Group co-Chairs held consultations in Vienna to try to stop the conflagration, Russia became the main architect of the cessation of hostilities. As soon as violence broke out on 1 April, President Putin and his Defence and Foreign Ministers exerted great direct pressure on the warring sides demanding them immediately to stop the violence, while a few days later, on 4 April, Russia held large-scale military exercises not far from the Azerbaijani border in order to send a clear message to the sides not to escalate the hostilities further. Finally, on 5 April, after Putin personally persuaded both sides to put an end to the violence, a ceasefire agreement was signed in Moscow by the Armenian and Azerbaijani Army Chiefs of Staff (ICG, 2016, p. 3). Many commentators saw Russia's actions as initiatives implemented 'in spite of, rather than through, the Minsk group' (Broers, 2016, p. 26). Yet, because of its regional proximity, geo-strategic weight and ability to exert effective pressure on the sides, Russia proved to be the most effective actor, capable of putting an end to the war and bringing the sides to the negotiating table.

After the April 2016 violent flare up, the Kremlin again promoted negotiations among the sides in order to reduce regional tensions and prevent a return to violent conflict. Putin worked both within the OSCE Minsk framework, and also directly with the conflicting sides. In May 2016, the OSCE co-Chairs succeeded in brokering a meeting with the Azerbaijani and Armenian Presidents in Vienna, where the sides agreed to implement a series of confidence-building measures (CBMs) to avoid a sudden escalation of violence. Russia's role at the Vienna talks, as noted by Oleg Matveichev (2016), 'proved decisive', although concerted efforts by the all OSCE co-Chairs also turned out to be determinant. The Minsk co-Chairs reached out to the sides and urged them to agree to the various de-escalating measures being proposed. Thereafter, Putin resumed his direct encounters with the Azerbaijani and Armenian sides, and also succeeded in orchestrating a trilateral encounter with the two Presidents, Ilham Aliyev and Serzh Sargsyan in St Petersburg on 20 June 2016 (ICG, 2016 p. 15). At the meeting, the sides reiterated their support for the agreements reached at the OSCE talks in Vienna, which were aimed at stabilising the situation in the conflict area and creating 'an atmosphere conducive for moving the peace process forward' (PRA, 2016). Yet no additional substantial commitments were made. The sides, however, agreed to continue meeting in this trilateral arrangement to supplement the existing OSCE Minsk co-Chairs' set up.

It remained unclear, however, whether the new Russian-led format would actually support, or instead, undermine the OSCE efforts (ICG, 2016, p. 17). The St. Petersburg meeting had been brokered primarily by President Putin, while the Minsk co-Chairs had been invited to take part only in the final part of the encounter. Theoretically, there had been coordination with the Minsk co-Chairs, but according to the *International Crisis Group* (ICG), France and the US were not fully involved in the planning of the meeting. As noted by the relevant ICG Report, 'This manifested the prima inter pares role Russia seems to pursue in the conflict settlement process: leading on diplomatic initiatives and committing heavyweight political resources to back them up, while formally keeping the Minsk-Group format' (ICG, 2016, p. 17). Russia was clearly displaying its hegemonic power in the region, although it could as well be argued that Russia had a legitimate interest in avoiding a resurgence of violence. At the same time, Moscow was forced to adjust its relations with Armenia, which resented Russia's behaviour and sharply criticised the Kremlin's sale of sophisticated military equipment to Azerbaijan, as well as Russia's military and economic rapprochement with Baku, which was seen as endangering their strategic partnership.

Moscow had by then established a strong military alliance with Armenia and kept an important military presence in that country, which reinforced their strategic bilateral and multilateral partnership within the CSTO framework. Armenia also hosted on its territory sophisticated Russian defence systems, effectively under the control of Russian forces based in Armenia, as part of the CSTO pact. Furthermore, Russian state companies had invested and owned several key strategic assets in Armenia, including railways, electricity networks, nuclear power stations and gas pipelines, and this allowed Moscow potentially to exert strong influence over Yerevan (de Waal, 2008). At the same time, Russia also developed a comprehensive partnership with Azerbaijan, which was sealed in an agreement reached in Baku by Presidents Medvedev and Aliyev in July 2008. To Azerbaijan's satisfaction, the agreement emphasised that the Nagorno-Karabakh conflict had to be resolved 'on the basis of international law, through the OSCE's Minsk group and with due respect for national sovereignty and territorial integrity' (Kuzmin, 2008). Russia also became an important source of military equipment for Azerbaijan – between 2010 and 2013, Russia delivered Baku an estimated total of $3billion–$4billion worth of Russian-made weaponry (ICG, 2013b, p. 5). To Russia's concern, however, Azerbaijan simultaneously also expanded its cooperation with NATO – it participated since 2008 in NATO's defence education programmes and in 2014 it joined NATO's Partnership Interoperability Initiative, together with other partners which participated in NATO operations. Within NATO's Planning and Review Process (PARP) process, Azerbaijan trained military units in accordance with NATO standards, and provided force contributions for NATO-led peace-support operations in Iraq and Afghanistan. In the energy sphere, Azerbaijan continued to sell most of its oil and gas to Western and global markets by-passing Russia, despite repeated efforts by Moscow to link Azerbaijan's gas sector closely to Russia.[3] In other words, Azerbaijan was able, because of its energy resources, and economic growth, to remain more independent from Russia.

On the other hand, in order to keep a strategic balance between the two South Caucasus states, Russia also sent a significant amount of armaments to Armenia, Russia's key regional ally and Azerbaijan's opponent, leading many to argue that Russia was effectively fuelling an arms race in the region, and therefore was responsible for the outbreak of violence in 2016. There seems to be no significant evidence, however, indicating that Russia tried to manipulate the situation around Nagorno-Karabakh in order to provoke an escalation of tensions and produce an outbreak of conflict, despite what eventually occurred in April 2016. Yet, it can be convincingly argued that Moscow's sales and deliveries of weaponry did exacerbate regional tensions and heightened concerns. Nevertheless, Russia remained the undisputable dominant actor in the region, the only one capable of enforcing a cessation of hostilities. Russia was simultaneously the mediator, the main arms supplier to both sides, and the holder of several leverages of influence, especially over Armenia, but also over Azerbaijan (de Waal, 2008).

The fate of Transdniestria

In the spring of 2008, the situation around Transdniestria became tense again, in view of developments in Georgia, and the expansion of official ties between the

Kremlin and the separatist entities of South Ossetia and Abkhazia. However, while the Russian Duma issued a declaration in March 2008, in support for Abkhazia's and South Ossetia's independence, the Russian Lower House declined to make similar calls for Transdniestria, most probably because Moldova was not seen as reaching out for NATO membership and for strategic alignment with the United States (Allenova, 2008; Hill, 2012, p. 175). Furthermore, a 'peaceful resolution' of the dispute was seen as more probable given the lower level of tensions on the ground in Transdniestria. Nevertheless, Moscow continued to provide economic and diplomatic support to Transdniestria while also increasing the level of diplomatic and governmental contacts with separatist officials in Tiraspol (Hill, 2012, p. 175). With the change of government in Chisinau, and the appointment of a new Prime Minister, Vlad Filat in September 2009, the process of CBMs implementation within the OSCE framework gathered speed, as Filat adopted a much more pragmatic approach and focused its efforts on resolving practical issues. During 2010 and 2011, over 20 meetings were held by the OSCE Joint Expert Working Groups on CBMs, 'in a contrasting atmosphere devoid of political wrangling'. This resulted in the implementation of several CBM measures that expanded bilateral ties (Neukirch, 2012, p. 141). Progress was also facilitated by the various bilateral high level encounters between Moldovan Prime Minister Filat and Transdniestria's de facto leader, Igor Smirnov, which were held in 2010 and 2011.

A major opportunity for the political resolution of the conflict presented itself in 2010 with the launch of the *Meseberg Initiative* by German Chancellor Angela Merkel and Russian President Dmitry Medvedev. The agreed Memorandum proposed the establishment of a pan-European institution – a *EU-Russia Political-Security Committee* (PSC) – intended to establish a dialogue of equals between the Russia and the EU on fundamental questions of European security, including finding a resolution to the Transdniestrian conflict (Devyatkov, 2012, p. 56). The objective was to set up an institution which would make Russia feel less isolated and more integrated in Europe, to be accompanied by further trade promotion and visa liberalisation policies between Russia and the EU. Advancement on this proposal, however, was made conditional upon progress on the resolution of the Transdniestrian conflict. Russia saw this as a unique chance to institutionalise its presence and influence in the European security framework, and therefore collaborated quite actively with the OSCE, within the 5+2 format, in order to ensure a final settlement of the Moldovan/Transdniestrian dispute. Strong pressure was exerted by the Kremlin on the Transdniestrian leadership to accept a compromise solution which kept the region inside Moldova, going as far as supporting an alternative leadership to de facto President Igor Smirnov to guarantee that a final agreement on status could be reached. Moscow also made it abundantly clear to Transdniestria that the region's independence was no longer a possible alternative, significantly altering Russia's long-held positions. Russia even showed a readiness to change the peacekeeping format of troops deployed in Transdniestria, place its forces under OSCE mandate and, if required, replace its troops with police forces. The withdrawal of Russian troops belonging to the OGRF from Transdniestria if the separatist conflict was solved was also considered by the Kremlin.

All this indicated that Russia was much more interested in securing for itself an influential place in the European security framework, than ensuring the 'independence' and 'well-being' of Transdniestria, even at the expense of abandoning its presence in the separatist region. It confirmed the view that Russia's actions in Moldova, and in Transdniestria more specifically, were closely intertwined with developments in the European continent, primarily in the security field. Russia's efforts to keep Moldova and Transdniestria under its sway had above all an instrumental role – to guarantee Russia's military security, prevent NATO's enlargement and ensure Moscow's influence in European affairs. Yet, despite substantial efforts by all sides – the EU, Germany and Russia – the Transdniestrian negotiations, however, failed to make any progress, because of persistent disagreements over the question of the separatist region's status inside Moldova. Furthermore, fundamental differences remained between Moscow and Berlin over the EU–Russia PSC's nature and its functions. While Germany envisaged the PSC as a 'deliberating' body, which would address pressing security issues and provide methods of cooperation on resolving 'conflicts and crisis situations', Russia, instead, was proposing a 'commission' of 27 + 1, which would operate on the basis of consensus, thus potentially granting Russia a veto over European security affairs (Remler, 2013). This proved to be unacceptable to Germany, and to Europe as whole. Key differences between Russia and Europe on the nature of the PSC made it hard for the project to advance. The whole Meseberg enterprise eventually floundered with the return of Vladimir Putin to the Russian Presidency, given his increased scepticism of the West, and even of Europe's best intentions.

During President Putin's third term, the Kremlin once again altered its policy and returned to a more obstructionist stance on Transdniestria. This entailed keeping a strong Russian military presence in the separatist region and ensuring a political arrangement that gave Tiraspol – and indirectly Russia – a strong say in Moldovan affairs. In March 2012, Russian nationalist politician Dmitry Rogozin was named Russia's Special Representative to Transdniestria. His appointment was accompanied by Kremlin's commitments to increase Russian economic aid to the region. It also followed plans to establish a more formalised institutional relationship between Russia and the separatist region, which entirely bypassed Moldova's jurisdiction (Socor, 2012b; Gamova and Roks, 2012). Rogozin also put forward a comprehensive plan which involved granting Transdniestria 'equal rights' (*ravnopravnyi*) as a partner in the negotiations, while conferring the separatist region 'federal or confederal' status. Russia wished to see Transdniestria as a 'special district', within 'a Moldovan neutral state', in the words of Russia's Deputy Foreign Minister Grigory Karasin (Solovyov, 2012). This new policy was interpreted by Chisinau as an attempt to force Moldova into agreeing very unfavourable terms on Transdniestria, which could potentially lead to the recognition of the region's independence by Russia. Russia's actions were also intended to put pressure on Moldova to join the Russian-led Eurasian Union, in a clear display of Russia's hegemonic power (Gamova, 2012b).

Moldova, however, continued to insist on a negotiated solution to the Transdniestrian conflict, which granted broad autonomy to the separatist region within a unified Moldovan state. Furthermore, Chisinau persisted in its calls for a replacement of the Russian peacekeeping forces by civilian observers to be deployed under international supervision (Khimshiashvili, 2012; *Nezavisimaya gazeta*, 2012). Chisinau also asked for the withdrawal of the Russian troops – the OGRF (Operational Group of Russian Forces), previously the 14th Army – from Transdniestria (Gamova, 2013a). While Russia expressed a readiness to start removing once again the ammunition of the OGRF that had remained stored in the region (Gamova, 2012b), the Kremlin's special envoy made it clear that Moscow refused to accept any changes in the peacekeeping format. In Rogozin's own words, 'We will never allow anyone to dispute Russia's mandate in this matter, or the exclusive rights [of Russia] to provide security in this region [Transnistria]' (Socor, 2012b), in a clear testament to his neo-imperialist mindset. Rogozin's April 2012 proposal also recognised Russia 'as the only country with political and military authority in the region', while at the same time it reduced the role of other 'external' actors, such as the EU or the United States in the negotiations, to a secondary position (Socor, 2012a). Furthermore, the Kremlin expected – or more precisely demanded – that Moldova refrained from joining any external 'blocs', such as the EU or NATO, and that it desisted from uniting with Romania (Socor, 2012a). Russia made it very clear that if unification with Moldova occurred, or if Moldova joined NATO, Russia would revisit the question of Transdniestria's right to self-determination and most probably would recognise Transdniestria's independent status (Gamova and Roks, 2012; Gamova, 2012d).

Russia's renewed attention to Transdniestria, however, reflected Putin's concerns over developments in neighbouring Romania, where President Traian Băsescu – a strong supporter of the reunification of what he called the 'two Romanias' (Romania and Moldova) – had at the time expressed clear wishes to reinvigorate the 'unification' project. Although the project was not officially promoted by Romanian Prime Minister Victor Ponta, closer economic and military ties between the two countries were fostered, especially after the pro-Western Alliance for European Integration (AIE) came to power in Moldova in the autumn of 2009 (Gamova, 2014a). Russian leaders also remained concerned over Romania's NATO membership which had brought the alliance closer to Russia's and the CIS' south-western borders (Gamova, 2012a). The accession of Romania and Bulgaria to NATO in 2007 had been accompanied by an increased military presence of the United States in these two countries (Moldovan *et al.*, 2009; Kaufman, 2010). In 2007–2008, Romania and Bulgaria agreed to share 'forward operating sites' with the USA, which the American military could use whenever it is considered necessary with the consent of their respective governments (Moldovan *et al.*, 2009, p. 15).[4] Russia also worried over the potential inclusion of Moldova into NATO, if the unification of Moldova with Romania moved ahead. Not only was Moldova strengthening military ties with Romania, it was also expanding its military cooperation with NATO, despite its official neutrality (Gamova, 2013a). Furthermore, when tensions around Transdniestria significantly increased in 2013, the possibility of Moldova's membership of NATO started to be openly discussed. In view of Russia's involvement in neighbouring Ukraine in the winter of 2013/2014 and in response to the increased pressures exerted by Russia on Moldova over its EU Associate membership, Defence Minister Vitale Marinuta openly stated in January 2014 that Moldova should abolish its neutrality and become integrated into NATO (Gamova, 2014b).[5]

With the Russian annexation of Crimea in March 2014, Chisinau began seriously discussing the possibility of abandoning its neutrality and joining NATO to protect the country from a potential Russian military incursion (Gamova, 2014e). Concern over Moldova's future grew after Tiraspol demanded that the Russian Parliament include provisions on Transdniestria's integration into Russia, in the Russian legislation drafted to facilitate the annexation of Crimea into the Russian Federation (*Moscow Times*, 2014). There was talk in Moscow and concern in the West at the time, that after annexing Crimea, the Kremlin would move its forces all the way to the Moldovan border, occupying not only the Donbass, Kherson, Zaporozhie and Odessa but eventually also Transdniestria. Russia, however, refrained from such an undertaking. It did not move ahead with the incorporation of additional regions of Ukraine and Transdniestria into Russia, if only because of the challenges it was encountering in eastern Ukraine. Its efforts to influence developments in its favour in Kharkiv, Lugansk and Donetsk and in other Russian-speaking regions of Ukraine became extremely difficult, and at the same time, the violent conflict in the Donbass became increasingly intractable. Furthermore, the new government in Kiev no longer allowed Russian troops to access Transdniestria through Ukrainian territory, and all this made Russia's ability to operate and defend Transdniestria a lot harder (de Waal, 2016).[6] Russia, however, succeeded in keeping a foothold in the Transdniestrian region. It not only maintained a military presence in the form of 400 peacekeeping troops and over 1,500 servicemen belonging to the OGRF. It also remained the main provider of state funding – it helped pay local pensions and government salaries, and continued subsidising the sale of Russian gas (de Waal, 2016). Moscow also retained a capacity to influence political Transdniestrian affairs – it successfully diffused an internal struggle between two groups vying for power in December 2016, and the summer of 2017 it sent Federal Security Service (FSB) operatives to take up positions in the Transdniestrian security apparatus (Popșoi, 2017). Moreover, as military ties between Moldova and NATO allies, particularly with the United States, expanded in 2016–2017, Russia increased the intensity of its military drills in Transdniestria, with the full involvement of the OGRF, in order to send a clear message to Moldova not to join NATO, and to the West, to stay out of the region and not infringe upon Russia's traditional sphere of influence (Popșoi, 2018; Gamova, 2017b).

The OSCE, in turn, concerned over a potential spill over of violence, orchestrated the adoption, during the German Presidency in 2016, of the Berlin

Protocol – a series of CBMs intended to defuse tensions and improve the daily life of citizens across the mutual border (de Waal, 2018). More significantly, in February 2016, an agreement was reached with Brussels which ensured that trade between the EU and Transdniestria would continue unhindered after Tiraspol's especially negotiated preferences with the EU expired on 1 January 2016, as a result the entry into force of Moldova's Association Agreement with the EU. Tiraspol agreed to a two-year transition period before it adopted a new trading regime which met key aspects of the Moldovan-EU 2014 free trade deal (de Waal, 2016). While an effective and pragmatic solution was found by the EU to this predicament, tensions over the geo-strategic direction of Moldova and the fate of Transdniestria remained. By the mid-2010s, there was an increased overlap of the EU and the Russian 'Near Abroads' in this region, with Moldova developing closer ties with the EU and NATO, and Moscow enhancing ties with Transdniestria. Interestingly, while Transdniestria's inhabitants felt close cultural affinities and political allegiances to Russia, they increasingly fostered commercial ties with Moldova and the EU. In 2012, 29 per cent of the region's exports went to the EU, while only 22 per cent were directed to Russia (Beyer and Wolff, 2016, p. 343). The election of Igor Dodon, a pro-Russian candidate to the Moldovan Presidency in December 2016 seemed to alter, at least temporarily, the country's geo-strategic paradigm. Dodon supported the restoration of a strategic partnership with Russia and called for Moldova's membership of the Eurasian Economic Union (EAEU). He insisted on upholding Moldova's 'neutral' status, while also trying to block Moldova's military cooperation with NATO. More significantly, Dodon did not call for the withdrawal of Russian forces from Transdniestria, and instead proposed the 'federalisation' of his country, through the establishment of a tripartite internal state structure involving Transdniestria, Gagauzia and the rest of Moldova. However, Dodon's ability to implement his pro-Russian foreign policy vector was impaired by Moldova's internal institutional arrangements. His authority was restrained by the Moldovan Constitution, which granted only limited powers to the Presidential office. The Moldovan government, instead, remained in charge of policy, and was able, despite the reduced support that it enjoyed at the time among the local population, to push ahead with its pro-Western agenda, which entailed enhancing cooperation with NATO and the EU, keeping, in this way, Moldova outside Russia's sphere of influence. Furthermore, after the Russian annexation of Crimea and outbreak of war in the Donbass, Ukraine emerged as a new key regional actor directly challenging Russia's policies in Moldova and promoting Transdniestria's full reintegration into the rest of Moldova – in 2017, Kiev introduced joint police and customs checkpoints together with Moldova along the Transdniestrian segment of the Moldovan–Ukrainian border, helping Chisinau to restore control over the separatist region's external trade (Gamova, 2017b; Popșoi, 2017). Russia, in turn, insisted on keeping its troops in Transdniestria, and pushed for the granting of 'special status' to the region inside Moldova, emulating its proposals for the Lugansk People's Republic (LNR) and Donetsk People's Republic (DNR) in Ukraine, as a way of keeping the Transdniestrian region, and Moldova, under its sphere of influence.

Assessment and concluding thoughts

In August 2008, Russia for the first time since the end of the USSR attacked a FSS, in clear violation of international law. The Kremlin conducted a massive campaign in the Georgian separatist regions of South Ossetia and Abkhazia, ostensibly to protect the South Ossetian and Abkhaz minorities, but essentially to further its geo-strategic objectives. Moscow's actions were intended to prevent Georgia from becoming a member of NATO and joining the Euro-Atlantic institutions in full. As such, Russia's military actions embodied a clear neo-imperialist project and indicated a readiness by Russia to go as far as using military force to fulfil its strategic objectives. While it could well be argued that Russia was pursuing legitimate state interest when engaging militarily in Georgia – stopping the violence, avoiding additional casualties among the South Ossetians, and preventing an exacerbation of tensions along its sensitive southern borders – such a line of argument does not stand up to scrutiny, as Russia was also partly responsible for the rise in tensions around the separatist regions of Georgia. Although immediate responsibility for the outburst of violence in August 2008 remains difficult to ascertain, there is little doubt that hostility and exchanges of fire had been escalating in the separatist region since 2006, with Russia contributing quite significantly to such enduring instabilities.

Similarly, while it could also be contended that Russia had a legitimate right to intervene in Georgia in order to ensure that the NATO alliance did not reach its most sensitive borders in the North Caucasus, its responses – a large-scale military action – were certainly disproportionate when measured up to the immediate threat faced by Russia. More importantly, Russia's actions did not conform with acceptable international practices and undoubtedly violated international law. As such, they reflected a clear neo-imperialist behaviour. Yet, as a result of its military intervention, the Kremlin succeeded in fulfilling its most immediate strategic aims – Georgia's membership of NATO was postponed indefinitely, its armed forces were significantly weakened, if not totally destroyed, and it was forced out of its two separatist regions, Abkhazia and South Ossetia. Furthermore, Moscow managed to keep a strong foothold in Abkhazia and South Ossetia, almost open-endedly, thus allowing it to exert pressure over Tbilisi and keeping, to a certain extent, Georgia under its influence. Right after a ceasefire was signed, Moscow moved ahead with the recognition of the separatists' regions' independence, and immediately proceeded with the stationing of substantial military forces in the new 'republics'. Thereafter, Russia initiated a process of almost complete absorption of these regions into Russia, in contravention to the September 2008 ceasefire agreements, and in clear violation of international law. Russia's neo-imperialist paradigm, therefore, reached full circle, and appeared almost complete. However, while South Ossetia and Abkhazia became to all intents and purposes Russian 'protectorates' and almost fully integrated into the Russian state, Moscow undoubtedly lost control over the rest of Georgia. Thereafter, Tbilisi strengthened its alignment with the West, enhanced its ties with NATO and fully developed its economic cooperation with the EU, thus moving out of the Russian sphere of influence and showing the limits of Russia's strategic reach. Although a more pliant leadership came to power in Tbilisi in October 2012, the country remained essentially within the Western geo-strategic orbit.

The outbreak of war in Georgia brought a renewed sense of urgency to the Nagorno-Karabakh conflict, located in the South Caucasus neighbourhood. Starting in 2009, President Medvedev engaged in a sustained and tireless effort to find a negotiated outcome to the dispute, by presenting to the sides a series of alternative versions of the previously agreed OSCE *Madrid Principles*. While the work of the Minsk Group was severely hindered by the outbreak of the August 2008 war, the improvement in US–Russian ties under President Barack Obama in 2009 helped to break the deadlock. Significant advancements in the dispute-resolution talks were initially made, as both Armenia and Azerbaijan agreed to cooperate constructively in the resolution of the Nagorno-Karabakh conflict, bilaterally and within the OSCE Minsk framework. As former US Minsk co-chair, Deputy Assistant Secretary of State for European Affairs, Matthew Bryza, echoed in May 2009, 'As difficult as our relations are with Russia with regard to Georgia, they are equally positive with regard to Nagorno-Karabakh' (ICG, 2009, p. 4) All OSCE co-Chairs, including Russia, shared the vision that the conflict had to be resolved peacefully, through negotiations, and in compliance with the Madrid Principles, and this seemed to indicate that Russia was ready to discard its imperial legacy in the region. Russia, moreover, did not press ahead with the introduction of a Russian peacekeeping force, although there was little doubt that Russia would have remained a key guarantor state in any future settlement that was reached, and this would have given it strong leverage.

Yet, despite these collaborative efforts and in spite of Medvedev's relentless support and direct engagement in the process, the various proposals presented to Armenia and Azerbaijan in 2010 and 2011, failed to get the support of the conflicting sides. Instead, the mid-2010s saw a significant escalation of violence which resulted eventually in the outbreak of full-fledged war in early April 2016. The Kremlin directly intervened in the dispute and successfully mediated an end to the violence, through the exercise of Putin's strong diplomatic pressure. This episode once again showed Russia's overriding influence over both Armenia and Azerbaijan and its ability to exercise effectively its regional hegemonic power. It clearly indicated that both Armenia and Azerbaijan were firmly placed under Russia's sphere of influence, if only because of their significant dependence on Russia for their own security and for regional stability. Armenia, furthermore, remained strongly attached to Russia both economically and geo-strategically. Russia controlled key sectors of the Armenian economy and the country was firmly entrenched within the Russian-led CSTO security arrangement. Once violence de-escalated, President Putin remained fully engaged in the negotiations, trying to reduce tensions and prevent a resumption of violence in a clear display of Russia's hegemonic strength in the region. While Vladimir Putin played lip-service to the OSCE negotiating format, it was he who took the initiative in the talks to end the hostilities and who engaged in direct bilateral and trilateral diplomacy with the conflicting sides in order to reduce tensions. Yet, Moscow's active engagement in the Karabakh dispute permitted violence on the ground to stop and tension to be kept in check. It can, therefore, be argued that the Kremlin's actions not only followed neo-imperialist ambitions, they also, quite undoubtedly reflected legitimate state security concerns – guaranteeing stability in the South Caucasus region – besides fostering Russia's geo-strategic ambitions. Yet, it must be noted that Russia's unscrupulous sale of significant sophisticated equipment to both Armenia and Azerbaijan during the 2010s did exacerbate regional tensions. This raises questions regarding Russia's real intensions and its objectives in the region, all of which remain hard to precisely decipher.

In the aftermath of the 2008 Russian/Georgian war, the situation also became tense around Moldova's Transdniestria. Yet, a new opportunity for a full resolution of the conflict presented itself in 2010 with the Meseberg Initiative proposed by the German government. The initiative foresaw the establishment of a pan-European security institution, intended to establish a dialogue of equals between Russia and the EU on fundamental questions of European security. While the setting up of a new institution was made conditional upon the resolution of the Transdniestrian conflict, Russia saw the proposal as a unique opportunity to institutionalise its presence – and influence – in a new European security framework. It therefore collaborated quite actively with the EU and the OSCE in the resolution of the Transdniestrian conflict, going as far as exerting strong pressure on Tiraspol to accept a compromised solution that kept the separatist region inside Moldova. Moscow's actions clearly showed that Russia's efforts to keep Transdniestria under its sway had primarily an instrumental role – namely to keep Moldova under its influence in order to strengthen Russia's security, prevent the advancement of 'hostile' military alliances near the CIS frontier and avoid the deployment of military infrastructure close to Russia's borders. Above all, the objective of Moscow was to rule out Moldova's accession to the EU and NATO. Yet, the pan-European security initiative failed to see the light of day, if only because of fundamental disagreements between Russia and the EU over the nature and functions of the new body, the PSC. As a result, the entire Transdniestrian conflict-resolution project floundered. When Putin returned to the Presidency in 2012, the Kremlin, reverted once again to its traditional more assertive policies towards Moldova – it expanded its military, security and economic ties with Transdniestria and exerted great pressure on Moldova to stay away from any close collaboration with NATO. In an evident display of neo-imperialist behaviour, Moscow made it clear that if Moldova joined NATO or the EU, or if it united with neighbouring Romania, Russia would revisit the question of Transdniestria's status and recognise the secessionist region's right to self-determination (Gamova and Roks, 2012; Gamova, 2012d). Furthermore, Moscow made sure that its peacekeeping and military forces in Transdniestria were not dislodged from the region, as was being demanded by Moldova, while at the same time, its troops collaborated actively with the local Transdniestrian 'armed forces'. Russia's actions, therefore, undoubtedly followed a neo-imperialist design. Yet, it could as well be argued that the Kremlin's actions also reflected legitimate security concerns – in 2008, Romania's (and Bulgaria's) had acceded to NATO and this created great concern in Moscow, as the process was accompanied by the deployment of the United States' military infrastructure in both countries territories. Furthermore, close economic and military ties between Romania (now a NATO member) and Moldova were established after right-wing governments in both countries reached power in the late 2000s, and Moldova adopted a clear pro-European foreign policy vector. This created great concern in Russia. The Kremlin worried that the further expansion of NATO (and of the EU) would also engulf Moldova, directly infringing upon Russia's vital interests in the south-western CIS region. By then, there was a clear overlap between the EU/NATO and Russian 'Near Abroads', with Moldova developing closer ties with the EU and NATO and Moscow expanding ties with Transdniestria. Yet, it must be noted that while Russia's concern over NATO and EU enlargement may have been legitimate, its actions and its assertive behaviour proved disproportionate. It reflected a neo-imperialist mindset among operatives in the Kremlin, who saw Moldova as belonging within Russia's sphere of influence.

Russia's involvement in all these separatist conflicts clearly shows that Moscow saw a Russian military presence and a strategic partnership with all CIS states, including Armenia, Azerbaijan, Moldova and Georgia, as essential for its own security. Russia's vast geographical extension, its ill-defined boundaries, and the difficulties of defending such an immense and unprotected landmass created, among Russians, a strong sense of strategic vulnerability (Eitelhuber, 2009). This perception of weakness and exposure along its borders was reinforced by a history of countless foreign invasions which had befallen the country throughout its existence, more recently during the Second World War. The end of the Warsaw Pact and the withdrawal of Soviet forces from eastern Europe in the early 1990s significantly weakened Russia's strategic defences. Yet, the collapse of the USSR in 1991, and the significant loss of territory which resulted from such an event, eviscerated Russia's defensive capabilities even further, and heightened Moscow's perception of strategic vulnerability. More importantly, it led to concerns that the Russian state itself could also implode if its defences were not strengthened and its internal cohesion was not substantially reinforced. In addition, Russia's NATO's enlargement eastward which began in the late 1990s and continued well into the 2000s, and was accompanied by the deployment of NATO military infrastructure in the close proximity of Russia's borders, further strengthened Russia's perception of being a 'besieged fortress', fully encircled by the West. Within this unfavourable geopolitical predicament, a strategic partnership with the former USSR states, which also included a military presence in those territories, was deemed essential. Only through a tight alliance with the ex-USSR states could Russia's weakened security be reinforced, as these countries were expected to grant Russia an additional layer of security and increased strategic depth. While from a Russian security perspective, such an approach can be seen as legitimate, it nevertheless placed all USSR countries, maybe with the exception of the Baltic States, squarely under Russia's 'natural' sphere of influence. It reinforced the notion that all these countries belonged to a Russian 'neo-Empire'.

Notes

1 Personal interview with local reporters, Tbilisi, September 2009.
2 More controversially, the agreement also called for the establishment of an intergovernmental bilateral commission, which would include both local and international experts, to examine the 'historical dimensions' of the two countries' relations – and this included the Armenian genocide.
3 Agreements were reached on the purchase of Azerbaijani gas by Russia's Gazprom at world market prices, but the volumes were much smaller than those sold via the BTE line.
4 The USA's military were authorised to deploy up to 2,500 soldiers to either Romania or Bulgaria at a time, 'with the possibility that two such groups could overlap for a total of 5,000 for up to 90 days' (Moldovan et al., 2009).
5 Transdniestrian leaders therefore shifted their external priorities in 2012, with emphasis being placed on developing closer relations with Russia and joining the Eurasian Economic Union (EAEU), rather than negotiating a final settlement over their status with Moldova. They turned to Russia for assurances on their security, and proposed Russia to station a military base in Transdniestria (Gamova, 2012c).
6 Ukraine's imposition of tougher restrictions on the entry of individuals on all its borders, including its borders with Moldova's Transdniestria, in order to prevent the entry of armed groups, complicated the lives of Transdniestrians, who found it harder to cross the border into Ukraine. All these factors of contention prompted Tiraspol to suspend its participation in the 5+2 OSCE talks – under the pretext that Chisinau had failed to waive import tariffs on Transdniestrian products, which had been previously introduced.

Bibliography

Alekperova, I. (2009). *Vremya novostei*, 14 October, p. 5.
Allenova, O. (2008). *Kommersant*, 22 March, p. 1.
Allenova, O. (2011). *Kommersant*, 24 November, p. 7.
Allison, R. (2008). Russia Resurgent? Moscow's Campaign to 'Coerce Georgia to Peace', *International Affairs*, 84 (6), 1145–1171.
Belov, P. (2008). *Kommersant*, 26 April, p. 4.
Beyer, J. and S. Wolff (2016). Linkage and Leverage Effects on Moldova's Transnistria Problem, 32 (3), 335–354.
Broers, L. (2016). *The Nagorny Karabakh Conflict Defaulting to War*. London: Chatham House. July.
Civil Georgia (2008a) Russian MOD: Troops in Combat Readiness in Abkhazia, 11 July. Available at: www.civil.ge/eng/article.php?id=18758&search= [accessed 7 October 2018].
Civil Georgia (2008b). Russia Blocks Georgia OSCE Mission Extension. 22 December. Available at: www.civil.ge/eng/article.php?id=20171 [accessed 11 October 2018].
Devyatkov, A. (2012). Russian Policy Toward Transnistria: Between Multilateralism and Marginalization, *Problems of Post-Communism*, 59 (3), 53–62.

Dubnov, A. (2008). *Vremya novostei*, 14 August, p. 1.
Dyomkin, D. (2011). *Reuters*. 21 November. Available at: www.reuters.com/article/idINIndia-60645720111121 [accessed 8 October 2018].
Eitelhuber, N. (2009). The Russian Bear: Russian Strategic Culture and what it Implies for the West, *Connections*. 9 (1), 1–28.
European Union (EU) (2009). *Report: Independent International Fact-Finding Mission on the Conflict in Georgia*. September. Brussels: European Union.
Fawn, R. and R. Nalbandov (2012). The Difficulties of Knowing the Start of War in the Information Age: Russia, Georgia and the War over South Ossetia, August 2008. *European Security*, 21, 1, 12 March, pp. 57–89.
Fuller, L. (2008). 'Moscow Declaration' A Victory For Armenia. Radio Free Europe/ Radio Liberty. 3 November. Available at: www.rferl.org/content/Moscow_Declaration_A_Victory_For_Armenia/1337592.html [accessed 10 October 2018].
Gamova, S. (2012a). *Nezavisimaya gazeta*, 17 April, p. 1.
Gamova, S. (2012b). *Nezavisimaya gazeta*, 18 April, p. 1.
Gamova, S. (2012c). *Nezavisimaya gazeta*, 31 July, p. 1.
Gamova, S. (2012d). *Nezavisimaya gazeta*, 16 October, p. 1.
Gamova, S. (2013a). *Nezavisimaya gazeta*, 25 March, p. 1.
Gamova, S. (2014a). *Nezavisimaya gazeta*, 13 January, p. 7.
Gamova, S. (2014b). *Nezavisimaya gazeta*, 15 January, p. 1.
Gamova, S. (2014e). *Nezavisimaya gazeta*, 4 March, p. 1
Gamova, S. (2017a). *Nezavisimaya gazeta*, 18 July, p. 1.
Gamova, S. (2017b). *Nezavisimaya gazeta*, 3 August, p. 1.
Gamova, S. and Y. Roks (2012). *Nezavisimaya gazeta*, 26 March, p. 2
Gerrits, A.W.M. and M. Bader (2016) Russian Patronage Over Abkhazia and South Ossetia: Implications for Conflict Resolution, *East European Politics*, 32 (3), 297–313.
Hill, W.H. (2012). *Russia, the Near Abroad, and the West: Lessons from the Moldova-Transdniestria Conflict*. Washington DC: Woodrow Wilson Center Press.
International Crisis Group (ICG) (2008). *Russia vs Georgia: The Fallout*. Brussels/Tbilisi, 22 August. Available at: www.crisisgroup.org/europe-central-asia/caucasus/georgia/russia-vs-georgia-fallout [accessed 10 October 2018].
International Crisis Group (ICG) (2009). *Nagorno-Karabakh: Getting to a Breakthrough*. Europe Briefing, 55. Baku/Yerevan/Tbilisi/Brussels. 7 October.
International Crisis Group (ICG) (2010a). *Abkhazia: Deepening Dependence*, 202, Brussels/Tbilisi. 26 February. Available at: www.crisisgroup.org/europe-central-asia/caucasus/georgia/abkhazia-deepening-dependence [accessed 13 October 2018].
International Crisis Group (ICG) (2010b). *South Ossetia: The Burden of Recognition*. Europe Report. 205. 7 June. Available at: https://d2071andvip0wj.cloudfront.net/205-south-ossetia-the-burden-of-recognition.pdf [accessed 10 October 2018].
International Crisis Group (ICG) (2011). *Georgia-Russia: Learn to Live like Neighbours*. Europe Briefing, 65. 8 August. Tbilisi, Moscow, Istanbul, Brussels.
International Crisis Group (ICG) (2013a). *Abkhazia: The Long Road to Reconciliation*, 224, Brussels/Tbilisi. 10 April, Available at: www.crisisgroup.org/europe-central-asia/caucasus/abkhazia-georgia/abkhazia-long-road-reconciliation [accessed 10 October 2018].
International Crisis Group (ICG) (2013b). *Armenia and Azerbaijan: A Season of Risks*. Europe briefing, 71. Baku/Yerevan/Tbilisi/Brussels, 26 September.
International Crisis Group (ICG) (2016). *Nagorno-Karabakh: New Opening, or More Peril*, 239, Baku/Yerevan/Tbilisi/Brussels. 4 July.

Izvestiya (2008). 27 August, p. 1.
Kaufman, S. (2010). Romania Agrees to Host Ballistic Missile Interceptor. America (US Department of State). 4 February. Available at: https://web.archive.org/web/20100210222720/www.america.gov/st/eur-english/2010/February/201002041554 05esnamfuak0.8593866.html#ixzz5QcRY18kw [accessed 8 January 2020].
Khimshiashvili, P. (2012). *Vedomosti*, 19 March.
Kuzmin, V. (2008). *Rossiiskaya gazeta*, 4 July, p. 2.
Latynina, Yu. (2008a). *Ezhednevnyi zhurnal*. 20 November. Available at: www.ejnew.com/?a=note&id=8587 [accessed 13 October 2018].
Latynina, Yu. (2008b). *Ezhednevnyi zhurnal*. 21 November. Available at: www.ejnew.com/?a=note&id=8589 [accessed 10 October 2018].
Matveichev, O. (2016). *Izvestiya*, 19 May, p. 6.
Moldovan, D., P. Pantev and M. Rhodes (2009). *Joint Task Force East and Shared Military Basing in Romania and Bulgaria*. Occasional Paper. 21. George C. Marshall. European Center for Security Studies. August.
Moscow Times (2014). 19 March, p. 1.
Mukhin, V. (2015). *Nezavisimaya gazeta*, 30 September, p. 2.
Neukirch, C. (2012). From Confidence Building to Conflict Settlement in Moldova? Yearbook on the Organization for Security and Co-operation in Europe (OSCE). January.
Newsru.com (2008). 2 November. Available at: www.newsru.com/russia/02nov2008/karabah_print.html#1 [accessed 10 October 2018].
Nezavisimaya gazeta (2012). April 26, p. 2.
Nezavisimaya gazeta (2013). 28 November, p. 2.
OSCE (2009). Statement by the OSCE Minsk Group Co-Chair countries. L'Aquila. 10 July. Available at: www.osce.org/mg/51152 [accessed 10 October 2018].
OSCE (2010a). Statement by the OSCE Minsk Group Co-Chair Countries. Muskoka. 26 June. Available at: www.osce.org/mg/69515 [accessed 11 October 2018].
OSCE (2010b). Joint Statement by the Heads of Delegation of the Minsk Group Co-Chair Countries. 16 July. Available at: www.osce.org/press/72085 [accessed 10 October 2018].
OSCE (2010c). Joint Statement by the Heads of Delegation of the OSCE Minsk Group Co-Chair Countries and the Presidents of Azerbaijan and Armenia. 1 December. Available at www.osce.org/home/74234 [accessed 10 October 2018].
OSCE (2016). Joint Statement of the Minister of Foreign Affairs of the Russian Federation, Secretary of State of the United States of America and State Secretary for Europe Affairs of France. OSCE Minsk Group. 16 May. Available at: www.osce.org/mg/240316 [accessed 10 October 2018].
Percy, N. (2012). *Putin, Russia and the West. Part 3*. Documentary. BBC.
Popșoi, M. (2018). Moldova's Cooperation With NATO—Strategic Choice or Political Tactic? *Eurasia Daily Monitor*, 15 (19), 7 February. Available at: https://jamestown.org/program/moldovas-cooperation-nato-strategic-choice-political-tactic/ [accessed 18 November 2018].
Popșoi, M. (2017). Former Transnistrian Leader Finds Refuge in Moldova Amid Growing Tension in the Region, *Eurasia Daily Monitor*, 14 (91), 12 July. Available at: https://jamestown.org/program/former-transnistrian-leader-finds-refuge-moldova-amid-growing-tension-region/ [accessed 18 November 2018].
Preobrazhensky, K. (2009). South Ossetia: KGB Backyard in The Caucasus. The Central Asia-Caucasus Analyst. 3 March. Available at: www.cacianalyst.org/publications/analytical-articles/item/11799-analytical-articles-caci-analyst-2009-3-11-art-11799.html [accessed 10 October 2018].

President of the Republic of Armenia (PRA) (2016). In Saint Petersburg Presidents of Armenia, Russia and Azerbaijan Made a Joint Statement. 20 June. Available at: www.president.am/en/press-release/item/2016/06/20/President-Serzh-Sargsyan-meeting-with-Presidents-o-Russia-Azerbaijan/ [accessed 10 October 2018].

Remler, Ph. (2013). Negotiation Gone Bad: Russia, German and Crossed Communications. Carnegie Europe. 21 August. Available at: https://carnegieeurope.eu/2013/08/21/negotiation-gone-bad-russia-germany-and-crossed-communications-pub-52712 [accessed 15 May 2018].

Remler, Ph. (2016). *Chained to the Caucasus: Peacemaking in Karabakh, 1987–2012*. New York: International Peace Institute.

RFE/RL (2009). Moscow Signs Defense Pacts With Breakaway Georgian Regions. 15 September. Available at: www.rferl.org/a/Moscow_Threatens_To_Seize_Georgian_Ships_Signs_Defense_Pacts_With_Breakaway_Regions/1823404.html [accessed 11 October 2018].

RFE/RL (2014). Putin Urges Karabakh Peace as Aliyev, Sarkisian Meet in Russia. 10 August. Available at: www.azatutyun.am/a/26523369.html [accessed 10 October 2018].

Sapir, J. (2015) La Guerre d'Ossetie de 2008. Les causes (II). Qui a piege qui?. Blog de Jacques Sapir sur la Russie et l'Europe. 8, August. Available at: https://russeurope.hypotheses.org/4192 [accessed 11 October 2018].

Socor, V. (2012a). Rogozin Details Preconditions to Transnistria Conflict-Resolution. *Eurasia Daily Monitor*, 9 (79), 20 April. Available at: https://jamestown.org/program/rogozin-details-preconditions-to-transnistria-conflict-resolution/ [accessed 10 October 2018].

Socor, V. (2012b). Rogozin Institutionalizing Direct Relations with Transnistria. *Eurasia Daily Monitor*, 9 (79), 20 April. Available at: https://jamestown.org/program/rogozin-institutionalizing-direct-relations-with-transnistria/ [accessed 12 October 2018].

Solovyov, V. (2012). *Kommersant*, 30 July, p. 6.

Solovyov, V. and G. Dvali (2008). *Kommersant*, 7 May, p. 1.

Sozayev-Guryev, Ye. (2015). *Izvestiya*, 19 March, p. 2.

Sukhov, I. (2008). *Vremya novostei*, 8 August, p. 1.

Sysoyev, G. (2008). *Kommersant*, 18 April, p. 9.

The Kremlin (2014). 24 November. Available at: http://kremlin.ru/supplement/4783 [accessed 10 October 2018].

United Nations Security Council (UNSC) (2008). S/2008/480. *Report of the Secretary-General on the Situation in Abkhazia, Georgia*. 23 July. New York: United Nations.

de Waal, Th. (2008). The Karabakh Trap: Dangers and Dilemmas of the Nagorny Karabakh Conflict. *Conciliation Resources*. December. Available at: www.c-r.org/downloads/The%20Karabakh%20Trap_Undated_ENG.pdf [accessed 12 October 2018].

de Waal, Th. (2013). *Black Garden: Armenia and Azerbaijan through Peace and War*. Revised edition. New York and London, New York University Press.

de Waal, Th. (2016). An Eastern European Frozen Conflict the EU Got Right. *Politico Europe*. 16 February. Available at: www.politico.eu/article/transnistria-an-eastern-european-frozen-conflict-the-eu-got-right-moldova-russia-ukraine/ [accessed 10 October 2018].

de Waal, Th. (2018). Moldova's Conflict: Unfreezing, In a Good Way? Carnegie Europe. 6 March. Available at: https://carnegieeurope.eu/strategiceurope/75712 [accessed 11 October 2018].

14 The annexation of Crimea and the war in Ukraine's Donbass

Russia's neo-empire expands

The Russian annexation of Crimean in 2014 and the outbreak of war in the Ukrainian Donbass, with the active, albeit covert, support of the Russian leadership, represented another watershed in the relations of Russia with the former Soviet states (FSS). Not only did Russia once again intervene militarily beyond its borders in clear violation of international law, its actions resulted in the acquisition of neighbouring territory and the escalation of tensions in the eastern regions of Ukraine, which led to the outburst of large-scale fighting. As had occurred in Georgia in 2008, Russia became engaged in Ukraine, allegedly to protect a Russian-speaking minority, in this case from the attacks of Ukrainian far-right forces. While there is little doubt that instances of far-right violence occurred in post-Maidan Ukraine, they did not justify Russia's military intervention. The Kremlin's actions were primarily intended to keep Ukraine within Russia's sphere of strategic interests and prevent it from turning completely to the West by thwarting its Euro-Atlantic aspirations, namely becoming a member of NATO and signing an Association Agreement (AA)/ deep and comprehensive free trade agreement (DCFTA) with the EU. Russia's military actions, as was the case in Georgia, only partly managed to fulfil the Kremlin's strategic aims – Ukraine's membership of NATO was temporarily postponed while Russia succeeded in incorporating Crimea into Russia, its Black Sea Fleet (BSF) at the naval base of Sevastopol indefinitely. Yet, Ukraine continued in its turn to the West, by enhancing its ties with NATO and strengthening its cooperation with the EU, as shown by the AA signing of it AA/DCFTA with the EU in 2014/2015.

Towards the annexation of Crimea

In the summer and autumn of 2013, Russia exerted great pressure on Ukraine to abandon its AA/DCFTA package with the EU, and instead join the Russian-led Eurasian Union, in a clear sign that it wished to keep Ukraine within its sphere of influence. Ukrainian President Viktor Yanukovych's decision in November 2013 to postpone the signing of the EU's AA/DCFTA, however, provoked massive demonstrations in Kiev and several Ukrainian cities, which ultimately led to his fall in February 2014, in what came to be known as 'the revolution of dignity' or EuroMaidan. Circumstantial evidence indicates that Russia played a significant part in pushing Yanukovych to use force against protestors in the Maidan, in the winter of 2014 (Ivzhenko, 2014a, 2014c; Musafirova, 2017), with Russian FSB operatives directly assisting the Ukrainian security service (SBU) counterparts, and helping them forcefully to address the imminent crisis (Ivzhenko, 2014b). The Kremlin's actions had the support of the official Ukrainian authorities, and as such cannot be seen, technically, as an unlawful interference in the internal affairs of Ukraine and as an infringement of its sovereignty. Nevertheless, Russia's actions were all part of an effort by the Kremlin to ensure a Russia-friendly regime, which would keep Ukraine within the Eurasian Union and within Russia's sphere of influence, remained in power in Kiev. To that end, Russia also reduced gas prices to Ukraine by 30 per cent and awarded Ukraine a $15 billion loan through the purchase of Ukraine's Eurobonds (Polukhin, 2014).

The Kremlin called the collapse of the Yanukovych regime an 'armed coup' instigated by the West, named the new Ukrainian government a 'Junta', and withdrew all its monetary support to the new authorities. Throughout the protests, Moscow strongly condemned the violence of 'radical elements' and interpreted their actions as an illegal rebellion. Russian leaders also constantly emphasised the 'fascist' nature of the revolt and its extreme nationalist undertones (Lavrov, 2014b). While there is little doubt that radical 'proto-fascist' forces were part of the anti-government rebellion, it must also be noted that the overwhelming majority of protestors on the Maidan were peaceful, unarmed citizens who had braved months of bitter cold to overturn their extremely corrupt government (Afineevsky, 2015). Yet, the EuroMaidan upheavals produced a series of counter-demonstrations among ethnic Russians and Russian-speakers in several southern and eastern Ukrainian cities, including in the Crimean city of Sevastopol, home to the Russian BSF, which enjoyed Russian support. Worried over the nationalist and 'anti-Russian' undertones of the new leadership and concerned over the spread of 'right-wing' militias, protestors appealed to Russian President Vladimir Putin to protect ethnic-Russians and Russian-speakers in Ukraine from nationalist Ukrainian attacks. While the threat posed by the new Ukrainian leadership to the overall well-being of ethnic Russians and Russian-speakers in Ukraine was often blown out of proportion by pro-Russian agitators, there is little doubt that there were legitimate issues of concern. The new government led by Arseny Yatsenyuk included several members belonging to far-right parties, such as *Svoboda*, and nationalist parties such as Yatsenyuk's *Batkivshchina*, who espoused strong anti-Russian views (Sakwa, 2015, p. 95). Furthermore, as soon as it deposed Yanukovych, the Ukrainian parliament, the *Verkhovna Rada*, tried on 23 February 2014 to rescind the 2012 Language law, which had granted citizens the right to use Russian as an official language in Ukraine's Russian-speaking areas (Ivzhenko, 2014d), to the worries of ethnic Russians. The *Svoboda* faction in the parliament introduced a resolution intended to prohibit the transmission of Russian media, and another one calling for 'overcoming the consequences of Soviet occupation in Ukraine', which included the dismantling of 'Soviet' monuments (Sabitova, 2014). To make matters worse, armed right-wing militias became responsible for patrolling the streets and they often abused their position, creating great concern among ethnic Russians.

This predicament gave the Kremlin an opportunity – and a pretext – to orchestrate a change of leadership in Crimea and proceed with the annexation of the peninsula to Russia, in blatant violation of international law. Immediately after Yanukovych fell from power, Russian sent special forces and paratroopers to Crimea, who immediately took control of the peninsula, while a 'referendum' on the region's future status was organised on 16 March 2014, at which a majority of the inhabitants voted in favour of joining Russia. Putin himself, in the documentary *Crimea: The Way Back Home* (2015), recounted that the decision to 'return Crimea to Russia' was taken on the evening of 22 February 2014, in a meeting with his closest advisors – Defence Minister Sergei Shoigu, Security Council Secretary Nikolai Patrushev, FSB head Aleksandr Bortnikov and chief of staff Sergei Ivanov. Yet, according to Mikhail Zygar, the Kremlin had already begun discussing a plan to take over Crimea in December 2013, when the Chairman of the Crimean Parliament, Vladimir Konstantinov, had visited Moscow and had told Patrushev, that Crimea would be ready to 'joint Russia' if Yanukovych lost power (Zygar, 2016). The issue of Crimea and of Ukraine's fate as a state if Ukraine joined NATO had also been raised by Putin already in April 2008 during the NATO Bucharest summit. Putin had hinted that if NATO enlarged and absorbed Ukraine, 'it may put the state [i.e. Ukraine] on the verge of its existence', while making reference to the fragility and 'artificial character' of the Ukrainian state (Unian, 2008). The Crimean peninsula occupied a key strategic place in Russia's geopolitical map due to its geographic location in the middle of the Black Sea and its hosting of the BSF at the naval base of Sevastopol. The prospect of the Russian fleet being evicted from Crimea and being replaced by NATO vessels, if a new pro-Western government took power in Kiev, became a great worry for Putin. His decision to intervene therefore followed clear geo-strategic concerns, and was not the result of sudden improvisation, as has been argued by Daniel Treisman (2016), although an element of 'improvised gambit' may well have been part of the decision-making process.

Russia's actions in Crimea were presented as 'a historic territory re-joining the motherland' and as 'the correction of an arbitrary and capricious historical wrong' (Toal, 2017, p. 237). While there is little doubt that clear geo-strategic concerns lay behind Putin's decision to annex Crimea, an imperialist project and a nationalist mindset also existed behind the Kremlin's actions. Putin attached great symbolic value to Crimea, as an emblem of Russia's past glory, as the representation of Ukraine's and Russia's shared history, and as the location where Russian Prince Vladimir had been baptised into Orthodox Christianity in the year 988 (Putin, 2014). Such a surprising and risky undertaking – the forceful annexation of Crimea – could not *only* reflect geopolitical concerns, especially given that the imminent threat of a Russian eviction – of its BSF – from Crimea had not yet materialised (Treisman, 2016). Neo-imperialist drivers *also* figured prominently behind such a daring act, which was conducted in clear violation of international law. As a result of such behaviour, Putin shifted the 'intellectual foundations of his foreign policy practice from great-power geopolitics (competitive statecraft conducted within the existing territorial order) to revisionist imperial geopolitics (competitive statecraft that seeks to remake the existing territorial order)', as correctly argued by Toal (2017, p. 245). More importantly, while Putin achieved a tactical victory – Russia acquired additional, vitally relevant territory, and he succeeded in 'bolstering his charisma by mobilising nationalist sentiments' (Malashenko, 2014) – Russia, to a great extent, lost strategically. The vast majority of the population in Ukraine turned against Russia, and this led to the 'loss of Ukraine', especially as war in Donbass loomed in the horizon.

The outbreak of war in the Donbass

The events in Crimea gave added impetus to developments in eastern Ukraine and created the spectre of Russia annexing an entire section of Ukrainian territory – Donetsk, Dnepropetrovsk, Luhansk/Lugansk, Kharkiv/Kharkov, Zaporozhe, Odesa/Odessa and Nikolaevsky – allowing Russia to build a land bridge in order to access Crimea and link it territorially to the rest of Russia. The eastern and southern regions of Ukraine were primarily inhabited by Russians and Russian-speakers, who shared close cultural and linguistic ties with Russia. As opposed to western Ukrainians who viewed Communist rule in a negative light and saw their incorporation into the USSR as an occupation, many in eastern Ukraine had a positive interpretation of the Russian and Soviet historical pasts (Frolov, 2014). This however, did not always translate into a desire to become part of Russia. While a series of pro-Russian parties, whose purpose was to draw the eastern and southern regions of the country into Russia, had emerged in Ukraine, these organisations did not prove to be very influential in the east of the country (Aslund, 2017). Even in Crimea, the pro-Russian party garnered only a couple of voices in the local parliament during the 2000s. At the time of the Euro-Maidan upheavals, polls indicated that the wishes among eastern and southern Ukrainians for secession and unification with Russia were not particularly strong (Toal, 2017). These communities had not suffered from serious discrimination, nor were ethnic Russians or Russian-speaking Ukrainians in the east of the country seriously at risk of violence from Ukrainian nationalist and far-right groups.

However, with the fall of Yanukovych and the rise of nationalist sentiments in Ukraine, concerns among the Russian-speaking population in east Ukraine increased, fuelled by the aggressive rhetoric of some Ukrainian far-right groups, such as the *Right Sector*. Although these groups were clearly in a minority, they exercised a loud voice and their open threats were quickly picked up by Russian propaganda channels and re-transmitted in east Ukraine. This explains why, during the Maidan upheavals, several anti-Maidan demonstrations were held not only in Kiev but in other parts of Ukraine, primarily in the eastern and southern parts of the country – in Donetsk, Kharkiv, Odessa, Luhansk, Nikolayev.

Although these protests were much smaller in number than the pro-Maidan demonstrations, they still indicated significant support for Yanukovych and for closer trade and business links, as well as close cultural ties with Russia, among eastern and southern Ukrainians (Toal, 2017). The protests were generally called by the Party of Regions (PoR), and also by the Ukrainian Communist Party, and often had the support of local government structures (Barabanov and Chernenko, 2014). More importantly, as violence in the Maidan escalated, many of the anti-Maidan demonstrators in east and south Ukraine expressed solidarity with the Berkut police and with other Ukrainian law-enforcement organs, concerned over the use of force by Ukraine far-right groups. As had happened in Crimea, many Berkut officers were greeted as heroes when they reached Donetsk in east Ukraine, after the collapse of the Yanukovych regime (Hilsum, 2014).

On 6 April 2014, the conflict entered a new, different phase, as crowds of lightly armed pro-Russian protestors seized government buildings and SBU offices in Donetsk, Luhansk, and Kharkiv, and raised Russian flags. They declared themselves the new authorities and called the new political organisations 'People's Republics', formally replacing the Ukrainian elected authorities (Toal, 2017; Ivzhenko, 2014e; Dvali, 2014). The rebels expressed their intention to hold referendums on 11 May on the regions' future status, and to organise the secession of these regions from Ukraine and their incorporation into Russia. They called on Russia and Putin to support their aspirations and to protect them from potential reprisals from Kiev (Toal, 2017). On 12–13 April 2014, as unrest was starting to die down in Donetsk, Luhansk and Kharkiv (Ivzhenko, 2014f and 2014g) a major turning point in the conflict occurred. A group of about 200 armed military men, calling themselves the *Donbass People's Militia*, seized government buildings and the headquarters of the security forces in several smaller eastern Ukrainian towns in the Luhansk and Donetsk Provinces – Slavyansk, Krasny Liman, Kramatorsk, and Makeyevka. These rebels arrived directly from Crimea, and were led by Igor Girkin (Strelkov), the main intelligence directorate (GRU) officer who had led self-defence forces in the Crimean peninsula during the Russian take-over in February 2014 (Ivzhenko, 2014g). At the same time, small, well-prepared armed groups, led by FSB operatives, were deployed in many other towns in the Donbass inciting the local population to revolt (Ivzhenko, 2014h). By mid-April, these rebels groups, which were subordinated to Russian special forces, had taken control over government agencies, police stations and SBU departments in about ten cities in Ukraine's Donetsk and Luhansk provinces, including Kramatorsk, Slavyansk and Gorlovka, and were inciting people to revolt (Ivzhenko, 2014h; *New York Times*, 2014).

Ukraine responded to this predicament by launching a major anti-terrorist operation in April 2014, commanded by the Ukrainian armed forces but supported by several nationalist militias, like the Azov and Dnieper battalions. Separatists in Donetsk and Luhansk, in turn, organised 'referendums' on independence on 11 May 2014, and established new government institutions for the 'Donetsk' and 'Lugansk' People's Republics (DNR and LNR), in the hope eventually of joining these territories into Russia. While Ukraine tried to negotiate a way out of the crisis, the separatists instead proceeded with reaffirming their authority by co-opting many local deputies, strengthening their defence capabilities and developing the external attributes of 'statehood', even though the actual status of these entities – whether as independent states or as autonomous provinces – remained blurred. (Kudelia, 2016, pp. 15–16). While Russia condemned Ukraine's use of force in east Ukraine, it neither supported the referendums, nor did it immediately send its own troops to support the pro-Russian rebels in these regions, although Russian volunteers did start arriving in big numbers. On the eve of the referendum, Putin actually called on the organisers to postpone the ballot, in what was seen by the rebels as a betrayal by the Kremlin of their 'Novorossiya' project – the annexation of these regions into the Russian state as the new Novorossiya province, in reference to the regions that had been first incorporated into the Tsarist Empire by Catherine the Great in the late eighteenth century.

In early July 2014, however, as the Ukrainian armed forces finally started to make significant inroads into rebel territory, Russia decided to become much more deeply militarily engaged in the conflict. Moscow began providing increased cover military support to the rebels, concerned over a full victory of Kiev over the DNR/LNR and over a potential loss of Russia's influence over developments in Ukraine. In mid-July pro-Russian fighters started receiving new weapons and ammunition from Russia, including heavy weaponry, modern artillery and rocket launchers (Mitrokhin, 2015, p. 240). The conflict mutated from a 'guerrilla warfare' to a full-fledged military engagement of conventional forces fighting against the Ukrainian Armed Forces (UAF), involving heavy equipment brought in from Russia (Kudelia, 2016, p. 19). Russia also started deploying special forces in the Donbass to engage in reconnaissance and assist pro-Russian rebels in military operations (Petlyakova, 2014), while fighters also received strategic and logistic support from Russian military advisors (Mitrokhin, 2015, p. 240). Furthermore, starting in May 2014, a high number of volunteers ready to defend the 'Novorossiya' project joined in the fight, ranging from neo-Imperialists and Eurasianists, to sympathisers of the National Bolsheviks of Eduard Limonov, and members of Sergei Kurginian's neo-Stalinist sect *Sut' vremeni* (The essence of Time). In principle, the recruiting process was being organised by Cossacks, but the FSB ensured the secrecy of the operation, while the Russian Ministry of Defence (MoD) provided training and weaponry near the Ukrainian border (Kostiuchenko, 2014). At the same time, though, the UAF were under constant attack from Russian artillery and rocket fire originating from Russian territory, especially in August and early September 2014 (Case and Anders, 2016; Scales, 2016).

At the end of the first week of August 2014, after the Ukrainian side managed almost completely to cut off Russian supply lines, Russian armed forces started becoming directly involved in the conflict – although only covertly – while the separatist militia deployed effective battlefield defence systems it received from Russia (Felgengauer, 2014a). At the same time, Moscow orchestrated a change of leadership in the separatist regions – Russian politicians and military leaders

Aleksander Borodai and Igor Girkin in Donetsk, as well as Valery Bolotov in Luhansk, were replaced by 'respected field commanders' holding Ukrainian passports. This was done in an attempt to show that the insurgency was locally driven (Mitrokhin, 2015, p. 242). Russia's direct, albeit covert, involvement in the fight proved decisive for the LNR/DNR rebels, as Kiev started suffering severe defeats in late August 2014, most particularly at Ilovaisk on 25 August, forcing the Ukrainian government to negotiate a halt to the hostilities. A temporary ceasefire was agreed on 5 September in Minsk, between representatives of the DNR and the LNR and the Ukrainian leadership (Felgengauer, 2014a). A more comprehensive agreement, drawn up by the Contact Group on Ukraine (Russia, Ukraine, and the Organisation for Security and Co-operation in Europe or OSCE), and brokered by former Ukrainian president Kuchma was reached in Minsk on 19 September 2014. The agreement was also signed by the OSCE envoy and the Russian Ambassador to Kiev, turning Russia and the OSCE into its key guarantors. This agreement put a temporary halt to the fight and called for a withdrawal of all armed forces from the line of contact (LoC), while it also established the creation of a 30 km security zone where no heavy weaponry could be deployed (Felgengauer, 2014b).

The deal also stipulated for the creation of security zones along the Russian–Ukrainian border; the permanent monitoring by the OSCE of that border; and the withdrawal of all illegal armed groups and military equipment as well as fighters and mercenaries from Ukrainian territory. All this was done in an attempt to put end to Russia's involvement in the conflict. But the difficulties of fulfilling such requests soon became apparent, as Kiev failed to restore control over its external borders with Russia in the east. Implementation of the ceasefire also proved difficult to achieve. The sides had agreed that the ceasefire, to be implemented immediately, would be monitored by international OSCE observers. The September 2014 agreement, however, did not envisage the sending of external peacekeeping troops to monitor the ceasefire, nor were any attempts made to establish a fully demilitarised zone along the LoC, thereby undermining the efficacy of the ceasefire enforcement operation. Furthermore, Russia's denial of its involvement in the war, and the insistence of rebel leaders that their militias were composed of 'local self-defence forces fighting for independence', made the point on disarming foreign fighters harder to implement (Ivzhenko, 2014k). Instead, in mid-January 2015, the separatist militias, led by Aleksandr Zakharchenko, conducted a major military offensive in an attempt to acquire control over Mariupol in the south, and over Debaltsevo and the Donetsk airport in the west, which resulted in fierce battles that again saw a significant involvement of Russian forces (Sutyagin, 2015).

A second Minsk agreement was reached on 12 February 2015, which established a comprehensive ceasefire, whose implementation however, only started on 15 February. This gave the separatists and their Russian backers an opportunity to complete the full conquest of Debaltseve, after having taken control of Donetsk airport in mid-January 2015. The deal also stipulated for the withdrawal of all heavy weaponry from the security zone, which for Ukrainian forces meant withdrawal from the de facto contact line, while for the DNR/LNR forces it meant the line agreed on the 19 September Minsk Memorandum. The OSCE was given full responsibility for effectively monitoring and verifying the implementation of the agreement. The Ukrainian government was to regain full control over its national borders with Russia along the entire conflict zone, starting on the first day after local elections were held in these two separatist regions. The process would be completed once a comprehensive political settlement was achieved by the end of 2015, and after Constitutional reform was carried out in Ukraine as envisaged in this new agreement. On the political front, the agreement envisaged the start of a dialogue with representatives of the DNR/LNR regions, 'to determine the modalities of local elections' based on Ukrainian legislation and on the September 2014 'Special Status Law'. A dialogue was also to be established with representatives of these regions to determine the future status of these regions, based on the 'Special Status Law'. The local elections had to comply with OSCE standards and had to be monitored by the OSCE. Ukraine was also expected to conduct a Constitutional reform, which would see decentralisation enshrined in the new Constitution. Decentralisation would take into account 'the special situation of certain areas of the Donetsk and Luhansk oblasts, in agreement with representatives of these areas' (Financial Times, 2015). This meant that the regions would have a say in the definition of their new status, which would become enshrined in the new Constitution. These areas would be granted the right officially to use their own language, participate in local self-government structures, and appoint chiefs of prosecution and judicial bodies. They were also given the right to create their own people's militia to maintain public order. Furthermore, these regions were allowed to develop close cross-border cooperation with Russia, while also being able to establish economic, cultural and social ties with the rest of Ukraine. Furthermore, Kiev was expected to assist them in their socio-economic development.

While Russia failed to enshrine Ukraine's federalisation in the agreement, it achieved some important objectives. Ukraine was expected to conduct a reform of its Constitution, which would enshrine a special status to the DNR/LNR regions. These regions would be able to develop cross-border cooperation with neighbouring Russian regions and officially use the Russian language. Elections in the DNR/LNR regions would previously involve a dialogue with Kiev, while control over the borders with Russia would be delayed for almost a year, and, more significantly, made dependent upon the holding of elections in these separatist regions and on the reaching of a comprehensive political settlement. This potentially left the Russian–Ukrainian border question unresolved for a long period of time, as it eventually occurred. At the same time, though, Kiev succeeded in preventing Ukraine's federalisation and instead managed to keep a unitary state structure intact. This theoretically allowed Ukraine to pursue unhindered its European choice and, potentially, its NATO membership, if it so wished. Kiev also ensured that Ukrainian remained the state language, although the Donbass regions were also allowed to use Russian as their official language, if they so wished. More importantly, the new agreement once again reaffirmed the full respect for the sovereignty and territorial integrity of Ukraine and Crimea was not recognised as part of Russia, as Moscow had desired. The separatist leaders however, succeeded once again in having their signatures attached to the final agreement, and this gave them increased status, and a higher degree of 'legitimacy'. However, Ukrainian President Petro Poroshenko made it clear that he would not negotiate with the current LNR/DNR leadership, as he did not consider these 'separatist institutions' as legitimate. As he rightly pointed out, the elections that had been held on 2 November 2014 in the LNR/DNR regions had actually been conducted in violation of the Minsk I protocols (Ivzhenko, 2015).

The Minsk II agreement helped to put an end to large-scale battles between Kiev and the Russian-backed separatists but clashes along the ceasefire line continued (Associated Press, 2016). OSCE observers often faced difficulties when trying to exercise their monitoring mission, and the ceasefire was constantly broken by skirmishes along the LoC. Progress towards a political settlement also stalled. Although Ukraine adopted a new Special Status law, it made its implementation conditional both upon the holding of elections in the separatist regions in accordance with Ukrainian legislation, and upon the withdrawal of Russian troops from the Donbass. This drew strong criticisms from Russia and from the separatist leaders, who argued that the Special Status Law had not been 'mutually agreed' (Zinets and Balmforth, 2015). Instead the DNR/LNR area became increasingly integrated into Russia. Moscow restored rail links between Donetsk and Luhansk, provided the regions with financial support – Russia allegedly delivered the Donbass seven billion roubles, or US$185 million, a month in cash – while Gazprom and InterRAO supplied free gas and electricity (Zygar, 2016).[1] Furthermore, the Kremlin directly interfered in the internal affairs of the new 'republics'. According to sources inside the LNR/DNR administration, Vladislav Surkov, President Putin's special advisor on Ukraine, controlled the situation through his handpicked proxies, 'who give him regular situation reports' (Zverev, 2017). Surkov 'used aides to arrange elections there, and has worked to build power structures that are responsive to Moscow's wishes' (Zverev, 2017). There was a clear sense that the uprising had been hijacked by Moscow (Zverev, 2017). Yet, while Russia brought these regions under its direct control, it lost its influence over the rest of Ukraine, alienated most Ukrainians, and, above all, it failed to ensure a durable geo-strategic alliance between Kiev and Moscow.

Concluding thoughts

Russia's forceful annexation of Crimea in 2014 represented a major turning point in Russia's behaviour towards Ukraine and a significant watershed in its policies in the former Soviet space. Not only did Russia intervene militarily beyond its borders in clear violation of international law, its actions resulted in the acquisition of neighbouring territory and the escalation of tensions in the eastern regions of Ukraine. This, in turn, led to the outbreak of large-scale fighting in Donbass, which produced a high number of casualties and saw Russia's undisputed overt and covert involvement. There is little doubt that Russia's actions in Crimea reflected clear geo-strategic and security concerns – the possible eviction of its naval forces (the BSF) from Crimea followed, potentially, by the deployment of NATO forces in a key strategic section of the Black Sea region. However, a strong neo-imperialist mindset also figured prominently among decision-makers in Moscow, especially when engaging Ukraine. With the annexation of Crimea and the involvement in Ukraine's Donbass, Russia's neo-imperialist paradigm, once again, reached full circle. It transformed Russia from an upholder of the status quo into a revisionist power, ready to adjust its external borders to suit its geo-strategic interests, with little regard of the consequences that followed from its daring actions. As other countries in the past, Russia violated the sanctity of internationally recognised borders, significantly threatening the stability of the European continent. Furthermore, as this chapter has shown, the Kremlin was undoubtedly an instigator of the Ukrainian upheavals in east Ukraine. While the full extent of Moscow's involvement in *initiating* and *supporting* the Donbass insurgency remains hard to discern, there is little doubt that its covert military and political engagement proved crucial. It transformed the initial rebellion into a full-scale conventional war, which also saw the direct – albeit covert – participation of Russian troops, tanks and artillery. Furthermore, the conflict also witnessed a high number of former soldiers, Cossacks and far-right radical adventurers joining in the fight, with the explicit support and engagement of the Russian MoD and the FSB. The Kremlin, however, soon distanced itself from the political 'Novorossiya project', which was being promoted by many of the fighters involved, which would have seen the direct annexation of the Donetsk and Luhansk regions to Russia. Moscow most probably remained concerned over the risks that such an additional undertaking could entail, and was possibly worried over the potential backlash that such a significant redrawing of Ukraine's borders could produce. Instead, in May 2014, Moscow supported the emergence of pro-Russian 'People's Republics' in the Donbass region, which would, however, remain as part of Ukraine's territory.

Putin soon realised that the acquisition of additional Ukrainian land would, most certainly, have resulted in the further alienation of 'the rest of' Ukraine, pushing it increasingly towards NATO and the EU. More importantly, such actions could have potentially produced an anti-Russian insurgency in the Donbass, with high costs for the Kremlin in terms of 'blood and treasure'. Furthermore, such actions would have most certainly produced an even stronger reaction from the West – resulting most probably in the introduction of additional economic sanctions and potentially also the deployment of military forces. Russia's actions, instead, revealed the true essence of the Kremlin's objectives in Ukraine – to keep the country under Russia's influence through its presence and influence in the LNR/DNR republics, in order to ensure, first, that the country did not turn against Russia and second that it did not become a full member of NATO, the EU and the West. Such a predicament would not only have weakened Russia's geo-strategic posture, it would have also created a cleavage between the Russian and Ukrainian 'brotherly' nations. Most Russians identified Ukraine with 'Small Russia', and saw the two peoples – Russians and Ukrainians – as belonging to a single 'divided' east Slavic nation (Tspiko, 2014). Vladimir Putin, in particular, clearly saw Ukraine as belonging to the same civilisational, cultural and economic space as Russia. He, therefore, wished to see Ukraine becoming a member of the same geo-strategic Eurasian bloc that Russia was promoting and that he so much cherished – the Eurasian Economic Union. Yet, Russia's actions in Ukraine did not entirely produce the expected results – while Ukraine neither joined the EU nor NATO, it nevertheless established a close strategic partnership with the West. Kiev developed very close military ties with Northern Alliance, from whom it received military training and support, which proved helpful in its fight against Russian-supported forces in the Donbass. Furthermore, Ukraine also developed very close economic and political ties with the EU, through the implementation of the AA and the DCFTA. These agreements not only established a free trade zone between Ukraine and the EU, they also foresaw the close regulatory alignment of Ukranian law with the EU Acquis Communautaire. However, Ukraine's rapprochement with the West had its limits. The transformation of the Donbass region, to all intents and purposes into a Russian protectorate, of the likes of Abkhazia and South Ossetia, allowed Russia to keep a foothold in Ukraine and, in this way, influence events in this country. While Russia did not succeed in turning Ukraine into Russia's neo-imperial domain, it nevertheless managed to retain some residual, albeit relevant, power over Ukraine though the LNR/DNR separatist regions and the looming threat of additional annexation of territory. Russia's actions, moreover, made full display of its hegemonic military and economic power in its efforts to keep Ukraine within its sphere of influence. As such, Russia's actions entirely fitted into the neo-imperialist paradigm.

Note

1 According to ICG (2017, p. 5), Russia spent over $1 billion in pensions, social benefits and salaries for officials in the Donbass, and even more on the military. Details of the funding, which is presented as 'humanitarian support for individual territories', have been provided by RBC (2017).

Bibliography

Afineevsky, E. (2015). *Winter on Fire* [film]. Netflix.
Aslund, A. (2017). Ukrainian Oligarch Could be Missing Link in Trump-Russia Probe. *The Hill*. 22 May. Available at: http://thehill.com/blogs/pundits-blog/the-administration/334139-ukrainian-oligarch-may-be-missing-link-in-trump-russia [accessed 10 October 2018].
Associated Press (2016). Ukraine Peace Process: Leaders Agree Roadmap to Revive Talks. *Guardian*. 20 October. Available at: www.theguardian.com/world/2016/oct/20/ukraine-peace-process-leaders-agree-roadmap-to-revive-talks [accessed 5 October 2018].

Barabanov, I. and Ye. Chernenko (2014). *Kommersant*, 25 January, p. 1.
Case, S. and K. Anders (2016). Putin's Undeclared War: Summer 2014 – Russian Artillery Strikes against Ukraine. Bellingcat. 21 December. Available at: www.bellingcat.com/news/uk-and-europe/2016/12/21/russian-artillery-strikes-against-ukraine/ [accessed 10 October 2018].
Crimea: The Way Back Home (Krym. Put' na Rodinu) (2015). Directed by Sergei Kraus, Produced by Andrey Kondrashev [film]. Russia. Rossiya1.
Dvali, N. (2014). Eks-nachal'nik Luganskoi SBU Petrulevich: Terroristicheskie gruppy GRU Rossii uzhe v Kieve i zhdut signala. Gordonua.com. 2 July. Available at: https://gordonua.com/print/publications/petrulevich-terroristicheskie-gruppy-gru-rossii-uzhe-v-kieve-i-zhdut-signala-29825.html [accessed 11 January 2020].
Felgengauer, P. (2014a). *Novaya gazeta*, 3 September. p. 2.
Felgengauer, P. (2014b). *Novaya gazeta*, 8 October, p. 2.
Financial Times (2015). Full Text of the Minsk Agreement. 12 February. Available at: www.ft.com/content/21b8f98e-b2a5-11e4-b234-00144feab7de [accessed 12 January 2015].
Frolov, V. (2014). *Moscow Times*, 18 February.
Hilsum, L. (2014). Fighting Fascism from Ukraine's Russian Enclave. 25 February. Available at: www.channel4.com/news/by/lindsey-hilsum/blogs/fighting-fascism-sevastopols-russian-enclave [accessed 11 October 2018].
International Crisis Group (ICG) (2017). *Can Peacekeepers Break the Deadlock in Ukraine?* Europe Report, 246. 15 December.
Ishchenko, V. (2016). Far Right Participation in the Ukrainian Maidan Protests: An Attempt of Systematic Estimation. *European Politics and Society*, 17 (4), 453–472.
Ivzhenko, T. (2014a). *Nezavisimaya gazeta*, 24 January, p. 1.
Ivzhenko, T. (2014b). *Nezavisimaya gazeta*, 13 February, p. 1.
Ivzhenko, T. (2014c). *Nezavisimaya gazeta*, 21 February, p. 1.
Ivzhenko, T. (2014d) Nezavisimaya gazeta, 5 March, p. 1.
Ivzhenko, T. (2014e). *Nezavisimaya gazeta*, 8 April, p. 1.
Ivzhenko, T. (2014f). *Nezavisimaya gazeta*, 9 April, p. 1.
Ivzhenko, T. (2014g). *Nezavisimaya gazeta*, 14 April, p. 1.
Ivzhenko, T. (2014h). *Nezavisimaya gazeta*, 15 April, p. 1.
Ivzhenko, T. (2014j). *Nezavisimaya gazeta*, 22 April, p. 1.
Ivzhenko, T. (2014k). *Nezavisimaya gazeta*, 8 September, p. 1.
Ivzhenko, T. (2015). *Nezavisimaya gazeta*, 13 February, p. 2.
Kostiuchenko, E. (2014). *Novaya gazeta*, 3 September. Available at: www.novayagazeta.ru/articles/2014/09/03/60981-armiya-i-dobrovoltsy [accessed 20 October 2018].
Kostiuchenko, E. (2015). My vse znali, na chto idem i chto mozhet byt. 5 March. Available: www.novayagazeta.ru/articles/2015/03/02/63264-171-my-vse-znali-na-chto-idem-i-chto-mozhet-byt-187 [accessed 10 October 2018].
Kudelia, S. (2016). The Donbass Rift. *Russian Politics and Law*, 54 (1), 5–27.
Lavrov, A. (2014a). Russian Again: The Military Operation for Crimea. In: C. Howard and R. Pukhov, eds. *Brothers Armed: Military Aspects of the Crisis in Ukraine*, Minneapolis: East View Press, pp. 157–184.
Lavrov, S. (2014b). *Kommersant*, 13 February, p. 1.
Malashenko, A. (2014). *Nezavisimaya gazeta*, 18 March, p. 3.
Mitrokhin, N. (2014). Transnationale Provokation. *OstEuropa*, 64 (5–6), 157–174.
Mitrokhin, N. (2015). Infiltration, Instruction, Invasion: Russia's War in the Donbass, *Journal of Soviet and Post-Soviet Politics and Society*, 1 (1), 219–249.

Musafirova, O. (2014). *Novaya gazeta*, 5 September. p. 2.
Musafirova, O. (2017). Interview: 'Ia gotov slushat' evo dnyami...' 16 May. Available at: www.novayagazeta.ru/articles/2017/05/16/72455-aleksey-donskoy-kreml-spasaet-yanukovicha-no-tsenu-emu-znaet [accessed 10 September 2018].
New York Times (2014). Pro-Russian Separatists take Kramatorsk Police HQ in Ukraine. 13 April. Available at: www.nytimes.com/video/multimedia/100000002822894/pro-russian-separatists-take-kramatorsk-police-hq-in-ukraine.html [accessed 12 September 2018].
Nezavisimya gazeta (2014). 1 April, p. 2.
Petlyakova, N. (2014). *Novaya gazeta*, 5 September, p. 4.
Polukhin, A. (2014). *Novaya gazeta*, 22 January, p. 9.
Putin, V.V. (2014). Direct Line with Vladimir Putin. 17 April. Available at: http://en.kremlin.ru/events/president/news/20796 [accessed 12 September 2018].
RBC (2017). Krym vmesto DNR: kak v pravitel'stve obsuzhdaiut otkaz ot pomoshchi Donbassu. 15 September. Available at: www.rbc.ru/economics/15/09/2017/59b84cc99a7947ce896ad25c
Sabitova, A. (2014). *Kommersant*, 23 February. Available at: www.kommersant.ru/doc/2414951 [accessed 11 September 2018].
Sakwa, R. (2015). *Frontline Ukraine: Crisis in the Borderlands*. London, I.B. Tauris.
Scales, R.H. (2016). Russia's Superior New Weapons. *Washington Post*. 5 August. Available at: https://www.washingtonpost.com/opinions/global-opinions/russias-superior-new-weapons/2016/08/05/e86334ec-08c5-11e6-bdcb-0133da18418d_story.html [accessed 8 September 2018].
Sutyagin, I. (2015). Russian Forces in Ukraine. Briefing Paper, RUSI. 9 March Available at: https://rusi.org/publication/briefing-papers/russian-forces-ukraine [accessed 11 September 2018].
Toal, G. (2017). *Near Abroad: Putin, the West and the Contest over Ukraine and the Caucasus*. Oxford: Oxford University Press.
Treisman, D. (2016). Why Putin Took Crimea. The Gambler in the Kremlin. *Foreign Affairs*, May/June. Available at: www.foreignaffairs.com/articles/ukraine/2016-04-18/why-russian-president-putin-took-crimea-from-ukraine [accessed 10 September 2018].
Tsipko, A. (2014). *Nezavisimaya gazeta*, 5 February, p. 1.
Unian (2008). Text of Putin's Speech at NATO Summit (Bucharest, 2 April). Available at: www.unian.info/world/111033-text-of-putins-speech-at-nato-summit-bucharest-april-2-2008.html [accessed 10 September 2018].
Zinets, N. and R. Balmforth (2015). Ukraine Parliament Offers Special Status for Rebel East, Russia Criticizes. *Reuters*. 17 March. Available at: www.reuters.com/article/us-ukraine-crisis-status-idUSKBN0MD1ZK20150317 [accessed 10 January 2018].
Zverev, A. (2017). Ex-rebel Leaders Detail Role Played by Putin Aide in East Ukraine. 11 May. Available at: www.reuters.com/article/us-ukraine-crisis-russia-surkov-insight-idUSKBN1870TJ [accessed 10 January 2018].
Zygar, M. (2016). *All the Kremlin's Men: Inside the Court of Vladimir Putin*. New York: Public Affairs.

Conclusion

This book examined the nature of Russia's relations towards the former Soviet states (FSS), and more specifically towards the Commonwealth of Independent States (CIS) member states, from the time of the USSR collapsed in 1991 to the present day. In particular, it partly challenged the validity of the commonly held view that the new Russian state that emerged in 1991, having lost vast amounts of land and over 25 million ethnic nationals, would prove unable to discard its imperial legacy and establish normal state-to-state relations with the new republics; and that, instead, its leaders would attempt to restore a sphere of influence or informal empire over Russia's former colonies, as the French did in sub-Saharan Africa after decolonisation. This book has shown that there is clearly support for the 'neo-imperialist' hypothesis, especially during Putin's third term as President of Russia, which began officially in May 2012. Neo-imperialist policies also became prominent during the mid-to-late 2000s, as disappointment with the West grew and Russia engaged in an increasingly assertive behaviour in the former Soviet space. However, the evidence of a neo-imperialist conduct is not always overwhelming, and this is especially the case in the first decade of Russia's life as an independent state after the USSR disintegrated. During the 1990s, Russia underwent a massive internal transformation, which involved both handling the legacies of the Soviet era, establishing new institutions, transiting to a market economy, and engaging in the process of nation- and state-building. Consequently, Russia's policies in most fields, including relations with its former Soviet neighbours, were often characterised by improvisation and by the lack of a consistent pattern of behaviour. A clear neo-imperialist agenda was absent in Russia's actions and there was hardly an attempt by the Kremlin to hold on to Russia's 'former colonies,' although Russia did behave quite assertively in certain opportunities, especially when violence erupted along its borders. Yet, these actions were more reflective of a slow withdrawal from Empire rather than an attempt to restore a new informal imperial entity in the ex-USSR space. In the Yeltsin era, therefore, Russia's actions in the Near Abroad did not fully resemble France's neo-imperial behaviour in sub-Saharan Africa. The latter was characterised by a coherent policy aimed at keeping a sphere of influence in the region, through a network of military bases, bilateral defence agreements and preferential trade agreements; the transfer of investment and economic aid; the establishment of the Franc Zone; and the development of cultural ties. Russia's policies, instead, although neo-imperial in many ways, did not follow a coherent strategy of informal empire building.

In the early- to mid-2000s, however, the Kremlin increasingly engaged in attempts to create a sphere of influence around its neighbouring states, although its policies were not necessarily characterised by an extremely assertive behaviour in all spheres of policy-making. As the decade progressed, though, Moscow's actions in the Near Abroad became more forceful, were increasingly distinguished by the use of *hard power*, and were often conducted in direct violation of international law. In the mid-2000s, and especially during Putin's second Presidency, the Kremlin made growing use of Russia's hegemonic power, resulting from its renewed economic and military strength, to bring countries in the former Soviet space under its sphere of influence. Russian leaders began defining the former Soviet territory not only as an area of 'special interests', but also as a common 'civilisational space' – an area that brought together the peoples of the USSR, untied by a common history, culture and tradition, and where Russia's influence was expected to remain predominant. Concerned over the growing penetration of the West in Russia's Near Abroad, and worried over China's rise in Central Asia, Moscow tried to create an alternative, Russian-led, geopolitical bloc, which would align most of the FSS closely to Russia. This, in turn, would allow Moscow to become one of the leading poles of a new 'multipolar world'. Furthermore, in the late 2000s and during 2010s, the promotion of the 'Russian world' concept – understood as a supranational community of people who associated themselves closely with Russia, with its values and its culture – became the guiding principle of a Russian foreign policy, which was increasingly endowed with a Messianic mission – Russia as the global leader of a 'Conservative' world.

While in the 1990s and early 2000s, Russia's policies reflected the notion of *post-Imperium*, namely a prolonged exit from Russia's imperial condition, in the 2010s, Russia's neo-imperial tradition was revived more forcefully. Russia became, to all intents and purposes, a revisionist state, which annexed Crimea, became engaged military in Ukraine, and encroached on Georgia's territorial integrity by recognising independence of the separatist regions of Abkhazia and South Ossetia. However, its actions did not go as far as revising the entire post-Soviet map, and more importantly, many of its policies did not produce the desired results. By the end of the 2010s, Russia had, to all intents and purposes, 'lost' the key strategic states of Ukraine and Georgia, its influence in Armenia was being increasingly questioned, Moldova hesitated between joining the EU and aligning itself with Russia, while Belarus – Russia's closest ally – engaged in efforts to adopt a more independent foreign policy and break its over-reliance on Russia's economic support. Even close allies such as Tajikistan, which depended heavily on Russia's economic and military assistance, hesitated strongly when it came to joining the Russian-led Eurasian Union project. Furthermore, Russia had difficulties in constructing an effective and successful economic bloc around its leadership, while its military hegemony in the former

Soviet space faced growing challenges from the West (represented by NATO and the EU) in the eastern Europe and the Caucasus, and from China in Central Asia. While Russia's policies undoubtedly produced some important results – Belarus, Kazakhstan, Kyrgyzstan and Armenia, for example, joined the Russian-led Eurasian Economic Union (EAEU); a more-effective CSTO (Collective Security Treaty Organisation) military organisation was put in place; NATO's further enlargement into the EU was averted – in many instances, Russia's actions did not produce the expected outcomes, as many CIS countries tried to turn away from Russia. Its policies can, therefore, best be described as those of an *aspiring hegemon*, rather than those of a fully accomplished neo-imperialist power.

The first Yeltsin years

During the first half of the 1990s, some elements within the Russian leadership, such as the Defence Ministry, the Vice President, and the majority of members of the Russian parliament, found it very difficult to totally dismiss the country's imperial heritage, and instead, attempted to reassert the country's influence over the FSS – although in an erratic and somehow incoherent fashion. Many of these individuals considered the post-Soviet space as a sphere of Russia's natural interests, and therefore believed that Russia had to retain a predominant position in the area. President Yeltsin and his Foreign Minister Andrei Kozyrev, instead, embraced a strongly anti-imperialist vision, especially during the early 1990s, and tried, quite actively, to disengage Russia's presence from the Near Abroad. In the spring of 1993, however, their foreign policy discourse underwent a major change – it become more assertive, especially as far as the former Soviet space was concerned, under pressure from more nationalist and imperialist figures in the Russian parliament and the Russian government, such as Vice President Aleksandr Rutskoi. In the autumn of 1993 and winter of 1994, Foreign Minister Kozyrev openly talked about the need to keep the FSS within Russia's 'sphere of influence', while the Russian government gave growing priority to the settlement of conflicts in the Near Abroad, the protection of the rights of Russian minorities in the Baltic States and the deepening of military and economic ties with the CIS states. However, despite a more stringent neo-imperialist rhetoric, the record of Russia's behaviour in the Near Abroad remained rather mixed. Russian leaders did not pursue in practice a clearly defined strategy of 'informal empire building', intended as the creation of an area over which Russia would have a substantial capacity to influence both external and internal developments, and over which other countries would be denied a hegemonic presence; an area in which countries would be forced to surrender part of their sovereignty to a former imperial power. Instead, in many instances, Russia disengaged itself from the former Soviet space, and proved ready to treat the new countries as sovereign and independent entities.

Nevertheless, elements of a neo-imperialist outlook were present in Russia's actions. Russia managed to retain a military presence in all CIS states, with the exception of Uzbekistan, Turkmenistan and Azerbaijan; to maintain control over most of the former Soviet air defence and early warning infrastructure located in the newly independent states; and to protect most of the external CIS borders with Russian troops, except for Ukraine, Moldova and Azerbaijan. Moreover, Russian leaders signed bilateral treaties with the vast majority of CIS states which foresaw the development of close military and military-technical cooperation between the Russian army and the armed forces of the states concerned. Russia also became deeply involved in the military conflicts that erupted in the post-Soviet space – in Nagorno-Karabakh, Abkhazia, Transdniestria and Tajikistan – by mediating between the warring parties, providing military support, and deploying peacekeeping forces in the conflict zones – all of which helped Russia to reinforce its military presence in these key strategic areas of the former Soviet space. Russian behaviour proved particularly assertive in the South Caucasus, where the Russian MoD, by providing military support to the Abkhaz, coerced the Georgian leadership to accept a long-term military presence in the country, in the form of three military bases and four naval ports. Similarly, Russia managed to delay the withdrawal of the 14th Army (in 1995 the Operational Group of Russian Forces) from Transdniestria, in contravention of what had been agreed, thus perpetuating its military presence in Moldova. The Kremlin also exerted strong pressure on the Azerbaijani leadership through the use of *coercive diplomacy*, to obtain approval for the establishment of military bases on Azerbaijani territory and to ensure the introduction of Russian-dominated peacekeeping forces in Nagorno-Karabakh. Yet, its actions did not produce the desired results. In Tajikistan, instead, Russia's active military involvement in support of the Rakhmon regime resulted in a prolonged military presence which turned the country almost into a Russian protectorate, given its heavy reliance on Russian financial support and military protection.

The evidence of Russia's behaviour in the 1990s, however, fails to support the neo-imperialist argument completely. There is no evidence indicating that the new Russian leaders in Moscow, which had gained power in 1991, purposefully exacerbated tensions and violent conflicts in the Near Abroad in order to intervene militarily and keep Russia's forces stationed in these regions. But, as a result of Moscow's engagement, Russia did succeed in keeping a military presence in Georgia, Moldova and Tajikistan, and this allowed Russia to extend its influence over these countries. The Crimean example, in this respect, is quite telling, as the Kremlin did not take advantage of the political crisis that erupted between the Ukrainian government in Kiev and the staunchly pro-Russian Crimean authorities in the early and mid-1990s to take control over the peninsula. Instead, in a sign that the Russian government in the 1990s had succeeded in discarding Russia's imperial legacy, the Kremlin recognised both Crimea and the 'glorious' city of Sevastopol, as part of Ukraine territory. However, this moderate stance came hand in hand with Russia being granted the right to lease the port of Sevastopol and with the possibility to keep its naval forces stationed in the peninsula for a long period – allowing Moscow to project its power in the Black Sea and expand further its strategic reach. The evidence, thus, seems to indicate that military-strategic concerns rather than imperial nostalgia guided the Kremlin's actions in the former USSR. Similarly, Russia's decision to increase oil and gas prices to Ukraine, Moldova and Belarus in the early- to mid-1990s reflected efforts to correct unfavourable terms of trade inherited from the Soviet Union, rather than attempts to exert coercive pressure on these countries to keep them under Russia's sphere of influence.

A clear examination of Russia's behaviour shows that Russia's policies in the economic sphere did not really fit into the neo-imperialist pattern. Most of the integration projects failed to materialise because Russia proved unwilling either to subsidise deeper integration projects through financial support or to enforce integration through the use of *coercive methods* or *imposition*. The Kremlin's actions therefore cannot be described as reflecting a *neo-imperial* paradigm but instead seem better to fit the model of *voluntary contracting*. The Kremlin, contrary to what happened in the mid- to late-2000s, did not show a willingness to use *hard power* instruments to force a union with either Belarus or with the other CIS states. Furthermore, Russia's policies often followed legitimate state concerns. Russia's readiness to provide huge subsidies to the CIS states resulted primarily from the close ties that existed between the FSS industrial, agricultural and energy complexes. Russian support was intended, above all, to avoid the total collapse of FSS' economies and of Russian industry. Even though re-establishing control over the former Soviet energy complex may have remained a key foreign policy objective, Russia's actions, in this respect, also followed a clear economic logic – Russia depended on several former Soviet states – primarily Ukraine, but also Belarus and Moldova – for the transit of its oil and gas to European and global markets. The evidence provided, therefore, indicates that as opposed to Russia's policies in the military sphere, Russia's actions in the economic field proved to be much less assertive than is usually assumed, and tended to follow primarily an economic and commercial logic. Successful economic transformation, including macro-economic stabilisation, became *the* top priority of the Russian government in the 1990s. Although these policies were certainly not conducted in a coherent fashion, and at various stages the objective of macro-economic stabilisation was temporarily abandoned, the overall goals of market transformation and financial stabilisation were preserved.

Primakov at the Foreign Ministry

With the arrival of Yevgeny Primakov at the Foreign Ministry in 1996, Russia's foreign policy became more coherent and increasingly more effective. Russian leaders succeeded in reaching agreements on the creation of a Customs Union (CU) and a common economic space (CES) with Belarus, Kazakhstan, Kyrgyzstan and Tajikistan, while the bases for a close economic and political Union between Russia and Belarus were also set. However, as the evidence shows, by the end of the 1990s, Russia had not entirely succeeded in establishing a tightly coordinated CU and a properly functioning CES with a selected group of CIS partners – primarily because of the reluctance of all CIS countries, including Russia, to subordinate their economic policies to supranational institutions. Russia hesitated to make the necessary investments 'in blood and treasure' to establish a powerful CIS economic bloc around its leadership, which would have allowed it, potentially, to exert significant influence over the ex-USSR region. Similar reasons also explain the lack of substantial progress in the establishment of a properly functioning Russian–Belarusian Union – particularly high implementation costs and strong disagreements between the leaderships of the two countries over the nature of the future Union prevented any serious advancement towards deeper integration. While Russia provided financial and energy subsidies to Belarus and may have exerted soft pressure on Minsk to agree to a Union state, it did not go as far as using hard power instruments to coerce Belarus into an agreement, in a clear sign that it was not ready to engage fully in a neo-imperialist policy.

The same can be said regarding CIS military integration. Despite Russia's efforts to strengthen military cooperation within the Collective Security Treaty (CST) framework, the Kremlin failed to transform the CST into an effective military organisation capable of addressing the new security challenges facing the CIS/CST region. Many of the CIS states, such as Georgia and Azerbaijan, moved away from the Russian military orbit and instead began developing closer ties with NATO countries. In Central Asia, China emerged as an alternative centre of power and influence, within the Shanghai forum, challenging Russia's geo-strategic hegemony in the region. Although Russia remained the main provider of security and military assistance to most CIS states, Russia's influence was primarily of a residual and 'post-imperial' nature. CIS states moved ahead with establishing their own armed forces, developing their own security structures and conducting their own independent foreign policies. Russia's actions, therefore, cannot be described as fitting entirely into the neo-imperialist paradigm. Russia's integration projects were generally supported by the other CIS signatory states, and therefore relations in this sphere resulted primarily from *voluntary contracting* rather than from *coercion* or *imposition*. Many CIS states had much to gain from cooperating with Moscow in the security and economic field, by expanding trade and investment and obtaining Russian assistance to address more effectively the newly emerging threats to their security. Furthermore, no strong pressure was exerted by the Kremlin on those countries less supportive of integration, such as Uzbekistan, Georgia or Azerbaijan, as opposed to what had occurred during the early- to mid-1990s. Instead, all these countries were able to abstain from joining the various Russian-led CIS integration projects – several even abandoned the military CST in 1999 – in a clear sign that Russia seemed reluctant to fully embrace a neo-imperial project. There is little evidence then that in the late 1990s Russia engaged in an assertive neo-imperialist policy to keep the Near Abroad countries within a Russian sphere of influence.

In several other areas of CIS policy Russia adopted a more conciliatory tone. Moscow engaged in active mediation efforts in the various Near Abroad military conflicts, in cooperation with other external actors, such as the OSCE and the

UN – an indication that Russia seemed ready, at least in theory, to discard its imperial legacy. However, in most instances, the Kremlin's resolution proposals awarded Russia the role of key guarantor of the agreements signed. They also generally foresaw the deployment of Russian peacekeeping forces in the conflict zones. Such stipulations showed that Russia felt it necessary to keep a military presence in the CIS volatile regions to prevent a resumption of violence and to ensure for itself a predominant military presence in the area. While Russia's military forces were welcomed by governments in countries such as Armenia and Tajikistan, which saw Russian troops as guarantors of regional peace and stability, other states such as Georgia and Moldova rejected Russia's military presence out of hand. By the end of the Yeltsin's presidencies, therefore, the record of neo-imperialism remained a mixed one. As the capabilities of the Russian state shrank, impaired by financial constraints, Russia's strategic reach diminished. Russia increasingly looked like a *post-imperial* state, whose hegemony was primarily of a residual nature.

Instead, as the decade progressed, Russia increasingly adopted a 'Russia First' policy, intended to ensure that its actions fulfilled, above all, Russia's national interests, especially in relation to those countries less inclined to cooperate with Russia. In this respect, Russia decided to increase gas prices to those CIS states, such as Ukraine, Georgia and Moldova, which were fully aligning themselves geo-strategically with Russia. While these actions may be interpreted as revealing a neo-imperialist design, they actually followed primarily a commercial logic – the need to adjust exports prices to world market prices. Moscow also exerted pressure on various CIS states to acquire equity shares in their industrial and energy assets, in exchange of the cancellation of their energy debts. This again reflected the necessity to ensure the continued flow of energy resources to foreign markets through the control of CIS export infrastructure. Furthermore, it must be added that Russia was at the time facing severe financial difficulties, which were exacerbated by the 1998 financial crisis that hit the Russian economy particularly hard, and this argued against granting subsidies to the CIS states unless some kind of economic, political or strategic benefits could be obtained in return. Such financial challenges also explain why Gazprom handed over to the intermediary company *Itera* the sale and distribution of gas to all those CIS countries which faced severe financial difficulties. While Belarus, a key Russian strategic ally, was able to buy gas at lower prices, such advantages were related to the readiness by Minsk, at least in theory, to establish a Union State with Russia, and were tied to the acquisition by Gazprom of Belarus' energy assets – in a clear sign that Russia's actions were also becoming increasingly *transactional* in nature.

Vladimir Putin reaches the Presidency

With the arrival of Putin to the Russian Presidency in the year 2000, the Kremlin's actions in the former Soviet space, received once again strong impetus. Most members of the Russian political elite still found it hard to accept the end of the

USSR and view the new states as truly independent and sovereign. For many the idea of 'Russia' remained closely linked to the USSR and the former Russian Empire in terms of territorial dimension and population composition. Positive notions of Empire as models to organise Russia's relations with the former Soviet states became increasingly fashionable, clearly showing the difficulties that many in Russia were having when trying to discard the country's imperial legacy ten years after the end of the USSR. Furthermore, most still considered that Russia had to aspire to regain its Great-Power status in the international arena. While President Putin became a strong promoter of Russia's Greatness, and an advocate of a multipolar world, he did not initially embrace an imperialist project in its entirety. Putin viewed Russia and the FSS as sharing a common civilisational space, which had to be organised under Russian leadership and influence. Yet, the idea of recreating a territorial empire out of the remains of the USSR was discarded. Instead, the former Soviet republics were seen as linked together by a common history, a similar culture, and the same Russian language – all these elements made of this space, a *common civilisation*. Through tight collaboration and deeper integration among the CIS states, a common economic, humanitarian and legal space was expected to emerge.

The arrival of Putin to the Russian Presidency therefore saw a determined attempt by the Kremlin to establish a properly functioning economic bloc with those countries traditionally most eager to integrate their economies with that of Russia – Belarus, Kazakhstan, Kyrgyzstan and Tajikistan. Russia's policies in the early 2000s were characterised primarily by a pragmatic approach – Russia's objective when promoting EvrAzES was to create an economic union which would expand Russia's markets and shield its products from external competition, while ensuring the unhindered transit of its products to external and internal EvrAzES markets. Russia tried to re-establish the economic ties that had existed during the Soviet era but on the basis of more efficient, market-footing arrangements. Yet, it also made sure that the new economic agreements would be beneficial to Russia, and to that end, the Kremlin made use of its *hegemonic* power. The Eurasian Economic Community (EvrAzES) project, however, cannot be entirely described as a neo-imperialist scheme, as member states *voluntarily* agreed to join the organisation (there are no signs in the early 2000s of Russia's coercion), in view of benefits that could be obtained in terms of the expansion of trade and freedom of transit. The 2003 *Single Economic Space* initiative, in turn, was actually promoted by the Ukrainian government, rather than by Russia, in order to appeal to domestic constituencies in the east of the country, and potentially create a bigger market for Ukrainian products through the full implementation of a Free Trade Area (FTA).

As the decade progressed, however, Russia's policies in the realm of economic integration began to evolve. Moscow proved increasingly reluctant to subsidise the economies of countries closely tied to Russia, such as Belarus – unless it obtained some tangible benefits in return. Furthermore, the Kremlin also began employing *hard power* instruments – in the form of economic sanctions, embargoes, restrictions and quotas – when pursuing its foreign objectives in the Near Abroad. As economic integration with Belarus stalled, Russia proved ready to exert significant economic pressures, including demanding substantial increases in energy prices – to draw Belarus into a closer union with Russia and to gain access to Belarus' coveted industrial assets, in a clear display of neo-imperialist behaviour. Russia's engagement with Ukraine was also characterised by a neo-imperial approach, as Russia directly interfered in presidential elections in 2004 to ensure the victory of a pro-Russian candidate, cultivated ties with Russian minorities, and dreamed of the 'reunification' the two big Slavic states around the SES project. The Kremlin's actions, however, also followed a clear economic logic – the unwillingness to continue subsidising the economies of countries which were not willing to open up their markets to Russia's products, as was the case with Belarus. As far as Ukraine is concerned, the possibility of creating a vast market of producers and consumers with neighbouring states also underpinned the SES initiative.

Under President Putin, Russia also actively promoted military integration within the CSTO framework, in order to create an effective security organisation capable of addressing the newly emerging regional security threats – the spread of Islamist fundamentalism, the resilience of drug trafficking and organised crime, and the challenges of NATO enlargement into Russia's Near Abroad. Yet, the CSTO was also expected to enhance Russia's own protection and security, by allowing Moscow to deploy its military troops in the CIS/CSTO area and by helping Russia to acquire additional strategic depth. In this respect, it can be argued that the CSTO project had, to a certain extent, a neo-imperialist design, namely ensuring that the CIS/CSTO states remained closely aligned militarily to Russia and that no foreign military alliance be allowed to encroach upon the CIS/CSTO space. While the Kremlin succeeded, to a certain extent, in its endeavour, there were clear limits to Russia's geo-strategic reach in the CSTO. In the 2000s, and especially after 9/11, CSTO member states began developing much closer military ties NATO and the USA, as well as with China, whose influence in Central Asia expanded through the strengthening of the Shanghai Cooperation Organisation (SCO). This new predicament directly challenged Russia's military predominance in the former Soviet space. Yet, it must also be noted, that all those countries which formed part of the CSTO, welcomed Russian military support, and therefore Russia's actions cannot be seen as entirely fitting the neo-imperialist model. All CSTO states, and especially the weaker ones – Tajikistan, Kyrgyzstan and Armenia – were consumers rather than providers of security, eager to obtain Russian military assistance whenever deemed necessary. As such, Russia's policies did not fully fit into the neo-imperialist model.

Russia's actions, however, were not devoid of *neo-imperial* undertones, especially in the energy field. When Putin reached the Russian presidency, he gave the energy sector in Russia centre stage. Not only were Russia's abundant energy resources supposed to support and underpin Russia's economic development, the energy complex was supposed to become an effective instrument of CIS integration. This in turn, was expected to allow Russia to emerge as an influential energy power, capable of conducting an independent foreign policy. While such an approach clearly reflected a neo-imperialist project, Russia's actions also followed, to a certain extent, an entirely legitimate commercial rationale – Russia and the CIS states could benefit quite significantly from common CIS energy systems, if properly managed, while Russia's Gazprom could also profit from the acquisition of market shares in the CIS internal gas distribution businesses. Furthermore, Russia's control over CIS transit pipelines could ensure the uninterrupted flow of Russian gas resources to consumers in Europe – one of Russia's key strategic and commercial objectives. The instruments utilised by Russia to achieve its aims, however, did not always correspond to legitimate commercial practices. During Putin's second and third term in office, and during the Medvedev interregnum, Russia's policies were instead characterised by a growing reliance on *hard* coercive methods, in contravention to international law – sudden substantial price increases, threats and cuts of energy deliveries, and the imposition of obscure business schemes in the energy trade. Russia was able, in this way, to obtain control over coveted energy assets in 'debt-for-equity' swaps in several CIS countries such as Moldova, Armenia and Belarus, and thus enhance control over the CIS energy complex.

Russia undoubtedly took advantage of its hegemonic position as the main CIS energy provider to set policies and prices. In some instances, Russia's continued dependency on Ukraine and Belarus for the transit of gas, reduced the Kremlin's leverage capacity, but Russia generally remained the stronger partner, able to determine export quantities and prices charged. More importantly, the Kremlin increasingly utilised gas prices, and the reliance of countries such as Ukraine and Belarus on the delivery of Russian gas, as policy instruments to achieve *political* objectives – for example, to weaken the pro-Western Orange coalition in Ukraine, or to compel Belarus to join Russia in a Union State. Russia, therefore, made increased use of its *hegemonic power* to try to keep these two countries under its sphere of influence in a neo-imperial space. In Central Asia, instead, Russia exploited its geographical position and took advantage of the transport infrastructure inherited from the Soviet era, to ensure that most of the gas produced in the region transited through Russian pipelines and was sold either inside Russia or the CIS space. Such a predicament compelled Central Asian gas-producing states to look for alternative markets for their sales, and CIS energy-consuming states – Ukraine, Belarus and Moldova – to find alternative gas providers, thus reducing Russia's hegemonic reach.

With Putin in the Kremlin, Russia also adopted a much more assertive policy vis-à-vis the conflicts in Georgia and Moldova. The early 2000s witnessed a significant deterioration of Russia's relations with Georgia in view of the resumption of large-scale violence in Chechnya, which turned the North and South Caucasus once again into areas of utmost concern for the Kremlin. Furthermore, the establishment of tight military cooperation between Georgia and NATO was seen by Moscow as challenging directly Russia's presence in Georgia – an area of key strategic significance to Russia on the Caucasus and the Black Sea. Concern over Russia's displacement from this traditional region of influence grew as Western pressure mounted on Russia to close its military bases in Georgia. To compensate for Russia's forced military withdrawal from its southern neighbour, the Kremlin established close 'unofficial' partnerships with Georgia's separatist regions of Abkhazia and South Ossetia, which effectively turned these areas into Russian *protectorates*. This allowed Russia to keep a foothold in Georgia, in the hope that it could exert its influence over Tbilisi's foreign policy decision-making, although it did not always succeed in its endeavour. Similarly, Russia also established very strong ties with Moldova's Transdniestria – in the form of financial subsidies and energy support, military assistance and the issuing of Russian passports. While Russia's actions in Transdniestria clearly showed Russia's eagerness to keep Moldova under its sphere of influence, they also reflected Russia's legitimate concerns over the enlargement of NATO into Romania and Bulgaria in 2004. Moreover, in a clear indication that the EU and Russia's Near Abroad increasingly overlapped, the EU became further engaged in the 2000s' resolution of the Transdniestrian conflict, while it also deployed a border assistance mission along the Transdniestrian section of the Ukrainian–Moldovan border in 2005, to Russia's great concern. When Ukraine, following on EU instructions, enforced customs regulations along its border with Moldova, Russia sided openly with Transdniestria and imposed a ban on Moldova's agricultural products, showing a readiness to use hard coercive power to ensure its objectives in the region – preservation of a foothold inside Moldova.

Russia's behaviour in Georgia and Moldova contrasted, quite sharply, with the positions adopted in relation to the Nagorno-Karabakh conflict. During the 2000s, and especially during the Medvedev interregnum, Russia took a positive stance in the negotiations and collaborated actively with the other OSCE Minsk co-Chairs on the Nagorno-Karabakh dispute, never engaging in overt obstructionism – in a sign that it had, at least apparently, discarded its imperial legacy in this region. Russia resigned itself to the fact that any deployment of Russian peacekeepers would be accompanied by the presence of other – most probably Western – troops. Yet, during the 2000s and 2010s Russia partly succeeded in achieving its key objectives in the region – it strengthened further its robust military-strategic partnership with Armenia while it also revamped Russia's relations with Azerbaijan, with whom it also established a military partnership. Russia, nevertheless, remained extremely concerned over the growing ties between Azerbaijan and NATO, and the increased military support provided by the United States to Azerbaijan's – and Kazakhstan's – naval forces in the Caspian Sea region, as such actions challenged its military predominance in the Caucasus/Caspian region.

Putin's more forceful foreign policy in the Near Abroad was underpinned by significant improvements in the country's economic conditions. This, in turn, generated high approval ratings for President Putin, which by the mid-2000s, exceeded 70 per cent. Foreign and security policy-making became increasingly concentrated in the hands of the President, who took an active and special interest in topic. Furthermore, a marginalised opposition and greater political stability gave Putin greater confidence, and pushed him to behave much more assertively, not only within the former Soviet space, but also in global affairs, and to directly confront the United States. Putin's self-assured behaviour was accompanied by attempts to modernise and strengthen the country's armed forces. The objective was to utilise Russia's military potential to project power and enforce policy more effectively. All this helped Putin to materialise his policies of greater engagement and assertiveness in the former Soviet space.

The arrival of President Dmitry Medvedev at the helm of Russia, did not really represent an end to Vladimir Putin's presence and influence in the Russian political scene. Putin remained in many respects the dominant actor, of the Medvedev–Putin *tandem*. Nevertheless, Medvedev did introduce a significant change of style in politics, which was characterised by a less confrontational approach, especially in the international arena. Yet, the Medvedev Presidency was soon marked by Russia's military intervention in Georgia – a watershed in Russia's foreign policy towards countries in the Near Abroad. For the first time, Russia openly utilised military force to protect its interests in the former Soviet space, and unilaterally modified the borders of a neighbouring sovereign state, by recognising the independence of Georgia's South Ossetian and Abkhaz separatist regions. Russia's intervention succeeded in putting a halt, at least momentarily, to NATO's continued enlargement into the former Soviet space. Yet, Russia's actions were conducted in clear violation of international law, and came at the expense of a significant deterioration of Russia's relations with the West. More significantly, Russia prolonged indefinitely its military presence in the Abkhazia and South Ossetia – in a clear sign that it viewed these areas, and Georgia as a whole, as falling under its exclusive sphere of influence. Through a series of bilateral agreements reached with Sukhumi and Tskhinvali, Russia not only guaranteed for itself a long-term military presence in Abkhazia and South Ossetia, it de facto incorporated these separatist regions almost fully into Russia. This, however, came at the expense of Russia's loss of influence over the rest of Georgia – the Georgian leadership described Moscow's presence in the separatist regions of Georgia as an 'occupation', and increasingly turned to the EU and NATO for support.

Putin's return to the Presidency

With the return of Putin to the Presidency in 2012, Russia adopted a significantly more assertive policy both internationally – in Syria and in the Balkans – and regionally – in the former Soviet space. Russia's policies not only responded to new geo-strategic realities and potentially legitimate state concerns – EU enlargement and the potential spread of Islamist fundamentalism in the Middle East – but also reflected concerns over 'regime change' in Russia. More significantly, Putin fully embraced a 'civilisational' narrative, as the driver behind Russia's policies in Eurasia. This translated into efforts by the Kremlin to establish a powerful Russian-led economic and military bloc in the CIS space which would turn Russia once again into a Great Power in the international arena. Putin's understanding of the CIS as unique civilisational space where Russia was expected to play a hegemonic role, came hand in hand with a vision of Russia as the leader of the Christian civilisation in the global arena. While the Medvedev interregnum had seen an attempt by the Kremlin to suppress the more extreme dimensions of the Russian nationalist narratives, the return of Putin to the Kremlin witnesses once again a revival of nationalist and imperialist ideologies, as well as the promotion of Russian conservative philosophers such as Nikolai Berdyaev, Vladimir Solovyov and Ivan Ilyin. More importantly, Putin placed Russia at the centre of a global conservative movement which upheld moral and traditional conservative values. He actively promoted such views in European countries of the Near and Far Abroad, in an attempt to challenge the EU's growing presence in the former Soviet space.

The late 2000s and early 2010s, thus, saw the emergence of a much more coherent and effective project, promoted by the Kremlin, to pursue economic integration within the EvrAzES framework – the Eurasian (Economic) Union. The project was spearheaded by Russia's desires to create a powerful economic bloc, which could counter the growing presence of the EU on the western fringes of the CIS and the rise of China in Central Asia. Clear geo-strategic objectives, therefore, lay at the heart of the project – the Eurasian Union, in the Kremlin's eyes, allowed Russia to establish its 'own regional centre of influence', and promote the emergence of a multipolar world. However, economic drivers also lay behind the establishment of such a bloc – the 2008 global financial crisis had shown the vulnerabilities of the CIS economies, including of the Russian economy. In the Kremlin's eyes, it had created the immediate need to enhance economic ties within CIS framework. This indicated that there also existed clear legitimate considerations, from Moscow's point of view, which argued in favour of closer economic integration – increased trade, bigger investment and/or protectionism against stronger external competition or monetary devaluation. Furthermore, many of the ECU/EAEU members themselves also supported such an economic project in the aftermath of the global financial crisis. Therefore, although the EAEU initiative reflected Russia's geopolitical ambitions, the project was also partly a result of *voluntary contracting*, especially as far as CIS countries like Kazakhstan and Kyrgyzstan were concerned.

The Kremlin, however, did not conceal its readiness to utilise coercive methods and threats – in clear violation of international law – towards those CIS countries more reluctant to join the bloc, such as Ukraine, Moldova, Armenia and Georgia. Russia even used coercive methods, including threats to end subsidies, against its all-time ally Belarus, in order to compel Minsk to join the Russian-led Eurasian integration projects. All this showed that Russia was ready in the early- to mid-2010s to engage in coercive diplomacy to restore a 'neo-empire' in the former Soviet space, which kept the CIS states tightly aligned to Russia. Furthermore, while Russia, in theory, accepted to engage in 'legalized forms of integration', it nevertheless behaved unilaterally, whenever it considered it necessary to further its own national objectives – clearly displaying its *hegemonic power* in a 'Russia First' approach. More importantly, as the dominant economic power, Russia was able to establish an economic project very much to its liking. Moscow made sure that the ECU's common external tariffs (CETs) were based on Russia's external tariffs, as this allowed Russia to expand its products in the ECU/SES space unhindered, and at the same time, shielded from external competition – although external tariffs were expected progressively to fall in line with Russia's World Trade Organization (WTO) membership commitments.

Russia proved particularly concerned over Ukraine's readiness to sign an AA/DFCTA with the EU and over its reluctance to join the Russian-led Eurasian Economic Union. Close historical and cultural ties brought the two countries together, as well as the existence of deep commercial and industrial links, which Moscow feared would be impaired if Ukraine signed up to the EU's free trade agreement. Moscow therefore exerted strong pressure on Kiev to ensure that it abandoned the EU's Association Agreement and, instead, joined the EAEU, clearly indicating that Russia was ready to use all instruments at its disposal to keep Ukraine within its sphere of influence. However, Russia's aggressive policies very soon backfired – the Ukrainian population rejected President Yanukovych's decision to abandon Ukraine's pro-EU course, and instead mobilised in a massive uprising against the Yanukovych regime. The fall of Yanukovych, and the prospect of a staunchly pro-EU leadership coming to power in Kiev, with a strong nationalist agenda, created great worries in Moscow. It led to concerns that Russia's naval forces could be evicted from the Crimean peninsula, and that Moscow would be forced to deploy its strategic Black Sea Fleet elsewhere in Russia. Russia also worried that if Ukraine joined NATO, the Atlantic Alliance's military infrastructure would be deployed very closely to Russia's borders, thus increasing Russia's geo-strategic vulnerability.

More importantly, the prospect of Ukraine integration into a different geo-strategic bloc than the one being promoted by Russia was a predicament that the Russian leadership – and the Russian population at large – could not accept. Russians still viewed Ukrainians as not only belonging to the same civilisational space as Russia but also as being the same 'people', in a clear indication that they proved unable entirely to discard Russia's imperial legacy. This predicament prompted President Putin forcefully to annex Crimea, and to foment unrest in southern and eastern Ukraine, in order to weaken the new Ukrainian authorities in Kiev. While geo-strategic imperatives certainly lay behind Putin's decision to incorporate Crimea into Russia – to secure Russia's military presence on the peninsula, and ensure Russia's ability to project its power in the Black Sea region – an imperialist idea and a nationalist mindset also directed the Kremlin's actions, especially as far as integration of eastern and southern Ukraine was concerned. Influential nationalist/imperialist circles in Russia promoted the *Novorossiya* project, which foresaw the incorporation of Crimea, the Donbass and southern Ukraine – the 'crown jewels' of the Russian Empire – into Russia. In the first days and weeks of the Donbass unrest, Russia toyed with the idea of incorporating Novorossiya into Russia, although Putin eventually decided to reject such an undertaking.

Instead, Russia's actions during May to September 2014 revealed the true essence of the Kremlin's objectives in Ukraine – to keep the country under Russia's influence, in order to ensure that it did not fully embrace the Euro-Atlantic institutional structures. Such a predicament – Ukraine's membership of NATO – was seen by the Kremlin as weakening Russia's geo-strategic defences and creating a cleavage among the Slavic 'brotherly' Russian and Ukrainian nations. As events in Kiev unfolded in February 2014, Russians increasingly questioned the territorial integrity of Ukraine – clearly attesting to a neo-imperialist mindset. Russia's military engagement in Ukraine, however, backfired – although Ukraine did not join NATO, Kiev nevertheless developed very close military ties with the Atlantic Alliance and established a close economic and political partnership with the EU. Furthermore, Russia's behaviour in Ukraine not only clearly violated international law, it upset the existing territorial order in Europe and reinforced Russia's behaviour as a revisionist power in the international arena. Yet, the transformation of the Donbass region, to all intents and purposes into a Russian protectorate, of the likes of Abkhazia and South Ossetia, allowed Russia to keep a foothold in Ukraine and partly ensure its influence in the region.

To summarise, this book has displayed that evolution characterised Russia's policies in the former Soviet space, moving from disengagement to hegemony. It has shown that Russia's policies towards the former Soviet space are much more complex and multi-faceted than usually assumed. They reflect a combination of legitimate state interests, enduring Soviet legacies, and genuine concerns over events unfolding along Russia's borders. The book, however, also shows that at times, great power nostalgia and a genuine difficulty of discarding Russia's imperial legacy does shape Russia's behaviour in the former Soviet space.

Index

9/11 attacks, impact on Russia 137–8
14th Army (Operational Group of Russian Forces): involvement in Transdniestria; 112, 116, 118–19, 123, 319; withdrawal 60, 118, 123, 216, 218, 220, 224, 317–19, 345
201st Motorised Rifle Division (MRD) 78, 79, 117–19, 121, 181, 186, 187, 203, 204
366th Motorised Infantry Division (MID) 112, 114

Abkhazia 14, 82–3; agreements with Russia 309–10, 321; EU Monitoring Mission in Georgia (EUMM) 309; recognition by Russia 305, 307–8, 321; Russia's military presence 307–8; United Nations 211–12; Upper Kodori 214, 306; war and Russia's involvement 111–14, 118, 121–2, 125, 126, 210–14, 304–7, 321–2
Afanasiev, Yury 27
Afghanistan 78, 84, 117, 137, 180–1, 188, 192, 201, 235, 315
Akhalkalaki military base 82, 85, 115, 123, 212, 213
Aliyev, Ilham 222–3, 310, 312, 314–15
Al-Qaeda 137, 196
Ambartsumov, Evgeny 28, 52
annexation of Crimea 199, 261, 293, 310, 313, 319–20, 329, 329–32, 337–8
Arbatov, Aleskei 22, 27–8, 34, 141, 200
Armenia: bilateral military cooperation with Russia 81–2, 181–2; cartels andmonopolies in 261; CIS border protection role 51; and the CIS/ Russian gas trade 100–1, 279–80, 284–6, 289–90; and the conflict in Nagorno-Karabakh 114–15, 121–3, 210, 220–3, 225, 227–8, 310–13, 315; and the EAEU 263–4, 269–70; and EvrAzES 158; border protection 60; relationship with the European Union 263–4, 279; relationship with NATO 192, 201; relationship with Russia 50, 60, 81–2, 84, 112, 115, 118, 123–4, 181–2, 187, 190, 199–200, 210, 221, 223, 314–15; relationship with Turkey 311–12; and the Russian-Georgian war 306; WTO membership 162
ArmRosGazprom (ARGP) 101, 106, 279, 285, 286, 289
ASEAN Regional Forum (ARF) 194
August 1991 coup 23
Azerbaijan: and the CIS/Russian gas trade 94, 103, 280–4, 289, 298; CST membership 58–9, 83; GUAM membership 81; introduction of national currency 54; relationship with NATO 124, 138, 223, 315; relationship with Russia 84, 111, 112, 114–15, 118, 122–4, 126, 199–200, 210, 221, 223, 314–15; relationship with the West 83; and the Russian-Georgian war 306; and the separatist conflict in Nagorno-Karabakh 111–12, 114–15, 118, 121–3, 220, 222–3, 310–15; withdrawal from CIS military alliance 124

Baburin, Sergei 26
Bagapsh, Sergei 2013
Balakhonov, Vladimir 1–2
Baku Tbilisi Ceyhan (BTC) pipeline 123, 221
Baku–Tbilisi–Erzurum (BTE) pipeline 103, 221, 281–2
Balkhash radar station 84

Index

Baltic states: and access to Western markets 17; achievement of independence 44; and the Adapted CFE Treaty 216; discrimination against Russian minorities in 30, 35; inclusion into the Atlantic Alliance (NATO) 138
Baranovichi missile warning station 84, 199
Băsescu, Traia 217, 318
Batumi military base 60, 82, 85, 123, 212, 213
Bediurov, Brontoi 26
Beissinger, Mark 11, 16
Belarus: 'Belarusian corridor' 58; bilateral military cooperation with Russia 60, 81, 182, 184, 198–9; and CIS trade 73, 153–63, 248–59, 260–2, 269–70; CST membership 58; and the CSTO 184, 185, 187, 189, 190, 197–202; customs union agreement 57–8, 155, 162, 288; devalues currency 261; and the EAEU 257–8, 269; and CIS economic integration 153–6; economic policy 56–7; and the ECU 248, 250, 253–4, 256; and EvrAzES 154–6, 158–9, 160–2; and the future of 'Russia' 22, 24; gas distribution 254, 279; border protection 51, 60, 184; relationship with NATO 192, 201; relationship with Russia 50, 84, 163–71, 181–2, 248–62, 269, 279, 284–8, 290–3, 296–7; relationship with the European Union 143; Russian-Belarusian monetary integration 55–7, 75–6, 167–9; Russian-Belarusian political and economic integration 74–8, 81, 163–7, 167–71, 173–4; and the Russian gas trade 75, 94, 97–100, 168–70, 266, 279, 284–9, 290–3, 296–7; and separatist conflicts 189–90, 200; SES agreement and implementation 156–7, 248, 251, 254; siphoning of gas 61; trade dispute with Russia 261; and the WTO 252
Belkovsky, Stanislav 243
'belt of good-neighbourliness' 24, 29
Beltransgaz 98, 105, 165–6, 168–70, 254, 279, 286, 290, 296, 297
Bendery 112, 116
Besançon, Alan 11
Beslan school siege 142
Black Sea 82, 102, 113, 170, 283, 288, 306–7, 331
Black Sea Fleet (BSF) 60, 66, 82, 90, 95–6, 98, 104–5, 214, 235, 291–2, 329–31, 338

Blue Stream 102, 283
Boden, Dieter (SRSG), 121
Borodai, Yury 26Borodai, Aleksandr 335
Bordyuzha, Nikolai 189, 198
Bosnia 35
British Commonwealth 5
Bulgaria 138, 210, 279, 288, 295, 318, 352
Bush, George W. 220

Caspian Sea 221
Central Asia – Center pipeline 284
Central Asia – China pipeline 283, 294
Central Bank of Russia (CBR) 54, 56, 76, 163
Central Bank of the USSR (Gosbank) 52
Chechnya 37, 83, 121, 138, 142, 210–11, 221
Chernomyrdin, Viktor 57, 94, 108
China 4–5; and multipolarity 36, 137; and military cooperation with Central Asian states 80, 191, 193, 201; Russia's overall trade with 160, 191, 242, 297; Central Asian gas trade with 102, 107, 283, 288, 294, 298; economic relationship with Central Asian republics 193–6, 201, 255, 259, 263; Russia's military cooperation with 139; Silk Road project (OBOR) 259–60; and the Shanghai Cooperation Organisation (SCO) 139, 192–6, 201, 203; and the Shanghai Five 85–6, 88
CIS integration: administrative bodies 71; air defence system 84–5, 182; anti-terrorist centre 182; border protection 51; economic integration moves ahead 153–6; establishment of a customs union 162–3; as evidence of neo-imperialism 86–9, 171–4; FTA implementation 71–3; military cooperation efforts 78–82; Primakov's encouragement 70; progress on EvrAzES 158–62; renewed attempts at economic integration 70–4; Russian-Belarusian integration 74–8, 163–7, 167–71; Russia's behaviour 82–6; a single economic space with Ukraine 156–7; treaties 70; visa regime 89; *see also* Commonwealth of Independent States (CIS); Eurasian Customs Union (ECU); Eurasian Economic Community (EvrAzES); Eurasian Economic Union (EAEU)
CIS military integration *see* Collective Security Treaty Organisation (CSTO)

'civilisational' view of the CIS space 3, 145, 238–9, 239–42
coercive diplomacy, the concept 9
collapse of the Soviet Union 1–2, 16, 21–2, 27, 49, 61, 144; and the fate of ethnic Russians 2; impact on Russia's traditional defence strategy 49; new geopolitical situation created by 49; and questions about 'Great Power' status 2; role of non-Russian republics 45–6; role of the RSFSR leadership 44–5; trigger 23; Ukraine's role 46; view of Russian imperial nationalists 26
Collective Security Treaty (CST): air defence system 84–5; Armenia 81–2, 181–2; Belarus 81, 181, 184; Central Asia 78–80, 180–1; Concept 59; Council 59; establishment 51; military exercises 180; renewal 83; signatories 51; under Primakov 78–86; under Putin 179–83; under Yeltsin's first Presidency 51, 55, 58–9, 63, 65
Collective Security Treaty Organisation (CSTO): aims 185–6; air defence 187–8, 198–9; assessment of the CSTO in the 2000s 190–3; assessment in the 2010s 200–1; background 179; birth of 183–6; Central Asian Collective Rapid Deployment Forces 184, 186–8, 190–1, 197, 204; Charter 183, 197; collaboration with NATO 192–3; Collective Aviation Forces 198; counter-terrorism efforts 182, 187, 193; establishment of an inter-state agency 191; as evidence of neo-imperialism 201–3; further strengthening 186–90; and internal security/intelligence 188, 190, 197; KSOR 197, 199, 200; military exercises 184, 187, 197; military integration moves ahead 179–83; peacekeeping forces and operations 189–90, 197, 198; plans for a joint standing conventional army 188; post-9/11 developments 191–2; as potential instrument of Russian hegemony 190; Rapid Deployment Collective Forces 180; Regional Coalition Group of Forces 180–1, 183, 185; regional systems of collective security 180; regional security complexes 199; reinforcement under Medvedev and third Putin presidencies 196–201; role of neo-imperialist designs 184–5; and Russia's nuclear weapons 182; and the Shanghai Cooperation Organisation (SCO) 193–6
'colour' revolutions 143, 168–9, 186, 189–90, 193, 195; *see also* Orange Revolution
common external tariffs (CETs) 58, 71, 76, 155, 158, 248, 252, 255–6, 262, 264
'Commonwealth of Democracies from the Baltic, Black Seas and Caspian region' 286
Commonwealth of Independent States (CIS): assessment 62–4, 88–9; aims 44, 48; asymmetrical confederation proposal 22; the Belarus-Russian monetary union project 56–7; Charter adopted 53; Charter details 62; concerns about Ukraine's reluctance to join 47; consensus-based decision-making 62; Council of Heads of Government 62; Council of Heads of State 62; creation 44, 46–8; customs union agreement 57, 63; Defence Ministers' Council 59; deeper integration efforts 56–62; and defence strategy 49–51; development of multilateral forms of cooperation with 29, 88; differentiated membership 62; disintegration 52–6, 153; disintegration of economic space 33; economic sphere 51–2, 54–6; Economic Union Treaty 57; energy and transport sphere 61–2; establishment of national armies 50, 55; as evidence of neo-imperialism 64–5; evolution of Russia's policy towards 48–50; factors in the decision to create 46–8; free trade and monetary union efforts 54, 56–7; Free Trade Area (FTA) 249, 251; incorporation of former Soviet states 33; 'informal empire' as objective of Russia's policies in 3; Inter-state Economic Committee 54; Intra-CIS trade 160–2; Joint Armed Forces (JAF) 50–1, 55, 66; military cooperation with Russia 58–60; military cooperation under Primakov 78–86; military disintegration and restoration 34; military doctrine 51; military integration under Putin 179–203; military sphere 55–6; performance assessment 62–4; rethinking of Russia's policy 153; Russian leaders' view of 24–6; Russia's objectives 44–8; Russia's policies in the early 1990s 48–2; technical credits 52; unified air defence system 59–60, 63, 66; voluntary nature 48–50; Yeltsin on the need for closer integration 30–1; *see also* CIS integration; gas trade in the CIS

Community of Sovereign States (CSS) 71, 75, 99; Supreme Council 74; Executive Committee 74; Parliamentary Assembly 74
Conference for Security and Cooperation in Europe (CSCE) 4
Conventional Forces in Europe (CFE) Treaty 89, 112, 123, 140, 142, 149, 213, 216, 224, 226
'Covenant on the Suppression of Terrorism, Separatism and Religious extremism' (2001) 193
Council for Foreign and Defence Policy 34
Crimea 82, 85, 96, 98, 332–3; annexation of 199, 261, 313, 319, 329, 329–32
Czech Republic 81, 140, 142, 217, 234, 335; joins NATO 37

Dashichev, Vyacheslav 34
derzhavnost' 35, 132
Dodon, Igor 320
Donbass region 319–20, 334; outbreak of war 332–7
Dostum, Abdul Rashid 78–9
Doyle, Michael 10
Druzhba pipeline 98, 99, 107, 279
Dubossary 116
Dugin, Aleksandr 137, 242
Dunlop, John 11

empire, definitions 10–11
energy prices, impact on the Russian economy 140
Energy Strategy of Russia 1994 62
Erdogan, Recep Tayyip 295
ethnic Russians 2, 16, 22, 146, 239, 330–2
Eurasia, Putin's civilising mission 144–7
Eurasian Customs Union (ECU) 248, 250–6, 260, 263, 266–7, 287, 290; Customs Union Commission (CUC) 162, 248, 249; Eurasian Economic Commission (EEC), 249–50; Customs Code 250
Eurasian Development Bank 158
Eurasian Economic Community (EvrAzES): assessment 171–2; common external tariffs (CETs) 155; Community Court of Justice 154; Court of Justice 155, 250; Customs Union 162–3; decision-making mechanisms 154; establishment and member states 153; Free Trade Area (FTA) 158–61; integrated foreign exchange market 158; Integration Committee (IC) 154, 171; Inter-State Council (ISC) 154, 162, 171; intra-EvrAzES trade 159; observers 158; progress on 158–62; single economic space with Ukraine 156–7; structure 154; tariff harmonisation 158; trade diversification 160; trade restrictions 161–2; and WTO accession 156
Eurasian Economic Union (EAEU): assessment 268–70; creation 248; Eurasian Customs Union (ECU) and Single Economic Space (SES) implementation 249–51; ECU and SES rationale 251–6; enlargement to new members 262–8; Eurasian Inter-Governmental Council 258, 262; as evidence of neo-imperialism 268–70; formal establishment 258; functioning of the EAEU 260–2; launch of Eurasian Union project 256–9; movement towards a single economic space 249–50; Russia's unilateral trade restrictions 261–2; and the Silk Road 259–60; Supreme Eurasian Economic Council 258, 262; 'trade wars' 261
Eurasianism 8, 22, 26–7, 135, 243
Eurasian Union (EuU) 153, 253, 256, 256–9, 318
EuroMaidan 268, 291, 330, 332
European Security Treaty (2009) 236
European Union (EU): Eastern enlargement 143–4, 217; Eastern Partnership 242, 243, 253, 263, 270; EU-Russia Political-Security Committee (PSC) 316–7; Neighbourhood Policy 143–4; Monitoring Mission in Georgia (EUMM) 309; and Russia 226, 238, 241, 257, 261, 270, 271, 317, 352; sovereignty transfer model 5; and Turkish Stream 288, 293, 295

Filat, Vlad 316
financial crisis (1998) 73, 76
financial crisis (2008/9) 160, 236, 238; *see also* global financial crisis
Finland 1, 12
Foreign Policy Concept (2008) 237
Foreign Policy Concept (2013) 240
foreign policy of the Russian Federation: active foreign policy debate (1992) 25–8; *Basic Provisions* 31; broad consensus (1994–1995) 31–5; criticisms 34–5; conservative nationalists 35; and the debate on 'What is Russia?' 22–4; Eurasianist perspective 26–7; as

evidence of neo-imperialism 38–41; imperialist nationalist perspective 26, 24; leaders' more assertive policy (1993) 28–31; moderate liberal arguments 27–8; moderate nationalist perspective 28; 'multipolarity' doctrine 35–8, 70, 121–2, 134, 215, 240–1, 269, 346; Russia's pro-Western orientation (1991–1992) 24–5; *see also* Russian foreign policy
foreign policy under Medvedev and Putin: background and overview 233–6; concluding thoughts on the civilisational narrative 242, 244; Medvedev's foreign policy outlook 236–9; Putin's return to the Presidency and reinforcement of civilisational paradigm 239–42
former Soviet states (FSS), reintegration proposals 22
France: arms sales to Georgia 265; assistance to Tajikistan and Kyrgyzstan 80; Group of Friends of Georgia 121; Minsk co-Chair 210, 220–3, 225, 311, 310–14, 322, 352; Neo-Empire 12–13, 342–3; *France d'Outre Mer* 12
French African Colonies 12–13
Fyodorov, Boris 33

Gabala radar station 84, 199
Gaidar, Yegor 33
Gamsakhurdia, Zviad 44
gas trade, Russian *see* Russian gas trade
gas trade in the CIS: acquisition of CIS energy infrastructure by Russia 278–81; Armenia, Georgia and Moldova 100–1, 289–90; assessment 103–7, 295–9; Belarus and Ukraine 95–100, 290–3; Central Asian-Russian gas trade 101–3, 281–4, 293–5, 298; Eurasian Gas Alliance 281; Gazprom raises prices 284–8; impact of the global financial crisis 288–9; relevance 94; siphoning of gas destined for Europe 61, 97, 100; *see also* Russian gas trade
Gazprom 94, 96–103, 168–70, 254, 266, 279–88, 290–1, 293–4, 337; interests in CIS states 61; raises prices 284–8
Georgia: CIS air defence cooperation 60, 84; and the CIS/Russian gas trade 100–1, 280–1, 284, 286, 289–90; 'colour' revolution 143; CST membership 58–9, 83; and the EAEU 264–5; GUAM membership 81; introduction of national currency 54; military ties with Russia 60, 82, 85; border protection 60; relationship with the European Union 244, 262, 264–5, 305, 309, 310; relationship with NATO 83, 124, 141, 210, 214, 265, 305, 308; relations with Russia 111–14, 121–4, 211–15, 224, 226, 264–5, 304–10; relations with the United States 211, 308; Russian military bases in 60, 82, 85, 113–14, 212; Russian blockade 113; Russia's overall trade with 161, 264–5; Russian withdrawal 216; wars in Abkhazia and South Ossetia 111–12, 114, 118–20, 121–4, 161, 210–15, 304–10; withdrawal from CST 83; WTO membership 162; *see also* Russian-Georgian War
global defence system, Yeltsin's proposal 25
global financial crisis: impact on CIS gas trade 288–9; impact on Eurasian economies 252; impact on GDP of CIS countries 248; impact on Russian economy 97; Medvedev presidency's focus on managing 234
GUAM/GUUAM (Georgia, Ukraine, (Uzbekistan) Azerbaijan and Moldova) 81, 84
Girkin, Igor (Strelkov) 333, 335
Goncharov, Sergei 27
Gorbachev, Mikhail: New Political Thinking 25; and disagreements with Yeltsin 45
Gosudarstvennichestvo 35
Great power status 2, 7, 8, 11, 29, 33, 34–6, 38, 41, 77, 133, 136, 141, 146, 148, 237, 241, 242, 253, 332, 349, 353, 356
Gyumri military base 60, 115, 181, 187, 199, 204, 221

Hamas 140
hard power, the concept 9
hegemony: the concept 5–6; Russian aspirations for the FSS 342–4; *see also* neo-imperialist hypothesis
Helsinki principles 4, 27
Hrazdan thermal power plant 279, 286
Hungary 37, 81, 217

illegal migration/immigration 4, 189, 249–50
imperialist argument: comparisons with the French experience 12–13; definitions of empire 10–11; testing the argument 13–17; *see also* neo-imperialist hypothesis

imposition, the concept 9
India 36, 102, 137
informal empire: definition 6–7; as objective of Russia's CIS policies 3; *see also* neo-imperialist hypothesis
Intermediate-Nuclear-Forces (INF) Treaty 140
International Monetary Fund (IMF) 26
international law 1, 3–5, 15, 25, 29, 37–8, 39, 44, 80, 120, 134, 163, 197, 215, 237, 240–1, 296, 304–5, 315, 321, 329, 331–2, 337, 343, 351, 353–6
international system: defensive structural realist argument 8; motivational realist argument 8; social constructivist perspective 8; structural realist beliefs 8
inter-state relations, Helsinki principles 4
Ionescu, Ghita 10
Iran 78, 101, 120–2, 137, 140, 182, 221, 223, 225, 235, 259, 279, 286, 288, 297
Iraq 37, 84, 137, 241, 315; US invasion 138
Islamic Movement of Uzbekistan (IMU) 79–80, 179–80, 193
Islamist-*jihadist* extremism: Moscow's concerns 183–4; Putin's view 137; and security in Central Asia and the Caucasus 79–80, 179, 184, 186, 188, 193, 236
Itera 98, 100, 101, 103, 106, 108, 284, 296
Ivanov, Igor 37–8, 186
Ivanov, Sergei 131, 137, 149, 153, 192, 331

Japan 80
Joint Armed Forces (JAF) 50–1

Kahler, Miles 6, 10, 13
Kaliningrad 17, 141, 169, 235
Kant military base 184, 186, 190, 199
Karachaganak field 103, 282
Karasin, Grigory 317
Karev, Roman 243
Karshi-Khanabad military base 192, 193
Kazakhstan: and China's OBOR initiative 259; and the CIS/Russian gas trade 103, 281–4, 293; and the CSTO 180, 184, 186–8, 197–9; customs union agreement 57–8, 155, 162, 288; discrimination of Russian minorities 35; and the EAEU 248, 250, 254–7, 260–2, 269–70; and EvrAzES economic integration 153–4, 158, 160, 163; oil and gas transit problems 161; 'potato war' 261; border protection 60; relationship with China 194, 201; relationship with NATO 192, 201; relationship with Russia 60–1, 79, 84; relationship with the United States 192; and the war in Tajikistan 118, 120; SES agreement and implementation 156–7, 248, 251; *Shanghai Five* membership 85; and the Shanghai Cooperation Organisation 193–6; WTO negotiations 252; WTO membership 262
KazRosGaz 103, 281
Keohane, Robert 5
Khadjimba, Raul 213
Khodjali 114
Khristenko, Viktor 157, 249, 283
Kochariyan, Robert 222
Kokoity, Eduard 212
Kolesnikov, Mikhail 59
Kolstoe, Paul 11
Kosachev, Konstantin 146
Kosopalov, Nikolai 25
Kosovo 37, 80, 214, 220, 234
Kosovo crisis 37
Kosyrev, Dmitry 2
Kozak, Dmitry 217
Kozak Memorandum 217, 219–20
Kozyrev, Andrei: pro-Western orientation 24–5, 29, 39, 48, 50; Draft Foreign Policy Outline 29; assertive tone 29, 32, 344; and rights of Russian minorities 29, 32; and CIS integration 32, 48, 50, 56; foreign policy consensus 33; criticism of Kozyrev's policies 34; assertive policies in the Near Abroad 39; support for territorial integrity 120; anti-imperialist vision 27, 344; Russia as the 'continuer state' 17
Kravchuk, Leonid 95
Kuchma, Leonid 97, 156, 174, 335
Kyrgyzstan: and the CIS gas trade 103; 'colour' revolution 195; and the CSTO 180, 184, 186–8, 200; EvrAzES customs union agreement 155–6, 162–3; and the EAEU 262–3; and EvrAzES economic integration 153–6, 158; IMU incursions 80, 179; outbreak of violence in southern Kyrgyzstan 197; 'potato war' 261; border protection 60; relationship with China 193–4, 201; relationship with NATO 201; relationship with Russia 190, 199; Russian military presence 184, 186, 190, 199; and the war in Tajikistan 118; *Shanghai Five* membership 85; and the Shanghai Cooperation Organisation 193–6; United

States bases 191, 193; WTO membership 158, 162, 262

Lavrov, Sergei 139, 141, 267; Russia's civilisational mission 240, 238–9; and the Nagorno-Karabakh conflict 308, 311, 313
Layne, Christopher 5
legitimate state interests, definition 4
Lebed, Aleksandr 116
Leontyev, Konstantin 240
Leontyev, Mikhail 243
Liberal Westernisers 25, 33, 34, 38, 136
Libya 241
Lieven, Dominic 10–11
Limonov, Eduard 26, 334
Lukashenko, Aleksandr 75, 77, 99, 105, 163–9, 171–4, 192, 202, 254, 257–8
Lukin, Vladimir 27–8

Madrid Principles 222
Main Lines of Development of Energy Policy until 2010 62
Main Provisions of the Energy Strategy of Russia for 2002 (2000) 278
Massoud, Ahmad Shah 78–9
Mearsheimer, John 8
Medvedev, Dmitry: assessment of his policies 351–4; becomes president of Russia 233–4; and the CSTO 196–7; emphasis on Russia's European destiny 238; and European security 236; foreign policy outlook 236–9; and the global financial crisis 234; Nagorno-Karabakh conflict resolution efforts 310–15; political style 233; and the Russian-Georgian War 234; and USA relations 235; 'privileged interests' 238; Meseberg initiative 316–17
Merkel, Angela 316
migration/immigration, illegal 4, 189, 249–50
Migranian, Andranik 22, 28, 33, 52
military conflicts: conciliatory stance under Primakov 121–4; as evidence of neo-imperialism 124, 126; Russia's involvement as neo-imperialist paradigm 112–20; in separatist regions 111–12
Moldova: and the annexation of the Crimea 319; and the CIS/Russian gas trade 100–1, 279, 284–5, 287, 289–90, 296–7; and overall CIS trade 73, 161; possible demilitarisation 218; discrimination against Russian minorities 35; and the EAEU 265–6, 270; and EvrAzES 158; Gagauz minority 266; GUAM membership 81; introduction of national currency 54; and the Kozak Memorandum 217, 219; Russia's military involvement in 112, 116, 118, 123; border protection 60; relationship with NATO 318–9; relationship with Russia 122–4, 161, 210, 216–21, 224–7, 265–6; relationship with the European Union 144, 217–19, 225–6, 265–6, 289, 290, 297, 316, 318, 319–20; relationship with the West 83; and the Transdniestrian conflict 111–12, 116, 118, 121–4, 215–20, 316–18, 320; Russian military presence 60, 85, 116, 219; Russian military withdrawal 123, 216, 220, 316–18, 320; WTO membership 162; *see also* Transdniestria
Moldovagaz 100, 279, 285, 289
'multipolarity' doctrine, Primakov and 35–8; Putin and 134, 137
Myalo, Ksenia 22, 243

Nabiev, Rakhmon 117
Naftohaz Ukrainy 266, 286, 291
Nagorno-Karabakh 14, 37, 83, 190, 200; April 2016 violence 313–4; assessment of Russia's role in 118–19, 227–8, 322; the conflict during Primakov's tenure 121–3; the conflict during Putin's first and second Presidencies 210, 220–3, 225, 227–8; the conflict during Medvedev's Presidency and during Putin's third Presidential tenure 310–13, 315; and the European Union 313; Key West talks 221; *Madrid Principles* 222, 310–11, 313, 322; Minsk co-Chairs 210, 220–3, 225, 310–14, 322, 352; outbreak of the war 111–12; *Prague Process* 222, 225, 310; Russia's role in the war 114–15; and the United States 220–1
Narotchinskaya, Natalya 243
nationalism, contrasting ideologies of 23
National Security Strategy (2009) 236
NATO: accession of Eastern European states 138; Armenia's relationship with 192, 201; Azerbaijan's collaboration with 223; Azerbaijan's relationship with 83, 124, 138, 223, 315; Belarus's relationship with 192, 201; CSTO's collaboration with 192–3; Eastern expansion plans 237; enlargement 34–5,

NATO: *continued*
37, 80, 100, 182–3, 200, 217; Founding Act with Russia 80; Georgia's relationship with 83, 124, 141, 210–12, 214, 226, 235, 265, 305, 307–8; Kazakhstan's relationship with 192, 201; Kyrgyzstan's relationship with 201; Moldova's relationship with 83, 217, 220, 224, 227, 318–9; NATO-Russia Council 138; 'out-of-area' operations 80; Partnership for Peace programme (PfP) 83, 192; Permanent Joint Council 80; Russian agreement with 37, 80, 123; Russia's relationship with 80–1, 141–2, 234, 235–6, 237, 241; Tajikistan's relationship with 201; Ukraine's relationship with 83, 214, 235, 286; Uzbekistan's relationship with 83

Nazarbayev, Nursultan 153, 171, 254–5, 257–8, 269

neo-imperialist hypothesis: and the former Soviet states 342–4; and Primakov's Foreign Ministry 346–8; and Putin's presidency 348–53; and Putin's return to the Presidency 353–6; the Yeltsin years 344–6

non-tariff barriers (NTB) 249–51, 259
Nord Stream gas pipeline 266, 288, 293
North Korea 137, 235
North Ossetia 113, 212, 215, 228, 310
North Caucasus 40, 121, 123, 137, 142, 183, 184, 214, 226, 236, 306, 307, 321
Northern Lights pipeline 98, 99, 165, 279
Novorossiysk 107
Novorossiya 334–5, 355
nuclear forces, locations of 51
nuclear power stations 95, 315
nuclear weapons: CIS and 44, 49; CSTO and 182
Nye, Joseph 5, 9

Obama, Barack 235–6, 310
One-Belt-One-Road (OBOR), China's initiative 259–60, 270
Orange Revolution 146, 157, 168, 195, 217, 285; *see also* 'colour' revolutions
Organization for Security and Co-operation in Europe (OSCE) 40, 81, 236; Istanbul Summit 82, 85, 123, 212, 216; and the Nagorno- Karabakh conflict 115, 119, 121–2, 123, 125, 210, 222–3, 227, 310–14, 322–3, 352; and the South Ossetian conflict 113, 119, 121, 122, 211–12, 309; and the Transdniestrian dispute 121, 125, 215–20, 224, 226, 316–17, 319–20; and the war in Ukraine's Donbass 335–6, 347

Pakistan 78, 102, 120, 201, 294
Paris *Charter for a New Europe* 4
Parrot, Bruce 6, 12
patriotism, Putin's view 132
peacekeeping operations, involvement of Russian troops in 29
Pleshakov, Konstantin 26–7
Poland 1, 81, 97, 99, 100, 106, 140, 142, 184, 217, 234–5, 266, 290; joins NATO 37
Poroshenko, Petro 337
post-Imperium, definition 7
Power of Siberia pipeline 294
Primakov, Yevgeny: and American predominance 134; assessment of his policies 86–9, 124–6, 346–8; and the doctrine of multipolarity 35–8; and CIS integration 70–86; at the Foreign Ministry 35, 346; and military conflicts in the former Soviet space (FSS) 121–5; post-imperial paradigm 85–8; views on Russia as strong state 35, 132; and the war in Transdniestria 215, 220
Prokhanov, Aleksandr 26, 136
Putin, Vladimir: advent and return to the Presidency of Russia 3, 239, 256, 353; annexation of Crimea 331–2; approval ratings 140; assessment of his policies 348–56; civilising mission in Eurasia 144–7; efforts to streamline the Russian administration 131–2; and the Eurasian Union project 256–9; foreign policy assertiveness and 'Russia First' approach 139–44; multipolarity 134, 137, 269; Munich Security Conference speech 139, 141; post-9/11 pro-Western turn 137–9; promotion and identification of Russian traditional values 132; Russia as a strong state 132–4; Russian nationalism 132, 136; return to the Presidency and reinforcement of civilisational paradigm 239–42; support for the views of Putin among Russian elites 136; on the unique nature of Russia's political development 143; views on CIS integration 136, 164; views on Russia and its place in the world 132–7; views on the Eurasian

dimension of Russia 135; views on Europe 134–5, 145–6, 256–7; views on Russia's energy potential 278; views on the West 134–5, 140–2, 241–2

Rakhmon, Imomali 117–18
Rebuilding Russia (Solzhenitsyn) 22
Regional Anti-Terrorist Structure (RATS) 193–4
Regional Coalition Group of Forces (RCGF) 180–1, 183, 185
religion, as integral part of Russia's identity 240
Remizov, Mikhail 243
Rice, Condoleezza 142, 149
Rogozin, Dmitry 265–6, 317–18
Romania 111, 138, 210, 217–18, 279, 290, 295, 297, 318–19, 323–4, 352
RosUkrEnergo (RUE) 284, 286, 287, 291, 296
rouble zone 52–4, 63
rubel' (Belarus) 55, 57, 77
Russia: increasing adoption of hegemonic and neo-imperialist approach 8; old and new ideas on what is Russia 22–4; One-Belt-One-Road 259–60; relationship with Armenia 70, 81–2, 84, 89, 100–1, 106, 111, 114–15, 118, 123–4, 181, 182, 184, 187, 190, 199–200, 210, 221–3, 225–7, 263–4, 279–80, 284–6, 289, 296–8, 314–15; relationship with Azerbaijan 84, 199–200, 210, 221, 223, 314–15; relationship with Belarus 50, 84, 181–2, 287; relationship with the European Union 37, 135, 138, 143–4, 145–6, 147, 236–8; relationship with Kazakhstan 60–1, 79, 84; relationship with Kyrgyzstan 190; relationship with Moldova 210, 216–21, 265–6; relationship with Tajikistan 79, 120–1; relationship with Ukraine 329–39; relationship with the United States 137–8, 141–3, 234–6, 237, 241, 310–11; relationship with Uzbekistan 188; WTO accession 248, 251–2; *see also* China; Belarus; Ukraine; Moldova; Kazakhstan; Kyrgyzstan; Tajikistan; Uzbekistan
Russia at the Turn of the Millennium (Putin) 133
Russia First policy 3, 23, 139–44
Russian Armed Forces 49–50, 59, 81, 83, 112, 113–17; Law on Defence 196–7

Russian Federation 1; as legal successor of the USSR 2
Russian foreign policy: as evidence of neo-imperialism 147–8; *see also* foreign policy of the Russian Federation; foreign policy under Medvedev and Putin
Russian gas trade 61, 94; acquisition of CIS energy infrastructure 278–81; assessment 103–7, 295–9; background 94–5; with Belarus 75, 98–100, 279, 290–1; with Central Asian and Caspian producers 103, 281–4, 293–5, 298; Central Asian gas triangle 101–2; with China 294; Eurasian Gas Alliance of Producers 281; with Moldova, Armenia and Georgia 100–1, 289–90; with Turkmenistan 101–2, 281–4, 293–4, 298; with Ukraine 95–8, 280, 290–3
Russian-Georgian War: assessment 321–2; aftermath 308–10; background 308–9; 'borderisation' process 265; ceasefire agreements 305, 309; Georgia's preparations for 306; global implications 237; and international law 304, 321; outbreak 305–8; Russia's objectives 304–5, 307; Russia's preparations for 306–7
Russian military doctrine 66, 179, 182, 183; Ivanov military doctrine 185
Russian minorities: discrimination against in the Baltic states 30; Russia's defence of the rights of in the Baltic states 34
Russian nationalism, anti-imperial 23; liberal 23
Russian Soviet Federative Socialist Republic (RSFSR) 1, 11, 21, 23, 38, 44–7; contrasting ideologies of nationalism 23
Russian world (*Russkii Mir*) 146
Russia's conduct towards Ukraine: annexation of Crimea 329–32; as evidence of neo-imperialism 337–9; war in the Donbass 332–7; and the EAEU 266–8
Rutskoi, Aleksandr 26

Saakashvili, Mikhail 212–13, 215, 286, 305, 308
sanctions: imposed on Russia by Europe and the US 289; Putin concerns about Western use of 241; Russian sanctions against Turkey and Ukraine 261–2
Sargsyan, Serzh 263–4, 310, 314

Schweller, Randall 8
separatist conflicts in Eurasia: and the future of Transdniestria 215–20; the Georgian conflicts 210–15; the Kremlin's approach under Putin 224–8; the Nagorno-Karabakh conflict 220–3, 310–15; participants in the resolution of 210
Sevastopol 82, 96, 98, 235, 291–2, 330–1
Seventh Congress of People's Deputies 52
Shafranik, Yury 94
Shah Deniz gas field 103, 107, 281, 282, 283, 294, 298
Shanghai cooperation organisation, and the CSTO 189, 193–6; Shanghai Five 85–6, 88, 347; calls to close military bases 139; and 'coloured revolutions' 189; military exercises 195
Sherr, James 9
Shevardnadze, Eduard 114, 124, 212
Silk Road project 259–60
Single Economic Space (SES) 156–7, 172, 249–51; and free trade area (FTA) 156–7, 172, 174, 249–50
Skokov, Yury 30, 31
Slavneft 105
Slavophiles 25
Slovakia 97, 138, 217
Slovenia 138Smirnov, Igor 215, 316
soft coercion, definition 9
soft power, the concept 9
Solzhenitsyn, Aleksandr 11, 22
South Ossetia 14, 28–9; war and Russia's involvement 111–13, 118–19, 121, 125, 210–14, 304–9, 321–2; peacekeeping forces 116, 118; recognition by Russia 305, 307–8; Russia's military presence 309; agreements with Russia 309–10, 321; EU Monitoring Mission in Georgia (EUMM) 309
South Stream pipeline 170, 288, 295
sovereign democracy 143
sovereignty transfer, EU model 5
Soviet Union: breakup 1 (*see also under* collapse and under USSR); exercising of monopoly of control 10; public nostalgia for 24
Spruyt, Hendrik 4, 6
Staff for the Co-ordination of Military Co-operation SCMC 55, 59, 185
Stankevich, Sergei 22
Starovoitova, Galina 24
state powers, ultimate goal 8
state sovereignty, Westphalian model 5

Strategic Course of the Russian Federation towards the member-states of the CIS 32, 61
Sudan 84
Surkov, Vladislav 143, 337
Syria 137, 140, 241

Tajikistan 14; and the CIS gas trade 103; and the CSTO 180, 184, 186–8, 200, 203; EvrAzES customs union agreement 155–62; and the EAEU 71, 263; and EvrAzES economic integration 154–6; and the IMU 79–80; introduction of national currency 55; border protection 60; relationship with NATO 201; military and strategic cooperation with China 201; relationship with Russia 79, 120–1, 184, 186, 263; Russian military presence 117–21, 123, 181, 184, 186, 190–1, 199; civil war 111–12, 117–20, 121–125; *Shanghai Five* membership 85; and the Shanghai Cooperation Organisation 193–6; Tajik-Afghan border 79, 184; and the Taliban 79; Treaty of Friendship with Russia 79
Taliban 78–9, 83, 137–8, 180–1, 196
Timoshenko, Yuliya 267, 268, 291–2
trade dispute, between Russia and Belarus 250
Trans-Adriatic pipeline 294
Trans-Anatolian Natural Gas Pipeline (TANAP) 294
TransCaspian pipeline 102, 106, 282, 283
Transdniestria 14, 28–9; conflict resolution negotiations 121–4, 215–20, 224–5, 279, 304, 315–20, 323–5; outbreak of war 111–12, 116, 118; relationship with the European Union 320, 323–4; Russian military presence 60, 85, 116, 219; Russian military withdrawal 123, 216, 220, 316–18, 320; Ukraine's conflict resolution efforts 121, 216–20, 224, 226, 320
treaty of Pereyaslav 1
Treaty on the Deepening of Integration in the Economic and Humanitarian Fields 70–1, 73–4, 89, 99; Inter-State Council 71; Inter-state Economic Committee (IEC) 54; Integration Committee 71; Inter-Parliamentary Committee 71
Treaty on the Union of Russia and Belarus 75; Charter 75
Treaty on the Creation of a Union State 163
Trenin, Dmitry 7, 41, 139, 253

Tsipko, Aleksandr 21–2
Turkey 82–3, 102–3, 115, 118, 123, 182, 199, 263, 281–3, 294–5; and the CIS gas trade 283, 288; relationship with Armenia 311–12; Russian sanctions against 261
Turkmenistan 60, 201, 259; and the CIS 62–3, 89, 182; and the CST 79; and the CIS/Russian gas trade 94–5, 101–2, 106–7, 120, 281–4, 286, 293–4, 298; introduction of national currency 54
Turkmenistan-Afghanistan– Pakistan–India (TAPI) pipeline 294
Turkmenrosgaz 101, 106

Ukraine: asymmetrical dependency on Russia 107; and the Black Sea Fleet 60, 66, 82, 90, 95–6, 98, 104–5, 214, 235, 291–2, 329–31, 338; and the CIS/Russian gas trade 95–8, 267, 279–80, 282, 284–5, 286–8, 290–3, 296–8; and the EAEU 266–8, 270; EuroMaidan 330, 332; European aspirations 157; and EvrAzES 158; GUAM membership 81, 84; Orange Revolution 195, 217; relationship with Russia 60, 84, 95–8, 266–8, 284–5, 286–9, 291–3, 329–39; relationship with the European Union 143, 157, 172, 244, 266–8, 286, 293, 297, 329, 338–9, 355–6; relationship with the West 83; relationship with NATO 83, 214, 235, 286, 329, 336, 338; reluctance to join CIS 47; role in the collapse of the Soviet Union 46; Russian military presence after the end of the USSR 60; Russian sanctions against 261–2; SES agreement and implementation 156–7, 248; siphoning of gas 61, 97; Treaty on Economic Cooperation with Russia 97; Turkmenistan gas trade with 101–3; see also Russia's conduct towards Ukraine; Ukrainian Donbass; annexation of Crimea
Ukrainian Donbass, outbreak of war in 332–7; anti-Maidan demonstrations 332–3; Donbass People's Militia 333; Donetsk People's Republic (DNR) 333–8; Lugansk People's Republic (LNR), 333–8; Minsk I agreement 335; Minsk II agreement 335–7; Novorossiya project 334–5, 355; Ukraine's Anti-Terrorist Operation 333–4

UkrGazEnergo (UGE) 286, 287, 291, 296
United Nations Security Council (UNSC) 2, 25, 38, 211, 214, 236, 306
United States: domination of the international system 36; Minsk co-Chair 210, 220–3, 225, 310–14, 322, 352; Yeltsin's intentions for Russian cooperation with 25
UNOMIG 114, 126, 309
USSR: hierarchical authority 7; *see also* Soviet Union
Uyghur separatist groups 193
Uzbekistan: and CIS air defence 188; and the CIS/Russian gas trade 103, 281–3, 293–4; and the CST 79; and the CSTO 180, 188, 200; EvrAzES customs union agreement 162; and EvrAzES membership and trade 158–61; GUUAM membership 84; IMU incursions 80, 179; introduction of national currency 55; relationship with China 201, 298; relationship with Russia 188; relationship with the USA 186, 192–3; relationship with the West 83; and the Shanghai Cooperation Organisation (SCO) 195; Treaty of Allied Relations with Russia 188; and the war in Tajikistan 118
UzTranGaz 181

Vasiliev, Aleksei 27
Vaziani military base 82, 212, 306
Verkhovna Rada 330
The View from the Kremlin (Yeltsin) 45
Vileika submarine communications facility 84
voluntary contracting, as basis of FSS relations 4, 10, 65, 78, 87–8, 225, 346–7, 354
Voronin, Vladimir 216–17, 220, 224

Westphalian state 5, 9
Westerners 25 Wilkinson, David 5–6
World Trade Organisation (WTO) 72, 156, 158, 248, 251–2, 254–5, 262

Xi Jinping 259
Xinjiang Uighur Autonomous Region (XUAR) 86

Yamal-Europe pipeline 98, 100, 108, 266, 279, 293
Yanukovych, Viktor 146, 157, 158, 168, 172, 235, 267, 291–3, 330–3, 355

Yatsenyuk, Arseny 330
Yeltsin, Boris: anti-imperialist approach 24, 39–40, 111, 119–20, 342; assertiveness in foreign policy 28–31, 33; assessment of his policies 62–5, 86–9, 103–7, 118–20, 344–6; and Belarusian-Russian integration 75, 77–8, 163; and CIS integration 31–2, 33, 53, 56, 60–2; and cooperation with the United States 25; decision-making under 34, 120, 143; military support to Armenia 115; role in collapse of the Soviet Union 44–8; and Russia's co-operation with Ukraine 97, 101; and the Russian-Ukrainian gas trade 104; and the war in Tajikistan 118; and the war in Transdniestria 116

Yugoslavia 37, 84
Yuriyev, Mikhail 243
Yushchenko, Viktor 157, 168, 280, 286, 296

Zakharchenko, Aleksandr 335
Zatulin, Konstantin 22
Zaslavsky, Viktor 22
Zhirinovsky, Vladimir 33, 35
Zyuganov, Gennady 35

Printed in the United States
By Bookmasters